ALSO BY COLIN FLETCHER:

The Winds of Mara (1973)
The Man Who Walked Through Time
(1968)
The Thousand-Mile Summer (1964)

THE NEW COMPLETE WALKER

THE NEW
Complete
WALKER

*The joys and techniques
of hiking and backpacking*

SECOND EDITION, REVISED,
ENLARGED, AND UPDATED

COLIN FLETCHER

Illustrations by VANNA PRINCE

ALFRED·A·KNOPF

New York · 1977

This Is a Borzoi Book
Published by Alfred A. Knopf, Inc.

Library of Congress Cataloging in Publication Data:
Fletcher, Colin, date.
The new complete walker.
1. Backpacking. 2. Hiking. I. Title.
G504.5.F55   1974   796.5   73-20763
ISBN 0-394-48099-6

Manufactured in the United States of America
PUBLISHED SEPTEMBER 24, 1976
REPRINTED FOUR TIMES
SIXTH PRINTING, MAY 1977

TO MY MOTHER
who understood that walking for fun
is no crazier than most things in life,
and who passed the information along.

Now shall I walk
Or shall I ride?
"Ride," Pleasure said;
"Walk," Joy replied.

W. H. Davies

Acknowledgments

Several fibers woven into this book have been plucked from *The Thousand-Mile Summer,* published by Howell-North Books, Berkeley, California, and from *The Man Who Walked Through Time* and *The Winds of Mara,* both published by Alfred A. Knopf, New York. To protect readers of these books from echo trouble, I have identified the rare passages in which I found it necessary to reuse any lengths of fabric.

A few strands also come from articles of mine that have appeared in *Field & Stream, Sports Afield, Reader's Digest* and the San Francisco *Chronicle,* and I wish to thank their publishers for permission to rework the material.

See also the preface to this second edition.

C. F.

Contents

Preface to the Second Edition

Second thoughts are ever wiser.
Euripides

This revised edition appears because five more years of backpacking revolution have rolled over us.

Equipment has improved—often radically, sometimes to the point of overengineering. Its manufacturers and distributors have multiplied, specialized, diversified, conglomerated, grown fat. In the kitchen, freeze-dried foods have come into their own and the "organic" movement has unfurled its puritan standards; indeed, the whole lightweight food scene is today a cornucopia that even spills out into the supermarkets. At the receiving end, our numbers have exploded. So has our literature. And we now suffer those slightly unfortunate battle cries, "Ecology!" and "The new ethic!"

"Yes," you say. "But is this really a revised edition, facing such changes? Or has the wretched man just cosmeticized?"

I have revised.

In places I have rebuilt: see, for example, almost the entire "Walls" chapter and the food and stove cupboards of "Kitchen." Where necessary, I have reassessed—as in "The current state of the mart." And I have injected innumerable minor and several major passages, embracing such items as hypothermia, an emergency solar still, the new literature and "Getting in shape" (for the omission of which I had rightly been taken to task).

Then there is feedback from the first edition. That edition brought me not only a splurge of unexpected affluence and offers from manufacturers to try out their wares but also readers' letters that ranged from joyous through serious, solemn and delightfully nutty to nutty. Most manufacturers were extremely helpful. But one of them, in response to a mildly critical report on his equipment, taught me a cautionary lesson in human nature by whipping back a gem of a reply that after four pages of mounting calumny rose to this peroration: "Your distortions, misuse, and lies are totally wasted, except to reveal to me the character of you, which I must say comes out quite disgusting." Readers proved gentler and more usefully informative, and I have fed back into this edition a number of their suggestions. I have not named names, but I would like to say "thank you," again, to everyone—and for the first time, to the man who sent me the most rewarding thank-you-for-the-book letter I have ever received and who had the delicacy to give no address and to sign himself only "Monty."

I do not call ecology and the new ethic "slightly unfortunate" because I disagree with what they stand for. Far from it. I offer up regular thanks for our recent success, at least on a lip-service level, with today's most urgent idea: that we must all learn to live in decent harmony with the rest of the planet. But I have trouble with current labels. "Ecology" is a striving polysyllable with a hard, intellectual, pseudoscientific ring to it; what we need is a warm, simple, poetic word that will eloquently reflect deep and imperative human needs. And there is a sententious smack to "the new ethic" —that altogether praiseworthy and indeed vitally necessary idea that backpackers must now treat the wilderness with tender loving care because our exponentially increasing numbers have turned many once-harmless practices into crimes. In any case, the "new" ethic is only an encapsulation, or at most a sharpening, of attitudes long held by aware walkers. I like to think that an awareness of both ecology and the new ethic was there all right, though un-labeled, in the first edition of this book. Then, I prudently soft-pedaled. This time I have mounted sundry wayside pulpits. But I hope I have continued to avoid the trap that always lies in wait for those of us who believe passionately: the whipping up of backlash by a messianic, holier-than-thou attitude. With "the movement" now out and running, I deem such an attitude our deadliest danger, against which we must stand daily and vigilant guard.

In discussing equipment I have carefully avoided considering the possibility, now glanced at sideways two or three times in the course of the book, that we may be over the hill and that we—the great tool-using species—therefore cannot assume we shall always have on tap our present wonderful wealth of tools. Already there is doubt about the supply of butane cartridges and white gas for stoves, and by publication time this edition may in part be a nostalgic monument to how things were, in one small field, at our peak. As for the years ahead, we shall see. Well, somebody will see.

In this edition I have not altered personal details—such as my flat, grassy hilltop retreat—when they merely illustrated a point and it is irrelevant if they no longer apply to my life. But I have struggled, through copious amendments and deletions, to bring everything else up to date: prices, practices, even prejudices (there are a couple of new, arcane uses for my beloved but much derided walking staff). The illustrator has furnished 32 new drawings and amended 21; and she has, we hope, kept the faith. Throughout the book I have tried to improve all writing that no longer satisfied me. Finally, I have refurbished Appendix I, brought II and III as up-to-date as sweat can bring them, and have tinkered about with IV by inserting several tidbits of joy I've recently stumbled on. When it was all done, after eighteen months' hardish labor, the number of pages had grown from 353 to 470 rather larger ones; and when I checked my work copy of the first edition I found that —apart from the brief opening and closing chapters, which stood virtually untouched—only 8 pages remained *virgo intacta*. And that, I think, argues a genuine, organic revision.

Yet in a sense nothing I wrote about has changed in the five years since the first edition appeared—even though I could then lie in my sleeping bag and watch the moon slide over a line of peaks and still wonder, with no boundaries except those of my imagination, what it would be like to be the first man to walk on that shining surface. I do not mean only that my publishers continue, amiably but firmly and no doubt rightly, to veto the subtitle I have long hankered for: "How to Succeed in Walking Without Often Crying." I do not mean only that although a great deal of equipment has mutated, much more has not; and that principles persist. Or that techniques evolve only slowly. I mean that equipment and techniques are mere means to an end, and the things I was writing toward are timeless. Cloud shadows still scud across sunlit peaks. Fleeing lizards still corner frantically around creosote bushes, flinging out little spurts of sand. I now have another familiar hilltop to which I can conveniently walk and on which I can sit for two days when I need space and beauty and silence so that I can sweep the daily clutter aside and penetrate surfaces and consider what I want to do with the rest of my life; or perhaps—as happened last Friday—so that I can wrestle with the preface to a new edition of an old book. A couple of years ago, deep in an Arizona mountain range, I was awakened near dawn by a soft, mouselike rustling—and soon impaled on my flashlight beam, less than two feet from my eyes, peering over the top of my pack, the sharp and nose-quivering features of an undoubtedly astonished coati-mundi. No, if you back off just a little ways, nothing much has changed. Essentially, the old book stands.

Because we backpackers now threaten with our numbers the quality if not the existence of the green world, and because books like mine may encourage the invasion, I suffered misgivings about a second edition. Then someone said, "Oh, but the trouble isn't really the numbers of people in the wilderness—it's the numbers that don't know how to live there properly and decently. We need more books like yours." I'm not sure this pleasing sentiment is sound, but I accepted it gratefully. And here is the new-old book.

C. F.
Summer 1973

WARNING! PRICES

As this edition goes to press in late 1973, prices are restless in the direction of up, and by the time you read the figures I quote they will no doubt be fond memory. So please extrapolate.

WHY WALK?

Why Walk?

Sanity is a madness put to good uses.
George Santayana

I had better admit right away that walking can in the end become an addiction, and that it is then as deadly in its fashion as heroin or television or the stock exchange. But even in this final stage it remains a delectable madness, very good for sanity, and I recommend it with passion.

A redeeming feature of the condition is that no matter how heavily you have been hooked you can still get your kicks from very small doses.

Ten minutes' drive from my apartment there is a long, grassy ridge from which you can look out over parkland and sprawling metropolis, over bay and ocean and distant mountains. I often walk along this ridge in order to think uncluttered thoughts or to feel with accuracy or to sweat away a hangover or to achieve some other worthy end, recognized or submerged. And I usually succeed—especially with the thinking. Up there, alone with the wind and the sky and the steep grassy slopes, I nearly always find after a while that I am beginning to think more clearly. Yet "think" does not seem to be quite the right word. Sometimes, when it is a matter of making a choice, I do not believe I decide what to do so much as discover what I have decided. It is as if my mind, set free by space and solitude and oiled by the body's easy rhythm, swings open and releases thoughts it has already formulated. Sometimes, when I have been straining too hard to impose order on an urgent press of ideas, it seems only as if my mind has slowly relaxed; and then, all at once, there is room for the ideas to fall into place in a meaningful pattern.

Occasionally, you can achieve this kind of release inside a city. One day when I had to leave my car at a garage for an hour's repair work, I spent the time strolling through an industrial area. I crossed a man-made wasteland, then walked up onto a little-

3

used pedestrian bridge over a freeway. Leaning on its concrete parapet, I watched the lines of racing, pounding vehicles. From above they seemed self-propelled, automatic. And suddenly, standing there alone, I found myself looking down on the scene like a visitor from another planet, curiously detached and newly instructed.

But no one who has begun to acquire the walking habit can restrict himself for long to cities, or even to their parks. First he explores open spaces out beyond the asphalt. Then, perhaps, he moves on to car camping and makes long all-day treks, out and away. But in due course he is almost sure to start dreaming of the truly wild places, far from any road. And at this point he is in danger of meeting a mental block.

Even in these mercifully emancipated decades, many people still seem to become alarmed at the prospect of sleeping away from officially consecrated campsites, with no more equipment than they can carry on their backs. When pressed, they babble about snakes or bears or even, by God, bandits. But the real barrier, I'm sure, is the unknown.

It was only a few years ago that I came to comprehend the reality of this barrier. To be more exact, I recomprehended it. I was taking a four-day walk over some coastal hills. (I was taking it, as a matter of fact, in order to sort out ideas and directions for the first edition of this book.) One warm and cloudless afternoon I was resting at a bend in the trail—there was a little triangular patch of shade, I remember, under a rocky bluff—when some unexpected tilt of my mind reexposed a scene that I had completely forgotten. For all the vividness of the vital features, it is a curiously indistinct scene. I am not at all clear when it happened, except that it must have been more than fifteen years ago. I do not even remember for sure whether it happened in Africa or America. But the salient contours stand out boldly. I had come to some natural boundary. It may have been the end of a trail or road, or the fringes of a forest or the rim of a cliff, I no longer know which. But I do know that I felt I had gone as far as a man could go. So I just stood there looking out beyond the edge of the world. Except for a wall of thick, dark undergrowth, I am no longer sure what I saw, but I know it was wild, wild, impossible country. It still looms huge and black and mysterious in the vaults of my memory.

All at once, without warning, two men emerged from that impossible country. They carried packs on their backs, and they were weatherbeaten and distilled to bone and muscle. But what I remember best of all is that they were happy and whole. Whole and secure and content.

I talked to them, briefly and in considerable awe. They had

been back deep into the wilderness, they said, away from civilization for a week. "Pretty inaccessible, some of it," admitted one of them. "But there's a lot of beautiful country in there—some of the finest I've ever seen." Then they walked away and I was left, still awestruck, looking out once more into the huge, black, mysterious wilderness.

The awe that I felt that day still hangs in my memory. But my present self dismisses it. I know better. Many times in recent years I have emerged from wild country, happy and whole and secure and content, and have found myself face to face with astonished people who had obviously felt that they were already at the edge of the world; and I know, now I have come to consider the matter, that what I have seen on their faces is exactly what those two men must have seen on mine, many years ago on the edge of that other wilderness. And I know now that the awe is totally unwarranted. There is nothing very difficult about going into such places. All you need is the right equipment, a reasonable competence in using it, a tolerable degree of physical fitness, and a clear understanding of your own limitations. Beyond that, all you have to do is overcome the fear of the unknown.*

Once you have overcome the fear of the unknown and thereby surmounted your sleeping-out-in-the-wilderness block, you are free. Free to go out, when the world will let you slip away, into the wildest places you dare explore. Free to walk from dawn to dusk and then again from dawn to dusk, with no harsh interruptions, among the quiet and soothing cathedrals of a virgin forest. Or free to struggle for a week, if that is what you want at that particular time, toward a peak that has captured your imagination. Or free, if your needs or fancies of the moment run that way, to follow a wild river to its source, fishing as you go, or not fishing. Free, once you have grasped the significance of this other reality, to immerse yourself for two months in the timeless silence of a huge desert canyon —and to learn in the end why the silence is not timeless after all.

* You will see that I tend to write of walking as if it is something that must be done alone. Most people prefer company, and by all reasonable standards they are right. For efficiency and comfort and the rewards of sharing, and above all for safety, a walking party, like a political party, should consist of at least two or three members.

But I like to walk alone. And therefore, when I am being honest, that is how I tend to write. It does not matter, though: if you choose, sensibly, to travel in twos or threes or twenties, just about everything I have to say still applies. You miss something, that's all. You never quite learn, for instance, that one of the riches a wilderness has to offer is prolonged and absolute silence.

There is one notable exception to my rule. When you and your companion are newly in love, the two of you walk with minds interwoven, and the bond enriches everything you see. And that is the best walking of all.

But long before the madness has taught you this kind of sanity you have learned many simple and valuable things.

You start to learn them from the very beginning. First, the comforting constants. The rhythm of boots and walking staff, and their different inflections on sand and on soil and on rock. The creak of harness as small knapsack or heavy pack settles back into place after a halt. And the satisfactions of a taut, controlled body. Then there are the small, amplified pleasures. In everyday life, taking off your socks is an unnoticed chore; peeling them off after a long day's walk is sheer delight. At home, a fly is something that makes you wonder how it got into the house; when you are lying sprawled out on a sandbar beside a remote river you can recognize a fly as something to be studied and learned from—another filament in the intricate web of the world. Or it may be a matter of mere money: five days beyond the last stain of man, you open the precious little package of blister-cushioning felt pads that is marked "45¢" and discover, tucked away inside, a forgotten and singularly useless $5 bill. Yet two days later you may find your appetite suddenly sharp for civilized comforts that a week earlier had grown flat and stale. A few years ago, toward the end of a week's exploration of a remote headwater basin, I found my heart melting at the thought of hot buttered toast for breakfast. And once, in the final week of a summer-long walk, I even found myself recalling with nostalgia the eternal city hunt for parking.

But long before such unexpected hankerings arise, your mind as well as your body has been honed. You have re-remembered that happiness has something to do with simplicity. And so, by slow degrees, you regain a sense of harmony with everything you move through—rock and soil, plant and tree and cactus, spider and fly and rattlesnake and coyote, drop of rain and racing cloud shadow. (You have long ago outgrown the crass assumption that the world was made for man.) After a while you find that you are gathering together the whole untidy but glorious mishmash of sights and sounds and smells and touches and tastes and emotions that tumble through your recent memory. Then you begin to connect these ciphers, one with the other. And once you begin to connect, only to connect, nothing can stop you—not even those rare moments of blackness (when all, all is vanity) that can come even in the wilderness.

When you get back at last from the simple things to the complexities of the outside, walled-in man-world you find that you are once more eager to grapple with them. For a while you even detect a meaning behind all the complexity. And that of course is the way it has to be. We are creatures of our time; we cannot escape it. The simple life is not a substitute, only a corrective.

For a while, I said, you detect new meanings. For a little while. That is where the hell comes in. In due course the hot buttered toast tastes like damp sawdust again and the parking hassle is once more driving you crazy and the concrete jabs at your eyes and the din and the dirt sicken you, and all at once you realize that there is no sense to be discovered, anywhere, in all the frantic scurryings of the city. And you know there is only one thing to do. You are helplessly trapped. Hooked. Because you know now that you have to go back to the simple things.

You struggle, briefly. But as soon as the straight-line world will let you slip away, or a little sooner, you go. You go in misery, with delight, full of confidence. For you know that you will immerse yourself in the harmonies—and will return to see the meanings.

That is why, on balance, I can recommend walking with passion. It is an altogether delectable addiction. Sometimes nowadays I find myself wondering what in God's name I would have done with my life if I had failed to fall an early victim.

Naturally, not everyone understands.

At a cocktail party some time ago, a smooth and hyper-satisfied young man boasted to me that he had just completed a round-the-world sightseeing tour in seventy-nine days. In one jet-streamed breath he scuttled from St. Peter's, Rome, via the Pyramids, to a Cambodian jungle temple. "That's the way to travel," he said. "You see everything important."

When I suggested that the way to see important things was to walk, he almost dropped his martini.

Walking can even provoke an active opposition lobby. For many years now I have been told with some regularity that by walking out and away I am "escaping from reality." I admit that the statement puts me on the defensive. Why, I ask myself (and sometimes my accusers as well) are people so ready to assume that chilled champagne is more "real" than water drawn from an ice-cold mountain creek? Or a dusty sidewalk than a carpet of desert dandelions? Or a Boeing 747 than a flight of graceful white pelicans soaring in unison against the sunrise? Why, in other words, do people assume that the acts and emotions and values that stem from city life are more real than those that arise from the beauty and the silence and the solitude of wilderness?

For me, the thing touched bottom when I was gently accused

of escapism during a TV interview about a book I had written on a length-of-California walk. Frankly, I fail to see how going for a six-month, thousand-mile walk through deserts and mountains can be judged less real than spending six months working eight hours a day, five days a week, in order to earn enough money to be able to come back to a comfortable home in the evening and sit in front of a TV screen and watch the two-dimensional image of some guy talking about a book he has written on a six-month, thousand-mile walk through deserts and mountains.

As I said, I get put on the defensive. The last thing I want to do is to knock champagne and sidewalks and Boeing 747's. Especially champagne. These things distinguish us from the other animals. But they can also limit our perspectives. And I suggest that they—and all the stimulating complexities of modern life—begin to make more sense, to take on surer meaning, when they are viewed in perspective against the more certain and more lasting reality from which they have evolved—from the underpinning reality, that is, of mountain water and desert flowers and soaring white birds at sunrise.

Here endeth the lesson.

But perhaps you are an unbeliever and need proof—a no-nonsense, show-me-some-practical-results kind of proof.

I can tell you now that I have had an unholy awful time with this introductory chapter.* I wrote it a dozen times, over a period of several months, and a dozen times it utterly refused to say what I wanted it to say. In the end I drove an hour out of town, parked the car on a dirt road, heaved the pack onto my back, walked for another hour, and then camped on the flat, grassy summit of a familiar hill. That was two evenings ago. I am still there. In front of me the long grass is billowing like the sea. Far beyond it and far below sprawls the city. It is very gray. But here on my hilltop there is only the grass and the wind and the sky.

From time to time since I climbed up here I have strolled around my domain. Once, I went down a few hundred feet with the pack on my back and filled all four canteens at a spring. But mostly I have sat up here in the shade of my poncho awning. I have looked at the billowing grass. I have looked beyond it at the sprawling gray city and have listened to the roar from a freeway that feeds it. I have consulted with a number of hawks, mice,

* I have let this little story stand as it appeared in the first edition, because that is the way it happened, sort of inside the book.

beetles, and trees. And this morning—after two nights and one day of bitter, bitter struggle and many, many words—I suddenly relaxed and began to write. I do not say that I am yet satisfied with what I have written. But I think it will do.

Words of warning

I am down off my hilltop now, but before we move on to consider the ways and means of walking I must point out two pitfalls that you should bear in mind, always—or as always as you can manage.

First, make sure the ways and means remain just that. They will always be threatening to take over. They will tend, particularly at the start of a trip, to imprison your thoughts on a treadmill of trivial worries: "Is that a blister forming on my right heel?"; "If the storm breaks, will that little tarp really keep me dry all night?"; "My God, is the water going to last out?" And any sudden small problem is liable to inflate without warning and fill the horizons of your tight little world. It all sounds very silly, I know; but anyone who has traveled on foot, especially alone, will recognize the syndrome. I should like to report that experience cures such nonsense. Unfortunately, it doesn't. It helps; it helps a lot. But I still find, especially on long trips with a sharp physical challenge, that I need at least a few days of "shakedown cruise." On a two-month journey I made some time ago through Grand Canyon, it took me all of two weeks to break free.

Whether you like it or not, the trivia are always there. And never underrate them; either you subdue them or they subdue you. A single blister can blacken the most shining day. And if you are miles from anywhere, soaked through and shivering and with no confidence in your ability to contrive a warm, dry shelter for the night, you will be deaf to the music of raindrops drumming against your poncho and blind to the beauty of clouds swirling around sawtooth peaks.

The important thing, then, about running your tight little outdoor economy is that it must not run you. You must learn to deal with the practical details so efficiently that they become second nature. Then, after the unavoidable shakedown period, you leave yourself free to get on with the important things—watching cloud shadows race across a mountainside or passing the time of day with a hummingbird or discovering that a grasshopper eats grass like spaghetti or sitting on a peak and thinking of nothing at all except perhaps that it is a wonderful thing to sit on a peak and think of nothing at all.*

The second pitfall is more subtly camouflaged. Naturally, your opinions on equipment and technique must never fossilize into dogma: your mind must remain open to the possibilities of better gear and to new and easier ways of doing things. You try to strike a balance, of course—to operate efficiently and yet to remember, always, that the practical details are only a means to an end. But I am not altogether convinced that after years and years of it—when you have at last succeeded in mastering most of the business and people have begun to call you an expert and someone may even ask you to write a book on the subject—I am not at all sure that it is then possible to avoid the sobering discovery that you have become, ex officio, a very tolerably accomplished fuddy-duddy.

---

* It would probably be a good thing if you reread this paragraph at least once—and tried to remember it later on. This is essentially a "know-how" book, but we must never lose sight of the fact that what matters in the end is the "feel-how" of walking.

HOUSE
ON YOUR BACK

Ground Plan

As long as you restrict your walking to one-day hikes you are unlikely to face any very ponderous problems of equipment or technique. Everything you need can be stuffed into pockets or if necessary into a convenient little pouch slung from waist or shoulders. And if something should get left behind, why, home is always waiting at the end of the day's road. But as soon as you start sleeping out you simply have to carry some kind of

A house on your back.

Obviously, there is a difference between the kind of house you need to carry for a soft, summer weekend in the woods and for a month or more in wild mountain country. But it is extremely convenient and entirely possible to devise a standard structure that you can modify to suit a broad range of conditions. In this book I shall describe in detail the fairly full-scale edifice, very simply modifiable, that I have evolved over a considerable number of years. If some of the architecture seems too elaborate for your needs, all you have to do is simplify toward harmony with those needs.

Similarly, I shall discuss most techniques as they apply to trips of at least a weekend. Often I will talk in terms of more ambitious journeys. Again, if my suggestions seem too elaborate for what you have in mind, simply simplify.

I make no apologies for writing a highly subjective book—a book that will give many experienced walkers a whole slew of satisfying chances to snort with disagreement. For backpacking is a highly subjective business. What matters to me is what suits me; but what matters to you is what suits you. So when I describe what I have found best, try to remember that I am really saying that there are no truly objective criteria, and the important thing in the end is not what I or some other so-called expert happens to use or do, but what *you* find best. Even prejudice has its place: a technique or piece of equipment that you have devised yourself is much more satisfying to use than an "import"—and in your hands it may well prove more efficient. The most a book can do, then, is to suggest guidelines.*

Guidelines are all I can offer for another reason too:

The current state of the mart.

In 1968 I wrote in the first edition of this book that backpacking was "in a stimulating if mildly confusing state of evolution —or perhaps I mean revolution—in both design and materials" and also in distribution methods. The ev- or rev-olution continues. Foam sleeping pads are still undergoing sea changes. Two potentially pregnant sleeping-bag fillers have floated over the horizon. Cunning new packframe designs now surface with every tide. And big things are going on in the kitchen: look, especially, on the freeze-dry and natural food shelves. As a result of all the competition, we are being offered more varied products of keener design at an increasing number of sources—a state of affairs that is known, I understand, as capitalism.

All this means that some of my solemn, carefully updated advice will soon be outmoded again. But it does not matter. Although I shall often be describing specific items, the essence will lie not so much in the items themselves as in the principles that govern choice —in those vital factors an intelligent backpacker should keep his eyes skinned for.

Custom suggests that I avoid trade names. But only by discussing brands and models can I adequately indicate the details. And if I recommend one brand of soup over another it is because I find it suits my needs better, not because, for crying out loud, I adore Mr. Maggi and deplore Mr. Knorr.

It should be borne in mind, though, that geography often plays a part in my own choices. You will find that a lot of my equipment is made by Trailwise of Berkeley, California. Now I consider their products to be excellent. But the fact remains that for many years I lived a dozen blocks from The Ski Hut, makers of Trailwise equipment. And the fact is obviously relevant. If you live in Centralia, Illinois, your druthers may be different. But the fact also remains that Ski Hut–Trailwise are the makers-retailers who have for many years offered perhaps the fullest range of backpacking equipment—though they are now challenged and sometimes equaled by a number of companies (some of them primarily or exclusively retailers) that also produce comprehensive catalogues

---

* Frankly, my advice to those genuinely interested in walking has always been to forget the books and to get out and get on with it, relying on the two finest teachers in the business, trial and error. I'm not at all sure a piece of me doesn't still stand by that advice.

and maintain nationwide mail-order services: Recreational Equipment Incorporated, a cooperative enterprise of Seattle, Washington, that sells many items at highly competitive prices; Eastern Mountain Sports of New England; Moor and Mountain of Concord, Massachusetts; Holubar of Boulder, Colorado; Sierra Designs of Berkeley, California; and The Smilie Company of San Francisco. Many other firms carry a fairly full range of equipment, and some of these specialize in certain products and have established themselves as leaders in their field of specialization. Names that spring to mind are A. I. Kelty of Glendale, California, and Camp Trails of Phoenix, Arizona, for packs and L. L. Bean of Freeport, Maine, for "Maine Hunting Shoes" (page 39).

Even this short list has changed considerably since 1968. Then, the distribution of backpacking equipment was expanding in an energetic but generalized way. We have now moved into a period of more diversified change. Retail outlets are still mushrooming, particularly in the East; and some firms are still expanding both their general manufacturing and retailing operations (Eddie Bauer of Seattle, for example). But a few have drawn in their horns. At least one (Gerry) has quit the retail business in favor of wholesaling through far-flung dealers. Others have undergone major internal reorganization (Alpine Designs—formerly Alp Sport—of Boulder, Colorado, now sells wholesale nationwide, but retails through a mail-order service, Wilderness Ways of Cleveland, Ohio). This last change is an eddy of the current tide race toward conglomeration. Once-independent concerns already assimilated by conglomerates include not only Alpine Designs but Gerry, Eddie Bauer, Holubar, Himalayan Industries, Kelty, and Sierra Designs.*

Sierra Designs' history shows how quickly things have been evolving. The firm began in 1966 as a small outfit tucked away in Point Richmond, California, that specialized in making down sleeping bags and clothing. In 1968 they moved into Berkeley and expanded to offer a full range of backpacking gear. Within a couple of years they had equaled and at times surpassed the nearby and long-established Ski Hut in quality and service—though not, perhaps, in range. In 1972 they were conglomerated (though they prefer to say "merged with the CML Group"). Time will tell what effects—good, bad or neutral—such take-overs provoke.

The grass roots are diversifying too. If you want a sleeping bag built to your own specifications you can now order it from at least two places, both in California, that specialize in such custom work: Yeti Enterprises of Topanga and Bugaboo Mountaineering of

---

* Bulletin: The Ski Hut has now succumbed to the avalanche. *Et tu, Hut-e!*

Monterey. Mountain Traders of Berkeley have recently opened a
kind of multispecialized operation: they make certain packs and
down gear, sell new mountaineering and backpacking boots as
well as used backpacking equipment—bought outright, accepted
in trade-in, or taken on consignment at 20 percent commission—
and claim to be "the only volume boot repair shop in America
specializing in Vibram, Galibier and other exotic climbing soles."
But, by general consensus, the best-known specialist repairer—
and supplier—of high-quality mountaineering boots is Steve Komito of Estes Park, Colorado. In the East, Stow-A-Way Sports
Industries of Cohasset, Massachusetts, will now supply people
making extended trips along the Appalachian and other eastern
trails by mailing packages of food and equipment to U.S. post
offices "as they proceed, and according to their schedules." They
have worked out suggested schedules. And Sugarloaf Ski Specialists
of Kingfield, Maine, will meet travelers along the Appalachian
Trail "at trail/road crossings with supplies, mail, etc. . . . transfer
cars, etc." For all I know there may be other small specialized
concerns in other places, news of whose germination has failed
to reach me down any grapevine. In fact, I'd be surprised if there
were not.

Then there is the do-it-yourself field—or, rather, the do-the-
last-part-yourself paddock—within which you can sometimes cut
costs by half. In 1968 Frostline Outdoor Equipment was a new
and somewhat tentative business that offered premarked do-it-yourself kits of good-quality lightweight gear: tents, sleeping bags, and
down-filled and other clothing. They have maintained high quality
standards, expanded, honed—and prospered. And they are no
longer alone. Somebody, exhibiting the sincerest form of flattery,
started a similar operation, also in Boulder, called Carikit Outdoor
Equipment, which has now been absorbed by Holubar. Eastern
Mountain Sports now offers a limited range of Emskits. And Adventure 16 of El Cajon, California, has Pack Kits (everything for
making a complete pack). I have not grappled with any of these
do-it-yourself kits, but there seems to be a reasonable consensus
that if you are on the all-thumbs sewing team you might be wise to
conscript a pinch hitter; that if you know how to operate a sewing
machine you should be able to cope with a relatively simple challenge like a sleeveless down jacket; but that for such creations as
sleeping bags you need unlimited time and patience, a genius's infinite capacity for staking pins, and—above all—an ability to
follow written instructions accurately and to the last letter. A
possible source of assistance in all such matters is a little paperback
volume, *Light Weight Camping Equipment and How to Make It,*

by Gerry Cunningham and Margaret Hansson (Gerry Division, Colorado Outdoor Sports Corporation, 5450 N. Valley Highway, Denver, Colorado 80216; 7 ounces; $2.50).

"To every revolution there is a counter-revolution, and so it has been with mountain gear," says Daniel Ford in an article in the January 1973 issue of *Wilderness Camping* Magazine. "Twenty years ago, you bought your hiking gear at the local Army-Navy store. . . . Then came the era of the mountain specialty shops . . . and . . . price tags that were astronomical." Now, he says, it's back to Sears Roebuck and the discount department stores. He makes at least a mild economic case for the movement too. But if you explore the possibilities—and they may be worth exploring—keep a wary eye open not only for poor-quality equipment but also for such standard merchandising tricks as "loss leaders" to lure you in— and on. And remember that you're unlikely to get the kind of follow-up service normal in good "mountain shops"—service tendered by people who are not basically salesmen but who know how to use what they are selling, and want you back, regularly.

For details of all the firms I have mentioned, and many more, see Appendix II—a list of retailers throughout the United States and Canada who specialize or deal extensively in backpacking equipment and maintain countrywide mail-order services. The list is as complete and current as I can make it. But remember that the field remains in a state of flux. Every month still brings new expansions, reorganizations, mergers and takeovers—or at least rumors of them. So please treat my list as a guide, not a gospel.

Most of the firms listed in Appendix II issue catalogues. Don't ignore them: they've become quite a phenomenon. They range from down-to-earth, complete-but-no-nonsense affairs like those put out by The Smilie Company and Moor and Mountain to such sumptuous and highly informative color creations as The Ski Hut's (they've set the standard for years) and the recent encyclopedic works of art and instruction produced by Eastern Mountain Sports (their superbly produced 1972 edition was probably the high-water mark of the entire genre). Along the way lie such experiments as recent Sierra Designs mood catalogues.

Catalogues are only the beginning of the new

Helpful literature.

Since 1968, backpacking has drawn upon itself a stream, going on a flood, of new books. Most of them try, roughly speaking, to do what this book tries to do. I shall not attempt to review them. After all, only a fool would accept me as a disinterested critic.

If you covet a list—exhaustive to the numbing point—of books and pamphlets, ancient and modern, on walking and ancillary matters, write to *Walking News* (see Appendix II, New York) for a free copy of *The Great Outdoors Book List* (1700 titles, yet).

The "Nomadics" section of *The Last Whole Earth Catalog* (and its earlier editions) contains much fresh and unbiased opinion on backpacking matters. (Nomadics aside, the *Catalog* offers some of the most delightful and nutritious browsing material I have ever gotten bogged down in. For my money, the 31-line extract from *Architectural Design* called "This Graded Universe" [page 88] is alone worth your $5.) *

At least one local backpackers' newsletter has prospered and grown. *Signpost* Magazine (started 1966) specializes in "news and articles about the northwestern United States, with emphasis on current backcountry conditions in Washington state." It publishes guidebooks and technical bulletins for individual or educational use. Also maintains a formidable card index of hiking and similar clubs. Quarterly magazine and bi-weekly newsletter. ($7.50 a year. Editor: Louise Marshall, 16812 36th Avenue W., Lynnwood, Washington 98036.)

Nationally, the old stalwart magazines—*Field & Stream & Co.*—have always run occasional backpacking articles. *Camping* runs rather more (of uncertain quality), but is primarily for vehicle campers, including those who travel on trail bikes and other mechanized horrors. *Better Camping* used to fall in the same category but now, as official journal of the National Hiking and Ski Touring Association, it is directed primarily to walkers—with nods toward skiers, canoeists and cyclists. The ads still Winnebago you, though. A monthly, available on newsracks ($.75) or by subscription ($6.50 a year: Woodall Publishing Company, 500 Hyacinth Place, Highland Park, Illinois 60035).

Off Belay now calls itself "a mountain magazine"—no longer strictly for climbers but also for "all those backpackers who leave the trails and move cross-country." A highly comprehensive study of backpacking stoves was scheduled for its December 1973 issue

---

* Late news: *The Whole Earth Epilog,* successor to the *Catalog,* and by the same people, is due out in the fall of 1974. And the old *Supplements* will be succeeded, starting this spring, by *The CoEvolution Quarterly,* available on newsstands ($2) or by subscription ($6 a year: Box 428, Sausalito, California 94965). *Epilog* and *Quarterly,* like the old *Catalog,* are both subtitled "Access to Tools."

Just out in this genre: *The Explorers Ltd. Source Book* (Harper & Row; $4.95)—40 pages on Backpacking, 340 more on everything from First Aid, through Ballooning and Ski Touring and Weather, to Two- and Four-Wheeling (trail bikes, jeeps and other shaitans).

(see page 169). A monthly, available at selected mountain shops ($1) and by subscription ($6 a year; 2 years, $11; 3 years, $15; 5 years, $20: 12416 169th Avenue S.E., Renton, Washington 98055).

Mountain Gazette (*Skiers' Gazette,* 1966–72) now embraces backpacking as well as other mountain foot deeds. Unglossy (newsprint), unhidebound, literate, interesting. Recently: a human yet informative little piece about the patina on an old Sierra Club cup; and a table of statistics, features and prices for over 100 boot models. A monthly, by subscription only ($5 a year; $8 for 2 years; $10 for 3 years: 1801 York Street, Denver, Colorado 80206).

Wilderness Camping, born 1971 and apparently gaining strength, is "for the self-propelled wilderness enthusiast": it carries down-to-earth articles on backpacking, ski-touring, canoeing and bicycle camping. It is sharply conservation-conscious, abominates off-the-road vehicles. A bimonthly, available on newsstands ($1) or by subscription ($4 a year: 1255 Portland Place, Boulder, Colorado 80302).

The first magazine exclusively for backpackers appeared early in 1973. Judging by the first three issues, *Backpacker* Magazine will be a product of distinction. It plans to cover all aspects of wilderness and not-so-wilderness walking. A quarterly ($2.50 a copy), available by subscription ($7.50 a year: 28 W. 44th Street, New York, N.Y. 10036).

Outdoor Magazine's first issue is due to appear soon. With several ex–*Sports Illustrated* staffers at the controls, it promises to be a thoroughly professional operation. Although embracing "the whole outdoors," it will definitely serve the backpacker—and share his ecological outlook. A monthly, available on newsstands ($1.50) and by subscription (charter, $10 a year; regular, $15: 516 Fifth Avenue, New York, N.Y. 10036).

Preparing this book has shown me at least one task that such magazines can perform. There are now so many models of certain equipment items, such as packs and sleeping bags, and they change so fast, that one man can no longer pretend to have meaningful experience with even a representative selection. And interested and competent groups tend to be beholden in some way to a manufacturer or distributor, or at least a region. A book has a built-in time lag, anyway. But a magazine, with a staff at its command, and timeliness an ever-present spur, can conduct a somewhat objective and vaguely scientific survey of many models and maybe make some kind of sense. The first three issues of *Backpacker* have done just that with packs, sleeping bags and tents. I'm by no means happy that walking—our simple, delightful, intended-to-be-liberating-from-the-straight-line-coordinates-of-civilization pastime—should have reached this pass, but there it is.

I hasten to add that one experienced man may still be well qualified to describe in detail the equipment he uses—not necessarily to make you buy any particular model but to point out important things to look for. And I regard that as a valid alternative instructional approach. Hell, I have to.

What with all these books, magazines and catalogues, there is now enough walking literature around to lure anyone into forgetting from time to time that the object of the exercise is not reading but walking. Let us, while still reading, get back on the trail.

When planning the house on your back, the weightiest matter is

Weight.

The rules are simple:
1. If you need something, take it.
2. Pare away relentlessly at the weight of every item.

In paring away you will find that if you look after the ounces the pounds will look after themselves. Any good sports store that specializes in backpacking equipment will list in its catalogue the weight of each article to the nearest ounce, and will also keep an accurate arm scale handy. When shopping in other stores I often take along a postal scale and weigh every item like gold dust. I still like to remember the bewilderment of one sales damsel when I produced my scale and insisted on comparing the weights of two rival pairs of jockey shorts.

I find that the paring process never ends. At home, such foods as raisins that come in cardboard containers get repacked in plastic bags. At the start of a trip, margins and unneeded areas are trimmed off maps. And when I'm laboring along under a knee-buckling load I'm never really happy until I've eliminated the last eliminable fraction of an ounce. Once or twice, in really frenetic moments, I've even found myself tearing the labels off tea bags.

Unfortunately it seems impossible to predict just what your load will be for a given trip. No matter how carefully you plan, you have to wait for an answer until you hoist the fully furnished pack onto your back on the first day. The only thing you can be sure of is that it will weigh more than you had hoped. If you want a meaningful figure, don't rely on the way the pack feels; get it onto a trustworthy scale. And memorize the reading. When it comes to talking about the loads they carry, lamentably few backpackers seem to restrict themselves to confirmed objective, unembroidered fact.

Men (or women*), such as Himalayan Sherpas, who have toted huge loads all their lives, can carry almost their own weight all day long. And even a halfway-fit, fully citified man can pack very heavy loads for short distances, such as canoe portages. Again, people whom I trust implicitly talk of having to carry eighty or one hundred pounds or even more on slow and painful approach marches of five or ten miles at the start of mountain-climbing expeditions. But this kind of toil is hardly walking, in our sense. The heaviest load the average man can carry with efficiency and enjoyment for a long day's walking seems to vary within rather wide limits, but a rough guide would be "up to one third of body weight." Naturally, this figure assumes an efficient pack frame and a reasonably fit and practiced body. Practiced, mark you. The only way of getting used to heavy loads is to pack heavy loads. (But see page 27 for reasonable short-circuiting facsimiles.)

People often express horror at the weights I seem to carry. But remember that on the rare occasions I quote figures I am almost always referring to long and often arduous journeys on which it would be foolhardy to leave anything unnecessary to chance. On the other hand, I habitually seem to carry rather more than many people I see on mountain trails. I notice, though, that most of the serious—as opposed to solemn—backpackers I know also seem to travel rather heavily laden. The answer may be that if you travel in a group or stick to well-traveled trails where "rescue" is simple and sure if something goes mildly wrong with equipment or weather, then you can cut corners. But if you tend to travel alone, avoid well-traveled trails, head naturally for remote areas, and are achingly aware of potential treacheries always lurking, then you'll probably take everything along, including the kitchen sink.

One of the few occasions on which I have weighed my pack, operationally stocked, was at the start of the two-month journey I made through Grand Canyon. Then, with a week's food supply and two gallons of water, the pack turned the scale at 66½ pounds. At the time I weighed 194 rather flabby pounds (20 more than I did at the end) and the load felt appallingly heavy. But the start is always the worst of it. Each day you use up not only food but also such items as stove fuel and toilet paper. And beyond each

* Everything I have to say in this book about men applies equally to women. Well, almost everything. And almost equally.

refill point the water diminishes steadily, hour by hour. By the end of my first week in Grand Canyon, when I took an airdrop of food beside a big rainpocket in the rock, my pack must have weighed less than 30 pounds. And that made a tremendous difference.

It always does. People often say, "I guess you get so used to the pack that after a while it doesn't worry you any more." But only when the load falls below 40 pounds can I sometimes forget it. At 50 I can't. At 60 it always feels desperately heavy. At 66½ it just about takes the joy out of walking. And short sidetrips with no load on my back are always like running into the sea after a hot and bothersome day in the city.*

Cost

The only really satisfactory way to approach the price problem is to ignore it. Good equipment always seems expensive, but whenever you find yourself in a store scowling at a price tag, try to remember that out in the wilds, where money is meaningless, the failure of a single item can easily ruin a trip. It may even endanger your life.

"Ignore the cost" is easier said than done, of course (though I should like to add, at the risk of sounding smug, that I am perfectly content to drive to the mountains in my reliable nineteen-year-old Plymouth but would not think of walking away from it with any equipment in my pack that fell short of the best available).† In the end, naturally, everyone has to establish his own standards, with due consideration for other responsibilities. But when it comes to such critical items as sleeping bags the only safe rule is to buy the best you can afford—and then another grade better.

I have indicated a price for almost every article I mention. Generally speaking, the figures in this edition represent a fairly high catalogue average for late 1973, but as I have warned after the preface, inflation is with us (as is devaluation) and you may have to do some sums. The Ski Hut—and perhaps other firms by now—have stopped listing items as "$2.49" or "$2.99" and have

---

* I shall be taken to task, even more resoundingly than before, for the weight of this bloated second edition. "You blabber about paring ounces," say the critics, "and then come up with a tome." But this book is intended primarily for pre-walking study. Of course, if you want to put it in your pack . . .

† This is a first-edition brag that has now burst. My beloved old Plymouth woody gave way at last, in its twenty-second elegant and still-shining year, to one of the behemoths I excoriated in the footnote on p. 337—and that beautiful but energy-guzzling dinosaur is now giving way to a machine more tailored to the times.

substituted the more honest "$2.50" or "$3," and where applicable
I have followed their courageous and praiseworthy lead.

Renting

If you live near a good mountain shop (I guess I'm a convert
to that pleasant and useful misnomer) you may be able to rent
certain items, such as packs, tents and sleeping bags (and perhaps
ice axes and crampons—though when you start using such gear
you're perilously close to the limit of what can reasonably be called
"walking"). It is possible, but unlikely, that you will also be able
to rent boots.

Renting is well worth consideration if you want a tent, say,
for only one week in the year. It is also a useful way of testing
equipment. It makes every kind of sense to rent for a trial run a
tent or pack of a kind you are thinking of buying outright. Sample
rental rates: two-man tent—$7 a weekend, $20 for two weeks;
pack—$5 a weekend, $20 for two weeks.

It would probably be a good thing to take a brief look, here,
at the general considerations to be borne in mind when deciding on

EQUIPMENT FOR A SPECIFIC TRIP.

Most decisions about what to take and what to leave behind will
depend on the answers you get in the early stages of planning when
you ask yourself "Where?" and "When?" and

"For how long?"

The length of the trip makes rather less difference than many
people imagine. The amount of food you can carry is what mostly
determines how long you can operate without some kind of outside help, and even on long journeys I normally plan once-a-week
replenishments. Occasionally I travel self-contained for ten days,
and I suppose I could if necessary stretch it to two weeks. But
even on my rather Spartan menu I would have to carry more than
30 pounds in food alone, and with all the other gear that normally
has to come along—not to mention water in some kinds of country
—that would mean a prohibitively heavy load. (For replenishment

methods—by outposts of civilization, caches, airdrops, etc.—see pages 389–98.)

As far as equipment is concerned, then, even a very long journey boils down in essentials to a string of one- or two-week trips. Besides replenishable items, all you have to decide is whether you'll be aching too badly before the end for a few extra comforts. A toothbrush, a paperback book and even camp footwear may be luxuries on a weekend outing, but I imagine most people would think twice about going out for two weeks without them.

What does make a difference is that the longer the trip the greater the uncertainties about weather; but here we begin to ease over into

"Where?" and "When?"

The two questions are essentially inseparable. Terrain, considered apart from its weather, makes surprisingly little difference to what you need carry. The prospect of sleeping on rock or of crossing a big river may prompt you to take an air mattress, as opposed to an insulating pad for snow, or nothing at all for sand (pages 241–9). In cliff country you may elect to take along a climbing rope, even when on your own (page 355). Glaciers or hard snow may suggest ice ax and crampons (page 54). But that is about all. And snow and ice, in any case, come close to being "weather."

In the end it is weather that governs most of the decisions about clothing and shelter. And weather is not simply a matter of asking, "Where?" and answering, "Desert," "Rainforest," or "Alpine meadows." You must immediately ask, "When?" And from the answer you must be able to draw accurate conclusions.

In almost any kind of country, the gulf between June and January is so obvious that your planning allows for it automatically. But the difference between, say, September and October is not always so clear—and it may matter a lot. The most convenient source of accurate information that I know is the series of booklets issued by the U.S. National Climatic Center under the title *Climatic Survey of the United States—Supplement for 1951 Through 1960*. Each booklet covers one state (exceptions: one booklet each for New England, Maryland–Delaware, Hawaii and the Pacific area, and Puerto Rico–Virgin Islands–West Indies). For every weather station with records for more than five years, the summaries list monthly figures for total precipitation, snowfall, and temperature (mean, mean maximum, mean minimum, highest, lowest, and mean number of days with readings below freezing and above 90° F.). Where records exist prior to 1951, averages are given. An index locates each station on a sketch map and gives its latitude and longitude and elevation. These booklets are available, at prices ranging from $.25 to $1 from The National Climatic Center, Federal Building, Asheville, North Carolina 28801. (Booklets periodically go out of print, but Xeroxes are then available at about twenty times booklet cost. A new series, for 1961–70, is in the works, with reported "drastic improvements.") From the same source you can get a lot more weather literature, including *Climates of the States* ($.10–$.60), that offer some non-essential but possibly useful information. Promised soon: a precipitation report for several stations along the Appalachian Trail.

In Canada, the equivalents to the U.S. *Climatic Survey* booklets are *Temperature and Precipitation Tables* (one booklet each for British Columbia, Yukon and the Northwest Territories, Ontario, Quebec, and the Atlantic Provinces [$.50 each] and for the Prairie Provinces [$1]) that give roughly the same information but unfortunately include no maps for identification of the weather stations. The booklets are available from the Assistant Deputy Minister, Atmospheric Environment Service, 4905 Dufferin Street, Downsview, Ontario M3H 5T4 (checks payable to the Receiver General of Canada). From the same gentlemen you can get two volumes covering all Canada for 1941–70: *Temperature Normals* ($1.50) and *Precipitation Normals* ($2). Also a free list of *Selected Publications in Climatology* that summarizes many local and general information sources.

Monthly figures can never tell the whole story, but these booklets (or at least the U.S. ones, which I use regularly) can be a great help in planning a trip. In deciding what night shelter you need, it may be critical to know that the lowland valley you intend to wander through averages only 0.10 inches of rain in September (20-year high: 0.95 inches), but 1.40 inches in October (high: 6.04 inches). And decisions about what sleeping bag and clothing to take on a mountain trip will come more easily once you know that a weather station 8390 feet above sea level on the eastern escarpment of the 14,000-foot range you want to explore has over the past thirty years averaged a mean daily minimum of 39° F. in September (record low 19°) but 31° in October (low, 9°); by applying the rough but fairly serviceable rule that "temperature falls three degrees for every 1000-foot elevation increase," you can make an educated guess at how cold the nights are going to be up near the peaks. Remember, though, that weather is much more than just temperature. See especially "windchill" chart, page 414.

A wise precaution before any trip that will last a weekend or longer is to check on the five-day forecast for the area. The weatherman at my nearest international airport is always amiable, often right. A similar public service is available in many areas. Look in the telephone book under "U.S. Government, Department of Commerce, National Weather Service."

But the finest insurance of all is to have the right friends. Or, to be more exact, the right friend. I have one who is not only a geographer with a passion for weather lore but also a walking computer programmed with weather statistics for all the western United States and half the rest of the world. I try to phone him before I go on even short trips to unfamiliar country. "The Palisades in early September?" he says. "Even close to the peaks you shouldn't get night temperatures much below twenty. And you could hardly choose a time of year with less danger of a storm. The first heavy ones don't usually hit until early November, though in 1959 they had a bad one in mid-September. Keep an eye on the wind, that's all. If you get a strong or moderate wind from the south, be on the lookout for trouble." By the time he has finished, I am all primed and ready to go.

Unless you have the only infallible memory on record, you ought to have a couple of copies of a

Check list of gear.

It should be a full list, covering all kinds of trips, in all kinds of terrain, at all times of year. On any particular occasion, you just ignore what you don't want to take along.

Eventually, everyone should evolve his own list. But many local and national hiking organizations (see Appendix III) are happy to supply beginners with suggestions. So are some commercial firms. But don't be misled by the skimpier lists into imagining that you can really get away in comfort and safety with ultralight loads. Appendix I of this book (page 433) is a very full list that might be a useful starter. But as soon as experience permits, draft your own list.

I'm afraid I have no advice to offer on what to do when you lose your list—especially if, as will very likely happen, you simply can't lay hands on the spare copy you filed away in an infallibly safe place.

FURTHER PLANNING

Unless you are fit—fit for backpacking, that is—you should, at least as early as you start worrying about equipment for a trip, worry like hell about

Getting in shape.

I repeat that the only real way to get used to heavy loads is to pack heavy loads—though what you mean by "heavy" will depend on your experience, ambition, frame, muscles and temperament. I try to keep in something not too far removed from backpacking shape by occasionally loading my pack with anything convenient and heavy, and heading for a nearby, undeveloped, hilly park. I certainly try to fit in one or two practice hikes in the week or two before any long wilderness trip. Sometimes I even succeed. Whenever possible, I make the exercise seem less hideously Spartan by stowing lunch in the pack and eating it on a suitable peak, or by adding typewriter and papers and setting up temporary office under a tree. Or I may carry the pack on one of the walks I regularly take in order to think, feel, sweat or whatever (page 3). As far as the exercise goes, I find that it makes no difference— well, not too much difference—whether I walk in daylight or darkness.

Even if your regimen does not permit such solutions, make every effort to carry the pack as often as you can in the week or two before you head for wilderness. Details of distance and speed are your affair, but take it easy at first and increase the dose until at the end you are pushing sweaty hard. If possible, walk at least part of the time on rough surfaces and up hills. Up steep hills. Not everyone, of course, has the right kind of terrain handy, but at a pinch, anywhere will do. The less self-conscious you are, the freer, that's all. You may blench at the thought of pounding up Main Street with a 40-pound pack (all those damned traffic lights would wreck your rhythm anyway), but, pray, what are city parks for?

If the pressures of time, location, family and *amour propre* combine to rule out fully laden practice hikes, attack the problem piecemeal. Your prime targets are: feet, legs, lungs, shoulders, hips, skin—and perhaps stomach.

For feet, see pages 43 ("Breaking in new boots") and 57 ("Getting your feet ready").

Legs are best conditioned by walking, jogging or running. Especially running. And especially up hills. For those with limited time at their disposal, running is almost certainly the answer. I suspect that a not inconsiderable number of those pent-up citizens who pant around Central Park Reservoir at their various rates and gaits may be preparing for a week or weekend along the Appalachian Trail. I know at least one who often is. Frankly, I find a much more pleasurable, though possibly less effective, regimen is tennis —singles, not doubles—played often and earnestly.

The finest conditioner for your lungs—probably even better than carrying loads—is, once again, running, especially up hills, up steep hills.

Because all the weight of a pack used to hang from the shoulders, people still connect backpacking with "sore shoulders." There is a certain residual truth in the idea: even a modern pack-frame, properly adjusted, can leave unready shoulders a mite stiff. But with the waistbelt that is the crux of today's packframe (page 71) it is on your hips that the real load bears. And, brother, does it bear! I have a sumptuously padded belt and I'm fairly often in harness, but I still find, on the second morning of most trips with heavy loads, that I wince as I cinch the belt tight—the way it must be cinched—on hip muscles still complaining about yesterday. And on that second morning, if not earlier, any hips that have never undergone the waistbelt trauma under a heavy load, or have not done so for a long time, are just about guaranteed, I hereby warn, to complain fortissimo. Unfortunately, there is no way I know of to prepare shoulders and hips for a load except—wait for it—a load.

Even if your skin, like mine, is reasonably sun tolerant, don't overlook the sunburn danger, particularly if you are going up high —and if your skin happens to be going-on-black, don't kid yourself you're immune. A severely peeled nose can be painful. A raw red back or shoulders can bring the whole outfit to a screeching halt. Ditto habitually shod feet exposed too long around sun-drenched camps. So in the days and weeks before you leave for desert or seashore or mountains or almost any place else, expose yourself to the sun as often and as flagrantly as you can. If you expect to walk stripped to the waist, bask or wander around in a swimsuit or less. Failing sun, I guess one of the plastic-tan machines, whatever they're called, would do the job.

That leaves the stomach. It now appears that you may be able to help yourself get in shape by careful attention to diet in the weeks before you leave. See page 125.

I'm afraid all these strictures end up sounding ferociously

austere. But Arcadian ends can justify Spartan means. Many a beautiful backpacking week or weekend has been ruined at the start by crippled city soft muscles—because their owners had failed to recognize the softness, or at any rate to remedy it.

Harbor no illusions about how much difference fitness makes to backpacking. There is a certain forest to which I retreat from time to time for a two- or three-day think-and-therapy walk. Normally I go when mentally exhausted from work and muscularly out of practice. I start, mostly, in the evening. And I am glad to camp a little way up the first, long hill and then to plod on next morning until I reach a little clearing on the first ridge, where I often stop to brew tea. Sometimes it is time for lunch. But once, in order to think out the shape of a book, I went to my forest only ten days after returning from a week spent pounding up a Sierra Nevada mountain. I was therefore fit and alert. And that purgatorial first hill flattened out in front of me. I stayed in high gear all the way; although I had started as usual only a couple of hours before dark, I reached the ridge clearing in time to choose a campsite by the last of the day's light.

So even if you cannot manage practice hikes, try to do something. Start early. Start easy. Work up. You may find that you actually enjoy what you are doing, especially if you organize the right palliatives (hilltop lunches, subarboreal offices, daydreams, tennis). And when you stride away from roadhead at last, out into Arcady, you will almost certainly discover that getting in shape has made the difference between agony and ecstasy.

Getting in shape for high altitudes

Up high, your body works less efficiently, especially at first—though the point at which mild inefficiency becomes distress may vary widely in different individuals, even in the same individual on different occasions. You'll certainly do better fit than flabby, probably young than old, and also, I'm inclined to think, practiced than unpracticed—though experience may benefit mind more than body. But the important thing, for everyone, is to acclimate.

These days, if I'm going over about 10,000 feet, I take pains to arrange that I cannot get out of the car and immediately, with my body still tuned for sea level, start to walk toward those beckoning peaks. When checking gear at home I leave such details as rebagging food and waxing boots to be done at roadhead. Other things being equal, I choose a roadhead as high as possible. And I tend to drive until late at night to reach it. Sometimes I drive clear through the night. Then I more or less have to sleep up high for at least one night, or part of a night (or day); and by the time

I've slept late and then gotten all my gear ready there is normally only an hour or two of daylight left—just enough for a leisurely walk and then another night's sleep up high before I can even begin serious walking.

If you know you are liable to feel distress at the elevations you'll be tackling, don't underestimate the importance of those two nights' sleep. Time is what the body demands to acclimate to high altitude—primarily to allow the number of red blood corpuscles to increase. So try to give it that time. Not everyone will want or even be able to apply my particular built-in brakes at roadhead, but try to devise your own version. If time and terrain permit, it is naturally better to start low and let the body adjust slowly, as you gain elevation. But the slope must be reasonable or the pace slow, or both.*

The body does most of its adjusting to a sudden altitude change in the first three days. Some people need longer. And the red blood cells take 10 days or more to adjust completely. So unless you are one of the ultra-hearty bunch that gets over the change in 24 or 48 hours, plan to take it easy for at least the first three days. And try to keep some kind of grip on your plan. If you've never been high before, pay particular attention to this pearl of wisdom. I know one family that on its first Sierra backpack trip ignored warnings and tried too much, too high and too early, so that everyone suffered headaches and the other malaises of "mountain sickness" and came down vowing never to set pack on back again. Even when you ought to know better you can still do stupid things. Only a few years ago, after sleeping one night at a 9000-foot roadhead and a second night just above it, I pushed too hard on the third day, with a very heavy load, and was pretty tired by the time I camped at dusk on a 13,000-foot peak. That night, for the only time in my life, so far, altitude ruined my sleep. All night I kept coming awake to find myself gasping for breath. It was not pleasant. And as soon as dawn broke I betook my shaken self down a talus slope that ended at 10,000 feet. There I camped. All day I sat. Next morning I felt fine. For the rest of that week—walking along a ridge, camping twice at 13,000 feet, only once below 12,000—I experienced no further distress. I had learned, vividly, what I had long known in a general way: for the first three days up high, you take things easy.

Even after those first days, you still take things much easier

* Dr. Fred T. Darvill, in the latest edition of his booklet *Mountaineering Medicine* (p. 353, this book), says that "it is now generally accepted that Diamox is of benefit in the prevention of acute mountain sickness" and suggests that in certain cases the drug might be taken prophylactically, "if adequate time for acclimatization is not available."

than at sea level. But that is a walking rather than an acclimating matter, so see page 66.

Be prepared, by the way, for your body to make readjustments when you return quickly, as you often will, to sea level or thereabouts. For two or three days you may feel decidedly sleepy.

The planning question that seems to haunt almost all inexperienced hikers is

"How far can I expect to walk in a day?"

For most kinds of walking, the question is wrongly put. Except along flat, straight roads, miles are just about meaningless. Hours are what count.

Naturally, there is a connection—of sorts. I have only once checked my speed with any accuracy, and that was more or less by accident. It was during my summer-long walk up California. One afternoon I followed the Atchison, Topeka and Santa Fe for nine arrow-like miles into the desert town of Needles. It so happened that I began at a mileage post, and I checked the time and jotted it down on my map. I traveled at my normal speed, and I recall no difficulty about stepping on ties (as so often happens when you follow a railroad track), so it must have been straightforward walking on a well-banked grade. I took a 10-minute halt at the end of the first hour; and exactly 1 hour and 55 minutes after starting I passed the six-mile mark. I would guess that this 3-miles-per-roughly-50-minutes-of-actual-walking is about my norm on a good level surface with a pack that weighs, as mine probably did that day, around 40 pounds. In other words, 7 hours of *actual walking* are roughly the equivalent of a 20-mile day on the flat, under easy walking conditions.

But cross-country you will rarely come close to 20 genuine miles in 7 hours. Even on trails, 2 miles an hour is good going. Over really rough country the average can fall below half a mile. The nonsense that hikers commonly talk about mountain miles walked in one day is only equaled, I think, by the drivel they talk about loads.

But if you now ask the amended question, "How many hours can I expect to walk in a day?" it remains difficult to give a straightforward answer. The thing is seamed with variables. On any given day—provided you are well rested and not concerned with how you will feel next morning—you can, if you are fit and very powerfully motivated, probably keep going most of the twenty-four. But what really matters in most cases is what you are likely to keep up, fully laden, day after day. Even a rough estimate of this figure demands not so much a grasp of arithmetic as an understanding of human frailty. I have published elsewhere a table representing a typical day's walking on the desert half of my California trip—a day on which, beset with all the normal and fascinating temptations of walking, I pushed tolerably hard, though not even close to my limit. Mildly amended to fit more general conditions, that table may help explain the difficulties of computation:

	Hours	*Minutes*
Walking, including ten-minute halts every hour	7	
Extension of half the ten-minute halts to twenty minutes because of sights, sounds, smells, ruminations and inertia		30
Compulsive dallying for photography and general admiration of the passing scene—4²⁄₇ minutes in every hour		30
Photography, once a day, of a difficult and utterly irresistible object (this will seem a gross overestimate to non-photographers, an absurd underestimate to the initiated)	1	
Conversations with mountain men, desert rats, eager beavers or even bighorn sheep	1	
Cooking and eating four meals, including tea	3	30
Camp chores		30
Orthodox business of wilderness traveler: rapt contemplation of nature and/or navel		30
Evaporated time, quite unaccountable for		30
Sleep, including catnaps	8	59
Reading, fishing, additional rest, elevated thinking, unmentionable items, and general sloth		1
Total	24	

Always, before you walk out into any kind of country, whether for a few hours or for several weeks,

Let some responsible person know where you're going and when you'll be back.

This registration should be automatic. It is not merely a question of your own safety. If you do not return, people will eventually come out to look for you; and if they have nothing to go on except the place your car was parked and perhaps the vague recollections of someone you happened to chat with, they will waste a great deal of time searching in useless places. And they may expose themselves to unnecessary dangers—on the ground and in the air.

In national or state parks and forests, leave full information with a ranger. In other places, cast about until you find someone that strikes you as thoroughly reliable (your life may depend on his reliability). If possible, leave a map marked with your proposed route. Above all, state a date and hour by which you will return— or will emerge elsewhere and immediately check back by phone. Let it be clearly understood that if you have not reported back by the time specified, then you are in trouble. In fixing the deadline, allow yourself a little leeway. And, once you've fixed it, make hell-and-high-water sure you meet it. I repeat: make hell-and-high-water sure you meet it.

Foundations

The foundations of the house on your back are your feet and their footwear, and the cornerstone is a good pair of

BOOTS.

Although some "serious" hikers own two or more pairs of boots, to meet different conditions, one pair should be enough to fill most people's walking needs. But they must be carefully chosen.

First, they must be stout enough to protect and support your feet with the heaviest load you expect to carry. Your feet are used to supporting your full bodyweight, and provided you do not add much to it they will, once hardened by practice, carry you comfortably over long distances even on thin soles and uppers. Soles for this unladen kind of walking, though they must be stouter than those of city shoes, need be no more than $\frac{5}{16}$ inch thick. The uppers can be thin leather, suede, or even canvas. For my money, the uppers should protect and support the ankles, but there are some walkers who go in for oxfords. A fair number, including a few backpackers, manage to cover long distances in basketball or even tennis shoes. They're welcome.

As soon as you carry a pack and so add appreciably to the burden on your feet, they need extra protection and support. Remember that you may be increasing their normal load by a third. For cushioning effect as well as for durability and traction, by far the most popular soles today are heavily lugged rubber-and-synthetic compound types such as the Vibram and Galibier. The $\frac{1}{2}$-inch thickness is probably best for general use. (This measurement is of the sole itself, with lugs; it does not include the softer mid-sole embodied in most good hiking boots, which helps the cushioning effect.) If you expect to do any rock climbing or to operate a great deal in snow, thicker soles might be an advantage —for rigidity in rock climbing, insulation on snow.

Vibram soles come in two types: the Roccia is a relatively thin, soft sole, fine for lightweight walking boots; the Montagna is thicker,

34

harder and less flexible, and will take rougher wear. These names are always stamped on the sole's Vibram label. Labels may be yellow or black: yellow means a high-carbon sole of the finest quality; black indicates a lower carbon content, but still a very good sole. Vibram soles are now made under license in Switzerland and the United States. A few years back, American-made Vibram soles were said to wear out faster than their European counterparts (as reported in earlier printings of this book) but they now seem to be of comparable quality. Every article imported into the United States must bear an imprint stating country of origin, and you will find it somewhere on the sole, though not necessarily on the Vibram label. The U.S.-made version that is sold here may show no country of origin. The British Commando, once fairly popular, no longer seems to be generally available in the United States. The French Galibier is comparable to the best Vibram. (For the pedantic use of "Vibram soles," vice the widely used "Vibrams," please blame the U.S. makers, who insist. Really!)

Some lightweight, less expensive boots now have molded soles, bonded direct to leather uppers. Because there are no stitches around the welt—the line along which sole and uppers meet, the line along which water is most liable to infiltrate a boot—this system has theoretical advantages. But aside from residual doubts about the effectiveness of the bonding, there is the difficulty that worn soles are at present not replaceable. Worse still, neither are heels, which form a single unit with the soles. So it seems doubtful whether bonded soles will ever become worthwhile on high-quality boots, which should outlast several soles and heels.

Turned-in welt　　　　　　　　**Standard (or Goodyear) welt**

The standard (or Goodyear) welt has exposed stitching. It lies along a narrow ledge that encircles the boot where sole joins uppers—a ledge that might have been designed to collect moisture and dirt. That is one reason the welt is a danger point: unless proper precautions are taken—and sometimes even then—water seeps into socks and feet; and dirt and other abrasives can play havoc with the stitching. At least one bootmaker, Vasque, sells a special device for applying epoxy to exposed welt-stitching. And some good boots designed for wet conditions have a strip of leather known as a storm welt sewn in along the junction line. Look, and ye shall find.

There is another kind of welt that some people consider better. Count me in—I've used it for ten years now, on Pivetta boots, with zero travail. In this welt, the uppers are turned inward and then sewn to the sole. Stitches are therefore protected from abrasion. And the boot has no ledge to collect water and dirt. Lacking a ledge, the sole ends almost flush with the uppers, is less flexible at the edges, and therefore gives you better purchase for rock climbing—and for the kind of scrambling you're sure to do from time to time in cross-country walking. Unfortunately, this in-turned kind of welt cannot be made by a fully mechanized process and is therefore found only on certain rather more expensive boots, including, for example, some made by Fabiano and Vasque.

Uppers must be stout enough to support foot muscles that are being strained by an abnormal load, and to afford adequate protection. But they must be pliant enough to allow feet to bulge outward slightly when under a heavy load. They must also, when properly treated (page 44), be very close to waterproof.

There is still no substitute for good leather uppers—smooth-finish, rough-out or suede. Smooth-finish boots come with the smooth, outside-of-the-animal surface facing outward. Rough-outs have the leather reversed. Suede is generally the inside half of a split hide; it therefore has two rough sides—and has been further roughened by an abrading machine.

The first edition of this book stated: "Virtually all really high-quality boots have smooth-side-out uppers." Even in 1968 that may have been a questionable statement. Today it is nonsense: the majority of hiking boots now seem to come with rough-out uppers. Untreated, they are said to be more waterproof than smooth-finish boots. Treated, smooth-finish uppers may seal a shade better; but they leave the thin "skin" of the hide—which forms the leather's most effective water barrier—highly susceptible to rupture from normal wear and tear. The surface of rough-outs is less tough, but scuff marks or even shallow cuts matter very little because the vital "skin" remains protected, way inside. Rough-outs, assert some pundits, are therefore better. Other pundits counterassert, fiercely. In the end, what seems to count is the quality of the leather. Above all, it should be "full grain" (i.e., unsplit, whole, intact). Because most of today's high-quality boots are lined, checking for full grain is difficult. Like it or not, you mostly have to rely on the integrity of maker and retailer.

Suede boots are relatively inexpensive, light, and cool to wear. But the porosity that makes them cool also makes them difficult to waterproof. They are useful for dry, not-too-rugged use—and for certain kinds of rock climbing.

The fewer seams in the uppers, the more rugged the boot (because it is at the seams that most boots first show wear). A single-seamed boot is the strongest kind—and also, because it demands the very best leather, in large pieces, the most expensive. A many-seamed boot will probably stand up well enough if you keep to trails. If you do much cross-country work, especially on talus, it probably won't.

A thin leather lining increases a boot's warmth and may possibly reduce friction. A thin padding such as foam rubber between uppers and lining makes the boot very easy to break in and comfortable and warm to wear. It also gives your feet extra protection. But there is some danger that in deserts and other fiery places it may make them uncomfortably hot. A Los Angeles firm, Bare/Foot/Gear, makes foam-padded boots with sweat-resistant leather linings and recommends—but does not insist—that you wear them without socks.

In extreme cases, terrain can affect your choice. Jagged volcanic rock or steep talus will soon knock hell out of thin or poor-quality material, both soles and uppers. And tough going like that can also bruise poorly protected feet. So if you expect to cross a lot of really rough country it may be as well to increase stoutness and/or quality a notch all around.

But extra stoutness means extra weight, and that can be critical. It is all too easy to pare away at the ounces that go into your pack and to overlook the boots. Yet the successful 1953 Mount Everest Expedition came to the conclusion that in terms of physical effort one pound on the feet is equivalent to five pounds on the back. As usual, then, you have to compromise. But remember that although it is obviously stupid to wear unnecessarily heavy boots, choosing too light a pair is asking for trouble.

Many people consider that ankle boots—six or seven inches high—are too low. But it seems to me that, except in heavy brush country, taller boots do not add enough protection to warrant the extra weight. They are also hotter—though that means "warmer" in cold weather. Even more seriously, they tend to restrict your calf muscles.

A few boots incorporate gaiterlike structures built onto the tops to seal the gap between boot and sock against snow, pebbles, or even water. These scree collars or snow protectors (they also go by other names) are clearly worth considering if the boots will be used exclusively or even largely under conditions that cry out for such protection. For a less specialized alternative, see "Gaiters," page 292.

The requirements I have outlined do not really restrict you very much. Today's equipment catalogues list and illustrate such an array of boots that studying them can cause severe mental indigestion.

The simplest way out—once you've grasped, roughly, the range of boots available—is to find a store with a salesman you feel you can trust (easier said than done, of course) and tell him what you expect to use the boots for, and also (if that's the way you operate) how much you're prepared to spend. If you plan to walk unladen, and only on civilized surfaces, you can probably skip the store and wear whatever has always been most comfortable for you, from tennis shoes on up. If you'll be carrying only mild loads and sticking to well-manicured trails, look at what the catalogues call "light" or "medium hiking boots," or perhaps "trail boots." For heavy loads, very rough or soggy trails, or cross-country work, consider only those listed as "heavy hiking boots" or something similar. Be careful of "climbing boots." They may or may not be suitable for prolonged walking.

Among boots generally acknowledged as first class are the German Lowa and Bass, the Italian Fabiano and Vasque (formerly Voyageur), and the French Galibier. I'm afraid I can report first-hand on none of them: it is a long time since I wore anything but Italian Pivetta boots. For a decade I have used the heaviest Pivetta, the Eiger, described as "a heavy mountaineering boot." The black, smooth-finish uppers are seven inches high and protect my ankles very adequately. The latest models have a soft, padded cuff designed to reduce the sad, supra-ankle soreness endemic to most boots that are new or have not been worn for some time. The uppers have only one seam—on the inner side of each boot. Nowhere does any stitching go all the way through the boot. The heel—where seams are particularly liable to split—is, except for a small incision for the pull-loop, solid leather. The boot has a hard toe and strong heel counter. A steel shank built into the center sole imparts necessary stiffness. Lacing is through eyelets. The calfskin lining is padded around the ankle section with thin foam rubber. Sole: Vibram Montagna, cemented on; the bond reinforced at heel and toe with brass screws. Welt: turned-in type, and sole trimmed flush with uppers. My size 10 Eigers weighed 5 pounds 12 ounces when new. Present cost: $45.

Now I don't want to suggest that these boots are necessarily "the best" on the market, whatever that might mean. Like most people, I have actually tried very few different kinds. And I came to these by the orthodox route: a combination of chance and whim and experience and personal prejudice, mitigated by a salesman's advice. But I've used successive Eigers in daytime shade temperatures ranging from 20°F. to over 100°F., on snow and sand, in places as different as Grand Canyon and Kilimanjaro. And I'm satisfied. I have yet to come across a pair of boots that looked as though they would prove better for all-around use.

My only possible complaint is that the foam padding perhaps makes them rather hot for desert use; but I do not really have a yardstick by which to measure this factor. The padding certainly makes for greater comfort and for warmth in snow and reduces both the time and trauma involved in breaking in a new pair.

When I described my Eigers in the first edition of this book I did not realize that the only place in the world they are sold is The Ski Hut. The Pivetta line of boots has been developed over the past twenty years by Trailwise (Ski Hut) in conjunction with the Italian maker, working from a modified U.S. marching last, and is not sold in Italy or anywhere else except the United States. Most Pivetta models are now increasingly available at retail stores across the United States, but so few Eigers are made that they are never wholesaled.* Still, I shall let my description stand—because Eigers are the only boots I know cuff to sole; because the important things, anyway, are the factors governing choice; and because boots very similar to Pivettas are now beginning to appear on the U.S. market.

Naturally, special conditions may call for special boots.

Two summers of slogging through trailless tracts of western Vancouver Island convinced me that for cross-country travel in rainforests, where your route often lies over or along slippery fallen tree trunks, and where undergrowth is always snatching at your legs, the only satisfactory footwear is a pair of caulked knee boots. By no means everyone agrees; but then, who would expect them to?

Another summer in the muskeg-and-lake country of Canada's Northwest Territories taught me that in such places you need a stout and roomy pair of leather-topped rubber boots (worn with thick insoles and two pairs of socks). The Maine Hunting Shoe made by L. L. Bean of Freeport, Maine, is the standard, though

* News just in is that a few will in future be wholesaled. But that will push their price up to around $60.

there are others. A generic name for the breed is "Shoepac." Ten-inch boots are probably the most popular, but they come in all heights from 6 to 16 inches. I understand that boots of this type are admirable for much eastern wilderness—the sort of flat, soggy terrain in which old tote roads skirt or even run through spruce and cedar swamps. They're especially good when hiking is largely a means to camping or hunting or fishing, and a day's backpacking may amount to no more than five miles and is unlikely to exceed twelve. In recent years, leather-topped rubber boots have been challenged by rubber boots heavily insulated with fiberglass or some similar material. Opinion seems to be divided. Some people find them unbearably hot.

In certain parts of the country—because of local conditions or innate human conservatism or both—a specific style of boot may remain as traditional as the dialect. You can always ask a reputable dealer about parochial preferences. Of course, there's no law that says you have to take his advice.

In really cold weather—especially at high altitudes—it may be necessary to wear extra-thick boots (a size or two larger than usual, to accommodate more sock). You may even need overboots. Recently, Ocaté and other firms have come up with foam boots ("mukluks") for ultracold conditions. But here we are coming close to the fringe of "just plain walking."

Insoles

Many boots—and especially those with hand-stitched soles (because the stitching may protrude and chafe your feet)—need insoles. In emergencies I have used cardboard cutouts from cereal boxes (they last about six hours), regular foam-rubber insoles of the kind you can pick up at a drugstore (intolerably hot), and makeshift devices fashioned from asbestos gasket sheeting bought at a wayside garage (effective, though they tend to curl). The best material I've tried so far is plain leather, but Dale Vent/O/ Soles ("woven saran—ventilates at each step"; $2.25 a pair from *Walking News,* New York [Appendix II]) look as if they just may have possibilities.

It is probably an advantage to glue the insoles in. If they are left loose, though, you can transfer an old pair, already well molded to the contours of your soles, into a new pair of boots and so cut down appreciably the grief of breaking them in.

Laces and lacing

Braided nylon laces are extremely strong. I have never had one break on me. They do not rot, absorb water, dry out stiff, or become brittle in extreme cold. Unlike leather laces, they are never eaten by mice or their allies. And the newer, flattened kind have largely overcome the annoying tendency of the old, round version to slip out of the top eyelets when your boots are unlaced.

I used to follow tradition and carry a spare pair of laces, but long ago decided to rely on a length of my ubiquitous ⅛-inch nylon cord (page 368).

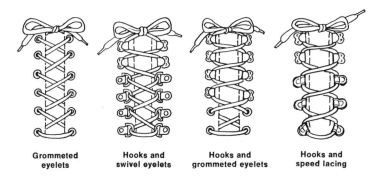

| Grommeted eyelets | Hooks and swivel eyelets | Hooks and grommeted eyelets | Hooks and speed lacing |

There are four distinct systems for lacing boots: grommeted eyelets; swivel eyelets (small D-rings attached by the straight side to clips fixed to the outside of the uppers); open hooks (similarly attached); and "speed-lacing" (closed, tunnel-like hooks through which the laces pass easily and can be tightened, bottom to top, with a single sharp pull). Some boots have speed-lacing or eyelets—grommeted or swivel—partway up, then hooks to the top. And there are other combinations.

Boots with speed-lacing, hooks or swivel eyelets are easier to take off or put on than those with grommeted eyelets, and also lace quicker and more simply. Indeed, if you are wearing big gloves in severe cold, open hooks may be the only practical solution. But under normal conditions I prefer the old-fashinoed and almost indestructible grommeted eyelets. Even if a grommet wears through or works loose, the hole is still usable. Hooks and swivel eyelets, on the other hand, can and do break off and pull loose—leaving you miles from Godknowswhere with a boot that is not only imperfectly laced but may also let water in. What's more, hooks can snag on undergrowth and other boot laces; somehow I can rarely get this danger, which is no doubt very slight, clean out of my mind. Still, grommeted eyelets are now perhaps the least common lace system on hiking boots—a fact that may be not unconnected with their being the most troublesome for manufacturers to install.

Laces should not be drawn too tight in the lower eyelets or hooks: the pressure can block the necessary wiggle-freedom of your toes and may even constrict circulation. But on the vertical part of the boot the laces must be tight enough to prevent your foot from sliding forward under the kind of pressure you generate when walking downhill.

Tall boots should be normally laced up to the ankle, but if the calf section, especially when of soft leather, can be left rather looser, then you get better ventilation and less muscle constriction. A reader suggests using separate laces, top and bottom. Or you can block the transfer of tension from tightly to loosely laced sectors by crisscrossing the laces three or four times at the ankle.

Fitting new boots

Think of yourself as trying to put a glove on your foot. But do not picture a skintight glove. What you need is a boot that fits snugly at the broadest part of the foot (the trick is deciding exactly what "snugly" means, and in the end you have to make your own decision, based on experience) but which leaves one finger's width of free room in front of the toes. You check this toe space by unlacing the boot, standing up without a pack, and pressing forward until your toes meet the end of the boot. If you can just slide a forefinger down into the gap left at the heel, that part of the fit is about right. With the boot laced, you should be able to wriggle your toes fairly freely (the shape of the toe cap is important; for most feet, the broader and squarer the better). But it is vital that, with the boot laced tightly up the vertical part, there is as little movement as possible at the heel, upward or sideways. The difficulty is that new boots are relatively stiff, and that with wear all boots mold themselves to the shape of your feet. You simply have to guess how much change will take place—how much the sides will "give," and how well that stiff-feeling heel will conform to the contours of your particular foot. Cheaper boots tend to alter more than good-quality ones, especially if they are unlined; buy them a little on the tight side. I find that with my Pivettas—presumably because of their lining and foam padding and high-quality leather—a good fit in the store seems to mean a good fit on the mountain.

Do not, by the way, pay too much attention to sizes. Base

your decision on the feel of the boot. If the size is not the same as last time, it doesn't matter a damn. Different boots marked as the same size may vary appreciably.

If you feel confident that the salesman is an experienced backpacker and knows what he is talking about, lean heavily on his advice. Even if you hike like crazy, all year round, you buy new boots only once every few years, and you tend to forget the rules. But the salesman is at it all day and every day. Frankly, I found when I came to write this section that I really couldn't quite remember what I looked for. So I talked to a backpacker-salesman I trusted and—after checking with other sources—have gratefully incorporated most of his testament. All I can say about the way I've managed to apply the rules in the past is that I've only once been dissatisfied with any hiking boots I've bought—and that was probably due to a manufacturing defect. Mind you, it may take me an hour to select the pair I want.

If you live far from any dealer that carries the kind of boot you want, you may have to mail-order. I hear that the best firms are very good at matching outline sketches of feet. Follow their instructions meticulously, that's all—particularly in making the foot sketches. And deal only with reputable people who offer what seems to be an honest guarantee.

Breaking in new boots

All new boots need slow and careful breaking in. Until some of the stiffness has gone and insoles and uppers have begun to conform to the contours of your feet, they are almost sure to be uncomfortable. And they'll be great at generating blisters. I have heard people advise: "Just put your new boots on and soak them in water for a while and then go out and walk. You'll never have any trouble." It sounds like pretty drastic treatment to me, and I have never tried it. (But one experienced mountaineer I know, who had always felt as I do about the soaking theory, once tried it out as a crash program and found that it worked. Perhaps it's relevant, though, that he says he hasn't repeated it.) All I do is take short, easy walks, with little or no load at first, and gradually increase load and distance. At the very beginning, even wearing the boots around the house helps (advantage: most good stores will change a poorly fitting pair that has not been worn outdoors). Naturally, boots should be well waxed as soon as you buy them (page 44).

For a major backpacking expedition—the kind that threatens to wear out a pair of boots—you obviously have to start with new ones. After all, you wouldn't set out on a transcontinental road rally with worn tires. For such expeditions, breaking in the new boots can become a problem. The theory is simple: the boots will take care of themselves during those practice hikes you plan to take for several weeks beforehand in slowly increasing doses that will painlessly harden your feet and muscles. But I have found that in practice the press of administrative arrangements just before the start rises to such a frantic peak that there is no time for any practice hikes worthy of the name. So you start with flabby muscles, soft feet—and stiff boots. And this is no laughing matter. It is not simply that sore feet soon take the joy out of walking. They can make walking impossible. Just before my Grand Canyon trip, while putting out a food cache and at the same time trying rather belatedly to harden my feet and soften a new pair of boots, I attempted too much in a single day, generated a blister, developed an infected heel, and had to postpone the start for a week. Fortunately, I had planned an easy first week's shakedown cruise. But even with an old pair of insoles in the boots, my feet barely carried me through the second critical and much harder week of the trip. I offer no solution to this kind of problem (which can also crop up on shorter journeys), but I suggest that you at least make every effort to allow time for a gentle shakedown cruise at the beginning. As we have seen (page 9) there is an even more important reason for such an arrangement. See also page 57.

Care of boots

Leather uppers must be conditioned with wax or oil. But which conditioners should be used and which avoided on what kinds of leather is something that dissolves the experts into raucous disagreement. As far as I can make out, the tentative current gospel reads: on "dry-tanned" leather (which forms the uppers on most hiking boots), use wax and/or silicone, *but never use oil or grease;* on oil-tanned leather (which is normally softer and more flexible, as on the upperworks of many calf-length boots), use oil or grease. Moral: when you buy new boots, make sure you know what treatment they demand.

For summer use, the ideal is to apply the conditioner lightly so that your feet can "breathe" through leather that will be reasonably water-repellent. In snow or wet, condition heavily. The leather will become waterproof; but it cannot then "breathe." That's the theory, anyway. Frankly, I find that in hot weather I need plenty of conditioner to keep the bloody boots soft.

For many years I used Kiwi neutral wax on my Pivettas but

found that they tended to dry out too fast on long journeys, even though I applied an average of one 2½-ounce can a week. Then I switched to Sno-Seal, a wax and silicone mixture, and found that it kept the leather supple for very much longer. Recently I have begun using Leath-R-Seal, a wax and shellac combination with several apparent advantages: it is reputed to penetrate the leather more deeply than Sno-Seal; it is apparently an effective seam-sealer; it does not weaken the cement that bonds the various layers of the soles (as the solvent in certain silicone mixtures can do); and it can be applied cold. It is the cold application that really attracts me. You are supposed to apply Sno-Seal "over direct heat," and I find it a damned nuisance. Even at home, let alone in the field, the chore tends to get put off. There is also some danger of "cooking" your boots (though one reader suggests heating the Sno-Seal instead of the boots, spooning or brushing it on, then standing the boots in direct sunlight for two or three hours).*

Whenever your boots show the slightest sign of drying out—and also when you get home after a trip of any magnitude—clean and dry them and rub the chosen dressing well into the leather with fingers or a rag, particularly at seams and welts. With silicone and oil, avoid the sole. Sample dressings: Sno-Seal—$.85 per 8-ounce can, $.55 per 4-ounce can; Leath-R-Seal—$1.40 per 5½-fluid-ounce bottle (heavy and breakable, unfortunately, and with a fragile plastic cap); Herbert's Leather Dressing (neat's-foot oil)—$.40 per 8-ounce can.

If your boots get thoroughly wet, dry them slowly. Packing loosely with newspaper or toilet paper helps absorb internal moisture. Never put wet boots close to a fire: the soles may curl up and the leather lose some of its life. Somebody once gave me a pair of cunning devices for preventing wet soles from curling. Called "stretchers," they're made of light alloy and plastic-covered cord, and are designed to apply tension that counteracts the tendency of drying soles to curl toward their uppers. Unfortunately, you cannot use them on boots that, like my Pivettas, have turned-in welts and therefore no ledge.

The interiors of boots left standing for any length of time may sprout a green mold. I have yet to try, as a reader suggests, prophylactic spraying with a fungicide powder (B.F.I., Quinsana, Desenex), but it sounds like a far from sterile idea.

---

* Now, the newest Sno-Seal has been "improved with silicones," and you no longer need heat your boots, only "keep warm" until the Sno-Seal is fully absorbed.

SOCKS

The best sock thickness depends on whether you tend to suffer from hot feet, cold feet, tender feet, or none of these afflictions. In theory, it would seem obvious to put on a thicker pair of socks in cold weather. But if your boots fit perfectly with the socks you normally wear they will pinch with a thicker pair. You are left with two alternatives: buying a second pair of boots, or getting by with the usual socks. (If conditions are severe enough to justify overboots, you probably need two pairs of thick socks and big boots anyway.) I normally wear only one pair of socks at a time, but many people, perhaps even a majority of backpackers, find that two pairs—the thinner ones inside—help reduce friction between feet and boots.

On almost every count—resilience, sweat absorption, insulation, and general comfort—wool is the material. But nylon reinforcement—a small percentage throughout, with a boost at heels and toes—increases durability without detracting appreciably from the other qualities. At least, this is what I believed for many years. And I wore medium-weight wool socks (4 ounces) that met these requirements and were also shrink resistant. Then these socks ceased to be available. As a stopgap, and also to give a trial to a new product, I turned with some skepticism to Wick-Dry (4½ ounces; $2.60). These socks have two layers. The inner layer of moisture-repellent orlon and nylon is designed to "wick" perspiration to the outer layer of moisture-absorbing yarn (the socks are 10 percent cotton), where it evaporates. The first trials turned out to be less than stringent, but the new socks seemed about as efficient as the old ones. So I went on using them. They've not yet had a really tough test under fierce desert conditions or in temperatures below about 20° F., and I retain a sort of residual skepticism; but on the whole I still don't seem to find any marked difference from wool. I guess I ought to have something firmer to report on such a fundamental matter. At this point, though, I'm afraid I don't.*

Whatever socks I'm wearing, I want them long enough to turn down over ankle boots when I'm wearing shorts—which is

---

* I've now gone back to wool—to the gray "Norwegian boot socks" that are almost standard western hikers' wear (4½ ounces; $3.50 a pair). Funny thing, though: I'm damned if I can produce any stunningly convincing reasons for my reconversion. I needed a new pair of boots and had to decide what thickness sock I'd fit them with, that's all. Sorry.

almost always. An ordinary rubber band keeps stones and dirt from falling down between socks and ankle.

I carry three pairs of socks at a time. The two spare pairs travel in the flap pocket of the pack—or if it lacks such a pocket, in some other easily accessible place. In very hot weather I often change socks every hour and tie the sweat-drenched pair on top of the pack to dry. A 3-foot length of nylon cord knotted to the upper crossbar of the packframe secures the tops of these socks with a clove hitch; and tucking the socks under the pack's closure strings prevents them from slipping off to one side. (Well, usually prevents.) When not in use, the cord tucks down behind the nylon-mesh back support (illustration, page 69). In cooler country I may wear the same socks all day, or almost all day, but any dirty pairs hang purifying on top of the pack. If a dirty pair have to go inside the pack for any reason (such as rain or snatching tree branches or recently washed socks that monopolize the outside dryer) I segregate them hygienically in a plastic bag.

A pair of socks no doubt lasts longer for some people than for others. In the six months and thousand-plus map-miles of my California trip (many more on the ground) I wore out nine pairs.

Care of socks

Woolen socks must be washed carefully. Some backpackers carry packages of Woolite, specially made for washing wool in cold water. But you eliminate one item and do almost as good a job if you use soap, which may be in your toilet gear anyway. Avoid detergent; it removes vital oils from the wool. Trak (page 347) is safe for wool, and a most convenient maid-of-all-work. But whatever you use, rinse the socks thoroughly. An advantage of Wick-Dry socks is that you need exercise less care.

If no washing agent is available, plain rinsing out of dirty socks, even in cold water, does a surprising lot of good.

Strictly speaking, socks should be dried away from the sun and lying flat rather than hanging, but even with wool I have often broken both rules without apparent penalty. I find, in any case, that drying out socks on top of the pack as I walk is often the only way I get to dry them out at all. (Warning: wet socks are heavy, and when spread out to dry on a rock will stay put in moderate winds; but as they dry out, so the tendency to flight increases. Solution: always hobble them with rocks, full canteens, or what have you.)

Try to wash your socks fairly often. In hot weather that may mean once a day. Dirty socks insulate poorly, absorb little sweat, and because they are no longer soft and resilient can quickly cause abrasions.

The only time I wore a hole in a sock while out and away, I patched it with a small foam-rubber disk cut from a sheet of "moleskin" (page 60). The repair turned out to be astonishingly effective.

CAMP FOOTWEAR

Wearing boots around camp is usually a nuisance, can often be uncomfortable, and may even amount to a serious inefficiency. (Toward the end of my first week's traveling in Grand Canyon my feet became so sore that I rested a day and a half beside a spring. Because I had moccasins, which slip off and on very easily, I was able to expose my feet almost continually to the air and never to the painful pressures of boots. If I had had to wear the boots for the many small chores that always need doing around camp, I am sure my feet would not have recovered as quickly as they did.)

Unless you feel confident that conditions will allow you to go barefoot in camp—and they almost never will—the only answer is to carry lightweight campwear.

I have found nothing to equal moccasins with an external composition sole about ¼ inch thick—not the hard and slippery kind but a softer, lighter, off-crepe type that grips almost any surface, wet or dry. Such soles add little weight but keep out thorns and blunt the cutting—and bruising—edge of almost any stone. They wear well too. My last pair died only after a long career culminating in months of hard use in Africa, day after day, driving and around camp. I'm finding it difficult to buy a replacement pair light and nonslip enough but I'll keep trying. Those old moccasins were ideal. Among other things, I could, by adjusting the laces, vary their fit: loose for slipping on and off sore feet in camp; firm and safe if the feet were in good fettle and took me exploring up a nearby rockface.*

If the weight problem becomes acute, consider light unsoled moccasins (average 9 ounces; $7). But in stony country don't expect too much from the unprotected underleather. The pair I carried in Grand Canyon just about lasted out the two months.

When your feet are really sore, even camp moccasins can feel

* Later: just found a pair—Minnetonka Buffalo Moccasins (17 ounces; $10).

uncomfortable, particularly if they're new. One solution: pad toes and heels with toilet paper.

For down booties, see page 295.

AIDS AND ATTACHMENTS
Walking staff

Although the vast majority of walkers never even think of using a walking staff, I unhesitatingly include it among the foundations of the house that travels on my back. I take my staff along almost as automatically as I take my pack. For many years now it has been a third leg to me—and much more besides.

On smooth surfaces the staff helps maintain an easy rhythm to my walking and gives me something to lean on when I stop to stand and stare. Over rough going of any kind, from tussocky grass to pockety rock, and also in a high wind, it converts me when I am heavily laden from an insecure biped into a confident triped. It does the same only more so when I have to scramble across a chasm or a big boulder or a mildly obstructive stretch of rock and keep reaching out sideways for a balancing aid or backwards for that little extra push up and over. And it does the same thing, even more critically and consistently, when I cross a steep, loose slope of talus or gravel or dirt, or wade a fast-flowing creek, or cross it on a log. In marshland or on precarious rock or snow, and in failing light or darkness anywhere, it tests doubtful footing ahead. It reconnoiters bushes or crevices that I suspect might harbor a rattlesnake. After rain, it knocks water off leaves that hang wetly across the trail. It often acts as the indispensable upright needed to rig a shelter from rain or sun with fly sheet (page 226) or groundsheet or poncho (pages 236 and 237). Occasionally, held down by a couple of heavy stones, it serves as ground anchor for the windward side of such a shelter (illustration, page 238—in lieu of canteen). It has performed successfully as a fishing rod. It has acted as a marked measuring stick to be checked later, when a rule is available, for the exact length of fish, rattlesnakes, and other dead animals. It forms a rough but very ready monopod for steadying binoculars if my hands are shaking from exertion, or for a camera if I need to shoot with a shutter speed slower than 1/60 second. And day in and day out, at almost every halt, it props up my pack and gives me a soft and stable backrest (page 92). (As I am lazy enough to believe that being able to relax against a soft backrest for even a ten-minute halt is no minor matter, I am almost inclined to regard this function of my staff as one of its most vital.) Although I had never really considered the matter until this minute, I think the staff also gives me a false but subconsciously comforting feeling that I am not after all completely defenseless against attack by such enemies as snakes, bears and men.

The staff still surprises and pleases me from time to time by accomplishing new and unexpected chores. I can pluck at least three from recent memories. Once, I decided halfway up a short rockface that it was unclimbable with the heavy pack on my back. I slipped the pack off and held it with knee pressure in a sloping crevice and took a short length of nylon cord from an outside pocket and tied it to the head of the staff and then to the packframe. Then I jammed the foot of the staff on a convenient ledge and angled its head up against the bottom of the pack so that it held there without my knee and thereby freed the knee and the rest of me for the short and relatively simple climb (unencumbered) to the top of the rockface—where I had a safe stance from which to reach down without difficulty and pull up the pack and attached staff. One cool and windy afternoon, when I was booted and fully clothed, the staff rescued, with about an inch to spare, an empty plastic water canteen that the wind had blown into a river no less wet than any other river and a good deal bigger and stronger than most. And one night when I was camped in a cave I tied the staff onto the nylon cord from which my candle lantern (page 318) was suspended—and thereby furnished myself with a convenient handle by which I could, without moving my lazy butt an inch, adjust the candle lantern into the various specific positions I wanted it for cooking, writing notes, or contemplating cave or universe.

The staff I used until recently was nothing much to look at: ordinary stout bamboo with an average diameter of 1⅜ inches—just right for a firm but comfortable grip.* After years of use, small cracks developed up and down its whole length, some of them decidedly threatening. Mostly, they stopped when they came to a knot mark, and the general structure remained sound. But each

---

* I don't know what kind of bamboo it is, but the man who gave it to me —near the start of my California walk, beside the Colorado River—said he had cut it on his own property near Los Angeles.

When I told him that I wanted the bamboo to replace a yucca staff I had broken in killing a rattlesnake he said, "Well, I hope you get a rattler with it. One of them killed my brother." But one of the few things the staff has never done is to kill a rattlesnake—at first because I did not want to risk breaking it or getting venom on it; and soon because, growing up, I came to realize that there is no reason except fear for killing rattlesnakes that live in places where they are unlikely to meet people (pp. 399 and 407).

end section had split so severely that, left to itself, it would flap like an empty banana skin, and over the years I bandaged the wounds with several rings of Rip stop tape (page 363.) Yet I have to confess that when I looked at the bamboo's weatherbeaten surface, and especially at the brown patina that had formed around the second knot, where my hand usually gripped, I felt sad at the thought that it would not last forever. In other words, I had come to regard the staff with a warm affection. I suppose some people would call it a soggy sentimentality.

But a dozen years of grinding toil wore away the foot of the staff, inch by inch, until at last it measured only 3 feet 10 inches. Reluctantly, I retired it. Its replacement, also bamboo, is 5 feet long—the original length of the old one—and weighs 15½ ounces. But it has already split rather severely, and although a couple of years' use have now pounded the beginnings of character into its shiny newness it has not really begun to command the affection I felt for the old one.

A possible but vanishing source of unimproved bamboo is your friendly neighborhood rug store, where they may still use bamboo poles instead of cardboard rolls as the inner cores of rolled carpeting.

I gather that my staff fixation has generated a bemused merriment among many readers of the first edition. But by no means among all of them. Two were even kind enough to send me staffs. One was the replacement bamboo. The other is an elegant aluminum job, complete with rubber foot and removable knurled top that screws onto a fitting the same size as the screw fitting of a camera tripod, thereby making the staff an instant monopod. Although I can all too easily imagine the metal becoming too hot and also too cold for comfort, the staff has proved entirely efficient. Yet I find I do not use it often: it is too mechanical-looking, somehow, for the back country. (Yes, pack-frames are also aluminum and shiny. I know, I know. But still . . .)

Several readers have sent stavic suggestions. A New Yorker writes that he bought from Honda Associates (485 Fifth Avenue —"Your Judo-Karate Service Center") an *aikido bo*, or wooden defense stick (48 inches; 18 ounces; $6. 60 inches; 27 ounces; $7). The kind of wood seems uncertain, but the 5-foot model, well treated with linseed oil, has given good service. It apparently pays, though, to check very carefully that a new *bo* is not warped.*

---

* A letter I received from Vermont deserves special mention for more than its data on how to make an ultrastrong staff. The staff is interesting enough: a 6-foot bamboo, about 1¼ inches in diameter, wrapped spirally with a single

Several outdoor suppliers now list staffs in their catalogues. Adventure Horizons of San Diego (see Appendix II) makes aluminum ones (5 feet and 4 feet, $8 post free). L. L. Bean offers a ¾-inch aircraft alloy tubing model that folds into three equal sections, has an internal heavy-duty elastic cable that "positively locks extended sections and cannot accidentally come apart," tungsten carbide tip, molded polyvinyl grip and adjustable leather strap. (Color, black. 56 inches, 13¼ ounces; 58 inches, 13¾ ounces; 60 inches, 14¼ ounces. Any length, $10.) Bean, Moor and Mountain, The Ski Hut, and maybe other catalogues offer a wooden model, hand fashioned from kiln-dried ash and finished in weatherproof walnut color, that has a leather wrist thong and is bound at the foot with a tapered brass ferrule fitted with an abrasion- and slip-resistant urethane tip (46 inches, 50 inches, 54 inches, and 58 inches. Average weight, 13 ounces. All lengths, $7. See, by looking closely, upper illustration, page 235).

There are many other kinds of staff. One reader was kind enough to send me a Wanderstock, or German walking stick. He says its metal tip "makes it almost prehensile on boulder fields and as a wading staff," and adds that the hooked end means you can "let it hang from the wrist for taking a picture or a leak." The Ski Hut, and perhaps other suppliers, catalogue these sticks. Then

---

layer of 3-inch glass cloth tape in a 50 percent overlap and bonded with epoxy or polyester resin (from a boating supplies store); the top capped with a large rubber chair-leg tip; the foot fitted with a large natural-rubber crutch tip (Safe-T-Flex by Guardian of Los Angeles) that "lasts for many years and is a very good gripper on wet rocks, ice, etc.":

Butt of staff

2½"

2½"

This tip, says the writer, "stops the clatter of the stick on rocks; prevents the foot from wearing and splitting; provides mass near the ground that gives the stick a good 'pendulum' action—I find it easy to 'throw' forward and, while light (1.4 pounds), to have good dynamics." But the letter's meat lies in the asides that keep popping up at you: "I have to use a staff for propulsion because I go on one common and one wooden leg. . . . The only failures have been to have them stolen, and one that went over a waterfall (before me). . . . I have used it for [among other things] poling canoes down rapids. The rubber cap keeps me from getting bruised in case I fall on it when pole vaulting down steep slopes. . . ." The letter ends: "Try this design," and I am sure the modest man was talking only about his staff.

there's the Wauk-o-Long Survival Staff (42-, 48- and 54-inch lengths; $7.49, $7.98 and $8.49 respectively from Springhart Corporation, Dayton, Ohio [see Appendix II]). Made of anodized aluminum, it "contains a set of plastic canisters for storing your own selection of survival gear or food [tare weight: 2½ pounds]. It also has a rubber crutch tip at each end, a nylon wrist strap and dayglo grip pads." My Technological God!

One small but constantly recurring matter: you cannot conveniently lift a pack onto your back while holding a staff. Where possible, lean the staff against something before you lift the pack, so that once you're loaded up you can easily take hold of it. But even in open places there is no need to waste the not inconsiderable energy expended in bending down with a heavy load on your back: just hook one foot under the staff, lift it with your instep, and take hold of it when the top angles up within reach of your hand. With practice, you'll probably find yourself flipping the head of the staff up with your foot and catching it at apogee. You'll soon get used to laying the staff ready for this maneuver on a low bush or stone across a depression in the ground before you hoist up the pack, so that afterward you can slide a toe under it. If you forget the precaution and can't get a toe under, simply roll the staff onto your instep with the heel of the other foot. It sounds gymnastic but is really very simple.

There are, I admit, times when a long staff becomes a nuisance.

If you have to swim across a fast river, for example, it can tangle dangerously with your legs. In calm water it's easy enough to pull the staff safely along behind on a length of nylon cord (illustration, page 379). But when a fast-water situation was plainly going to arise on a 1966 trip beside the Colorado River I left my regular staff behind and on the first day cut a four-foot section from the stem of a dead agave, or century plant. With the thicker end carefully rounded it made a very serviceable third leg. During river crossings it tucked conveniently out of the way in the bindings of my packframe, protruding only very slightly at the top (page 382). The odd thing was that by the end of two weeks I was feeling for this little staff the same kind of affection that I lavished on my regular one—so much so that when it broke on the next-to-last day and I had to cut a fresh length of agave, I stuffed the scarred, foot-long stub into my pack and carried it all the way home. I guess "soggy sentimentality" is about right.

A staff is also a nuisance, even a hazard, if you have to do any climbing that demands the use of two unencumbered hands. Oc-

casionally, on short and unexpected pitches, I've pulled the staff
up after me on a nylon cord, or lowered it ahead. If you know
you're likely to face some rock climbing, it may be worth leaving
your regular staff behind and cutting a temporary one that can
be discarded and replaced (climbing was a contributory reason
for my doing so on that 1966 Colorado trip). If you expect to do
very much climbing, there are two solutions. Either do without a
staff of any kind; or take along an

Ice ax.

Even if you use the ax little if at all for ice work, it will
serve as a reasonably efficient staff, even in its pack-prop role. And
while you are climbing you can tie it out of the way on your
pack. An ice ax (1¼–2 pounds; $24–$35) is, incidentally, a
splendid instrument for extracting stubborn tent pegs from packed
snow (page 223)—and in its old age, I'm told, for gardening.

When walking, hold the ax by the head with the pointed part
of the head forward so that in case of a fall the danger to you is
reduced. A rubber protector for the base tip can be used on
hard surfaces, and definitely should be used when the ax is in the
car or at home (1 ounce; $.50). You can also get rubber covers for
the ax head (1½ ounces; $1.75).

The technical use of an ice ax does not fall within the scope
of a walking book.

Two other walking aids that lie close to the fringes of walking deserve brief mention:

Crampons

Although crampons are essentially ironmongery for climbers,
they are sometimes worth carrying if you expect to cross ice or
hard snow. And not only steep snow. A flat snowfield that has
weathered hard may develop basins and ridges and even savage
pinnacles that in naked boots create considerable and potentially
dangerous obstacles. And I once discovered by accident, when
I climbed out onto the lip of an ice-covered gully on Mount
Shasta, that when you are carrying a heavy load crampons can
transform a sloping slab of very soft rock from a nasty barrier
into a cakewalk.

For beginners, ten-point crampons are said to be best (22
ounces; $21). Twelve-pointers, with a pair of spikes protruding

forward, can easily trip unwary users. Novices should exercise great care with *any* crampons; indeed, some experts suggest that a tyro may be better off with an ice ax alone. When you buy crampons or rent them (at, say, $2 for a weekend or $8 for two weeks), take pains to ensure that they fit your boots exactly, for both width and length. A loose pair can be extremely dangerous. Make sure too that you learn how to strap them on properly. I will not try to describe the correct method here: it is a complicated thing to verbalize but very simple to learn from a salesman.

Weighted down with stones, crampons make excellent tent pegs on hard surfaces that more orthodox pegs refuse to penetrate.

Snowshoes

My experience is meager, but I have learned that snowshoes permit you to move over the very surface of snow into which your booted legs plunge knee deep—and that immediately after a storm they will allow you to travel (sweating hard, but sinking in less than a foot at each step) across snow into which you would otherwise go on sinking forever if God had not arranged that human legs eventually converge. I have also learned that if you have an old hamstring injury, snowshoeing may let you in for some nagging discomfort. Also that, short of a shovel, there is nothing like a snowshoe for digging out your tent during and after a storm.

When I first inquired about the technique of snowshoeing, several people said, "Oh, you just put them on and go." And that seems to be about right. The vitally important thing is not to splay your feet out. At the very start, keep looking down to see how close together you can slide your feet without entrapping one snowshoe under the other; or after a little practice, how far forward you must step in order to get away with lifting the edge of one shoe *just* over the edge of the other at the bulging widest part. Soon you find yourself moving along without thinking about how to put your feet down. Naturally, the closer the movement comes to normal walking, the less tiring it is.

Without a pack, the thing soon becomes simple. But if you are backpacking the chances are that the pack—what with tent and warm clothing and big sleeping bag—will be hippopotamic; and although snowshoes make movement possible under conditions that would otherwise bog you down, you should be prepared for the discovery that snowshoeing can be a pretty laborious, not to say boring, business. But it has its moments. In really deep, soft, new snow you may get the disturbing notion that if you lose your balance and fall with that huge load on your back you will "drown."

At one end of the snowshoe spectrum lie little tear-shaped "bearpaws" (average 13 inches by 30 inches, weight 6 pounds), too awkwardly wide for normal cross-country use but apparently valuable around cabins or in thick brush where maneuverability is vital. At the other end come prodigious structures 5 feet long and more that look as if they would support an elephant on detergent foam. Terrain dictates the type. On the West Coast, long-tailed models are most popular; in New England, smaller, tailless, "modified bearpaws." Check locally. The only kind I have used are "trail shoes" measuring 10 inches by 56 inches and weighing 6 pounds. On them I was able to move comfortably over deep snow with a crust too weak to support my boots, and to move rather laboriously through a storm that had already dropped more than four feet of powder-soft snow. This was when I found out about the drowning threat. It was pretty hard work with a heavy pack anyway, and my solution was to break trail unladen, back-track, and then pack forward over an easy, trampled trail. I can imagine experienced snowshoers extracting considerable amusement from this admission. But at least I emerged undunked.

When not in use, snowshoes can in reasonably open terrain be tied horizontally on your pack. Laying them across the top of the open pack and just pulling tight on the flap is often the simplest way. Where trees or brush are likely to snag the protruding ends, strap the shoes vertically.

Standard ash-and-rawhide-thong snowshoes need occasional revarnishing. (Spray varnishes are now available.) An alternative to buying your own (around $45) and having to maintain them is to rent a pair (say, $5 a weekend, $18 for two weeks) and let the store look after the varnishing.

Some wooden snowshoes now come with nylon or neoprene thongs, and they are said to be good. So are aluminum-framed models, provided they are kept well varnished. There are also all-plastic versions, and they are still said to be, roughly speaking, terrible: they break. But they're improving. One cognoscente suggests that they've already gone from terrible to bad, and that given time and research they may well carry the day.

The way to move across snow country is to ski. But on skis you are no longer walking. At least, that clearly used to be so. With Nordic skiing, which I have yet to try, the distinction seems less definite.

CARE OF FEET

Some people seem to have naturally tough feet. But if you are like me you know that it pays to take stringent precautions before and during any walk much longer than you are currently used to, or with a load much heavier than you have very recently carried. If you do not yet understand the value of such precautions, then you've never generated a big, joy-killing blister with many miles still to go.

Getting your feet ready

This vital task is best achieved by practice—by taking time out beforehand to work up slowly from a few gentle miles, unladen (if you are in really bad shape), to a long day's slog with a load as big as you mean to carry (page 20). But somehow (page 44) you rarely seem to have the time to take out, and even more rarely the determination to take it. The only substitute I know, and it's a poor one, is to toughen up the skin (soles, toes, and heels particularly) by regular applications of rubbing alcohol for a week or so beforehand. If you put the alcohol bottle beside your toothbrush it is not too difficult to remember this simple half-minute chore, morning and night. It helps too, if you cannot get out for any serious walking, to wear your boots—especially new ones—as much as you can for a week or so beforehand, even if only around the house.

Some people who habitually get blisters in certain places on their feet say they ward them off by covering the sites in advance with tape or moleskin (page 60). And one reader writes: "If you go barefoot whenever you can, you'll most likely develop lovely leathery feet." I think she's got something too.

On the march

The important thing is to begin easily. Men—and whole families—who backpack into the bush for once-a-year vacations all too often find the whole week or fortnight ruined at the very beginning by too much ambition and too little discretion. Their feet never recover from the pounding of the first day or two. A gentle shakedown cruise (pages 9 and 44)—a day or a week, depending on the total length of the trip—can make all the difference. On my thousand-mile California walk, although I be-

gan with stiff new boots and soft city feet, I suffered only one
blister—a minor affair generated by an ill-advised insole experiment. But I took great care in the first week and averaged barely
seven miles a day, over very easy going. In Grand Canyon my
feet fared less well. But I began with a barely cured infected
heel, and because of it had worn nothing but very soft moccasins for almost two weeks. If it had not been for two days of
easy ambling at the start and a further four days of taking it fairly
easy, I should probably have been crippled before I got fully
started.

It's essential that you continue to take precautions until your
feet are comfortably lasting out the longest day and the heaviest
load—even with steady downhill work, which gives feet a much
more brutal hammering than they get on the level or uphill. I
rarely seem to reach this point for at least a week or two. Until
then I go on applying rubbing alcohol. For years I carried about
5 ounces of it in a flat plastic bottle, but have now switched to
one of those little plastic squeeze-bottles that drugstores sell for
use with all kinds of liquids, from hand lotion to insect repellent.
These bottles (¾ ounce; $.40) have long, thin, internal tubes
attached to their caps, and when squeezed they eject liquid contents in a fine spray. They are therefore much more economical
than open-mouthed bottles, which tend to slosh too much alcohol
onto your feet. For a normal week's walking I find the 2-ounce-
size bottle adequate. But there are larger sizes. Before you pass a
bottle for "combat" duty, try it in every position, including up-
side down, to check that the spray cap never leaks alcohol. A
technical adviser assures me that "a useful source for good bottles
(for this and other uses) is the nasal spray counter. The inner
tops come out, they are the right size, and you can always pour
the junk down the drain." My alcohol bottle travels, immediately
accessible, in an outside pocket of the pack (page 376). Normally
I rub my feet with a little alcohol morning and night, and in hot
weather or when my feet are really sore I may do so several
times a day. I also carry a 3-ounce or 1-ounce can of foot powder,
in the same pocket of the pack. I always sprinkle the insides of my
socks with it in the morning, and may do so again several times
during the day.

Many experienced hikers deplore all this messing around.
"Unless something is seriously wrong," I once heard an expert advise a beginner, "keep your boots on until you stop for the
day. You'll have far less trouble with your feet that way." And
no doubt such advice is sound enough for some people. I go to the
other extreme. In hot weather I often take my boots off at each

halt and let the air get at the perspiring feet. When my feet
are really sore I anoint them with alcohol and powder at almost
every hourly halt and also change socks, repowdering the pair
that has been drying out on top of the pack. I sometimes used,
if water was available, to wash my feet at almost every halt—a
practice that a lot of people regard as skin-softening idiocy. I am
now inclined to regard it—with considerable conviction, on the
flimsiest of evidence—as skin-softening idiocy.

Taking your boots off and airing your feet whenever you can
certainly makes good theoretical sense. Heat is the cause of all
blisters. Locally, the heat comes from the friction of a rucked
sock or an ill-fitting boot. But it seems reasonable to suppose that
the overall temperature of your feet makes a big difference. I certainly find deserts the hardest places on feet. And it is not really
surprising: few people realize how hot the ground underfoot can
be. In Grand Canyon I repeatedly checked air and ground temperatures. With air temperature about 85° F. I would get a ground
reading on unshaded rock (and that meant just about any rock)
of around 115° or 120°. On unshaded sand the mercury would
go well past the last gradation of 120°. When air temperature
climbed over 90° I had to be careful where I left the thermometer,
for fear the mercury would blow off the top.*

Remedial treatment

If, in spite of all your care, your feet need doctoring, start it
early. The moment you feel what may be the beginnings of a
blister, do something about it.

First remove any obvious and rectifiable local irritant, such
as a fragment of stone or a rucked sock. Then cover the tender
place. Cover it even if you can see nothing more than a faint
redness. Cover it, in fact, if you can see nothing at all. Being a
"hero" is being a bloody fool. The covering may only be needed
for a few hours; if you take it off at night and let the air get at
the skin you may not even need to replace it next morning. But
if you do nothing at the first warning you may find yourself inside the hour with a blister that will last a week.

* An article by A. Court in the *Geographical Review* (1949, No. 2, pp.
214–20) gives these figures for extreme conditions in American deserts: air at
5 feet, 125° F.; at 1 foot, 150°; at 1 inch, 165°; at ground, 180°.

This kind of heat layering is by no means confined to deserts. See, for example, p. 362.

Interesting temperatures recorded during World War II at a naval research
center in Imperial Valley, California, on a day when the official air temperature
touched 120° F., include 145° in the gasoline in a 50-gallon drum left in the
sun, 155° in the vapor above the gasoline, and 190° on the seat of a jeep.

For covering, a piece of surgical tape or a Band-Aid will do, provided its adhesive surface is efficient enough to prevent rucking—a requirement not always met when the trouble is on your toes.

By far the best patches I know are those cut from the oddly miraculous devices known as "moleskins." They're sold in most drugstores. Now it used to be that a moleskin was a moleskin was a moleskin. No more. These days you must choose between five variants. The original Moleskins, still sold under that name, are sheets of thin white felt, adhesive on one side. Kurotex ("A Superior Moleskin") seems to be the same only flesh colored (well, flesh colored for pinkish Caucasians, anyway). Kiro Felt is flesh colored and double thickness. In Adhesive Foam ("Softer than Moleskin!"), latex foam replaces felt. In Molefoam, you get felt over foam. I've unfortunately failed to extract from the makers any coherent information about the advantages and disadvantages of each variant, so for the moment I'll stick to Moleskin and Kurotex. I mistrust the foam: it must surely hold the heat. But I see that Eastern Mountain Sports calls Molefoam the "greatest thing for blisters ever invented." (Moleskins and Kurotex come in convenient flat 1-ounce packages of four 3-by-4-inch strips, $.45; and in rolls in cans—7 by 10 inches, $.50; 7 by 30 inches, $1.15. Kiro Felt: two strips, 4⁵⁄₁₆ by 2⅞ inches, $.45; roll in can, 7 by 10 inches, $1.10. Molefoam: 4¾-by-5-inch sheet, $.43. Adhesive Foam: 6-by-6-inch sheet, $.33.)

Moleskins—and, I assume, the variants—stick to skin like glue even after your feet get wet. In fact, it is sometimes quite a business peeling the thin protective layer of plastic off new patches. (The makers leave a helpful projecting band of this layer and advise you to remove the plastic before cutting patches to the required shape. But in order to preserve the adhesive qualities—which can be rather easily damaged by handling—I shape the patch first with a pair of scissors, carefully beveling all edges, then lever up one corner of the plastic with the scissors' point, and peel it off.) But mere adhesion does not begin to explain the extraordinary efficiency of moleskins. I suppose their secret has something to do with the resilience and sideways-sliding quality of the felt. Anyway, I know for a fact and with gratitude that they can stop embryonic friction trouble dead; can stifle the pain from any surface blister and often keep it from getting worse; and can even, apparently from mere cushioning, deaden the worst pain from those deep, dismal, often invisible blisters that occasionally form under heel or ball of foot.

My moleskins travel in my "office" (page 359), and conveniently protect both scissors and signaling mirror (page 354).

If you generate a blister in spite of all your care—or because you were not careful enough—and if it is either very deep or is not yet very bulbous, the best treatment is probably just to cover it. But if the blister is close to the surface and has already inflated you will need to burst it before you can walk with comfort. Pierce it with a needle, from the side, down near the base of the balloon, so that all the liquid can drain away. (I carry several needles, primarily for repair work, in my waterproof matchsafe [page 363]. Sterilize the needle first, in a sterilizing agent if you carry one (rubbing alcohol won't do), but failing that in a flame—far better than nothing, in spite of the carbon deposits. If you have got to keep walking and if the loose skin of the balloon does not ruck up when deflated, it is probably best to leave the skin in place and cover it, and to cut it away only when the skin beneath has had time to harden. But if you can rest long enough for the skin to harden—which it does more quickly if exposed to the air—or if the deflated outer skin puckers so badly that it seems likely to cause further damage as you walk, remove it by scissoring carefully around the edges of the blister. Take care to keep the exposed area clean. And leave no dead skin likely to cause new chafing. If you must keep walking, and apply a moleskin or other adhesive cover, use a thin fragment of gauze to prevent the cover from sticking directly to the exposed and tender skin. A sprinkling of foot powder helps reduce friction further, and so does an antiseptic of a kind that will lubricate as well as reduce the danger of infection.

But never forget that a blister is a sign of failure. The efficient way to deal with foot trouble is to avoid it. Pre-harden. On the march, and especially in the early days of a trip, attend assiduously to preventive measures. And nip tribulations in the bud.

THE FOUNDATIONS IN ACTION

A book on walking should no doubt have something to say about the simple, basic, physical act of walking.

On the most fundamental level, advice is probably useless. Anyone old enough to read has almost certainly grown too set in the way he puts one foot in front of the other to alter it materially without devoting a great deal of time and determination to the task. Unless, of course, there is something correctably wrong with his feet.

On the other hand, it is very easy to improve by a little conscious thought what I regard as the most important single element in the physical act of walking: rhythm. An easy, unbroken rhythm can carry you along hour after hour almost without your being aware that you are putting one foot in front of the other. At the end of a really long day you will be aware of the act all right, but as long as you maintain a steady rhythm very little of your mind need be concerned with it. And your muscles will complain far less than if you have walked all day in a series of jerky and semi-coordinated movements, sometimes pushing close to your limit, sometimes meandering.

With experience you automatically fall into your own rhythmic pace. (At least, mostly you do. There will still be days when you have to fight for it, and not always with total success.) But when you first take up real walking you may have to think deliberately about establishing a stride and a speed that feel comfortable. And both stride and speed may be rather different with and without a load.

You will almost certainly have to concentrate at first on the important matter of not disrupting the rhythm unless absolutely necessary. This means stepping short for a stride when you come to some minor obstacle such as a narrow ditch, or even marking time with one foot. I cannot emphasize this unbroken rhythm business too strongly.

Of course, rhythm is not always a simple matter of constant stride and speed. In fact it remains so only as long as you walk on a smooth and level surface. The moment you meet rough going underfoot or start up or down a gradient, you have to modify stride or speed or both.

Climbing a gentle slope means nothing more than a mild shortening of stride, though leaning forward slightly may help too. But long before a mountainside gets so steep that you start reaching out for handholds, stride becomes a meaningless word. Now, you put your feet down almost side by side at one step, a foot or more apart at the next, depending on the immediate local gradients and footholds. Even the rate at which you move one leg past the other—slowly and deliberately and almost laboriously, though not quite—may vary in response to changes in the general gradient. But the old rhythm persists. I am not sure where the relationships lie. It is not—though I have sometimes thought so

—that you continue to expend the same amount of energy. Steep climbing takes more out of you, always (page 101). But the fact remains that although you must change gear in an almost literal sense at the bottom and top of a steep hill you can maintain the deeper continuity of the old rhythm. The pulse is still there, somewhere, if you know where to feel for it.

Downhill walking, though less sweaty than climbing, is less easy than it ought to be. In broad theory you merely relinquish the potential energy you gained with such labor as you climbed; but in practice you do no such thing. At every step you expend a great deal of effort in holding yourself back—and this effort too demands a deliberate change of gear. If the gradient is at all severe you reduce both stride and speed as much as you think necessary to prevent yourself from hammering hell out of knees and ankles and feet (especially feet). Again, though, you find with practice that it is possible to maintain the essence of the old rhythm.

You may also have to apply a conscious effort to maintaining your rhythmic pace when you come to certain kinds of rough going —soft sand or gravel that drags at your feet like molasses; talus that slides away from under your feet like a treadmill; rough rock or tussocky grassland that soon disrupts an even stride; or prolonged sidehill work that puts an abnormal strain on foot and leg muscles and may also present something of a problem in balance.

Walking after dark, especially on pitch-black, moonless nights, can also destroy your customary rhythm. If you have been walking in daylight and simply keep going, little trouble seems to arise. But if you get up in the middle of the night and hike out into darkness you may have a surprise in store. I wrote in *The Thousand-Mile Summer* about the only time I traveled at night on my California walk. It was in Death Valley. The first night inside the Valley I had no sleeping bag, and I failed, dismally, to stay asleep (see page 261, this book). At 3:30 I got up from the gully in which I had camped and headed north into the darkness. There was no moon. From the start I found myself walking in a curious and disturbing state of detachment. The paleness that was the dirt road refused to stay in positive contact with my feet, and I struggled along with laborious, unrhythmic steps. All around hovered hints of immense open spaces and distant, unconvincing slopes. Time had lost real meaning back in the gully; now it lacked even boundaries. When dawn gave the landscape a tenuous reality at last, I was still two hours away from my next cache. In those endless two hours I completely failed to reestablish my usual rhythmic pace.

Next night I was on the move by 9:30. This time, bright moonlight made the physical world something real and conquerable. I could plant my feet firmly and confidently on the solid white road. But soon after eleven o'clock, the moon set. The world narrowed to hints of colossal open space, to a blur that achieved reality only through jabbing at my feet. Distance degenerated into marks on the map. Time was the creeping progress of watch hands. All through the long and cold and dismal night that followed I had to struggle to hold some semblance of my usual daytime rhythm. I succeeded only marginally. But I succeeded far better than on the previous night.

A delicate sense of balance is vital to good walking. And it's not just a matter of being able to cross steep slopes without tightening up. Your body should always be poised and relaxed so that you put down your feet, whatever their size and whatever your load, with something close to daintiness. Before I walked through Grand Canyon I met the one man who seemed to know much about hiking away from trails in its remote corners. Trying to get some idea of whether I would be able to cope with the rough, steep country that he crossed with such apparent ease, I asked him to tell me, honestly, if he was a good climber. "No," he said, "definitely not. I'd say I was a very mediocre climber indeed. But in the Canyon it's mostly walking, you know, even though it can be pretty tricky walking at times." He smiled. "I guess you could say, come to think of it, that maybe I don't dislodge quite as many stones as the next guy." And I knew then that he was a good walker.

One of the surest ways to tell an experienced walker from a beginner is the speed at which he starts walking. The beginner tends to tear away in the morning as if he meant to break every record in sight. By contrast, your experienced man seems to amble. But before long, and certainly by evening, their positions have reversed. The beginner is dragging. The expert, still swinging along at the same easy pace, is now the one who looks as though he has records in mind. One friend of mine, a real expert, says, "If you can't carry on a conversation, you're going too fast."

The trap to avoid at all costs, if you want to enjoy yourself, is spurious heroism—the delusion that your prowess as a walker rests on how dauntlessly you "pick 'em up and lay 'em down." It's a sadly common syndrome.

The actual speed at which you walk is a personal and idiosyncratic matter. Settle for whatever seems to suit you best. It is really a question of finding out what you can keep up hour after hour in various kinds of terrain carrying various loads. Until you know your own limits, aim for a slow, rhythmic, almost effortless pace. You'll be surprised, I think, at the ground you cover. The miles will come to meet you. In time, you'll learn that, generally speaking, the way to hurry is not to hurry but to keep going. To this end I have two walking speeds: slow and slower. See also page 31.

The halts you choose to take are a matter of personal preference, but frequent and irregular halts are a sure sign of an inexperienced hiker. Unladen, it may be a good thing to keep going hour after hour without disturbing your rhythm. But if you're carrying a sizable pack you will almost certainly find that, no matter how fit you are, you need to get the weight off your back for a short spell about once an hour. I halt every hour with fairly mechanical regularity, modifying slightly to suit terrain. I like

to get to the top of a hill before I stop, for example; and I often halt a few minutes early or late to take advantage of convenient shade or water or a pleasing view. In theory, I rest for ten minutes. When I have a map, I sometimes mark the halting place and pencil in the exact time I stopped. I am no longer sure why I began doing this, but I do so now because I know only too well that it is horribly easy to let a halt drift on for fifteen, twenty, or even thirty minutes, and the penciled figures on the map act as a reminder and a spur. They also help me to judge how I am progressing across a given kind of country, and make it much easier to estimate how far I should be able to travel in the next hour or afternoon or day or week.

At each halt I take off the pack and prop it against a rock or a tree or my staff and lean against it with my back resting comfortably between the protruding outside pockets (page 91). I try to relax completely. Sometimes, warding off the attractions of scenery, animals and the map, I succeed. I may even doze off for a few minutes. Getting started again may demand considerable will power, especially toward the end of a long day; but within a few paces I slip back into the old regular rhythm. With luck I will hold it, unbroken, for another fifty minutes.

Walking at high altitudes

Even if you acclimate properly (see page 29) you must, once you get up high, walk differently. "How high" is not really answerable with a figure: your body, on any given day, will respond more accurately. But as a guideline it is probably safe to say that most people will have to adjust over 10,000 feet, and that many will have to do so a lot lower.

First, you must learn to modulate your rhythm—to dead slow. Even at sea level, there's nothing so becomes a walker as modest slowness and languidity;

> But when the mountain air blows in your ears,
> Then imitate the action of a tortoise;
> Slacken the sinews, throttle down the blood,
> Deflect ambition with delib'rate pace,
> And lend the legs a loitering aspect;
> Let them creep through the hours of the day
> Like a brass clock; let the body dawdle
> As languidly as doth a smoker
> Drag slow-foot through the grass, like a tippler
> O'erfilled with mild but tasteful potion.
> Now ope the teeth, and stretch the nostril wide;
> Draw slow the breath, and suck down every intake
> To his full depth!—On, on, you noble Walker,

whose blood is thin from scaling this full height, and remember that not only during the first three days of your body's readjustment but on, on into the fourth and fifth, Henry, and beyond that for as long as you stay up high, you must strive to keep moving in this consciously imposed, almost ludicrous slow motion. If you do it properly you will not get breathless unless you go very high indeed. And your heart will not pound. (I maintain that if your muscles feel the strain of walking when you are up high then you are asking too much of your heart.) If you forget to hold your legs in check, and revert to something like your normal pace, you will begin to gasp and to feel your heart triphammering. You will therefore rest—and lose time and momentum. But if you tortoise along you can often keep going for the full regulation hour with no more distress than at sea level.

Remember too about those deep, slow breaths—preferably taken in rhythm with your steps: by dragging each breath down into the full depths of your lungs you will at least in part make up for the reduced oxygen-absorbing efficiency of your blood. If you find your brain is not functioning very well—and up high there will assuredly be times when it does not—stop and drag down several extra-deep breaths that expel every lurking unoxygenated residue from your lung cellars. You may begin to think better at once. And this treatment will as often as not remove or at least moderate the headaches that are apt to afflict you for a spell. I keep at headaches with such deep breathing and find I very rarely need resort to aspirins, which I regard as something to be avoided—even in bed, certainly on the move.

Once you have mastered these simple lessons you will be ready to sample the simple joys of walking around on top of the world.

There remains the matter of what you do with your mind while your body walks. Mostly, I find that everything takes care of itself. My mind soars or grubs along or meanders halfway in between, according to the sun or cloud, the wind or rain, the state of my metabolism, the demands of the hour, or other elements beyond my control. But there are times when, in the interests of efficient walking, you need to discipline your thoughts. If the way ahead looks long and tiresome, and above all if it slopes steeply and inexorably upward, on and on, then you are liable to find that the prospect presses heavy on your mind and that the depression acts as a brake on your body and that its lethargy further depresses your mind—and so on. The syndrome is pandemic to mountains, and especially to those high enough for the thin air to brake directly on mind and body. In early November 1971 I went up Mount Whitney. I wandered up, acclimating slowly, savoring the emptiness and silence of the country (I had chosen November for horde avoidance); but I was carrying a considerable load—my plan, soon scuttled by weather, was to camp on the summit—and on the long, final pull, each step became a wearisome, mind-demanding effort. Ahead, the trail curved on and up, on and up. As I climbed, the air grew thinner, even less sustaining. My mind sagged under the burden of step-by-step effort. And then I remembered something. My paperback for the trip was *Zen and the Art of Archery,* and while reading it in my tent the night before I had decided to try applying one of its lessons. I immediately began to do so. "I am the summit," I told myself. "I am the summit. I am the summit." I focused my mind on the statement, close. And very soon, very easily, I believed it: my insignificant self and the apex of that huge blade of rock *were* the same thing—or at least they occupied the same point in space and time. Yet the space was in another sense still above me. The time, I think, was a nudge ahead in the future. Or perhaps it was the present. Anyway, I held the concept tight and firm, so that there was no room for anything else. (Excluding other ideas was not too difficult: at 14,000 feet you can rarely cope with more than one at a time.)

It seemed to work. The effort of climbing—of pulling self and load on and up, on and up, step by laborious step—faded away. To say that I floated upward would, I guess, be hyperbole; but when I reached the summit in a physical sense I was, I think, less tired than I have ever been at such a high and crowning moment.

Walls

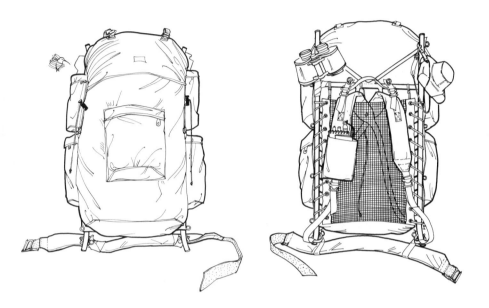

The walls of the house on your back (the outside walls, that is—the shell that contains and protects everything else) are your pack-frame and packbag; and there is no item of equipment, except perhaps a bad pair of boots, that's so certain to ruin a walking trip as an inadequate or ill-fitting

PACKFRAME.

On one-day trips, the kind of small pack you carry, if you carry one at all, does not really need a frame (page 87). And for light-load weekends a tolerably comfortable solution may be a Bergans-type rucksack that puts most of the weight on the shoulder straps but transfers a little of it to a band bearing against your hips. Such packs are lightweight and reasonably inexpensive. What's more, the soft and somewhat amorphous bags do not tend to catch too often in thick brush; and (a critical matter for climbers) they do not push you unexpectedly away from steep rock or ice. But ruck-sacks are not designed for heavy loads. The limit of real comfort for most people is probably around 35 pounds. Beyond that, and perhaps well below it, you need a pack with a rigid frame.

For many years, the only rigid type available was the Yukon or Trapper Nelson packboard with a straight wooden frame and wrap-around cloth or canvas that distributed the load efficiently over your whole back. But these packboards were heavy and cumbersome. And the wrap-around material, fitting snugly the whole length of your back, was abominably hot, even in temperate climates.

Today, by far the most widely used frame is the contoured aluminum type (illustration, page 69).

These welded frames have all the advantages of the old packboards and few of their disadvantages. The tubular aluminum structure is rigid and extremely light. Contrary to appearances, it is remarkably strong. At least, it is in the best (and most expensive) models. The two uprights curve in a very gentle "S" that echoes the contours of your waist, back, shoulders, and neck. The frame therefore sits close to your body throughout its length and holds the load far forward, where it exerts the least possible leverage against your muscles. But the construction leaves plenty of air space between load and back for ventilation. And the outward-curving lower ends never bear on your rump in the uncomfortable way that a straight frame can. These aluminum frames, like the old Trapper Nelson, are versatile. You can take off the packbag if you want to and tie on a slaughtered deer, or a five-gallon can containing a cache of food or water. With one of the several kiddie seats now on the market (page 88) you can even convert the frame into a rickshaw for Junior.

There are certain disadvantages to tubular packframes—though they are marginal compared with the advantages. In dense brush, frames with projecting side members tend to catch in branches and creepers. Curved-across-the-top frames, such as Jan Sport's, avoid this curse; frames with projecting side members demand only a removable closed-loop top that in clutching country can be slipped over the projections—which are, as we shall see, very useful for other things. When you're climbing, the almost rigid frame of any tubular model may also bear unexpectedly on solid rock or ice and throw you dangerously off balance. But it is worth noting that most high-altitude climbing expeditions—for which load-carrying is as vital as actual climbing—now use tubular frames. Hornbein and Unsoeld did so on their technically difficult final assault up the West Ridge of Everest.

I have let the last three paragraphs stand much as they appeared in the first edition. In essence, they remain true. But I have spoken only of *welded* aluminum frames.

The weakest points of almost any frame occur at the joints between uprights and crossbars. For many years after Kelty introduced aluminum frames in the 1940s, most high-quality models were heliarc welded at the joints. (You can tell heliarc welding by its uneven, obviously handmade look, distinctively different from the smooth, machined finish of other welds.) Heliarc welding remains perhaps the strongest and most popular system (Kelty, Trailwise, Mountain Master, Sunbird, Universal, Alpenlite, Adventure 16 [in part], and the more expensive Camp Trails models). But there have always been alternatives, and you now see more and more of them in the catalogues and even the mountains: arc welding, soldering, or brazing (Recreational Equipment, some Camp Trails models); bolts of various kinds (Gerry, Antelope); and adjustable metal or plastic couplings (Alpine Designs, see page 86). Jan Sport packs have a "unitized" frame: a single tube bent in a "U," with a curved bar across the open ends joined to them by pinned ferrules, and with two crossbars held in place by metal couplings. Cannondale have just brought out a series of "internal/external frame" packs that seem to eliminate crossbars—and joints.

Until now, the only alternative to aluminum for modern packframes has been magnesium alloy (some Camp Trails models and a discontinued North Face line). Although it is lighter than aluminum, doubts about its strength persist. North Face recently tried a one-piece injection-molded frame of a polycarbonate plastic, the kind used in football helmets; but it failed to withstand outdoor scrimmaging under certain conditions, including extreme cold, and they have discarded the project. Now they report "a new concept in frames," still secret but hopefully to be unveiled in early 1974.

Waistbelts—and beyond

Experiments aside, the main current changes in packs are taking place around your waist.

It began in the early 1960s, when either Trailwise or Camp Trails (there is some doubt who was first) introduced a waistbelt broad enough to transfer most of the pack's weight from shoulders to hips.

The uninitiated never really believe that waistbelts have revolutionized backpacking. A nonhiking friend once slipped my pack on when it held about 55 pounds and was appalled at the dead weight on his shoulders. I told him to fasten the waistbelt. "Why," he said when he had done so, "it practically takes the sting out of the load!" It does too. The belt removes almost all the weight from the shoulders and puts it on your hips.

That is where it belongs. The human backbone has evolved from a system designed primarily for horizontal use, with the weight taken at anchored end-points. Our newfangled upright stance has therefore assured us a rich legacy of back trouble. Old-type packs put most of the load on your shoulders and imposed fierce vertical pressure on the easily damaged spine. They also put a heavy strain on the muscles of shoulders, neck, and back, hastening fatigue. A waistbelt removes this pressure and strain and transfers the weight to the simple, strong, and well-muscled structure of hips and legs. It also lowers your center of gravity—often a material help.

And yet—predictably, backpackers being the quirk-ridden creatures we are—you still find a few merry individuals who persist in ignoring waistbelts, or at least in leaving them half slack and so doing no more than dampen their packs' slip and sway.

For a decade the waistbelt evolved slowly toward bigger and mostly better things: from a simple 2-inch-wide belt of cotton or nylon webbing, through broader Ensolite-padded affairs covered with nylon fabric, to sumptuous foam creations, 4 inches deep or more at the back. If you carried heavy loads you welcomed each advance: the broader and better-padded the belt, the less sting to the load, and the less second-morning waistbelt trauma (page 28). Still, there is a limit beyond which added weight and increased heat in the small of the back will block further progress in this direction. Many packs still have narrow webbing waistbelts. For light loads they are probably adequate. Most of these belts are made of nylon, and provided you wear thick pants they are fine, but if you ever walk without pants or wearing only a swimsuit or some such thin garment, the nylon will cut you. A softer belt of woven cotton or some such fabric does the trick. So does a temporary padding, such as folded underpants, worn as a band under the belt.

A waistbelt, no matter what its width, should encircle you: there now seems to be fairly general—though not total—agreement that sidestraps from the base of the frame fail to do a satisfactory job.

For cinching up the waistbelt, see page 87.

An innovation already appearing in several forms gives promise of carrying the weight-on-your-hips-instead-of-shoulders movement to its logical conclusion. The basic idea is to extend the foot of the frame forward in some way and suspend the waistbelt from points level with the hip sockets (junctions of pelvis and femurs or thigh bones). The line joining these sockets is the axis around which pivot the major movements of the walking human body, and a packframe suspended from the waistbelt at approximately these same points should also pivot around this axis. Frame and back therefore move together, in harmony. And that is clearly the way things ought to be. Well, fairly clear. I guess.

At least three different systems are already on the market:

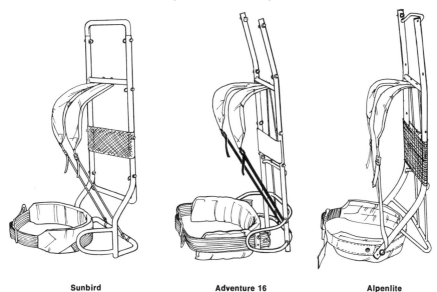

Sunbird   Adventure 16   Alpenlite

Similar designs are marketed by Universal and Jan Sport.

So far, I have tried only the Adventure 16, and that for only an overnight trip, but I was sufficiently impressed by the way the pack rode to feel that it deserves, at the very least, further trials.

Mind you, I glimpse certain disadvantages in any such design. Because the metal projections must lie close to your hip sockets, fit is critical, and a slightly wrong size—or even putting on bulky clothes—could throw things awry. My brief trial also suggested that even with a good fit the more-or-less unyielding pressure of the metal projections may, until your body gets used to it, cause soreness or even muscle cramps. Other users have voiced similar misgivings. And there are reports that with really heavy loads these packs do not ride well.

The makers of some side-projection models claim that their packs stand upright, unassisted. On flat surfaces—living room floors, meadows—they will. But on wilderness surfaces they often will not—and then the projections become a minor nuisance: they make it difficult to lean the pack backwards against a tree or other convenient prop. For me—because I regularly convert the pack into a backrest by propping it against my staff (page 91)—this is a serious drawback. And the projections inherently project—and so are liable to damage when the pack is off your back. I am not thinking only of rests and camps: many packs have to withstand repeated man- and machine-handling into and out of car trunks, the backs of pickups and the brutal baggage compartments and conveyors of buses and airliners. (Adventure 16 frames circumvent this difficulty with detachable projections: you can slide them out of the main frame and carry them, or stow them inside the pack.) *

But in all these matters I am only voicing misgivings. It may well be that the "hip-socket" packframe is here to stay. Improved designs may overcome the apparent difficulties—or the difficulties may pale to insignificance beside proven advantages. Time will tell. Meanwhile, catalogues and magazines and newsletters and convocations of backpackers everywhere are having a ball as they gnash over the merits and demerits of standard and hip-socket frames. The weight of scientific-sounding evidence is intimidating. To no one's surprise, it leaves us with two sets of utterly contrary conclusions.

Adventure 16 now offers a conversion kit that enables you to fit its hip-socket attachment to Kelty packs. And a Sunbird kit fits all frames with 1-inch tubing (i.e., most frames; but not Trailwise or Antelope).

The shoulder yoke, or harness

When waistbelts appeared, the work of a pack's shoulder yoke or harness underwent radical change: instead of taking almost all the weight, it had to do little more than hold the pack in the correct position against your back. (With a well-fitting pack [page 85] and properly tightened waistbelt [page 87], your shoulders should take little if any of the load: standing still, you should be able to slip at least one finger under the yoke strap where it passes over your shoulders.)

Yet in the first decade of effective waistbelts, the design of

---

* One peregrinating mountaineer—his letter came from South America— writes: "I feel that I have solved the problem of taking a chance of having my frame bent or pack damaged by airlines people, etc. (which it was once) by having a 'suitcase' made for my pack. The case is a stiff leather but a heavy canvas would probably work equally as well. My case was designed large enough to accommodate a loaded pack plus have room to hold my boots on top. It has 4 large handles and 2 zippers which meet in the center with a lock. This saves wear and tear on the pack and also makes for easier handling. Just leave it at your car or the starting point."

Similar contraptions have now appeared in one or two catalogues.

harnesses underwent zero change. Trailwise, though, has now introduced a yoke specifically designed to do its new work. There are three separate adjustments. One need be set only the first time you put the pack on, and ensures correct fit at the shoulders. The other two can be changed—even when you are on the move—to allow for variations in load, slope, slippage, expansion, sagging muscles, and any of the other mysterious but undeniable factors that can affect the way a pack rides on your back. The theory behind the system has been explained to me. It concerns body movement, and slip and sway. Mostly, the words flowed over my head; I was wondering, anyway, if this was not a bad case of over-engineering. But when I tried the pack out I changed my tune. And I'm certainly not alone. One of the most experienced and also skeptical backpackers I know says that with really heavy loads the new harness makes the pack ride better than any he has ever tried. Each pack fitted with the new harness comes with explicit instructions for fitting and adjustment. Follow them.

Most packs still have simple shoulder straps, attached to a crossbar. Often, there are spare holes in the crossbar for lateral adjustment—holes that you can also use, incidentally, for attaching a small nylon web handle of the kind now fitted to all Trailwise packs (page 81; illustration, page 69). You may also be able to make a minor vertical adjustment by moving the attachment above or below the crossbar.

No matter what kind of yoke you use, you will—unless you never carry heavy loads or walk stripped to the waist—probably find wide, foam-padded shoulder straps far more comfortable than plain webbing. The difference is less achingly acute than with waistbelts. But it exists. Like hell it exists.

Back supports

In all tubular packs some system of tautly stretched fabric support (or supports) will hold the frame away from your back. It cushions the pressure and applies it at strategic places—and also ensures ventilation between back and pack.

The most common arrangement is still a pair of woven nylon bands, 4 or 5 inches wide. One rests against your shoulder blades. The other, which does the real work, fits across your hips. (The bigger and better your waistbelt, the less work the lower band does. With Rolls Royce belts it can be discarded.) The gap between the bands is normally about 8 inches, and in this gap air can circulate freely. In hot weather, if you walk bareback or with only a thin shirt, such ventilation can make a world of difference. But with loads of more than about 40 pounds the lower band may begin to press uncomfortably; sometimes it even rucks.

Now when the weather is even mildly warm I like to walk stripped to the waist; and where weather and privacy are both right (as often happened in Grand Canyon) I like to strip to hat, socks and boots. When Trailwise replaced the double-band arrangement some years ago with a single nylon mesh support, 17 inches high, I at first resisted the change because I felt that the harsh-feeling material would rub a bare back raw, and in spite of the open mesh would prevent adequate ventilation. But when I tried out the new support I found that even in temperatures well over 100° F. my fears on both counts proved unjustified. And the long single support vastly improves the pressure distribution on your back. Nowadays, if I try a pack with the old double-band support, I find myself longing for the extended mesh system. I see that several makers have now adopted it.

End-buttons

Small plastic buttons that plug the four open ends of the tubular frame are now standard fittings on most packs. You need them. Open ends at the bottom pick up samples of any soft ground that you put the pack down on; and when you walk on again the samples neatly decant, if you are wearing shorts, into waiting sock tops. The buttons also protect the interior of car and home.

A spare button travels in my "Odds-and-ends Can" (page 371).

A 150-page report of an engineering study on the strength of selected packframes, conducted at Arizona State University—no doubt a valid engineering project, but one that unfortunately seems to ignore most realities of practical backpacking—finally generated as its prime design suggestion the fitting of "a soft rubber tip for the bottom of each side member. Not only would this better support the frame on rock or slick surfaces but would absorb much of the force otherwise transmitted to a frame when it is put down hard or dropped." Good idea. In fact, a reader—apparently unassisted by a 150-page engineering report—recommended foiling packs that delight in skidding on hard surfaces by fitting rubber crutch tips ($.15 each; estimated weight, ½ ounce). But there should, I think, be a standard plastic button underneath to protect the frame when the rubber cuts or wears through, as it assuredly will.

A reader has suggested removing an end-button and using a section of the frame as a kind of "mailing tube" for storing such

items as hacksaw blades. I'm not sure the idea is furiously practical
but it does open up fragrant possibilities.

PACKBAG

Any good packbag is big, tough, as close to waterproof as you can
make it, and multi-pocketed.

Generally speaking, the bigger the better. A cavernous sack
weighs only an ounce or two more than a middle-class job, and it
will accept and protect just about everything you can carry, even
on winter snow trips, when the bulk problem looms largest.

As we shall see, I continue to use one of the old-style, un-
divided type, usually called "expedition bag," that runs the full
length of the frame. But few backpackers agree with my choice.
The three-quarter-length packbag, with sleeping bag strapped on
underneath, is now vastly more popular. In fact, many firms no
longer make full-length bags. I remain skeptical, though, about
the three-quarter-bag-with-sleeping-bag-underneath system. It's not
only that I have yet to be convinced about the load distribution
advantages most makers claim (page 89). I dislike the loss of
valuable space. And I wonder about the sleeping bag, even when
it's protected by a stuff bag. No backpacker's sleeping bag is a
robust article, and it is the one piece of equipment you just have
to keep dry. Yet it seems to me that every time you put your pack
down, the sleeping bag receives the maximum quota of both wear
and moisture. Stuff bags may be protective and waterproof when
new, but I wonder how long they remain so under this kind of
treatment.

I repeat, though, that—in spite of a reported trend back
toward big sacks—the three-quarter bag now has the field largely
to itself. To some people, that's the only reasonable place. Not long
ago I was starting on a wilderness trip when a young boy—golden-
haired, bright, "almost eleven"—walked with me a few hundred
yards toward the reservoir he was going to fish. When I responded
to one of his questions by saying that I'd be back in the wilderness
for several days, he looked hard at my bulging pack and said: "Oh,
I see—I didn't think you were staying overnight, but you must have
your sleeping bag inside."

Many packs—perhaps most of them—now have the main
sack compartmented. The theory is fine: neat little "cupboards" to
keep everything tidy. My first experience with simple dividers convinced me that they were a perishing nuisance: many bulky though

light items I always carry simply would not fit in. I've since softened my dislike a little—after trying out a well-designed Jan Sport two-story bag. An increasing number of bags feature such upper and lower compartments. There are even multi-layered jobs, like mid-rise parking lots. I look on such structures with horror. I have never used one, and I base my contempt squarely on prejudice. The savage divergence of views among experienced backpackers on this subject (and oh so many others!) may stem from accidents of evolution as well as common human orneriness: if you developed your gear and techniques while using a multi-pocketed marvel you'll likely look with supreme contempt on my cavernous, undifferentiated sack.

No matter what kind of pack you use, its fabric must be tough enough to withstand the sudden grabbing onslaughts of the sharpest rock outcrop and the most viciously pointed branch. It must not crack in extreme cold, as some of the older synthetics do. And the bottom must resist constant scuffing. (One reader reports that he sews a "2-ounce leather patch" onto his packbag bottom.)

"Water-repellent" is a term that fills me with distrust. Like "hi-fi" and "psychosomatic," it can mean almost anything or almost nothing. But your packbag must at the very least repel water. The ideal bag is waterproof, but even waterproof fabrics that stand up to hard wear do not ensure a waterproof bag: most untreated seams leak through the stitching holes—though a new self-sealing thread may reduce or even eliminate the "wicking" effect. Any seams can be waterproofed, but it is a tedious job that must be done by hand and I know no makers who do it. In downpour country—and also if you may have to swim across a river (page 380)—you should certainly do it yourself with one of the specially made brush-on solutions suitable for the fabric of your particular bag. You might be wise to do it anyway. If you mean to do a good job—and no other kind is worth considering—do not expect to get through with it under an hour or two. Frankly, I am not yet convinced that any waterproofing job, no matter how carefully done, stays totally waterproof for very long. For a possible solution, see "rain cover," page 85.

It is hardly possible to have too many outside pockets on your packbag. In them you put all the things you are continually wanting, and the items you may need in an emergency, such as a first-aid kit; also a stack of small articles that you could never lay hands on if they languished at the bottom of the main sack. Kelty now offers loose pockets for attachment to the main bag. See page 376 for the Jan Sport color-coded-pocket idea; and for suggestions on packing.

The pocket zippers on most good packs—and also on other equipment—are now usually nylon. They run more smoothly than metal ones and do not so easily become iced up—though they will fuse if you somehow succeed in dropping a hot coal on them. For words on the coil zippers that may soon replace the lug type, see page 255. People who operate in very cold weather and therefore have to wear large and clumsy gloves will sometimes thread loops of nylon cord through the zipper tabs of their pack pockets. The advantages are obvious—though it is difficult to imagine a more efficient way to snag trees or bushes or damn near anything than by festooning your pack with five or six loops of nylon cord.

Many bags now have a rigid aluminum bracket that holds the mouth squarely open, for easier loading. (And also, perhaps, for easier selling: it makes the bag look very neat and shipshape.) I've removed my bracket—because it prevents me from reaching back and down into the lower fastnesses of the bag when the pack is propped up behind me; because it ruins the empty pack as a backrest; and because discarding it saves 2 ounces. It also hinders rather than helps in the struggle to get everything in when the pack is full to overflowing—as most packs manage to be most of the time. On this score, and also for protection from rain, I still like the old sleeve-and-drawstring system with which you simply push down on everything with one hand while pulling the drawstring tight with the other.

Do not underestimate the importance of the method by which the pack's flap is battened down. You probably open and close your pack many times a day, and if you have to bend or kneel down every time to the foot of the bag—perhaps into mud or snow—in order to release or retie a knot, your back and language will soon reflect the exercise. Current available systems run from good through fair to diabolical. The best I have found is on Kelty packs: nylon cords adjusted by small, simple, spring-loaded toggles. Fortunately, you can fit such toggles to many other bags.

The bag itself must be anchored to the frame like a super-limpet. The most common device is a series of clevis pins that run through holes bored in the side tube. Grommeted holes along the edge of the packbag are secured to the pins by a variety of cunning or bizarre methods. Most of them presumably work. For one that certainly does, see page 81.

CHOOSING A PACK

You will have gathered by now—even if you have never cata-
logue-browsed or done more than glance at the packs on people's
backs or at their hitchhiker feet—that we are today confronted
with a mind-boggling array of packs. If you are in the market for
one you can narrow the field by accepting my prejudices or those
of some other writer or of an acquaintance—or your own, if you
have chalked up some experience and therefore achieved prejudices. You can heed the makers' passionate pleas. You can, to
much greater purpose, check some dependable and informed independent survey (page 83). You can even put several models
through trial by rental. But unless you are a congenital experimenter you are unlikely to subject more than a couple of packs to
really exhaustive tests. I am not sure it matters all that much: you
cannot, I think, go tragically wrong. Thanks to the severe competition, most of the packs sold by responsible suppliers (though
not, I suspect, by many quick-buck general stores) are fair value
for the money. Some are fairer than others, that's all.

The price range slides all the way down from the new Sunbird (which on paper looks a good pack—and ought to be, at
$85), through the very high-quality $50 to $60 class, past a slew
of intermediate candidates, down to the smallest, cheapest, stripped-
down models made by Recreational Equipment, Camp Trails and
Antelope ($24, $21.50 and $14.50 respectively) and by several
Japanese firms. I have mentioned most of the names on page
71. As in other walks of life, you get—by and large—what you
pay for.

There is one injunction you should bear steadily in mind when
choosing a pack. It applies to all equipment, and to techniques as
well, and it advises: "Keep things simple." Backpacking, even more
than most human activities, falls under the stern sway of Murphy's
Law: "If things *can* go wrong, they will." But much of today's
equipment is so finely developed that improvements, especially in
zealot hands, are apt to develop into bad cases of over-engineering.
So every time you see an alluring packframe that's a jury rig of
split rings and couplings and other adjustable festoons, or a packbag that's an architectural dream but has more zippers and flaps to
the square inch than a concourse of crotches, ask yourself, "Yes,
but could it go wrong?" Ask it several times, searchingly. And ask
it in the store, not in the cold bite of a mountain dawn.

Fifteen years ago a great deal of chance, a little prejudice and almost no informed opinion put a Trailwise pack on my back. I had the original frame, with successive improved bags, for more than ten years, and it did me proud. It withstood three long treks totaling about twelve months of walking. Every year it came on a couple of week- or two-week-long wilderness trips, perhaps half a dozen two- to four-day jaunts, and many one- or half-day walks. It also endured, fully loaded and without murmur, untold heavings into and out of cars, buses, airliners and those sadistic airline conveyors. I don't think I treated the frame particularly brutally, but I took no very great care of it and it never gave me a moment's trouble. At the end of the ten years it was still in perfect condition, and I would probably still be using it had Trailwise not evolved new and improved models. The combination I am using now is essentially the original rig modified by the years. For illustration, see page 69. (R101 frame, large size: 2 pounds 8 ounces, $30; R172 bag, large size: 1 pound 9 ounces, $29. The equivalent three-quarter-length bag—capacity only 2924 cubic inches [see next page for comparisons]—comes complete with accessory straps and sack for sleeping bag, weighs and costs 3 ounces and $2 less.)

The frame is ¾-inch aluminum alloy tubing, heliarc welded, S-contoured, tapering slightly from shoulders to waist. It is simple and very well constructed. The Ensolite-padded yoke embodies a new design said to reduce "the localized pressure on shoulders inherent in all ordinary shoulder strap suspensions" (page 75). The full-length nylon-mesh back support gives excellent weight distribution, good ventilation. The foam-padded, full-circle waistbelt is 2¾ inches deep at the back. The nylon hand strap on the top crossbar, which you may, like me, dismiss at first glance as en effete fussyism, turns out to be a jewel. The packbag is secured to the frame by ten eyebolts that screw into recessed, easily replaced devices called Riv-nuts. (Easily replaced in the store, that is. I've never tried it in the field.) The Riv-nut system means that the frame has to be drilled from only one side and this, according to Trailwise, means a strength advantage over the usual clevis pin and wire attachment. I have never had a Riv-nut pull out, though one or two eyebolts that I've removed for some reason have partly stripped their threads. The eyebolts never seem to snag on anything and are occasionally useful as lashing points.

My packbag is the "expedition," or single-bloody-great-sack type, innocent of compartments. It is made of heavy nylon duck, coated on the inside with waterproof urethane. It has two long pockets on each side, and a large one on its rear. The bag is mounted on the sides of the frame—as opposed to the uprights' rearward surfaces in earlier models (see illustrations, pages 92 and 379)—and is therefore a shade wider. It is also less deep, so that the load hugs your back more closely (page 90). Dimensions at the top are 17 inches wide by 8 inches deep; length, 29 inches; capacity, 4429 cubic inches. I find this bag good but imperfect.

Above all, it is too small for my particular regimen. The catalogue dimensions make it sound bigger than earlier equivalents, but it tapers from top to bottom, and in fact you can get less gear in. I am hoping to persuade Trailwise to make a larger, truly "expedition" model.*

The "map pocket" sewn onto the flap in earlier models has been replaced by a pair of straps for lashing on foam pads or other items. I deplore the change. While accepting The Ski Hut's contention that flap pockets are especially liable to leak and their zippers to break, I now feel destitute. You can no doubt chalk that one up to habit. But as for the straps on top, I loathe the popular habit of lashing gear (usually a foam pad) on top of the pack: it gets in the way every time you open the bag, and wet every time it rains; it tends to bang against your head; in high winds it acts as a sail; and the moment you turn off open, turnpike trails it seeks to embrace every passing tree, bush and creeper.

Finally, the two nylon cords that hold the flap closed are tightened and held by double D-rings attached halfway down the bag. This is an improvement over earlier models, which had a down-on-your-knees-in-the-mud-or-snow-brother-and-tie-a-knot system. But although the double D-rings are excellent for closing the bag—you just pull, and when you let go the rings jam the cord tight—trying to unjam them, even without gloves, is a pain in the fingertips. I long ago fitted a pair of Kelty toggles (see page 79). I'm delighted to report that Trailwise is at last considering a similar arrangement.

Until recently, these packs, like most Trailwise equipment, have been on sale only at The Ski Hut, in Berkeley; but they are now available at certain other retail stores, mainly in the West but increasingly across the country.

For fifteen years now, the only backpack I have owned has been this combination of one of the successive Trailwise frames and big bags. I suppose such a house is really too elaborate for short trips, but it has proved so comfortable and efficient, and I

---

* They've now done so. The new version is 3 inches deeper, front to rear, and the mainsack's capacity is 5423 cubic inches (pockets additional). Although I've yet to give it a genuine bulky-load field test, it looks good. Better, anyway.

handle it now with so little thought, that it rarely occurs to me to turn to something else, even for a one-day jaunt.

Alternative assessments of currently available packs

For an exhaustive and knowledgeable examination of the relative merits of fifteen leading pack models, see *Backpacker* Magazine No. 1 (Spring 1973). The survey is a meticulous and largely objective comparison of a representative selection of the models available (in 1972, 334 varieties from at least 15 manufacturers, says the article). This approach is diametrically opposite to my subjective description of one intimately known pack in the hope of indicating the essential features to bear in mind. And, predictably, the editorial preferences are not identical to mine. Yet—although all but a few final corrections of this revised chapter were written well before I saw the article—we do not, I think, fundamentally disagree. I suppose I should admit that the survey probes more deeply into some corners than I do. But there are limits to honesty.

MODIFICATIONS

I have made two minor modifications to my pack, as I did to its predecessors:

Office-on-the-yoke

Because I often walk without a shirt and therefore without a front pocket, I have had a 5-by-6-inch pocket sewn onto the front of my yoke strap, roughly where the shirt pocket comes. Into it go notebook and map, and sunglasses when not in use. Pen, pencil and thermometer (page 361) clip onto the rear, between pocket and strap, where they are very securely held—not, as they used to, in front, where removing map or notebook can flip them out unnoticed. I cannot imagine how I ever got along without such a pocket. Mine is made of ordinary blue-jean material, but anything stout will do. Moor and Mountain now make a nylon fabric "Guide and Map Pocket" based on this idea, but including a flap, that does much the same job (1 inch by 5 inches by 7 inches; 2 ounces; $6). I've tried the pocket out, and it works—though the slick nylon does not hold pens and pencils well. It suspends by

adjustable webbing from the shoulder-strap clevis pin and fastens
to the yoke with Velcro-closed loops.*

For which side to put your office, see page 90.

Binocular bump-pad

My binoculars normally travel slung on a short cord over the
projecting top of the frame, at my left shoulder (page 69). At
each step they bump, very gently, against the frame. For years I
accepted the slight metallic sound without thinking about it. Then,
one summer when I was out with a party in the Washington
Cascades, a young fellow who had been following close behind me
for several days said, "You know, I can't understand how you toler-
ate the rattle of those binoculars just behind your ear. Even walking
several feet back of you like this, it nearly drives me crazy." After
that, of course, it began to drive me crazy too, so I finally stuck a
thick wrap of air mattress patching fabric around the frame's upright and crossbar, just where the binoculars bump (illustration,
page 69). Soon I was happily back to not noticing the muffled
sound. I imagine fewer animals are scared out of my view, too.
Naturally, the pad needs a patch from time to time, when it wears
through.

For further notes on carriage of binoculars see page 326.

* Velcro tapes, used as closures on much clothing and a few pack pockets,
come in pairs. One tape is a mass of small, stiff, contorted loops: through a
magnifying glass it looks like the innards of old-fashioned horsehair furniture.
The mating tape wears row upon serried rank of tiny nylon hooks: magnified,
it looks like a broad but ill-designed tank barrier, or perhaps a crooks' cemetery.
When you press the tapes together, hooks snag loops—and cling fairly tena-
ciously. But you can easily peel the tapes apart.

A modification I have in mind is a

Removable top-of-frame loop.

Mostly, I'm glad my packframe has projecting ends: from them I sling binoculars, camera and sometimes hat (pages 84 and 326). But in thick country, especially when you have to crawl and the projections point forward, they're a menace. They continually grab vegetation, often pull you up dead. A ferruled loop joining the projections and fitted when the country demanded it might at time be a worthwhile thing to carry. Later: The Ski Hut now makes just such a loop for Trailwise packs. It looks a bit fussy, but I'll probably give it a go.

Two pack modifications I have never tried are:

Tumpline

A tumpline is an adjustable band that runs around your forehead and attaches to the packframe, usually to its sides, and helps take some of the strain of heavy loads off back and shoulders. A friend of mine who occasionally uses one says it is an appreciable help, especially on steep upgrades. Unfortunately, he says, you cannot really use one effectively until your neck muscles have grown accustomed to the unfamiliar strain.

Tumplines should apparently be attached to packframes as low down as possible. At a pinch they can, in an emergency, be used alone. The women in parts of Africa use them that way all the time for huge loads.

Rain cover

Kelty now makes a waterproof nylon shell that fits over the entire pack, "for those sleeping hours or in a downpour." Though designed for Kelty bags (which are uncoated nylon, and therefore porous) and made to fit specific sizes, they—or facsimiles—seem a possibility for almost any pack (4 ounces; $5).

FITTING A PACK

Choosing the right size frame for your frame is largely a matter of matching the distance between upper shoulder-strap connection and waistbelt on the packframe with the distance between your shoulders and hips. Any competent mountain shop salesman will set you straight. The Alpine Designs packframe has cross-members secured to the uprights with polycarbonate plastic couplings that are adjustable and so "allow you to custom-fit the frame to your own back by repositioning the adjustable bar." Although I've yet to see one of these frames, I rather wonder if I don't hear a distant Murphy rumble (page 80); but there are good reports—and the system certainly sounds like a very viable proposition for bean-stalking teen-agers, and for cases in which one pack must fit several individuals.

Choosing the make and model that works best on your particular body—apart, that is, from the cerebral and emotional choices among the features we've already discussed—has to be a matter of trial and error. At least, I think so. Hip shape may be one big factor, body length another; but the rest tail away into such barely quantifiable subtleties as dynamic muscle relationships and idiosyncratic gait. In practice, the choice, though possibly confirmed by rental trial, will mostly be made in the store by trying on various packs. Load each with at least 20 pounds of gear, and preferably as much as you habitually carry. Select the one that feels most comfortable when you walk.

It is important that you adjust and fit the pack correctly. For that first trial you'll likely have a salesman to help. But thereafter, forevermore, rock and forest, desert and mountain, morning and afternoon, you must fit the monster correctly and without thought. To avoid bad habits, make sure you start right. First follow any instructions that come with the pack. (They may—as with the new Trailwise yokes [page 75]—supersede the instructions I give here.) Then, with your waistbelt undone, adjust the shoulder straps until their point of attachment to the frame is roughly level with the tops of your shoulders. (Some packs have several holes punched in the shoulder-level crossbar, and you can space the yoke straps to the most comfortable position.) Next, hunch your shoulders so that the pack lifts a little, and cinch the waistbelt tight.

At this stage, it is important to remember that "waistbelt" is a misnomer: the belt should bear not on your waist but on the protruding bones of your hips. Once the load has settled down on your back, the belt will slant slightly upward and forward. On some packs you can adjust the waistbelt so that it bears in the right place by moving the belt attachment to the frame up or down. In others, you adjust the yoke-to-frame attachment point. In some you can adjust at both sites.

Wear the belt tight. First, pull firmly. Then hoist the pack higher on your back and tighten again. Now take a deep breath and pull even harder. If the belt almost hurts, it's about right.

At first you may find that the tight belt, taking almost the whole weight of the pack, tends to constrict your hip muscles. It may even cause mild cramp pains. But persevere. In a day or two the muscles will accept their new work. And the ease with which you now find yourself carrying the load will soon make you forget any temporary discomfort. If you want to, you can ease the strain from time to time by loosening the belt and returning the load to the shoulders. At least, I understand that is the theory. In practice, I find I almost never do so.

On packs with a single long nylon-mesh backband, keep it as tight as possible. On packs with double solid-fabric bands, keep the lower one tight as a drum. If you keep the top band tight you will improve ventilation behind your back; if you slacken it a shade you may improve the riding qualities of the pack slightly by angling the frame somewhat further forward.

For weight distribution in pack, see page 89.

ALTERNATIVES TO TUBULAR PACKFRAMES

In advanced rock climbing—when you hammer hardware into the rock and haul your baggage up sheer faces—an aluminum frame would continually snag. Some kind of soft bag is needed. I can offer no advice, so see the catalogues. (Such plumber's work has nothing to do with walking, of course, but you may have to walk long and sweaty to reach your place.) A little old-style climbing —when you reduce the world to yourself and the clean, simple rock, and then leave it as it was, undefiled—is something you may run into in the course of a walking trip; and at such times an aluminum frame can become a protruding and perishing nuisance. Ditto when you have to crash hour after hour through brush (though for a palliative, see page 85). Another alternative, assuming you are to carry any kind of a load, is a rucksack, with or without a small frame. Some people seem to find such bags bearable, even for heavy loads.

The catalogues now teem with neat little packs of various sizes, designed for day or overnight trips. Some of them look very good (see, especially, Cannondale of Connecticut).

Belt bags

These cunning little nylon pouches that belt around your waist seem to offer a sensible alternative to the small orthodox shoulder-restricting pack both for day strolls and for sidetrips away from your main pack. Some of the best are designed for skiers (around 6 ounces; $6). For a makeshift alternative, see page 298.

Child carriers

Tubular-frame carriers that distribute the load much like an ordinary frame pack (without waistbelt) apparently make carrying small children a relatively painless business. The Gerry models, in which the child faces forward, seem to be the most popular. (Kiddie Pack, with adjustable seat and storage space underneath—stated load 35–45 pounds: 1 pound 4 ounces, $15; deluxe version, better padded, with airy, easy-clean seat: 1 pound 8 ounces, $20; Kiddie Seat—similar to Kiddie Pack, but with nonadjustable seat, no storage space:—1 pound, $10.)

I claim no experience, but I'm told that although most children seem happier facing forward, a few won't keep their cotton-picking fingers out of Mom or Dad's hair. One solution: a model in which the little darling faces backwards. Disadvantages: possible temper tantrums due to isolated position—and a load with its center of gravity inefficiently further from the carrier's back. If you'd like it both ways, consider Himalayan Industries' "Easy Rider" models, in which the loved one can face either fore or aft, depending on state of love (Model 7000: 1 pound 14 ounces; $14.95. Model 7040—fancier, with sub-buttock storage sack: 2 pounds 2 ounces; $24.95).

For very short hauls there are frameless fabric affairs such as the Gerry Pleatseat (5 ounces; $3.50).

For very long hauls—or children grown agonizingly heavy—you can lash a framed carrier to your regular packframe.

A dog's life

Gerry now makes—wait for it!—a Doggie Pack: two zippered, nylon-duck panniers, leather-reinforced at corners, held in place by a chest-encircling yoke (11 ounces; $20).

Remember, though, that dogs are forbidden on National Park trails and in many other places. Also that, joyful companions though they may be, few of them are reliably enough disciplined

to avoid being on occasion a pain to other people and a danger
to wildlife and themselves.

THE WALLS IN ACTION

Packing

It is too early to consider ways of stowing gear into your
house: we have not yet discussed the furniture. See page 374. But
we should at this stage take a look at the general principles of
weight distribution.

It was always said, and I think rightly, that with the old
shoulder-load packs you should keep the weight as high as possible.
Most makers maintain that even with a waistbelt, high loading is
still an advantage. That is one reason they make three-quarter-
length bags: the main load rides high; your sleeping bag, which
weighs precious little, sits at the foot. I remain in a state of mild
skepticism (even though it is undoubtedly true in theory that because most packs ride most of the time with their tops tilted slightly
forward, a high load rides closer to your center of gravity). I made
a few rough and ready experiments by moving twenty pounds of
full canteens to points as high and as low as they would fit in my
otherwise normally loaded packbag, and found little or no difference between the feel of the two loads. A later trial when I was
carrying a heavy load of canteens from a river to a distant camp—
with almost nothing else in the bag—did seem to suggest at first
that lashing the canteens up high made a great deal of difference;
but reflection convinced me that the change could well have been
a result of holding the load closer to my back. Carrying the load
low obviously lowers your center of gravity, and the greater stability can be important: in skiing, snowshoeing and difficult climb-

ing, for example, and when crossing rugged terrain or battling high winds. Several makers have now followed Kelty's lead and recommend that under such conditions you consider carrying the sleeping bag on top and moving the bag down to the lower part of the frame.

There is no doubt about the value of keeping a load close to your back. At one stage of the California walk I got into the habit of tying my sleeping bag on the back of the pack. When rain forced me to stuff it inside again one day, I was amazed at the improvement in the way the pack rode. As far as possible I now stow all heavy articles close to the packframe, or at least keep them away from the back of the bag (page 374). And the contouring of the frame, combined with the pull of the waistbelt, holds the load as close to my back as is consistent with adequate ventilation.

Getting the pack onto your back

You carry out this operation in the field many times each day, and the total energy consumed is considerable. At the end of an exhausting day it might even be crucial. So it pays to give the matter some thought.

The easiest way to load is to use a loading platform—a convenient rockledge or bank or fallen tree trunk—and just slip your arms though the yoke straps.

Failing a loading platform—and rest assured that you will almost always fail—you can sit down, enyoke, and then stand up with an easy if inelegant sidle. With a back-breaking load this is about the only possible method. I believe it is the one the time-and-motion sages agree is the least expensive in energy.

Yet for all but the very heaviest loads I find that the simplest method is to hoist the pack up into position with an easy swinging motion, one hand gripping the yoke and the other the small nylon hand strap on the upper crossbar of my packframe (illustration, page 69). Swing the pack up from whichever side comes naturally; but if you use an office-on-the-yoke (page 83) make sure you have it stitched on the yoke strap that slips onto your shoulders first. On the other side it will infallibly foul things up.

The question remains: "At what stage should I switch from the easy-swing-up to the sit-and-enyoke method?" My own answer is: "Not until somewhere around sixty pounds, and not even then for sure." I find that by swinging the pack up onto a raised upper leg first, and then onto the shoulders without ever quite stopping, you use surprisingly little energy. Yet one experienced friend of mine sits-and-enyokes with a load as low as 40 pounds. To find out what suits you, experiment.

Pack, sweet pack

Whenever I am out on my own, free from civilization, and my pack is in every way my home, containing everything on which my continued existence depends, I find that I develop a reluctance to move very far from it. Even a sidetrip of an hour or two involves a battle with this reluctance—an almost physical tearing away. For a long time I assumed that mine was an idiosyncratic caution, but I find—hardly to my surprise, come to think of it—that other lone backpackers quickly arrive at the same sensible state of mind.

THE WALLS AS NONWALLS

Your more or less empty pack may from time to time act as windbreak on one side of a tent or bivouac, as ground insulation for your feet when they protrude out beyond a three-quarter-length air mattress or pad (pages 244 and 248), or even as a pillow. If it is big enough, and uncompartmented, it could make a water- and windproof cover for the foot of your sleeping bag—though you would have to check that it did not soak the bag in the moisture escaping from your body. It could certainly make an emergency footsack in the horrendous event you burned or otherwise lost the use of your sleeping bag. On such occasions, sleeve-with-drawstring tops are obviously best. I recently found an experimental sack by Bergan of Norway with a 25-inch sleeve that came up to my armpits.

But for my money by far the most important auxiliary use is

The pack as backrest.

If you prop the full pack at an angle and lean against it so that your back comes between the side and center pockets, it makes a very comfortable chair back. When the bag has been emptied or part-emptied, prop the frame at right angles to your axis and lean back on it, with or without the luxury padding of an air mattress or foam pad (pages 243 and 248).

When you can, simply prop the pack against a tree or rock. But if, like me, you believe in resting on the smoothest and softest piece of ground in sight, there will nine times out of ten be no such convenience. So mostly you use your staff as the prop. It soon becomes almost automatic, the moment you halt—even for a ten-minute rest—to look for a rock or crevice or a tree or even just a clump of grass to wedge the butt of the staff against. Failing all these—and here again you will fail regularly—just angle-prod the staff down into the soil until it holds firmly, with or without an assist from a stone, and then jam the top of the staff between the yoke and the top crossbar of the pack, hard up against the bag. (The nylon hand strap on my pack holds it perfectly.) Fine-adjust the angle of the packframe, sit thankfully down, and lean back. But lean so that your back thrust is along the staff's axis. Otherwise the pack will assuredly skew. It will skew anyway, from time to time, no matter how careful you are. But care helps. This all sounds rather complicated, I know; but after a while the whole operation takes about four seconds—and virtually no conscious thought (unless your packframe has a rounded foot that skews and skids at a touch on almost any ground: no amount of conscious thought will teach such mavericks a lasting subservience).

Kitchen

FOOD

There is an altogether delightful simplicity about the idea of just walking out and away and living off the land, and the system's allure is stiffened by obvious practical advantages: no heavy food in your pack; constant variety; fresh, vitamin-rich products at every plucking. It seems as if you could hardly ask for a more perfect fusion of romance and efficiency.

Forget it. Above all, forget the efficiency. There are no doubt a few places in which certain select souls could live off the land and still find time to do one or two other things as well, but my advice is to leave the happy dreams to those who have never tried it.

That does not mean ignoring what the land drops into your lap (see, especially, Euell Gibbons's *Stalking the Wild Asparagus* and other books; and two little decks of cards—one for *the Western States,* one for *the Eastern States*—with color photographs and text on *Edible and Poisonous Plants* [each deck 3½ ounces; $4.95 post free from Plant Deck Inc., 2134 S.W. Wembley Park, Lake Oswego, Oregon 97034]). I often supplement my regular rations with trout, and occasionally with mushrooms or watercress or a few wild strawberries. And not long ago I came close to eating my first rattlesnake steak. But in most cases and places, the time and energy you would have to expend in shooting, snaring, catching or otherwise gathering in a day's food and then preparing it are simply better applied elsewhere. Anyway, such hunting and cropping have little place in today's pressured wilderness: even where not illegal, they're mostly immoral.

An emergency is a different matter (see, for example, page 401 for rattlesnakes as emergency rations). And a deliberate attempt to live off the land may be well worth it for the spiritual effect of sheer primitive simplicity. But for normal walking, when one of your objects is to get somewhere or to do something when you get there, like climbing or looking or lazing, I recommend unequivocally that you carry just about everything you expect to need.

In choosing what foods to take, consider:

1. Nutritional values, especially stick-to-guttability
2. Weight
3. Ease of preparation
4. Palatability
5. Packaging (with a special thought for litter)
6. Cost

On every count, except cost, the only answer is dehydrated food—either freeze- or vacuum-dried. Less than 2¼ pounds of it can satisfy your nutritional needs for a highly energetic day. You can, if you want to, concoct complicated, multi-flavored dishes. On the other hand—and this may sometimes loom large in your planning—you can keep the cooking childishly simple and still have a palatable and nourishing meal. What's more, although a steaming mass of meat bar and dehydrated potatoes is hardly the kind of dish you would want to find on the table at home, I assure you that at the end of a twenty-mile hike it can taste better than a filet mignon in any city restaurant.

Modern packaging of such foods is convenient too. Vacuum-dried items mostly come in strong, ultralight, moisture-resistant envelopes made of some material such as polyethylene that can be burned after use. Because freeze-dried foods must be kept from contact with the air until used, they—and some vacuum-dried foods too—come in foil packages. The foil cannot be burned, but it is very light to pack out. See also pages 120 and 187.

Dehydrated food, properly processed and packaged, is stable. Its flavor does not become haylike. (Freeze-dried food, in particular, stays highly sapid.) Provided the water content remains below 5 percent neither bacteria nor mold will grow on it and insects will not eat it. It is not perfect, of course. It tends to be expensive, makes you fart like a bull, and may demand a certain quota of tender loving care to make it consistently palatable. But if you are carrying any considerable number of days' rations it is the only practical solution.

In America we now have—for the present, anyway—such a wealth of special backpacking foods, and of other foods eminently suitable for backpacking, that there is no longer any real problem about finding something that will do, only about making suitable decisions. But before we dip into our cornucopia we had better examine some general considerations.

There are two possible approaches to backpacking gastrology:

Trial and Error, in which you follow personal preferences and are guided only by rules of thumb; and

The Scientific Nutritional Method, in which you calculate in calories and try to balance the carbohydrate-protein-fat intake against your energy output.

Trial and error

The advantage of this approach is that, although it involves a lot of built-in chance, your answers begin with a bias toward your individual requirements and evolve along the same axis. This is important, physiologically and psychologically. Each individual's alimentary system works in its own idiosyncratic way. And different men have very different philosophies of outdoor eating. Some like to make a meal out of making a meal. Some almost seem to make each trip one long making of meals. At the other extreme lie those who, like me, were born British and therefore, as far as food goes, barbaric.*

I began, the way most people do, with the trial-and-error method. That is, I stood and looked at the packages in the stores and listened to a little advice and even took some of it. If I found I was at all hungry on a trip, I took a bit more next time. If—as was far more likely—I had a lot left over, I retrenched. If an item tasted good and/or seemed to keep my legs going like pistons, I tended to take it again. If not, not. Anything that turned out to be a nuisance to prepare, I promptly dropped. Continually, though never lavishly, I experimented. And in the course of time I developed a well-tested backpacking menu, entirely adequate for a barbarian.

But one day it occurred to me that the logical approach was the strictly rational, quantitative,

Scientific nutritional method.

It seemed to me that by tailoring a diet to my exact nutritional requirements under specified conditions and by paring vigorously away as usual at the half ounces I could hardly fail to come up with the most economical menu—economical, that is, in terms

___
* Hell has been described as a place in which the politicians are French, the policemen German, and the cooks British.

of weight and energy. I might have to allow for a few personal fads and fancies, but that was all.

First I disposed of the often-raised mineral and vitamin questions. I knew that the public mind has been obfuscated on both counts by dense, dollar-delivering Madison Avenue smokescreens, and I confirmed, as I expected, that unless you are going to walk for a year or more in country known to be deficient in some vital mineral such as iodine or cobalt and are going to live on nothing but locally grown produce (a pretty unlikely combination of events), you can forget the minerals. If you are in normal health you can forget the vitamins for at least a month and probably forever, though on a trip longer than a month you can, if you like, take along multi-vitamin pills. They weigh very little and may protect your peace of mind.*

Next I looked at fat and protein requirements. It seems, though it cannot yet be fully explained, that certain minimum amounts of each are essential. Accepted guideline minima are: fats—20 percent of total caloric intake; protein—45 grams per day per 100 pounds bodyweight (though your body cannot assimilate the protein properly if you eat the full requirement at a single sitting).

Fats contain approximately 9 calories per unit of weight compared with 4 calories in the same weight of protein or carbohydrate, and they therefore form by far the most efficient food in terms of calories per unit of weight. Although no meaningful figures exist (the technical literature hedges, even cites "fast and slow stomachs"), it seems to be accepted that the energy from fats and protein is released over longer periods than that from carbohydrates, and that they are therefore less efficient for booster snacks but excellent for what might be called all-day or all-night background. The body has to work hard to digest them—much harder than with carbohydrates—so they should in general be avoided during or immediately before very strenuous exercise. As far as is

---

* When I wrote the first edition of this book I was a firm unbeliever in the vitamin jag.

But I have since read the gospel according to Saint Linus (*Vitamin C and the Common Cold*, by Linus Pauling [San Francisco, 1970]), and after a little experimenting I'm inclined to think that at least the suppression system works. So now, dammit, I carry vitamin C pills. I have also noted, but chosen to disregard, the fact that the gospel—though this time without visible supporting evidence—also preaches multi-vitamin supplementation of your diet.

In addition I have discovered that when I am struck down by certain fell diseases, and especially by Fletcheritis (a debilitating if opaque somatic affliction typically induced by extreme worry about writing a book), then certain potions based on vitamin B will, especially when bestowed intramuscularly, work bloody wonders.

In other words, I am no longer so scathingly sure. At the very least, I must redraw your attention to the words "If you are in normal health . . ."

known at present, there seems no purely nutritional reason why calorie-efficient fats should not make up at least 35 percent of a diet, and perhaps much more.*

Remember, though, that fats may raise a palatability problem, especially at high altitude. Up high, anyone's appetite is liable to falter. In particular, you may revolt against the very thought of fats and proteins. The elevation at which such awkward things happen varies widely from person to person, even from trip to trip. It may start as low as 8000 or 9000 feet. It's apparently rather likely to happen above, say, 17,000. Slow acclimation helps but does not necessarily cure. All you can really do is take along a fair variety of foods and hope there's always something in your pack that appeals to you. Sweet things are probably the best bet, but the range of sudden demands is unpredictable. Frank Smythe, struggling on and up, alone, toward the summit of Mount Everest, longed for frankfurters and sauerkraut; Ed Hillary, high on Cho Oyu the year before he climbed Everest, for pineapple cubes. I had always thought these reports a bit farfetched. But on one trip I found myself feeling, at a mere 14,000 feet, the same craving for pineapple. Such vagaries of appetite are the results of a particular kind of stress. A soldier may face a similar situation, and the U.S. Army Food Service recognizes the palatability problem that can arise under combat stress. They have a saying, "It doesn't matter how many calories you give a man if he won't eat." In the mountains, the trick is to guess right—short of pineapple cubes— and still keep your menu practical. It's as simple as that. And as difficult.

Unfortunately, I cannot let you read the passage drafted for this space. It gave sage scientific reasons, with contradictions, for the apparent reluctance of many people to eat fats at high altitude or in extreme heat. I was terribly proud of my research. But by the time it had been gnawed at by two unimpeachable experts—both genuinely helpful people too—my mind was in turmoil. Frankly, the experts also admitted a degree of confusion—or at least of doubt. Which is perhaps where we presently stand.

With these preparatory matters out of the way I turned, in my search for a scientific nutritional method, to the first part of the basic problem: computing total energy supply.

* I am being deliberately vague. At present, the full facts about fats (or "lipids" as nutritionists usually call them) are simply not understood. Neither are the facts about human idiosyncrasies. When I was in the nutritional sciences department of a university checking some figures for this chapter, I saw on the blackboard in a room of delightfully unstuffy researchers the plaint: "Lipids are inscrutable." But someone had struck out "lipids" and substituted "guinea pigs."

First I set about learning how to calculate the nutritional content of various foods. Almost at once I discovered *Agricultural Handbook No. 8: Composition of Foods*, published by the U.S. Department of Agriculture. I recommend this book to anyone at all interested in a scientific approach to outdoor eating (or, for that matter, indoor eating). Most of its 190 pages consist of two vastly comprehensive tables headed "Composition of foods, 100 grams, edible portion" and (better still for our purposes) "Nutrients in the edible portion of 1 pound of food as purchased." These tables analyze in detail the nutritional make-up of everything from abalone (raw and canned), through muffins, to zwieback. It is worth remembering, though, that the figures for many foods can be only approximations. As a nutrition expert warned me: "No two wheat germs are quite alike." (See, I suspect, the rather surprising figures the table gives for different kinds of trout.)

The book also contains several supplementary tables (Table 6 gives accurate calories-per-gram figures for selected foods) and some mildly useful notes. It does not contain, as it should, the information that 1 gram = 0.357 ounces, and that therefore 100 grams = 3.57 ounces; or that 1 ounce = 28.35 grams. Even if you are not about to use these full and rather forbidding figures, you need a rough conversion rate.

Public libraries—except, perhaps, very small ones—are likely to have reference copies of *Handbook No. 8*. There is sure to be one in the nutritional science library of any university, and with luck you'll be able to buy a copy from the student union bookstore or its equivalent. Failing that, you can, in the due course of bureaucratic time, get one for $2 from The Superintendent of Documents, U.S. Government Printing Office, Washington, D.C. 20402.

By studying *Handbook No. 8,* consulting various manufacturers, and reading much small print on many labels, I managed to calculate the caloric, protein, and fat content of each item on my standard food list for a seven-day period—the normal basis on which I plan. (Because my original calculations were based on this list, it must obviously stand; but as we shall see, both my tastes and the available foods have now changed.) In one or two cases, where figures were unobtainable, I substituted guesswork for calculation. There's a certain amount of it involved in any such game. It is often difficult, for example, to assess from available figures exactly what percentage of the caloric content of a food is in fat form: two sources of information may supply widely divergent figures. But a nutrition expert has checked the following table and detects no flagrant errors.

Lbs.	Oz.			Energy value Calories	Fat energy value Calories	Protein Grams
2	0		Dry cereal mixture (Fini or Familia)	3200	700	90
0	12	3	Pkg. dehydrated fruit (4 oz.)	1200	30	14
0	9	6	Energy bars	1200	480	48
0	4		Beef jerky	410	40	98
1	4	8	Pkg. dried soup (average)	2400	680	85
0	1	1	Pkg. instant gravy powder	100	10	5
1	5	7	Meat food product bars	3590	2420	283
1	4	5	Pkg. dehydrated beans (4 oz.)	1930	90	127
0	8	2	Pkg. dehydrated potatoes (4 oz.)	800	10	19
0	4	1	Pkg. dehydrated mixed vegetables (4 oz.)	400	10	9
0	1		Herbs and spices	0	0	0
1	6		Powdered nonfat milk	2230	40	223
1	8		Granulated sugar	2620	0	0
0	8	1	Bar semisweet chocolate	1150	640	10
1	5	3½	Bars Kendal Mint Cake candy (6 oz.)	2290	0	0
1	0		Dry raisins	1310	0	11
0	3	30	Tea bags	0	0	0
0	6	2	Pkg. fruit-drink mix	600	0	0
0	4		Margarine	820	810	1
0	3		Salt	0	0	0
0	1		Salt tablets (about 40) (30 percent dextrose)	30	0	0
0	3		Emergency ration: 1 meat bar	510	350	40
			Total for one week	26,790	6310	1063
			Average daily total	3830	900 (23.5 percent)	152

At first glance, the 3830 daily caloric total struck me as a little low, but I postponed judgment. Naturally, I was relieved to find that my diet provided more than the guideline minima for both fats and protein: fats, 23.5 percent of total caloric intake as against a recommended minimum of 20 percent; protein, 152 grams as against the recommended minimum requirement of 85 grams, based on my bodyweight (190 pounds).

With these intake figures established, I turned to the second part of the food-to-output tailoring process: calculating what my body needed for maintenance and exercise under various conditions. If I had been starting from scratch, without a food list to evaluate, I should probably have begun on this tack. I'm glad I didn't.

I soon learned that for maintenance alone (basal metabolism) the average person needs about 1100 calories per day per 100 pounds of bodyweight. In city-slob shape—which is the way I seem to start just about every backpacking trip—I weighed around 190 pounds. So mere maintenance drained off 2090 calories from my daily total of 3830.

During the process of digestion, the body consumes a certain amount of energy as heat. This factor is called, for some reason, "specific dynamic action." It fluctuates between 6 percent and rather more than 10 percent of the total caloric intake. For simplicity, it is usually averaged at 10 percent. So in my case specific dynamic action accounted for another 380 calories. 2470 of the total gone; 1360 left. I began to wonder.

Next I got down to assessing energy output over and above these constants. I quickly ran to earth a table of fascinating figures. The moment I began to read the table I thought, Ah, *this* is the answer. Now, nothing can stop me.

THE ENERGY COST OF ACTIVITIES*
(exclusive of basal metabolism and influence of food)

	Calories per 100 lbs. per hour
Walking: on hard, smooth, level surface, at 2 mph	45
at 3 mph	90
at 4 mph	160
(For walking on rough trails, multiply each figure by a rather arbitrary figure of 2.)	
Standing relaxed	30
Sitting, quietly	20
Eating	20
Dressing and undressing	30

* Most of these figures are derived from T. M. Carpenter: *Factors and Formulas for Computing Respiratory Exchange and Biological Transformations of Energy* (Carnegie Institute, 1948 edn.), p. 136.

Lying still, awake	5
Sleeping (basal metabolism only)	0
Shivering, very severe	up to 220
Sawing wood	260
Swimming, at 2 mph	360
Writing	20
Dishwashing	45
Laundry (light)	60
Singing in a loud voice	35

This table lists several other activities that make interesting reading, and all of them might, at a pinch and on a highly diversified walking trip, become ancillary pursuits:

	Calories per 100 lbs. per hour
Typewriting, rapidly	45
Driving an automobile	40
Bicycling (moderate speed)	110
Horseback riding, walk	65
trot	200
gallop	300
Running	320
Boxing	520
Rowing	730

Come to think of it, campfire concerts often feature harmonica and recorder accompaniment, and I suppose there is no reason why it should stop there. So:

	Calories per 100 lbs. per hour
Violin playing	25
Cello playing	60
Piano playing, Mendelssohn's songs	35
Beethoven's *Appassionata*	65
Liszt's *Tarantella*	90

Almost all walking includes some uphill work. And it seems that, assuming a body efficiency of 30 percent, you use about 110 calories in raising every 100 pounds of bodyweight each 1000 feet of elevation. For practical purposes, you can add the weight of your pack direct to bodyweight.

Armed with all these figures (but already suffering misgivings)

I began to work out energy sums for an average fairly hard day's wilderness walking. I pictured myself, at 190 pounds, carrying a 50-pound pack, walking on a rough trail for seven hours (with halts), gaining a total of 3000 feet in elevation, and otherwise doing all the things you do on an average day. Juggling with the figures I had gathered, and trying to pin down the hours of a wilderness day along the lines of the table on page 32, I came up with:

	Calories
Basal metabolism (190 lbs. @ 1100 cals. per 100 lbs.)	2090
Climbing 3000 feet (240 lbs. @ 110 cals. per 1000 ft.)	760
6 hours actual walking, at 2 mph (240 lbs. @ 45 cals. per hour per 100 lbs., times a factor of 2 for roughness of trail)	1250
3 hours dishwashing, laundering (light), making and striking camp, photography, compulsive dallying, and unmentionable activities (average: 50 cals. per 100 lb.-hours)	290
3 hours dressing and undressing, standing (relaxed), singing in a loud voice, cooking, and such items as evaporated time (quite unaccountable for) (average: 30 cals. per 100 lb.-hours)	160
3 hours eating, writing notes, and sitting quietly (halts, rapt contemplation, worrying, elevated thinking, general sloth) (average: 20 cals. per 100 lb.-hours)	110
1 minute lying still, awake (to nearest cal.)	0
8 hours 59 minutes sleeping (including catnaps	0
Total	4660
Plus specific dynamic action, 10 percent	470
Total day's energy output	5130

Even before I arrived at this figure and stopped to contemplate with dismay the gulf between it and my theoretical daily food consumption of 3830 calories, I knew something was going wrong with my neat little sums. Some of the figures in the energy output table were obviously very rough approximations indeed. The efficiency with which you walk, saw wood, do laundry (light), or sing in a loud voice may vary drastically from day to day, even from hour to hour. And you perform most wilderness activities much more efficiently after you have been out for a week. Altitude tells, too.

But the biggest variable is the individual. All the figures are for average people, and although rough theoretical allowances can apparently be made for discernible differences due to age, build, sex, and even race, the critical question remains, "How do I, personally, function?" The spread, even between apparently similar individuals, can be wide. About 70 percent of people fall within a fairly narrow central efficiency range; but if you belong to the 30 percent in any one function—and the chances are that you do— then any computation may give highly misleading results.

At this point in my investigations I began to suspect that the right approach to the food question was, after all, *trial and error* and not the strict, rational, quantitative, *scientific method.* With considerable misgivings, I voiced this thought to several experienced research workers in the field of human nutrition. To my surprise, they tended to agree. Present knowledge, they said, left too many variables for any very meaningful quantitative balancing of energy input and output. The best way was to "get out in the field and establish bases for your own personal nutrition requirements." To do, in other words, just about what I had done in the first place.*

Now the last thing I want to suggest is that the scientific method turns out to be useless. If I thought so I should hardly have inflicted eight pages of it on you. Nowadays I routinely apply what I have learned to make rough calorie counts and even esti- mates of protein and fat content for almost any food list I assemble. And I'm convinced that even a little knowledge of the principles of human nutrition can be an invaluable aid to anyone striving to evolve a backpack diet that suits his needs. Had I known what I know now, my early trials would have been less tribulatory, my errors less gross. I could have ensured much sooner, for example, that my diet contained enough fats and protein. Early menus, as on the six-month California walk, were almost certainly low in both. The caloric content was considerably lower, too, than in the later diet I used for calculation, and I remember feeling a little faint at the end of one or two really long days.

So please do not write off my energy input and output tables as stillborn theorizing. Apart from anything else, what I've learned

---

* A Texan who read this paragraph was good enough to send me a sup- porting quote from *Changing Times* Magazine of August 1969: "Even the best- laid systems analysis can go agley. Charles J. Hitch, formerly with the RAND Corp. and the Department of Defense [and now president of the University of California], tells about a sophisticated systems analyst who was told by his doc- tor to lose weight. He consulted with experts to discover his minimum require- ments for proteins, carbohydrates, fats, vitamins, minerals, etc. Next he obtained the quantities of these food elements in each of the 500 or 600 foods on his list. Then, on the plausible theory that mass is filling and that most dieting attempts fail because the subject feels hungry, he maximized, subject to various con- straints, the weight (not counting water content) of the diet that would give him his minimum caloric requirements. Finally, he fed the data into a com- puter and asked it for the perfect diet. The answer supplied by the computer was that, in addition to minor quantities of various foods, he should drink 80 gallons of vinegar per day."

According to *Agricultural Handbook No. 8*, that makes 35,964 calories a day in vinegar alone—enough to keep Goliath bounding along. But, at 666 pounds, it unfortunately falls short of being the ideal backpacking menu.

about nutrition in the course of preparing them has helped me build some solid-looking bridges across the gap they have revealed between my actual intake and apparent needs.

On long trips, I usually take one day of almost total rest in every week of walking. Often I take two. On these days I normally eat less than on the others. So for the days that really demand energy I have rather more than the standard quota available—more than 4000 calories, almost certainly.

In addition, I tend to nibble away at small quantities of food throughout the day, and this little-and-often kind of intake turns out to be the most efficient, especially for quick-burning carbohydrates. And experiments suggest that as you get progressively more tired, so your muscles need more and more carbohydrate, as opposed to fat, to keep them going.

But the really big factor, in more ways than one, may be my spare tire. I know from happy experience that my midriff begins to deflate after just a few days of walking with a load. On the California and Grand Canyon trips the tire vanished. The Grand Canyon trip was the only time I have ever done a before-and-after weighing, and in those two strenuous months I dropped from 194 to 174 pounds. I am fairly sure that almost all the loss came in the very strenuous first half—a conclusion borne out by nutrition experts who say, "Weight loss is usually most marked at the start of any stepped-up exercise." I lost, then, something approaching 20 pounds in thirty days. Up to two-thirds of this loss, or about 14 pounds, is likely to have been fat. (Water would account for most of the balance.) Now it seems that the body uses this fat just as efficiently as it does fat ingested by mouth. That is, it extracts 9 calories per gram, or about 4000 calories per pound. In other words, my 14 pounds of fat gave me an additional 56,000 calories in thirty days, or close to 2000 calories per day! Too many imponderables are involved in reaching this rather astonishing figure for us to accept it as at all accurate. But to say the least, it makes the theoretical daily gap of 1300 calories between my apparent needs and actual intake yawn a great deal less capaciously.

In conclusion, then, it seems to me that the way to work out a good backpacking diet is to go on a shakedown cruise and find out by trial and error what suits you. If this sounds too unscientific for your temperament, call it "going out in the field and establishing personal nutritional bases." A good starting point is the U.S. Army allowance of 4400 calories per man for heavy work. (Allowance for "normal" work, 3600; for sedentary jobs, 2800.) To translate calories into ounces of food, consult *Agricultural Handbook No. 8* or some simplified list. Remember that most backpackers, including me, tend to err on the side of taking too much food. From there, play it by ear. But keep the ear carefully cocked in the direction of calories and proteins and fats and the like. Think like a rough-and-ready slide rule. And don't forget to sing in a loud voice.

Dipping into the food cornucopia

You must buy backpacking food differently from and much more carefully than the food you use at home. Compare all weights, of course, and packaging. Read the cooking instructions and choose the simplest, always. Ignore cost, to the limit of purse and temperament. Above all, make sure that each item will give you a maximum of either quick energy or stick-to-guttability. In other words, forget the "zesty richness" and "tangy flavor" and other alluring horseradish printed on the packages; what you want to know above all is how quick and easy this particular item is going to be to prepare when you're tired and hungry, how much better it is going to make you feel, and how long it will go on making you feel better. Advice on this score is useful only up to a point: what really matters, remember, is how the food suits *you.* And the only way to decide that is to experiment.

For our experimentation we now have a palate-boggling array of foods.

In the vacuum-dried field, competition has generated a rich potpourri of complete meals, separate courses and individual items. In the East, the best-known names are Stow-A-Way, Chuck Wagon, and Seidel; in the West, Rich-Moor, Dri-Lite, Trail Chef, and Bernard. On the whole, these firms tend to serve their own regions—though Rich-Moor, with its wide selection, permeates the East, and most Seidel products are stocked by Recreational Equipment of Seattle. Rich-Moor is to be congratulated on giving, in its comprehensive yet single-sheet food list, nutritional values for nearly every item (calories, and grams of protein and fat and carbohydrate).

Freeze-dried foods have now come into their own: instead of a few fussy-to-prepare oddments we have a full range of precooked meals, courses and items. They cost rather more than equivalent vacuum-dried foods but are simplicity itself to prepare and often taste good even at home. When exposed to air, though, their taste and nutritive values soon deteriorate; so once opened they should be used fast. Most of the firms I have named now offer freeze-dried products—sometimes a full range. Oregon Freeze Dry Foods of Albany, Oregon, makers of a broad selection of the excellent Mountain House and Tea Kettle foods, sell nationwide. So do Wilson's of Oklahoma City, who concentrate on meat products (freeze-dried and otherwise) and make the 3-ounce Meat Food Product Bar that in my opinion is still the finest fat-and-protein source for Spartan menus—and not-so-Spartan menus too (pages 122 and 124). Neither of these firms sells retail by mail order, but both will supply lists of local suppliers. For lightweight food suppliers that operate direct mail-order services, see Appendix II, page 446.

A recent interesting trend is toward foods so packaged that you need carry only the most rudimentary kitchenware. Mountain House freeze-dried foods come in cunning cardboard and plastic fold-down "plates," wrapped in protective, airtight foil. You merely add boiling water, wait five minutes, and eat from the unfolded "plate." The plate is burnable. The foil must be packed out. The same company makes freeze-dried Tea Kettle entrées that come in very light, covered aluminum dishes and demand only the addition of a little hot water, a minimum of stirring and a wait of five minutes. Plate and foil cover must be packed out. I find the Tuna à la Neptune outstanding. Trail Chef now packages its foods in plastic bags that you add cold water to, reseal, and immerse in boiling water. You can use the cooking water for washing up, or a hot drink. If water is scarce you can empty the food out and cook normally. For both the Trail Chef and Mountain House systems you still need some kind of pot and a heat source, but you can cut your kitchen load to the bone. For the kind of considerations that can affect your decision, see page 198.

To no one's astonishment, the "organic foods" movement has infiltrated backpacking. Several small firms now put out neat packages of soups, vegetables and supporting items, all more or less guaranteed to be innocent of preservatives, chemicals, chocolate and Spiro. The names, at least, are often delectable: "Juniper Bark," "Survival Fudge," even "Nature's Nuts." The best items seem to taste as good as ordinary, polluted foods, and no doubt they supply just as much energy. Now you can't help feeling a great deal of sympathy for the ideas, or at least emotions, that prompt this revolt against industrial buggering about. But it becomes a little wearying to be warned ad nauseam that consuming fouled-up "commercial" food is the reason you have warts, are impotent, and died last week. Worse, organic food seems to generate not only energy but also halos—the same appallingly human halos that always lurk, ready for conspicuous wear, behind the knowledge that you have "seen the light"; and it makes no difference whether your "truth," hidden from all lesser eyes, concerns "natural food," Christianity, the cooperative movement, or "ecology." Anyway, the point is that the "organic" movement generates a backlash. I confess that I sometimes find it very difficult, faced by certain food purists, to stop their goddam halos from blinding me to real advantages that "natural" foods may offer. But if you are immune to such choler, or can survive it, and want to live on a preservative-free, unpesticided, health-and-halo-inducing diet, and also to backpack, then know ye that the world is now full of little packaged jewels.

Another expanding field is what Chuck Wagon calls "Shirt Pocket Foods": nourishing, "easy-to-eat" bars or similar items you can carry in your pocket and eat cold, even while you're on the move. I await the future with semibated breath.

But it is not only specialist foods that have proliferated in the last five years: most supermarkets now carry a selection of dehydrated items whose nature and ease of preparation qualify them for almost any pack. A few do not even need repackaging—only the shucking of cosmetic outer skins. See especially soups, pastas, vegetables and Lipton's one-pot main dishes (try the Beef Stroganoff first: 6¼ ounces; 760 calories; protein 22 percent [36 grams], fat 14 percent, carbohydrate 55 percent—but you can always boost the protein with meat food product bar [page 113] and the fat with butter or margarine). Although such items tend to contain fewer calories per ounce than their best specialist equivalents, they certainly cost less (Wilson's meat food product bar is almost 50 percent more efficient, ounce for calorie, than Lipton's Stroganoff; but it costs almost twice as much). So remember—especially if cost is a major consideration or you do not live near a specialist store—that today's supermarket is definitely a part of our cornucopia.

The following meal-by-meal review of present backpacking foods, though it seems necessary, poses difficulties: I am undoubtedly ignorant of many first-class items, particularly those sold only in the East; taste is perhaps the most wildly idiosyncratic corner of the idiosyncratic backpacking field; and attitudes toward meal-making run it a close second. So while I shall follow my normal practice of stating personal preferences you'll find that I try to take a rather more objective view than usual. Remember, too, that personal tastes and attitudes toward meal-making can change. I remain, at rock belly, a Britannic barbarian. But the years have taken their toll: America has corrupted me. I have to confess that at times, even far from civilization, I now yearn for parti-civilized food. And I often pander to this treasonable weakness. So my needs have evolved well beyond the list on page 99. Have evolved—but not necessarily progressed. A backpacker with a cuisine that is simple going on depraved can perhaps claim survival advantages.

Breakfast

I find this the most difficult meal. The basic requirements are at odds with each other. Nutritionally, you want something that will keep you going through a long morning's walking; but you often want to start walking immediately after eating, so the slow-digesting fats and proteins that fill the first requirement are the very items that, because of their demands on the body's energy output (page 96), should be avoided immediately before strenuous exercise. Even more to the point, the meal should, except on rest days, be very simple to prepare. I find that I eat most breakfasts in at least a mild hurry, sometimes in darkness, and nearly always in that pseudocatatonic post-wakening period when no one in his right mind would describe me as awake. And I have yet to discover the perfect meal to accompany the hot tea that is the only catalyst reasonably sure to jolt me toward interaction with a new day. It is worth remembering, though, that starch is digested more slowly than sugar: some people even say that oatmeal or pancakes for breakfast keep them unhungry longer than bacon and eggs do.

For many years I ate 4 ounces of cold dehydrated fruit, soaked overnight. Later I used to alternate it with one or the other of those two excellent Swiss cereal-fruit-and-nut mixtures, Fini and Familia, neither of which needs cooking; but eventually I grew so tired of the cereal's cloying sweetness that for a while I could face neither. Now I once more use them—but sparingly. Recently, the very similar Swissy and Alpen have joined the originals on supermarket shelves. You can, of course, ring the changes with any of them by mixing fruit and cereal, and by crumbling a little chocolate onto them. One young reader of seventy-five, still going up, suggests adding an ounce or so of shredded coconut to $2\frac{1}{2}$ or 3 of Familia for a breakfast mix. "We tried it," he writes, "on an ascent of the Grand Teton and it was voted slightly terrific." He also suggests cooking the cereal if you get tired of that cloying taste.

Some of the organic mixes based on oats are worth trying. So is Rich-Moor's Instant Sunrise Cereal. And All-Bran can be useful in the first days of a trip if, because of the suddenly changed way of life, your bowels need prompting. An alternative, I'm told, is dried fruit, especially white figs.

If I expect to face a really long morning's walk—and particularly if I can afford a digestion pause before starting—I sometimes boost fat and protein intake by breakfasting on a half or whole Wilson's Bacon Bar (35 percent protein, 35 percent fat, 22 percent moisture; 3 ounces; $1.10) eaten either straight out of its wrapper, like a banana, or gooed up, with perhaps a dash of dried onion flakes and herbs, in a little hot water. But I find that the banana method can make even a barbarian gag; and the goo, although concoctable with spare tea water, does demand a little preparation. The bacon taste also tends to keep burping up during the morning. From time to time, under certain conditions (page 198), I substitute a half or whole Wilson's Meat Food Product Bar, which tastes and burples less than the bacon bar and clearly nourishes more (nutritional data, page 113). Mountain House freeze-dried sausage patties (49.5 percent protein, 35.5 percent fat, 5.5 percent carbohydrate; 2.3 ounces; $2.35) are very simple to prepare and taste good; I have yet to try walking directly after eating them. I often mean to beef up the breakfast protein with jerky, but my glazed morning mind almost always seems to overlook this overnight intention. Occasionally I remember to suck a stick while striking camp.

Some backpackers—perhaps most—demand a full, home-style cooked breakfast. There are plenty of dried-egg preparations on the market now—plain or in fancy omelettes, even "organic" style—and many people proclaim them excellent. But a big drawback is the time-and-trouble factor. And you more or less have to carry a frying pan. If you absolutely must have a big, city-type breakfast, consult the catalogues. You'll find Campsite, Ranch Style, and even Rib Sticker breakfasts, with such alluring subtitles as "scrambled eggs, sausage patties, and hash brown potatoes." But read the instructions before you buy them. If you like multi-course menus, see, especially, Bernard's Kamp Pack series. Sample: Breakfast #4—giant pitted prunes, sweet cream buttermilk pancake, boysenberry flavor syrup, golden clear no-stick (pan coating), and hot chocolate. Dri-Lite produces similar meals. I steer clear of such blatant time-consumers—and not only for breakfast. But alfresco Julia Childs no doubt revel in them.

An experienced backpacker once spoke to me, with something close to ecstasy in his voice, of a Chinese noodle breakfast; but I found I just did not walk well on it. Carnation Instant Breakfasts (128 calories per 1.2-ounce envelope, 6 envelopes for $.69; 21 percent protein, 4 percent fat, and 60 percent carbohydrates) seem a natural; but although I occasionally carry one I find I can rarely face it. (And purists recoil in horror from the additives in these concoctions.) On rest days, of course, you can let yourself go: my favorite is small trout, caught either the evening before, or better still, that same morning. But don't kid yourself that trout are fuel fit for long-distance walking.*

Lunch

I am always a little surprised that, whenever I can, I heat soup for lunch. Yet I do so even in the desert, almost every day there is enough time—and water. Hot food seems to recharge me best.

The Swiss soup powders get my vote, every time. I used to favor Maggi heavily over Knorr because their soups were markedly simpler to prepare. Knorr have now drawn about level on that score but I still prefer the Maggi foil packaging. These soups demand almost no stirring or other fancy work, and at the end of a long, long morning that makes a monumental difference. Herbs improve any soup. So does a dab of margarine. Don't forget

---

* Postscript: a reader who failed to send his address and whom I am therefore unable to thank personally has just written drawing my attention to "MPF" —variously called "Multi-Purpose Food" and "Modern Protein Food." This extremely low-cost protein formula, based on defatted soybean, was developed by Dr. Henry Borsook of the California Institute of Technology and is made in the United States exclusively by General Mills, under an arrangement with the Meals for Millions Foundation of Los Angeles. Designed for "underdeveloped" nations and for emergency use in case of nuclear attack or other diseases of overdeveloped nations, it seems to offer distinct backpacking possibilities—for breakfast and way beyond.

MPF comes completely precooked, in near-powdery granules, and you can blend it with almost anything, from orange juice through soup to spaghetti and meatballs. At a pinch you can eat it alone—as a hot or cold drink or mush, or even dry, as is. Said to have a "delicate toasted flavor," it has. Roughly speaking. But it amply meets the injunction (page 112) about the taste of often-repeated items of a diet being bland.

I have not yet tried MPF in the field, but my informant extolls its stick-to-gutability. One tablespoonful in beef bouillon at lunch, he says, "satiated my hunger until I had dinner, usually about six hours later. MPF expands in the soup and it also seemed to expand in the stomach."

MPF comes in hermetically sealed 4½-pound cans that keep it "virtually non-perishable." Even in an opened can it "remains stable . . . providing normal precautions are taken to protect the contents from dust, water, insects, and fall-out." (50 percent protein, 31 percent carbohydrate [half of it "available"], 2.2 percent fat; madly mineralized; vibrant with vitamins; 75 calories per ounce; $4.50 per 4½-pound can, or $24.30 for 6 cans, postpaid, direct from General Mills Inc., Box 175, Minneapolis, Minnesota 55440.)

that different soup flavors, even of the same brand, may have widely different nutritional values.*

Not many backpackers seem to cook their lunches, but for those who do the alternatives to soup include "bowl of chili," Tea Kettle tuna casserole, and maybe sausage patties. If you don't want to cook but appreciate a medium-long halt, you'll find that many catalogues now list freeze-dried salads that demand only cold water, mixing and a 15-minute wait.

If, like most people, you make the lunch stop little more than an excuse to get the pack off your back for rather longer than usual, you can carry bread—as a surprising number of people do— and spread goodies on it to your stomach's content. Finally, lunch can be no more than another helping, perhaps bigger than normal, of your routine "trail snacks" (page 115). In practice you often have to operate this way, like it or not. I find myself doing so, for example, if it is too cold to stop for long without making camp, or if I am really pushing for miles, especially when days are short. At such times I often chew half a Wilson's meat bar. Its nutritional values (page 113) suggest why I find it excellent for all-through-the-afternoon walking.

Britannic afternoon tea

Tea. Thirty bags see even me through the thirstiest week. A little to my surprise I find plain, straightforward Lipton bags best for sheer resuscitation—though I nearly always take a few fancier jobs, such as orange- or mint-flavored, for rest-day kicks.

* Here are the figures for Maggi Soups, kindly supplied by the Nestlé Company:

Soup flavor	Net pkg. wt. Oz.	Protein %	Fat %	Carbo-hydrates %	Food energy value per pkg. Calories
Peas with smoked ham	2¾	17.4	14.2	48.5	334
Onion	2⅝	10.2	12.5	56.2	309
Egg macaroni shell	2⅝	14.2	11.9	54.5	309
Oxtail	2⅝	18.5	13.8	43.2	305
Asparagus	3⅜	14.6	11.4	53.4	276
Mushroom	2⅜	12.2	10.9	56.0	263
Vegetable	2	11.4	13.6	39.0	197
Chicken noodle	2¼	4.2	11.4	53.4	176

I apologize for not having updated this list to match the flavors currently available; but repeated inquiries have failed to raise a whisper from any Maggi source.

Dinner

Even more than at home, this is the main meal of the day, and probably your main protein intake: the day's walking or exploring or fishing or what-have-you is over and you have both time to cook and also freedom from the inhibiting prospect of immediate strenuous exercise. The catalogues offer a wild array of dinners (full menus, single courses, separate items) and most are now pleasant tasting and easy to prepare. But don't panic if you delight in juggling four different ingredients through a maze of stirrings and simmerings, not to mention "patting with a paper towel": you can still have yourself a ball with some of Armour's or Wilson's freeze-dried concoctions. These days I often use such well-sauced main courses as Rich-Moor's Spaghetti with Meat Balls, Beef Stroganoff, and Spanish Rice Dinner. The packaging, usually for "four," is mildly inconvenient if you travel solo but I find it easy enough to use only half the package for a meal and then rubber-band the balance away for another day. The protein content generally seems low (no doubt because protein is the most expensive component) so I often boost such dinners with up to half a bar of Wilson's Meat Food Product or, occasionally, bacon. With all dinners—and other meals too—ignore such printed fiction as "serves four." If you need the kind of evening meal I do, allow a total of at least seven ounces, dry weight, and include adequate protein and fat.

You will have gathered by now that I am big on meat bars. They are, I suppose, the modern equivalent of pemmican—a Cree word meaning "fat meat." Old-style pemmican was made by pounding dried lean meat into a paste with fat and preserving it in the form of cakes or bars. The cakes sometimes included raisins, sugar, and even suet. The object was to concentrate as much nutrition as possible into a convenient form that would keep almost indefinitely.

The word "pemmican" seems to have slunk out of favor—except, oddly enough, in various vegetable and even fruit-and-nut "pemmicans" (page 116), but meat bars still flourish. One reason most makers no longer call them pemmican may be the connotation of hardship. Also, perhaps, because a regular diet of the old, strong-flavored pemmican grew horribly monotonous: it's a sound general principle—likely to avert considerable suffering —that if some items of your diet are frequently repeated you should try for bland-tasting versions that can be "swamped" by varied additives.

Wilson's meat bars are bland unto tastelessness. So you can add them to almost any dish and leave its flavor unimpaired. And even if the bars form the foundation of every dinner for a week you can ring the changes by using a variety of vegetables, gravies, herbs and spices, and so dine off a different dish every night. Well, vaguely different, anyway.

I'm aware that many experienced backpackers turn up their noses at mere mention of these meat bars. "Taste like sawdust," they mutter.* But such critics miss the important point about easily submersible flavor in frequently repeated foods. I readily admit, though, that a meat bar chewed banana-fashion out of its foil wrapper is about as interesting as daytime TV.

The easily crumbled bar is austerely labeled "Wilson's Certified Meat Food Product." (An identical bar made by Wilson for Rich-Moor is called plain "Meat Bar.") It contains nothing but dehydrated beef and pork, rendered beef fat and salt, and is a highly efficient source of fat and protein (48 percent protein, 41 percent fat, 8 percent moisture; 478 calories; 3 ounces; $1.30. Yes, I know these figures differ from those in the table on page 99; I let those stand because that was the information I worked with at the time. These are more recent, revised data, supplied by Wilson's, and I shall use them when we examine a more current menu [page 122]). One 3-ounce bar is said to be the equivalent of a pound of fresh meat. It certainly satisfies. And the satisfaction lasts.

Hence Fletcher Stew. For years this was my dinner, six out of seven backpacking days, and I still fall back on it fairly often, particularly when I know I'll be tired and will want an easily prepared meal that will restore the day's ravages. The basic recipe for Fletcher Stew is 1 meat bar and 4 ounces of vegetable boiled in water; but the switcheroos are almost limitless. You can vary the vegetables and mixtures thereof. You can ring gravy changes. You can shuffle and reshuffle your mixtures of herbs, spices and onion flakes. And you can modulate the amount of water so that you serve yourself anything from thickish soup to amorphous meat loaf. Now I have never thought of Fletcher Stew as a gourmet's delight. But not long ago my literary agent— who is an experienced backpacker and also an apparently civilized

---

* One reader recommended "machaca" as an alternative. She describes it as "a very thinly sliced, unsalted dry beef used in Mexico, requiring no refrigeration. Although it looks rather like wood shavings and would be unpalatable as is, it can be fried with onions, mixed with scrambled eggs or added to soup, rice or beans." ¡Olé?

Manhattanite—spent a week striding around the High Sierra with me, discussing business and the state of the universe, and on the last evening he demanded that we swap dinners so that he could sample Fletcher Stew. (It was he, by the way, who had christened it.) He was pleasantly surprised. In fact, his compliments waxed so warm that I have considered dropping the plebeian name "Fletcher Stew" and anointing my creation with a gracious outdoor living title. What price "Boeuf Gallois Alfresco"?

Vegetables. Although some retail stores—notably Smilie's in San Francisco—still sell straightforward, unjazzed-up dehydrated vegetables in small, simple polyethylene bags, they are, by and large, no longer easy to find. The big producers such as California Vegetable Concentrates of Modesto tend to think in railroad cars of a single item, rarely in orders smaller than 20 gallons, and so are hardly a source for backpackers other than expedition organizers. But Mountain House, whose freeze-dried vegetables normally come in very small amounts, rather copiously packed, also sells them in gallon-size cans. And at least some of the regular lightweight food producers, including Stow-A-Way in the East and Dri-Lite in the West, put up bulk orders on special request: write defining your special needs, and ask for a price. Because of the very short storage life of any freeze-dried foods after opening, you cannot satisfactorily repack them. But if you buy vacuum-dried products in bulk you can repackage into small amounts that suit your requirements by buying small polycel heat-seal bags and sealing along the open edge by pressure with a warm iron.* That way you can concoct mixtures too—of fruits as well as vegetables (try apple and date, for example). But almost your best bet for unjazzed vegetables these days are supermarkets. See especially beans, rice in a dozen flavors, and such exotics as couscous.

Gravy masculates any stew. I alternate between one of the instant gravy powders and a package of soup (usually oxtail or mushroom). And a reader stresses the value of chili powder, curry powder and garlic powder as antidotes for any mistakes one might make.

---

* The plastic called Mylar affords a better air-and-moisture barrier than polyethylene, which is somewhat permeable. But Mylar is not readily heat sealable. Laminated Mylar/polyethylene bags, eminently heat sealable, can be bought in ½-pint, 1-pint and 2-pint sizes in some department stores. A recent Sears Roebuck catalogue lists (on the same page as the electric toasters, fry pans, etc.) a small household heat sealer kit including 30 boilable pouches of assorted sizes for about $15.

Herbs and spices can vivify any dish, including lunch. I carry very small bags of ground cumin seed, oregano, thyme, and an "Italian" herb mixture. Also dried onion or garlic flakes.

Desserts rarely feature on my menus, but you'll find them in every food catalogue. Some are good, too. Try Mountain House freeze-dried strawberries flavored with Rich-Moor banana chips and a little sugar, and lubricated with water and powdered milk.

Trail snacks

Sugar is the big thing, because it gives you a quick, easily digested energy boost, but a little fat and protein help the boost linger. Ideally, the snacks are small, conveniently packaged items that do not melt, crumble or make you thirsty. They travel in an accessible outer pocket of the pack—or even of shirt or pants ("nibble pocket," page 376). I nibble at every hourly halt, except perhaps the first of the day.

My staple snack remains the English bar candy known as *"mintcake,"* very popular with mountaineering and caving expeditions. There are several brands now, but they all come in 6-ounce bars that contain six-sevenths sugar and one-seventh glucose, taste good in both white and brown variants, and do not seem to induce thirst. I allow myself half a bar a day. But I eat none on stay-in-camp days and very little on easy days, and thereby conserve stocks for days when I'm pushing hard.

Raisins are good but you tend to get tired of their cloying taste. I still carry them occasionally. To avoid goo-coated fingers, buy the dry type, always.

Chocolate contains about 35 percent fat and in theory is therefore highly imperfect for use during or just before strenuous exercise. But I find that it always—any place, under any conditions —tastes damned good, and so gets eaten. I always carry it and just about always finish my stock. So, I gather, do most walkers. Hershey have for some years put out a small and convenient 1-ounce bar of "tropical chocolate" (2 for $.15) but have just informed me that they've had to stop making them "for this season and probably for a long time due to high cost and shortage of cocoa beans." Half-pound bars of supermarket semisweet chocolate, used mostly for cooking, are just about as good but less convenient. Both kinds melt less readily than ordinary chocolate. Still, they melt. In deserts, avoid.

Alternative snacks—both specialist and supermarketed—run to a wild variety: Lifesavers; hard candies (preferably individually wrapped); the German Tex-schmeltz traubenzucker (2 ounces; $.30); "gorp"—beloved by many but not by me; fruit and vegetable "pemmicans" and their fellow travelers (Running Bear's Pemmican by the Inter-Mountain Trading Company of Berkeley is palatable, well balanced, without additives, and reasonably priced [honey, nonfat dry milk, wheat germ, soy flour, raisins, almonds, soybeans, walnuts, grape juice, wheat bran, malt, filberts, safflower oil; dripping with vitamins, etc.; less than 1 percent moisture; 4-ounce wad, $.75, 676 calories, 16 percent protein, 48 percent carbohydrates, 36 percent fat. Also in 2-pound wad for $5.30]); Muesli Fruit biscuits (Familia in biscuit form: 6⅓ ounces; $.75); Space Sticks, in four flavors (⅓-ounce, 44-calorie sticks; 4⅞-ounce pack of 14 sticks, $.59; 10 percent protein, 13 percent fat, 68 percent carbohydrates. "Exorbitant!" wail the consumer-eagles. Maybe. But close to nutritionally balanced—though short on protein—and also nonsticky, neatly encased in long-lasting individual wrappers, and resistant to both heat and prolonged bottom-of-the-pack buffeting); Mountain House freeze-dried "ice cream," in solid form (2⅓ ounces, $1.25, 375 calories. Not too much like ice cream perhaps, but sure as hell tastes good—though it lingers on fingers as well as palate); marzipan (Odense of Denmark makes convenient little candles—sugar, almonds, liquid glucose, certified color added; by appointment to the Royal Danish Court: 7 and 3 ounces, $.79 and $.39); sundry fruits, vacuum- and freeze-dried, jazzed and unjazzed; nuts (which I nearly always take now because they're fat-rich and therefore highly efficient in weight-calorie terms, though not the best thing, in theory anyway, just before heavy exercise); and beef jerky (those same thin brown strips, very tasty, that the barman sells you. A protein-rich snack [1 pound reputedly equals 3½ pounds of fresh steak] for any time of day, or for dropping into soup or stew—though it will not rehydrate because, unlike most dehydrated foods, it has been heated past the point at which tissue structure is irreversibly damaged, and no amount of soaking will soften its leathery soul).

If you want to extend this list to truly unmanageable proportions, let your imagination wander around a supermarket, and if that's not enough consult some of the lightweight food catalogues. You'll find, for example, that Chuck Wagon now puts out compact, calorific, nonmelting, long-lived, "shirt-pocket foods" called Hi Energy bars, in five fruit-and-nut flavors—such as pineapple-orange-almond and fig-orange-walnut (150 calories per 1½-ounce bar, 3 bars for $.89; average 3½ percent protein, 5 percent fat, 74 percent carbohydrates). And the thing doesn't end there. One reader, who "found mintcake horribly sweet and sick-ening," recommended "the ancient food *halvah*," which Webster elucidates as "a Turkish confection consisting of a paste made of ground sesame seeds and nuts mixed with honey." It is readily available, I understand, in Istanbul.*

Another reader—that same onward-and-upward septuagenar-ian who swore by a coconut-and-Familia breakfast for the Tetons —shared this home-made energy bar recipe: "I throw raisins, dates, coconut, figs, prunes, pecans, walnuts and filberts in a heteroge-neous mixture into the food chopper. I pack the dubious-looking mess which the chopper spews out into a 1-inch metal tube, ram-ming it down hard with a close fitting rod. When the tube is nearly full I lay it on waxed paper and push the cylindrical rod of 'gorp' out, wrap it in the paper, wrap that in foil, and stow it in the refrigerator. I suppose it would go rancid eventually at summer temperatures but I haven't noticed it after it has been out a week or so. On a hike one merely peels it like a banana."

As you see, there is almost no end to this subject. And trail snacks are not only for trail snacks: they may form your entire lunch; they can round off any meal; and for people who dine early, they make the most convenient warming-effect-last-thing-at-night snacks (page 261). So whenever need strikes, delve into your personally evolved nibble bags of trail snacks, come up with what-ever catches your fancy, serve to taste and continue singing in that loud and cheerful voice.

A few words on some staple items:

Milk. Adding cream to nonfat milk (that is, milk from which the cream has been removed) sounds crazy; but with Milkman dried milk it seems to work. At least, that is what Foremost say they do before drying their product; and the resulting powder dis-solves at least as quickly as the Carnation Nonfat I used to favor, tastes distinctly better, contains about 25 percent more calories, and somehow seems to go appreciably further in normal use. A single foil envelope (3.44 ounces; 384 calories; 35 percent protein, 5 percent fat, 50 percent carbohydrate, battalions of vitamins; 6 en-velopes for $1.37) makes 1 quart of reconstituted milk (butter-fat: .5 percent), neatly fills (with a little shaking down before

* I've just discovered that, in addition, a plant has grown in Brooklyn (The Joyva Corporation). And that their little 1¼-ounce bars, in both chocolate and vanilla flavors ($.15; 198 calories; 12.7 percent protein, 16.3 percent fat, 46.4 percent carbohydrates) just melt in your mouth. My mouth, anyway. Beau-tiful.

the final topping up) my plastic milk-squirter (page 146), and unless used ultralavishly lasts me much more than a single day.

Beverages. Tea: see page 111. Coffee unfortunately makes me sick, but I hear that Mountain House freeze-dried is both good and convenient (2-ounce cans [40 cups]; $.90. 1.2-gram foil packets [1 cup]; $.50).

Granulated sugar. The simplest quick-energy food. Pure, stable and cheap. Use with everything. Warning: There is fierce current controversy over whether you should eat much—or any—sugar in the form of sucrose. For the answer, wait until next reincarnation.

Margarine (rather than butter, because it keeps) improves almost any dish. And because it is almost pure fat it has a higher energy/weight ratio than any food you can lay sticky hands on (204 calories per ounce—compared with 203 for butter, 159 for Wilson's meat bar and for halvah, 126 for space sticks, 112 for Milkman dried milk, 109 for granulated sugar, 105 for spaghetti, 100 for Chuck Wagon's Hi Energy bar, 99 for dried red pinto beans, 75 for MPF, 28 for raw brook trout [flesh only], 14 for raw brook trout [whole] and also for yogurt made from partially skimmed milk, 3 for watermelon [raw, whole] and 120 for zwieback). Yet I find that I often and stupidly don't take margarine. In trout country, though, I sometimes carry an extra 4 ounces for frying.*

Fruit-drink mix. A pleasant quick-energy source. Valuable in killing the taste of alkaline or otherwise unpalatable water: makes even the Colorado River eminently drinkable. Wyler's fruit-ades, complete with sugar, come in convenient foil packages that make 1 quart (3 ounces; 2 for $.25; 340-calorie average). Flavors: orange and lemonade (the two best); pineapple-grapefruit (pleasant); strawberry, raspberry, cherry, and grape (also-rans). Ratings are my own, but seem to be widely shared. Kool-Aid, which used to make only sugarless powders, now puts out a similar range to Wyler. The Rich-Moor equivalents come in polycel bags (6¾ ounces; $.40; 776 calories; vitamin C everywhere, but everywhere) and seem about the same in taste and dissolvability. The polycel

---

* This paragraph set me toying with the idea of a new appendix listing calories per ounce for a wide range of backpacking foods. In the end I decided "no." And not only because the job would be a pain in the butt. Such a list might dangerously mislead earnest people who ignored such vital factors as nutritional balance, minimum protein requirements, possible upper fat and sugar limits, the need for some fiber and at least some variety, and the vagaries of taste. Anyway, if you really want such figures, consult *Agricultural Handbook No. 8* (which, as you have no doubt zwiebacked out, is what I did). Scan Table 2, Column D, and divide by 16.

bags can be burned and don't seem to leak but are in all likelihood slowly permeable to oxygen and moisture. The Wyler and Kool-Aid foil envelopes cannot be burned, and will crack after much storing and bending in a pack and will therefore leak; but while uncracked they shut off all oxygen and moisture and therefore ensure a longer shelf-life.

Salt and salt tablets. When you sweat you lose salt, and unless you replace it you may suffer from heat exhaustion. So use it more lavishly on food than you would at home, especially in low humidity when sweat dries quickly and you often fail to realize how much liquid you have lost. Only experience will tell you whether you also need tablets. Individual requirements vary widely. A Death Valley Ranger once told me, "When it reaches 110° F. I take one tablet a day. I need that one, but my stomach won't accept more. Yet there's a guy at Park HQ who has to take twenty a day. If he doesn't he ends up in the hospital."

Salt deficiency may cause mild or acute exhaustion, or produce other, highly variable, symptoms. I've only once been sure I was suffering from it. As I approached Death Valley on my California walk, in temperatures around 100°, my leg muscles began to ache and my head to flutter. Several hours passed before it occurred to me that the trouble might be salt. Soon after I swallowed a few tablets, legs and head returned to normal. From then on, in really hot weather, I took eight tablets a day. Now, I always carry enough for at least a four-a-day dosage. Some people need more, some less. If in doubt, overdose yourself. It seems that the only people to whom too much salt can be dangerous are those with relatively weak hearts or with kidney trouble. Normally, though not always, that means older people. The Death Valley Ranger told me he suspected too much salt might cause a mild skin rash. He may be right; but if so it's a price worth paying.

Extra table salt will do instead of tablets, but tablets are very convenient—and more likely to get taken. Buy them in any drugstore. Most brands now include some sugar as an energy boost.

Emergency ration. It is probably wise to carry a small emergency ration of some sort, just in case of trouble. Its nature depends on what you expect to do if things go wrong. If you are always going to be able to get out to civilization within one day, some quick-acting high-energy food may be best. Horlick's rum fudge bars are no longer available. I now carry an extra Wilson's meat bar.

Morale boosting: goodies. If you have been living on dehydrated food for days or weeks or months you will not hesitate, given half a chance, to call in at a café (as I could occasionally on the California walk) and order a red-blooded steak. Even under more Spartan conditions you may be able to engineer a change of pace. I do not mean only such delicacies as small trout so fresh that it's a problem to keep them from curling double in the frying pan. Occasionally I take along Tea Kettle Tuna (page 106) for rest days—small size (1.2 ounces; $.75; 175 calories) for lunch, or large size (3.6 ounces; $1.59; 525 calories) for dinner. The vivid taste is always a treat.

On my Grand Canyon walk I included in each cache and airdrop one can of delectables—oysters, lobster, cocktail meatballs, fish appetizers, or frog's legs—and a small bottle of claret. The goodies were great. But the claret, oddly enough, did not really fit in. You simply don't need alcohol in the wilderness. Not when you're on your own, anyway.

But if you feel the need for alcohol (and a little Scotch or bourbon in a group can be very welcome at the end of a day, especially in a group of two) a good container is an aluminum bottle similar to the one I use for white gas (page 173). Get the kind that's anodized and noncorrosive and so protect both the inside of the bottle and the taste of the booze. In addition, the bottle's bright outside color will obviate (or almost obviate) possible dire confusions. (Anodized bottle; 1⅓ pint; 4¼ ounces; $2.70.) Back home after a trip, wash the bottle carefully and leave open until next time. Hard plastic hip flasks (10-ounce capacity; 2 ounces; $1.25) apparently taint drink only very little.

Packaging. Most of today's systems are effective and conven-ient, but as we have seen, each has its advantages and drawbacks. To summarize:

The foil envelopes in which freeze-dried foods come (because air must be rigorously excluded until they're used) have a very long shelf-life; but they will sometimes crack under bottom-of-the-pack buffeting—though the best are now becoming very tough indeed. The foil cannot be burned, cannot be burned, cannot be burned and must be packed out, must be packed out, must be packed out (page 189).

The polyethylene that houses most vacuum-dried foods can be burned; but although it is moisture proof for reasonable periods there is some degree of porosity (for an alternative, see footnote, page 114). In damp climates the packages should if possible be stored or cached in airtight cans. In the first edition I suggested including some desiccant such as calcium oxide, but I now find that when calcium oxide absorbs moisture it becomes corrosive. Instead, use silica gel or Drierite (anhydrous calcium sulfate), which come with moisture indicators and can be regenerated by baking. (Silica gel from VWR Scientific Company, Box 3200, San Francisco, California 94119; Drierite from W. A. Hammond Drie-rite Company, Xenia, Ohio 45385).

For no-pot-needed packaging, see page 106.

Specimen food list

There is no such thing as a perfect food list for every trip. And it's not only that you have to meet the varying demands of weather, terrain, load and trip length: your theories, tastes and prejudices change; and you probably like to experiment. So my immediate reaction to the prospect of compiling a current personal list was to say, "The hell with it!" But I guess I had better have a go.

Now look, I specifically do not say that the list overleaf shows what I am nowadays likely to carry for a typical week's trip. But—notated experimental items aside—it includes only things I have tried and found satisfactory. It is offered primarily as an up-to-date starting point from which beginners can work out their own salvations, and the actual selection is designed to suggest ideas and sources and at the same time to convey as much information as possible about quantities, nutritional values and costs of items fairly readily available to western backpackers. Easterners, I'm afraid, will need to translate a few items.

Net wt. Oz.	Quantity	Item	Brand	For # days	Energy value Calories	Prot.	Fat	CH.	Protein Grams	Cost $	Based on price of
		BREAKFASTS									
4	—	Cereal mix (cold)	Familia	2ª	452	56	83	313	14	.31	.98/13 oz.
4	1	Apple slices	Rich-Moor		428	4	7	417	1	.90	.90 ea.
11.75	1	Sunrise cereal (cold)	Rich-Moor	3ᵇ	1520	300	72	1148	75	.90	.90 ea.
3	1	Bacon bar	Wilson	2ª	388	120	268	0	30	1.50	1.50 ea.
2.3	1	Sausage patties	Mountain House		324	120	193	11	30	2.00	2.00 ea.
				7							
		LUNCHES									
13.2	5	Soups (various flavors)	Maggi	5	1533	240	463	830	60	2.00	.40 ea.
1.2	1	Tuna à la Neptune	Tea Kettle	1ᶜ	175	56	44	75	14	.75	.75 ea.
3	1	Ham salad	Rich-Moor	1ᵈ	480	96	316	68	24	1.90	1.90 ea.
				7							
		DINNERS									
12.75	1	Stroganoff w/beef	Rich-Moor	2	1524	296	432	796	74	2.75	2.75 ea.
13	1	Chicken Pilaf	Rich-Moor	2	1404	276	200	928	69	2.75	2.75 ea.
6	2	Meat bars	Wilson		956	324	632	0	81	2.56	1.28 ea.
4	—	Rice (flavored)	(Supermarket)	2ᵉ	412	32	5	375	8	.23	.35/oz.
4	—	Pinto beans	(Supermarket)		386	100	12	274	25	.20	.50/10 oz.
3.4	1	Chicken Chop Suey	Mountain House	1	408	76	122	210	19	1.59	1.59 ea.
1.8	1	Peas	Mountain House		200	60	6	134	15	.85	.85 ea.
1	1	Gravy powder	(Supermarket)	—	100	20	10	70	5	.19	.19 ea.
1	—	Herbs and spices	(Supermarket)	—	0	0	0	0	0	—	—

TRAIL SNACKS

Qty		Item	Source								
21	3½	Mintcake bars	Kendal	—	2290	0	0	2290	0	2.28	.65 ea.
16	2	Semisweet chocolate	Baker	—	2300	80	1280	940	20	1.20	.60 ea.
4	1	Running Bear's Pemmican		—	676	104	313	259	26	.75	.75 ea.
7	20	Food sticks	Inter-Mountain	—	880	84	241	555	21	.79	.55/14
1	1	Strawberries (frz.-drd.)	Pillsbury	—	115	8	9	98	2	.95	.95 ea.
1	1	Banana chips	Mountain House ⎫ a		652	8	400	244	2	.65	.65 ea.
4	1		Rich-Moor ⎬		410	392	18	0	98	1.98	1.98 pkg.
4	1	Beef jerky	(Supermarket)	—	1350	160	1020	170	40	.99	1.99/lb.
8		Nuts (mixed)	(Supermarket)	—	220	0	5	215	0	.20	.10/oz.
2		Candies	(Supermarket)	—							
		STAPLES									
32		Granulated sugar	(Supermarket)	7	3493	0	0	3493	0	.33	.83/5 lbs.
17.2	5	Milk powder (envelopes)	Milkman	7	1910	640	220	1050	160	1.07	2.57/12
4		Margarine	(Supermarket)	7	820	4	811	5	1	.10	.40/lb.
ca. 30		Tea bags	Lipton et al.	7	0	0	0	0	0	.39	.62/48
3	3	Fruit-drink mix (pkgs.)	Wylers	7	1020	0	0	1020	0	.38	.25/2
3		Salt	(Supermarket)	7	0	0	0	0	0	.03	.13/12 oz.
ca. 40		Salt tablets (30 percent dextrose)	Thermotabs	—	30	0	30	30	0	.32	.79/100
ca. 30	1	Vitamin C tablets	(Supermarket)	7	0	0	0	0	0	.40	1.29/100
14 lbs. 0 oz. [g]	**2 lbs. 0 oz.**		Total for One Week ⟶		26,856	3656	7182	16,018	914	34.19	
			Average Daily Total ⟶		3837	524 (26.8 per-cent)	1026	2287	131	4.88	

a. Maybe mixed.
b. Also a trail snack.
c. Rest day.
d. Sheer experimentation.
e. Fletcher stew.
f. May also be used with meals, mixed or as corner-fillers.
g. Gross weight (with packaging) probably about 1½ pounds extra.

Occasionally, when conditions demand or at least indicate extreme simplicity, I subsist on a

Rock-bottom, tin-can menu.

Using no stove or pot, only a medium-size tin can fitted with a makeshift wire handle (text and illustration, pages 198–200), I "cook" solely with water boiled in the can over a very small open fire. In the past I have grounded this menu—to the sinking point—on Wilson's meat bars. The basic one-day list reads:

| Wt. | | | | Total | Calories | | | Protein | Cost | Based on |
Oz.	Qty.	Item	Brand	cals.	Prot.	Fat	CH.	Grams	$	price of
9	3	Meat bars	Wilson	1434	484	950	0	121	3.84	1.28 ea.
1	1	Herbs, dried onions and garlic	—	0	0	0	0	0	—	—
6	1	Mintcake bar	Atkinson	654	0	0	654	0	.65	.65
6	—	Other trail snacks	(Various)	650	76	238	336	19	.90	avge.
1	⅓	Fruit-drink mix	Wylers	113	0	0	113	0	.04	.25/2
½	5	Tea bags	Lipton	0	0	0	0	0	.07	.62/48
3	1	Milkman milk	Foremost	382	128	44	210	32	.21	2.57/12
4	—	Granulated sugar	—	436	0	0	436	0	.04	.83/5 lb
1 lb.				3669	688	1232	1749	172	$5.75	
14½ oz.					(33.5 percent)					

Breakfast: one meat bar. Lunch: one meat bar. Dinner: two meat bars. Mintcake, trail snacks and fruit drink: often. Tea, hot and very sweet: with every meal except dinner—and resuscitatively as needed.

Mostly, the meat bars are rendered passing palatable by crumbling them into your cup, adding a different medley of herbs and spices and onion or garlic flakes at each meal, and then anointing the amalgam with enough boiling water to create the soup or stew or mid-range salmagundi that you fancy—or happen to end up with. At times, though, you just bite pieces off the bar, banana fashion, and chew.

Provided motivation and stomach are strong enough, you can repeat this rather austere menu ad nauseam, with or without such thrilling additions and variations as bacon bar, dry cereal, or even dried fruit. I once ad nauseamed it for ten days in some Arizona mountains and came out fit and happy with lots of miles and no vomiting behind me. The only cheating was a rest-day lunch of Tea Kettle tuna. It tasted transcendentally ambrosial.

Nowadays, Mountain House no-pot-needed packages (and to a lesser degree the Trail Chef equivalents) mean that you can manage a more varied diet with this stalwart regimen. And although you'll lose some simplicity in preparation and a point or two on your ounce/calorie rating, you may find that these delightful decadencies convert the rock-bottom, tin-can kitchen into a palatable as well as useful proposition.

We now face the prospect of being able to use

Diet as a means of getting in shape for walking.

In the June 1968 issue of *Nutrition Today* Magazine, Dr. Per-Olof Åstrand—a Swedish physiologist, cross-country skier and Olympics watcher—decries the "protein myth" for athletes' diets and says:

"The proper preparation for a competition in any endurance event exceeding 30–60 minutes would be to exercise to exhaustion the same muscles that will be used in the event. This should be done about one week in advance to exhaust glycogen stores. Then the diet should be almost exclusively fat and protein for about three days. This keeps the glycogen content of the exercising muscles low. As the big day nears, the athlete should add large quantities of carbohydrate to the diet. 'Add' is the word, because the intake of fats and protein should be continued. This regimen is recommended for anyone preparing himself for prolonged, severe exercise (in hiking, mountaineering, or military operations). We have found it works. Right before the competition the athlete should be permitted to eat whatever he wants, whatever he thinks will make him win."

As the final sentence shows, Dr. Åstrand is a human sort of guy. He even admits that skiers "are often one or two steps ahead of the experts in the practical applications of the nutritional aspects of exercise." But some of his supporting data, as presented in the article, leave room for doubt. And remember that for the moment his ideas remain unproven: they will have to stand up to time and the predictable questions. From our point of view, among the questions might be: "Maybe that's fine for one-day efforts, but what is the effect on the seventh day of a 7-day effort? Is it good or bad?" Also: "But what about those soft city muscles that in practice simply don't get adequately exercised except in the week before the suddenly looming trip?" And: "What about the man or woman to whom the prospect of losing weight is an important attraction of backpacking?"

Still, as Konrad Lorenz says, "Truth, in science, can be defined as the working hypothesis best fitted to open the way to the next better one." And for the time being, anyway, I shall try to pay at least some attention to what the man says.

WATER

You can if necessary do without food for days or even weeks and still live, but if you go very long without water you assuredly die. In really hot deserts the limit of survival without water may be barely forty-eight hours. And well before that your brain is likely to become so addled that there is a serious risk of committing some irrational act that will kill you.*

Dangers of dehydration

Too few people recognize the insidious nature of such thirst-induced irrationality. It can swamp you, suddenly and irretrievably, without your being in the least aware of it.

I described one such case in *The Man Who Walked Through Time*. In July 1959 a thirty-two-year-old priest and two teen-age boys tried to follow an old trail down one side of Grand Canyon to the Colorado. They carried little or no water. More than half-way down, hot and tired and already very thirsty, the priest made the barely rational decision to climb back to the rim. Before long

* The length of time a man can survive without water, or with very little, will clearly depend not only on how much exercise he takes and on his build, health and state of mind but also on ambient temperature, humidity, wind and available shade. Still, the following table—which you will notice assumes *no walking at all*—makes interesting reading:

WATER REQUIREMENT CHART
(from "The Physiology of Man in the Desert," by Adolph & Associates)
Number of Days of Expected Survival in the Desert, No Walking At All:

Available water per man, U.S. quarts	0	1	2	4	10	20
Max. daily shade temp. F.	Days of expected survival					
120 degrees	2	2	2	2.5	3	4.5
110 degrees	3	3	3.5	4	5	7
100 degrees	5	5.5	6	7	9.5	13.5
90 degrees	7	8	9	10.5	15	23
80 degrees	9	10	11	13	19	29
70 degrees	10	11	12	14	20.5	32
60 degrees	10	11	12	14	21	32
50 degrees	10	11	12	14.5	21	32

the trio lost their way. Next morning, desperately dehydrated, they tried to follow a wash back to the river. Soon they came to a sheer eighty-foot drop-off. The priest, apparently irrational by now, had all three take off their shoes and throw them to the bottom. Then he tried to climb down. A few feet, and he fell to his death. The boys soon found a passable route, but one of them died on the way down to the river. The other was rescued by helicopter a week later, eight miles downstream.

I know only the bare outline of this story. But a few years ago I interviewed many times, and eventually wrote a magazine article about, two boys who were trapped in the Mojave Desert. This is not a walking story, but it is the only case in which I know full details of the kind of irrationality that any dehydrated hiker could all too easily develop. The boys were Gary Beeman, eighteen, and Jim Twomey, sixteen. Their car bogged down near midnight in soft sand, 200 feet off a remote gravel side road. It was June. Daytime shade temperatures probably approached 120° F. Humidity was virtually zero. The only liquid foods in the car were two cans of soup and one of pineapple juice, plus two pints of water. By the end of the first day—during most of which the boys rested in the shade of some nearby rocks—they had finished all the liquid. That night, working feebly, they moved the car barely fifteen feet back toward the firm gravel.

The second day, back among the rocks, both boys suffered delirium. At sunset, Jim Twomey staggered toward the car. Suddenly he sank to his knees, pitched forward, and lay still. The older boy, Gary, saw him fall. In midafternoon he had staggered irrationally out from the shade of the rocks into blazing sunlight in order to "try to find some water," and had finally dug himself into the cool sand. Now, he felt less lightheaded. He went over to his friend and bent over him. Jim's face was deathly pale. His mouth hung open. Dried mucus flecked his scaly white lips. Gary hurried to the car, searched feverishly through the inferno inside it, and at last found a bottle of after-shave lotion. He wrenched off the top and put the bottle to his lips. The shock of what tasted like hot rubbing alcohol brought him up short. He had a brief, horrible comprehension of his unhinged state of mind. Afterward, all he could think was, "We need a drink. We both need a drink."

Desperately, he ran his eyes over the car. For a moment he considered letting air out of the tires and somehow capturing its coolness. Then he was thinking, "My God, the radiator!" He had always known that in the desert your radiator water could save you; yet for two days he had ignored it! Again he had that terrible momentary comprehension of his state of mind. Then he grabbed a saucepan, squirmed under the front bumper, and unscrewed the drainage tap. A stream of rust-brown water poured down over the greasy, dust-encrusted sway bar and splashed into the saucepan. "That water," he told me later, "was the most wonderful sight I had ever seen."

After he had drunk a little, Gary found himself thinking more clearly. He went back and poured some water into Jim's open mouth. Quite quickly, Jim revived. All at once Gary saw what should have been obvious all along: a way to run the car clear, using some old railroad ties they had found much earlier. He spent almost the whole night aligning the ties—five or six hours for a job that would normally have taken him twenty minutes. At sunrise he helped his half-conscious friend into the car and made what he knew—because they had now finished the radiator water— would have to be their last attempt, however it ended. Moments later, with wheels spinning madly and the bucking car threatening to stall at any second, they shot back onto the gravel road. Four hours later, after many sweltering halts for the now dry motor to cool, they hit a highway.

Since that day, Gary has never driven into the desert without stocking up his car with at least 15 gallons of what he now calls "the most precious liquid in the world."*

Conservation of body fluids

You can very easily, in your minute-by-minute behavior, take sensible steps to conserve your body's precious water. People brought up in hot climates often train themselves, early, to reduce losses on torrid days by keeping their mouths closed. Talking is reduced to the minimum. The moist membranes of the mouth certainly lose a lot of water if exposed to free air, and such precautions are well worth taking.

Theory and folklore suggest you wear clothes that cover almost all your skin and so reduce perspiration loss. But other factors come into it, and in practice I tend to do exactly the opposite (page 310).

For recycling of body fluids in a solar still, see page 135.

---

* When I asked Jim Twomey how he had felt when his friend came with the radiator water, he said, "Oh, I just wanted him to leave me alone. I was so tired. You know, I'm fairly sure I'd never have regained consciousness if Gary hadn't brought that water, and I guess it sounds a pretty horrible way to die. But it isn't. I wasn't suffering at all—just terribly tired. All I wanted to do was to lie down and go to sleep, quite peacefully, and never have to wake up again."

How much water to carry

When you're backpacking you can't play it as safe as Gary Beeman now does, and carry 15 gallons of water (1 U.S. gallon weighs 8⅓ pounds); but in any kind of dry country you'll have to carry more than you would like to.

In the mountains you may not need to pack along any at all—though even in the mountains there are often long, hot stretches without a creek or lake or snowbank, and unless I am sure of a regular supply I tend to carry at least a cupful in a canteen. In deserts, water becomes the most precious item in your pack—and often the heaviest. In the drier parts of Grand Canyon I left each widely spaced water source carrying at least two gallons. Together with the four canteens, that meant a 19¾-pound water load. At the start of several long dry stretches I carried a third gallon in a disposable plastic liquid-bleach bottle from a food cache. On such occasions I would walk for a couple of hours in the cool of evening, drink copiously at dinner and breakfast, then leave in the morning, fresh and fully hydrated, on a long and waterless stretch that was now two critical hours shorter than it had been.

The amount of water you need under specific conditions is something you must work out for yourself. As with food, requirements vary a great deal from man to man (though see page 126 *fn.*).*

For me, half a gallon is under normal conditions a comfortable ration for a dry night stop, provided I am sure of finding more by midmorning. In temperatures around 90°, and in near-zero desert humidity, a gallon once lasted me thirty-six hours, during which I walked a flat but rather soft-surfaced thirty miles or so with no appreciable discomfort, though with no washing or tooth cleaning either. But I was steely fit at the time, and well acclimated; I would not dream of attempting that stretch "cold" with so little water.

I always lean toward safety. I can recall only three occasions on which I have been at all uncomfortably thirsty, even in the

* Small, wiry men are generally regarded as better adapted to living in deserts than are big, muscular ones. In a sense this is true. As any solid increases in size, its volume is cubed every time its surface area is squared. So the bigger a man's body, the less surface area it has for each unit of volume; and the surface, or skin, is where we lose excess heat, mainly through perspiration. Small men are therefore able to keep their body temperature down more efficiently than are big men. But this extra sweat efficiency also means that small men tend to drink more water for their size than big men do. And because a rough relationship exists in most cases between bodyweight and acceptable load (see page 21), big men can normally carry heavier weights—and therefore more water.

desert; and lack of water has never even threatened to become a real danger. It pays to remember, though, that only a hair's breadth divides safety from potential tragedy. If you are alone, one moment of carelessness or ill luck could send you stumbling across the threshold: a twisted ankle miles from water would probably be enough; certainly a broken leg or a rattlesnake bite. I try to make some kind of allowance for such possibilities, but in the end you have to rely mostly on caution and luck. Perhaps the two are not altogether unconnected. An ancient Persian proverb has it that "Fortune is infatuated with the efficient."

How often to drink

The old Spartan routine of drinking water at infrequent intervals, and rarely if ever between meals, is perhaps necessary for military formations: only that way can you satisfactorily impose group discipline. But for individuals the method is inefficient. For one thing, you tend to drink unnecessarily large quantities when at last you get the canteen to your lips. And although thirst may not become an actual physical discomfort, you often walk for hours with your mind blinkered by a kind of dehydrated scum that seals off any vivid appreciation of the world around you.

In well-watered country I take a drink at almost every convenient creek or lake, and I often suck snow or ice as I walk along. In deserts I drink a few sips of water at each hourly halt, swilling it around my mouth before swallowing. I am almost sure I use less water this way. I certainly know that the little-and-often system keeps washing the first traces of that blinkering scum away from the surface of my mind, and so rehones the edges of my appreciation. And appreciation, after all, is the reason I am walking.

Water sources

In assessing the purity of any water supply, the only safe rule is: "If in doubt, doubt." All still water should be suspect—except perhaps recent rainpockets in rock, and really remote mountain lakes. So should rivers and creeks, no matter how clear, if there seems any chance at all of a permanent settlement upstream, or even an often-used campsite. Most springs are safe. But it is possible for mineral springs, especially in deserts, to be poisonous. One culprit is arsenic. What you do if you suspect an unposted bitter-tasting spring, I really don't know—though a marked lack of insect life would be good reason for doubting its safety. I would guess that if you're in danger of dying from thirst you drink deep; and that if you're not in danger you stand and ruminate for a few minutes, then walk on. Perhaps I should add that in out-of-the-way places I've come across some remarkably evil-looking springs, bubbling and steaming and reeking, and have discovered that the water was drunk regularly by some hardy local. But the only safe rule remains: "If in doubt, doubt."

Do not rely on maps, by the way, for information about springs. Even the excellent USGS topographical series often show springs that dry out each summer or have vanished altogether due to some subterranean change. Other springs may fail in extra-dry years. Rely only on recent reports from people you feel sure you can trust (page 345). If any doubts linger, carry enough water to take you not only as far as the hoped-for spring but also back to the last water source.

Sometimes, of course, snow will be your surest, or only, source of water (page 200).

Water purification

Consult the purity rule: "If in doubt, doubt," and either boil all doubtful water or treat it with purification tablets.

Ten minutes of boiling should make any water safe, though longer will be needed at high altitudes. But boiling consumes time and energy and fuel, and leaves you with a hot, unquenching drink. So I almost always use chlorine-liberating halazone tablets. I carry them in a 35 mm. film can, with some cotton wadding to stop them from being pounded to powder. The tablets are stable, light and cheap (100 tablets weigh less than ½ ounce, cost $1.50). One tablet disinfects one pint of ordinary water. Heavy pollution may require a double dose. (It's not a bad idea to jot the dosage down on a scrap of paper and keep it in the container you use for the tablets.) To purify water, simply fill a canteen, drop in the tablets, screw down the stopper, and wait thirty minutes.

Some people seem to find the chlorinated water objectionable. Most if not all the taste can be removed by shaking the canteen vigorously and then opening it and allowing it to stand a while. Or you can mask the taste with fruit drink mix.

Water in an emergency

Cunning ideas are always being propounded about what to do if you run out of water. Typical examples are "Catch the rain in a tarp" and "Shake condensed fog off conifer trees" and "Dig in a damp, low-lying place." Then there are various crafty systems for distilling fresh water from the ocean. Just the other day, in an Armed Forces Research and Development publication, I ran across a description of what at first seemed a practical rig for sea-skirting backpackers: a series of foil sheets between which you heat salt water, either in the sun's rays or "by sitting on them." But right at the end came the killer: "With additional sheets, a survivor can obtain about one pint of water in 16 hours."

Unfortunately, the occasion on which you're really in desperate straits for water is pretty darned sure to come just when there is no rain, no fog, no damp place, and no ocean (not to mention no sheets of special foil). In other words, in the desert, in summer.

Until recently, the only advice I'd heard that sounded even vaguely practical was "Cut open a barrel cactus." An experienced friend of mine says he rather imagines you'd "extract just about enough moisture to make up for the sweat expended in slashing the damned thing open."

But I have now learned of something that seems thoroughly practical. Not long ago a California reader sent me a copy of an article describing an emergency solar still. I have drawn the following account from that article and other sources.*

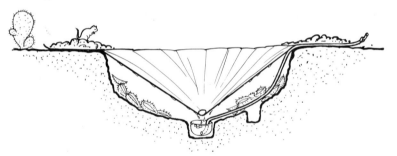

The beauty of the device is that it works best in the time and place you're most likely to need it: summer desert. The hotter the sun, the more water you get. And the water is as pure and clear as if it had been distilled in a laboratory. An Air Force medical

* Sources:

1. "Solar Distillation of Water from Soil and Plant Materials: A Simple Desert Survival Technique," by Ray D. Jackson and C. H. M. van Bavel. *Science,* 149, No. 3690 (September 17, 1965), pp. 1377–9.

2. Private correspondence with Dr. Ray D. Jackson of the U.S. Water Conservation Laboratory, Phoenix, Arizona.

3. "Water, Water, Everywhere," by Frank James Clifford. *FAA Aviation News,* 5, No. 1 (May 1966), p. 10.

4. "Water, Water, Everywhere," by Joe Bailey. *The Airman,* 10, No. 8 (August 1966), pp. 24–5. (Less technical detail than above, but one or two additional findings.)

    Articles on the still have appeared in many other places, including these: *The American Rifleman,* July 1970, p. 35; *Outdoor Life,* August 1965, p. 14; *U.S. Army Aviation Digest,* October 1965, p. 18; *The Flying Physician,* July 1966, p. 37.

colonel has called this still "the most significant breakthrough in survival technique since World War II"—and the colonel has headed a team that experimented with the still for twenty-five days in the southern Arizona desert. Judging by the team's findings, which essentially confirmed those of the original researchers, there seems no reason why this still should not save your life, or mine, if either of us ever gets in water trouble while backpacking in the desert—provided we have a clear understanding of what to do.

The still's only essential components are two items we might seem reasonably likely to carry: a container to catch the water; and a 6-foot square of clear or almost clear plastic sheeting. Up to a point, the container is easy: cooking pot or cup or Svea stove cover or a plastic bag or even a small piece of plastic sheet or aluminum foil (page 142) shaped into a hole in the ground. But the container should be wide enough to catch all drops falling from the sheet—as a cup would not. And a metal container will get very hot and "boil off" some of its precious water. So a cooking pot will do, but a plastic bowl or bucket (page 308) will do better. At first blush, the 6-foot square of plastic sheet looks easy too: we should simply get used to taking a *clear* plastic groundsheet on desert trips, and carry a poncho as sun awning (page 237). But because plastic groundsheets are almost always polyethylene, a difficulty arises; as we shall see, though, there is a way out.

A desirable but not essential component for the still is a piece of flexible plastic tubing, 4 to 6 feet long (the kind sold for aquariums is fine). Hardly a likely thing to be in your pack, you say? For other reasons you might consider taking it, see pages 140 and footnote on page 184.

Constructing the still sounds a simple enough job for even a weak and scared man, provided he has kept a modicum of his cool: Dig a hole about 40 inches wide and 20 inches deep. Dig the sides straight down at first, then taper them in to a central cavity (see illustration). Failing a toilet trowel (page 386) or a staff or stout stick, your bare hands will do the job, provided the soil is not too rocky. When the hole is finished put your container in its central cavity. If you have plastic tubing, tape it inside the container so that one end lies very near the bottom. Lead the other end up out of the hole and seal it by knotting or doubling and tying with nylon. Next, stretch the plastic sheet over the hole and anchor it around the edges with soil. Then push the sheet down in its center until it forms an inverted cone with sides 25 to 40 degrees from the horizontal. The plastic should run 2 to 4 inches above the soil and touch it *only* at the hole's rim. Place a small, smooth stone or other weight dead center to hold the conical shape and reduce wind flutter. Pile extra soil around the edge to hold the sheet firmly in place and block off *all* passage of air. In high winds, reinforce with rocks or other heavy articles. Leave the free end of the plastic tubing uncovered—and clean. Estimated construction time: 15 to 30 minutes.

This simple structure works on the same principle as a conventional still: solar energy passes through the clear plastic and heats the soil (or added plant material); water evaporates, condenses on the plastic (which is cooled by wind action), runs down to the point of the cone, and drops into the container. It takes one to two hours for the trapped air to become saturated, so that water condenses on the plastic and begins to drip into the container. With a plastic tube you can suck up water at any time; without it you have to keep removing the container—and each time you do so you lose ½ to 1 hour's water production.

It is the apparently simple business of the water running down to the point of the cone that raises the first groundsheet difficulties. Plastic groundsheets are polyethylene, which is slick, especially when new, and therefore sheds many drops before they reach the cone's apex, thereby reducing yield by about half. Any used groundsheet will be scratched, and water will adhere rather better. And scouring the sheet's undersurface with sand might make a critical difference. (I don't suggest you do it ahead of time: just file the idea away in your mind for emergency use.) But there are other groundsheet difficulties. A sheet punctured in any way, even with small holes, will drastically reduce the still's yield. Possible remedy: patch with Rip-stop tape (page 363). Again, the thinner the sheet, the more efficient: 1 mil is ideal. But a 1-mil groundsheet is close to useless; mostly, they're at least 3 or 4 mil. Finally, any loss of transparency, such as accidental or deliberate scratching, will further reduce the still's yield. In other words, a transparent groundsheet, somewhat scratched and with all holes patched, will do at a pinch. But a thin special plastic, such as Du Pont's Tedlar, will do far, far better. Unfortunately, Tedlar is twenty times as expensive as polyethylene and is not readily available to the public. One solution is to buy and carry one of the kits listed at the end of this section (page 136, first footnote).

A sandy wash makes the best site for your still. Next best is a depression where rain would collect: months after a shower, such places still retain more water than nearby high ground. The finer the soil the better. Make every effort to site the still where it will get day-long sunlight.

After long droughts you may be able to collect only small

amounts of water from even favorable soil; but—and it's a gigantic "but"—you can probably save the day by lining the sides of the hole, under the plastic, with vegetation *cut open so that its moist interior is exposed.* Cactus is best. Prickly pear and barrel cactus yield most; saguaro comes next, cholla a poor fourth. Creosote bush helps very little.

The vegetation should not touch the plastic; it may flavor the water slightly. Small ledges made in the sides of the hole may make it easier to keep the vegetation in place.

Seawater or brackish water (as found in many desert lakes) can be purified by building the still where the soil is kept moist by the underlying water table. Or keep adding the polluted water —either into a trough (see below) or by pouring it well down in the hole, not up near the rim, where condensing water could touch the soil and carry impurities down into your container. If the soil is badly contaminated on the rim (by strong alkaline deposits, say) your precious harvest of water may be fouled, so raise the plastic slightly with small rocks placed underneath it, all around the hole. With these precautions, you can even—cozy thought—operate in a region made radioactive by fallout.

Slightly modified, the still will purify water polluted by almost anything *except* antifreeze from a car radiator. So your body wastes become recyclable. To make full use of polluted material, dig a trough halfway down the hole (see illustration), line it if possible with a plastic sheet and pour the material in.

Yield will depend on many factors, but it seems reasonable to expect at least a quart a day from a properly constructed still dug in desert sand containing some moisture or lined with cut cactus. And although there seems to be an upper production limit of about 3 quarts a day for such stills, that yield can in relatively moist soil or with a good vegetation lining be maintained for four or five days. After that, make a new still or replace the vegetation. These 40-by-20-inch stills are the optimum size: if you need more water—and have the necessary materials—make more stills rather than a bigger one. Given fleshy plants or polluted water, *two* stills should provide adequate drinking water for one person *for an indefinite period.*

If rain falls, your plastic cone will naturally capture it. It may capture other things too. In the desert, water always attracts animals, and the Air Force colonel's team found that "many small rodents and snakes became trapped in the middle of the plastic"— unable to escape over its slick surface. If you're hungry these poor little bastards are obviously going to end up in your gut. (For

136 *House on Your Back*

thoughts on rattlesnake steak, see page 400.) And even if you don't feel hungry, remember that the animals contain precious fluids.

A word of warning: it occurs to me that the quoted yields of water were achieved by men practiced in the technique and operating with minds and bodies in good shape. Don't underestimate the possible effects of weakness and irrationality (page 126). But you can take care of the technique problem by personal experimentation. (If you experiment, make sure you fill the holes afterward.)

To me, this simple solar still sounds like a practical proposition for backpackers. (And for car and airplane users its components should henceforth be standard emergency equipment, kept stowed aboard against a nonrainy day). I look forward to testing it—experimentally.*

Water caches

On both California and Grand Canyon walks I had to establish several water caches. Bottles, I discovered, kept the water clear and fresh. Whenever possible I buried them—as protection against the hoofs of inquisitive wild burros and the fingers of other thirsty, thieving, or merely thoughtless mammals.†

Unburied bottles are liable to crack from extreme heat (if you

---

* A kit of materials for this still is available from Harbor Scientific, Box 2129, Costa Mesa, California 92626 (5½ ounces; 7½ by 4¼ by ¾ inches; $2.49 postpaid). It contains a thin 25-foot-square plastic sheet to which drops adhere well, a collapsible plastic container, a 42-inch plastic "straw," a plastic liner for the polluted-water trough, a spare container bag, and an instruction booklet.

† On the California walk, at the southern end of Death Valley, an amateur rockhound operating from a pickup truck kindly gave me a gallon bottle of good drinking water that he had "found under a pile of stones, back up in the hills." The water tasted far sweeter than the alkaline spring water I had camped beside. But it brought on a bad case of the worries: I became highly conscious that for three days ahead I would be relying on water I had cached out as I drove south through the valley two months earlier, and I hoped no thoughtless, light-fingered rockhound had stumbled on any of my caches. Fortunately all the caches were buried and camouflaged. I found each one safe.

I also found them without difficulty. People often ask me how you can be sure of finding a cache again. The safest way is to draw in your notebook a sketch map showing important features such as gullies and bushes and rocks, and to pace out and record a few measurements from obvious landmarks. And then to mark the exact spot with a big stone. I did all these things. But I never actually used the maps. Each time, memory took me directly to the right place. City people sometimes express amazement at such a "feat." But once you have lived for a while in any wilderness, its landmarks stand out quite clearly. Even a moderately practiced eye will detect at least as much difference between two neighboring desert gullies as between two neighboring downtown streets.

leave them in the sun) or from extreme cold (wherever you put them, if temperatures fall low enough for the water to freeze solid). I worried a good deal about the freezing danger in Grand Canyon, but found the bottles at both caches intact, in spite of night temperatures several degrees below freezing. The bigger the bottles you use, the less danger that they will freeze solid. One-gallon wine bottles, thoroughly washed, are good; 5-gallon bottles, though cumbersome, are better. Plastic bottles such as those used for liquid bleach or for distilled or spring water are lighter and perhaps stronger, but they leave me worrying about rodents.

Water left for even a few weeks in 5-gallon metal cans seems to take on a greenish tinge, apparently from algae, though I have no idea why. On the other hand, these 5-gallon cans are light and strong, and easily lashed to a packframe when caches have to be made on foot. Twice in Grand Canyon I used 5-gallon cans in which my food had been stored (page 390) to pack water a half day ahead and so break a long waterless trek into two much safer segments.

Canteens

In buying canteens, take no chances. If you find one leaking badly, miles from the nearest desert spring, it may well be about the last thing you ever find.

Metal canteens, which I used for years, are, for backpackers, essentially things of the past. Today's polyethylene bottles are far lighter and cheaper—and in many ways tougher.

Good polyethylene quart-size canteens weigh about 3½ ounces and cost less than $1; aluminum equivalents weigh at least twice as much and cost close to $3. In ½-gallon models, the best polyethylene kind average around 7 ounces and something under $2; if you can still find a good ½-gallon aluminum canteen, it's likely to weigh 13 ounces or so and cost at least $6 or $7. The old, beloved, "western round" steel canteens are now only of interest, really, for packsaddle use (½-gallon: 1 pound 9 ounces; $6.50. One-gallon: 2 pounds; $7.50). A modernized version, with felt cover and metal band around a polyethylene container, still comes out at 12 ounces and $3.70 in the ½-gallon size, 1 pound 4 ounces and $4.50 in the one-gallon.

On the score of toughness, metal naturally impresses you with greater immediate confidence. But on my Grand Canyon trip the felt covers of both my metal canteens developed gaping holes, and when the canteens came on sidetrips—slung from my belt by their convenient little spring clips—the bared aluminum banged against rocks and developed seep holes. I fixed the leaks with rubber air mattress patches—but my confidence had been punctured too. The polyethylene canteens I also carried on that trip showed no sign of wear, and since that time I have used only plastic canteens. They have given no trouble—with one exception.

The exception has been leaky stoppers. But the stoppers of all-aluminum canteens were an even greater source of grief: the threads of both neck and stopper tended to wear away; cross-threading became horribly easy; in the end the stoppers even threatened to flip off. Plastic stoppers, though not immune to this infirmity, seem less susceptible. But eventually they may begin to leak a little. Padding the stopper's inset rim-fitting with string—much as you pad a sleeve-fitting with asbestos string—stops the leaks all right, but in time the always-damp string apparently harbors bacteria and begins to reek. Inserts cut from automobile inner tubes work better. But the likeliest solution I've heard comes from a reader who suggests cutting liners or gaskets from the plastic lids of coffee cans—preferably colored plastic, so that if the gasket drops out it is easily found.

When new, and to a lesser degree after being stored for long periods, the polyethylene of the canteen tends to smell. It may even taint water. As with many things in life, time cures.

There is one feature of metal canteens that plastic cannot match. If metal canteens with felt jackets are wetted and put out in the sun, evaporation from the felt soon cools the water. You can with advantage rig a makeshift jacket for a plastic canteen with almost any article of wettable clothing, but because plastic is a poor conductor of heat it does not work nearly so well.

Most old metal canteens had good, solid spring clips for attaching to your belt—a valuable feature on packless sidetrips. I long ago rejected the traditional idea that in thirsty country you carried a canteen clipped outside your pack, readily available:

thirsty country almost always means sunny country, and direct sunlight soon turns even cold spring water into a hot and unquenching
brew. In thirsty country I carry my canteen near the top of the
pack, but insulated under a down jacket. In any case, a canteen
clipped outside your pack, especially if swinging loose, is pretty
sure to be a poorly placed load (page 89). A few good plastic canteens now come with small spring clips, or at least with holes for
attaching them; but I've yet to see one that looked strong past
doubt. The best plastic canteen for sidetrips now seems to be the
green, 1-quart Oasis—comparatively expensive but widely available
—that has a stout metal slip-over-your-belt clip (and a shoddy
screwtop) (4½ ounces; $2.75). Oasis also makes a flat, circular,
plastic, quart-size model with a fabric cover and carrying strap
(7½ ounces; $3). It has, no doubt, certain advantages.

A new alternative to clip-on canteens is a neat little woven-
nylon bag by Sierra West (1 ounce; $2). A small stuff sack with its
mouth rimmed by elastic instead of a draw cord, it has a strong belt
loop stitched to one side. On sidetrips, or even when wearing your
pack, you can slide the bag onto your belt, and into it stuff a small
canteen—or anything else you please. The elastic holds the contents safely in place. With luck, such canteen bags will become
widely available in assorted sizes.

A stopper attached to its canteen is virtually unlosable. A less
obvious profit in this arrangement, but one I rate almost as high, is
that the thong or chain attachment gives you something to hook
finger or thumb through when you're carrying several canteens back
from water source to camp or pack—a convenience you may learn
to bless at least once a day.

The catalogues feature many well-made canteens, and provided
you go for the features that seem important to you and settle for
nothing less than highest quality materials, especially in the stopper threads, it probably does not matter too much which you buy.
Round bottles are no doubt the strongest; rectangular ones are said
to pack better. Perhaps the best models—usually of somewhat
flattened shape—now come from Europe. The canteens I presently
use most are French: two each, 1- and 2-liter size (3 and 7 ounces).
I bought them outside the United States, and I no longer have any
idea how much they cost. One of the green, clip-on, quart-size
Oasis models also comes along fairly often, for sidetrips. (For
coarse practical purposes, a liter is a quart. In the catalogues, liter-
size European canteens are often labeled "quart-size." Yes, Ralph,
one liter = 1.0567 quarts.)

Flattened canteens—the kind I favor—make tolerably comfortable pillows, especially if padded with clothing. In weather no

worse than cool, the pillow routine also keeps the stopper from freezing (and for an infuriating minor frustration few things equal waking up thirsty in the middle of the night and finding yourself iced off from your drinking water). Simply putting the canteens on air mattress or foam pad may be enough to keep the stopper ice-free, but in really cold weather take one canteen to bed with you. If you think there is any danger at all of the others freezing solid, make sure they are no more than half full. That way, they can hardly burst.

In Grand Canyon I carried, to boost the capacity of the four big canteens to a full two gallons, a wide-mouthed 250 cc. poly-ethylene Evenflo baby feeder bottle (1 ounce). It turned out to be highly important. Without it I should have been hard put to find an efficient way of collecting water from the shallow rainpockets I often had to depend on. These little bottles are tough too. Once, when mine held my last precious half pint of water, I dropped it on a boulder. It bounced quite beautifully.

A baby bottle is also useful if you're walking in hot weather along river banks or lake shores. Fill it at every halt, add one halazone tablet and a little fruit-drink mix, and slip it into a pack pocket. At the next halt you have, immediately available, just enough safe, palatable water to see you through another hot, dry hour.

The baby bottles are also convenient for short sidetrips. Failing a canteen bag (page 139), one will slip into your pants pocket—though it can also slip out. The two-piece lid (for fitting baby's rubber nipple) is a mild nuisance. To hold it in one piece and so prevent the inner disk from dropping off every time you remove the lid, just slap a piece of Rip-stop tape on top (page 363). Renew it occasionally. The tape will allow the disk to turn a fraction when you replace the lid, and so jam into a water-tight joint—provided you keep the rubber nipple in place.

Collapsible water bags and bottles of various shapes and sizes (see most catalogues) take up little room in your pack and will fill you with gratitude as well as water if you have to camp far from the latter.

Possible canteen accessory: rubber or plastic or metal tubing

A "survivalist" reader writes that "a ¼ inch piece of brass tubing 8 inches long makes a good metal drinking straw. You can suck water drippage out of a rock fissure that normally you cannot get your lips at," or you can suck water drippage up with the straw and blow the mouthful of water into a canteen. You can buy the tubing at a hobby shop.

It occurs to me that rubber or plastic tubing would do the job almost as well; would be lighter, and less liable to damage; might even come in useful for siphoning into the canteen; and, most important of all, would mean—provided it was 3 feet long—that you had a highly desirable component for an emergency solar still (page 133) and for an "exhilarator" (page 184 *fn.*).

A reader has recently volunteered yet another use for such tubing. "I'm very proud of my water support system," he writes. "I carry a baby bottle, like you do, in one of my upper pockets. Connected to the bottle is a yard of aquarium tubing. If I get thirsty while I'm hiking along, I don't have to stop. I just reach for my tubing."

KITCHEN UTENSILS

Keep your utensils as few and as simple as you can, consistent with your personal requirements of weight, comfort, convenience, and obscure inner satisfaction. Naturally, no two backpackers are likely to make identical choices. I know one man-and-wife hiking team who never carry more than one cup and one spoon between them. At least, so they say. Other people like to pack everything along, including the kitchen sink. My own list reads:

	Lbs.	Oz.
2 nesting cooking pots	1	4
Stainless steel cup		3
Spoon		2
Sheath knife		6
Salt and pepper shaker		1
Sugar container		2
Margarine container		2
Milk squirter		1
Bookmatches—7 per week		1
Waterproof matchsafe		1
Miniature can opener		⅛
Total	2	7⅛

For a simpler, lighter, de-potted version, see "Rock-bottom, tin-can kitchen," page 198.

In trout country I often add:
A *steel frying pan* with detachable handle (8¾ inches diame-

ter; 12 ounces; $4.25). Aluminum pans, though lighter, are much less efficient heat spreaders. Teflon is said to be better. For a flame-spreader that promises to make frying on a stove a practical proposition, see "Wire-and-asbestos wundergauze," page 180. Aluminum foil is a good makeshift "pan" for baking fish in their skins—and maybe even for other cooking.

My *nesting cooking pots* (3½- and 2½-pint capacities; see illustrations, pages 182 and 198) are polished aluminum, with lids that double as plates or pans. The bail handles lock firmly into an upright position.

These are simple, highly practical units: the corners are rounded and easily cleaned; the low profiles and broad bases promote rapid heating. And these pots are tough. The smaller one, which travels protected inside its mate and also gets less cooking use, is now fifteen years old and still looks like new. My original larger one withstood a dozen years of brutal use (it once bounced 150 feet down a steep talus slope in Death Valley and pulled up with only a couple of minor dents) and then had to be retired only because it got so dented that cleaning became difficult. Its replacement has after three years begun to mature—though hardly to usurp, yet, the place in my affection once held by that old and honored friend.

Some people say they have difficulty lifting the lids of these pots. I seem to do so easily enough, with almost no thought and one end or other of my spoon. The spoon may simply hold the lid ajar for me to insert a tea bag, or may lift it so that I can grasp and remove it with my other hand—insulated if necessary by a bandanna (page 302).

These Swiss-made pots, by Sigg, also come in 5¼-, 7-, and 8¾-pint sizes (15, 17, and 20 ounces). The catalogues sometimes call them "kettles." (My sizes, 1 pound, 4 ounces the pair; $9.75.)

A popular alternative for one, two or even three people is the Sigg Tourist Cook Kit—a nesting set of 2½- and 3½-pint aluminum pots, lid that doubles as fry pan, and stove base and windshield (2 pounds; $10). (Beware of Taiwanese equivalent: it is reported to contain dangerous levels of lead and copper.) This high-rise set that encages the stove and seems to shield it effectively from wind is normally used with a Svea or Optimus 80 (illustrations, page 157) in "naked" condition—that is, stripped of all removable, windshielding extras.

A convenient newcomer for solo backpackers is the new but similar Optimus 88 stove-with-cook-set—1½-pint-capacity pot, lid that doubles as fry pan, stove base, windshield and pot lifter (complete with "naked" Svea: 1 pound 4 ounces; $19.95). Without a stove, the unit is called Cooking Set 124 (9 ounces; $7.95).

See also Optimus 77A Storm Stove, page 171.

Cups. The Sierra Club stainless steel cup (the latest, slightly enlarged version: capacity 10 fluid ounces; weight 3 ounces; $1.30; see illustration, page 199) is one of those simple but gloriously successful devices that man occasionally invents. It is tough. It cleans easily. Its rim rarely burns your lips, even with the hottest food or drink—a feature that anyone who has suffered an aluminum cup will appreciate. The open-end steel wire handle stays cool too, hooks over belt or bough or cord, and snaps easily and securely onto a belt clip (page 371). (A reader writes: "Have you ever found an efficient way, or even an inefficient way, to stop the occasional intolerable rattle of Sierra cup in belt clip?" The answer is simple: "No.")

Beware of cups that look like the Sierra Club version but cost half as much. They may be lip-burning aluminum abominations.

Unfortunately the Sierra Club cup has in certain wilderness circles become a badge of conformity: you are not considered "in" if you do not sport one dangling from your belt. A dismal fate for a first-class article. But it is entirely possible, I assure you, to be a member of the very worthwhile Sierra Club and to carry one of their excellent cups and yet not qualify as what has been aptly called a cup-carrying member.

For a reserve cup in case of loss or unexpected company, see cover of Svea stove (page 165, and illustrations on pages 157 and 210—where it is acting, the way mine often does, as a cup stand). The cover is aluminum, though, and a guaranteed lip-scorcher.

Although there have always been pretenders, a real competitor to the Sierra Club cup has only recently surfaced: the Palco plastic cup (illustration, page 146). Color: green or white. It holds 20 percent less than the Sierra cup (8 fluid ounces), but is much lighter and cheaper (1 ounce; $.25), seems very tough and clean-able (flexible polypropylene), cannot burn your lips, is measure-marked in 2-ounce (¼-cup) increments, and unlike the Sierra cup, has no protruding and dirt-collecting lip. Also, being deeper and less heat conductive, it keeps food hotter.*

Unfortunately, the Palco's extra height and weight mean less stability (a real factor, this, and perhaps the main reason I continue to carry a Sierra cup: I find that when close to empty the Palco tends to tip over if you rest a spoon on it). The smaller top area also means less convenience with the lumpy stews and even hamburgers that the Sierra cup handles with such surprising grace. And you cannot cook in the plastic Palco. Again, you cannot hang the cup as presently made onto a belt clip, though I understand it is possible to cut or burn a hole for this purpose in the rather small handle— which will not, unfortunately, hook over your belt with anything like the Sierra cup's security. Finally, gung-hoers complain that the Palco is not in the same class as the inverted Sierra cup when it comes to digging handholds in snow slopes.

The collapsible stainless steel "Bob Lane" cup—which a reader was kind enough to send me—folds flat, fits in your shirt pocket, does not rattle, and snaps open into a cone (capacity 4 fluid ounces; weight ½ ounce; $1.75 in the L. L. Bean catalogue). Un-like telescopic folding models, it looks easy to keep clean. Another reader says that he carries a plastic cup, but because it will not clip on his belt, supplements it with a "Bob Lane." After all, he says, the pair weigh less than one Sierra Cup.

Spoon. Any tough, light spoon will do. One from a clip-together knife-fork-and-spoon set will have two little protuberances

* I have just conducted a rather elegant experiment to prove my point. I several times filled both cups, side by side, with water of known temperature and then exposed the cups, still side by side, to cool environments of known temperature. Summary of results:

Water at start	Cool environment	Minutes exposed	Water temps. ° F. Sierra	Palco
Boiling	Garden, 58° F., windless	15	120	126
		18	112	118
		20	109	115
122° F.	Freezer box, 15° F.	5	96	100
Boiling	Freezer box, 15° F.	10	120	126

I assume that any impartial observer would accept these figures, which were supported by lip-service tests, as clear demonstration (taking into account the time and temperature parameters probable in field use, and reducing all readings to two decimal places) that the Palco is, as a heat conserver, superior to the Sierra Club cup by a factor remarkably close, all expectations considered, to zero.

that are not only ideal for hooking on pot rims when you leave the spoon standing in one, but also unbeatable for collecting dirt.

Fork. Redundant.

Knife. I am sometimes a little surprised to find myself still carrying a 6-ounce sheath knife. On the rare occasions I use it for eating, a much lighter tool would do. Even for other jobs, I find I use it rather infrequently. But I can recall several occasions when, lacking such a solid blade and handle, I should have been hard put to it to gouge out dry kindling, or even to clean especially large fish. It would certainly be great for cactus cutting (page 135). And there is no denying that, especially in game country such as East Africa, it is comforting to have some sort of defensive weapon along. I would guess, though, that I go on carrying my old friend mainly because I couldn't bear to cast it out.

Most outdoor equipment catalogues feature ultrafunctional knives festooned with gadgets. Swiss army model #16935 embodies large blade, nail file, scissors, saw, magnifier and fire-starting glass, can opener, screwdrivers, reamer, file, metal file, tweezers, toothpick, Phillips screwdriver, fish scaler with hook disgorger, and lanyard shackle—all for 4¾ ounces and $21. But color TV is extra.

Small carborundum stone (3 inches; 1 ounce; $.50). For knife sharpening. An alternative is a small tungsten-carbide steel shaft, four-sided, hollow-ground, with handle. It is said to be highly efficient as well as very light. Of course, some people rarely seem to get around to sharpening their knives, and mostly make a hash of it when they do. Others keep their knives razor sharp. With mine, on a hot day, you can cut butter forever.

Salt and pepper shaker. I use a strong plastic shaker, the "Tokyo-Top," made in Japan, that lets you see how much salt and pepper is left (1 ounce; $.70). But I hear whispers that it may be going off the market.

Containers. The strongest and lightest, not to mention the cheapest, are polyethylene. The best, such as Tupperware, wear surprisingly well. My sugar container is now fifteen years old.

Before switching to Trak (page 347), I used to carry detergent powder, and it once taught me to make sure all my containers were easily distinguishable, by sight and touch: I can heartily unrecommend predawn cereal sleepily sweetened with detergent powder. My sugar now travels in a square container that holds 1¼ pounds; the margarine in a round one that just takes a squeezed-down ¼-pound bar. If you carry detergent, make sure you put it in a bottle of some other distinctive shape.

Some people carry food items in wide-mouth plastic bottles of various sizes, now featured in many catalogues. An alternative for margarine and also for such potential pack wreckers as jam, honey and peanut butter is a poly-squeeze tube (¾ ounce; $.40)—a plastic version of a large toothpaste tube, refillable by disengaging the end clip. You can carry exactly the amount you want in such a tube, and so escape the limitations of prepackaged products. (Warning! Recent reports suggest that certain substances, such as mayonnaise, may cause these tubes to disintegrate.)

I'm told you can break eggs into squeeze tubes and halfway trust the yolks to be intact for morning fried eggs. Alternatively, buy yourself a hard plastic egg box, biovular through duodecimovular (1 ounce, $.45, through 6 ounces, $2). I did so once, with profit, on a summer-long walk up England when I could often drop into a farmhouse in the evening and buy a couple of eggs for breakfast.

Milk Squirter. One of those pliable, squeezable polyethylene containers in which honey and mustard are sometimes sold. For refilling with milk powder, unscrew main top. For making milk, remove only the little dunce-cap top and squirt powder down onto water, tea or coffee. Even in a raging gale you suffer virtually no loss. A simple but valuable device—and one that lasts. The Sue Bee honey container (12-ounce size) that I started with ten years ago is still squirting strong.

Bookmatches, though useless in a high wind, are otherwise more convenient than wooden ones. I find a book a day more than enough.

A *waterproof matchsafe* holds about twenty large wooden strike-anywhere matches for use in wind or wet. I'm always rather surprised at how rarely I use mine. The matchsafe is also a safe place to keep needles and a little thread (page 363).

My matchsafe is the screw-tight metal kind (1 ounce; now $.85). I've carried it for years, but at one time grew unhappy with both the difficulty of opening it and also the way the metal attachment loop can pull loose. If it weren't for the usefulness of this loop, which permits you to tie the matchsafe to your belt, or to an inflatable vest on river crossings (page 382), I would probably switch to a simpler plastic model (¾ ounce; $.45), though I mistrust the screw-on lid. 120-size film cans are said to be useful makeshift matchsafes—but judging by my experience with them in other capacities, I'd have thought they were bound to dent around the screwtop and let moisture in.

A reader writes: "Through accident I discovered what has proven to be an airtight, light, buoyant and free matchsafe. Just take any square, 3-inch-high spice can of the type that bay leaves come in (not the ones with the shaker tops) and you'll find enough room for matches, needle and thread, safety pins or whatever. You have to pry the lid off with a knife, coin or strong thumbnail (not advisable), but it's lighter than any other I've tried. And again, it's free."

A *can opener*—U.S. Army type—is worth carrying, even though ordinary canned foods make hopelessly inefficient backpacking fare. You may need the opener for canned goodies that you include in cache or airdrop, or buy as a welcome change at a wayside store, or are given by some kind, heavy-toting, back-country horseman. One end of the opener doubles as a screwdriver. It's not particularly effective. But as can openers these tiny instruments (⅛ ounce; 2 for $.25) are astonishingly efficient. The Ski Hut catalogue used to call them "one of the noblest products of the U.S. Army." Recently, they went off the market for a while, and the similar-looking civilian substitutes were almost useless. But the originals are back now, in all their glory.

Warning: These can openers are easily lost, especially in sand, so thread a small piece of red rag through the key-chain hole. My opener goes into the office (page 359), wrapped in its own small plastic bag.

A *prospector's magnifying glass,* most often useful for examining rock samples and such sights as the horrifying head of a dragonfly, forms an emergency reserve for fire-lighting (page 185). Mine is 10-power, weighs 2 ounces.

A reader recommends a camera lens—removable from my Pentax (page 327) and many other cameras—as both magnifier and emergency fire starter. Trouble is, I rarely carry a camera these days. But binoculars might do the fire job.

Flint stick. This catalogue item—now "the official Boy Scout fire-starter"—caught my eye some time ago (and halfway convinced me, especially as I was told it's a very effective little device). It gives off a fat, high-temperature spark that will ignite flammable gases or tinder. At least, so the instructions say. The kit now comes in a neat little plastic case: flint, striker, tinder, small wax fire-starter and key-ring (1 ounce; $.98; from the Flint Stick Company, 4803 Snowden Avenue, Lakewood, California 90714). "The size of a house key," says the catalogue, "but it could save your life." Maybe it could too. But I've now carried one of the older, plastic-boxed versions around for five years, always meaning to test it in a quiet moment, never getting around to the job. It's still lurking in a pocket of my pack—a monument, rather battered now, to my remarkable powers of procrastination.

Keeping utensils clean

Nowadays I generally carry a single "paper" washrag (actually rayon or similar, sold as "Miracloth," "Wash 'n Dri" or the like) for wiping pots clean (maybe ½ ounce; around $.20). Several readers write that they always take scouring pads of various kinds (Chore Girl, Tuffy, or Dobie) which they swear will clean anything instantly with cold water in cold weather.

For soaps and detergents see page 347.

For notes on the actual practice of cleaning utensils see "A sample day in the kitchen," page 194.

HEAT SOURCES

Fires

The campfire is one of man's most ancient traditions (indeed, you could define man as "the fire-lighting animal"), and even today a fire is to many people half the fun of camping. Understandably so. For cheer and warmth as well as for cooking—not to mention for drying out you and yours—there is nothing quite like it.

The warmth is not very efficient—you tend to be toasted on one side, iceberged on the other—but there's no doubt about the cheer. Beside your fire, you live in a private, glowing little world. All around you, fire-shapes dance across rocks and bushes and tree trunks. A grasshopper that you have been watching as it basks on one verge, motionless, leaps without warning clear over the flames and out into the darkness. But most of the time you just sit and gaze into the caverns that form and crumble and then form again between the incandescent logs. You build fantastic worlds among those pulsating walls and arches and colonnades. No, not quite "build," for that is too active and definite a word. Rather, you let your mind slip away, free and unrestricted, roaming wide yet completely at rest, unconnected with your conscious self yet reporting back at some low, quiet, strangely decisive level. You sit, in other words, and dream. The East African has an almost limitless capacity for this masterly and delightful form of inactivity, and when his friends see him squatting there, lost, they understand and say in Swahili, poetically, *"Anahota moto"*—"He is dreaming the fire."

But there is another side to this shimmering coin. For many years now, in places it was both easy and reasonable to build campfires, I have, far more often than not, done without one. Perhaps laziness has a lot to do with it. But I am very aware that a fire cuts you off from the night. I do not mean only that it makes most night animals give your camp a wide berth. Within the fire's domain you exist in a special, private, personal, isolated world. It is only when you walk away and stand for a while as part of the silence and immensity beyond that you understand the restriction. And then you find that the silent, infinite, mysterious world that exists beyond the campfire is truer than the restricted world that exists around it—and that in the end it is more rewarding. I walk out into wilderness primarily, I think, to reestablish a sense of unity with the rest of the world, with the rock and the trees and the animals and the sky and its stars—though perhaps I mean only that when I return to the city a renewed sense of this affinity is, above all, what I bring back with me. Anyway, a campfire, by its very charms, disrupts my sense of inclusion.

But if I do not build a fire I build no lasting barriers. After I have cooked my evening meal on the little stove I use instead, and have switched off the stove and registered the unfailing astonishment I experience at the noisiness of its hissing, I am alone in and with the night. I can hear, now, the magnified sounds of its silence: a field mouse thinly complaining; a dry leaf rustling; a wedge of wind sliding down the far slope of the valley. And I can look deep into the shadowy blackness or the starlit dimness or the moonlit clarity. Or best of all, I can watch the moon lever itself up and flood the starlit dimness into landscape.

Always, over each of these separate mysteries, spreads the sky, total. And I, at the center—my center of it—am small and insignificant; but at the same time a part of it and therefore significant.

Then there are the ethical considerations.

A thousand charred forests bear black witness to the dangers of open fires. These dangers are as old as the dry summer hills; but in recent years new imperatives have crowded in on us. They depend, as do so many things, on numbers. Even half a dozen years ago, popular wildernesses like the High Sierra were so lightly used that a backpacker could, within reason, light a safe, properly controlled cooking- and campfire every night with a clear conscience. No longer. And it is not only that round black fire-site pockmarks have in places become so common they rupture the sense of wilderness that people are presumably there to capture; or that too many fires—even small, safe fires—in such fragile places as meadows may seriously damage root systems. The fundamental and inescapable fact is that wood fires consume wood.

This slow consumption by humans does not at first seem to matter much. If you like tidy, parkland sort of country rather than genuine wilderness—which is rarely tidy, close up—then you may even like the result. I can do no more than differ with your esthetic judgment. But dead and decaying wood is a component of the mechanism that has built what you find in the

corner of the planet you have camped in. At moving margins—
a meadow's edge, a forest's flank, the battlefront between soil and
sand dune—it may be the most important component of all. It
provides shade; holds soil and moisture; becomes food for grasses,
plants and insects—and so sets off new chain reactions that soon
employ more grasses and plants, more insects and birds, then
reptiles and mammals too. And eventually—dust to dust—it re-
becomes soil. A new, richer, more productive soil. Reduce the
wood available for decay, and you slow down this process. Reduce
it a bit more, and you halt all progress. Reduce a bit more, and
you begin to impoverish the corner of the planet you have camped
in. And never forget that the accretion is slow: it moves by the
decade, the century, the millennium. But the depletion is rapid:
man consumes by the year, the day, the hour, the minute. And
when he can find no more dead wood to consume, he begins to cut
green wood. . . .

And now I have a confession to make. To make with reluctance. My draft of this new section ecologized along to considerably beyond this point. When it was written I sent copies
of it, for a check on facts and arguments, to two qualified outdoorsmen friends—one a geography professor and the other a
doctor of ecology who drives Boeing 707's for a living. To my
surprise, both came up fighting. Both suggested—independently,
but with one voice—that I had employed a common current
ploy: using tenuous and questionable "ecological" arguments to
justify what was really a gut feeling. On reflection, I pleaded
guilty. Each of them then proceeded to demolish my "ecological"
arguments with an expertise beyond my grasp. In particular, they
zeroed in on my use of the word "impoverish." In some areas it
might be applicable; but fire-lighting man might equally be said
to stimulate growth by releasing the nutrients bound up in dead
wood. More had to be learned about the chemistry of such burning. Again, in much prime backpacking country, decades of successful fire prevention had created such an accumulation of fuel
in the form of choked bush that when the inevitable fire came at
last it was, instead of a clean-up operation, a holocaust. Hence
my "charred forests."

Both my friends then said at some length that to them campfires were, anyway, "a part of it all." They extolled the warm skills
and traditions of woodcraft. They listed all the campfire pleasures
I had listed. They added more. And for groups, they said, the
pleasures multiplied: there is nothing like a campfire to promote
community spirit within a heterogeneous party. My "sense

of inclusion" idea had some merit in bright moonlight; but "what about a dark night?" Anyway, you only had to move away from a fire to see the stars. And too damned often there was a "hair shirt" element in doing without a fire. Maybe a campfire was even one of man's "deep evolutionary needs." And so it went on.

Now, both my friends are honest men, and both readily admitted that they were no doubt doing exactly what I had done: justifying gut feelings with any "logic" that came to hand. But both remained adamant. They were very much attached to fires. They disagreed with me "one thousand percent." And they disagreed with terrible competence.

I am slightly intimidated but not, I find, convinced. I fail to detect the faintest tickle of a personal hair shirt. And I continue to feel that the building of campfires in much of today's wilderness is harming that wilderness. On further reflection, I think I am talking less about genuine ecological damage than about fires' charring effect on the "natural," harmonious, non-human timbre of true wilderness—the quality I probably value above all. My opinion is no doubt based on gut feeling rather than logic. But I make no apologies for that. Rather the reverse. Few people accuse me of clear thinking, but I like to consider that on occasion I can *feel* with some accuracy.

Finally, I call for support on another backpacking friend who has spent long months striding around the High Sierra. He is a man who dotes on wilderness cooking and drools over smoke-tanged steak. He sees stoves as "revolting, noisy, heavy little bastards." But he has reluctantly concluded that in heavily used back-country areas all wood fires should be banned. Such a ban would be a deplorable step in many complicated ways (see, for example, page 233), and I am not sure I would really approve of it; but I might well come to regard it as the lesser of two looming evils.

All this is very sad. As I have said, there is nothing like a fire for warmth and cheer. In real cold and wet, drying you and yours can be a crucial matter. And let us not forget such soft delights as "dreaming the fire" (or of being choked by billows of smoke, or of watching red-hot sparks spit onto hapless sleeping bags). Fortunately, there are still places in which even a protectionist more rabid than I would condone campfires: below high-tide mark, for example, on a beach littered with logging debris, as so many Pacific beaches are littered. And there are occasional times and places, even now, when I light my own small campfire.

. . .

When it comes to cooking fires, I find myself in the same minority position—for the same reasons (a properly handled stove poses no fire hazard), plus others that are perhaps simpler to explain.

Cooking outdoor food on an open fire is the obvious as well as traditional way. (For operating with one, see page 182.) But fifteen years ago I bought a small gas-burning stove for use in a fuelless mountain area above timberline, and the stove turned out to be so efficient that very soon I virtually gave up open-fire cooking.

For me, a stove wins on every count except weight. When selecting a campsite you no longer have to worry about fuel supply or to hunt for wood as soon as you stop—an important advantage when you want to push ahead until dark, and always a comfort in rattlesnake country. Instead, you light up the stove (an operation that takes only a minute or so, even with the less convenient kinds, once you're competent), then leave the meal to cook by itself while you set up camp—another sharp gain, especially when you're flop-down tired. And heat control is almost as easy and instant and exact as on the gas stove back home. On a stove, too, the outside of your pot stays bright and clean. You won't write this off as a minor benefaction if you've ever discovered that the plastic bag sheathing your fire-blackened pots in the pack has sprung a leak, next door to the sleeping bag; or if you have woken up one morning to find that you unsuspectingly went to sleep the night before with one hand soot-black from handling a cooking pot in the dark. A stove allows you greater freedom in choosing campsites too: you need not worry about having fire-wood available, or about that appallingly combustible layer of pine needles. What's more—and this is vital to me—a stove makes it possible to cook and eat all meals comfortably cocooned in a sleeping bag (page 190). For groups, though, a fire yields one important practical advantage: you can heat more than one pot at a time—especially if you carry a grill or grate, as many experienced backpackers do.

It is true, of course, that even a small cooking fire offers, in miniature, any campfire's glowing, pulsing mysteries. It is at once a relaxing and yet stimulating change from modern home life—including its own emasculated shadow, the suburban barbecue. Then there are the smells. And food cooked on it can pick up a delightful tang. But to my mind these attractions hardly begin to offset the practical and ethical drawbacks. And nowadays, for cooking, I almost always rely on my

Stove.

The standard rig I carry, complete and primed for a week, consists of:

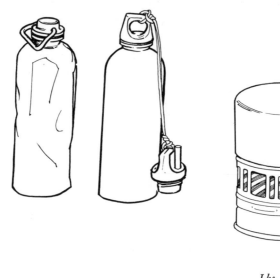

	Lbs.	Oz.
Svea 123 stove, with cover	1	1½
⅓ pint white gas in stove		4
Stove cover handle (for use when cover acts as cup or pot) (see page 157)		¼
Aluminum white gas bottle (holds 1⅓ pints) (see page 173)		3
1⅓ pints white gas	1	
The Canedy cap (see page 174)		½
Total	2	9¼

If I expect to have to melt much snow or ice for water, I carry a second bottleful of white gas.

I chose my Svea on the advice of an experienced backpacker—in other words, by that combination of chance and sagacity that is the route most of us slide along in choosing equipment—and although I may use other stoves to meet special conditions I still rely mostly on my little Svea. But we must examine alternatives.

Gasoline stoves have long been standard for backpackers. "White," unleaded gas (page 173) is led from tank to burner jet by a wick that, abetted by a strainer, prevents dirt from reaching and clogging the nozzle. In heavy models, a hand pump pressurizes the tank. In lightweights, pressure comes initially from preheating, then is maintained by the stove's own warmth.

Butane cartridge stoves have in recent years challenged the gasoline burners. These stoves offer advantages that are eyecatching to the inexperienced; but they suffer from several serious defects. Until recently, butane stoves were vapor-fed (Bleuet and Ranger), but at least two models (Mini-Stove and Mousetrap) now operate on a new liquid-feed system. The two types behave differently, especially in cold and at high altitudes.

Let us look at vital statistics and performance figures for the most popular stoves.*

Please remember that although controlled "kitchen" tests such as I made are necessary for the kind of table that follows (you can't control a damned thing in a gale at 12,000 feet), the figures have value only for *comparisons* between stoves. They give precious little indication of what any stove will achieve in the field.

I suppose I must try to convince you that my figures, though hardly rockbound scientific, are essentially valid.

The stoves tested were brand new, except for a slightly used Bleuet and Primus Ranger, and all were weighed at a post office on an official scale. I checked all gasoline fuel capacities by pouring and repouring several times. Fuel for gasoline stoves came from two new, sealed, gallon-size cans of Camplite camp fuel ("white gas"). Whenever a stove's performance became even slightly suspect, its burner jet was cleaned. All timings were read from a starkly clear digital clock.

* Similar figures for many of these stoves have appeared so often in retail catalogues and books, including the first edition of this one, that they assumed the glow of gospel truth. But for this edition I have done some tests of my own. And lo and bedamned, the gospel turns out to be laced with errors! Some are marginal. All are small. But they add up to significance: innocents everywhere have been laboring under minor misapprehensions that could affect their choice of stoves. I certainly have.

Please don't assume that the manufacturers issued deliberately misleading figures: over the years, design changes have probably been made while the statistics—already muddied by translation from the metric system—have by and large been allowed to stand. Recently published tables also suggest that independent investigators, seeking only the truth, can generate disparate figures, all susceptible to challenge. I therefore rest confident that, in spite of the care I took, somebody somewhere will do similar tests, come up with different answers, and be able to revile me. It is rewarding to know that your work will bring so much happiness into the world.

Tests were conducted in six sessions spread over ten days. Burning-time figures are averages of *at least* seven complete-tank burns for each gasoline stove, three complete-cartridge burns for each butane stove. In boiling-time-for-a-quart-of-water tests, at least twelve boils were made per stove (times noted to nearest five seconds; averages corrected to nearest quarter of a minute).

For the first session, to stifle any personal biases (who said I had a yen for Sveas?) I press-ganged two friends as assistants. The lady sat and courageously clerked and pretended a cold was not half killing her. Her husband—a doctor, but not entirely innocent of science—kept an eye on me and did wise things to hold the waiting water at a constant temperature. (For the six sessions, water temperature averaged 52° F. and never exceeded 56° or fell below 50°. Ambient temperatures rarely rose above 70° or fell below 60°. None of the variations had any discernible effect on boiling times.)

Lacking a thermometer that went high enough to ensure an objective decision on the moment at which each quart of water boiled, I substituted for the first session a team of two grown men peering earnestly into pots and bleating about "big bubbles reaching the surface." For later sessions, one ditto, muttering to himself. Any errors of judgment inherent in this, er, system can hardly have invalidated the results: with the quicker-boiling stoves, the lag between "pretty damned sure it's boiling" and "obviously boiling now" ran to no more than four or five seconds; times for butane stoves at low ebb are more subject to question, but as we shall see, that scarcely matters.

The pots used were two Sigg 3½-pinters (page 142), kept at a reasonably constant temperature for each test by having a quart of water, usually from a previous test, boiled in them until a few seconds before use—a practice that raised the test water's effective temperature about 5° F. During boiling, pots were left uncovered. All tests were conducted about 300 feet above sea level, indoors, on a wooden table, in a place as windless as was consistent with safe ventilation for the gallant experimeters.

All in all, then, it is with some confidence that I characterize the tests as not only heroic (by the end, I never wanted to see another stove) but also valid.

And now the candidates . . . and the results:

GASOLINE STOVES

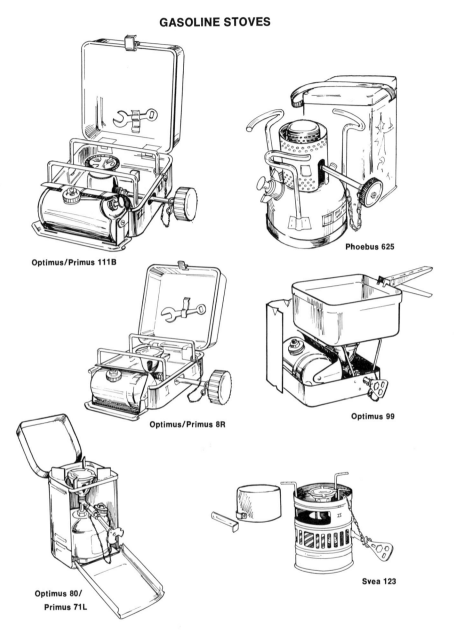

Optimus/Primus 111B

Phoebus 625

Optimus/Primus 8R

Optimus 99

Optimus 80/
Primus 71L

Svea 123

Note on name maze: On January 1, 1973 the makers of the
Optimus/Primus/Svea stove line discontinued use of the name
Primus for gasoline stoves sold in the United States and Canada.
Before that, the names Optimus and Primus (with the same num-
bers) had been interchangeable for models 111B and 8R, while the
Optimus 80 and Primus 71L were identical. The old names will
doubtless linger for years around every backpackers' hot stove
league.

BACKPACKING STOVES: VITAL STATISTICS

> WARNING! THESE DATA ARE FOR SHELTERED, SMIL-
> ING CONDITIONS. They do not indicate how any stove will
> perform in the unkind field. And no figure should be assimilated,
> raw, without a check for maddening qualifications in the text,
> above or below.

	Weight empty or w/o cartridges		*Fuel capacity*	*Burning time*[a]	*Boils qt. water*[b]	*Price*
	Lbs.	*Oz.*	*Pints*	*Minutes*	*Minutes*	
Gasoline stoves						
Optimus 111B	3	6	1.10	120[c]	4–4½	$27.00
Phoebus 625	2	9	1.45	(150)[h]	(3¾)[h]	$19.50
Optimus 8R	1	9½	.30	60	7–7½	$15.00
Optimus 99	1	6	.30	(35!)[i]	(3¾–6¼!)[i]	$16.25
Optimus 80	1	2½	.40	65[c]	5–5½	$13.00
Svea 123	1	1½	.35	55[c]	5–5½	$14.00
M.S.R. Model 9	—	12	1.3 or 2.2	(see page 165)		$19.45

Butane cartridge stoves			*Ounces*			
Bleuet S-200	1	2½[d]	—	60–220[e]	11–16[f]	$ 7.70[d]
C-200 Gaz cartridge:						
full/empty		10/3	6¾			$ .80
						($ 4.50/6-pack)
Primus Ranger		15½	—	90–240[e]	10–15[f]	$10.75
2201 cartridge:						
full/empty		10/2	8			$ .96
Gerry Mini		7½	—	100	5½–10[g]	$12.00
Mini cartridge:						
full/empty		10/3	6¼			$ .98
Optimus 731 Mousetrap		11¼	—	(see page 169)		$12.95
Optimus 702 cartridge:						
full/empty		10/3	6¼			$ .98

For Primus Grasshopper (propane), see page 170.

For Optimus 77A Storm stove (alcohol), see page 170.

　　a. At continuous full flame. In the field, with much simmering, stoves will assuredly burn longer.

　　b. Figures for gasoline-burners show brackets established by six fastest test boils.

BUTANE CARTRIDGE STOVES

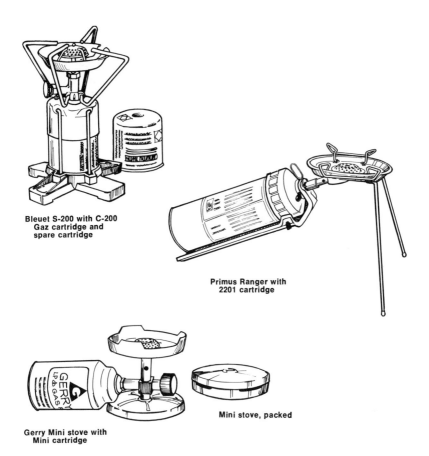

Bleuet S-200 with C-200
Gaz cartridge and
spare cartridge

Primus Ranger with
2201 cartridge

Gerry Mini stove with
Mini cartridge

Mini stove, packed

c. Readings are for full tank, not for ¾- or ½-full tank, as recommended. I find that, contrary to all lore, stoves burn equally well when full.

d. Weight and price include metal windscreen (4 ounces; $1) and plastic stand (1½ ounces; free).

e. First figure: the point at which an average cartridge took more than 16 minutes to boil its quart (rather arbitrarily designated the end of the cartridge's "effective life"). Second figure: time flame finally died.

f. First figure gives boiling time with new cartridge; second figure, time at end of estimated effective life. See, importantly, text and table on p. 160.

g. Bracket does not, as with Bleuet and Ranger, indicate pressure drop-off, but variable effectiveness of individual cartridges (p. 167).

h. Figures are not from main tests but from other people's results, supported by brief last-minute tests of mine.

i. These astonishing last-minute-test results, radically different from anyone else's, were confirmed by 4 full-tank burns and 15 boils. Fastest boils came at ends of burns.

Unfortunately, certain complications arise.

In the main tests I burned all stoves *without pause*. But as the Bleuet and Ranger burn—and lose pressure—their cartridges cool themselves, severely; and both stoves work far less efficiently when cold. So by operating them continuously, beyond a point normal in field use, I unfairly accentuated their negative feedback. I therefore conducted subsidiary tests. I burned each stove continuously for fifty minutes, noted how long it then took to boil a quart of water, and turned the stove off. Thereafter I conducted boiling tests in pairs: the first after a "rest"—at least one hour, often a day or two—that let the cylinder return to air temperature; and the second immediately afterward. In the "with rests" column of the following table, such pairs are bracketed.

AVERAGE TIME NEEDED TO BOIL ONE QUART WATER

Elapsed burning time from full	Continuous burning (main tests) Bleuet mins. secs.		Ranger mins. secs.		With rests Bleuet mins. secs.		Ranger mins. secs.	
10 mins.	10	25	10	5				
20 mins.	12	5	10	0				
30 mins.	12	5	10	45				
50 mins.					12	50	10	50
					Rest		Rest	
1 hour	15	40	13	25	{ 10 { 13	10 30	{ 8 { 12	40 30
					Rest		Rest	
1½ hours			14	30	{ 10 { 16	40 20	{ 9 { 15	55 0
					Rest		Rest	
2 hours	20	0			{ 15 { 35	15 40[a]	{ 15 { 18	40 30
					Rest		Rest	
3 hours	—	—[b]			—	—[c]	24	0[a]
4 hours			26	40[a]				
Flame out:	3 hrs. 40 mins.		4 hrs. 15 mins.		3 hrs. 8 mins.		3 hrs. 27 mins.	

a. *Almost* boiling.
b. Would not quite boil.
c. Flame soon out.

Conclusion: if the Bleuet and Ranger are burned continuously, performance soon tapers off; but "rests," such as occur naturally in most field use, improve performance spectacularly.

A summary of evidence in the heated case of

Gasoline stoves vs. cartridge stoves.

Heating efficiency. Gasoline outperforms vapor-feed cartridges (Bleuet and Ranger) roughly two to one. This apparent advantage is slightly reduced by the need to preheat gasoline stoves; but it is radically widened by the way the cartridges lose efficiency as they empty, while gasoline stoves (and liquid-feed cartridges) burn at peak to the end. Liquid-feed cartridges (Gerry and Mousetrap) seem to rival and perhaps equal gasoline's performance. The effects of cold and high altitude on gasoline and liquid-feed stoves are small—though not negligible. Cold radically reduces the efficiency of vapor-feed stoves; but high altitude—because it means lower external air pressure—makes them work better. As it is usually cold up high, performance becomes a seesaw balancing act. For effects of wind, see individual stoves, pages 163–69.

"But why all this fuss," I hear you mutter, "about a couple of minutes' difference in boiling a quart of water?" The grisly fact is that when the wind is iceberging and you are tired and cramped as well as aching cold, and everything you do is difficult and so tends to get done inefficiently, then the two or three minutes' difference registered under test conditions may run to ten minutes or twenty—or even to the difference between boiling and not boiling: as the water nears boiling point, loss of heat from stove and pot to a hostile environment increases and in the end may balance that generated by the stove, so that the outfit hunkers down into a docile but immovable state of equilibrium, maddeningly shy of boiling. Even in my cozy tests, this happened when Bleuet and Ranger cartridges ran low.

Heating efficiency is by no means the only admissible evidence. Even more significant (as a single stove failure miles and days from succor would undoubtedly convince you) is

Reliability. One stove expert writes: "Only many years of fooling with these little devils under many conditions will produce reliability information." I vouch for the Svea and, within its limitations, the Bleuet. On overwhelming testimony, the other gasoline stoves cited (though not necessarily all other models) pass with flaming colors. The Ranger and Gerry are relative newcomers: jury still out. Mousetrap: no data.

Weight. Two figures apply: what you start with; and what you pack out, empty.

My filled Svea cooks me through one full day, and with a liter-size Sigg container in support will do so for a week. Three Bleuet cartridges also last me a week. Assuming I would need three cartridges for both the Ranger and Gerry, and that all your requirements are the same as mine (which is a lot to assume, I guess, but we've got to start somewhere), and using weights from the table on page 158, then we have:

Length of trip	Day (*1 tankful or cartridge*)		48-hr. weekend (*half-liter of fuel or 2 cartridges*[1])		Week (*1 liter of fuel or 3 cartridges*)	
	Full	*Empty*	*Full*	*Empty*	*Full*	*Empty*
	Lbs. *Oz.*	*Lbs.* *Oz.*	*Lbs.* *Oz.*	*Lbs.* *Oz.*	*Lbs.* *Oz.*	*Lbs.* *Oz.*
Svea[2]	1 5½	1 1½	1 15	1 5	2 9	1 5
Bleuet	1 12½	1 5½	2 6½	1 8½	3 ½	1 11½
Ranger	1 9½	1 1½	2 3½	1 3½	2 13½	1 5½
Gerry[3]	1 1½	— 10½	1 11½	— 13½	2 5½	1 ½

1. If, like me, you lack the courage/stupidity to rely on any cartridge for a full 48 hours.
2. For Optimus 80 add 1 ounce; for 99, 4½ ounces; for 8R, 8 ounces.
3. For Mousetrap, add 3¾ ounces.
(*Note:* "empty" figures assume you will pack out all empty cartridges. If you expect to call in at a ranger station or some other place with garbage disposal, deduct three ounces for each empty Bleuet or Gerry cartridge, two ounces for each Ranger cartridge.)

Convenience. Cartridges win, nolo contendere. This is what catches the inexperienced eye: instant heat whenever you want it. Cartridge stoves are also cleaner and less noisy. And in cool weather you can relight them to heat chilled food—an unreasonable operation with any gasoline stove.

Beginners boggle at the imagined difficulties of preheating gasoline stoves, but once you achieve competence (page 175), it is in fact a minor chore.

Safety. Gasoline stoves have safety valves that prevent their tanks from exploding. You hear and read lurid but apparently true stories of these valves spouting jets of flaming vapor; but I know of no experienced user having such trouble. This is not, by God, to say that it can't happen; only that I'm suspicious of half-screwed-down filler caps and grossly overheated bowls.

The Bleuet and Ranger have positive cartridge-to-stove locking systems, and provided they are properly used seem very safe. I've heard of no accidents. Gerry cartridges connect more informally; yet the only accident I know of (page 168) apparently had nothing to do with the connection.

Fuel availability. Gasoline stoves have the edge in the United States and Canada. Overseas, probably not. See page 173. Bleuet cartridges are sold worldwide. For details, and for Primus and Gerry, see pages 166 and 167.

We cannot, of course, assume that we shall always have a ready supply of cartridges, or even white gas (Preface, page xiv; and also page 357).

Cost. Initial outlay: except for the very reasonable Bleuet, not much to choose. Running costs: gasoline wins, wallets down.

The *litter problem.* With gasoline stoves: nil. With cartridges: a growing menace. EMPTY CARTRIDGES MUST BE PACKED OUT. That seems no more than common sense, common decency. Yet many people either do not care or are too dim-witted to comprehend that they degrade the land, and themselves, when they toss empties away. For Gerry nickel refund, see page 167.

The *verdict.* If you must be able to cook, yea unto boiling, any place, any time, under all but the most bloodcurdling or heavenward conditions, or if you grudge every extra ounce on your back, pronounce judgment in favor of gasoline.

If you can be sure of benign conditions, place high value on convenience and cleanliness, do not demand particularly quick cooking, do not grudge every last ounce, and are not a litterlout, settle for a cartridge stove.

Riders.

1. The Gerry and the Mousetrap—provided they meet your other criteria—will, if they prove out in the field, form an exception to the weight clause, and perhaps the speed clause too.

2. Note that many experienced backpackers, after affairs with the seductive cartridge stoves, seem to return to the gasoline fold; but that others continue, like me, to use cartridge stoves for short trips when all suns shine.

CHOOSING YOUR MODEL

For illustrations, vital statistics and performance figures, see pages 157–8.

Gasoline stoves

(*Note.* All stoves cited except Optimus 80 now have self-cleaning jets: when you turn the valve fully open, a wire rises from inside and cleans the orifice.)

Optimus 111B (Primus 111B). Long the standard unit for high-altitude and uncivil temperatures because its built-in pressure pump enables it to roar defiance. Seems less affected by poor fuel than the lightweight four (see below), and at a pinch can use automobile gas (page 173). Stable and compact. But heavy. So no go for warm, low-down, solo backpackers. But maybe for parties.

Phoebus 625. Austrian. May be a "comer" for Spartan, 111B-type conditions. Increasingly available in the United States. Said to be "crude, but a trouble-free workhorse." Automobile gas o.k. if cooking area properly ventilated. Stable. Bulkier and less elegant than 111B, but lighter (1 pound 15½ ounces *without* protective can).

The following "lightweight four" are the standards for experienced, go-almost-anywhere backpackers—solo, duo or slightly more social. None has a hand-pump: after priming, heat of stove maintains pressure. Improved handle-chains on recent models kink and bedevil you less than earlier versions (I like to think a suggestion of mine to the makers prompted this change, but alas! I have no proof). Relative wind resistance of the various models very difficult to judge. Indeed, any comparison of quartet members tends to raise a storm of swirling personal loyalties. But I guess I must try:

Optimus 8R (Primus 8R). The 111B's little cousin. Very stable. And easier than Svea to prime by simple eyedropper method (page 177). Some say it "starts more easily than its rivals at high altitudes or in sub-zero weather." Others call it "stronger and more reliable." I remain unconvinced. The first one I tested performed so poorly that I rushed out and bought another: it performed, marginally but consistently, rather worse. This report will naturally raise howls from the 8R's faithful supporters. I'm sorry about that.

Optimus 99. A new, revised 8R with identical tank and burner but lighter, aluminum case. Top of case doubles as 1½-pint pot. Grip-handle included. Also simple aluminum windscreen for now very exposed burner. Maker's data and logic suggest performance identical to 8R's, but see table, page 158, footnote i!

Optimus 80 (Primus 71L). An old and well-tried favorite. Easier than Svea to eyedrop-prime (page 177). Marginally less stable, and has narrower support for pots. The only quartet member still without built-in self-cleaning needle—a decided debit in theory, marginally so in practice. Comes in metal box that's a windshield, heat reflector and pot stand. One reader writes that he has replaced the 8-ounce box with "a three-pronged aluminum pot support that weighs about zero" (no other details). Another reader substitutes "a 1-pound coffee can, properly cut for ventilation and flame adjustment, that weighs only 3 ounces."

Svea 123. The lightest and dead-heat hottest of the light-weight four, and probably the most popular. Fifteen years my trusted friend. Integral perforated windshield. Removable aluminum cover doubles as pot or cup (hellishly hot on lips, but a useful reserve in case of unexpected company or loss of regular cup). Recent models have built-in cleaning needle, of kind long installed in 8R. Frankly, I hardly ever had to use the old, separate cleaning needle (which some people maintain pushes dirt down into the burner), and find the new device's theoretical advantage offset by further reductions of arc in an already touchy flame-adjustment valve. Still, this is a wonderful little stove. It has roared sturdily away for me at over 14,000 feet and in temperatures around 10° F. And it has never let me down.

To me, one of the Svea's bonuses is that innocuous-sounding cover-pot-cup. I sometimes carry the pot on sidetrips away from my pack and brew tea in it over a small wood fire. But its main use is as a cup stand (illustration, page 210). By rotating the open end a couple of times on any rough surface except rock I can dig it in enough to form a raised, level, and stable platform. Even on rock you can experiment and soon find a firm base. Anyone who has watched precious tea or coffee spill from his tilted cup will understand the value of this instant table. In snow, where a hot cup quickly melts its own hole, I invert the cover and rest the cup in its hollow. The heat dissipates much more gradually, the food stays hot longer, and the cover, kept cool, sinks into the snow only very slowly. To correct even that minor fault, I put the stove's Ensolite pad (page 180) underneath once it is no longer needed for the stove. This cup stand may sound like the blatherings of a man blinded by personal loyalty to an old friend; but every time I use another stove I am re-amazed at the way I chafe at not having the Svea cover to put my cup on. In fact, I often take it along.

Phoebus 725. A mini-version of the Phoebus 625—without hand pump (2 pounds 3 ounces; $15.30). Has just entered U.S. market. I have yet to see one or hear field reports; but if it's to challenge the lightweight four at that weight it will have to burn like seven hells.

Gasoline stoves: postscript

Mountain Safety Research of Seattle now markets a 12-ounce stove (Model 9; $19.45) that operates directly from a standard Sigg Fuel bottle (page 173) fitted with a screw-in pump. I have yet to see one of these ingenious little rigs, but reliable reports suggest that performance is remarkable, even under bad conditions. Questions are raised, though, about some practical handling characteristics.

Cartridge stoves

Bleuet S200. Vapor-feed. French. The first widely available butane stove. Reliability now amply proven. With plastic stand, quite stable. Pot supports good and wide. With metal windshield fitted, has fair wind resistance. You can now buy stoves and cartridges all over the world: I've even found them in small African village stores.

Within the limitations of butane (page 161), the Bleuet is a workhorse. Although it produces the least heat of all stoves tested, it can surprise you. During a twenty-four-hour stay in a hut at about 16,000 feet on Kilimanjaro, with temperatures around freezing, mine once brewed me many cups of tea and all regulation meals. Admittedly, I seem to remember that it was pretty slow work.

Cartridges are attached to the stove by a strong pressure system that is leakproof, *provided* you clean the indented portion of each new cylinder and the rubber cone against which it will seat. But you are specifically warned not to remove cartridges until empty. So if you have a half-empty one on the stove when you want to start a trip, you either have to light it and let the cartridge burn empty or, alternatively, pack along an uncertain amount of fuel in an inefficient form, weightwise. And empty cartridges reek: you may get butane whiffs from your pack as you walk along. Remedy: seal exit hole with a piece of Rip-stop tape (page 363) or a plug of spiraled paper.

Primus Ranger. Vapor-feed. Swedish (but made by different firm from Optimus line: a separate offshoot of old Primus business). A relative newcomer to the United States. Promising, though reliability not yet proven. Consistently outperformed Bleuet in my tests by 10 to 20 percent. High stance means little or no site preparation needed, almost any place. Excellent stability. But the hinged-wire-loops pot stand is meager—even when pulled out, which the instructions do not clearly instruct you to do. Has little or no protection from wind. Cartridges sketchily but increasingly available in the United States; overseas, I don't know.

The screw-in cartridges have a valve fitting and can be replaced at any stage of burning—a clear gain, especially at the start of a trip. But I harbor misgivings about the screw fitting. It is very small and fine. Even at home you could cross-thread; in a storm, when you're cold and tired, it would be perilously easy.

And the cartridge valve sometimes sticks: although screwed home, it will not emit gas. Mostly, turning the stove valve half open *before* screwing on the cartridge will for some reason do the trick; or you may be able to loosen things up by depressing the cartridge valve briefly with a match or similar repair tool. This even worked for me once when a cartridge simply faded out while burning. Cartridges can leak too, though I'm not sure how commonly.

Do not confuse the Ranger with the similar-looking but propane-burning Primus Grasshopper (page 170). Thread fittings are different, and cartridges are *not* interchangeable.

Gerry Mini Stove. Liquid-feed, with wick inside cartridge. American. (Also sold, it seems, under these names: E.F.I. Model 200 Mini Stove; Universal Sierra Stove; and Medalist Sierra Stove.) Another relatively recent entry. Half the weight of its rivals (for a consequent rumination on use in modified tin-can kitchen, see page 200). Astonishing heating power—but reliability still unproven. New Mark II model may be less temperamental than its predecessor. Stability good. Wind resistance fair to good. Cartridges unfortunately still hard to find, even in the United States. Will work on similar Coleman cartridges (though see page 168), and on the new Optimus 702's (page 169) when they appear. Printed on all new Gerry cartridges is an offer of a nickel on a new cartridge for returning the old one empty. A commendable idea. But at least one store has tried it with Bleuets—as well as plastic groundsheets—and raised little response. I wish I could be more hopeful.

When I first saw this stove, packed up like a large but tinny yo-yo, it struck me as just the sort of damn clever, impractical little device I deplore. But assembling the stove and repacking the yo-yo turned out to be not the finicky business I'd feared but simplicity itself. And my tests taught me respect. Although cartridge performance for some reason varied widely (4 cartridges: 5½-, 6-, 7½- and 10-minute average readings for boiling their quarts), the stove did not, even without "rests," lose efficiency as a cartridge emptied.

The Mark I stove seemed temperamental, though. Even under the friendly test conditions it was liable when first lit to emit a high yellow flame. And when I lowered the flame it often went out. In theory, you just put a pot on the stove to protect the flame and over the next minute or so gradually open the valve. In practice, you fiddle. And even with the stove thoroughly warm, the flame may go out if you try to lower it. The Mark II is supposed to ameliorate this fault, and also a reported tendency for burners to clog.

The Mini's rubber cartridge valve is self-sealing. You moisten a smooth, protruding rod on the stove and slip it into the hole in the cartridge valve. The seating is not rigid, and the cartridge, which sits on its side, has a tendency to be forced outward by the taper of its top against the stove base. If it drops, performance can fall sharply. Cylinders removed from the stove apparently do not always reseal. Remedies: first, slide back onto stove and remove again; if this cure fails, push matchstick or nail or similar into hole. This could be dangerous. In fact, the whole valve ensemble fills me with less than bounding confidence.

One reason the Mini stove has not really caught on yet, in spite of its lightness and excellent heating powers, could be the fairly widely disseminated reports of an accident that occurred in July 1972. According to one report, a man "was preparing dinner for a group of Boy Scouts and had a large pot on the stove, which he was steadying by surrounding it with rocks. In use [on a Gerry Mini Stove Mark I] was a Coleman cartridge, which suddenly ruptured, enveloping the area in a ten-foot fireball." The man suffered third-degree burns over a large part of his body, but has fully recovered.

In an effort to pin down facts that we potential users clearly want to know, I have consulted with both the stove maker and the victim. A damages case has been filed, and everybody is cagey. But the following facts emerge: The cartridge in use was indeed a Coleman, not a Gerry. This is probably irrelevant. The victim reports that the cartridge burst apart at the point where the top is crimped to the main body. The makers say the accident was due to "enclosure of the fuel can and stove with rocks, which permitted an excessive [heat] buildup in the can. This type of operation is specifically warned against in our current instructions for operation. The large pot was not the direct cause of can failure . . ." The victim maintains that the rocks blocked off "no more than two fifteen-degree sectors around the stove."

Whatever the exact facts of this case, it has lessons for us. Unlike the tanks of gasoline stoves, which must be warm to generate pressure, butane cartridges should while operating be cool or even bloody cold to the touch. So check occasionally. If a cartridge feels hot, *turn the stove off*. And always make sure your stove is sufficiently ventilated to prevent heat buildup.

Other attachments for butane cartridges

Ranger. A lamp that has definite value under certain conditions (page 319). Also a heater (page 350).

Gerry. An infrared heater that the makers claim cooks well, but is reported to have bugs still. Currently, no lamp.

Bleuet. A lamp, but a very bulky one; and cartridge un-switchability reduces its value still further.

Butane stoves: postscript

Optimus has just advised me that in early 1974 it will market a completely new, liquid-feed butane cartridge stove:

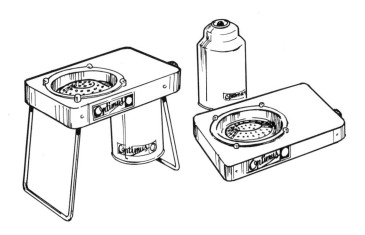

The *Optimus 731 "Mousetrap"* operates on an Optimus 702 cartridge, identical to a Gerry Mini cartridge. But the stove is said to perform markedly better because gas is *preheated* by being piped around the burner before emission.

Other features of the new stove: Upright cartridge said to "prevent flare-ups." One leg holds cartridge firmly in place, even if assembled stove is moved. Stove folds flat, like a mousetrap: 4¾ by 7⅛ by 1 inches. (For bloody big mice; but we'd better not follow that line of thought.) Stove alone: 12 ounces; $12.95. Full cartridge: 10 ounces (average burning time: 2 hours); $.98. Stove also works on Gerry and Coleman cartridges.

And now you know as much as I do about whether this may indeed turn out to be a better mousetrap that will soon have us all making a beaten path to the optimal door marked "731."*

* *Off Belay* Magazine (p. 18, this book) has kindly sent me advance proofs of part of a stove article scheduled for the December 1973 issue. As the magazine's figures are not strictly comparable with mine for other stoves, I will not quote them; but they suggest the Mousetrap is, to say the very least, a highly promising unit. They sustain the makers' claim that at sea level under "normal conditions" the Mousetrap boils its quart of water in 5½ minutes.

The *Off Belay* survey, incidentally, looks like being a wide-ranging and very worthwhile effort. It gives performance figures not only for "normal" conditions similar to mine but also for controlled "cold" and "windy" conditions.

Propane cartridge stove

The *Primus Grasshopper* burns propane and therefore operates on big, *heavy,* steel cartridges that will withstand the high
pressure under which propane is packed. So it is at best a marginal
backpacking stove. (Stove: 11½ ounces; $10. But slim #5931
cartridge holding 14.1 ounces of fuel weighs 30 ounces, costs
$1.75; and jumbo #5933 cartridge holding 16.1 ounces of fuel
weighs 40 ounces, costs $2.) Under my test conditions (page 156),
it boiled its quarts in an average of nine minutes.

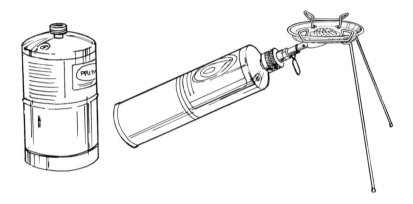

Propane works far better than butane at high altitudes (because of the high internal pressure) and low temperatures (it
vaporizes down to −40° F.), and might therefore be carried at
times by big parties. It's also a convenience in your car for use
at roadhead. Note again that, in spite of marked similarity, Ranger
and Grasshopper stoves and cartridges are not compatible: their
screw connections differ. But the Grasshopper takes such standard
propane cylinders as Bernzomatic, Turner, and Sears.

Alcohol stoves

The normal fuel is "denatured alcohol"—ethyl (or booze)
alcohol rendered poisonous by additives. It costs about $3 a gallon.
It generates only about half as much heat as the same weight of
gasoline or kerosene, but it is said to be "explosion proof and absolutely safe." And if you cock a jaundiced eye on the future, note
that it is not a petroleum product.

Until recently, alcohol stoves suitable for backpacking had
virtually vanished from the North American market. But now we

have one that may prove viable, even valuable—especially in deep winter or shallow energy crises:

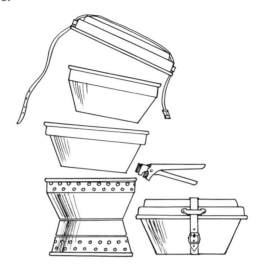

The *Optimus 77A Storm Stove* (complete with 2-pot cookset [2½ pints each] and pot-lifter: 1 pound 12 ounces; $15.95) burns denatured alcohol in an open bowl, not under pressure. In my quart-of-water tests, its average for three boils was just over 9½ minutes. The makers claim 8 minutes a quart—and say the stove consumes 0.35 pints of fuel an hour, or much the same as a Svea. They also say that "windy conditions, cold temperatures and high elevations will not affect the performance of this stove [which is] used by the Swedish Commando units." One experienced winter cross-country man I know confirms these claims. "You can light it anywhere," he says. Another demurs. "Though expensive to operate," he writes, "they [alcohol stoves] work well under the right conditions. They burn silently and efficiently if not subjected to wind or cold. . . . Try this simple experiment. Take a small amount of fuel alcohol and place it in a metal lid from a small jar. Place it in a freezer and allow it to sit for an hour or so. Remove it from the freezer and try to light it with a match. You will find that it cannot be lit until it warms up to 40 degrees or more." I have just obeyed—but putting the complete burner unit from a 77A in the freezer. With the alcohol at 26° F. and the garden air at 54°, I lit a large wooden match and let it burn out while it stood in the alcohol. The fuel lit first time.

I carried a 77A on a recent brief field trip during which temperatures never fell much below 40° and there was no wind.

It worked fine. I found not being able to adjust the flame a trial, but Optimus now supplies a brass ring that tethers the flame effectively at "low." A bonus: the stove indeed burns in absolute silence. A disadvantage: your pots get black, but black.

(Later: a friend who recently used the stove on a cross-country ski trip, at elevations over 9000 feet and in temperatures down to 10° below zero, had no difficulty lighting the stove with book-matches—and found it highly effective for a 3-day trip on which the high fuel consumption did not mean a prohibitively heavy load.)

Sterno (solid alcohol in a can) is a word that used to re-verberate around the woods. It conjures up pictures of cold, wet groups huddled hopefully around a small pot perched on a smaller can, waiting for water to boil. Waiting . . . and waiting . . . and waiting . . .

Kerosene stoves

Once well alight, these stoves burn persistently and very hot; but they tend to be heavy, smelly, and fiends to start. You have to carry alcohol or some other priming fuel. If you lose the stove's cleaning needle you're soon in trouble. And the pump leather must be kept oiled: it may balk for lack of a few drops. Although often obligatory for climbers (the stoves work well at high altitude and in extreme cold), they have in the past hardly entered our walking orbit.

But Optimus is now trying to promote the use of kerosene instead of gasoline and alcohol—on grounds of safety and cost. The flash point of kerosene is high; it rarely catches fire at all, unless preheated. And in the smelly, crude form in which you buy it in bulk (5 gallons or more) at gas stations, it costs around $.60 a gallon; but deodorized kerosene in gallon cans may run $1.75. (Coleman or similar "white gas"-type stove fuel is about the same.) Optimus will next year be marketing not only an odorless kerosene under their own label (no prices yet) but also a priming paste—"more or less alcohol in paste form"—reputed to "make the priming and general use of kerosene stoves just as convenient as gasoline."

Models. Best appears to be the Optimus 00 (1-pint tank; reputed to boil a quart of water in 3–5 minutes; 1½ pounds; $17.95), though it may be mildly awkward to pack unless you carry its tin box (6 ounces). The Optimus 96 weighs 3 ounces less but has only a ½-pint tank and is rated to boil its quart in 6–7 minutes (also $17.95). Then there is the Optimus 111, a kerosene version of the 111B (same vital statistics).

OPERATING YOUR STOVE

Safety. Don't be afraid of any stove. But each time you touch one, *exercise meticulous care in every little act.* Your first failure to screw a filler plug or cartridge fully home could be your last.

Convenience is the cartridge stoves' strong point, and you don't really have to learn much except how to put a match to a burner. But for such things as must or should be done see under each model, page 166 and onward. For "Protection from wind" and "Keeping cooked food warm," see pages 178 and 181.

To make any gasoline stove realize its potential you must know what you are doing. That is no doubt why, in spite of their unquestionably superior field performance, small gasoline stoves consistently trail cartridge stoves in sales.

Fuel

We shall ignore such chilling imponderables as the future may hold, and consider only the stable present.

In cities, bulk white gas has become less and less easy to find. But most sports stores now stock gallon cans of Coleman Appliance Fuel or Camplite or other similar equivalent—all distinctly more expensive than bulk white gas and maybe marginally more efficient. All these fuels deteriorate in storage. When I filled my new Svea with Camplite fuel that had been standing in the garage for God knows how many months or even years, boiling time for a quart of water rose from 5 or 5½ minutes to between 7 and 8.

Automobile gasoline contains additives, including lead, that will in time block a stove's jet. Use only in emergencies—even in 111B and Phoebus 625. And buy low-octane grades: they contain fewest additives. No-lead and low-lead gasolines are presumably best.

Overseas, you can rarely buy white gas. In Europe, a relatively common replacement is naphtha—a first distillate of gasoline that's very efficient but highly volatile.

Fuel containers

The most popular containers, and the ones I use, are the cylindrical, spun-aluminum Sigg bottles, made in Switzerland (1-

liter: 4½ ounces; $1.85 [illustration, page 154]. 2-liter: 6 ounces; $2.10). Buy the bare aluminum, non-anodized kind: the more expensive, colored, anodized versions are needed only for corrosive liquids such as, my God, whiskey (page 120). Slightly cheaper versions, made in Taiwan, are now appearing. I have no reliable reports.

The Swiss bottles are extraordinarily tough. My original one, though battered like a pug, was still sound after a dozen years; but dents finally reduced its capacity so severely that I retired it, with honor. After three years, its replacement remains pretty pristine. You may have to replace a worn gasket every few years, but that's about all. Not long ago the makers switched from metal to plastic stoppers, and difficulties arose over fit; but the contretemps has now mercifully subsided. If a stopper is hard to remove, apply overwhelming leverage by twisting a spoon or stick pushed through the stopper arch.

With care, a full 1-liter bottle of fuel plus the starting tankful last me and my Svea a week. If snow or ice must be melted for water, I carry two bottles.

An Austrian-made series of tin-alloy, flat-type containers with pouring spouts and built-in filter screens (1-pint: 4 ounces; $3.50. 1½-pint: 5 ounces; $4. 1-quart: 6 ounces; $4.15) is sold as "leakproof." But I hear vehement reports that hard buffeting may split the seams. There are cheaper, Taiwanese versions of these, too.

A black-plastic miniature jerrican with reversible filler spout, made in Germany (2-liter: 5 ounces; $2.25) has its adherents. But it poors pourly—I mean, pours poorly—for me, anyway. And the stopper threads suffuse me with distrust.

Filling the stove

For years I carried a tiny plastic or aluminum funnel (⅛ ounce; $.50) and poured directly into it from my Sigg bottle. But when the bottle was full I always spilled a little gas, no matter how carefully I poured. Once the level dropped, the difficulty vanished; but that wastage of precious fuel hurt. Several readers suggested crafty arrangements of rubber tubing epoxied into spare stoppers, with fuel flow controlled by finger pressure. The ultimate in this idea came from Mr. Buck Canedy of Massachusetts, and is now commercially available.

The *Canedy pouring cap* (illustration, page 154) is made from a standard Sigg plastic stopper. Its pouring tube may be copper or plastic. You control fuel flow with a fingertip on the small drilled hole.

Although these clever little caps weigh and cost more than funnels (they average about ½ ounce), they work very well indeed and eliminate that wastage of precious fuel. I have carried one for over a year now, tied to the bottle's regular stopper with a short length of nylon cord. It has suffered no damage. Do not do as I did, though, the first time I carried it: forget to replace the normal stopper—and lose most of your fuel in the pack.

The caps fit both pint- and quart-size Sigg bottles, but *not* the older, metal-stoppered versions. They are now sold by a small but growing number of mountain shops, from Massachusetts to California, and are also available for $1.25 direct from S. Buck Canedy, P.O. Box 1685, Fall River, Massachusetts 02722. He will ship first-class mail. (He reports that as of October 1973 he has sold an astonishing total of more than 12,000 caps, all hand-modified.)

Sigg is reported to be about to introduce, with all its bottles, free of charge, a modified stopper that also pours. It is self-sealing, and eliminates the need for a second cap. The idea sounds simple and brilliant: two holes—one larger than the other—are drilled on opposite sides of the stopper, up near the top of the threads. To pour, you simply unscrew the stopper to the last thread and pour through the larger hole, while controlling flow with a fingertip on the smaller hole. I have just tried out what is said to be an exact copy of a Sigg original, and I regret to report that it simply doesn't work. The pouring hole lies so close to the bottle lip that fuel spills down the side of the bottle. The small controlling hole is so recessed that not even a half-grown Hobbit could get a fingertip on it; and even if he could, the slack fitting of the almost-unscrewed stopper would allow air to pass—and nullify the control effect. What's more, the loosened stopper is liable to pop off. A pity.

Priming (preheating)

Before lighting any gasoline stove you must prime it by preheating the generator. The theory is simple. First you fill the little bowl at the foot of the generator with fuel. (Although almost everyone uses the white gas that fuels the stove, because that saves carrying something else, you *can* use alcohol, which is reputed to deposit less dirt but certainly puts out less heat [see, though, alcohol paste, page 172].) You light the liquid (or paste) in the bowl. When it has almost finished burning—thereby heating the generator and vaporizing some fuel—you open the stove valve. If you time it dead right, the dying flame lights the jet. If not, you apply a match. And once the jet is alight its heat will maintain pressure for as long as there's fuel in the tank.

What causes dismay among beginners and ecstasies of disagreement among pundits is the apparently simple business of filling the bowl. The makers' instructions tell you to open the valve slightly and then cradle the tank in the palms of your hands: they will warm the fuel and cause it to expand and emerge from the nozzle and run down the generator and fill the bowl. But the fact is that, except when temperatures are cool but not cold, you run into difficulties. At one extreme, the cold metal murders your hands. At the other, the gasoline is already so warm that the increase in temperature, if any, is too small to force out fuel, and you sit there for minutes on end, solemn and expectant as Aladdin, and nothing happens.

I rarely bother with the warm-hands routine. Sometimes I just put the stove in the sun or on a hot rock for a few moments and just sometimes it works. More often I light a fragment of paper under the bowl. Toilet paper does fine, but—in one of those old-womanish habits that seem so important in the wilderness, and are—I hoard in a pants ticket-pocket every discarded paper wrapper from tea bags and meat bars and mintcake and the like, and I reach for one automatically when I want to light the stove. The system works well, especially if you remember, as I almost never do, to open the valve when the stove has cooled after use, and so nullify the internal vacuum. Occasionally no heating is necessary: when temperature or altitude is much higher than on the last occasion you used the stove, especially if you refilled it then or remembered the devacuum business, the fuel often wells out as soon as you open the valve.

But there are, as one correspondent writes, "a million ways to prime." The one you select will depend on chance and on your general character, specific prejudices, and model of stove. My paper-burning method works well with a Svea, not quite so well with an Optimus 80 (because you have to remove the stove from its can and then replace it), and is hardly possible with an 8R or 99. Alternative methods work better with the other stoves.

There are two currently sanctified alternatives—both promulgated in several readers' letters, and now bruited about, I see, in other literature.

One is to carry a small plastic eyedropper. To prime stove,

remove filler cap (automatically devacuuming tank), fill eyedropper with gas, and transfer it to preheating bowl. Repeat if
necessary until bowl is full, and preferably overflowing. Close
filler cap firmly—and you're all set. This system works well with
an Optimus 80 (you need not remove the stove from its can),
even better with an 8R or 99. And the eyedropper can travel
in the can of either. If it has a white or bright red rubber bulb,
or a piece of bright material attached, the danger of losing it is
no doubt reduced. The dropper can travel inside a Svea's windshield; but because Svea lovers have to remove the windshield to
get at the filler cap, they may, like me, find paper-burning better.

Describing the second method, a reader points out that "there
is no rule that says you can't take off the cap and blow gently.
Gas comes squirting out of the nozzle and into the bowl." He
adds that he uses an 8R, which has "easy oral access," and admits
that with a Svea or 71L "a little gas might dribble down onto your
nose." Worse, it seems to me, is the damned nuisance of having
to remove these stoves from can or windshield and also the near-
certainty that they will transfer to your lips and nose some of the
soot they'll assuredly have accumulated from repeated priming.
Still, the method seems to work well with the 8R. And as the
reader tartly reminded me, "it eliminates the messing around with
lighting little bits of paper."

There are other, less publicized, priming tactics. A 75-year-old
reader confides: "It took me ⅔ of a lifetime for this idea to hit me
so best I pass it on while yet there is time. . . . Next time you fill
your Svea, screw the filler cap on, then unscrew the conical burner
from the vaporizer stem, open the valve, put your mouth tight over
the nipple (no bum cracks, pliz) and apply all the breath-pressure
you can (it will be about 2½ lbs. p.s.i.) for about 20 secs.
Close the valve before you relax the pressure or you'll get 'gassed.'
Your stove now is pressurized. If you now opened the valve, fuel
would shoot 8 inches high so replace the burner. From here on
proceed as heretofore. You will add the pressure due to heat to that
you already have built up by breath and Svea will take off like a
747. You'll find this especially useful in cold weather."

Another reader, scorning details, simply says: "Mountaineers
discovered years ago that the only way to light [gasoline stoves]
was to douse the whole thing with gas and then stand back and
throw a match in. A stove lit in this manner will light 'first time
every time.' "

Yet another reader writes: "Open the valve a few turns, then
turn the stove upside-down and let it rest there a minute or two.
. . . Holding the match, or as I use, a cigarette lighter, under the

nipple will cause the stove to light within a couple of seconds. Only a rapid return to uprightedness and closing the valve somewhat, and the stove is ready to go." I wish you better luck than I've had.

Finally, if you have just refilled the stove, then you can—given a suitable filler, such as a Canedy cap (page 174)—pour direct from container into bowl. This method is inadvisable at other times, not only because getting the container out of your pack would be a nuisance, but also because there is a remote chance of fire or even explosion—not, obviously, when the stove is cold, but if, as can happen, the first priming was not fully effective and you decide to give the partly heated stove another dose. At such a moment you could, especially when weary at the end of a long day's walk, overlook a lingering spark. Or the heat could cause spontaneous combustion. If the flame flashed back into the container it could conceivably explode. And that is not a chance to take.

Now choose the priming method that suits your stove and temperament.

Protection from wind

Wind is a major difficulty in lighting a stove. A guttering warm-up flame does precious little warming up, and the stove will burn feebly, if at all. So make sure you shield it adequately. Cupped hands work well.

But wind remains a problem even when the stove is well alight. It drastically reduces the effective heat. And because this is something you cannot see, the only way you know about it is that after a while you find the wretched water still hasn't come to a boil. Most of us, I fancy, tend to become careless about protecting our stoves from wind. Every now and then I get a reminder. Not long ago I spent a night on a mountain in winds that I later learned had gusted to 50 miles an hour, and was forced to sleep in a sheltered rock crevice. At the back of the crevice I found a beautiful little grotto of a kitchen that might have been made for my Svea. Although I was over 12,000 feet, the stove burned in that perfectly protected place with the healthiest and boomingest roar I have ever heard it make, as if overjoyed at being given this chance to defy the rage outside. And my dinner stew that night seemed to start bubbling and steaming much more quickly than usual.

Sometimes a gust of wind will blow a stove clean out, particularly before the burner ring becomes red hot, or when you lower the flame for simmering. At such times, and especially when you are relighting it, a match left across the burner helps keep a reluctant flame alive.

To shield your stove you can build a makeshift structure with pack, boots, clothing, spare pots or anything else you can lay hands on. (But take care not to overheat a cartridge stove [see page 168].) Or you can, as I often do nowadays, carry a

Windscreen.

For years, the only screen widely available was a cloth affair (3 ounces; $2.25).

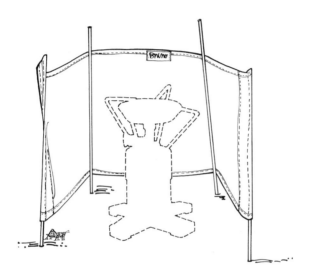

Provided the ground is soft enough to accept the aluminum-alloy legs, this screen works fairly well. The simplest way to keep its sides reasonably taut is to remove the two middle legs from the fabric, plant the two outer legs firmly, leaving the screen slack, and then force the screen outward as you plant the middle legs.

In the first draft of this revision I wrote: "Frankly, the device falls lamentably short of perfection. It's time a great brain got to work on this problem. . . ." One has. The Ski Hut now sells an excellent, simple little folding aluminum screen designed specifically for Sveas but usable with other equally squat stoves (three 5-by-6-inch panels; 4 ounces; $5).

This screen works well, folds down flat, and seems almost exempt from Murphy's Law—except with a Gerry Mini Stove, when you would clearly have to keep checking that the cartridge had not overheated (page 168).

Unsung uses: folded flat under a gasoline stove when priming it in a high-fire-hazard place, to make sure no gasoline leaks down onto deck; and, in an emergency, as a sun reflector to air or land rescue team if no mirror available (pages 392–4 and 396).

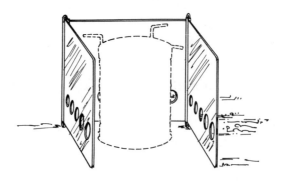

See also, if keen-eyed, illustration, page 198.

Protection from cold feet

Snow (or very cold rock or earth) may cool a gasoline stove so severely that even after it has been burning well it will lose pressure and finally go out. If I foresee any such danger I carry a small square of Ensolite cut from a foam bed pad (page 246). At night, if you're sleeping on a pad, you can put the stove on one corner of it. Use the same methods to slow heat loss from pots of hot food.

Wire-and-asbestos wundergauze

I years ago gave up trying to fry on a stove: its concentrated heat makes most food—and especially fish—stick to the pan. But an Army Medical Corps colonel stationed in Germany has just sent me a 6-inch-square wire gauze with a 4-inch-diameter asbestos center (1 ounce). "Like we used in chemistry lab to attenuate Bunsen burner heat," says the colonel. "With corners folded down it can be packed in almost any cooking rig or stove. And it allows the thickest slop to be cooked without burning, even in a wind . . . acts as a fine toaster, and is good to put your cup on to save heat, especially in snow. . . . It's a standard item in all laboratory supply catalogues."

I have tried it for frying, just laid across the top of my Svea, and it works like a charm.

Keeping cooked food warm

With a gasoline stove, this chore can pose problems. You can't leave the stove on low indefinitely: fuel is too valuable. And relighting any stove that needs priming is next door to unthinkable. In cold or windy weather you can wrap the cooking pot in the sleeping bag or some other spare insulator; or you can stand the pot on the small Ensolite stove pad (page 180) or on a corner of your sleeping pad. The one really satisfactory solution arises when it is both desirable and reasonable to light a large campfire (not for cooking [page 183]) and you can put the pot of cooked food beside it—close enough to keep warm, far enough away to keep clean. You have to keep reversing the pot, so that half the food doesn't get cold, but you can do this very simply each time you pour or ladle out another cupful of food.

Maintenance

The new Sveas and all Optimus 111B's, 8R's and 99's have built-in cleaning needles (page 163). Optimus 80's come with a little wire pricker. You won't need it often, but when you do you'll need it bad. My Svea pricker used to travel in my "office" (page 359), wrapped in its own small plastic bag (page 187).

Any of the little gasoline stoves will eventually begin to show its age, and once it starts giving trouble no amount of replacing doubtful items such as generator or wick seems to work. The only remedy is to ditch it and buy a new one. Several people confirm this apparently illogical fact. I use my Sveas a fair amount, and five years seems to be about their life span. Specific troubles are not the only signs of aging. I have long suspected that heating efficiency eventually declines, and during my recent stove-test orgy I checked my third Svea, already booked for retirement, against its new replacement: the new one boiled its quart in 5½ minutes; the old one took 7½.

Or was that my fourth Svea? I'm not sure. Rather surprisingly, I don't seem to generate a warm affection for individual stoves. For Sveas as a tribe, yes. Very definitely. A reliable stove earns your gratitude time without number, at the most God-awful moments. Don't forget that. And if you're wondering whether 27 pages of print tell you a hell of a lot more about stoves than you wanted to know, ruminate afresh on the nature of that gratitude, and of its anguished opposite—and also on the pockmarking of wilderness by rampant woodcutters and by the scars of open fires.

OPERATING YOUR FIRE

Cooking fire

Nowadays, I find that except when stove fuel runs low or I brew tea on sidetrips away from my pack or I'm operating on a rock-bottom, tin-can menu (page 124), almost the only time I cook on an open fire is for frying—which generally means frying fish. And the colonel's wundergauze (page 180) may sandbag even that. But I shall light a fire occasionally, and so will other people, so we had better take a look around.

For frying, I find that the best hearth is a two- or three-stone affair with a shallow trough for the fire. The stones must be flat enough to form a stable rest for the pan, and deep enough to leave space for a sizable fire. Wind direction and strength dictate the angle of the trough. A light breeze blowing down its length keeps flame and glow healthy; a high wind is best blocked off by the side stones, perhaps with an assist from others.

On the rare occasions I use an open fire with my cooking pots—and the last was years ago—I usually make a two- or three-stone hearth. A useful alternative that makes it easier to build and replenish a sizable fire and to control its heat is a double-Y-stick-with-crossbar rig:

The two forked (or more often, branched) sticks must be planted firmly, and far enough apart to be safe from burning. As a precaution, I may splash them from time to time with water. The crossbar must be tolerably straight and either green or wet enough not to burn too readily.

If there is any hint of fire hazard, I carefully seal off my fire, no matter which kind, with a circle of stones (page 186).

The hottest fire comes from small sticks; the best are those that burn fairly slowly and/or remain glowing for a long time. (See also "Rock-bottom, tin-can kitchen," page 200.)

Another satisfactory cooking method that I occasionally use, especially for frying, is to build a small extension to the stone ring around a big campfire. It's simple, then, to transfer a few glowing embers from the main fire, and to keep replenishing them.

If you build a fire in an untouched place, try to keep it small; then you can remove all, or almost all, traces when you leave. Pockmark sears, remember, are a major objection to open fires.

For fire precautions, see page 186.

Lighting a fire

An outdoorsman's ability to start a fire—anywhere, anytime—is the traditional criterion for judging his competence, and I suppose I have always accepted the criterion in an unthinking, uncritical sort of way. But now that I try to assess my own competence I find it surprisingly difficult to award a grade. Perhaps it is just because I am not a prolific lighter of fires. But I suspect that the traditional criterion has outlived its validity.

Every modern outdoorsman should be able to light a fire, but the act is not, it seems to me, a particularly important or testing part of his life. There are exceptions, of course. In cold, wet country where you are always needing a fire for warmth or for drying out clothes, getting one alight quickly is both a testing and an important business. And doubly so in an emergency, without matches. But the generalization stands.

I certainly seem to have survived without undue discomfort on a meager and rather incoherent grab bag of fire-lighting rules that I've made up as I went along:

Carry plenty of matches, and *keep them dry*. The kindling is what matters; once you've got a small but healthy fire going, almost anything will burn on it. Unless your kindling is very dry indeed and very small, use paper as a starter. If the whole place is dripping wet, look for big stuff that will be dry in the center and from which you can cut out slivers that are easily split and shaved into serviceable kindling (the dry side of a dead cedar is a good bet, and so are the dead and sheltered twigs at the foot of many conifers), but don't overlook sheltered rock crevices and hollow trees (mice or other small animals will often store small sticks there, and you can rob them with remarkably little guilt). If you anticipate real trouble in starting a fire (if, for example, you had just one hell of a time doing so last night), carry along some kindling from wood that you dried out on last night's hard-won fire; and don't just stuff it into your pack; wrap it in a plastic bag and keep out the damp air. If necessary, do the same with some fire-dried paper too; in really wet weather, even paper can be hard to light. Some people, when they expect bad conditions, take along some kind of starter: candles (which are dual purpose tools), heat tablets, or tubes of barbecue igniter paste, such as Redifire.

The basic rules for the actual lighting of a fire are simple and fairly obvious: Have plenty of wood ready in small, graduated sizes. Arrange the sticks of kindling more or less upright, wig-wamwise, so that the flame will creep up them, preheating as it climbs. Keep the wigwam small. Apply your match at the bottom. In the first critical moments, carefully shield the flame from wind. If in doubt what to do with a just-started fire that looks as though it may go out, leave it alone. If a fire with plenty of hot coals under it happens to go out, put small sticks or tinder on the coals, uprightish, and wait. Often, the heat will recombust them spontaneously. A mild blowing applied after a decent interval will almost always convert them into a sudden small inferno.*

With these simple rules I seem to have got by without serious trouble. Oddly enough, the only real difficulties I can recall have been in the desert. Lighting a fire there is normally simple: you just break off a few twigs of almost any growth, dead or alive, and it lights. But desert plant life must, to survive, be adapted to absorb every drop of moisture. And it does so alive or dead. One sharp shower of rain, and every plant or fragment of plant you break off will feel like damp blotting paper. I vividly remember one cold and windy evening in Grand Canyon when a day of inter-mittent rain had ended with a snowstorm. At dusk I found a shallow rock overhang that offered shelter from both wind and snow but fell appreciably short of coziness. Tired and damp and cold after a long day, I wanted a fire more than anything else. But every piece of wood I could find under the thin blanket of snow was soggy, clean through. I made a few abortive attempts at

---

* "In the old *Outing* magazine of about 1898 or 1899," writes a reader who was fifteen or sixteen at that time, "Stewart Edward White, one of the most experienced hunters and campers, gave a lot of sound tips. I made one of his *Exhilarators,* and used it to start balky fires successfully for many years. It's a little blow torch, made from a piece of small brass tubing, flattened out at one end, and the other inserted in a rubber tube about 3 feet long. Blow through it to make balky wood burn or to expedite a blaze."

For reasons you might be carrying a piece of tubing, see p. 140.

starting a fire with the driest wood, but even the scraps of paper from my pocket did little more than smolder. I was running desperately short of white gas, too, and could not afford to use the stove as wood drier. Eventually I found the fairly thick stem of a cactus-like century plant or agave and managed to whittle some shreds of dry kindling from its center. It lit first time, and I spent a cheerful and almost luxuriously warm evening.

It is only common sense to site a fire so that the smoke from it will blow away from your campsite—but it is also common sense to expect that the moment you light the fire the wind will reverse itself. Objective research would probably confirm the existence of something more statistically verifiable behind this expectation than the orneriness of inanimate objects: campfires tend to be lit around dusk, and winds tend to change direction at that time, particularly in mountain country.

Some men speak learnedly about the virtues of different firewoods. Frankly, I know almost none by name. But it does not seem to matter too much. It is no doubt more efficient to know at a glance the burning properties of each kind of wood you find; but you have only to heft a piece of dead wood to get a good idea of how it will burn. Generally speaking, light wood tends to catch easily and burn fast. Heavy wood will last well, though the heaviest may be the devil to get started, even in a roaring blaze.

I have never, thank God, had to produce a flame without matches. I have not even given the matter the thought it deserves. The magnifying glass that I carry primarily for other purposes (page 148) is always there as an emergency concentrator of sunlight onto paper or tinder, but I have never, in spite of intermittent good resolves, actually tried it out. A reader suggests that a detachable camera lens might do a better job. But the uncomfortable fact is that the day on which you need a fire most desperately is likely to be wet and cold, and even a camera lens would then be about as useful as a station wagon in outer space. A flint stick (page 148) might be just the answer. I really must find out.

In an emergency, it is theoretically possible to do the trick with a piece of string or bootlace that you wrap around a rotator of a stick whose end is held in a depression in a slab of wood. The idea is to twirl the stick fast enough and long enough to create by friction enough heat to ignite some scraps of tinder dropped into the depression. Simple, primitive men certainly started fires this way; but I have an idea that we clever bastards might find it extraordinarily difficult.

To be honest, I'm singularly unimpressed by the woodsy

fanatic who's rich in this kind of caveman lore, especially if he'll pass it all on at the drop of a snowflake. I always suspect that he'll turn out to be the sort of man who under actual field conditions can stop almost anywhere, any time, and have a pot of water on the very brink of boiling within 2 hours and 35 minutes—provided it isn't actually raining, and he has plenty of matches. But maybe you'd be right to chalk my cynicism up to plain jealousy.*

Fire hazards

These days, the way a man guards and leaves his fire (on those occasions he judges it reasonable to light one) may well be a more valid criterion for judging his outdoor competence than the way he starts one. A deliberately apprehensive common sense is your best guide; but the Forest Service lays down some useful rules:

Never build a fire on deep litter, such as pine needles. It can smolder for days, then erupt into a catastrophic forest blaze.

Clear all inflammable organic material from an area appreciably bigger than your fire, scraping right down to bare earth. (This destructive suggestion is unacceptable in much of today's tramped-over wilderness; but the need for it as a safety measure is another reason for forgoing fires.)

Generally speaking, and where possible, build a ring of stones around your fire. It will contain the ash and considerably reduce the chances of spread.

Never leave a fire unattended.

Where a fire hazard exists, do not build a fire on a windy day.

Avoid wood that generates a lot of sparks. The sparks can start fires in surrounding vegetation—and your sleeping bag.

Above all, *don't just put your fire out—kill it, dead.* Stir the ashes, deep and thoroughly, even though the fire seems to have been out for hours. Then douse it with dirt and water. You can safely stop when it's so doused you could take a swim in it.

Oddly enough, you can forgo such precautions in most kinds of desert. The place is curiously immune to arson. I have only once

---

* At least one reader shares my cynicism. She writes:

"A terribly procedure-conscious walker from Stanford once told me, 'One evening in the Sierras, I lighted a fire in a snowstorm, WITH ONLY ONE MATCH!'

" 'Yes,' said his long-suffering wife. 'And it only took him an hour and twenty minutes to prepare it.'

"I call this sort of nonsense 'One-match Machismo.' "

seen an extensive "burn" in treeless desert. Individual bushes may catch fire rather easily, but vegetation is so widely spaced (a necessary adaptation to acute moisture shortage) that the fire rarely spreads. The heat and dryness of deserts would seem sure to cause fires in mass-inflammable vegetation, so perhaps susceptible species have been selected out by the natural process of destruction by fire.

General fire precautions

Cultivate the habit of breaking all matches in two before you throw them away. The idea is not that half a match is much less dangerous than a whole one, but that the breaking makes you aware of the match and conscious of any lingering flame or heat. Bookmatches are rather difficult to break, but as I use mine only for fires or the stove, I always put used matches into the former or under the latter.

The big match danger comes from smokers (with a seven-year nonsmoking halo now tilted rakishly over my bald patch I feel comfortably smug*). In some critical fire areas you are forbidden to carry cigarettes at certain times of year. In many forests you are not allowed to smoke while on the move, and can do so only on a site with at least three-foot clearance all around—such as a bare rock or a broad trail. Increasingly, smoking is restricted to posted locations that have been specially cleared. Make absolutely sure you put your cigarette stub OUT. Soak it in water; or pull it to shreds. If you doubt the necessity of following such irritating rules to the letter, make yourself go and see the corpse of a recently burned forest.

THE KITCHEN IN ACTION

Packaging and packing

My kitchen travels, almost exclusively, in plastic freezer bags. The most useful sizes are small (pint and quart), medium (half gallon and gallon) and capacious (the thick, pillow-size kind you can get for 25 cents from machines in some laundromats). Before knotting small and medium-size bags with food in them, expel most of the air. And secure them as high as possible, so that bag and contents can adjust to external pressures and occupy the minimum and most convenient space. To avoid frustration, knot bags loosely. If bags are too full for knotting, secure with a rubber band.

---

* It breaks my heart to correct that boast from the first edition—but at least I am now 3 months into a 50-year trial period abstention.

Or you can try the small, reusable plastic closures called Locka-bags (made by West Products Corporation, P.O. Box 707, East Boston, Massachusetts 02128; featherweight; $.85 a dozen).

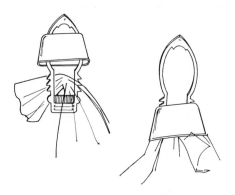

They're an attractive idea, and very secure; yet I found that after brief experimental use I no longer bothered with them.

Ziploc plastic bags, now on sale in most supermarkets, at first struck me as godsends. They have a plastic zipperlike closure that you simply press home and can reuse indefinitely. But the closure turns out to be a finicky thing: you have to get the opposing parts neatly aligned before you press. And although these bags have their uses, especially when you need to fill them almost completely and will not have to reclose too often, I have by and large gone back to ordinary plastic bags.

For iron-seal plastic bags, less permeable than the standard polyethylene kind, see footnote, page 114.

Into small bags go herbs and spices, spare salt, bookmatches, can opener and stove nozzle cleaner. Just about everything else goes into medium-size bags: dry cereal mixture (emptied from its heavy cardboard box); soup and gravy packages (they tend to split open); powdered milk packages (they split too, and you can picture, I'm sure, a faintly milk-coated kitchen on a rainy day); the week's supply of meat bars (for convenience rather than protection); the complete collection of little bags containing herbs and spices; spare sugar; dry raisins in bulk; the various trail snacks that travel in my "nibble" pocket; trail snacks for the rest of the week; tea bags; fruit-drink mixes; and margarine container (always mildly greasy). Also, sometimes, the stove—though I now tend to use a stuff bag. The more rebellious items (cereal, soups, sugar, milk, chocolate) get double-bag protection. The blackened frying pan, when it comes along, slips inside two medium-large bags.

All the food, bagged and unbagged, is then divided between

two pillow-size bags. Into one bag goes everything needed for the current day. Into the other goes the balance of the week's rations. (If you put the whole lot into one bag you'll never be able to find what you want.) Because it is difficult to find pillow-size bags that are strong enough, you may have to use doubled bags—at least for the much-handled day's-ration bag. Once a day I choose the morrow's menu and transfer the rations (page 194).

Into one of the pack's upper outside pockets (my "nibble pocket"—page 376) go the between-meals trail snacks (page 115), the film can of salt tablets, and one meat bar—so that if there's no time to stop for a regular lunch I need not unpack the main food.

Into one of the lower side pockets go my baby-feeder water bottle (page 140, and illustration, page 137), a package of fruit-drink mix, and the film can of halazone tablets.

Large canteens travel in the main compartment—loaded back or front, high or low, haphazardly or meticulously, according to whether full or empty, needed next halt or next day, requiring or not requiring insulation from hot sun.

The nesting cooking pots travel in a large plastic bag, folded around so that no residual water can escape. Well, not much, anyway. Spoon and cup fit inside the inner pot, though in well-watered country I often carry the cup ready for use on a belt clip (page 371).

Garbage

In recent years the wilderness litter problem has reached grotesque proportions, and food wrappings are the most obvious—though not always most serious—source. No matter how carefully you select food that comes in burnable packages, you'll always find small items that can't be burned. And burying is no solution to litter: animals will soon smell the adhering food and dig it up. I stow all unburnable garbage into doubled, medium-size plastic bags that travel, easily get-at-able, in the back pocket of the pack. Into these bags go empty foil wrappers from freeze-dried foods, soups, meat food products, energy bars, milk and the like. Also, on the rare occasions I use them, cans. The weight rarely amounts to much. I've checked three times. Once, after ten days on a rock-bottom, tin-can menu that meant many foil-wrapped meat bars, my garbage bag weighed out at 10 ounces. Another time, at the end of seven days in desert back country, when I'd carried a lot of freeze-dried foods, the total came to 9 ounces. Recently, after seven days in the mountains, on a more standard menu, the total was only 4 ounces. Some national forest ranger stations now provide ingoing backpackers with plastic garbage bags (which tend to be unnecessarily huge).

For disposal of stove cartridges, see page 163.

I used to feel nothing but contempt for those who desecrate the countryside with litter. But nowadays I'm uncomfortably aware that once, in a mild alcoholic haze and pleasantly provocative company, I heaved an empty wine bottle out onto the virgin desert sand—and did it maliciously, with delight, and with satisfaction. Like a good, rabid antilitter man, I retrieved the bottle later. But the memory is still there, and although I continue to look on litter-louts with contempt and loathing, I can in my more charitable moments feel twinges of understanding. But only in the more charitable moments.

For further sermons, see pages 232–4 and 420–1.

A SAMPLE DAY IN THE KITCHEN.*

(Not to mention the bedroom, and most other departments too. Meticulously applicable only to those who operate on the Fletcher in-sleeping-bag culinary system; but embodying, I hope, suggestions useful to those who for good—or merely conservative—reasons persist in getting out of bed to cook.)

Something stirs inside you, and you half-open one eye. Stars and blackness, nothing more. You close the eye. But the something keeps on stirring, and after a moment you slide another inch toward consciousness and turn your head to the east and reopen the eye. It is there all right, a pale blue backing to the distant peaks. You sigh, pull up one arm inside the mummy bag, and check that the luminous hands of your watch say five o'clock.

After a decent interval you loosen the drawstrings of the mummy bag so that there is just enough room for you to slip on the

---

* There are several similarities here, to an account in *The Man Who Walked Through Time* (pp. 19–24) of how I prepared an evening meal.

Because the pith of this sample day is method, not details of diet, I have allowed the simple dishes I described in the first edition to stand. The only serious amendment I might have made was to have you (traveling this sample day under the name Fletcher) respond to such a chilly morning by putting on hat or even balaclava very much earlier. You might well, in fact, have been wearing the balaclava all night. These changes have been brought about by the passing of further years and residual hair.

shirt (which has been coiled around your shoulders all night, keeping the draft off) and the down jacket (which you have been lying on). Then, still half-cocooned in the mummy bag, you sit up, reach back into the pack (which is propped up against the staff, just behind your head) and take out your shorts (which are waiting on top of everything else) and the pillow-size bag containing the day's rations (which is just underneath the shorts). From the ticket pocket of the shorts you fumble out bookmatches and an empty Lipton tea-bag wrapper. You stuff the shorts down into the mummy bag to warm. Next you take the flashlight out of one of your boots (which are standing just off to the left of the foam pad or air mattress). Then you put the tea-bag wrapper down in the little patch you cleared for the stove last night (on the right side of the bed, because the wind was blowing from the left last night; and very close to the groundsheet so that you don't have to stretch). You set the tea-bag wrapper alight and hold the stove (which is waiting close by) by its handle with the base of the bowl just above the burning paper. Soon, you see in the beam of the flashlight that gasoline is welling up from the nozzle. You put the stove down on the tea bag, snuffing out the flame. Gasoline seeps down the generator of the stove and into the little depression in the bowl that encircles the base of the generator. When the depression is full, you close the stove valve and ignite the gasoline. When it has almost burned away, you reopen the valve. If you time it dead right, the last guttering flame ignites the jet. Otherwise, you light it with another match. The stove roars healthily, almost waking you up.

You check that the roaring stove is standing firm, reach out for the larger of the cooking pots (which you half-filled with water after dinner last night—because you know what you are like in the morning—and which spent the night back near the pack, off to one side, where no restless movement of your body could possibly knock it over). You put the pot on the stove. Next you put on your hat (which was hanging by its chin band from the top of the pack-frame) because you are now conscious enough to feel chilly on the back of your head where there used to be plenty of hair when you were younger. Then you reach out for the smaller cooking pot (which is also back in safety beside the pack, and in which you last night put two ounces of dehydrated fruit cocktail and a shade more water than was necessary to reconstitute it). You remove the cup from inside this pot (it stayed clean there overnight) and put it ready on the stove-cover platform (which is still beside the stove, where you used it for dinner last night). You leave the spoon in the pot (it too stayed clean and safe there overnight). You pour a little more water into the pot from a canteen, squirt in some milk powder (the squirter stood all night beside the pot), stir, and add about 2 ounces of cereal mix. Then you lean back against the pack, still warm and comfortable in the mummy bag (the hood tapes of which you retighten if necessary, just below your armpits) and begin to eat the fruit and cereal mixture. The pale blue band along the eastern horizon broadens.

Soon—without needing to use the flashlight now—you see steam jetting out from the pot on the stove. You remove the pot, lift its cover a little way with your spoon handle, and swing-flip one tea bag inside. (You put the tea bag ready on top of the pot at the same time as you took the cereal out of the day's-ration bag.) You leave the label hanging outside so that later, when the tea is strong enough, you can lift the bag out. Then you turn off the stove. And suddenly the world is very quiet and very beautiful, and for the first time that morning you really look at the silhouetted peaks and at the shadows that are the valleys. You swirl the tea-pot a couple of times to suffuse the tea, take a few more mouthfuls of fruit-and-cereal, then pour a cupful of tea, squirt-add milk, spoon in copious sugar (the sugar container also spent the night beside the pots), and take the first luxurious sip. Warmth flows down your throat, spreads outward. Your brain responds. Still sluggishly, it takes another step toward full focus.

And so, sitting there at ease, leaning back against the pack, you eat breakfast. You eat it fairly fast today, because you have twenty miles to go, and by eleven o'clock it will be hot. You keep pouring fresh cups of hot tea, and each one tells. Spoonful by spoonful, you eat the fruit-and-cereal. It is very sweet, and it tastes good. When it is finished you chew a stick of beef jerky. And all the time the world and the day are unfolding above and below and around you. The light eases from gray toward blue. The valleys begin to emerge from their shadow, the peaks to gain a third dimension. The night, you realize, has already slipped away.

Do not let the menu deceive you: there is no better kind of breakfast.

When the meal is over you wash up rather sketchily (there is plenty of water, but time presses). You re-bag the food and utensils and stove and stow them away in the pack. The light moves on from blue toward pink. Still inside the mummy bag, you put on your shorts. And (because this is a day in a book) you time it just right. The sun moves majestically up from behind those distant peaks, exploding the blue and the pink into gold, at the very moment you need its warmth—at the very moment that the time arrives for you to pluck up your courage and forsake the mummy bag and put on socks and boots.* Ten minutes later you are walk-ing. Another half hour and you are wide awake.

(This is only a sample morning, of course—a not-too-cold morning on which you know there is a hot and fairly long day ahead. If the night had been really cold, or the dew so heavy that it soaked the mummy bag and everything else, you would probably have waited for the sun to make the world bearable or to dry out all that extra and unnecessary load of water. If, on the other hand, the day promised to be horribly long, or its noonday heat burningly hot, you would have set the something to stir inside you even ear-lier—probably suffering a restless night thereby, unless you are a more efficient alarm clock than I am, or wear an alarm wristwatch —and would have finished breakfast in time to start walking as soon as it was light enough to do so safely. By contrast, this might have been a rest day. Then, you would simply have dozed until you got tired of dozing, and afterward made breakfast—or have woken yourself up first by diving into lake or river. But whatever the variations—unless you decided to catch fish for breakfast and succeeded—the basic food theme would have remained very much the same.)

You walk all morning, following a trail that twists along be-side a pure, rushing mountain creek. Every hour, you halt for ten minutes. At every halt you take the cup from the belt clip at your waist and dip it into the creek and drink as much of the sensuously cool water as you want. And at every halt—except perhaps the first, when breakfast is still adequately with you—you take one of the trail-snack bags out of the nibble pocket and munch a few frag-ments of the chosen delicacy. At each succeeding halt you tend to eat rather more; but without giving the matter much direct thought, you ration against the hours ahead. In midmorning, a stick of beef jerky helps replenish the protein supply. Later, you boost the quickly available energy, and the fats too, with a piece of chocolate.

Just after noon, you stop for lunch. You choose the place care-fully—almost more carefully than the site for a night camp, because you will spend more waking hours there. You most often organize the day with a long midday halt, not only because it means that you avoid walking through the worst of the heat but also because you have found noon a more comfortable and rewarding time than late evening to swim and wash and launder and doze and read and write notes and dream and mosey around looking at rocks and stones and

* Such perfect timing is not, I find, restricted to sample days in books. One reader, whose sole mentor for his first backpack trip was apparently this book, reports that on his first morning, at precisely the moment he was ready to emerge from his sleeping bag, the sun rose.

fish and lizards and sandflies and trees and panoramas and cloud shadows and all the other important things. A long lunch halt also means that you split the day's effort into two slabs, with a good long rest in between. Come to think of it, perhaps this after all is the really critical factor.

Anyway, you choose your lunch site carefully. You find a perfect place, in a shady hollow beside the creek, to prop up the pack and roll out the groundsheet and then the foam pad (and maybe, in cooler weather, even the mummy bag), and within three minutes of halting you have a setup virtually identical to the one you woke up in that morning.

The soup of the day is mushroom. The directions could hardly be simpler: "Empty the contents into 1 liter (4 measuring cups) of hot water and bring to the boil. Cover and simmer for 5–10 minutes." So you light the stove and boil as much water as you know from experience you need for soup (what *you* need, not necessarily 4 measuring cups). You stir in the soup powder, add a smidgen of thyme (after rubbing it lightly in the palm of your hand), replace the cover at a very slight tilt so that the simmering soup will not boil over, reduce the heat as far as it will go (a mildly delicate business), and meditate for five minutes, stretched out tiredly but luxuriously. After five minutes you add a dollop of margarine to the soup, stir, and pour out the first cupful. You leave the rest simmering. When you pour the second cup you turn off the stove and put the pot in the warmest place around—a patch of dry, sandy soil that happens to lie in a shaft of sunlight. Within half an hour of halting you have finished the soup and dropped off into a catnap.

When you wake up you wash all pots and utensils—thoroughly now, because there is time as well as water. You do so well away from the creek, to avoid polluting it. You use sand as a scourer, grass or Miracloth as a cleaning cloth, biodegradable detergent as detergent, and the creek for rinsing. (If the pots had looked very dirty and you had been "out" for a long time, or if an upset stomach had made you suspicious about cleanliness, you might —if there was fuel to spare—have put spoon and cup into the small pot and the small pot and some water into the big pot and boil-sterilized the whole caboosh.)

Next you do a couple of chores that you have made more or less automatic action after lunch, so that you will not overlook them. You decide on the menu for the next twenty-four hours and make the necessary transfers from bulk-ration bag to current-day's bag—including the refilling from the bagged reserve of the containers of milk (an everyday chore) and sugar and salt (once, in midweek). You also replenish the nibble pocket with trail snacks.

If necessary, you put a new book of matches in a ticket pocket of your shorts or long pants or both. (You carry a book in each.)

Then you refill the stove. You use the funnel and take great care not to spill precious fuel, but the aluminum bottle is brimful and some gasoline dribbles down its side. Still, you expected this slight wastage; and you know that it won't happen in a day or two, once the level in the bottle drops. Alternatively, you use a Canedy pouring cap and remember, smugly, how you always used to chafe at the wastage.

(Naturally, it does not matter much what time of day you choose to do these chores. In winter, for example, when the days are short, you'll probably just snatch a quick lunch or succession of snacks and will do the reapportionment and refilling during the early hours of the long, long darkness. But on each trip you try to get into the habit of doing the chores at about the same time each day, because you know that otherwise you may find yourself fumbling down into the pack for the bulk-food bag in the middle of a meal, and at the same moment hear the dying bleat of an almost empty stove.)

For the next two or three or four or even five hours you either do some of the many make-and-mend chores that always keep piling up (washing, laundering, writing notes, and so on), or you mosey around and attend to those important matters that you came for (rocks, lizards, cloud shadows), or you simply sit and contemplate. Or you devote the time to a combination of all these things. But eventually, when you know you ought to be walking again within half an hour, you brew up a sizable pot of tea (this particular day, remember, you too are walking on a British passport). And because there are still four hours to darkness and night camp and dinner, you chew a sampling of trail snacks. Then you pack everything away, hoist up the pack, and start walking—leaving behind as the only signs of occupation a rectangle of crushed grass that will recover within hours, and, where the stove stood, a tiny circle that you manage to conceal anyway by pulling the grass stems together. These are the only signs you leave at any of your campsites, day or overnight.

You find yourself walking in desert now (a shade miraculously, it's true, but it suits our book purposes better to have it happen that way), and it is very hot. Because you expect to find no more water until you come to a spring about noon the following day, you have filled all three ½-gallon canteens you brought with you. Now, you go easy on the water. You still drink as well as munch at every hourly halt. And you drink enough. But only just enough. Enough, that is, to take the edge off any emerging hint of thirst. At the first couple of halts this blunting process calls for only a very small sip or two. Later you need a little more. But always, before you swallow the precious liquid, you swirl it around your mouth to wash away the dryness and the scum.

One canteen has to be nonfumble available at halts. But direct sunlight would quickly turn its water tepid. So you put it inside the pack—on top, but insulated by a down jacket.

With an hour to go to darkness, and a promise already there of the coolness that will come when the sun drops behind the parched, encircling hills, you begin to feel tired—not so much muscle weary as plain running out of energy. So at the hourly halt you pour some water into the lid of one cooking pot, squirt-add milk, and pour in some cereal mixture. (Looked at objectively, this cereal snack has always seemed a highly inefficient business. It ought to be enough to take from the nibble pocket a booster bonus of mintcake or some other snack. But on the few long, hard days that such tiredness hits you, the cereal snack seems to work better.)

At this final pre-camp halt you empty into the inner cooking pot the dehydrated beans and mixed vegetables that are on the day's dinner menu, and add salt and just enough water to reconstitute them. (Presoaked like this, they cook in ten minutes rather than half an hour.) You know from experience how much water to add. It is surprisingly little: barely enough to cover them. You add as little as possible, to reduce the danger of spillage, and from now on, when you take the pack off, you are careful to keep it upright.

You walk until it is too dark to go on (keeping a canny rattle-snake-watch during the last hour, because this is their time of day —see page 402). You camp in any convenient place that is level enough, though it is a kitchen advantage, stovewise, to have adequate shelter from desert winds (usually *down* canyons at night).

Dinner is the main meal of the day, but it is very simple to prepare. It has to be. You are tired now. And because the rising sun will be coercing you on your way again in less than eight hours, you don't want to waste time. So as soon as you halt you roll out the groundsheet and foam pad and sleeping bag and sit thankfully down and set up the kitchen just as you did last night and at lunch-time, except that because of a hump in the ground and a gentle but growing crosswind you find it expedient to put everything on the other side of the bed. Even before you take off your boots, you empty the already soft vegetables out of the small pot into the big one, scraping the stickily reluctant scraps out with the spoon and swirling the small pot clean with the water you're going to need to cook the meal anyway. You add a little or a lot of water, according to whether you fancy tonight's stew in the form of a near-soup or an off-putty goo. (Only experience will teach you how much water achieves what consistency. For painless experience, start with near-soups that won't burn, and then work down toward goo. Your methods are rough and ready, so you will from time to time add the pleasures of surprise to those of variety.) You light the stove (using the flashlight to check when the gasoline wells up) and put the big pot on it, uncovered. Then you crumble one meat bar onto the vegetables and sprinkle in about one fifth of a package of oxtail soup and a couple of shakes of pepper and a healthy dose of hand-rubbed oregano. You stir and cover. Next you take off your boots and put them within easy reach, on the opposite side of the bed from the kitchen, and put your socks in one of the boots. Then you anoint your feet with rubbing alcohol, taking care to keep it well away from the stove. (If you were using an air mattress you would inflate it at this stage: you never leave that breath-demanding chore until after dinner.)

At this point, steam issues from the stew pot. You reduce the heat to dead-low or thereabouts (taking care not to turn the stove off in the process), stir the compound a couple of times, inhale appreciatively and replace the cover. While dinner simmers toward fruition you empty two ounces of dehydrated peaches and a little water into the small cooking pot and put it ready for breakfast, up alongside the pack, out of harm's way. Then you jot down a few thoughts in your notebook, stir the stew and sample it, find the beans are not quite soft yet. So you study the map and worry a bit about the morning's route, put map and pen and pencil and eye-glasses and thermometer into the second bedside boot, take off your shorts and slide halfway down into the mummy bag out of the rapidly rising wind, and stir the stew again and find all ready. You pour-and-spoon out a cupful, leaving the balance on the stove because the wind is distinctly cool now. And then, leaning comfortably back against the pack and watching the sky and the black peaks meld, you eat, cupful by cupful, your dinner. You finish it—just. Then you spoon-scrape out every last possible fragment and polish-clean the pot and cup and spoon with your Miracloth, or failing that, a piece of toilet paper. If you use toilet paper you put it under the stove so that you can burn it in the morning. Then you put the cup and spoon into the breakfast-readied small pot, pour the morning tea water into the big pot, set the big pot alongside the small one and the sugar and milk containers alongside them both, put the current day's-ration bag into the pack (where it is moderately safe from mice and their night allies) and your shorts on top of it, lean one canteen against the boots so that you can reach out and grasp it during the night without doing more than loosen the mummy-bag drawstring, zipper and drawstring yourself into the bag, wind your watch, belch once, remind yourself what time you want the something inside you to stir in the morning, and go to sleep.*

THE KITCHEN IN ACTION
UNDER SPECIAL CONDITIONS

Rock-bottom, tin-can kitchen

In recent years I have several times met conditions that demanded and also permitted a radically simplified kitchen. The demands concerned weight: I wanted or needed to pare every eliminable ounce, down beyond my normal comfort requirements. The permission concerned fires: in the country I would be walking through it had to be easy and ethical and preferably legal to build very small open fires any place I camped.

* The elapsed time between halting and going to sleep will obviously vary with many factors, including how eager you are to get to sleep. It is difficult to give meaningful average times. You just don't measure such things very often. The only time I remember doing so was under conditions markedly similar to those of our sample evening. I was in no particular hurry, but I did not dally. And I happened to notice as I wound my watch that it was exactly forty minutes since I had halted.

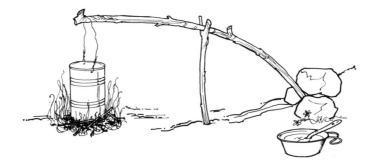

In one case I wanted to walk for ten days along a desert mountain range that offered no possibility of replenishing food stocks but every chance that I would at times need to carry 2 gallons of water. Faced with the prospect of a house that would put 25 pounds of food and 16 pounds of water on my back before I even began to install the standard furnishings, I cast around for ways to cut the load. Careful inquiries about the mountains revealed, as I had expected, that the country I would be walking through abounded with small sticks, presented no fire hazard at that time of year, and was so little traveled that small fire scars would probably heal before being seen by human eyes. I therefore opted for a rock-bottom, tin-can kitchen. I cast out my cooking pots and stove, and also the two gasoline containers (one of them half full) required for ten days' stove-cooking. That saved me 4½ pounds. As sole cooking utensil I took an ordinary medium-size, one-pound-of-fruit tin can with its top removed and a wire handle threaded through two holes punched with a nail near the carefully tamped-down rim. Total weight: 2 ounces. The simplified menu (page 124) meant a saving of about 1½ ounces a day, or a pound for the ten days; and the simpler packaging meant a further saving of at least half a pound. Total saving: 6 pounds—which feels like a hell of a lot, I assure you, when it means around 54 pounds on your back instead of 60. Anyway, it turned out to be a rewarding, unbackbreaking ten days, and I did not regret my decision.

Another time, conditions were different. I was planning one of my sudden, periodic, spur-of-the-moment, two- or three-day therapeutic disappearances into some local hills in which you are always, like it or not, going uphill or down. Mostly, I'm content to take it easy in there. But on that occasion I for some reason felt within me the urge to walk fast and, compared with the normal Fletcheramble, furiously. So to keep my load down I again opted for my tin-can kitchen. And again it worked: I indeed walked fast and far and furious, reveling in the light load, and emerged amply restored.

The fire for a rock-bottom, tin-can kitchen should be small and concentrated, so that when you have covered your traces Sherlock Holmes would be hard put to discover you had passed that way. You want fast, short-lived heat, so you use only very small sticks. And to make full use of their heat, you build them up around the sides of the can.

It has occurred to me that if I find the very light Gerry Mini-Stove proves out in the field, I might just use it in modified tin-can-kitchen situations.

High altitude

At sea level, water boils at 100° C. But the boiling point falls 1° C. for every rise of 1000 feet. At 5000 feet: 95°. At 10,000: 90°. At 15,000: 85°. (These figures are for pure water under average barometric pressures. When the water contains salt or other impurities, the boiling point rises slightly. Marked weather changes may raise or lower it.)

As most outdoor cooking depends on the boiling point of water, food therefore takes longer to cook at high altitudes than at sea level. With my simple menus, and at the maximum elevations I normally reach (little over 14,000 feet), I pay almost no attention to the differences. I just sample and go by the taste. But with more complicated dishes you should probably work out some kind of graduated compensation. The only time I ever noted any figures was at 14,246 feet. There, an egg boiled for ten minutes turned out to be still slightly underdone. It would be difficult, I imagine, to find a more superbly useless item of information.

For the vagaries of appetite at high altitude, see page 97; of stoves, page 161.

In snow

For keeping canteens deiced, see page 140; for insulation of stove tank and also pots with Ensolite pad, page 180; and for use of inverted stove cover as cup platform, page 165. But the big problem in snow—or, rather, the big labor—is water.

Even in midwinter you can, in clear weather and while the sun is high, often find little runnels of water on rock surfaces or at sharp drop-offs in the snow. And a few places that drip slowly but steadily will enable you, given time, to collect all the water you need by putting pots and pot lids and cups and canteens under the drips. Or you may be able to spread out a groundsheet or poncho or both, anywhere but on the snow, and scatter snow on it for the sun to melt. Sometimes you'll find a creek appearing intermittently at small openings, far down in deep drifts, and a cooking pot lowered on a nylon cord will land you all the water you need. Where such creeks are common, some backpackers carry tin cans with baling-wire handles.

Traveling up high in summer or fall, you may sometimes have to melt snow for water (though you naturally stand a good chance of finding the liquid form). The winter's snow will by then have compacted, and a potful of it may produce as much as a half potful of water. Under these amiable conditions you need adopt no tight melting techniques. Just pack snow into a pot, heat, and pour the water into your canteens.

But in winter, in powdery snow, you need to apply a little more thought. The object is to produce a reasonable volume of water with the least possible expenditure of time, fuel, energy and fret. From limited experience I have evolved this procedure for tent camping:

Before you crawl inside the tent, pile up a heap of snow just outside the entrance and within easy reach of your lying position inside (and on the opposite side from that on which the zipper opening has just jammed halfway). Stamp the pile of snow down to a reasonably compact consistency. When you are safely inside and have the stove set up, reach out and, using your cup as a scoop, fill both cooking pots with the compacted snow and also build tall piles on both inverted pot lids. (If you are carrying a toilet trowel [page 386], scoop with that. Because of its everyday role, you'll probably have to overcome a natural revulsion—but a little thought will convince you that there's no reason the trowel should be contaminated.) Tamp the snow in the big pot firmly down. Light the stove and heat the big pot. Wait until water appears at the surface of the snow—which will by that time have shrunk almost to the bottom of the pot—and then begin to add spoonfuls of snow from the small pot. (You wait for the water to appear because once it has a chance to permeate the new snow it conducts heat far more efficiently than the dry crystals do.)

Continue spooning in more snow. Keep matches ready for immediate use, because water tends to condense on the outside of the pot and drip down, and it may occasionally douse the flame. Replenish the lids from the snow pile outside the tent. When the pot is almost half full of water, stop adding snow. Just before the last snowbergs disappear, pour all the water except about an inch depth into the small and now empty pot. Quickly replace the big pot on the stove and refill with snow from the waiting lids. Replenish lids, rather feverishly, from the outside dump. At a convenient pause in the rush, pour the water with tremendous care from the small pot into a canteen. Leave small particles in bottom of pot. Restopper canteen and place on your Ensolite pad. (By transferring the water from big pot to small you reduce fuel wastage, keep the big pot hot, introduce a double-sedimentation process for removal of inevitable dirt particles, obviate the pouring hazard of floating snowbergs [if one or two flop down into the small pot, wait until they dissolve before filling the canteen] and also give yourself a more sharply curved and therefore better-pouring vessel with which to transfer water into the canteen.) Continue adding snow to big pot. When half full, transfer again. Continue ad nauseam.

Do not expect to do much all this time except melt snow. For one thing, you will find yourself fully occupied. For another, you can bet your bottom layer of clothing that if you take your mind off the stove and pot for more than ten seconds straight you are, in those cramped quarters, going to swing a careless arm and send the whole caboodle flying.

This kind of snow-melting is a long and tedious business. The time needed to produce a given volume of water varies with, among other things, the consistency of the snow and the efficiency of your stove and technique. As a guide on the first attempt, allow twice as long as seems reasonable. Then double this allowance. And don't be so naïve as to imagine you'll really do that well.

In a tent (especially, but not necessarily, in snow)

Two kitchen dangers must not be forgotten.

One is fire. In the cramped confines of a tent you are hardly likely to be absent-minded enough to drop a still-glowing match. But a stove—and especially a kerosene stove—being lit in low temperatures is apt to send an oversize flame shooting upward. So it is wise to be ready at any moment to hurl the complete fiery article outside. As you may have to batten down tight while lighting the stove in order to cut wind disturbance to the minimum, you cannot always leave a zipper or drawstring undone. But at least you can be mentally ready, somewhere in the far recesses of your mind, to pull them open at the first sign of trouble.

A more serious danger, and one more likely to occur, is carbon monoxide poisoning.

Unless you ensure adequate ventilation, a burning stove can very quickly consume almost all the free oxygen in your battened-down little world. And a stove burning in a confined space that lacks a free oxygen supply will give off carbon monoxide.

It is important to understand the distinction between asphyxiation (lack of oxygen; presence of too much carbon dioxide) and carbon monoxide poisoning. If you are starved of oxygen, your breathing will in time fill the space around you with carbon dioxide, and you will usually be warned of the danger of asphyxiation—even awakened from sleep—by being made to gasp for breath (page 225—though also page 240). But carbon monoxide is a colorless, odorless, highly poisonous gas—the gas that occasionally kills people in enclosed garages. It does not warn you of danger by making you gasp for breath. And it does not extinguish or even dim a flame.

Carbon monoxide poisoning is no mere theoretical hazard for campers—especially in snow, which can very effectively cut off all ventilation. Down the years there have been many tragedies and near-tragedies. Vilhjalmur Stefansson, in his book *Unsolved Mysteries of the Arctic* (1938), gives some graphic examples. The gas almost killed Willem Barents and his entire polar party when they holed up in a snow-encased cabin on Novaya Zemlya in the winter of 1596 and tried to keep themselves warm with "sea-coles which we had brought out of the ship." Stefansson himself was lucky to escape in 1911 when his four-man party found an old Eskimo snowhouse, sealed the doorway too tight, and began cooking on a kerosene-burning stove. A kerosene-burning heater almost killed a man on the first Byrd Antarctic expedition of 1938, when a blizzard partially blocked the flue pipe. Stefansson maintains that the two men of the ill-fated Andrée arctic balloon party of 1897, whose bodies were not found until 1930, probably died from carbon monoxide poisoning: a kerosene-burning Primus stove stood between their bodies, and there seems every reason to believe that their tent may have been partly covered by drifting snow.

Only a few years ago, two young men apparently died from carbon monoxide poisoning while camping in the Inyo National Forest of California. It seems almost certain that, in unexpectedly cold weather, they battened down their impermeable plastic tube tent (page 234) and for warmth left their Sterno stove (canned heat) burning when they went to sleep. They never woke up.

Now I do not want to make you afraid of cooking in a confined space. But I do want to make you keenly aware of the dangers. It is vital to remember that, as becomes clear from the accounts of survivors from near-tragedies, you get no warning of carbon monoxide poisoning beyond, perhaps, "a slight feeling of pressure on the temples, a little bit as if from an elastic band or cap." Unconsciousness may follow within seconds. Unless someone else recognizes the danger in time and lets in fresh air before he succumbs himself, you die.

The necessary precautions are simple. When you are cooking in a tent or other enclosed space, especially in snow, always make sure that you have adequate airflow. In a high wind, that is hardly likely to be a problem. But if snow is falling, keep checking that the air vents do not become blocked, and keep clearing away drifted snow, so that the entrance is never in danger of being completely buried (see also page 224).

Bedroom

THE ROOF

Under most conditions, the best roof for your bedroom is the sky. This commonsensible arrangement saves weight, time, energy and money. It also keeps you in intimate contact with the world you are presumably walking through in order to come into intimate contact with.

That world often mounts to its most sublime moments of beauty at the fringes of darkness; and the important thing, I find, is not just to see such beauty but to see it happen—to watch the slow and almost imperceptible transitions of shine and shadow, form and shapelessness. You cannot see such events by peering out occasionally from under a roof. Certainly you cannot lie under a roof and let yourself become a part of them, so that their meanings, or whatever it is that is important about them, move deep inside you. You must be out under the sky.

For me, the supreme place to watch beauty happen is a mountaintop.

I shall never forget a calm and cloudless autumn night when I camped roofless and free, yet warm and comfortable, on the very summit of Mount Shasta. Shasta is an isolated volcanic pyramid that rises 10,000 feet from a broken plain. Its apex stands 14,162 feet above sea level. From this apex, as the sun eased downward, I watched the huge shadow of the pyramid begin to move out across the humps and bubukles of the darkening plain. At first the shadow was squat and blunt. And its color was the color of the blue-gray plain, only darker. As the sun sank lower, the shadow reached slowly out toward the horizon until it seemed to cover half the eastward plain. Its color deepened. The pyramid grew longer, taller, narrower. At last the slender apex touched the gray and hazy horizon. There, for a long and perfect moment the huge shape halted; lay passive on the plain. Its color deepened to a luminous, sumptuous, majestic, royal blue. Then the light went out. The shadow faded. Night took over the gray but still humped and bu-bukled plain. And slowly, as the western sky darkened, the shape-less shadows moved deeper into everything and smoothed the plain into a blackboard. Soon, a few small lights bloomed out of the dusk. But the real happenings were over, and after a while I went to sleep, high above the stage and yet a part of it.*

But you do not have to climb a 14,000-foot peak in order to sleep above and yet in the night. Sometimes, when I feel the need for a new perspective on my tight little urban life, I go—often late at night—to the place in which I wrote the opening chapter of this book. I heave my pack into the car, drive for an hour, and park the car on a dirt road that winds steeply through a stretch of still-untrampled ranch country, recently set aside as a public park. An hour later, aided by a flashlight and the pleasurable excitements of change and darkness, I climb up onto the flat, grassy summit of an isolated and "unimproved" hill. This little tableland stands al-most 1700 feet above sea level, and from it I can see the sprawl-ing blaze of lights that now rings San Francisco Bay. I can watch tiny headlights creeping in and out of this web, like unsuspecting fireflies, along the freeways that link it, eastward, with the black and mysterious continent. And when I have rolled out my mummy bag and cocooned myself inside it against the cold wind sweeping in from the Pacific, I can sometimes see as well, quite effortlessly, in the moments before I fall asleep, both a time when the shores of the Bay were as black as the rest of the continent, and a time when the eastward view from this hill will blaze almost as brightly and beautifully and senselessly as the present thin ring around the blackness that is the Bay. I should find it almost pointless to camp on that hill in a tent.

But there is more to rooflessness than panoramas. Some worlds only come alive after dark, and my memory often cheers me with warm little cameos it would not hold if I always roofed myself off from the night. Deep in Grand Canyon, inches from my eyes, floodlit by flashlight, a pair of quick, clean little deer mice scamper with thistledown delicacy along slender willow shoots. On a Corn-ish hillside, with the Atlantic pounding away at the cliffs below, the shadowy shape of a fox ambles unconcernedly out of and then

---

* Important safety note: mountain peaks, although superb, are treacherous. The weather can change within minutes. So if you are going to camp on a peak you must know what you are doing. Mount Shasta, I understand, has killed a fair number of people; and before I decided to camp on its peak I made sure that (*a*) the weather pattern was stable in a way it rarely is in that part of the world; (*b*) I had a tent ready, should the weather change; and (*c*) a tentative evacuation-to-lower-elevations plan was always lurking ready at the back of my mind.

back into the darkness. On the flank of a California mountain, in sharp moonlight, a raccoon emerges from behind a bush, stops short and peers through its mask at my cocooned figure, then performs a long and comically exaggerated mime of indecision before turning away, and still not altogether sure it is doing the right thing, sea-rolls back behind the bush.

Without a roof, you wake directly into the new day. Sometimes I open my eyes in the morning to see a rabbit bobbing and nibbling its way through breakfast. Once I woke at dawn to find, ten feet from my head, a doe browsing among dew-covered ferns. Near the start of my California walk, camped beside a levee that protected some rich farmland that had been created from desert by irrigation with Colorado River water, I woke in a pale early light to find myself looking into the rather surprised eye of a desert road runner that stood on top of the levee, as still and striking as a national emblem. There was a light frost in my little hollow, and I lay warm and snug in my bag, only eyes and nose exposed, and watched the bird. It watched me back. After a while I heard a noise off to the left. The road runner came to life and retreated over the levee. The noise increased. Suddenly, sunshine streamed over the dike. Soon a tractor pulled up, twenty feet from my bedroom, beyond some low bushes. A large and cheerful and voluminously wrapped Negro got down and swung his arms for warmth and made an adjustment to the motor. Then, seeing me for the first time, he grinned hugely and enviously and said, "Well, *you* look warm enough. That's one of us, anyways."

Yet in spite of the obvious advantages of rooflessness a majority of indoorsmen—and quite a few outdoorsmen—seem to assume that camping means sleeping in a tent.*

TENTS

There are, of course, certain conditions under which a tent becomes desirable or even essential.

Very cold weather is one of them—the kind of weather in which you need to retain every possible calorie that your body generates. But unless a wicked wind is blowing, such conditions occur

---

* In this connection I always recall the instinctive remark of a young lady whose forte was indoor rather than outdoor sports but who was for a time the very close friend of an experienced outdoorsman. One close and friendly evening she lifted the sheets above them both with the tips of her pink toes so that it formed a neat little pup tent, and exclaimed, "Look! Camping out!"

No, come to think of it, it was a friendly afternoon.

only when the temperature falls really low. That night I camped on the peak of Mount Shasta, the thermometer read 9° F. at sunrise. Yet with nothing for a bedroom except an Ensolite pad and a good sleeping bag, I slept warm and snug. But that night was dead calm. In almost any kind of wind, even when the temperature is up close to freezing, you need walled shelter: all but the warmest sleeping bags, unprotected, lose too much heat. You also find it virtually impossible to cook food or do any other part-way-out-of-the-bag chores. A cave may be the best hideout, but in most places good caves are rare. When you're on the move, a tent is unfortunately the only dependable solution.

You also need a tent in any appreciable snowfall—if you want to be sure of reasonable comfort. And under really bad conditions of cold and snow a tent may be necessary for survival.*

But you do not really need a tent in rain, except perhaps when the rain is heavy and prolonged and wind driven. There are, as we shall see, better bedrooms. In heavy or hard-driven rain, anyway, a tent—except an impermeable one, which has grave drawbacks—needs a fly sheet: without one you simply can't keep dry. And a tent and fly sheet together tend to be heavy, even when dry—and therefore to be avoided unless absolutely essential.

If mosquitoes or other insects routinely mount mass-formation attacks at dusk—as they do, for example, in northern Canadian summers—then a tent may be the only way to retain your sanity.

There is one other occasion on which a tent may be worth packing along. If you are going to set up a semipermanent camp and move out from it each day—for fishing, hunting, climbing or whatever—it is convenient to be able to leave your gear unpacked and ready for use but still protected. Protected, that is, from any weather that may blow up, and also from animals. Naturally, no tent will keep out every kind of animal. Ants can usually find a way in. So, less certainly, can mice. But a properly battened-down tent, especially one with a sewn-in floor, will keep out most middle-size creatures that can be a daytime nuisance: birds (especially jays, which are sometimes called "camp robbers") and such inquisitive mammals as chipmunks and squirrels, and worst of all, pack rats. Fortunately, most of the big mammals—deer, coyote, bobcat, cougar—seem to steer well clear of anything that smells of man. There are two dire exceptions. One is man of the light-

---

* I suspect, though, that a safely constructed snow cave may be as good if not better. Once, in a Sierra Nevada storm that brought four feet of snow but left temperatures up around 25°, I found a U.S. Air Force survival training group dug in, apparently without sleeping bags, on a steep ridge. As far as I could make out (when I stumbled on them, visibility was down to about 10 yards), they seemed reasonably comfortable. They certainly sounded cheerful.

fingered breed; but although becoming more widespread in back-packing habitats, he remains rare. The other exception—extremely rare in most places—is bear; and a tent, especially if it contains food, will unfortunately do precious little to deter bear.*

Outside North America, the animal situation may be rather different. For some considerations in East Africa, see page 213.

Car campers often carry tents to give them privacy in crowded campsites; but if you go backpacking and camp in crowded places, don't worry about a tent. Consult a psychiatrist.

Kinds of tents

My experience with tents is not extensive, but I suppose I must attempt to lay down guidelines for those even less experienced.

Stores and catalogues offer a wide range of what might be called "fair weather" or "family" tents, and are sometimes termed "forest" tents. They come in many shapes and sizes. They may be floored or unfloored, reasonably well made or poorly made. With a fly sheet, they may possibly vanquish even heavy rainstorms. They are not designed to withstand really heavy winds. I'm afraid I can offer no useful advice. I have never used a backpacking tent of this kind: it seems to me that except for privacy and just possibly for mosquitoes, other devices that are both cheaper and lighter do the job better. Still, there is no doubt about the popularity of "forest" tents. Mind you, the reasons may not be purely practical: some people do not seem to feel they are camping unless they sleep in a tent.

The tents that fill an unquestionable need are the kind usually called "mountain" tents. They are floored, very strongly made (though still light), and are designed to withstand gale-force winds on exposed mountainsides, heavy snowfalls, and—usually with fly sheets—torrential downpours.

Most mountain tents are now "permeable": their upper fabric "breathes." That is, it allows air to pass through it—thereby reducing ventilation and condensation problems. But such fabric will repel only very light rain. So if there is any chance of something heavier you must carry a fly sheet. "Impermeable" tents are designed to repel any rain without the shield of a fly; and they

---

* But I have glimpsed a way out of the bear hazard. We carry insect repellent, why not bear repellent? Something neutral or pleasing to a human nose but obnoxious to a bear's. (Tincture of bear mother-in-law?) Just spread or spray the mixture lightly on your tent or packbag and then go fishing all day without a bear-worry in the world.

See also, and seriously, pp. 403–4.

sometimes achieve their aim. But they must then, by some means or other, overcome serious ventilation and condensation problems (see the Warmlite, page 217). No matter how good such a system, there are dangers (pages 224–5).

For many years I owned only one tent, a Trailwise "One Man Mountain Tent" (now discontinued; but similar models available from other makers). I used to pack this tent occasionally on high mountain trips. Very occasionally.

Made of bright yellow nylon fabric, with a lightweight coated nylon floor, it is 40 inches high and 40 inches wide at the head. At the foot it tapers to 16 by 16 inches. When the zipper is closed, a front alcove extends out about 22 inches from the head. In theory, you stow pack and gear into this alcove. In practice, you are hard put to it to fit the stove and pots in there. The tent does a fairly good job of conserving warmth in high winds, though I don't think I'd trust its stability in a full-scale storm. The whole structure lacks the necessary reserve of strength. Several times I have slept in sheltered rock niches rather than trust it—though part of the choice can be attributed to the difficulty of erecting a tent in high winds. In rain, without a fly sheet, this tent is several grades worse than useless: water seeps in, collects on the waterproof floor, and leaves you wallowing in a puddle.

But the tent is very light. The whole rig—tent, guys, alloy poles and pegs, and carrying bag—weighs just 2 pounds, 14 ounces. A fly sheet of waterproof Nylport-coated nylon weighs 20 ounces. Equivalents today cost about $80 for tent and fly.

Of its kind, this tent was excellent. But, ounce-parer though I am, I'm inclined to regard all such very small affairs as unsatisfactory for the sort of conditions under which you normally use a tent. To face a long siege from a winter storm you must have plenty of reserve strength in fabric and attachments. And strength means weight—even though some of today's tents are marvels of lightweight toughness. Remember, by the way, that in practice it's not just a matter of catalogue weight. The bundle that goes into your pack may be a snow-and-ice-caked mess, half again as heavy as the original.

Then there's the size question. A geographer friend of mine who does a great deal of winter mountain work maintains that for real efficiency, let alone comfort, a man on his own needs what the catalogues call a "two-man tent." I agree. Some years ago a snowstorm kept me more or less confined to my rented two-man tent for four straight days; but I was both warm and tolerably comfortable. I would not have liked to spend those four days cooped up in my little one-man tent.

Later, on a week's solo cross-country ski trip, I packed along a two-man tent. (Yes, you're right, skiing is not walking. But as far as the tent was concerned I could just as easily have been using snowshoes. And snowshoeing, we decided, *is* walking.)

The tent I used (see illustration) was a Sierra Designs prototype of a model they still sell in improved form under the name "Wilderness."

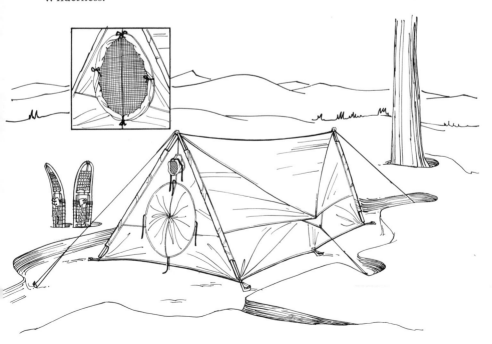

This tent proved highly satisfactory. I found the floor space (4½ by 7½ feet) plenty big enough for myself, my outspread gear, my pack, and my actions; and the headroom (45 inches) and footroom (36 inches) were entirely adequate.*

With side pullouts tight, the walls did not sag too markedly under one overnight snowfall of about a foot. The fabric of thin Rip-stop nylon stood up without sign of strain to the reasonably gentle weather I experienced (no howling winds, no heavy snowfalls, no temperatures below 16°). There was a certain amount of condensation on the walls, especially during two hours of unexpected rain, but it never became a problem. A projecting vent at each apex provided good ventilation. Each vent was fly-screened with fine nylon mesh, and could be tape-tied shut from inside or out. Later versions of the tent have a clothesline attachment in the ridge (page 309). The floor, and the sidewalls and endwalls up to a height of 12 inches, were made of tough, waterproof Nylport. All stitching was with nylon thread.

The two sets of aluminum A-frame poles were of a "self-erecting" type: a thick shock-cord ran through the three sections of each pole, preventing single sections being lost and also tending at all times to spring them into the joined, or erect, position. At first I scoffed at this fancy device. But the week's use made me a tentative convert. The poles seemed very convenient compared with the usual unattached sections, which acquire wills of their own as soon as you start trying to put up a tent in a wind or a hurry.

For me, the outstanding features of this tent—beyond the lightweight and apparently effective fabric—were the entrance and the cookhole.

The entrance was of the tunnel—or sleeve or drawstring— type, a foolproof, easily adjustable system that I had not used before but which I found a vast improvement over zippered doorways, which in foul weather can freeze, jam, break, and utterly infuriate—though tunnel entrances force you to crawl low and accurately, and are hardly worth such travail except in snow in foul

---

* The panels of virtually all modern mountain tents with any pretension to quality come with "catenary cut." The phrase stems from the Latin *catena* ("chain"). It refers to the curve caused by gravity in any chain or cord suspended freely between two fixed points not in the same vertical plane. A piece of fabric curves or sags in the same way. So the edges of fabric for tent panels are cut in curves that will, when the tensions of the erected tent are applied, compensate as accurately as possible for the tendency to sag. The tent therefore remains taut and does not collect water or flap unduly in wind (the key to stability). Catenary cut reduces, though never altogether prevents, the sagging caused by a heavy snowfall.

weather. (And see page 225 for dangers of tunnel entrances in very heavy snowfall.) The entrance had a zippered nylon mesh screen door that sealed off the tent completely, for insect country. I did not have to use it.

The cookhole was simply a 30-inch semicircular, nylon-zippered flap on the floor of the tent. I found it admirable, not only for cooking (to keep food scraps and condensed water off the floor) and for garbage disposal (just sweep snow and debris into it—see page 224) but also for indoor sanitation (though to perform you need to be half brother to a contortionist). The cookhole is normally put on the left side of the tent: if you are right-handed, you probably find it easiest to cook lying on your left side, using your right arm for most of the work. Many experienced people regard cookholes as abominations that reduce a tent's strength, especially in high winds, and provide ingress for snow and water. They could be right, too.

From my limited experience, I would say that a tent of this type comes pretty close to the ideal for one man operating in snow country or in cold, strong winds. And if there are two of you . . . well, this *is* a two-man tent.

Later, I gave a prolonged trial, under very different conditions, to Sierra Designs' topline "Glacier" tent—similar to the Wilderness but 45 inches high at both ends and with a drawstring entrance at one end, zipper door at the other.

I used this tent fairly often during a six-month return visit to East Africa, when I spent much of the time watching wild game in Kenya, Uganda and Tanzania. Because it is dangerous—not to mention illegal—to walk in most game reserves and all parks, I car-camped. Generally, I slept in the tent—not because you need protection from weather on most East African nights, but because it is unwise, on account of lions and hyenas, to sleep in the open on your own. You do not need much protection: almost anything that completely surrounds you seems to keep the predators off (a mosquito net is probably, though not quite certainly, enough). But it is important that you are *completely* surrounded. Lions, in particular, have been known to wander in through the open doors of tents. The point of all this is that I had to have a tent that would, even when closed, be well enough ventilated on nights that, although usually cool, occasionally remained fairly warm (most game areas of East Africa lie at elevations between 3000 and 7000 feet above sea level). The Glacier filled the bill. By closing the lower halves of both zipper and tunnel doors and fully closing their mosquito-net coverings, and by leaving the mosquito-netted air vent above the tunnel door open, I maintained adequate ventilation. And the lions and hyenas that often circled around camp at night never bothered me.

When there was a danger of rain I used the very simply erected fly sheet. With it, the tent withstood several tropical downpours. Once, when an all-night storm left the ground half an inch deep in water, there was some seepage through the cookhole, but a shallow drainage ditch around the tent's perimeter would have prevented this contretemps.

This was the first tent I'd used that dispensed with line tighteners. You just tied a loop in the nylon cord at a convenient place, passed the free end of line (coming up from its peg) through the loop, pulled to tighten, and jammed with a slip knot (page 220). Simple. Brilliant.

All in all, my trial convinced me that the makers were not exaggerating when they described this tent as "suitable for use in Alpine or Tropical conditions in all weather." I also became a full-blooded convert to the shock-cord-joined, self-erecting aluminum poles. And I bought the tent.

Makes and models

I have described these Sierra Designs tents in detail because they are the only two I have used over protracted periods, and because most of the best suppliers now put out basically similar models. My intent has been to indicate the features I found desirable in such tents, not to imply that the Sierra Designs versions were first on the scene or are necessarily the best: I regard them as very good indeed, but I cannot judge the relative merits of others with any vestige of authority. You will find that similar tents have sprung up in the catalogues like housing developments. See, for example, North Face, Ski Hut, Holubar and Alpine Designs. There are no doubt others.

Weights and costs for the current version of the Sierra Designs Glacier tent (with tunnel entrance at one end, double-zip at the other) are fairly typical: tent alone, 3 pounds 14 ounces; fly sheet, 1 pound; poles, 1 pound 9 ounces. Total, including pegs, 7 pounds 4 ounces; $142.

A new family of tents by The Ski Hut—a whole genetic line ranging from "two man minus" to "three man" and perhaps beyond—looks on inspection (I have yet to try one) as if it may signal a distinct advance in mountain tents.

The prime design aim was a tent with maximum space for minimum size of main panel—to reduce sag and its attendant

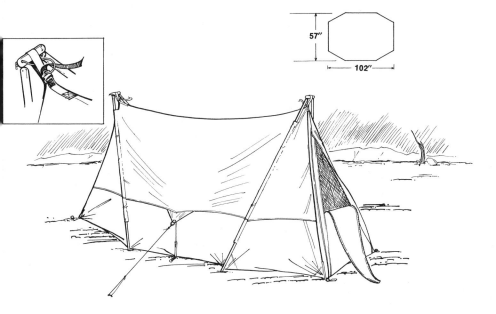

horrors. The A-frame poles were therefore placed a little in from the ends, and the whole tent outboard of them tapered somewhat. The result hits its prime target and several more. Above all, you need no guy lines (except under extreme wind conditions, when end guys may be advisable); you peg only the tent's four corners. The poles, pulled into slight tension by the fabric, hold the whole structure firm. In theory, the absence of guy lines means simpler erection, reduces peg load, permits smaller campsites, and protects shins and tempers from the old, traditional, circum-tential guy-line trip. Although absolute joy may be obstructed by the foul-weather end lines and by guyed side pullouts that are not essential but certainly improve internal space, the self-supporting feature remains very attractive.

All the tents in this family embody the normal features of current high-quality mountain tents. And they look as if they may really prove high enough for you to sit upright inside without getting the usual crick in your neck. The only models now in production are the two-man-plus Fitzroy (designed for two, could take three at a pinch—though without the third pack, that's for sure) and a smaller two-man version with the lofty title "Gothic." Others should surface soon. Fitzroy details: floor, 60 by 102 inches; ridge, 66 inches long; height, 51 inches at peak ends, dipping to 48¾ inches at center; two entrances—zippered triangular; and well-designed tunnel that promises a good crawl. Both with mosquito screens. Tent without fly sheet but with poles and pegs: 6 pounds 12 ounces; $115. Fly sheet: 2 pounds; $35. Total: 8 pounds 12 ounces; $150.* The Gothic, illustrated on page 215, is the same length, 4½ inches narrower and 5½ inches lower; has a single, zippered entrance; and is 1 pound 4 ounces lighter and $10 less.

Even if these new Ski Hut tents work out in practice (and they should: the prototype was built six years ago), their design is only another step forward in the evolution of the basic modern mountain tent. The same can probably be said of the Pack-Lite tents designed by Barry Bishop, one of the five Americans to have climbed Everest, and sold for some years now by his Bishop's Ulti-mate Outdoor Equipment of Bethesda, Maryland. I have not seen these tents, but I hear good reports.

High-quality lightweight tents that differ radically from the basic design are generally for expeditionary or other specialized use, but some of them might interest backpackers who push. Among such tents are the Ultimate line by Bishop.

The Ultimate tents have an external suspension framework. So do several recent "dome" tents. The Adventure 16, like the Ultimates, has aluminum poles; the CDC Igloo II (by Coworkers' Development Corporation of Brooklyn), fiberglass poles. The Jan Sport models come with optional aluminum or fiberglass poles; and the tents' upper works are Dacron Rip-stop—which it is claimed "will not deteriorate with exposure to ultraviolet rays of the sun." These are all backpackers' tents.

So are the Warmlite series—a genuinely "different" design— by Stephenson's of Woodland Hills, California. According to the catalogue, "Model 6 tents will comfortably sleep 2 adults with their gear, or 2 adults and a child. Model 7 will be roomy for 3 or snug with 4 adults. Model 8 tents are comfortable for 5 to 6 adults." I have bought a Model 6, primarily for solo use, and given it a few trials. Although impressed in some ways, I harbor mis-givings. But the tent is ultralight and undoubtedly cunning (it was designed by an aerodynamicist and aerospace engineer), and cur-rently enjoys some vogue among snowcampers in the West. So it deserves mention.

In its catalogue, the tent looks and sounds highly impressive (especially with the models used—who do not, I sadly understand, come with any of the models illustrated). Weight, complete with poles and sack (but without the pegs needed), 2 pounds 6 ounces. Height at peak, 40 inches. Price: $106. Loaded with such extras as screened side openings and special liners, it may run 3 pounds 3

---

* I've just seen Class 5's Uptite tents. The poles are less acutely angled, but the concept seems similar. I do not know which came first—Fitzroy or Up-tite. And if I asked the makers I'm afraid it would only make them Fitzroy or Uptite.

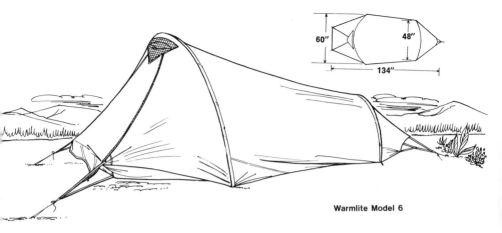

60" 48"

134"

Warmlite Model 6

ounces; $152. Model 7's run a pound heavier in all versions, cost $140–$189 according to extras. Model 8's weigh 4 pounds 12 ounces to 6 pounds 1 ounce; $188–$242.

None of these tents comes with a fly sheet. Indeed, you cannot fit one. The wall fabric for all models is 1.2-ounce Rip-stop nylon with what the catalogue calls "a special water repelling urethane rubber coating on it. . . . [It] is practically waterproof, yet has considerable porosity to water vapor. It is absolutely raintight against any amount of rain." These words frankly scare me (see the "holy grail" in rainwear, page 286). And even if they prove valid for a brand-new tent, both fabric and coating are so thin and apparently liable to damage that I cannot see them, unsheltered by a fly, *always* being waterproof. My suspicions have been borne out by three reliable accounts of Warmlites that have leaked in downpours. And a single failure per person is enough: once you begin to flood a floored tent, there is Noahscape.

Many people, when they first see the tent erected, share my doubts about its resilience under the rough and fumble of daily backpacking use. It is a beautifully constructed rig; but the reserve of strength seems marginal. It is tempting to blame the designer's aerospace background—and his instructions support the suspicion. "Sun deteriorates nylon," they say. "During the day unhook loops and place tent in a shaded spot." I am afraid I find such an outlook impractical. You must certainly look after your equipment; but hell, it is there to sustain you, not run your bloody life.

Still, you just cannot ignore a tent that weighs 2¼ pounds. I have yet to use mine in fierce winds but I understand that the curved structure does indeed seem to hug the ground. The tent is pretty easy to erect. And although I had minor condensation problems under poorish conditions and also damaged the floor first time out (sometimes you just have to camp on gravel), the ventilation system, with its screened floor-level vents at each end and another at the peak, seems to work well in spite of the impermeable fabric. So I shall persist with my trials—at least in snow, when the danger of rain seems remote.*

Filmgap

Stephenson's is now making "a unique new liner for the Model 7 tent which eliminates the need for sleeping bags." An insulating unit hangs inside the tent and provides a warm compartment for two, with foam pads underneath. The unit has "10 layers of aluminized plastic film with ¾-inch air gaps between layers. . . . An oversize end closure at the neck end permits the user to sleep with head outside of the liner but inside the tent."

Clearly, a new and crafty idea. But it sounds perilously susceptible to the slings and arrows of outrageous Murphy.

Fly sheets

Because fly sheets do not have to "breathe" (the "breathing" is done by the semipermeable main wall, 2 or 3 inches lower), they can be fully waterproofed. The current standard: urethane coating on woven nylon. If the coating suffers minor holes and abrasions from normal use (and rest assured it will), do not worry unduly. Small amounts of water that seep through will usually run harmlessly down the inside surface of the fly. And you can ignore an occasional drip onto the main tent: solid soaking or the force of driving rain are what breach it. But patch major breaks in the fly coating with Rip-stop tape (page 363).

Frost liners

In temperatures well below freezing, moisture from breath and body may coat your tent wall with ice crystals. I've had it happen as high as 20° F. One response is a detachable liner, usually of light cotton or some similarly absorbent material, that can be taken out and shaken, and will also absorb the moisture should the crystals melt.

Tent poles

Most modern poles are hollow aluminum tubes that break down into convenient sections of less than 3 feet. The best of them now tend to be joined together by shock cord for ease of erection and difficulty of loss. See page 212.

---

* For an up-to-date and altogether different kind of assessment of tent models, consult *Backpacker* Magazine No. 3 (fall 1973).

If poles won't conveniently travel in the tent's stuff bag, carry them tied to one side of your packframe. Autonomous sections, unjoined by shock cords, have a tendency to work loose, and could be lost. I find this tying method best: bundle the poles together as a unit with three rubber bands (at top, middle, and bottom) so that they will not slip and slide. Then lash the bundle tightly to one side of the packframe with a 3- or 4-foot length of nylon cord (page 368). Knot one end of the cord to the lowest aluminum eyebolt on the packframe (illustration, page 69). (For knot, see page 369.) Lay the bundled poles snugly along the packframe, upright, close to the packbag. Then, maintaining all possible tension, wind the cord upward around the packframe outer bar and the poles. Wind in open turns about 6 inches apart. Five or six turns bring you to the packframe crossbar. Make several securing turns around the bar and finish off with a knot through the nearest eyebolt. I find that, secured this way, the poles often stay firmly lashed without retightening for several days and nights on which I do not use them.

Tent pegs

Plain round Duralumin pegs (½ ounce; $.17) or light steel twisted skewer pegs (1 ounce; $.10) are probably still the best for most normal purposes. Angled or rounded (half-tube) aluminum pegs that nest to save space will hold better in loose soils but do more damage to fragile soil cover—and weigh 1½ ounces each and cost $.60. Plastic angled or I-beam pegs weigh about the same and cost half as much but can snap into sudden uselessness, while the aluminum versions simply bend.

If a campsite is too soft to hold your pegs firm (sand) or too hard for you to drive them in (yes, rock), and if the wind is not too strong (if it is, try to go someplace else), tie the guy lines to the middle of the pegs, lay them flat, and block them from sliding toward the tent with heavy rocks. For this job, strong sticks are even better than pegs: their greater friction reduces the chances of slippage. Either method works better than trying to tie guy lines directly onto all but ideally shaped stones. But it is often easier and safer to loop your guy lines around the lowest branches of a bush. Or you can tie a loop of nylon cord to the bush and thread the guy line through it so that you can more easily adjust the guy. Another alternative: crampons (page 55).

For tent pegs in snow, see page 222.

Guy line tighteners

Featherweight tighteners come in nylon and aluminum, in triangular and also in both flat and curved rounded-rectangular shapes. The triangles hold best, the curved versions next best. All are excellent at promoting snarls and at abrading packed tents. To eliminate them, tie a loop in the cord somewhere near the fabric. Use a figure-eight knot, to make undoing easier. Then thread the free end of the line (coming up from its peg) through the loop, pull to tighten, and jam with a slip knot:

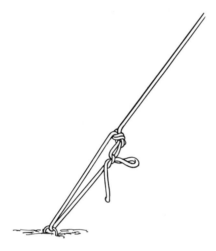

In driving snow, I'm not sure which would be the greater sonuva-bitch to adjust: frozen loop or frozen tightener. But I guess the tightener might prove safer.

Color

Green or pale blue tents mean a soft light inside in bright sunlight, and an inconspicuous camp. Orange or yellow fabric keeps the interior from getting too dark and oppressive in snowstorms and the like, stands out well in case of search-and-rescue (yellow is said to be best in dull weather, orange in sunlight), and catches the customer's eye in the store.

TENTS IN ACTION

Pitching a tent in a high wind

Every tent has its own stratagems for driving you to the brink of lunacy when you try to erect it in a high wind. But there are standard defensive measures with which you can counter. Before you unroll the tent itself and allow the wind to breathe berserk life into its billowing folds, have all the support weapons ready and waiting—poles, pegs, and an assortment of articles from pack or nature that are heavy enough to help hold down the wind-filled tent and yet smooth enough not to tear it. Then drive in the first peg, part way. For obvious reasons, wind- and door-wise, this peg should be the one for the center guy line of the foot end of the tent. If possible, hook this line over the peg before you unfold the tent. Drive the peg fully home, so that the line cannot by any devilish means flap free. Then take a deep breath and unfold the tent. Unfold it slowly, close to the ground, and onto each foot or so of unfolding fabric put one or more of the heavy, smooth articles. Their size and nature will depend on wind strength and campsite: sometimes all you can use is the full pack; big stones, when available, are godsends, but they must be smooth. Failing adequate heavy support weapons, sprawl yourself over the whistling, flapping bedlam. Slowly, painfully, drive in the pegs that hold down the edges of the stretched-out floor. If no stones are handy, drive in the pegs with your heels. Unless you've attempted this maneuver from the prone position in a thirty-mile-an-hour wind—brother, you haven't lived.

The sequence in which you tackle pole erection and the securing of the other guy lines will depend on the structure of your tent and the vagaries of your temperament, but in general you fix the windward end first and you try to keep everything flat on the ground until you are ready to lift the fabric quickly into a taut, unflappable position. You can't possibly accomplish such an act, but you might as well aim for it. Once you've come anywhere close, your troubles are almost over. But if you get the tent up within double the time you figured on, count yourself a candidate for the Tent of Fame.

Once the tent is up you should check several times that no pegs are threatening to pull out. And because even the tautest tent will flap in a very high wind, you may have to tighten the lines occasionally. End-to-end stability is the most vital factor, and it pays to place the head-end peg so that the line tightener or loop comes close to the apex of the tent and you can adjust it by simply reaching out from inside. If necessary, shorten the line by tying in a sheepshank.

Drainage moats

It was long the practice—and a wise one too—to dig a small ditch or moat around your tent even when there was little danger of heavy rain: if the rain came, you diverted all invading surface water. Tents without floors almost demanded such precautions. And in a real deluge even the best floored tents can, unless moated, begin to ship water through a cookhole, the foot of a zippered entrance, or a worn sector of the waterproof floor and lower wall; and once the flood begins there is, as I almost said before, Noah's Cape.

But times have changed. A single large party of well-meaning but unaware people that assume they are being good woodsmen by meticulously moating each tent in their little village can turn a beautiful meadow, almost overnight, into a scarred eyesore. In today's heavily used back country such a place rarely gets, as it used to, a year or so's rest. And the disruption to the delicate drainage and soil-binding relationships of a fragile place may turn it within a few years into a rutted, eroded mess. "Ah," you say, "but I always travel alone." Maybe. But one moat-minded person camping in a place every day of the month (which is the kind of usage many back-country campsites now suffer) is little different from thirty such people camping there for one night: although the damage will at first be confined to a smaller area, it will be locally more severe—and will soon force campers further and further afield. The result is the same.

So we must desist. What a man does in one of those fortunately rare cases when no amount of good site choosing and tent pitching can save him from the flood must be left to his own terribly human conscience. My guess is that, like me, he would reluctantly dig as small a moat as possible and fill it carefully when he strikes camp. But the routine digging of tent moats, though a perfectly reasonable practice when backpackers were few and far flung, is in today's congested wilderness no more acceptable than digging a septic tank for your downtown office.

Pitching a tent in snow

In hard snow, the only vital difference from pitching a tent elsewhere (unless you have to level a site) lies in the pegs. Ordinary round tent pegs are useless in snow. Use special angle pegs (1¾ ounces each; $.65). They're astonishingly efficient. Once you've driven them in, in fact, the only difficulty tends to be getting them out when you strike camp. The best extractor is the point of an ice ax. It is also a highly efficient tool for making holes in tent fabric.

For angle snow pegs as shit shovels, see page 386.

A new and increasingly popular alternative to the snow peg is the "deadman" snow anchor—a light alloy or fiberglass disk, 6 or 8 inches in diameter, with two central holes for tying in the guy line (or better still, for tying in a loop of nylon cord through which you thread your guy line). You bury the anchor and stamp the snow firm on top of it, or maybe slide it in sideways. You dig it out with shovel, ice ax, ski, snowshoe or whatever your ingenuity devises. Deadmen weigh 14 ounces each (and cost $6.50), so their use is restricted to the vital end guys.

In case of lost pegs or "deadmen," snowshoes or skis or ski poles or ice axes make good emergency replacements. Some people even use them regularly and so reduce their load; but that means, of course, that they probably can't move far from the tent without collapsing it.

In soft snow it is essential that before you attempt to pitch a tent you stamp out the site. Do the job before you take anything out of your pack, and make sure you know beforehand how many paces or boot lengths you need for length and for width, allowing room for you to move around outside the tent during the pitching operation. Stamp out narrow extensions for all guy lines, and a broad one around the entrance (illustration, page 211). In bad weather, this stamped-down entrance area will reduce the risk of drifting snow blocking all ventilation (pages 202–4 and 224–5). In good weather you'll find it invaluable as a place you can probably stand up in without snowshoes or skis. A little alleyway extension as a john is a worthwhile refinement.

The tent in action in snow

In snow camping, your tent is your castle. Outside, the world howls, white and hostile. Inside, you create a little domain of your own—cramped, imperfectly dry, and frigid by town-indoor standards; but livable and surprisingly snug. Of course, you have to work to keep it that way. Above all, you have to work at keeping things reasonably dry. Primarily, that means keeping the snow out. Before you crawl inside, brush all the snow you can off clothing and person. Stamp as much as you can off your boots too. And do not wear them all the way inside: swivel around before they come more than an inch or two over the threshold, take them off (less easily done than written), and immediately slip your feet down into the sleeping bag. Legs and body probably go into the bag too. (If you're covered with snowflakes or melted snow you must obviously brush off or dry or remove your outer layer before getting into the bag.) Then bang the boots together and get most of the remaining snow off them. In good weather hold the boots outside for this operation. In vile weather bang the snow onto something waterproof, laid out just inside the entrance, and empty it outside when you get a chance. A cookhole (page 213) makes it very simple to dispose of such snow as collects on the waterproof floor, and you can relax some of these precautions. But you still have to be careful not to get sleeping bag or clothing wet.

Boot desnowing is not the only reason for having a water-proof mat of some kind just inside the entrance (I use the large, tough plastic bag that wraps my cooking pots—see page 189). This doormat collects most of the snow that inevitably comes with you when you crawl in, and also the smaller but by no means negligible amounts that dribble in whenever you have a small opening for ventilation. It also serves as an interim garbage can for all the foreign matter you'd just as soon didn't lie around inside: gas spilled when you're refilling the stove; water spilled when you're filling canteens after melting snow; food fragments; even, if you're feeling house-proud, the inevitable stray feathers from sleeping bag and down clothing. At convenient intervals, you empty all this debris outside—or into the cookhole, if you have one.

Your waterproof mat also acts as a doormat when the weather is good enough for you to put on your boots outside: you tread on it in stockinged feet while you put on the boots. You can also stand on it in stockinged feet, just outside, when you have to answer the liquid calls of nature. The right kind of gloves make good short-service slippers (page 300). The ideal is a pair of down booties (page 295). For more on sanitation, see page 387.

For techniques and precautions when cooking in a tent, see pages 200 and 202.

The most vital precaution of all when camping in snow is to keep the tent from getting buried. You can even buy lightweight aluminum shovels (1 pound 7 ounces; $6) to carry along for the job—and, of course, for clearing tent sites, digging snow caves, or even clearing a route. But a snowshoe is a very efficient tool for keeping your tent unburied. In extremely heavy snow it may become necessary, if the snow keeps falling for a day or two, to take down your tent, raise the platform by shoveling in snow and stamping it flat, and then repitch the tent.

In mid-July 1958 a party of four climbers camped in stormy weather on an exposed Alaskan ridge at about 11,500 feet. They had two two-man tents: a Gerry model made of permeable material and with two entrances, and an impermeable army mountain tent with only a sleeve entrance. On the second stormbound night a very heavy fall of snow formed a 10-inch-thick windslab over the tents so quickly that none of the climbers appreciated the danger before morning. Around 6:00 A.M., one of the men in the army tent woke, breathing rapidly, and realized that the air was foul. Unable to find knife, boots or gloves in the semi-collapsed tent, he just managed to dig his way out through the clinging folds of the sleeve-entrance, barehanded, then had to slide back inside to rest and warm up. (The outside temperature was around −10°.) Suddenly, he and his companion found themselves gasping for breath. The first man immediately started out the entrance again, but was unable to free himself from the door, stopped digging to rest—and lost consciousness. Around 8:30 A.M., one of the men in the Gerry tent dug free and saw him lying halfway out of the entrance, with evidence of frostbite. Carried into the Gerry tent, he soon recovered consciousness. His companion was found, still inside the army tent, motionless and not breathing. Four to five hours' artificial respiration failed to revive him. He had died, of course, from asphyxiation (lack of oxygen, presence of carbon dioxide) due to the tent's being buried.

Extremely bad snow conditions caused this accident, but contributory factors included the impermeable tent fabric, the clinging nature of the only exit, and a guying system that failed to preserve adequate internal air space. (For full report and analysis, see "Accidents in American Mountaineering," Twelfth Annual Report of the Safety Committee of the American Alpine Club, 1959, pages 22–4.) The story is a vivid object lesson in how alert you must remain—under conditions horribly conducive to weariness and boredom—when there is any danger of your tent's being buried by snow.

For more on blocked ventilation, see pages 202–4.

Care of tents

A nylon tent needs far less looking after than the old canvas type with rope guy lines. In the field, you do not have to keep loosening and tightening the lines to meet humidity changes. And once the weather swings around on your side the tent dries out very quickly.

Damp does not harm nylon the way it does canvas and rope, but mildew can still form, and if you arrive home with a wet nylon tent you should dry it out. The simplest way is to erect it on the lawn, wash it if necessary with the garden hose, and just leave it to dry. If you have to do the job indoors, hang the tent by its normal suspension points. Some makers recommend washing nylon tents after use in a tumbler-type—not agitator-type—washing machine, with mild detergent, then drying them in a spin dryer. (To avoid grisly tangles, remove all guy lines.) Other makers cry, "Never!"

NON-TENTS

Your roof need not be a tent, of course. The several alternatives are all lighter than tents and easier to erect. All perform more efficiently as cool retreats in hot weather. And all are much cheaper. On the other hand, none can approach the efficiency of a tent in blocking out a really high wind or in conserving warmth (though it is often overlooked that all of them, except in a very high wind, reduce the rate at which warm air from your body can escape, and so increase your warmth at night to a surprising degree). Although some of them repel the average rainstorm as well as most tents do, or even better, nothing rivals a good tent *with* fly sheet for protection from prolonged rain, whether it is a heavy downpour or a swirling, penetrating mountain drizzle.

You choose your roof, then, to suit expected conditions.

A fly sheet alone

A few years ago I used nothing but a fly sheet for night protection during a four-month walk up England—through the very maw of what the British sportingly call summer.

I had a serviceable unit made up from two pieces of cream-colored, 3½-ounce, untreated nylon fabric, joined down their length:

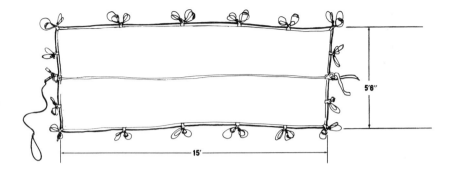

The center join and all edges were strengthened with ¾-inch herringbone twill tape. The center join was waterproofed. I had small aluminum rings attached by loops of tape, stoutly stitched. To all rings on the long edges I tied on 3-foot guy lines of ³⁄₃₂-inch braided nylon. To keep these thin lines from snarling, they had to be gathered up in rough slip knots every time the fly sheet was packed away. Each line had a small, ultralightweight aluminum tightener. They were of the old kind, straight but bent. (The newer triangular tighteners [twelve to an ounce] are more efficient. But see page 220 for a way of dispensing with tighteners.) To one of the rings at the ridge I tied on the two metal pole sockets from the apex of my one-man tent (illustration, page 210). To the other I tied on two 1-foot lengths of strong tape. The whole rig weighed 1 pound 10 ounces. I can't find a record of the cost, but it was very low.

Along with my fly sheet I carried the two aluminum tent poles from my one-man tent (each 4 feet long, but breaking into two sections), and sixteen of the small pegs from that tent (two as spares).

This bedroom was very simple to erect. My walking staff, tied to one end of the ridge by the lengths of tape (and held upright by three lengths of nylon cord attached to three pegs or other convenient points such as trees or bushes) held the ridge high at the head-end. The tent poles, inserted in their metal sockets, held the sheet high enough over my feet. The side lines kept the sheet spread wide and taut. The small aluminum rings on the short edges enabled me to pull one or both ends of the structure in with lengths of nylon cord, and so form rough endwalls that could be further buttressed, once I was inside, by a poncho.

The fly sheet made a surprisingly effective house, even in a soggy English summer. The side lines unfortunately tended to pull the ridge down into a depression midway between its ends, and in very wet weather moisture occasionally collected there and dropped off. But for the most part the roof was rainproof. When rain drove in from one side I could lower the ridge, drop the eaves on the windward flank, plug the small ground-level gap with anything handy (from brush to poncho), and stay remarkably snug. In extremely heavy rain the force of big drops sometimes drove a fine spray through the nylon. But on such occasions my outspread poncho kept the sleeping bag dry, and the spray was too fine to harm anything else. I remember in particular a nighttime thunderstorm just outside Nottingham when the rain lashed down for several hours with tropical intensity. I remember it vividly because it is the only time I have *heard* lightning hitting the ground all around me. The rain matched the ferocity of the flashes and crackling explosions, but under my little fly sheet I slept as dry as a dehydrated bean.

The fly sheet was strong enough to stand up to prolonged use and to strong winds (though not, of course, to full-scale mountain storms). And it was a reasonably flexible unit. I could make a high-roofed, airy bedroom or a low, snug retreat simply by raising and lowering the point at which I tied the tapes to my staff and by splaying the aluminum poles more or less widely. Once, when I stayed several days on a Cornish headland and a wind blew steadily in from the Atlantic, I used my poncho as a roof and the fly sheet as sidewalls.

All in all, the fly sheet setup made a good bedroom, especially where there were no trees or other hitching posts. Today, I would have the fly sheet made from coated nylon or would buy a regular coated fly sheet. I suppose I could have the old one treated, but nowadays I tend to use instead a

Plastic sheet with Visklamp attachment.

This cunning and convenient, though unlikely looking, rig is strong, light, and very cheap. The plastic sheet is smooth, white, translucent .004-inch polyethylene, known as Visqueen, that is absolutely watertight and a great deal tougher than it looks. (Make sure, though, that you buy good-quality sheeting. One sample that I tried soon began to tear. And check that the material is translucent, not semitransparent, or it will make a scurvy sun awning.)

The sheeting comes in several sizes including 6 by 8 feet (1 pound; $1), 8 by 9 feet (1½ pounds—according to the catalogue though my present one is 3 ounces lighter; $1.49) and 9 by 12 feet (2 pounds; $2.10). You can also buy it even more cheaply in 100-foot rolls, either 12 or 24 feet wide. With the

8-by-9 size, I live luxuriously, solo. For two people, the 9-by-12 is
fine.

The sheets are plain, without grommets or attachments of
any kind. You secure them with improbable little two-part devices
called Visklamps (¾ ounce and $.15 each).

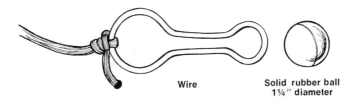

Wire

Solid rubber ball
1¼″ diameter

A Visklamp is extremely easy to use. At whatever point you
want to attach a guy line, you simply wrap the rubber ball in the
sheet and twist a couple of times so that the ball and the plastic
envelope around it form an isolated isthmus. Then you pass the
enveloped ball through the larger metal loop and slide the twisted
neck of the isthmus down the narrow connecting channel until
the ball is held in the smaller loop. Attach a nylon cord to the
larger loop, and you have a guy line that will take remarkable
strain. For easy adjustment, run the guy line back from tent peg
or substitute and thread through the Visklamp. Pull downward,
using the Visklamp loop as a pulley. When the guy is tight, knot
the free end at the Visklamp. You can then readjust the tension
on any line without leaving your shelter.

The great advantage of this system is its flexibility. You
can build an orthodox, tentlike bedroom:

or a sort of eccentric rotunda (though you have to be careful about the angles, or you end up with almost no roof—only folds):

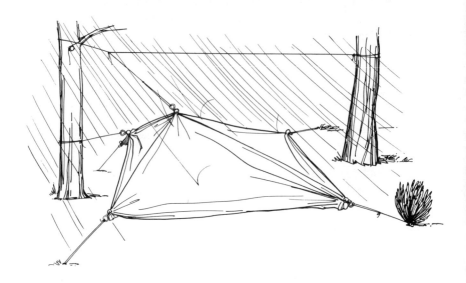

or a useful lunchtime shelter in wind-driven drizzle:

For further ideas, see variations on the poncho theme, pages 236–40.

An advantage of this rig is that you can, by moving one or

two Visklamps, very simply make a major readjustment to meet new conditions of wind or rain. And in most setups you can, while still in bed, slip one Visklamp loose and lift the roof aside for cooking or working or for looking around, and can immediately replace it if rain threatens or you want more warmth. Carrying this idea further, you can put up your shelter because you think it may rain or get cold enough to make you grateful for the roof's assistance, and can then remove one or more of the rubber balls (filing them in a pocket or some other instantly reachable place) and so enjoy all the freedoms of rooflessness and yet know that if it rains, even in the middle of the night, you can get the roof over your head in about ten drops flat. I find that nowadays I often rig such a ready-roof. It may be the prime reason I continue, despite raucous laughter from serious, haughty backpackers, to use my Visklamp shelter.

If you have not used this prophylactic system and rain catches you unawares, you can as an emergency measure simply spread the sheet over yourself. Or you can wrap it loosely around everything—taking care to leave an opening at your head for ventilation. (For details, diagram, and dangers, see pages 239 and 240.) This wraparound system, by the way, will help you keep warm, rain or no rain. Do not wrap yourself too tightly or your sweat may condense on the impermeable sheet and soak the sleeping bag.

I normally carry six Visklamps and six aluminum tent pegs for this setup, but in really cramped and awkward corners a couple extra of each can make all the difference. If you lose a metal attachment, just tie the nylon directly around the twisted isthmus below the rubber ball. The 4-mil polyethylene sheeting is tough enough to stand up to this makeshift arrangement. Once or twice, when I needed more attachment points than I had Visklamps, I have just twisted up a tumor of plastic and tied the nylon directly to its neck.

Once, a couple of summers ago, when a desert afternoon wind was blustering across the plateau on which I'd camped, it repeatedly tore the sheeting at a Visklamp. So, although that has been my polyethylene's only failure, I would certainly not trust this rig in a full-scale mountain gale. But I always take it now on summer trips of a week or so when there seems a chance of heavy rain. I am not sure I would rely on the sheeting for a really long trip when I could not replace it, but on short trips the wear factor can hardly become serious.

Because the sheeting is white, it does not make your den dark and dismal, even in oppressive weather. And because it is translucent-going-on-opaque it makes an excellent sun awning.

This sheeting is versatile stuff. It's exactly what you need for waterproofing your pack contents on major river crossings (pages 378–85). And if you have to swim across a river on a packless sidetrip you can wrap all your clothes and gear in the sheet, tie it with cord, and have yourself a buoyant, watertight bundle that you can push or pull along (page 379). In any kind of terrain not covered by snow, the sheeting also makes a first-class marker for airdrops (page 394).

Few mountain shops seem to carry either Visklamps or strong enough sheeting to use with them, but Recreational Equipment, Seattle, always seems to have both.

Some catalogues now represent adhesive grommet tabs (package of 10: 2 ounces; $1.35) as improvements on Visklamps. But although undeniably lighter and possibly stronger, they lack the Visklamps' shining flexibility: once fixed, they're immovable. Still, they may be worth putting at the most commonly used attachment points—the four corners and midway along each long side. Three or four Visklamps would then be enough for most styles of imaginative free-lance architecture. Many plastic groundsheets, by the way, now come with loose grommet tabs, and if, like me, you rarely attach them to the groundsheet, you can build a stock for use with your Visklamp shelters.

Tarp tents

A number of suppliers—including Moor and Mountain of Concord, Holubar of Boulder, and both Sierra Designs and The Ski Hut of Berkeley—now catalogue large coated-nylon tarps with a grommet at each end and doubled tapes attached at various points. They look as though they would be almost as flexible as the Visklamp setup and somewhat stronger. But they are heavier and much more expensive. (Range: from 1¾ to 3½ pounds; from $22 to $37.50.) I must try one.

A choice between Visklamp shelters and tarp tents involves a new and important matter of principle that applies even more stringently to other items but which we had better examine before we go any further:

The ethics of using disposable plastic equipment.

For several years now, disquieting reports have kept coming out of the more heavily used back country: campsites, whole meadows, even above-timber rock basins transformed into garbage dumps by discarded plastic groundsheets, tarps and tube tents.

The causes of this defilement seem clear: an exponential increase in the number of human visitors; the inability of uneducated newcomers to grasp the gulf that yawns between behavior acceptable in a human society still sick with the no-deposit-no-return syndrome and behavior acceptable in an essentially nonhuman society with its fragile economics totally dependent on recycling; and the cheapness, lightness, efficiency and wide availability of plastic sheeting molded to many backpacking uses. The remedies are less clear. One possibility is to limit, forcibly, the number of human visitors. Unless present trends reverse, such a step seems inevitable. But it is highly undesirable: among other things, it imposes petty human strictures on an experience with freedom at its core; and it guarantees joyful employment for the kind of person that has reveled in rasping domination of his fellows since long before Shakespeare bewailed "the insolence of office." One alternative is enlightenment of the uneducated (such as I am attempting now, I guess); or a more general attempt—that seems to be in hand, thank God—to eradicate the no-deposit-no-return mentality. Another approach would be to remove the plastic offenders from the marketplace. At least two firms have, to their eternal credit, made the attempt. Sierra Designs and The Ski Hut, horrified by the results of their legitimate business, at first tried charging refundable deposits for disposable plastic items; and when that scheme proved ineffective both firms ignored profits and stopped selling plastic groundsheets, tarps and tube tents. I applaud, long and loud. But I am not hopeful. It seems unlikely that all outdoor equipment suppliers can be persuaded to follow this public-spirited lead. And as long as the offenders are for sale the only people likely to refuse to buy them are precisely those people least likely to strew them around beautiful meadows and rock basins. Besides, even if all outdoor equipment suppliers embargoed plastic sheeting articles, the raw sheeting would still be available—and bought.

For all of us, the question arises, "What should I, personally, do about this plastic problem?" Should we stop using such vastly useful articles—you and I, who would never by God dream of ditching a plastic groundsheet or anything else in a wild place? (I mean, after all, would we?) The sacrifice would without doubt generate a cozy holier-than-thou feeling—which is always rewarding (and the reason self-denial remains so improbably but perennially popular). But would it do much good? I'm afraid I doubt it.

In my particular case the question arises, "Should I remove all reference to the offending items from this book?" Such a course would certainly ensure that cozy glow of holiness; but again I doubt its effectiveness. So for the time being I shall, unhappily, at least finish using the plastic items I own; and I shall let my plastic paragraphs stand. But I remain in a state of considerable confusion.

The trouble is, I think that the situation in those sad camp-sites and out in those desecrated meadows and rock basins is simply another manifestation of the current general human malaise: imbalance with the rest of the world. And the only way to correct that imbalance lies through a broad change of heart and actions. (See, for example, *The Limits to Growth,* page 357.) Still, the gaunt fact remains that only backpackers can stop this plastic defecation. It has got to be stopped, somehow.

The pivotal point, then, in a choice between plastic Visklamp shelter and coated nylon tarp is that the expensive nylon tarp does not wear out quickly or have a "disposable" feel. It is therefore unlikely to be tossed thoughtlessly aside. The same consideration arises with a

Tube or instant tent.

The traditional form of this popular device—which I have for some reason never tried—has been a tube of inexpensive polyethylene, usually 3.5 mil or lighter, about 9 feet long and 8 to 10 feet in circumference. The tube can be quickly strung up on any ridge line. The weight of your gear and body—perhaps

with an assist from smooth stones—anchors the floor. Some models have grommets at each end for drawing the openings more or less closed. Weight varies from 1 to 2 pounds, price from $2.50 to $3.50. Some catalogues now offer lengths of continuous 4-mil tube tent material that can be cut to any length.

Tube tents are obviously useful for thunderstorm weather. But if the ridge line sags beware of the suffocation hazard, and of carbon monoxide poisoning (page 203).

The Ski Hut, now that it refuses to sell plastic tube tents, offers "a durable, more sophisticated" fabric version, little heavier than a stout plastic one (2 pounds 2 ounces). It costs several times more ($22) but is said to "outlast ten plastic jobs."

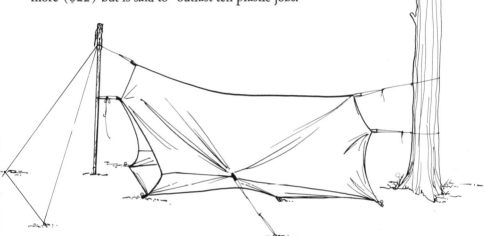

Other firms are now making similar fabric tube tents. And evolution along this hopeful line continues. Holubar offers a do-it-yourself Carikit for a highly flexible "Super Tube" with mosquito netting at the door end (2 pounds 10 ounces; $24.95). And The Ski Hut has now produced this mosquito-netting-at-each-

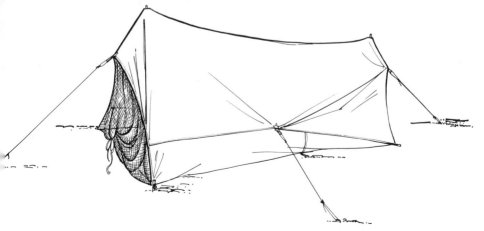

end version with two upright poles (3 pounds 6 ounces; $32.50) that comes close to being a large, light, simple one-man mountain tent.

Unless the rain threat is serious, I often rely for an emergency roof on my

Poncho or groundsheet.

Most heavy ponchos have grommets along their edges, and it is a simple matter to string them up with nylon cord. Lightweight ponchos often lack grommets, but I have up to six or eight specially inserted. To build your roof you can string a ridge rope between trees and make an orthodox tentlike bedroom (illustration, page 229), or you can attach the poncho by its corners to surrounding bushes and branches, or to sticks held in position by stones. In heavy or driving rain you can stay surprisingly dry if you keep the roof so low that there is only just room for you underneath. I often carry one Visklamp as a roof-lifter for the poncho: with the low-level, battened-down roof, it makes life much more comfortable.

If you suspend the roof by the poncho's hood cord you do not risk damaging the fabric with the Visklamp, but you put the roof's high point in the wrong place and probably get some rain in through the hood opening.

Under milder conditions you can use your staff either as an external upright or as an inside prop to force the roof pleasantly high

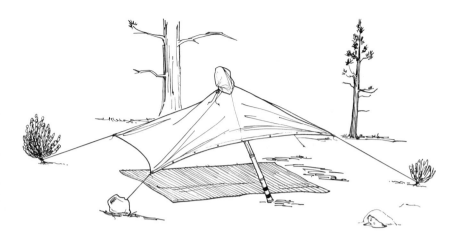

above your head and also to keep it taut, so that rain does not collect in sagging hollows. When you use the staff this way, pad it at the top with something soft so that it will not cut the poncho.

The poncho rig is especially useful in open desert, when you may find yourself in desperate need of an awning at midday halts. The difference between the sun-scorched ground and the little coffin-shaped patch of shade under your poncho will seem like the difference between hell and . . . well, something a comfortable half-hitch short of hell. (See figures for desert ground temperatures, page 59, footnote.) The awning will certainly make a critical difference to your sense of well-being and therefore to what you are capable of doing in the cool of evening. Under certain conditions it could even be the difference between life and death.

On desert afternoons a strong wind often blows for hour after hour. When it does, the continuous flapping of the poncho makes a

hideous din, always threatens to tear grommets loose, and sometimes does. One way of reducing both noise and strain is to secure
only three corners of the poncho to fixed points and to tie a large
rock on the downwind corner with a cord of such length that the
stone will just rest on the ground under normal conditions but
will lift, and so ease the strain, when the poncho billows under an
especially strong gust.

A grommeted *groundsheet* (page 240) can make as effective
a rain roof as a poncho. As it is usually bigger, it will when new
make an even better one—but groundsheets rarely stay unpunctured for very long.

Economy-size groundsheets (which in our peculiar modern
tongue are distinctly large ones) can be folded so that they act
both in their normal role and at the same time as an angled wall
that will protect you from driven rain (and from a cold wind,
dry or rainbearing). You can hold the angled edge down with
full canteens or other heavy equipment, with your staff (anchored
by large stones), or with smooth stones alone.

As awnings, clear plastic groundsheets are, of course, comprehensively useless—and translucent colored ones only a shade
better.

Whether you choose to use groundsheet or poncho as your
emergency rain roof depends on conditions. If you can race an
approaching storm you will probably be wise to consider rigging
your capacious groundsheet over a dry piece of ground and doing
without anything under your mattress. Then you'll be able to wear
the poncho when necessary. Try to resist the temptation to use it as
a groundsheet; it will certainly develop holes. If the ground is

already wet you will need the groundsheet as a floor, and the poncho goes up as roof.

Finally there is the problem of what to do about a roof when you go to sleep in the open, confident that no rain will fall, and wake up an hour later to the pitter-patter of tiny raindrops or the clammy drift of drizzle. One solution is to unwrap your groundsheet (which is doubled under you) and cover yourself over, with the open side to leeward. If the weather gets worse, you can quickly improve this makeshift cocoon by lacing the open side with nylon cord threaded through the grommets, if any (you get only mildly wet in the process). Another solution is to use the poncho in the same way, laced or unlaced. (If I harbor any doubts at all about the weather I go to sleep with the poncho ready, close at hand.) Better still is a combination of groundsheet and poncho: the groundsheet as main cocoon, the poncho wrapped like an elephant's foot around the bottom of your sleeping bag, which otherwise persists, steadfastly, in pushing out into the open. Provided the rain is not too heavy, such a makeshift shelter can keep your sleeping bag surprisingly dry, and yourself totally so. (One good friend of mine, an experienced backpacker, holds with ferocity to the childiotic notion that if he erects any rain shelter more complicated than a poncho-groundsheet cocoon he is pandering to his weaker instincts.)

The extent of the action you take when surprised by rain during the night depends on your sleepy estimate of the probable heaviness of the rain. If you think it is going to come down but good, it pays to make the hard decision early and get up and rig poncho or groundsheet into an adequate roof. Of course, any man with an ounce of sense will rig a roof whenever there's a hint of doubt about the weather. I have at last learned to rig a ready-roof (page 231) at such times—with poncho or groundsheet if necessary. Well, I've more or less learned.

The cocoon bedroom in all its variants is also a useful makeshift measure in unexpected light snow. Even in dry weather, it gives you a surprising degree of extra warmth, particularly in high

winds. Remember, though, that unless there is adequate ventilation your sweat will condense and soak the sleeping bag. An unventilated cocoon—or a tarp or groundsheet just spread over your sleeping bag—can be dangerous. In early April 1961, a co-ed from the University of New Hampshire camped beside the parking lot of a New England ski resort. She had considerable winter camping experience. The weather had been warm, and there was melt water on the packed snow. It rained during the night. Then the weather cleared, and the temperature fell. Presumably to keep the rain off, the girl had covered her sleeping bag with an impermeable plastic tarp. In the morning she was found dead. It was presumed that she had suffocated, for the edges of the tarp were frozen to the ground ice, and she had been sealed in. The carbon dioxide that would normally have awakened her by making her struggle for breath may have been absorbed by the moisture collected under the tarp. Lesson: always leave plenty of ventilation at your head, especially if there is any danger of the tarp's being frozen to the ground.

In the advertising material for old-type, open-mouth sleeping bags you still find, occasionally, neat little pictures of

Head roofs.

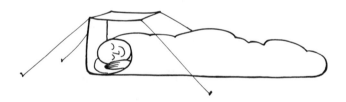

I suspect that the whole tradition is nurtured by advertiser-indoorsmen. I certainly can't remember seeing such a device actually being used. Yet heavy sleeping bags often have special flaps for just this purpose. I suppose they would help shield you from a head-to-toes wind, but anyone who uses an open-mouth bag rather than a mummy type (page 249) is presumably not too worried about keeping warm.

GROUNDSHEETS

It is entirely possible to operate without a groundsheet. But I find that I never do. You need one in most places to keep out the damp, in even more places to reduce wear and tear on such fragile items as air mattress and sleeping bag, and just about everywhere as a general keep-clean-and-keep-from-losing-things area for the gear you take out of the pack. A slippery groundsheet also forms a natural defense zone against ants and ticks and scorpions and their brethren. And on top of all this there is the groundsheet-as-roof-and-walls-or-even-cocoon (pages 236–40).

When your load problem is acute and the chances of rain slight (a combination that applied on my Grand Canyon trip) you can carry a light poncho that doubles as groundsheet. A groundsheet does highly abrasive duty, so do not expect the dual-purpose article to last very long as a waterproof poncho. In Grand Canyon, mine, sure enough, didn't. But all the rain and snow fell near the start, just as I had expected, and the arrangement worked out fine.

For a long trip on which you cannot get equipment replaced you need a strong, though still lightweight, groundsheet. Nylport or Nyltown (urethane-coated, fine-weave nylon) is at present the best bet. But it is expensive. A typical 5-by-7-foot sheet weighs 12 ounces, costs $12.50; the 7-by-9-foot size weighs 1 pound 8 ounces, costs $17.50. A few stores sell the fabric by the yard.

On short trips I have for years used the much cheaper 3- or 4-mil polyethylene sheets (4-mil size—5 by 7 feet: 1 pound; $1. 9 by 12: 2 pounds 4 ounces; $1.95). They normally come with four self-adhesive grommet tabs that you can either attach to increase the groundsheet's usefulness as roof or cocoon, or can hoard for other jobs (page 232). Again, you can sometimes buy this sheeting by the yard.

Most plastic groundsheets are semitransparent. All are waterproof when unpunctured—and are expendable. And that's the trouble. Because they so often get punctured and torn, they form a considerable part of the recent plastic desecration of wilderness by uneducated oafs (see, *please,* pages 232–4), and at least two stores have stopped selling them. Each of us is going to have to make up his own mind about his personal response.

MATTRESSES

When you are young and eager and tough, and the weather is not too perishingly cold, you do without a mattress. I did so all through the six months of my California walk (except for the first few days when, to cushion the shock of changing from soft city life, I carried a cheap plastic air mattress that I didn't expect to last long, and which didn't). I soon got used to sleeping with my mummy bag directly on all kinds of hard ground, but I often padded the bag inside with a sweater or other clothes. On that trip, temperatures rarely fell more than a degree or two below freezing, though on one occasion I slept on stones at 25° F. (That night I had a floored tent and a few sheets of newspaper, which make a very useful emergency insulator.)

But failing to use some kind of insulating mattress radically reduces a down or Dacron sleeping bag's efficiency: your weight so compresses the down directly beneath you that its air-holding—and warmth-conserving—property is cut almost to zero. And even when cold is no problem you are liable to find that if you have grown used to an ordinary bed the change to unpadded-mummy-bag-on-the-ground ruins your sleep for at least a few nights. This will reduce your efficiency, and also your enjoyment, and the saving in weight just isn't worth it—unless you can be sure of finding some soft, dry sand for a bed. Then, all you need is a couple of wriggles to dig shallow depressions for shoulders and rump, and you've got yourself a comfortable sleep.

The traditional woodsman and Boy Scout routine was to build a mattress from natural materials: soft and pliable bough tips, or moss, or thick grass. On the California walk I did for a while use branches from desert creosote bushes. But in today's heavily traveled camping areas the cutting of plant life is not merely illegal but downright immoral—an atrocity committed only by the sort of feeble-minded citizen who scatters empty beer cans. Besides, the method is inefficient. Even when you can find suitable materials, you waste time in preparing a bed. And the bed is rarely as warm or as comfortable as a modern, lightweight pad or air mattress.

For perhaps twenty years the standard equipment under almost all conditions was an

Air mattress.

An air mattress can amplify the efficiency of your sleeping bag, neutralize the sharpest stones, support your body luxuriously at all the right places, convert into an easy chair, float you and your pack across a river, and get punctures.

As far as the punctures go, all you have to do is keep a wary eye open for thorns, pray, and carry a repair outfit (2 ounces; $1). Traditionally, such outfits seem to include a wild selection of patches but nothing like enough adhesive. Consider carrying an extra tube of rubber solution—or two complementary tubes of epoxy, which will repair not only your air mattress but everything from sunglasses through boot soles to packbag and even aluminum packframe. But beware of crushed tubes! And keep the two tubes separated.

Inflating an air mattress is easy—but not quite as easy as it sounds. For sleeping, the mattress should be fairly soft. Inexperienced campers tend to blow their mattresses up far too tight, spend a night or two bobbing around like corks on a rough sea, then give up the great outdoors for good. The trick is to inflate the mattress just hard enough to keep every segment of you off the ground—and no harder. The easiest way to achieve this end is to blow the mattress up considerably harder than it will finally need to be, wait for the hot air from your lungs to cool and therefore contract, lie on your side on the mattress and press down unnaturally hard with your hip, and slowly let air out of the valve until your hip just touches the ground. Then close the valve. The mattress will now be firm enough to hold your hip clear of the ground when you're lying naturally, but soft enough to accept your body into its bosom rather than to send you bobbing around or rolling off to one side. And because the protruding portions of your body compress the air, the mattress will support the parts that need support: knees, small of back, and neck. If your mattress has a pillow section as a separate compartment, inflate it rather hard. Again, overinflate, and when you lie down reduce the pressure to what feels right.

Rather to my surprise, I have come to the conclusion that a separately inflatable pillow section is worth having. It certainly makes for a more comfortable bed. And it also means that you carry along, without extra weight, an excellent easy chair (see illustration, page 230). For the chair, reverse the inflation routine for the bed: blow the main section up hard but leave the pillow soft. Then reverse the mattress too, propping the main section up against your pack as backrest and laying the pillow flat as a seat. You can hardly make the backrest too firm. The best way to get the pillow right is once more to overinflate and then to fine-adjust with your butt in position. You may possibly classify a wilderness easy chair as rampant hedonism—until you have sampled the difference between eating the evening meal with and without a comfortable backrest, or have spent an afternoon leaning against a gnarled tree trunk while you tried to read or write.

For techniques of river crossing with an air mattress, see pages 378–85.

Air mattress materials. Unless you want an air mattress only for a night or two, avoid at all costs the cheap, thin, plastic jobs.

They puncture at the drop of a twig, tear almost without provocation, and often don't get the chance to do either before a seam pulls open. Most backpackers seem to find coated nylon mattresses satisfactory. They are certainly light and should be strong. But the only one I have owned gave me continual trouble with leaky seams, and I remain prejudiced. Rubberized canvas, though heavier, is very tough. It gets my vote.

Size. The choice lies between three-quarter or hip-length (supporting butt, shoulders, and possibly head; in cold weather you keep your feet off the ground with spare clothing or your pack or whatever else you can lay hands on) and full-length (accommodating the whole body, but weighing about half as much again). Some years ago, after several miserable nights on a hip-length mattress, I vowed a solemn vow that I would never again carry anything but a full-length. Today, the only backpacking air mattress I own is a small hip-length. And it is some time since I even thought about changing. I can offer no explanation for this phenomenon, unless it is that in time a man gets used to just about anything. There is no need, by the way, for a wide mattress. A flat width of twenty-four inches—rather less when inflated—is entirely adequate. Provided you keep the pressure down, you will not roll off. Not often enough to matter, anyway.

Valves. The simpler and stronger the better. Not too much can go wrong with stout rubber tubes and solid plug stoppers attached with stout nylon. Even if you lose a stopper, a makeshift wooden plug shouldn't be beyond your powers. One-piece metal screw tops fill me with distrust: I am always afraid they may jam, particularly in sand. And they let air out miserably slowly. The process may take three or four minutes. With the stopper type, you just pull the plug while lying on the mattress; within seconds the bulk of the air is out, you are more or less forced to get up, and the mattress is ready for packing.

Models. My choice has long been a rubberized canvas mattress (the Good Companions by Thomas Black) with separate pillow section and four longitudinal tubes that are "wave-joined" to help keep all parts of your body clear of the ground:

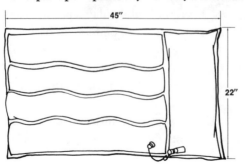

(Weight: 1 pound 14 ounces. Color: varies with vintage. Cost: $10.)

I carried a Good Companions all through the two-month traverse of Grand Canyon, and treated it brutally. Night after night it supported me in comfort on bedrock or gravel or sand. Sometimes a thin poncho protected it; sometimes, nothing. Day after day it was my easy chair for reading, writing and sloth. Five times it was my raft for river-detours around unclimbable outcrops; and once it floated me clear across the Colorado. The only puncture came three days from the end when I lived for twenty-four hours in a cliff dwelling; then, as I sat at ease in my chair on the chip-strewn floor, the pillow protested at last with an explosive three-inch rent. In more normal use I almost never seem to get a puncture.

There is a line of nylon mattresses (the Stebco Backpackers), rubber vulcanized on the inside, without pillows, that carry a two-year factory guarantee. Many experienced backpackers seem to find them good, though it was one of these that gave me trouble with leaking seams. They come green on one side, brilliant orange for emergency signaling on the other. (23 by 50 inches: 1 pound 8 ounces; $7.50. 28 by 72 inches: 2 pounds 8 ounces; $10.50.)

Air Lift of Berkeley has recently marketed a new kind of very compact, lightweight air mattress. Nine strong vinyl tubes—each inflatable by "a single breath"—fit individually into the compartments of a zippered, 1.9-ounce Rip-stop nylon cover. This system means you can inflate the outermost tubes hard, and so reduce the danger of rolling off; but to adjust the mattress to your requirements—and again to deflate in the morning—you have 9 separate valves to play with. (Model 9B: 20 by 42 inches; 1½ pounds; $14.50. Spare tubes: $1 each. Model 10-BL: 22 by 72 inches; 2½ pounds; $24.50 [includes patch kit]. Spare tubes: $2.) Each mattress comes with sack and spare tube.

There are any number of big, luxurious, and very strong models in every catalogue, with such refinements as large outer and foot tubes to give a cradle effect. But they weigh anything from 4 pounds on up. They are excellent for car camping, though, and I sometimes take one along when I drive to my starting point. That way, I save wear and tear on the lighter backpacking mattress, or avoid the less comfortable foam pad (see page 246), until I hike away from the car.

Inflators. Concertina-type pumps that "will inflate your mattress in a few minutes" appear in almost every catalogue. And the propaganda goes on to say that they are "very necessary at high altitudes and a big help at any altitude." A big help, possibly; but also 7½ ounces. I use my lungs, no matter what the altitude. But I always do the job *before* a meal.

I still use my air mattress sometimes when I judge the nights will not be cold enough to make sub–sleeping bag insulation a major problem; if I'm likely to need it for a river crossing; if bedsites promise to be very hard or rough and unsmoothable; if bulk poses a load problem; or if I want to spend a lot of time sitting and reading or writing, and like hell fancy the idea of an easy chair.

But nowadays, especially if night temperatures are likely to fall below freezing, I generally carry one of several kinds of

Foam pads.

The huge advantage of pads is that they insulate superbly—far better than air mattresses. They also tend to be lighter. And they're puncture immune. They have therefore largely replaced air mattresses for general backpacking. And no one in his right mind would still carry an air mattress for snow work.

But pads are not perfect. The thin kind (Ensolite and variations, see below) are truly comfortable only on snow or sand or a deep pile of leaves or other soft underlayer. They are bulky. They make inferior chairs. And they'll help you precious little on river crossings. These are mostly minor matters. But do not ignore the question of comfort: a body used to beds may sleep poorly for at least a couple of nights if laid out on a thin pad on anything but soft ground. Pads continue to evolve, though, and the comfort problem is receding.

Most early pads were *Ensolite,* a closed-cell foam synthetic that will not soak up water. It comes in thicknesses from ³⁄₁₆ inch up, and sheets can be laminated with any good adhesive. The ⅜-inch sheets seem a good compromise between insulation and comfort on one hand and weight and bulk on the other. The bulk is important. Ensolite compresses very little; that is one reason it insulates so well. When it is new, indentations made in it quickly disappear; but with age it becomes, like people, less resilient. You can buy Ensolite in various hip-length and full-length sizes. Or you can get a large sheet and tailor your own pads. I have two. See illustration. The hip-length pad is for general use under friendly conditions, when weight and/or bulk pose a problem. It folds down fairly well to fit flat inside my packbag. In cold weather I keep my

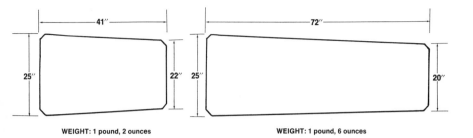

WEIGHT: 1 pound, 2 ounces   WEIGHT: 1 pound, 6 ounces

feet off the ground with whatever is handy—spare clothing, pack, food bag, anything the land will painlessly supply. The full-length pad is for snow country. (Many snow campers prefer to cut down on weight and bulk by carrying only a hip-length pad.) There is just too much of this big pad to fold, so I carry it rolled. It is bulky and a damned nuisance—until the time comes to lie down.

Thermobar is heavier and more expensive than Ensolite but is said to remain flexible down to −40° F. (compared to "below zero" for Ensolite).

You can now buy foam pads half the weight of Ensolite bearing such names as *Superlite, Polylite, Minilite, Microlite* and *Volarfoam*. This foam—also closed-cell and therefore nonabsorbent —comes in thicknesses from ¼ through ½ inch, and costs about the same as Ensolite. But it is less resilient and breaks more easily. Opinion on the severity of these drawbacks is sharply divided. In one store I visited it has replaced Ensolite. In another it disintegrated on the sales floor and has been discontinued. "Terrible stuff," says one backpacker I know. "You can stick your finger through it, especially in snow. Now Ensolite you can manhandle." "I'll never use it again," wrote another after a weekend trial. "It crushed easily, broke a couple of times, and was inordinately slippery." On a short trial I found it adequate but rather uncomfortable and, sure enough, slippery. Such discrepancies in performance may be due to variations in the different brands. The best of them—especially if they can be strengthened somewhat—may at the very least have a role when load is a crucial factor. After all, with what other piece of today's equipment can you cut the weight in half?

Thick *open-cell foam pads* have largely replaced Ensolite and its allies for general backpacking use. I now use one routinely. It compresses easily and therefore sleeps me far more comfortably, especially as the underside is convoluted, like an egg carton. But to achieve the same insulation as Ensolite, open-cell pads must be about three times as thick. They're therefore bulkier, heavier and more expensive. The bulkiness is more apparent than real: stuffed hard into a packbag, these pads compress halfway well. Unfortunately, the open-cell structure means that they soak up water. So they mostly come complete with covers—waterproof nylon underneath, cotton or cotton/Dacron on top to reduce slipping effect and permit perspiration to dissipate. A pleated pocket at the head of the cover may offer holding space for whatever pillow you chose to inject. (For more on pillows, see page 273.) Thomas Black claims that their Kampamat, which looks much like the other open-cell pads, is "practically immune to damp . . . [and] does not normally require a cover."

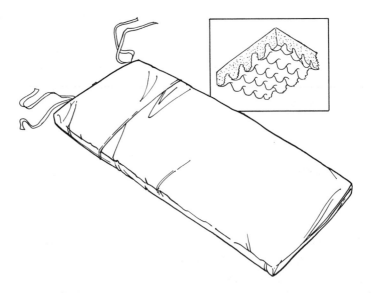

Most of these pads are 2 or 2½ inches thick, but they come as thin as ¾ inch. A typical hip-length version measures 2 by 21 by 38 inches and is said to roll into a bundle 9 by 6 by 20 inches. Complete with cover, it weighs 1 pound 4 ounces, costs $11. The same pad, uncovered: 1 pound; $3. Full length (21 by 76 inches): 2 pounds; $6.25 (though reputed rolled size has blown to 13 by 21).

I find my 2-inch, covered, hip-length Sierra Designs version as warm and trouble-free as Ensolite and almost as comfortable as an air mattress—though it hardly makes as sumptuous a chair, especially on a slope. I still use my mattress under the conditions listed on page 246. And in snow I would probably revert to

Ensolite: it is waterproof; and a full-length Ensolite pad, though bulky, is acceptable, while that hippopotamus of a full-length open-cell job daunts me (and I'm not sure you can buy one with a cover). But for a couple of years now, the covered, hip-length, open-cell pad has been my regular mattress. That may change, though. Foam pads are on the move: one big distributor reports all manner of cunning and not-so-cunning variations on the synthetic theme being better-mousetrapped hopefully and almost weekly at his door.

Finally, a thought from a reader: "Have a treat some time and put a foam pad on top of an air mattress—it's great for snoozing away the hours in luxury."

HAMMOCKS

You can now buy a nylon-net Auca hammock that rolls into what is described as "a pocket-sized ball" and damn near is. It reputedly "supports half a ton." (Extended net: 7 by 20 feet. Effective size: 4 by 6½ feet. Complete with tie ropes and metal tie rings: 8 ounces; $6.)

I find the device passing uncomfortable. But you may not. And I guess it could be useful as a bed if you want to keep cool (air all around you); if the ground, every place, is soaking wet; if you're petrified beyond sleep by the thought of rattlesnakes or scorpions or other things that might go chomp in the night; or if you're an old-style sailor, landlubbering but pining. Other suggested uses: for slinging food and gear from trees, high above the ground; as protection against flood, bears and other invaders; and, with poles, as an emergency stretcher.

SLEEPING BAGS

No modern backpacker would seriously consider carrying blankets, as the old-timer had to. Yet some people still carry old-style, rectangular, open-end sleeping bags, which are in my opinion as outdated compared with mummy bags as blankets are with the old-style bags.

It was natural enough that the first sleeping bags should be the rectangular shape of a normal bed: they obviously evolved from the idea of stitching two or more blankets together. But were it not for the innate conservatism of mankind, virtually all outdoorsmen would surely have switched long ago to mummy bags. They are, after all, designed to contain human forms rather than small upright pianos.

I have heard only two mildly valid objections to mummy bags.

Some outdoor lovers complain that mummy bags do not leave enough room for maneuver. Opportunists may certainly face a problem here. (Though a local Don Juan advises: "You'd be surprised what has been achieved. Where there's a will there's a way.") Those who plan their amatory operations with care should note that it is possible to order two side-zippered mummy bags with zippers on opposite sides that will join convivially together. There are also double mummy bags—lighter, less bulky, warmer and cheaper than two individual bags. At a pinch, one can be carried for solo use.

A few people say they feel uncomfortably confined in mummy bags; and claustrophobics are obviously going to have difficulties. But if you have given mummies a fair trial and just cannot get used to any real or imagined constriction, you do not necessarily have to put up with the inefficiencies of the old rectangular piano-envelope. The catalogues now teem with designs ranging from slim through mesomorphic to downright obese. Take your well-pondered pick. But remember that each size up means marginally greater weight and bulk. Worse, your body has to warm, all night long, a marginally larger volume of contained air. Still, if you really cannot abide a full, form-fitting mummy bag, you will have to settle for one of these bags that compromise between people and pianos.

Perhaps the most clearly defined of the continuum are the tapered but unshaped type called semimummies or barrel bags. A better name for them might—*pace* any liberational girlcott—be "daddy bag." But do not harbor wrong ideas about how mummy bags earned their name. It is simply that any human lying on his or her back in one of these roughly contoured bags, with the tapes on the rounded headflap pulled halfway tight so that only the face shows, is a dead ringer for an Egyptian mummy.

Mummy bags are more efficient than the old-style rectangular envelopes not only because they eliminate a great deal of superfluous material (though that is important) but, even more vitally, because they do a far better job of conserving your body heat.

It is not only that your body has to warm less air. The old-style bag gives your head no protection at all, and your shoulders precious little. (You can wrap the mouth of the bag around them neatly enough at first, and some bags have cloth flaps attached for

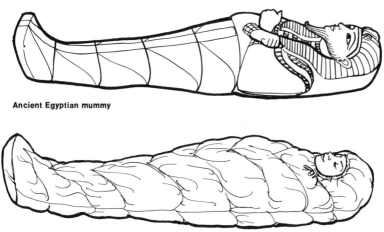

Ancient Egyptian mummy

Modern American mummy

the purpose; but on a cold night you're likely to wake up half an
hour later and find your shoulders exposed to the elements—
though a down-filled hood [page 272] looks as if it may help.)
This head-and-shoulders business is bad enough, but what matters
at least as much is that the bag's wide mouth allows a large though
unmeasurable amount of precious body heat to escape.

A mummy bag eliminates all these faults. It can cover your
head completely in the same all-inclusive envelope that conserves
the heat from the rest of your body. You just pull on the draw
tapes of the hood and tie them in a bow or other simple quick-
release knot—though the tapes of many bags now come fitted
with leather or spring-loaded plastic toggles or some similar secure
but quickly adjustable device. On a cold night you pull until the
opening contracts to a small hole around nose and mouth. If, like
me, you prefer to sleep naked because you wake feeling fresher,
you may sometimes find cold air seeping down through the hole
and moving uncomfortably around bare shoulders. All you need
do is wrap a shirt loosely around your neck. (But see also "Collars,"
page 273.) But this arrangement often holds the warm air in so
well that you soon find you are too hot. To reduce the inside
temperature (whether you are using a neck wrap or not), simply
slacken the hood tapes a little. That will make a lot of difference:
your head dissipates heat more quickly than any other part of the
body (page 414). (You will not question this statement if you
are balding fast into coot country: you'll probably, like me, have
taken to wearing a balaclava at night if there's even a touch of
chill in the night air.) In warm weather you can leave the tapes
undrawn, so that the mouth of the bag remains as open as in

old-style envelopes. In hot weather you can go two steps further—
if you have the right kind of bag.

Mummy bags designed for use only in cold weather (that is,
for polar exploration, high-altitude mountaineering and winter
hunting) do not normally have zipper openings: an uninterrupted
shell is not only the lightest possible design but also conserves
heat the most efficiently. But such a bag, though ideal for its job,
lacks versatility. In anything but chilly weather you are liable to
find yourself sweating even though the mouth of the bag is open—
with no alternative except getting partly or wholly out. A zipper
opening solves the problem. The modification is not pure gain. To
prevent air passage through the closed zipper, it has to be faced
inside with a down-filled draft flap—though some of the latest
bag designs seem to block the zipper zone even more effectively
with a broad extension of the main wall that snugs in tight when
you close the zipper. A 72-inch zipper and its flap also add several ounces to the weight of a bag, and no matter how good the
flap there is bound to be some slight loss in heat-conserving efficiency; but it seems to me that if you expect to operate at times
in temperatures much above freezing the very great gain in versatility is well worth such minor drawbacks. Many bags now have
zippers that open all the way around the foot so that you can
ventilate your feet as well as the rest of you—and can convert
the fully opened bag into a flat though markedly tapered down
cover, very useful for warm nights in the bush and cold ones back
home in bed. Double zippers are another increasingly popular
feature: you can open the zipper from both top and bottom and
so control your temperature much better, head and toe. Provided
these modifications do not significantly increase a bag's heat loss
with zippers closed, they are valuable aids for the almost nightly
game of adjusting your bed to suit different and changing temperatures (pages 282–3).

Sleeping-bag materials

The *fill* is what matters most. It must hold within itself as
many pockets of air as possible, to act as an insulant between the
warmed inner and cold outer air, and for backpacking purposes
the best material is that which does this job most efficiently for
the least weight. But there are subsidiary considerations: com-
pactibility (the packed bag should not be too bulky); fluffability
(the fill must quickly expand to its open, air-trapping state after
being tightly packed); efficiency when wet; even, for a few people,
possible allergic effects.

Reliable comparative insulation values for different materials are hard to come by, but there seems little doubt that the best fill is still good-quality *down* (especially goose down), even though it is useless when wet and may just possibly produce allergies in rare individuals. Much learned and no doubt justified talk goes on about white versus gray goose down (probable ultimate verdict: the difference is either nil or very little), the difficulty of quality control, the adulteration of down with fluff, and even the occasional perfidious sale of mere duck down under a "goose" label. (All new bags must bear a sewn-in label showing government specification of the fill, but classification tends to be general.) Some heretics even deny any practical difference between duck and goose down. It's all very illuminating—but about people rather than down. In the end, poor boobs like you and me frankly have to rely on the good name of the makers. Play it safe, and you're unlikely to go far wrong.

There have long been *synthetic fills,* complete with fancy names and low prices, that I would not touch with a walking staff. Although Dacron has for years been accepted as a satisfactory substitute for down when weight and bulk did not matter, as in car camping, you needed twice as much Dacron as down fill, and it remained only a marginal proposition for backpacking. But Du Pont has now marketed Dacron Fiberfill II, and it seems to represent a distinct advance. The makers claim that it approaches goose down in some properties, surpasses it in others: 1.4 pounds of Fiberfill II afford as much insulation as 1.0 pound of down; it compresses 90 percent as effectively as down and refluffs only marginally less well; it absorbs much less water, and if it gets wet retains its shape and insulating properties far better; it dries out quicker; and it costs considerably less. It can also, in well-made bags, be machine washed and dried, though only with safety in rotating oversize commercial machines (for questionable wisdom of this procedure with down, see page 276). Independent informed opinion, although tending to downgrade some of the performance figures slightly and to maintain that good lightweight winter bags cannot be made with Fiberfill II, tends to agree that it offers distinct possibilities for summer backpacking bags, especially when economics press. After one brief trial (page 267), I'm inclined to go along.

People sometimes say, "Yes, and you don't have to kill any ducks or geese for Fiberfill bags." But this understandable comment won't wash: it seems that all commercial down is stripped from the carcasses of birds raised and killed for food.

Foam bags (and also clothing, page 286) have received

much recent publicity. The sleeping-bag fill consists of two shaped foam sheets—compressible open-cell polyurethane, not closed-cell Ensolite—that is normally 1 inch thick. Both makes presently available come with orthodox Rip-stop nylon shells (attached to the foam at only a few places), and the mummy versions have orthodox shaped hoods with drawstrings that can more or less close it to encase your head.

Printed reports, not all of them partisan, indicate that these bags, though imperfect, offer impressive advantages. They cost about half as much as good down bags. They cushion you full length without pad or air mattress, even on rock and no matter how restlessly you roll. Except along the zipper, if one is fitted, insulation is uniform, with no cold spots, even at pressure points on cold ground. Because the foam does not fold around you as down fill does but instead stands away from your body, you can by leaving the neck and possibly the side zipper open assure good ventilation and therefore a cool sleep in temperatures up to 70° F. At least, that's the theory. And in theory you can also batten down zip and hood and keep thoroughly warm even in sub-zero weather. What's more, the foam is virtually windproof. But your body can "breathe" through it. Though not waterproof, it is markedly water repellent and will keep you dry, unprotected by any roof, in appreciable rain. The foam does not, as has been reported, "soak up water like a sponge." In fact, it is said to act for some time—until most of the cells flood—as a buoyant life preserver. But if a bag gets soaking wet you can wring it out and still sleep warm, even though you are damp; and your body heat will gradually dry the foam out. A foam bag is also rotproof, mildew resistant, non-allergenic, and tough. And you can wash it at home, boisterously: simply lay it in the bathtub and flush it out.

The drawbacks of foam bags are bulk, stiffness, and in some cases, flammability. If you carry your sleeping bag strapped to the packframe (pages 77 and 89), bulk poses no great problem; but if you carry your bag inside the pack, almost any foam bag will be too bulky. The stiffness makes rolling the bag for stuffing in its bag something of a struggle, and can also undo people who habitually sleep in the fetal position. Ordinary polyurethane foam, once lit, apparently blazes merrily—a disturbing thought beside campfires, lamps, or even stoves; but at least one bag maker claims his foam is fire retardant.

That leaves us with the really crucial sleeping bag question: weight vs. warmth. I can find no convincing comparative figures. It would seem, though, that present foam bags are appreciably less efficient than down bags. By what percentage, I cannot guess. But these are early days: foam bags will assuredly continue to evolve. My experience of them is slight, but I would hazard a guess that they may have a real future. For particulars on present models, see page 268.

Jan Sport recently experimented with closed-cell foam sleeping bags—and clothing—but tell me they've given up on it after two of them "almost froze to death last winter."

The *shells* of almost all high-quality sleeping bags are now made of woven nylon. Although less water repellent than the Egyptian cotton it has virtually replaced, and also less pleasing to bare skin, it is rather lighter, appreciably more wind resistant, and wears far better. Nylon linings tend to pick up a peculiar odor from the human body—an odor that I at first attributed to some terrible private uncleanliness, but later found, to my relief, was experienced by other people. It is a very minor problem. Out in the field I rarely notice the odor. If I do, spreading the bag out in sunshine soon dispels it. Back home, I put the bag out to air (page 275) and maybe wash the inside with soap (not detergent) and warm water and then wipe-rinse with clean warm water.

Most nylon shell fabric is Rip-stop—a weave reinforced every quarter inch or less by thicker threads, clearly visible, that indeed stop most rips but can cause puckers across strained cloth. The standard gauge weighs 1.9 ounces a square yard, and its weave just meets government specifications of "down proof." A 1.5-ounce Rip-stop saves roughly 4 ounces per bag and has a finer weave but is more expensive and wears less well. Some firms make their finest bags with nylon taffeta—a plain-weave fabric that lacks the thicker reinforcing threads of Rip-stop but has almost twice as many threads per square inch. It's softer on the skin than Rip-stop, and even more luscious to the buying eye. But it does not have Rip-stop's Madison Avenue word-magic.

The *zipper* must be of superb quality: a failure is sure to be infuriating, likely to be uncomfortable, might even prove fatal. Nylon zippers (or those made from the similar plastic, Delrin) have more or less replaced metal ones on sleeping bags: they run more smoothly and give less trouble. Some of the massive-lugged kind allow you to pluck out any folds of the fabric that may—indeed, will—sometimes get trapped in the zipper as you open or close it. A good coil zipper is said to be even better on this score—and also to trap the fabric less often, to back off more easily if it does, to resist wind and water better, to be less liable to damage, and perhaps to freeze a little less easily. But it must be a *good* coil zipper. So far, there are not many around. And a bad coil is a pain in the bag. The most common failure comes at the junction of spiral and tape, when the join is made with exposed thread and not "burned down" into the tape and so protected from abrasion. In time, coil zippers may well replace the lug type. But for the moment, buy with care.

Any sleeping-bag zipper should have a draw tab inside as well as out.

For around-the-foot and two-way zippers, see page 252; for conjoining two bags, page 250.

Construction

With use, any kind of fill except foam sheet tends to move away from the points of greatest wear, notably from under your butt and shoulders, and unless the bag is properly built you are eventually left with nothing to protect you at vital places except a couple of layers of the thin shell. To minimize this effect, the shell is divided into a series of self-contained tubes that keep the fill from moving very far. Because of a general tendency for fill—and especially down fill—to migrate from the head toward the foot of the bag, transverse tubes work far better than longitudinal ones. It is claimed by at least two makers (and predictably dismissed as poppycock by the rest) that an angled or chevron plan is even more effective than transverse tubing.

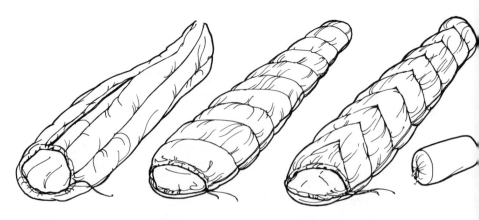

Longitudinal   **Transverse**   **Angled or chevron**

If tubes are made by simply stitching through the inner and outer walls of the shell,

you are obviously left unprotected at the stitch-through points.

If some form of batting is inserted at the stitch-through points (a simple and cheap system),

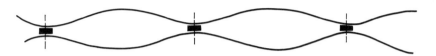

there is some improvement. But not much.

The difficulty can be overcome in two ways:

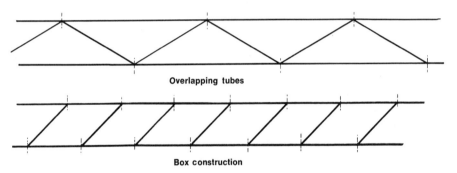

Overlapping tubes

Box construction

All good down sleeping bags now embody one or the other of these last two systems, or some variation.

To conserve weight and reduce the volume of trapped air that must be kept warm, the best mummy bags are now made widest at the shoulders and narrowest at the ankles, then flare out again to accommodate the feet. Until recently, "differential cut" was almost gospel among bag makers, especially for close-fitting bags: they cut inner shells smaller than outer, reputedly creating a "thermos" effect, permitting fill to "loft" freely (page 259) and keeping protruding knees and elbows from pushing tight against the outer shell and so losing virtually all insulation. But some revisionist makers now dismiss the "thermos" effect as applicable only to rigid bodies, and claim that inner and outer shells of the same size not only reduce costs but actually work better: the slack inner shell folds itself warmly around your body. Infighting between opposing factions can wax passionate. The people at Bugaboo Mountaineering, of Monterey, California, which uses both systems in its bags, say that "in all honesty, we feel the difference is almost academic."

Costs

Any good sleeping bag is an expensive item. The reasons: construction and materials. Simple, inefficient, single-tube bags can be stitched, with or without batting, by machine; a bag with box construction or overlapping tubes demands many hours of trained hand labor. Then there is the fill. In just about every case, cost varies in direct proportion to efficiency. A fairly good backpacker's bag filled with Dacron is likely to cost little more than one third of its equivalent with a down filling—though the down bag is likely to be much better made, because the makers know that a backpacker who wants a good bag is unlikely to settle for Dacron. Fiberfill II bags—which may cost only half as much as down equivalents—are a marginal and perhaps changing case. See page 267.

It is difficult to give any very meaningful sample costs without specifying the construction and materials of each bag, for the details are what count. But you can pick up a fancy-looking rectangular bag filled with several pounds of some reassuringly named synthetic material for $20 or less—and can shiver through many a long night regretting it. With luck and patience you may be able to buy a not-very-well-constructed mummy bag filled with 4 pounds of old-style Dacron for about $30—and maybe get away with it. The extra $10–$20 for a good Fiberfill II bag will almost certainly be worth it. Any really well made mummy bag with, say, 2 pounds of high-quality down fill, is going to cost around $80. The very best models, in which nothing has been spared in materials or construction, will run over $100. And there are intermediate models on every rung. (There are also some crummy bags on every rung—including the $100 one.)

As far as cost goes, you must as usual make your own decisions. Mostly, but not invariably, you get what you pay for—in reputable specialist stores or catalogues, anyway; "general" stores and catalogues can be a different matter. I am aware that many people who use their camping equipment only once or twice a year may not feel justified in view of other responsibilities in spending close to $100 on a sleeping bag. All I can say is that when you take a sleeping bag out of your pack as night falls on a frigid, windswept mountain slope, you understand without even having to think about it that dollars are meaningless frivolities.

Choosing a bag that will suit your purposes

The usual criterion for gauging the efficiency of a sleeping bag is the lowest temperature at which it can be used with comfort. "This bag is excellent for use down to 25° F.," the catalogue may proclaim. And the general rule is sometimes promulgated: "For summer use, with temperatures above freezing—2 pounds of high-quality down; for temperatures down to 0° F.—3 pounds."

Such generalizations have their uses. Beginners need guidelines. But there is a serious danger that people may accept the figures uncritically. Many factors other than temperature are involved, and a wide variation in one or more of them can throw out the whole works.

The first and simplest factor is construction. Two and a half pounds of down is not going to keep you warm in freezing temperatures, let alone down to 0° F., if the bag's shell is so constructed that the fill can migrate from the places it is most needed, or if single holding tubes are used, whether stitched with or without batting. You can check the construction of most bags light enough for backpacking by simply holding the shell up to a strong light.

One way sometimes recommended for checking the probable efficiency of both fill and construction is to measure what is called "free loft." Unroll the bag on a flat surface and shake its edges with a gentle fluffing action that allows air to become entrapped in the fill. Then measure the height of the bag at its midsection.

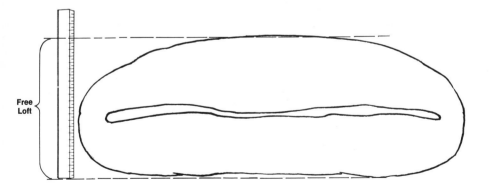

The amount of loft depends on both the quality of the fill and the efficiency of the shell construction (see differential cut, page 257). Unfortunately, different makers seem to measure loft in different ways; but it seems reasonable to assume that, as is claimed, a relationship exists between free loft and heat-retaining efficiency. What the exact relationship is I have no idea, and I'm inclined to doubt if anyone has.

It is important to remember that temperature tolerance figures for sleeping bags are now generally based on the assumption that you sleep in a tent with good insulation under you. A bag that keeps you comfortably warm at 32° F. on a full-length Ensolite pad will obviously not begin to do so if you roll it out on bare ground. And the same kind of difference exists between different roofs—tent, sky or intermediate. The temperature inside a tent may run 10° or 20° higher than outside. Again, much depends on what clothes, if any, you choose to sleep in. My solution to all this is always to carry a pad or air mattress and to take a sleeping bag that I judge will keep me warm under normal conditions for the time and place if I sleep without clothes or roof (except in snow), and will just about do so under the worst recorded conditions if I wear every garment in my pack and protect the bag with every form of shelter I am carrying—whether mere poncho or a Visklamp-and-polyethylene roof or a tent. Nowadays I seem to guess about right. I cannot remember a night in the past ten years when I have slept in a sleeping bag and been at all seriously cold.

A major difficulty with temperature ratings for sleeping bags is that the relationship between air temperature and what the human body feels is a remarkably tenuous one.

First, weather is much more than just temperature. Above all there is wind. A bag that keeps you snugly warm in the open on a calm 10° F. night may be frigidly inadequate at 32° in a 30-mile-an-hour wind. See, importantly, "windchill table," page 414. Humidity comes into it too. Dry air is a poor conductor of heat, damp air a good one. So in wet weather the air pockets held in the fill of your sleeping bag insulate less efficiently than in dry. This is no idle theorizing. Using equipment that has proved entirely adequate in dry weather at freezing and below, you may find yourself decidedly cool in a temperature of 40° after heavy rain has saturated the atmosphere, even though your bag remains dry. It is even possible for a drop in temperature to make you feel warmer. I remember one snow trip when my thermometer readings ranged from 24° to about 34°. At 34°, with the air full of water vapor, the weather was rawly cold. When the temperature fell a few degrees and the moisture that had been ruining the insulation froze, I felt appreciably warmer.

But the most variable factor of all is the individual.

Some people "sleep cold," others "hot." The theory—no more—is that the bigger you are and the more generally active, the warmer you tend to sleep. After camping under various conditions with other people using similar equipment you will probably get a fair idea of your own rating. Or you can tap indoor experience: do bedmates regard you as iceberg or hot water bottle? (This is a purely thermal rating, of course—nothing to do with the factor involved in that libelous dig, "Which would you rather have—an English lover or a hot water bottle?")

Remember, too, that no individual is a neat, predictable, laboratory-conditioned guinea pig. At different times he may react very differently to similar conditions. Tiredness, emotional state and fullness of stomach certainly come into it: a man who sleeps snugly in a given bag at zero when he is rested, secure and well fed is unlikely to do so if he is exhausted, worried stiff about a sick companion, and has not eaten since morning. (Don't overlook the eating business. High blood sugar, available for heat production, will mean you sleep much warmer than on an empty or half-empty stomach. So if you tend to dine early, consider a sugar-rich snack just before you go to sleep.) Again, personal variations may be simply a matter of not being used to the cold or the heat or the elevation or whatever prime stress the situation imposes. Our bodies need time to adapt to radically changed conditions. Two or three days' acclimation may be plenty; but if the change is too abrupt those two or three days can be distressing.

The solution is to get used to a new environment gradually. One word for this process is "training." In Europe during World War II we often used to sleep in the open or in slit trenches in subfreezing weather with nothing over our distinctly temperate-country clothing except a thin anti-gas cape. I don't say we liked it. And I don't say we slept very well. But we slept. We were young, we were fit—and we got used to it (mainly, perhaps, because we had to). By the time I made the California walk I was a dozen years less young; but after a month of walking I was probably just as fit. Yet I remember a night in Death Valley, when I had no sleeping bag, that might make you wonder if I were the same person. That warm desert night I put on all the clothing I had—which was certainly as warm, if not warmer, than British battle dress. Then I wrapped my poncho around me and curled up in a little gully. I had just finished a twenty-mile day, and I promptly fell asleep. But before long I came half awake and tried to pull the poncho more closely around me. There was no wind; nothing that could even be called a breeze. But cool night air was moving slowly and steadily across the desert's surface. Like the tide advancing across mudflats, it penetrated every corner. It passed over me. It passed around me. It passed underneath me. Soon it seemed to be passing through me as well. Minute by minute it sucked my warmth away. No matter how closely I cuddled to the gully wall, the cold bit deeper and deeper. For shapeless hours I fought the sleep battle. Occasionally I dozed. More often I lay three-quarters awake, telling myself I was half asleep. By two o'clock the dozes had become unreal memories. And at 3:30 I got up, packed my bag, and headed north into the darkness.*

Later, I learned that the temperature that night never fell below 58°. This is admittedly an official reading, taken 5 feet off the ground; but a thermometer lying beside my bed just before I left would probably have registered about the same. Now 58° is a very mild temperature. But the reason I felt so bitterly cold is simple: I wasn't used to it. I had been walking through deserts for more than a month, in day temperatures that had risen to a peak of 105°. Recently, the nights had been warm too, and the day I entered Death Valley the minimum temperature had been 80°. But what mattered most was that all this time I had been sleeping in a highly efficient 2½-pounds-of-goose-down mummy bag. Then, two days earlier—wanting to cut my load, and feeling I did not need a bag in night temperatures that seemed likely to fall no lower than 80°—I had given it to two Death Valley rangers who checked my arrival at a spring at the south end of the valley. I arranged to collect the bag when I passed through a ranger station a couple of weeks later. But that same night an unexpected storm sent temperatures plunging. The next night I found myself curling up in that miserable little gully with no protection except my clothes and poncho—and, what was even more important, with my body unprepared for the shock of sleeping in what seemed reasonably warm conditions. (Note, though [pages 413 and 414], that two-thirds of maximum windchill effect occurs when the wind is blowing at only 2 miles an hour.)

Acclimation can also work the other way. One September I spent a week walking along a mountain crest that rarely fell below 12,000 feet and rose at one point to 14,000. In clear autumnal weather the panoramas and the wind were both breathtaking. On the third night my route took me down off the crest for the only time all week, and I camped in a sidecanyon at 10,000 feet. At dusk, my bedside thermometer read a bare degree or two below freezing. Because I was trying out a very efficient experimental mummy bag that had been designed for Alaskan mountaineering (it had 3 pounds of down and no side zipper), I did not bother about shelter, except to camp just below some bushes. The bushes,

* From *The Thousand-Mile Summer,* p. 86.

I felt sure, would blunt the almost inevitable down-canyon wind. To my surprise, no wind blew. Soon, I was far too hot to sleep. I slipped into my wool shirt and a very thick, hooded, down parka, then eased up part way out of the sleeping bag and pulled on long johns and pants. With the sleeping bag pulled loosely up around my midriff and a pair of big leather gauntlets to protect my hands, I immediately fell asleep.

I woke at dawn, glowingly warm, to find the thermometer registering 22°. But what really surprised me was that during the night one glove had come off and my bare hand, lying unprotected on the grass, felt perfectly warm. The circulation in my hands has always been rather poor in cold weather, and I would not have believed it possible for one of them to feel pleasantly warm at 22°—even with the rest of my body glowing and the air very dry. The point is, I think, that I had been up in cold, windy country for two days. I very much doubt if the hand would have felt so warm under identical conditions on the night I left the car.

I hope this long discussion has not led you to believe that temperature ratings have no value as a means of expressing a sleeping bag's efficiency. I repeat: they're useful guidelines. But if uncritically accepted as absolute statements they can be dangerously misleading. Bear that danger steadily in mind when you are making your choice. And ponder ponderously. Buying a sleeping bag is a serious business. If you make a mistake you will have many long, slow, purgatorial hours in which to repent.

Makes and models

Down-filled bags seem to have leveled off onto a design plateau: until someone strikes out on a radically new line, they've gone about as far as they can go. And with the pioneering past, the flood has come. Stores and catalogues now teem with tough, convenient, super-efficient calorie-trappers—thistledown light, gleaming, curvaceous, almost demanding to be stroked. They're superb creations, even works of art. (Art can provoke artiness, though: one maker anoints its shell fabrics with such color labels as Heavy Cobalt Blue and Acapulco Gold.)

As far as design goes, choosing between the best of these bags is largely a matter of deciding which small variation seems to you to offer some advantage. But look closely at draft flaps inside zippers. See if the base of the flap is sewn right through and might cause cold spots. Check that the flap (or the continuation of the main shell) lies snug along the zipper line. If in any doubt on this score (and maybe even if not), take the bag into a strong light, put your head inside, and see whether, with the bag in the kind of position it will assume when full of you, any gaps show. If they do, take the bag back to a dark corner and leave it there.

In general, though, any real differences lie in materials, construction—and workmanship.

For criteria in materials and construction, see pages 252–8.

Meticulous workmanship is the key to toughness and long life in any first-rate backpacking bag, stripped as it must be of every unnecessary gram. It is no assembly-line product. To ensure high quality, at least one maker has each bag "constructed by a single seamstress who is personally responsible for that bag." In the finished bag almost the only outward and visible sign of this inward and invisible pride and expertise is the stitching. Check it carefully. Check it most of all in difficult places, and those that will undergo most strain—such as around the top of the zipper. But I suspect that most backpackers are as poorly qualified to judge the quality of workmanship as I am. (Note that, in spite of earnest consultation with manufacturers, I have not found it possible to describe just how you should rate stitching.) In the end the safest way is probably to check reputation. Don't just shop around; check around. Pay some attention to good reports, great attention to bad ones. Finally you may even want, if you can, to try out the model you favor by borrowing or renting one.

Fortunately—although I do not suggest that there is no difference at any given time between the design, materials and workmanship of the bags made by the best and most reputable firms—you cannot go diabolically wrong if you buy from any of them. The list of such firms is long, and lengthening. It includes such established names as Alpine Designs, Eddie Bauer, Blacks, Gerry, Holubar, Kreeger, Moor and Mountain, North Face, Recreational Equipment Incorporated, Sierra Designs, and The Ski Hut. Newer firms that may well be up and coming include Class 5 and Snow Lion. Eastern Mountain Sports, though they do not make their own bags, deserve mention because they carry an impressive selection and print an interesting comparative table in their catalogue. Quality do-it-yourself kits come from Frostline and also Carikit (of Holubar). Then there are specialist newcomers such as Camp 7 and The Pinnacle, who concentrate on sleeping bags; and Bugaboo Mountaineering and Yeti Enterprises who make custom bags. There are no doubt other names I should have included. And tomorrow there will be more.

Even if we restrict ourselves to this list, we face an awesome array of bags: from slender mummies, through barrelsome daddies, to unabashed biggies; bags with down fill ranging from 1½ to 4 pounds and more; bags built with an eye and a half on cost, and bags built with both eyes riveted on quality. And the catalogues are now beginning to feature "combination" bags: they can be used singly or in combination—one inside the other—and so fit you for an astonishing range of conditions. On the face of it, the idea looks good. I must try one out. But even without such complications, the time is long past when one man, even if he had the time and stupidity, could test and form valid judgments on anything approaching the full sleeping-bag spectrum. Anyway, his opinions would be out of date by tomorrow. As with packs (page 83), the place for such a comprehensive survey is, if anywhere, a magazine.*

So I shall not attempt the task. Instead, I will describe in detail the bag I use under almost all conditions short of the coldest. It is the second of the same model that I have bought, and both have done me proud. But although I have yet to detect anything that looks better, I do not suggest that this model is necessarily the very best of the whole magnificent bunch. I simply do not know. So read what I have to say, please, only as a guide to the features you might care to look for.

The bag is a Trailwise Slimline—a beautifully made, very close-fitting little mummy with Tenaya nylon shell (taffeta, not Rip-stop) differentially cut and chevron baffled. My overfilled medium size—for people up to 6 feet—incorporates 1 pound 14 ounces of white goose down, weighs 3 pounds 3½ ounces, and costs $105. (The same size with standard fill has 4 ounces less down and therefore weighs and costs 4 ounces and $5.50 less. There is also a 4-ounce difference between standard and overfill in the small and large sizes—for people up to 5 feet 8 inches and 6 feet 5 inches respectively. Fill, total weights and costs range from 1 pound 8½ ounces, 2 pounds 12½ ounces, and $96.50 through 2 pounds, 3 pounds 14 ounces, and $112. Colors: blue or orange.) My bag, like all current Slimlines, has a 72-inch double-slider nylon zipper that can be fitted on left or right side and will couple with a mate. The draft flap works. A drawstring pulls the hood around my head to any degree of enwrapment including everything-except-the-nose. The drawstring has leather toggles designed to hold the hood at its chosen position; but they tend to slide, and I tie a slip knot in any kind of battened-down hood position. Some bags now fit positive-locking plastic toggles, and I would guess they are an im-

* Sure enough, *Backpacker* has now published just such a survey (No. 2, summer 1973).

provement. I have not yet used my second Slimline on a very cold, windy night and am not yet sure that the small gap at the foot of the zipper, necessitated by the double-slide feature, is indeed properly draftproofed; but reports are good.

My first Slimline, even when "overfilled," held 4 ounces less down than the present one. But I took it confidently on all trips on which it seemed from weather records that the temperature (here I go already!) was almost certain to go no lower than about 15° F. and was unlikely to fall more than a few degrees below freezing. Around freezing I could normally sleep naked in it with total comfort. And once, wearing a wool shirt and down jacket and long whipcord pants and down booties (page 295) I slept warmly in it, roofed only by stars, at 10,000 feet on a windless night when the temperature fell to 11° F. I was carrying a large plastic sheet and a pair of down pants but used neither. My new Slimline would presumably do at least as well. In hot weather the bag zips almost completely open, leaving only the feet with an envelope, and I can spread it over me, partly or completely, and adjust during the night (page 283). In every respect, I'm entirely satisfied.

Ultralight mummy bags similar to the Slimline now come from many other makers. And if you find that a very slim mummy causes claustrophobia or unacceptable physical constriction, or if you tend to sleep "cold" (as I do not) or to need your bag for colder weather than I do, then you have only to leaf through catalogues until you find, somewhere among the plethora of bags that scale upward in almost insensible gradations of size, shape and fill, one that suits your requirements and fancy. If possible, go and inspect it. Inquire around. Choose. If you know pretty well what you want the difficulty will be not so much finding it as making up your ruddy mind between half a dozen rivals.

Stephenson's Warmlite bags are a slightly special case. The combination "solo-triple" (one person—three bags in one) incorporates such refinements as a shoulder collar (page 273) and double zippers in place of a draft flap, and also makes two radical departures from current standard design: the bottom of the bag is a large, down-free pocket into which fits a shaped, removable pad of 1½- or 2-inch, open-cell polyurethane foam (page 247), replaceable by Ensolite (page 246) if bulk looms too large; and a waterproof, aluminized coating is sprayed on the inner surface of the thicker of the two upper layers of the bag (both layers zip off all around and can therefore be used alternatively or together— giving you the "three bags in one"). The bag is beautifully made, and when I first saw one I was impressed—though suspicious of so much complex cunning in a Murphy-bound field. A five-day test up to 12,000 feet and down to a windless 16° F. confirmed my suspicions. In a tent, wearing little or no clothing, I found that with the waterproof inner surface above me I was far too hot, soon began to sweat, and failed to adjust the bag's various openings to an all-around comfort level. I normally lie first on one side, then the other, moving the whole bag with me and thereby keeping an opened zipper to my front; but because the Warmlite's built-in pad could not move with me, any opened zipper was, in one position, bound to run close and cold to my curved back. I experienced other minor difficulties too (though the makers assured me with heat that I misused the bag) and I reluctantly came to the conclusion that this was a sad case of overengineering, and that I would stick with simplicity: in backpacking, even more than in most walks of life, it is the key to happiness. But if you revel in gadgetry and also sleep cold—and therefore do not sweat much—and are entranced at the prospect of a bag in which someone was too hot, almost naked, at 16° F., then you know where to look. (Solo-triple [standard size, for 6 foot 1 inch sleeper]. Fill: 2.34 pounds. Foam pads: 1½-inch, 1 pound 3 ounces; 2-inch, 1 pound 10 ounces. Cost, with pad: $140. Standard color: "rich royal blue.")

Second-generation Dacron (*Fiberfill II*) *bags.* For general characteristics, see page 253. My experience is presently limited to four nights in a Coleman model 8125–600—a tapered semi-mummy (barrel or daddy) bag, 33 by 85 inches, with full-length zipper and 3 pounds of fill; "rated for 25°–45° F." Total weight: 4½ pounds. Cost: $38. Note that it weighs one third more than my Slimline (page 265) but is only about one third the price.

I found the bag slightly but not objectionably bulky. And in the main it passed a very easy test. On the coolest of the four nights, ground temperature was 40° F. at 8:00 P.M., 37° at 5:00 A.M. Humidity seemed high but there was little or no wind. I slept on my 2-inch open-cell foam pad (page 248), and because rain threatened I put up a Visqueen tarp roof (page 228). Wearing undershorts, and an unbuttoned Viyella shirt (page 289) to draft-proof my shoulders, I was comfortably warm.

But even four days' use revealed weaknesses in materials and workmanship. Before I left home, my stuff bag split along a seam. And one line of cross-stitching on the main shell has now failed. Because the stitching merely holds continuous sheets of Fiberfill in place, such failure is much less serious than with down; but it hardly inspires confidence. Worse, the zipper tape has already parted from the shell, up near the head. I also found that the zipper kept sliding down. Finally, the draft flaps—which I was able to give no trial in wind or cutting cold—seem inadequate. They are mere ⅞-inch extensions of the fill, protruding from each side and meeting directly over the zipper. Even in their present new and stiff condition, they fail my head-in-the-sack test (pages 263–4).

Clearly, none of these weaknesses is due to Fiberfill II itself. But it struck me at the time that they may reflect a bind inherent in its use in lightweight bags: a fill with cheapness as a prime advantage seems to demand an inexpensive shell; but a lightweight bag strong enough to stand up to even normal use currently seems to demand that very expensive commodity, meticulous hand-workmanship.

I am glad to report, though, that I seem to have been wrong. Several makers of high-quality bags, including North Face, Sierra Designs, and Yeti, now offer Fiberfill II models. And Paul Petzoldt's Wilderness Equipment has apparently been using Dacron 88 since 1965, and Fiberfill II since it appeared. The price range for all these bags is about $60–$80. Their shell quality should be good, the results interesting.

Foam bags designed for backpackers currently come from two makers—Trail Tech and Ocaté. I have yet to see a Trail Tech bag, but all of them feature foam that has been treated to make it fire retardant. (See general discussion of foam fill, page 253.)

After only three untesting test nights with an Ocaté bag I cannot say much. But there is, at the very least, something in the claim that you can use it comfortably even in high temperatures. One night, it was 60° F. when I lay down, dog-tired—and 62° when I resurfaced after 11 hours' pretty sound sleep. All night the bag was zippered at least halfway, but I felt only very slightly too warm. And I sleep hot: in even a very light down bag I would under such conditions have sweated blood.

I'm still worried by the tendency of foam bags to stand away from your body and so increase the volume of air that has to be warmed. And I dislike even more the gap that tends to open up at your neck, even with the hood pulled tight. But experiment may show that these problems are soluble. Certainly, the adjustable crisscross nylon cord fitting on Ocaté bags helps in pulling the foam closer around you:

This is the 6-foot 2-inch "Everest" Ocaté bag: 5 pounds 10 ounces; $64. The Trail Tech "Omni Temp" Mummy style Model 602 (for large adults up to 6 feet 3 inches) weighs 5 pounds, costs $52. Remember, in considering weights for foam bags, that with them you do not normally need to carry a foam pad or air mattress.

Oddments

"Bag One" is the name Kreeger of New York gives a creation with an inner of "perforated space age material" that "keeps you warm by reflected heat." Designed for mild weather or as a performance-improving liner for a regular bag, it weighs only 1 pound 12 ounces, costs $27.95 (regular, to 6 feet) or $30.50 (extra large, to 6 feet 6 inches). And now you know as much as I do.

Finally there are "temporary bags," made of paper or the like, with varying degrees of usefulness and uselessness and, sadly, of disposability.

Double mummy bags

See page 250. Said to be warmer for two than equivalent solo bags. Many makers now offer them.

Children's sleeping bags

These bags are usually made of cheaper materials than full-size ones, and are more simply constructed, no doubt on the reasonable assumption that if you are going to invest in a high-quality bag you are not going to buy something your children will grow out of within a year or two.

Yet the lower-quality children's bags apparently sell very well. One possible reason is that children tend to sleep warmer than adults. In theory, they should sleep colder: their smaller bodies, with a wider surface-to-volume ratio, should lose heat faster. But to balance this factor, their metabolism tends to operate at a higher rate. What happens in practice is a matter of opinion, but a limited poll I conducted among friends tended to support the opinion of one mother of five children ranging from four to thirteen years old, whose family seems to spend half its young life camping or cabining in the mountains. "Yes," said this seasoned troop leader, "I'd say there may well be something to the sleeping-warmer business—certainly when the kids are young and covered in puppy fat. I've found our four-year-old almost out of his bag on quite cold nights, still fast asleep. Once children start beanstalking up into their teens, though, it's rather different. It could easily be that at that stringy stage they tend to sleep somewhat colder than adults."

If you want a really warm bag for a child, one answer is a good small adult bag: it should last well beyond childhood. But some quality models specifically for children have now appeared. Frostline—the do-it-yourself-kit people in Boulder—offer an Add-on bag for "the growing years." The basic bag will sleep a child up to four feet tall, and 12-inch sections can be sewn on as needed (Kit for basic bag: 2 pounds 10 ounces; $29.95. Each add-on section: 7 ounces; $5.95):

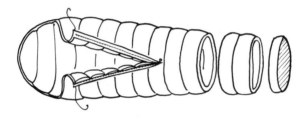

Carikit—the do-it-yourself-kit branch of Holubar—go what may be one better. Stage 1 of their Inchworm bag is a full 5-foot 10-inch shell with two lower section compartments closed off and stored inside by drawcords. Initially, you do not fill these compartments with down. And you have a bag 36 inches long. As the need arises, you buy down "packettes" for Stage 2 (52-inch bag) and Stage 3 (the full 70 inches), and activate the compartments. (Kit for basic bag: 3 pounds 6 ounces; $44.95. Down packettes for Stage 2: 7 ounces; $8. For Stage 3: 10 ounces; $9.)

The Pinnacle of Mountain View, California, now make a Mini Mummy that is the lower two-thirds of their regular slim mummy with hood added, and weighs only 1 pound 11 ounces ($39). Suitable for children up to 5 feet tall, it can double as adult bivouac bag or as a liner for a full-size bag. North Face, The Ski Hut, and Holubar make similar but rather heavier and more expensive models. Such bags are, in fact, almost indistinguishable from another solution to the children's sleeping-bag problem:

The footsack, or elephant's foot.

Essentially, a footsack is the bottom half of a slim mummy bag with a drawstring at the top. Good models are cut higher in the rear than in front—to protect the sensitive small of your back when you are lying down and also to keep it covered in the pull-apart sitting position. A footsack is designed as an emergency bag for use with a good down-filled parka (on occasions when you do not plan to sleep out but just might have to) or as a straight sub-stitute for a bag (when you really have to cut down the weight and think you can trust the weather). Don't forget that you need warm gloves with this rig—unless, like one friend of mine, you can sleep comfortably all night with hands deep inside the bag in a fig-leaf position.

A first-rate footsack, with baffled nylon shell and a pound of goose-down fill, weighs and costs around 1¾ pounds and $60.

A high-quality footsack—say 50 inches long in front and 60 inches in back—makes an excellent mummy bag for a child up to about 4 feet 2 inches tall. Two factors make this a popular choice for a really warm child's bag. The drawstring pulls the top of the sack into a hood just like that on an ordinary mummy bag. And parents can help justify the expense by reminding themselves that they are buying something that might come in useful later on— for both generations.

SUBSTITUTES AND SUPPLEMENTS
FOR SLEEPING BAGS

Convertible down pants/footsack

Holubar makes down pants that zip the full length of each leg and have foot extensions that snap up inside when not in use. You can zip the legs together and join the foot extensions to them with a Velcro strip (footnote, page 84) and so form a reputedly draft-free footsack (2 pounds 8 ounces; $80).

Cagoule-and-footsack bivouac

The knee-length parka or cagoule (page 299) is designed for use as a bivouac—either alone (when you draw your knees up inside it) or with a companion footsack.

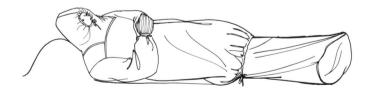

The idea is presumably to use the combination when nights are really warm, but there are few climates I would trust. As an emergency bivouac the rig looks ideal. But "emergency bivouac"

means sleeping out when you do not expect to—and therefore are unlikely to be carrying equipment for the job. Still, it is possible to imagine certain situations in which the complete rig might be worth packing along. Anyway, the world would be poorer without it. It is one of those intriguing items that make catalogue-browsing the dreamy, time-wasting, utterly delightful pursuit it is.

Packbag as emergency footsack

See page 91.

Sleeping-bag covers

You can buy covers of various designs to sheathe your bag. Mostly made of woven nylon, they come with and without side zippers, and waterproofed all around or waterproofed below but "breathing" above. It is claimed that they will increase insulation ("lowers temperature rating by 10 degrees"); ward off wind and light snow, even rain; replace groundsheet and even tarp; reduce abrasion and soiling of bag shell; keep bag and foam pad together —sometimes with a special pad pocket—in case you're a restless sleeper; provide a thin cover for hot weather, when you want to lie on top of your bag; "give you somewhere to put your clothes"; make an emergency stretcher; and act as a carryall "net" for all your gear when you want to haul it up out of bear reach. Maybe. A typical cover: 1 pound; $15.

Sleeping-bag liners

Removable, washable liners of Rip-stop, cotton, cotton-polyester, or cotton flannel will keep your bag clean, add a modicum of warmth, give you a choice of materials next to the skin, convolute like crazy (I hear) unless attached to the bag, increase your load by 6 or 7 ounces, and lighten your pocket by as much as $10 or even $15.

Down-filled hood

Said to be a useful supplement for any sleeping bag in extreme cold or wind. An intriguing item that looks as if it might almost convert a rectangular sleeping bag into an efficient unit, especially if there is some kind of drawstring at the mouth of the bag (6 ounces; $8). Certainly useful for people who feel claustrophobic in anything less spacious than an old-fashioned rectangular bag.

But it is not always easy to find a catalogue that lists one: they pop in and out.

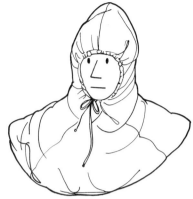

I sometimes wonder if a hooded down jacket does not do an equally good job—as well as being a darned sight more generally useful at no huge extra weight.

Collars

Some makers—including Holubar, Warmlite, Bugaboo, and Frostline—now incorporate into their bags, or offer as extras, on request, down-filled collars, attached to the inner shell, that can be pulled snug around the shoulders—usually by a drawstring, with Velcro fastener at the zipper opening—and in cold weather will clearly do a better job than a loosely wrapped shirt (page 251). Collars, other than on do-it-yourself kits such as Frostline, can normally be fitted to bags only by the maker. Whether they impede ventilation in hot weather, even if left open, I do not know; but I would guess that they may, at least in cold-weather bags, be a coming thing.

Pillows

Some people do not mind sleeping without a pillow; others even prefer it that way. Unless I am too tired to notice, I find it disconcerting not to have one. Minor back trouble has recently forced me to carry, almost always, a specially shaped foam pillow (my "security pillow"), but I still make do occasionally with older, more orthodox devices. For me, the little air mattress with pillow (page 244) is ideal. With an Ensolite pad I normally just roll up my long pants or down jacket or both and stuff them under my head. Sometimes I bolster the clothing with a plastic canteen or the day's-ration food bag. If the night is cold enough to make me wear all the clothes I have brought, I may use a canteen alone. This arrangement helps keep the canteen unfrozen; and because I am sure to be wearing my balaclava helmet and perhaps a hooded parka as well, it is tolerably comfortable. Or I may pad the canteen with the packbag or ration bag—making sure that soft food such as cereal is directly under my head. On sand or other loose soil the simplest and most comfortable pillow is a roughly banked-up guillotine block. No matter how much you want a soft pillow, there are precious few places left in which it is justifiable to use bough tips or moss or any natural material. Occasionally, manna falls. One reader reports that when, as member of a large party, he was the bearer of an inflatable plastic arm splint, he found it made "a luxurious pillow."

Stuff bags

For many years I used to stuff my sleeping bag loose into the pack or even tie it unprotected onto the outside. But I am now a convert to stuff bags. They are normally cylindrical affairs with drawcord closures, and they protect your bag—and down clothing and other items too—from unnecessary wear and tear and also from rain. If you're at all worried about the bag's getting wet, line its stuff bag with a large plastic bag (page 187), filched from almost any other use.

Stuff bags are often said to make packing easier because they reduce the bulk of whatever goes into them. I am skeptical. If your pack is stuffed tight, then any soft article is going to be compressed to its limit and also forced every which way to fill odd corners. A tightly wadded stuff bag cannot be so forced, and may therefore leave the odd corners empty. So I always try to buy a stuff bag big enough to take its load with room to spare, leaving it reasonably soft, malleable and odd-corner-fitting. There is another good reason for using oversize stuff bags: it does not matter much if you have to struggle a bit to persuade a mummy into its bag in a warm room back home; but it matters like hell—very much like hell—when you try to do so in a small tent, or in an icy wind, or even just when time presses. Still, a tightly packed bag is probably more resistant to rain and therefore might be better for people who carry sleeping bags outside their packs.

Most stuff bags are made of waterproofed woven nylon. (Typical range: 7 inches diameter by 18 inches long, 1¼ ounces, $2; through 11 inches diameter by 21 inches long, 3¼ ounces, $3.25.)

Carrying your sleeping bag: strapped on
frame or stuffed inside packbag?

See page 77.

CARE OF SLEEPING BAGS

Any sleeping bag should be aired after use. A nylon-shelled one
must be (page 255). Just open the bag and leave it spread out,
preferably up off the ground. With nylon bags, two or three days
is not too long. Outdoor airing, especially in sunshine, seems best.
Purists will warn you that sunlight is nylon's archenemy. Technically, they may be right. But life is too bloody short.

It is best not to store a bag for long periods compressed in its
stuff bag. Lay it out flat, hang in a closet, or roll loosely.

Normally, cleaning should amount to no more than sponging
lining and cover with a mild soap (not detergent) and tepid water.
Rinse, then dry thoroughly. If a bag becomes so soiled that it
demands more stringent cleaning, one way is washing. Take the
bag to reputable launderers, accustomed to down clothing, and have
them wash it in soap or mild detergent and then tumble dry.

An alternative is dry cleaning. The experts' advice on dry
cleaning or not dry cleaning your bag seems to change about as
often as skirt lengths. So I shall stick with my first edition advice
(though there does seem to be a tendency for more and more
makers to recommend dry cleaning at reputable cleaners).

Ever since one favorite old bag of mine lost a great deal of
its virtue after two or three widely spaced visits to the cleaners, I
have been inclined to avoid commercial cleaning. But so that I
should not pass on pure hunch, I made careful inquiries before writing this section. The manager of one dry-cleaning plant, who owns
both down and Dacron sleeping bags (the latter for car camping),
advised me that only dry cleaning will do a really satisfactory job
on badly soiled shells. And Dacron fill, he said, remains unaffected
by cleaning. No harm comes to down if the solvents used are
petroleum based and are not chlorinated hydrocarbons (which,
though excellent for most jobs, are just too efficient at removing
greases and therefore remove essential oils from the down). It
seems that only small cleaning firms use chlorinated hydrocarbon
solvents; the process is too expensive for big plants. So have your
bag cleaned, if at all, at a big plant. But make local inquiries first;

a good mountain shop should know which local firms do a re-strained but effective job on sleeping bags.

One reason it is sometimes advisable to have a bag cleaned is that in time the down begins to mat. Clumps of it coagulate, and large areas in each baffle tube are left empty. Dry cleaning certainly seems to redistribute the down effectively. But the plant manager I quoted (and he can hardly be accused of commercial bias in this opinion) maintained that the redistribution was purely the result of mechanical tumbling in the dryer. In other words, the way to redistribute the down in your bag, especially if it has been soaked, is to put it in the tumble dryer at low heat—back home or at a laundromat. It is rumored that a pair of sneakers thrown in with the bag will help pound clogged down apart; and that the rubber/nylon combination helps generate static electricity needed to loft the down fully.

Warning: almost any kind of patch will come off a bag during dry cleaning, and fill will escape. So if your bag has been patched, have the plant wash rather than clean it. Or you can wash the bag at home. Some people advise doing the job in a bathtub with tepid soapy water, provided you rinse carefully and then dry the bag outdoors—fluffing the down as it dries out—or in a tumble dryer, at low heat, with or without a sneakers assist. But you must not manhandle the bag: soaked, it is so heavy that its own weight can tear the internal baffles. Other people say you can safely wash down bags in tumble (though not top loading) washers; but, they mutter darkly, avoid washing products with enzymes.

All these washing instructions apply equally to down clothing. For washing Dacron and foam bags, see pages 253 and 254.

Repairing

Like it or not, small cuts and burns happen. Rip-stop tape is the remedy. It used to be that the adhesive was enough on its own, but this no longer seems to be so. Certainly not for permanent patches. My opinion, based on many years patching of one ancient cotton covered bag, is apparently not purely attributable to crabbed age: I recently forced one experienced salesman to admit that, owing to the slipperiness of the newest Rip-stop, the stuff really does not adhere the way it used to. The solution: sew permanent patches around all edges.

Pensioning off

There comes a time—no matter how much cleaning or tumble-drying or self-deceiving you do—when a patched and trusted old bag is no longer sure to give you a warm sleep anywhere within its temperature range. There is only one remedy. But it is always a sad moment when another old friend bites the Goodwill.

CHOOSING AND PREPARING A BEDROOM

Level bedsites

There are few simpler ways of ensuring a bad night's sleep than choosing a bed that slopes. If the slope is sideways you spend the night in a thinly conscious hassle with gravity; and you wake, tired and aching, to find yourself still pressing fiercely on the downslope with arms and knees and a battery of assistant muscles. If the slope is from feet to head you don't go to sleep at all. No matter how gentle the incline (and it is sure to be gentle, or you would never have overlooked it) you discover the horrible truth the moment you lie down. The feeling that all the blood is going to rush to your head is so disturbing that after a few feeble attempts at telling yourself that it's all imagination you gruntle up and switch head and feet.

If you can't possibly avoid a sloping bed, sleep with your feet downhill. That way, if the slope is not too severe, you spend a passably comfortable night: you may come half awake occasionally to find yourself a yard and a half downhill from pillow and ground-sheet, and have to do an undignified wriggle back uphill; but you wake with nothing worse than mildly aching leg muscles.

Do everything you can, then, to organize a level bed. I routinely check by lying full length on the bare ground (or on a groundsheet if it's wet), adjusting to the most comfortable position, and then lying still long enough to make sure my head is not too blood-collecting low. If you have to camp on generally sloping ground, try to do so on a trail or just above a tree or in some other place where there is a ready-made level platform. Or go to considerable pains to make a platform. Often, you can find a place with soil loose enough to kick away with your heels. You can always do so on talus. But in heavily used country you must these days accept a bedsite that needs leveling only if the construction work will do no damage to the ground and can be completely repaired before you leave. Sand, talus and a deep leaf-carpet qualify. Grass like hell does not: leveling it means removing the roots, and therefore killing it.

Choice of under-bed material

Grass is one of the poorer choices for a bedsite, anyway. Except when very long, it cushions you precious little; and even aside from the unacceptable scarring, it is difficult to contour to fit your form ("Improving a bedsite," page 281). An air mattress or thick foam pad takes the sting out of loose gravel or talus, and they are far easier to contour. Bare earth is often as easy, and appreciably softer. Sand rates higher still. A deep carpet of leaves, and especially of pine needles, offers the ultimate luxury in warmth and comfort—and also a monumental fire hazard. Leaves should never be chosen if you intend to light a fire. Even with a stove you must clear a hearth to bare soil—and still exercise meticulous care.

Shelter from wind

The level bed business is so important that when I camp at nightfall and expect to move on again first thing in the morning, it is often the only campsite feature I worry about. In fair weather, that is. But when the wind rises to gale force or feels like a disembodied iceberg, then shelter from wind supplants level ground as the one thing you absolutely must have.

Unless you have both a tent and confidence that you can erect it in the teeth of the gale, go to great pains to find natural shelter. I tend to do so anyway. It's much simpler, and often warmer. A clump of trees or bushes will deflect the full fury of any wind. And even in exposed places, quite minor irregularities, if themselves total windbreaks, make remarkably good refuges. I have spent comfortable nights, well sheltered from icy gales, in the troughs of shallow gullies, behind low walls, even tucked in close to a cattle trough. But the best hideout of all is an overhanging rockledge. (A full-fledged cave protects you better, of course; but caves tend to be both rare and unappetizing.) Even a very shallow ledge, provided it's on the lee side of a hill or rockpile, can be a snug place. The rock retains much of its daytime warmth, and after one comfortable night in such a place you understand why cold-blooded rattlesnakes like to live among rocks. The floor of the ledge is rarely as level as you would like it to be, but there are often small rocks lying around for a rough construction job. Such construction can rarely be justified in heavily used country. Even less can the still-general practice of camping in an unprotected place and then collecting boulders and building a wall or, sometimes, an embryo cabin.

Remember, by the way, that winds often die at dusk, then revive from a different quarter. Desert winds fairly consistently blow up canyons by day, down them (and cold) at night. The night downwind is also common on most mountains.

Shelter from rain

Rockledges make good shelters from rain too—and caves are even better. But beware of shallow caves in thunderstorms (page 415). Hollow tree trunks are traditional wilderness shelters, but to be honest I have never tried one. In rain I just tend to put up whatever roof I've brought along. Naturally I choose the most sheltered site I can find.

Shelter from snow

In heavy and prolonged snowstorms, an obvious campsite in the lee of a cliff or steep rise may just possibly be dangerous: drifting snow could bury your tent while you sleep. At least, so they say.

"They" also say that properly constructed snow caves are very warm and tolerably comfortable (footnote, page 208). I'm afraid my experience is zero.

Cold bedrooms

Meadows, especially when cradled in hollows, collect not only cold but damp air. They're delightful places to camp, though and —provided human usage is light (page 222)—should not necessarily be avoided. A hillock or rockslab a few feet above the meadow itself is often enough to ward off the worst of the cold, improve the view—and spare the fragile grass.

Riverbanks also tend to be damp and therefore cold places— and to provide richly rewarding campsites. But see page 387.

Siting your bedroom to catch—
or avoid—the morning sun

It can occasionally be important that your bed should catch the first rays of morning sunshine. Sometimes only the sun's warmth will make a bitter world habitable. Sometimes you go to sleep without a roof—because you are tired or lazy or just because you like it that way—expecting heavy dew during the night but knowing that morning sunshine will quickly dry it off and save you packing along pounds of water. Or it may be that a tent needs drying. And on days on which you are planning not to move camp, or to move late, it is always more pleasant to start the day in sunshine. At least, almost always. In deserts, in summer, you will want to avoid the sun. And some people prefer to avoid it, especially if they want to sleep late, in all but icebergial weather.

Anyway, whatever your reason for wanting to know where the sun will rise, the solution is simple: on the first day of the trip—or before you start, if you can remember it—measure with your compass the exact bearing on which the sun rises over a flat horizon. Pencil the bearing on the back of the compass. Then, at any night camp, all you have to do is take out the compass, sight along the correct bearing, make due allowance for close or distant heightening of the horizon, and site your camp in the right place. With a little experience you can prophesy accurately enough to make use of even narrow gaps in trees.

Minor factors in choosing a campsite

Your criteria for a good campsite will vary a lot with the kind of country, your probable length of stay, and your personal preferences. For the first day or two of a trip, especially in strange country, you may find yourself—as I did during *The Thousand-Mile Summer*—circling around a promising area like a dog stirred by ancestral memories. But before long you are once more recognizing a good site at a glance: not only a good, flat bedsite with reasonable protection from wind but also (if you want a fire) plenty of firewood and (where there's water) a bathroom.

Don't underrate the importance of a good bathroom. There is a yawning gap between a camp with running bedside water (where you can without effort scoop out drinking water, wash, wash up, and wash your feet) and a place in which you have to crash through tangled undergrowth and yards of sucking swamp to reach a tepid outpuddle of a river. By comparison, the difference between hotel rooms with and without a private bath is so much fiddle-faddle. Naturally, I'm speaking now of large lakes or rivers in genuinely remote places. In most of today's teeming wildernesses it's rarely possible to act with so little consideration for fellow-travelers (page 308).

You earn, by the way, an oddly satisfying bonus if you succeed in choosing a memorable camp from the map—as you can sometimes do once you grow used to a certain kind of country. If you play the percentages and the hunches and manage to get everything right—level bed, shelter from wind, firewood, water, morning sunshine, pleasing surroundings, even (and this is what makes a camp truly memorable) the stimulation or mystery or magic that can come from an isthmus of woodland or an oddly shaped hillock or a quietly gurgling backwater—if you get all these right, you experience the same slightly surprised pleasure as from finding that your checkbook total tallies with the bank statement.

Improving a bedsite

When I lie down to check the levelness of a bedsite, as I routinely do (page 277), I naturally discover any bumps, rocks and other body prodders. If I'm sleeping with nothing except a groundsheet between sleeping bag and ground (which nowadays is almost never) I work with bare hands or a stick or even my toilet trowel (page 386) until everything is smooth. If I'm carrying a thin Ensolite pad, I still exercise considerable care; with a thick foam pad, a good deal less; and with an air mattress, precious little.

Provided the country and the under-bed material permit (page 277), it often makes sense to contour a bedsite to fit your form—certainly if there'll be no cushion between bag and ground; probably with an Ensolite pad; possibly even with a thick pad or air mattress. The idea is to emulate a waterbed by digging or merely boot-scratching a shallow depression for your shoulders and a rather deeper one for your butt. Excavated material builds a pillow, or raises the legs a trifle. Determine your needs by trowel and error.

THE BEDROOM IN ACTION

We examined most details of how the bedroom operates in our "Sample day in the kitchen" (pages 190–3 and 196–8). For modifications under various kinds of roof, see their separate subheadings in this chapter. But several points remain unmade:

Keeping tabs on the flashlight

After dark, you must always know exactly where the flashlight is. Otherwise, chaos. My flashlight spends the night in an easy-to-feel position in one bedside boot. And I have a rule that when it is in intermittent use, such as before and during dinner, I never let go my grasp on it without putting it in the pocket designated for the night (*which* pocket depends on what I'm wearing). This rule is so strict that I rarely break it more than three or four times a night.

Come to think of it, it might be worth tying the flashlight to a loop of nylon cord large enough to slip over your head. (Later:

it *is* worth it. The new Mallory flashlight [page 312] has a small hole in its case, and if you thread a very thin nylon cord through it, tie the cord into a small loop, and use this loop to hold a big, neck-encircling loop of ordinary nylon cord, you may just find that your flashlight-losing days are over. See also "Dental floss," page 370.)

For more on flashlights, including head-strap models, see pages 312–17.

For candle lanterns and even fancier illumination, see pages 318 and 319.

Fluffing up the sleeping bag

Although I am told that many people fail to do so, it seems only common sense that before you get into bed at night you should always shake the sleeping bag by the edges and so fluff up the down and fill it with the air pockets that actually keep you warm. At this point in the first edition of this book, I wrote: "One of these nights I must try it out." I'm happy to report that the act of writing that sentence has prodded me into doing the job fairly often. It's good to know, firsthand, that the book has taught somebody something.

Adjusting to suit the night

With experience (and I guess there's no other way) you can usually gauge pretty accurately how much clothing, if any, you will need to wear in your sleeping bag. Or in warmer weather, how tightly you need pull the hood drawstrings, and whether you should unzip the bag part way. But you will never get so good that you always hit the nail dead center.

In general, be a pessimist: if in doubt, wear that extra layer of clothing, and pull the drawstrings tight. Sleeping too hot is uncomfortable; but sleeping cold is murder. In any case, the night will usually, though not always, get progressively colder (the coldest time typically comes either at dawn, or even more often, in the last few minutes before sunrise).

But the main reason you do better by deliberately looking on the bleak side is that boosting insulation is a major operation, reducing it a very simple one. When you wake up uncomfortably hot (and you will do so occasionally unless you consistently under-insulate, and then God help you) all you need do is slacken off the drawstrings. At least, that usually lets out enough heat, especially if you flap the bag in a bellows effect a couple of times to introduce some cold air. But if you find that to establish the right balance you have to slacken the drawstrings until there is a gaping hole around your head, you will probably find that the upper part of your body gets too cold and the lower part stays too hot. If you are wearing heavy clothes, take off one layer. (A minor disadvantage of a close-fitting bag like the Slimline is that putting on or taking off socks and pants "indoors" is a struggle. But it can be done. At least, taking them off can.) If you wake to find yourself too hot when you're wearing few or no clothes (which will mean that outside air temperatures are not too barbarously low) feel for the inside tab of the zipper and slide it part way or all the way down. A two-way zipper, now becoming almost standard, allows you to open up a breathing hole at your calves as well. Once again, only experience will tell you how far to go, and also how to tuck the opening under you, or to wriggle it around on top, or away from the wind, or whatever else achieves the balance you want. If you unzip, you may well have to rezip as the night grows colder, and/or to tighten the drawstrings; but you soon learn to do so without coming more than about one-eighth awake.

On really hot nights, the only comfortable way to use the bag may be as a cover—fully unzipped and just spread out loosely over your body. At such times it may be most comfortable to wear a shirt to keep your shoulders warm, and to tuck your feet part way into the foot of the bag. A little to my surprise, I find myself sleeping this way more and more often on windless nights when the temperature is over about 40° F. One advantage of using the bag instead of wearing a couple of layers of clothing is that as the night grows colder (which it mostly will) you can compensate, without coming one eighth awake, by pulling the edges of the outspread bag a little more firmly around you.

For use of bag covers in warm weather, see page 272.

Dealing with a full bladder at night

See page 388.

Getting to sleep

An experienced outdoorsman has suggested that I include in this chapter "the ritual of getting to sleep in a bag," and as he is my editor I suppose I had better attempt the task.

My technique is to lie down, close my eyes, and go to sleep.

Clothes Closet

The best dress for walking is nakedness. But our sad though fascinating world rarely offers the right and necessary combination of weather and privacy, and even when it does the Utopia never seems to last for very long. So you always, dammit, have to worry about clothes.

The most sensible way to set about deciding what clothing to take on a trip and what to leave behind is to consult weather statistics (page 24) and your own experience and so arrive at an estimate of the most miserable conditions of temperature, wind, exposure, humidity and precipitation that you can reasonably expect to suffer. The worst conditions recorded in, say, twenty years. Then, all you have to do is judge what you need take to keep you warm under daytime conditions when you are wearing everything and doing something, or at least are only sitting down and doing nothing for short intervals. If you hit this target around about center, you can feel reasonably sure that at night, with shelter and sleeping bags selected to match, you will sleep tolerably warm under the bitterest conditions possible if you wrap yourself up in every stitch of clothing you have brought along. During the day, if you stop doing anything for any length of time and begin to feel cold, or even to think that you might soon feel cold, you simply pupate inside the sleeping bag.

This kind of calculation involves not so much a precise balancing of conditions and clothing as an exercise in extrapolating from experience. But it seems to work. I do not think I have been seriously cold for at least a dozen years. Not, I mean, for more than the few minutes it takes me to do something about it. Mind you, I have never operated in bitterly cold conditions. Never below zero, in fact. But people who do so fairly often seem to apply much the same methods of choice and the same techniques.

Color

Generally speaking, it pays to choose clothes that are dark but bright. Dark, so that they will not advertise the inevitable dirt. And bright (especially red), because you can hardly walk away from camp and leave gaudy garments lying on the ground or hanging up to dry; because if you are brave enough to go out and walk during the hunting season, a plain-as-a-pikestaff exterior may save your life; because in case of accident, worn or waved clothing may attract rescuers' attention; and finally because a small splash of red or orange can crystallize an otherwise amorphous color photograph.

On the other hand, it is worth having one set of outer garments in some obscurantist shade of brown or green or gray for those occasions when you don't want to be seen: fishing, photographing game, keeping out of people's way, trespassing, Watergating.

Materials

Natural fibers tend to be a good deal more moisture absorbent than synthetics but less resistant to wear and wind. So in general it pays to wear natural fibers such as wool or cotton next to the skin, and to use synthetics for outer garments. Synthetics are being improved so fast that the best for any particular function seems to change with every storm. At the moment, for most purposes, woven nylon or a cotton/nylon combination such as 60/40 cloth still rules the roost.

A woven fabric can be treated so that it becomes "water repellent"—whatever you choose to take that to mean—but still breathes. The fabric can also be waterproof-coated, but it then breathes no more than does solid "plastic" polyethylene (which is what the coating is), and therefore soaks you in your own sweat. A search was long ago mounted, and continues unabated, for the ideal wet-weather fabric: something waterproof that breathes. The search seems to have perpetual motion potential: new miracle fabrics burst regularly on the scene—and consistently sink into oblivion. Five years ago it was Reevair, then Ventile. "The trouble is," one mountain shop man told me recently, "that everyone wants the stuff to defeat rain like a rubber sheet and to breathe like cheesecloth. And it won't do either really well." A current candidate is Bukflex, by Peter Storm of England and Connecticut— "guaranteed 100% waterproof" but also "water vapor permeable" and "condensation-free" and therefore "no-sweat." I devoutly hope so. Another interesting approach is a sleeved cape now made by The Great Pacific Iron Works: to absorb the sweat, it has a thin foam lining. But I confess I doubt that we have yet sighted the holy grail.*

A promising newcomer to the clothing scene is open-cell polyurethane foam—the stuff also used in some sleeping pads and bags. For general properties, see page 254. I have not yet been able to try any foam garments, but—in spite of bulk and stiffness—they clearly hold some promise for cold-weather wear, even if only on the score of cheapness and apparent effectiveness when wet. Open-cell foam "breathes," of course.†

For an unsuccessful experiment with closed-cell foam, see page 255.

The distaff wardrobe

I have co-opted an experienced subcommittee to advise me on important differences. She mentions that in hot weather many

---

* The 1973 Sierra Designs catalogue says, on p. 51:

We would like to give you our thoughts on how to interpret the magic word "waterproof." . . .
    The closest thing we know to really waterproof gear is yachting foul-weather stuff. And then only the *best* double coated, machine sealed seams—expensive, heavy stuff—keeps out the worst of the weather.
    The lightweight fabrics we use are laboratory tested to qualify for "waterproof" . . . a certain amount of pressure on a given area over a specific time tells us so. O.K.
    If you stay out in the rain long enough you are going to get wet—what you are doing and what you are wearing under your raingear will make a difference. The point is . . . raingear serves to keep off the worst until you can get the hell out of the rain. Water will come in at the neck, or face, sides of a poncho, splash up under the bottom, come through the seams (painting on seam sealant helps) or be forced through the fabric sometimes . . . e.g., by pack straps if pack is worn over the gear.
    Things that help you stay dry are to wear something soft and absorbent under a poncho—a light wool shirt will feel dry and stay drier under the rain layer than a thin cotton one. Try not to exert yourself to the point where you sweat profusely—raingear does not breathe and much body moisture will condense inside around the upper body. Try to keep the raingear loose . . . a tent flysheet works so well because it is kept away from the tent wall and only has to shed.

A pleasing change from standard catalogue Disney-speak.

    † Articles by Robert S. Wood in the final two 1973 issues of *Wilderness Camping* discuss an idea, promulgated by Jack Stephenson of Warmlite, that assumes "breathability" is all bunk and suggests an alternative cold-weather approach based on heat retention by a vapor barrier. You wrap your feet or whatever in impermeable baggies or whatever. Mr. Wood extolls the system. Other people damn it. Count me neutral, going on skeptical. But at least it's a pleasant bit of heresy.

women, like men, prefer to walk shirtless, and that to preserve the decencies they often carry a cotton sun- or swimsuit top (or halter). On a more fundamental level, she finds that by taking along one attractive garment ("something that makes me feel good"), she helps sustain her beleaguered sense of femininity. Otherwise, she says she can think of no mentionables worth mentioning.

Beyond these broad generalizations, choice of clothing is largely a matter of selecting each individual garment carefully for warmth in relation to weight, for toughness in wear, for versatility in use, and in some cases for water resistance. Also, whether you like it or not, in response to those obscure promptings, probably esthetic, that often lurk, shadowy and mostly unsensed, behind an apparently logical choice.

UNDERCLOTHING

Fishnet or string vests or shirts

These rather unlikely-looking garments are a lot of big holes tied together with string. At least, the original models were.*

Today, the string has been replaced by soft knitted cotton, but the holes are much the same—about ⅜ inch in diameter. And the holes are the important thing: they are what keep you warm when you want to keep warm and cool when you want to keep cool. To keep warm you button up all outer clothing and close neck and wrist openings. The holes of the fishnet weave then hold air in place close to your skin, and your body heat soon warms this air. The result is highly efficient insulation, mechanically much like that you create when you wear down or foam clothing.

To cool off, you simply loosen the neck opening of your outer garments and allow warm air to escape. Loosening wrist openings speeds up the process. If you get too hot, unbutton jacket and shirt and allow all hot air to be replaced by cold. When you are

---

* During World War II, I was for a time with a British unit that had been issued true fishnet vests as special mountaineering equipment. Eventually the unit was converted to cliff assault duty and moved to a Cornish fishing village. Our string vests astonished the fishermen and their wives. For several years they had, as experienced netmakers, been producing these strange devices for the war effort, in great secrecy, but they had never been able to guess what the peculiarly shaped nets were used for. No one, when sober, had seriously entertained the notion that they might be some kind of clothing.

unbuttoned like this, air circulates freely, and then a string vest is far cooler than conventional underwear.

Because of its dual efficiency, fishnet underwear is ideal when you are likely to work up a sweat while on the move, then cool off drastically the moment you stop, as when mountain climbing. It is also excellent when you get soaking wet: the wide fishnet weave holds little moisture and continues to provide good insulation. Scandinavian Knitters of Vermont now make all their fishnet garments of 50 percent cotton and 50 percent polyester. This combination absorbs less moisture than straight cotton, and dries out much faster. It therefore speeds up body heat evaporation. The new material is also lighter, softer, stronger and more durable than cotton, and shrinks far less.

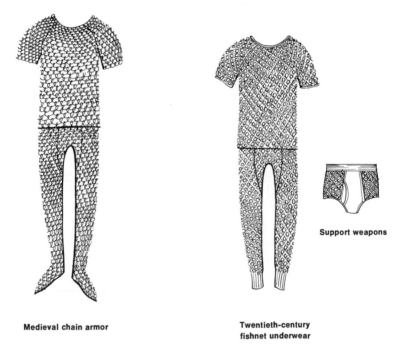

Support weapons

Medieval chain armor

Twentieth-century
fishnet underwear

To get full two-way benefit from a string vest, wear outer clothing that unbuttons completely down the front, and carry a scarf so that you can block off the passage of air at your neck.

A fishnet vest weighs about 6 ounces and costs around $5. So do a pair of

Fishnet longs.

They are made on the same principle, and I understand they are excellent. But on such occasions as I feel the need for undercovering on my legs, I use old-fashioned

Long johns.

Some people wear long johns in relatively mild weather, little below freezing. I am not sure I have ever worn them on the march; but I occasionally take them when cold or wind threatens to be extreme, and have several times worn them in bed with gratitude.

Fishnet shorts

Long a regrettable lack, fishnet shorts are now made by Scandinavian Knitters. On the strength of one trial, they seem fine.
I normally wear ordinary cotton

Jockey briefs.

But some people apparently experience rawness and itching with them, and prefer the boxer type.

On longish trips, if weight is not too acute a problem, you may feel like taking along spare briefs, or at least lightweight substitutes, for the times you wash the first-line pair—in case it is too cool or unprivate to wander around naked while they are drying.

If the weather is at all warm I tend to dispense with underpants once I'm away from civilization, thereby conforming, to within one step of its logical conclusion, with the Second Law of Thermodynamic Walking: "Give your balls some air."

SHIRTS

The choice is almost unlimited. Avoid synthetics. For cold weather, wool. The accepted quality names for thick wool shirts are Woolrich and Pendleton. For warm weather, any material that absorbs sweat will do: thin wool, cotton or a combination. The fabric I've used for years is the British Viyella (55 percent wool, 45 percent cotton), but it has become difficult to find in this country. Now very popular, and appearing in many catalogues, are "chamois" shirts—really "100% cotton chamois cloth that looks and feels like chamois leather." They are durable, warm and sweat-absorbing —and get softer with each washing. Around $11.

I usually take a fairly thick shirt, and always one with long sleeves: except in cold weather I tend to walk without a shirt, and when I stop I want something comfortably warm. Otherwise, my only criteria are that the shirt shall unbutton all the way down the front, have at least one breast pocket (preferably with button-down flap), not weigh too much, and be either a bright color-photography red or some soft camouflage color. But everyone has his own shirt preferences. One friend of mine will use only those with zippered rather than buttoned fronts. His specialties are blue jobs made for railroad workers (Hickory, Big Mac, or Lee), but the zippers reach only halfway down the front, and for me that's hopeless.

SWEATERS

In really cold weather, one or more thin sweaters between shirt and overclothing can make a lot of difference. Weight for warmth, there is said to be nothing to match an old cashmere sweater. Mine certainly seems to make a big difference. On the presumably sound assumption that many thin layers work better than one thick one (because they hold air between them and also afford greater flexibility), I suppose I should take it along more often than I do. But I never pack anywhere without at least a thin down jacket (page 293), and that usually seems enough. Down jackets are far more efficient than sweaters, anyway—except perhaps when you're liable to get soaking wet. Then, a wool sweater with some windproof outer shell might do a better job.

PANTS

Whatever you wear on your behind, the material must be tough: you'll be using unpadded chairs. And choose a color that hides the dirt.

Shorts

I'm a wholeheartedly bigoted devotee of shorts—so much so that I often find myself wearing them until the temperature drops into the thirties or the wind develops a really keen cutting edge. At least once I have arrived at a 14,000-foot peak in shorts; but I hasten to add that there are not too many places and days you can do such a thing in comfort. A few years ago I wore shorts up 5000 feet of snow, on a cloudless April day of icy winds, to the 12,000-foot rim of Fujiyama—and paid for my stupidity for the rest of the week every time I tried to force red, raw legs into the steaming hot baths that are the only form of ablution in Japanese inns, and which *noblesse* apparently obliges you to refrain from tempering with cold water. But I remain an unrepentant shorts man.

Shorts allow much more efficient ventilation than long pants do. See thermodynamic writ, page 289. And I've now reached the point at which I feel, or imagine I feel, dragged down by the restrictiveness of long pants. Fortunately, real cold seems to override the sensation. But several times I have started out on bitter mornings in longs and have realized later, after the day had warmed up, that I was making meager progress simply because I was still wearing them. A change to shorts has usually been enough to get me moving well again.

Really pesky insects might, I guess, drive even me to give up shorts for a while. See page 349.

Corduroy is the best material I know for shorts. It is warm and absorbent, washes well, and wears prodigiously. But it must be really good quality. The only way I've been able to get what I want is to have shorts made from material I've selected myself. I'm now using the second pair of corduroy shorts made by The Redmayne Suit Copying Service, Station Road, Wigton, Cumberland CA7 9AF, England. They're made to my careful specifications: leg openings wide, to the decency limit; built-in waistband reasonably adjustable so that it can conform to a midriff that, like many people's, fluctuates wildly in response to prolonged packing of heavy weights and to such other variables as food, love life and tennis; pockets strong, numerous and tailored to my fancies (two hip pockets, two side pockets, and two ticket pockets at the waistband, front—one for bookmatches and the other for fire- or stove-priming scraps of paper [page 176]. Weight: 1 pound 9 ounces). These are good shorts: my first pair held more or less together for six years. The snag is price: in 1966, less than £7 ($17) in England; in 1972, £15.45—which means, after clearing U.S. customs, something close to $50.

The Great Pacific Iron Works of Ventura, California (formerly Chouinard), now sells wide-legged British-made corduroy shorts for $18 (1 pound 5½ ounces). Although they lack some of the refinements of my custom-made pair, they seem good.

The G. P. Iron Works also forges heavy tent duck shorts that are machine washable (1 pound 3 ounces; $16).

Drill shorts are lighter, and are worth considering if you'll be using them only occasionally and they'll spend most of the time in your pack. Also for short trips in very hot weather. They last a little while.

Some multi-pocketed, off-the-peg lederhosen (and cotton variants) look tough and practical—but are too tight around the thighs for me.

Long pants

Even in the hottest weather, evenings are apt to be cool. So, except in low desert in high summer, I nearly always carry long pants. A stout whipcord pair, forest ranger style, all wool (1 pound 10 ounces; $20), is the only kind I have used for some years. But the choice is wide. Many people take nothing but a pair of blue jeans for all uses. Others wear climbing knickers, tight-fitting below the knees. Take your pick.

For extreme cold, consider pants with instep straps.

Belt

If possible, buy pants with built-in waistbands and avoid this unnecessary item. It is not only a question of weight; any belt is uncomfortable under the waist belt of your pack. When you go off on packless sidetrips and, lacking a belt bag (page 88), need something around your waist to which you can attach a poncho-wrapped lunch and a cup and camera tripod and so on, simply use a few turns of nylon cord (page 368).

Leg protectors

If you wear shorts you may find that in certain kinds of country, especially desert, you need something to stop your bare and vulnerable lower legs from being savaged by scrub, thorn brush and cacti. The best protection I've come across is a pair of Ace bandages (that I always carry anyway; see page 373), wrapped puttee fashion from boots to just below the knees.

Gaiters

Something to seal off the gap between boots and long pants is essential in soft snow and profitable in cold winds, heavy rain or wet undergrowth. I have a pair of coated, water-repellent-nylon gaiters with elastic inserts top and bottom to grip pants and boots. Cords fit under the instep and stop the gaiters from riding upward. Side zippers make them easy to put on and take off. They work very well indeed. (Height 6 inches; 3½ ounces; $8.50.) They come in various designs and sizes.

If you need gaiters almost constantly for your kind of walking, consider boots fitted with scree-gaiters (page 37).

DOWN-FILLED CLOTHING

When man woke up a few decades ago to the idea of taking a feather out of the birds' book and making down-filled clothing as well as sleeping bags, the result was so much more effective than anything he had used before that it revolutionized polar and high-altitude exploration. Men could operate with safety and even comfort where they once had to battle simply to exist. Even in much kinder environments it pays to accept this breakthrough with gratitude and both hands.

As with down sleeping bags, down clothing seems to have attained a design plateau of excellence. Excellent jackets and pants now come from virtually all the established bag makers (page 264), and again there is generally precious little to choose between them. I shall therefore not attempt to list recommended makes and models, only to indicate the features I have found desirable. If you select from a reputable catalogue or store a model that seems to meet your requirements of the moment, and check its workmanship as for sleeping bags (page 264), you're unlikely to go far wrong.

For my Grand Canyon trip, when I had to pare away every last half ounce, the one really warm upper garment I took was a

Lightweight down jacket.

Although snow fell twice during the early part of the trip and evenings were often decidedly chilly, I do not remember that I was ever cold. From then on I took the jacket on almost every trip, except in very cold weather (see heavy down jacket, page 294). When it at last demanded retirement, eight years later, I bought a new, improved version. This one, by Sierra Designs, is nylon shelled, waist length, long sleeved and front zippered. It has two outside patch pockets. Elastic inserts keep the cuffs reasonably snug, and they have snap fasteners for bitter cold. A drawstring means you can pull the waist tight and trap warm air inside. (Don't buy a jacket without some such closure, or at least the possibility of adding one: without it, a jacket loses half its effectiveness.) The current Sierra Designs equivalent, the Sierra Jacket, weighs 1 pound 6 ounces, costs $38—and has a snap-detachable down hood. That's a big improvement: the back of your neck is often a fiend to keep warm.

You can also buy ultralight, sleeveless and hoodless down vests, for over- or underwear. (Alpine Designs version: 10 ounces; $22.)

Heavy down jacket

Some such garment (often called a "down parka" if it has a hood, as it certainly should have) is essential if you are going to operate in real cold or in bitter winds. Such jackets average around 2 pounds, and are astonishingly warm. (Eastern Mountain Sports carries an excellent range.) Buy big, if not huge, so that you can if necessary wear your lightweight jacket underneath without compressing the down too much, and so destroying its efficiency. (A Ski Hut pair, designed for such nesting, together weigh 2 pounds 8 ounces, cost $94.)

I have a Sierra Designs model that is essentially a heavier version of the Sierra, above, but with detachable hood and snap-down storm flap over zipper. The current rough equivalent, the Whitney Parka, weighs 1 pound 11 ounces, costs $46. I am inclined to believe that such jackets, designed for really cold weather, are better with attached hoods. I've never lost mine, but I've worried.

You can buy heavier jackets, to meet almost any conditions—ranging up to the Eddie Bauer Kara Koram Parka, used by a party that wintered at the South Pole in temperatures averaging about 70° F. below (2 pounds 13 ounces; $69.50).

In extremely cold weather you may also need

Down pants.

If, like me, you are one of those unfortunates whose upper and lower clothes layers always seem to pull apart at the mid-section, make sure your pants come up high and have an effective built-in belt. Quality and warmth cover much the same range as for down jackets. Weights average about 1 pound; costs, about $30 or $35.

Down booties

Highly practical. Once, they kept my feet totally warm—perhaps even a shade hot—in a Slimline bag, unprotected, at 11° F. (page 266). On Kilimanjaro, when the temperature hardly fell below freezing but murkily miserable weather and the thin air at 16,000 feet made it seem colder, they kept my feet comfortable in a similar lightweight bag.

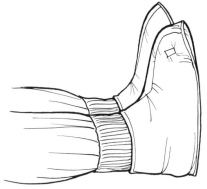

These booties—with light nylon shell and thick waterproof nylon sole padded with ¼-inch Ensolite—are also excellent for brief excursions from your tent out into the snow (page 224), provided the snow is cold and dry. Many makes and models (average: 8 ounces; $12).

As far as I know, every foam-soled down bootie comes equipped with a resident little devil whose sole aim in life is to slide the foam off to one side, where it becomes comprehensively useless. The latest Ski Hut models incorporate elastic inserts at the heels, intended to exorcise these devils. Intended.

Stuff bags

Worth considering for down jackets, pants and even booties. I use them, mostly. But see page 274.

FOAM CLOTHING

For a brief note on general considerations, see page 286.

Jackets, vests and mittens are now available, as well as mukluks (page 40). For mittens, see page 300.

WIND- AND RAINWEAR

In biting winds you may need a windproof jacket over your down clothing.

A windproof of this kind is often called a

Parka (or anorak).

"Parka" is an Aleutian word originally meaning "a fur jacket or heavy, long woolen shirt, often lined with pile or fleece, with attached hood." "Anorak" is the Greenland Eskimo word for a similar hooded garment, though it may be made of leather or cloth. In modern English the two words mean the same thing: a hooded jacket, windproof and waterproof to widely varying degrees. Anyone who has tried to operate without a hood in cold or very windy conditions will know why these jackets are so popular.

A parka that is windproof and at least somewhat water repellent may be necessary over a down jacket not only in cutting winds but also when snow falls in temperatures only just below freezing. Under such conditions, escaping body heat melts snowflakes that come to rest on an unprotected down jacket and soon turn it into waterlogged and useless pulp. With the snow at lower temperatures, no such problem seems to arise.

Many people say they find, especially in the mountains, that a parka is about the most useful and versatile garment they own. Frankly, I've yet to try one I consider worth carrying regularly. The trouble is the fabric. (See "holy grail," page 286: you drown in either rain or sweat.)

The other requirements of a good parka are relatively simple. To shut out the wind you need drawstrings at hood and waist, and some effective closure at the wrists. The warmest "expedition" kind have crotch straps. Big pockets are a convenience. But the really important thing is size. Again, buy big. A size larger, perhaps, than the biggest you think you need. You'll be wearing the parka over many layers of other clothing, often including a bulky down jacket. And as every garment is essentially there to hold pockets of air in place, the whole object is defeated if you compress the layers. Most parkas now have front openings. Be thankful. If you have never stood on a mountain ridge in a howling gale and tried to battle your way up and into a nonopening parka a size too small for you—I suggest you make every effort to avoid the experience.

Most parkas weigh around 1 pound. Cost can vary from $6 to $30.

As a garment that might be called a parka becomes more waterproof (for ruminations on that word, see page 285), and therefore "breathes" less, so it moves closer to being a

Rain jacket.

This is the solution in which you decide to soak in sweat rather than rain. Many people accept it. It is really the only one if you expect to be in prolonged heavy rain anything far short of tepid. But remember that you'll get almighty hot as well as sweat-wet.

An experienced friend who goes for the heavy stuff says the best comes from England, Japan and Scandinavia. Canadians may like to try the Pioneer line by Jones Tent and Awning of Vancouver (they do *not* export to the United States). The firm is honest enough to say that the line is not really very suitable for backpackers, owing to weight and stiffness; but I remember without horror that twenty years ago I used the pants and jackets for much cross-country footslogging on soggy Vancouver Island.

Rain pants

In really wet weather, an inseparable part of the soak-in-sweat solution.

Rain chaps

Because they cover legs but not butt and environs, chaps permit better ventilation than pants. Some weigh only 4 ounces, and could be worth carrying if you might have to slog for hours through sodden scrub. It is apparently difficult to make a pair that will withstand the inevitable abrasion; so pin your hopes low.

For normal, not totally sodden conditions, I find the best bet is a

Poncho.

A poncho is a waterproof sheet, 4 feet by 7 feet or a little bigger, with a head-hole and hood in the middle. In good backpacking ponchos the hole is placed somewhat off center, and the longer rear section covers your pack. At least, that's the theory;

but if a wind is blowing don't expect too much overlap from theory into practice. Most hoods can be tightened flush around your face with a drawstring. The rest of the sheet hangs down like a shroud, but snap fasteners on the edges allow you to make rudimentary sleeves that help keep the poncho from flapping too wildly in a high wind. Some heavier models have a drawstring at the waist that not only cuts down the flappage but also holds in warmth—too efficiently sometimes. A length of nylon cord around your waist will do the job almost as well, though its rubbing may damage the waterproofing.

A poncho is clearly not a superbly efficient device, but it gives you leeway. You can wrap yourself up reasonably well against most rain—and accept that you'll sweat a bit. Or you can leave matters loose and know that at least your body will get some air. A poncho is also one of the most versatile garments around. Those snap fasteners along its edges help, and so do the grommets sometimes put in at each corner. (I always have at least one other grommet—and probably three or four—inserted in the center of each long side; the short sides rarely have a wide enough hem to take even a small grommet.) With these simple fittings, a poncho can be much more than a waterproof garment. It can be a windbreaker—especially useful when a thin down jacket is the only warm garment you have with you. As we have seen (pages 236–9), the grommets allow you to turn it into a wild assortment of roofs and sidewalls and cocoons that will ward off snow, rain, wind or sun. With two ponchos snapped together by their fasteners you can build a big ridge-backed shelter. Under certain conditions (pages 238 and 241) you may be forced to use your poncho as a groundsheet; but if you do, do not expect it to remain waterproof for long. On packless side trips or on short walks from home or car, a bundled poncho secured around your waist with nylon cord makes a useful belt bag (page 88) for lunch and oddments, especially convenient if there is danger of rain. Cunningly molded to the landscape, it can form a wash basin (page 309). Finally, it will help waterproof your pack contents during a river crossing (page 380).

Poncho materials include heavy-duty rubberized fabrics, coated nylon and other synthetic fabrics, and thin plastic (vinyl). Rubberized fabrics are heavy but very strong. For years, when there was a danger of torrential or prolonged rain, I carried a thick U.S. Army surplus model.

Generally speaking, woven synthetic fabrics such as nylon are at present the best. They are very light and are becoming progressively stronger and closer to waterproof, though no cheaper. Not all of them stay waterproof for long.

Plastic ponchos are light, cheap, and when new, wholly water-proof. But they do not breathe and so are extremely hot. Worst of all, they tear. They tear almost without provocation; and once started they don't stop. But they have short-term, shallow-pocket uses—and a horrifying litter potential.

Weights run from around 2½ pounds for a rubberized poncho down to as little as 10 ounces for a nylon or plastic one. A tough, coated nylon poncho that breathes may cost $16 or $20, though a less fancy and less durable one may run only $6. The plastic horrors sell, unfortunately, for as little as $1.25.

An alternative to a poncho is a garment designed primarily for climbers—a

Cagoule.

The word is French and originally meant "monk's cloak" or "penitent's cowl." The modern outdoorsman's cagoule is a knee-length, sleeved cape with hood.

Some years ago I bought one, made of waterproof-coated nylon, but it leaked at the shoulders. A good model, though it could prove hot for walking, might make a practical wet-weather garment around camp. Drawstrings at hood and hem allow them to be drawn tight. Elastic keeps the wrist openings closed (19 ounces; $21.50).

A cagoule cannot, like a poncho, serve as a roof. But it is designed for emergency bivouac use: you can if necessary draw your knees up inside the long "skirt," and seal yourself off by pulling the drawstring tight. If you carry a companion footsack-

and-carrying-bag (6 ounces; $7) of the same material, you are in even better shape. See pages 291–2 for further thoughts, pro and con.

Cape

For an interesting innovation, see the Great Pacific Iron Works cape, page 286.

EXTREMITIES AND ANCILLARIES

Gloves

In big hiking parties, where heavy work such as digging and wood-gathering has to be expected, it is worth carrying a pair of leather work gloves. They're also useful in mild winds and cold. Some backpackers always take a pair—for firelighting, cooking, and protection against sunburn and insects (see also page 349) as well as the cold. Traveling on my own, I rarely carry them; but except in hot weather I usually take along a pair of light woolen gloves or mitts (2 ounces). For moderate cold, fleece-lined leather gloves or mitts are good. Mitts—which house all four fingers together and leave only the thumb on its own—are always warmer than gloves of similar construction.

In really cold weather your hands need greater protection. One satisfactory pair of mitts I've used has leather palm and thumb, cotton twill backing with fur pad (mainly, I'm told, for wiping off that cold, dripping nose), and a 9-inch twill gauntlet with an elastic insert at the end that forms a good windproof seal, well above the wrist. Current versions come with removable wool liners. A small metal loop at the end of each gauntlet makes it easy to join the gloves with a length of nylon cord that runs inside your outer clothing layer, up one sleeve and down the other, and keeps the gloves dangling and ready if you need to take them off for a short time—a useful arrangement with any cold-weather gloves. These G.I. gauntlet mitts (12 ounces; $5) also make pretty fair snow slippers for brief nature trips outside the tent (page 224).

Down-filled mittens have long been considered best for severe conditions. They come in many varieties, normally with deerskin shells (7–16 ounces; $14–$40). But foam gloves seem to offer a challenge. They are lighter and cheaper: Ocaté makes a 4-ounce, nylon-covered pair for $8. And I understand that if they get wet—for example, from handling snow—they are much better than down. Wet down pulps into uselessness; foam may let water through, but it stays windproof and your hands stay warm. Some reasonably abominable snowmen swear by a shuffleable three-layer system: silk liners (see below); wool mitts of the Dachstein breed; and an outer shell of Rip-stop or similar.

No matter how good your mittens, you probably need inner gloves: you have to remove the outer layer for any task that needs fingers, from taking a photograph to lighting the stove, and bare hands can quickly become frostbitten. Wool inner gloves are warm but soon develop holes. Thin silk inner gloves enjoyed a recent vogue. Although they look like something from a boudoir, they do not encumber your fingers at all, help a little in keeping them warm inside the mitts, wear better than wool, and are thick enough when worn alone to protect your hands for short periods and above all to keep the skin from sticking to cold metal (¼ ounce; $4). Some users, but not all, say that similar gloves, made of something as light as silk and lined or impregnated with tiny grains of metal, will reflect much heat back onto your hands but allow some moisture to escape, and will also last longer (½ ounce; $4). Perhaps better still is a newer, thicker silk glove that looks like woven cotton and is said to wear very well indeed (1 ounce; $3.35).

Balaclava helmet

Balaclavas come in both wool and orlon (3 ounces; $2.25). I have yet to decide which is better. Rolled down, they encase head and neck in most comforting fashion. Rolled up, they make warm hats that you can wear alone or under a parka or poncho hood, day or night.

Do not underestimate the importance of a balaclava or some such covering in cold weather. The head is the body radiator: at 40° F. it may, if unprotected, lose up to half your heat production; at 5°, up to three-quarters. See "Hypothermia," page 414.

Face masks

These entrancing, horrifying protectors against bloodcurdling winds come in leather from several sources (2 ounces; $6.95), and now in down from Eddie Bauer (unknown ounces; $14.95).

Scarf

The human neck is no doubt necessary, but it is a hell of a thing to keep warm. And it creates a weak point in almost any clothing system. Even in warm weather I always carry a small (1-ounce) wool scarf to block off the escape of precious warm air from the main reservoir that clothing has created around my body. Unless you have tried it, you will find it difficult to believe how much difference this small detail can make, especially when your clothing is on the light side. In particular, a string vest unsupported by a scarf is only half effective.

Swimsuit

Where there's a chance of a swim, you may, unless you're reasonably sure of privacy, like to take along a thin nylon swimsuit. On recent major river crossings with my pack (page 382) in rough water and hot weather, I wore mine every time, so that in the unlikely event of being separated from the pack I would at least have some protection from the sun (2½ ounces; around $4. "Ocean Speed" by Ocean Pool Supply Company, 17 Stepar Place, Huntington Station, New York 11746).

Bandanna

A large cotton bandanna or handkerchief, preferably bright colored and therefore not easily lost, is your wardrobe's maid-of-all-work. It performs as potholder, napkin, dishcloth, washcloth, towel, emergency headgear, wet inside-the-hat cooling pad in hot weather, Lawrence-of-Arabia neck protector (especially cooling if damp), hand pad for snow-peg-as trowel (page 386), snooze mask, and even fig leaf (page 311).
Wash frequently. Dries quickly if tied on back of pack. (20-inch square: ½ ounce; $.35. 27-inch square: 1 ounce; $.85.)

Hat

Hikers wear about as many different kinds of headgear as you'll see in a fully fashioned Easter parade. But the criteria that matter are lightness, protection afforded from heat, ventilation quotient, and ability to stand up to brutal treatment. (Rain resistance matters very little: presumably you always have a poncho or parka hood.) Otherwise, suit your fancy—though should you be thin on top but still able to enjoy the finer things of life it is

desirable that the hat be of such a nature that if it becomes dislodged during totally engrossing delights under a hot, hot desert sun it is easy, without any interruption at all, for her to reach up, if she really loves you, and replace it.

On occasion, you must be able to arrange things so that the hat will stay on your head in half a hurricane. The only way you can do so is with a chin strap. If the hat you like doesn't have one (and it probably won't) all you have to do is punch a hole in the brim on either side, close to the crown, then grommet the holes or have a shoemaker do the job, and thread through the grommets a suitable length of braided nylon cord. (Red cord dirties less objectionably than white, and also helps color photography.) When not in use, the chin strap goes up into the crown: you soon get used to flicking it up without thought as you put the hat on. Or, sometimes, you can tuck it into the hatband.

A little to my surprise I've recently favored an ordinary soft U.S. Army surplus fatigue hat. It is light, tough, eminently packable, brimmed, cool, and cheap—and also stands up clear of your dome (6 ounces; $1.89).

But for many years I used good-quality soft felts: Half Stetsons or reasonable facsimiles. Brims: about 2½ inches wide—so that they give adequate shade but continue to stand out for themselves after being crushed, soaked and trampled on, yet do not keep hitting the packframe. Crown: high enough to leave air space between bald pate and murderous sunshine. Color: brown or blue-gray, because they don't show the dirt and because I like the look of them (though I know that in theory a light-colored hat would reflect the heat better).

All these hats did their job well. But they took a continuous beating, and although each lasted several years, none looked pristine for very long. They not only got soaked and trampled on but spent long hours slung by their chin straps from my packframe or even stuffed into the packbag. (These days, for safety, I tend to clip the hat's chinstrap onto the belt-clip-on-cord-from-top-of-packframe that is primarily there for my camera [page 326].)

I bought one new hat just before the Grand Canyon trip. It soon reached maturity. At the halfway mark, when I met people for the first time since near the start, the month-old hat would hardly have done for church, and one bright girl asked, "But was it *ever* new?"

Reluctantly, I at last pensioned off that worthy hat. (It now hangs on the wall of my office, a pleasing memento. I have just looked up at it, as I often do, and smiled happily.) After two years' hard labor its crown had worn through around the fold and was only held in place by about 4 inches of material at the back. This unintentional ventilation kept my head pleasantly cool in hot weather—and the bonus gave me an idea.

In hot weather you want all the ventilation you can get for your head; in the wet or cold, you want little or none. This is a vital problem (see, on both counts, "Hypothermia," page 414), but not easy to solve. Straw hats, for example, are useless because although they ventilate your head well, they give no protection from wind or cold and do not stand up to more than a few days of the treatment any hiking hat must be able to absorb for months on end. It seems to me that the obvious answer is an adjustable hat—a sort of stilt-roofed affair that you open up in hot weather and close down in cold:

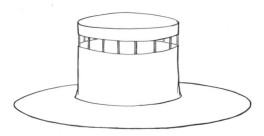

Generously, I fling this brilliant idea open to the public. All some ambitious man needs now is a little research into details. I will claim no more than a nominal 10 percent rake-off.*

Failing some such modification, the way you wear the crown of your hat in hot weather can be critical. From force of city habit we tend to indent the top, "stylishly." But doing so in hot weather radically reduces the vital air-insulation barrier between the top of your head and the sun's rays. The thing to do is to push the crown out to its rounded maximum.

* Soon after writing the above I discovered that my idea was not quite as original as I had thought. By chance, I happened on the following in a 130-year-old copy of an English publication, *The New Sporting Magazine* (Vol. 15, No. 87 [July 1838], p. 40):

HOW TO MAKE A VENTILATING HAT FOR SHOOTING, WITH A SLIDING SHUTTER, BETTER THAN ANY CAP.
Probatum est.

Take any light beaver or felt hat, and make, with a wadding punch, four, six, or eight holes in its circumference, and about half an inch from the top. You need not use a hammer; let your punch be sharp, and then if you support the felt inside with the ends of the thumb and three fingers of your left hand, and hold the punch firmly and pretty low down with the thumb and forefinger-knuckle of the right, twisting it backwards and forwards, and pressing steadily all the while, the hat will speedily be cut through. So much for ventilation.

Now for your shutter. Get an old hat of the same colour, as large or larger in the crown, and out of its circumference cut a ring or hoop, an inch and quarter, or so, in width. If it chances to fit *inside* the crown of your ventilator, so as just to slide up or down, your job is done; if not, and it be too large, cut it across, and place it in the ventilator's crown with its cut ends one overlapping the other, and while held firm in that position, mark with pen or pencil the extent of the overlapping—cut off the superfluous part, and then, if you have done your work well, it will exactly fit the *hat*-crown, and only wants the two ends joining—which you will effectively do by glueing a small piece of felt, or pasteboard, over the joint *inside*—to be as good a sliding shutter as if it had not been cut. Slipping it downwards you open your air-holes, either entirely or in part; slipping it upwards, you close them. You will meet sometimes a man whose wide-open eyes tell you plainly of bullets he supposes to have passed through your headgear; but *n'importe*, he will respect you "for the danger you have past," and your head will be cool with the thermometer at 100°.

Thomas Trigger

A rounded crown hardly helps you to look intelligent, but if appearance counts enough to force you to stay with a dented crown you had better confine your walking to the financial district.

Some sober and reliable people classify as pure myth the tradition that you need a hat in hot, sunny weather. But I know that if I go without a hat in any kind of hot sun I very soon feel dizzy. Or, at the least, I imagine I feel dizzy—and the two states are indistinguishable. So to me, in summer desert, a hat is no joking matter.

On my California walk, when I rested for a day at the southern end of Death Valley, the temperature was $105°$ in the extremely rare shade. During the morning of that day I climbed up into some stark hills to photograph the gray trough that was the valley—the trough I would within twenty-four hours be walking through. All morning a strong west wind had been blowing. As I climbed, the wind increased. But the heat lost none of its intensity. By the time I reached the first summit ridge, the wind had risen to a half gale. On the ridge I stopped to take a photograph, and used my hat to shield the camera lens from the sun. Afterward, in a careless moment, I forgot to slip the chin strap back under my chin. Before I could lift a hand, the wind had snatched the hat away and sent it soaring upward.

Suddenly the sun was battering down on my head like a bludgeon.

I cannot have stood there looking at the flying hat for more than two or three seconds. But I do not think I shall ever forget my feeling of helplessness as the twirling brown shape grew smaller and smaller. I stood still, watching it twist up and away into the hard blue sky.

Then the hat dived behind one of the fantastically colored ridges that stretched back and back as far as I could see.

Its disappearance snapped the spell. I broke into a run. As I ran I remembered how, only a couple of weeks before, a wise old desert rat had shown me a magazine picture of a corpse sprawled beside a bicycle out in the Mojave Desert. "No hat—not surprised," the old-timer had said. I raced on over bare rock. A makeshift hat in Death Valley? I might go days without seeing anyone. And I knew that I could hunt for hours among those endless ridges without finding the hat. I scrambled onto a chocolate-brown crest. And there, its strap neatly looped over a spike of rock, lay the hat.

I picked it up, chin-strapped it firmly onto my head, and then walked slowly back down the hill. Now the danger had passed, I felt thankful that the desert had reminded me how fine a line

divides safety from tragedy—and how easily a moment of carelessness can send you stumbling across it.*

Hat substitutes

Once, before instituting my clip-on-camera cord safety system
(page 326), I lost my hat and was forced to devise a substitute.
It happened during a two-week trip beside the Colorado River in
lower Grand Canyon, with the temperature up over 100° just
about every day. I not only lost the hat (I think it was plucked
off by a mesquite thicket while hanging on the packframe, un-
secured, during the cool of the evening) but somehow succeeded
in losing as well both my bandanna, which had been acting as a
wet-pad cooling system inside the hat and might have done as a
river-soaked substitute, and also, after they had done the job for
a couple of days, my jockey shorts. In summer, that part of Grand
Canyon is a huge, deep-cut, heat-reflecting rock oven. Except in
morning and evening, there is precious little shade, and I knew that
I had to have some kind of hat. My nylon swimsuit, I discovered,
dried out too quickly and was almost impossible to keep in place.
But after a while I devised a method of folding the lightly inflated life vest (page 381) and lashing it with nylon cord into such
a conformation that, with its web belt under my chin, it would
stay on top of my head. This unlikely rig, immersed every hour
in the river, and with the wet swimsuit stuffed into its hollow
center, turned out to be just about the coolest hat I've ever worn,
even if not the most becoming. I had to hold my head fairly upright to keep it on, but that was probably good for my posture or
something.

* From *The Thousand-Mile Summer*, pp. 82–3.

CARE OF CLOTHING

In the field

In civilized temperatures I generally try to wash most of my clothes at least once a week.* This works out well because I find— and I think most people find—that about once a week you need a day's more or less complete rest from walking.

Whatever soap or detergent you choose, it must, today, be biodegradable. The stuff you use for kitchen and personal purposes (page 347) will probably do fine for most clothes. For wool articles, see "Care of socks," page 47.

The time has now passed, almost everywhere, for washing clothes directly in a river or lake. Suds persist for more than a mile, and the chances are simply too great that someone a little way downstream will soon be drinking that same water. Besides, with today's heavy usage the accumulation spells undoubted pollution. (Exceptions: huge rivers, maybe; and genuinely remote country— now just about unfindable in the lower forty-eight.)

The solution is simple, cheap, compact—and light: a plastic or waxed-fabric bucket and bowl.

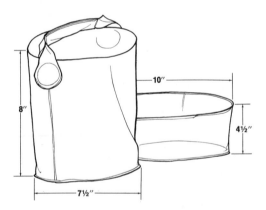

You scoop up water in the bucket and wash clothes (and yourself) in the bowl. Dirty water can safely be ditched 50 feet back from the river or lake: it will filter clean as it seeps down through the soil. The plastic bucket-and-bowl set illustrated weighs 8 ounces, costs $2, takes up almost no room in your pack, and is much more efficient than it looks—though the bowl walls tend to fold un-

---

* In really cold weather you simply don't do any washing of clothes—or of yourself; which means that when you get back to civilization that first hot shower is not only sheer heaven but highly necessary.

expectedly and disastrously inward. The walls of the waxed-canvas, French-made IT bowl (2 ounces) sometimes found in U.S. stores, do not. Failing bucket and bowl, you can improvise a bowl from any impermeable fabric—poncho, groundsheet, fly sheet, awning— by laying it in a natural hollow, by scooping a hollow out of sand or soil that will not be damaged, or by arranging stones or wood as under-rim supports. Fill from canteens.

To dry clothes, string them out on bushes or a nylon line. I'm indebted to a New York reader who apparently carries a light nylon line for what she calls her "twist-and-shove," which she maintains is simpler than it looks and has become a one-minute- or-so part of her evening camp routine. You loop the line around whatever two aids you can find—with the center of the line at one of them—twist tightly, then shove the clothes into two or more twist-loops.

For shirts, if you're fussy about looks, it's easy to make a clothes hanger out of a piece of stick and some nylon line. For socks, see page 47.

In wet weather, the only answer to drying out clothes that have been ill-advisedly washed or have just plain got wet is a fire. Sometimes you're reduced to using the cooking stove inside your tent—if there's enough fuel. A tent with a clothesline attachment— grommeted tabs at each end of the ridge for joining with nylon cord—may allow damp clothes to dry from a combination of stove and body heat. For final drying, take clothes to bed with you.

At home

Treat most articles of clothing like their everyday counterparts. For down-filled clothing, see sleeping bags, page 275. For foam, see page 254.

THE WARDROBE IN ACTION

Sartorially, hikers can be subdivided into two distinct breeds: the put-it-on-and-keep-it-on school and the keep-adjusting-your-clothing-all-day-long-so-that-you're-always-comfortable faction.

You undoubtedly save several minutes a day if you put on at the start what you judge is about right, and can then stick it out hour after hour without discomfort. But I belong, unreservedly, to the fussy, thermally responsive faction. With every variation of effort and environment I button and unbutton, unzipper and rezipper, peel and restore and then peel again. I find that in any but frigid weather it takes barely a mile of walking and a side glance of sunshine to strip me down to hat, underpants, shorts, socks, and boots. That, I find, is the way to walk. With air playing freely over your skin you feel twice as fresh as you did with a shirt on. And although you may lose precious body liquids more quickly this way, experience has convinced me that you walk so much more comfortably that you more than make up for any loss. At least, I do. Besides, I enjoy myself more.

On those rare but by no means unknown occasions when you are traveling beside a river or lake in very hot, low-humidity weather, you have a cooling system ready for use. On my two-week trip in lower Grand Canyon, when I hiked day after day beside the Colorado River, I learned to utilize this system to the full. I found that I could keep walking comfortably, even through the heat of the day, if at the end of each halt I dived into the river wearing my drill shorts and Dacron-wool shirt. For almost the whole of the next hour, the continuous evaporation from the rapidly drying clothes surrounded my body with a pleasantly cool "micro-climate." For the highly efficient hat I used, purely by accident, see page 307.

Occasionally on that trip, because of a cut on one leg that I wanted to keep dry, I just soaked the clothes in the river. At other times, when the heat was not too ferocious, I simply draped the dripping wet shirt around my neck and kept resoaking it with barely a check in my stride by dropping it in the river and in one easy movement pushing it under and lifting it up with the tip of my walking staff.

It is not often that you meet the right and necessary combination of weather and privacy and so can carry the keep-adjusting-your-clothing-all-day-long-so-that-you're-always-comfortable system to its logical conclusion. The first time I did so for any length of time was on my long Grand Canyon journey. Of course, I exercised due care for a few days with the previously shielded sectors of my anatomy. In particular, I pressed the bandanna into service as a fig leaf. But soon I was walking almost all day long with nothing above my ankles except a hat.*

Now nakedness is a delightful condition, and by walking naked you gain far more than coolness. You feel an unexpected sense of freedom from restraint. An uplifting and almost delirious sense of simplicity. In this new simplicity you soon find that you have become, in a new and surer sense, an integral part of the simple, complex world you are walking through. And then you are really walking.

* Warning! Not everyone can take such liberties with his skin in hot sun. And most people need a lotion (p. 349), at least at first.

Furniture and Appliances

No matter how grimly you pare away at the half ounces, you always seem to burden your house with an astonishing clutter of furniture and appliances. At least, I do. Each item, of course, is a necessary aid to some necessary activity. For example, there is the vital matter of

SEEING.

To lighten my darkness I mostly carry only a small

Flashlight.

The small plastic Mallory (empty, 1½ ounces; with two AA alkaline batteries, 3 ounces; $1.75) has become by far the most popular backpacking flashlight. I've used one for years. And now Mallory is about to market an improved version, the Duracell 805 (empty, 1 ounce; with batteries, 2½ ounces; $2.29). Both models are reputed to throw 250-foot beams, and their light is certainly adequate for most purposes.

When I first saw the old model, its plastic case and flimsy innards inspired me with zero confidence. But it turned out to be astonishingly tough. Its plastic lens seems virtually unbreakable, and it has few metal parts that can corrode either from dead batteries or from dampness or from being dropped in water. Also, because of its shape and lightness and plastic case, it is easy and reasonably comfortable to hold in the mouth, even in cold weather, while you use both hands to do something in its beam. What's

more, all parts are easily get-at-able for drying, cleaning or repair—though fixing those fragile innards can be a hell of a game.
Once one of these little lights begins to get battered, though, and
to keep the light steady I have to press on some part of the case,
I discard it. Some people apparently carry a spare flashlight, always.

So far I have used the new Mallory Duracell 805 only briefly,
but it looks like a genuine improvement. It is not only smaller and
lighter and more elegant, it seems simpler and stronger. The case
promises to flex rather less. And the switch mechanism looks less
likely to go wrong. There is also no little screw to hold the halves
of the case together (and to drive you down on hands and knees,
peering and cursing, if you have to change batteries after dark);
instead, you simply pry the halves apart by inserting the wilderness
equivalent of a coin (your spoon handle, for example) into a small
recess, and twisting. (Warning: once the batteries are removed, it
is possible for the bulb to fall out.) Finally and valuably, a small
hole through one corner of the case makes it very simple to rig a
nylon cord loop that at night will keep the flashlight conveniently
slung around your neck (page 282), and during repairs or battery
changes will hold the case's two halves together and unlosable.

Mallory also makes a larger plastic model (empty, 3 ounces;
with two C alkaline batteries, 7½ ounces; $2.50), but most back-
packers seem to regard it as too heavy for normal use. A metal
equivalent, of orthodox cylindrical shape, is the Ray-o-Vac Sportsman (empty, 3½ ounces; $2.99). It's very tough. I carried one
in my pack for years, and still use it around the house—and
even for backpacking occasionally when weight is no big deal and
long-lasting light may be. But as with all such models, the interior of the cylinder is virtually inaccessible, the switch mechanism
totally so.

Reliability, convenience, and ease of repair aside, choice of
flashlight depends on weight and effective light output. But it is
impossible to understand comparative figures without first grasping
the relative effectiveness of the different sizes and types of battery
most often used in flashlights.

The standard (carbon-zinc or Leclanché) flashlight battery is
entirely adequate for intermittent use. But if the light has to be
kept switched on for long periods—as can happen in an emergency
or through miscalculation or even by design on a long day—then
the battery quickly loses energy and the light soon dims to a useless
glow. A new heavy-duty general-purpose battery may last up to
twice as long under such continuous-drain service. But an alkaline

(or manganese) battery is far more efficient. According to the makers, it may give up to ten times more service. For normal field use, this table gives a fair idea of what to expect:

WEIGHTS, CONTINUOUS-SERVICE LIVES, AND COSTS FOR
PAIRS OF VARIOUS FLASHLIGHT BATTERIES *

Size:	AA	C	D
Name:	Penlight	¾-size	Regular
Diameter:	$\frac{9}{16}$ inch	$1\frac{1}{32}$ inch	$1\frac{11}{32}$ inch
Used in:	Mallory AA	Sportsman/Mallory C	Large flashlights
Bulb:	PR4 or PR2	PR4 or PR2	PR2
Standard:	1 oz. ½ hr. $ .50	3 oz. 1½ hrs. $ .60	6 oz. 2 hrs. $ .60
Alkaline:	1½ oz. 4 hrs. $1.40	4½ oz. 15 hrs. $1.60	9 oz. 12 hrs. $2.00

For continuous-service use, then, alkaline batteries are by far the more efficient, ounce for hour—though their sudden final blackouts are a minor disadvantage.

Service-life figures for the kind of intermittent use a flashlight gets in camp are so subject to imponderables that they would be close to meaningless. But it seems that in the larger cell sizes alkaline batteries might deliver two to three times the service of their standard equivalents. In the AA size, you could expect much larger advantages from alkaline batteries—perhaps seven or eight times.

* The Union Carbide Corporation, makers of Eveready flashlights and batteries, kindly supplied the facts and figures in this table and in the paragraphs of text that follow—with one important exception.

That exception is the service life given for AA batteries in a Mallory flashlight. The Union Carbide figures were ¼ hour for standard batteries and 3 hours for alkaline batteries. It seemed to me that I remembered better service. So I did some experiments—and came up with the figures of ½ hour and 4 hours.

The difficulty, of course, is to decide when a battery is no longer giving useful light. This turns out to be where Union Carbide and I differ. I tried to estimate, as well as I could in my garden, when I would no longer be able to find the way down a reasonably clear trail by flashlight alone. If anything, I tended to underestimate service life. And Union Carbide now agrees that, given the low end-point voltage I found acceptable, my figures are correct.

During my trials, temperatures averaged 66° F. The tests were for continuous life: batteries were switched on and left on, with no rest periods. I did not warm the flashlights by holding them in the palm of my hand. Standard batteries soon dropped off peak performance and lost strength gradually, to the useful point and beyond. The alkaline batteries held close to their peak for about 3 hours, and after 4½ hours were still giving enough light to read this print by. Then, quite suddenly, they blacked out.

Tested again after 11 hours—with no heating or other coercion—the standard batteries lasted about 5 minutes with a rather poor light, the alkaline for rather more than ½ hour. Tested four days later, the standards again lasted about 5 minutes (though more faintly than before), the alkalines for about 20 minutes.

Then there's the temperature question. Standard batteries are designed for use at 70°F. At lower temperatures their efficiency falls sharply. At 32°, AA sizes will function for only a very short time; C and D sizes give only poor light—for about 1 hour and 2 hours respectively. At 0° the figures are: AA—0; C—40 minutes; D—60 minutes. Exposed to temperatures above 125°, standard batteries rapidly disintegrate. Before dismissing the danger of your batteries being exposed to such temperatures, read the first complete paragraph on page 362 and then the footnote on page 59—and ruminate.

Alkaline batteries function fairly efficiently at low temperatures. At 32° F. the continuous-service life of AA, C, and D batteries is reduced to about 35 percent of their life at 70°. At 0° the figures are: AA—40 minutes; C—3 hours; D—2 hours. Temperatures up to 130° have little effect on alkaline batteries, though prolonged exposure to such heat will shorten their "shelf-life." (Mercury batteries are very expensive, 30 percent heavier than alkaline batteries, and last about 30 percent longer—at 70°. But although they work well in extreme heat, they're less than 10 percent effective at freezing, barely 1 percent at 0°. So they're not worth considering for normal backpacking.)

Because of all these factors, and also to keep the replacement situation simple, I nowadays carry only alkaline batteries. For a week-long trip I take two spares for the Mallory AA. I don't remember ever using them. They're essentially for emergencies, such as having to walk out at night. It is easy, though, to think of conditions under which it might be comforting to carry four spares for the Mallory AA—or two for the Mallory C or Sportsman. So let us go ahead at last and compare weights and continuous-service performances for these flashlights, based on the figures in the table on page 314 (remembering that the Mallory AA weighs $1\frac{1}{2}$ ounces empty and assuming for simplicity's sake that the Sportsman and Mallory C both weigh $3\frac{1}{2}$ ounces empty):

Mallory AA, with two spares: $1\frac{1}{2} + (1\frac{1}{2} \times 2) = 4\frac{1}{2}$ oz. — 8 hrs.
Mallory AA, with four spares: $1\frac{1}{2} + (1\frac{1}{2} \times 3) = 6$ oz. — 12 hrs.
Sportsman, with no spares: $3\frac{1}{2} + 4\frac{1}{2} = 8$ oz. — 15 hrs.
Sportsman, with two spares: $3\frac{1}{2} + (4\frac{1}{2} \times 2) = 12\frac{1}{2}$ oz. — 30 hrs.

Experience suggests that in a normal week's backpacking I get by easily on four hours' continuous-service use, or its equivalent in intermittent use, so the Mallory AA is clearly the choice. It allows me, from the spares, a reserve of 4 hours' continuous emergency use—probably plus some extra from rested or partly consumed first-line batteries. If you feel you will need more lighted time—such as when a planned night march will necessitate a flash-light—then the table should help you pick light and batteries to meet your expected needs.

Head-strap flashlights

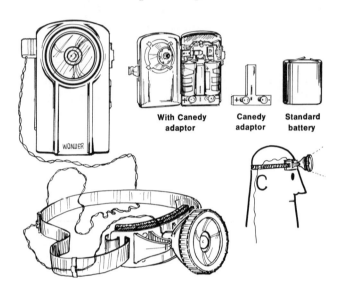

With Canedy   **Canedy**   **Standard**
adaptor   **adaptor**   **battery**

One of the lighest and neatest of these convenient devices is the French Wonder model (empty, 5 ounces; $5). The main hand unit operates alone or as clip-on-pocket source for the angle-ad-justable headlamp, which douses the main light when plugged in. I've tried it, and it works well. Some people say it gives them headaches, and I believe it. Still, even at that risk and that weight, it's a thought for special occasions and dispositions.

In the draft of this section I wrote: "Unfortunately, the 4.5-volt French Electra battery for this light is almost impossible to find, and American equivalents, such as the Eveready #703, not impressively easier." But now Mr. Buck Canedy of Massa-chusetts, who invented the Canedy pouring cap (page 174), has come to the rescue. He has made a simple but effective plastic adaptor that converts the Wonder to American "C" size batteries, and the bulbs to the low-drain (2.7 amp) G.E. #14 or L 233. It will also work with #222 bulbs, "creating a good spotlight." There's even a place to carry two spare bulbs on the adaptor, in-side the flashlight. Simple! Superb! Obtainable for $1.75 (with bulbs) from Mr. Canedy (address, page 175)—who rightly says that the lamp is particularly good "for winter hiking as the light can be comfortably carried in your pocket to keep batteries warm even while using the headlamp on those early climbs."

Stowing the flashlight

Naturally, you must always know exactly where your flash-light is. During the day, mine used to go into the inside pocket of the pack, where it was reasonably well protected and tolerably accessible. But my present pack has no inside pocket, and for some years the flashlight has traveled without damage in an upper outside pocket, padded by scarf or balaclava.

For use and storage at night, see pages 281–2.

Accidental battery drainage

This far from minor mishap is all too likely to happen in your pack when something presses against the flashlight switch. The surest way to prevent it depends on the kind of flashlight you use. With orthodox cylinder-shape, end-loader models such as the Sportsman, you simply reverse the lower battery. You soon come to do it automatically every morning. Restoring the flashlight to working condition is something you most often do at dusk or after dark, but again it's all very simple. You just unscrew the base, shake out the bottom battery, replace it right way up, and screw the base back on. In wet weather you can do the job in a few seconds with the flashlight held out of rain and therefore out of sight under your poncho. Ditto, though differently, with the French Wonder.

With the Mallory, such an operation is complicated, and rough on the mechanism; but fortunately, all you need do is put a piece of adhesive tape over the large-surfaced, rotating switch. With the tape in place, the switch cannot turn. At night, park the tape on a flat side of the flashlight. In the morning, replace it on the switch. A 2-inch length of the 1-inch tape from my first-aid kit does the job perfectly and lasts through a two-week trip.

Spare bulbs

Carry at least one spare. I carry two. They travel in a 35 mm. film can marked "odds and ends" (page 371). PR4's, or their equivalent, are the type for both the Sportsman and Mallory—or other lights with C or AA batteries. A PR2 or #222 bulb gives a somewhat brighter light but might be expected to have a rather shorter life.

Candle lanterns

For some years now I have often, when nights were long—and particularly if I needed to do evening reading or notetaking—carried a cylindrical aluminum French candle lantern (2 by 4½ inches folded, 11½ inches extended; 3¾ ounces; $5.50). Use stearene candles (pink; 2 ounces and $.07 each; 80 cents a dozen): they drip far less wax than ordinary household "plumber's" candles—which can, however, be used. The lantern has a spring in the lowest section, designed to keep the candle at a uniform burning height. Unfortunately, you cannot buy candles of the designated size in the United States. But if you cut about an inch and a half off the bottom of a stearene candle and then shave it for its entire length (except the very head) so that it fits *exactly* into its casing, it will indeed perform according to the book. Well, maybe. If you shave it roughly (and you have to shave it to get it in) then it almost certainly will not move. But you still get a passing good light —certainly enough to write by, just about enough to read by if you have big print and good eyes and plenty of time, and enough to cook and housekeep by if you can hang the lantern high so that household items do not cast too many concealing shadows. The glass chimney does a remarkable job of shielding the candle from wind. And it is tough: I've never had one break on me. You can suspend the lantern by its chain on a nylon cord without fear of burning the cord—and you can adjust it by an auxiliary sideways-pulling cord, perhaps with some such convenient handle as a staff (page 50).

There are also folding candle lanterns, with mica windows,

that some people find more effective, especially in the larger, stronger size.

Estimating how many candles you will need is a problem. All I can tell you is that a single stearene candle is rated to burn for three hours, and probably does; and that I always seem to take too many candles.

Gas-cartridge lanterns

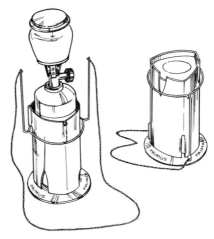

Both Primus and Bleuet—but not Gerry—now make lanterns that operate from the same gas cartridges as their backpacking stoves.

I cannot judge relative reliability; but the Primus 2220 defeats the Bleuet L200 on almost every other count: it weighs little more than half as much; it folds into a sturdy, compact unit; and above all, its valve system means you can switch partly-empty cartridges to and from stove and lantern—as you cannot with the Bleuet. Specifications:

Primus 2220: Lantern alone, 9 ounces; with cartridge, 1 pound 4 ounces; $13. Assembled, 11 inches high. Folds down to stout, compact 5½-inch-high package. Rated to burn 7 hours, full-on.

Bleuet L200. Lantern alone, 1 pound 11 ounces; with cartridge, 2 pounds 5 ounces; $11. 12 inches high. Does not disassemble—and is therefore a hell of a thing to pack. Rated to burn 4½–5 hours, full-on.

Both lanterns have frosted globes "for bright, glare-free light"; and both have fragile little mantles for easy breakage. I don't yet know, only fear, that mantles may be the lanterns' Achilles' heel. A spare Primus mantle is a backpacker's horror—a flimsy square job that looks almost as likely to break as the one on the lantern; but I'm told that a Coleman 100-candle-power propane mantle works fine, and it is the kind that is flat and pliable until burned, and is therefore easy to carry. The Bleuet spare is that kind of mantle, but will not fit the Primus.

To sum up, the Bleuet is hardly a backpacking proposition; but the Primus, though not worthwhile or even desirable for every trip, has its points. I carried one recently when I wanted to read after dark, and was distinctly glad of it. Many people might consider carrying that extra 9 ounces of lamp if they need cartridges for the stove anyway. But remember that a lantern screens you off from the night even more drastically than a fire does (page 149). And although it does not roar the way a stove does, the damned thing hisses, right there by your bloody earhole.

Sunglasses

Dark glasses are a comfort and convenience just about anywhere, almost indispensable in deserts, totally so in snow.

For all-around use, G15 lenses (Bausch and Lomb) are generally recognized as best. I've used a pair for years, and find them excellent under widely differing conditions. But Polaroids, even more than G15's, let you look through the surface glare of water—often a critical advantage in fishing. If you wear eyeglasses, either some or all of the time, prescription sunglasses are far better than either clip-on glasses or a large pair that will fit over your normal corrective glasses, though both these are useful as spares.

Other useful spares are the flimsy, frameless plastic affairs that oculists give you to protect your eyes after dilation. For permanence, patch them at the bends with Rip-stop. A pair always travels in my office. Once you've graduated to bifocals, they are invaluable if you want to read in bright sunlight.

In snow, failure to take sunglasses may mean snow blindness. I understand that in an emergency almost any opaque material with cross-slits or a small hole cut into it will let you see halfway adequately, and will ward off snow blindness. Possibilities: cardboard from the "office" (page 359), Rip-stop tape (page 363), cover from a paperback book (page 357), part of a map or food wrapper.

But if you know you'll be traveling in snow you should take

Goggles or special snow glasses.

You can buy a small, strong pair of round-lens goggles (2 ounces) for $3, and they'll see you through most situations. But they restrict your vision, and seem to come only with green or smoke lenses—necessary in sun glare—not with the amber kind that accent shadows and definitely help bring up shapes from the deceptive and dangerous flatness of a sunless "white-out"—which can conceal not only undulations but also big and potentially fatal drop-offs. Under such conditions, green lenses give the outside world a dark and depressing aspect; amber lenses impart surprising brightness and help keep spirits high. Do not underestimate this bonus.

Large and fancy goggles with interchangeable lenses are one answer to the problem; but they tend to be complicated and liable to damage. Vaurnet sunglasses overcome the difficulty with green zones at the top and bottom of each lens to filter glare from sky and underfoot snow, but with an amber zone in between. An experienced snow man tells me they work extremely well in both sunglare and flat light. Lenses are cadmium coated to screen infrared and ultraviolet rays. The frames are so pliable and tough that you can literally tie a knot in the temple and then let it spring back to normal. Unfortunately these glasses do not yet come with sidescreens. They weigh only 2 ounces but cost $18.50.

Such unsidescreened glasses fail to protect your eyes from cutting winds or driving snow; but at least they are well ventilated. At the other extreme, highly protective goggles tend to mist or fog as your perspiration condenses on the cold lenses. Some fancier goggles now have adjustable vents. But there is no final solution to the problem in driving snow: let in enough air, and you let in the snow. The standard compromise is to wear highly enclosed goggles but treat the lenses with an antifog paste or stick. My experience with antifog preparations on snow goggles is frankly small, but I've experimented widely in attempts to keep my eyeglasses from fogging as I sweat around tennis courts, and I've found nothing to compare with a glycerine-based paste called Neva-Mist (Tanasol Company, Berkeley, California. See Appendix II). It comes in ½-ounce tins of convenient size but fiendish unopenability ($.60). A makeshift substitute is wetted soap. Apply a thin film to goggles or glasses and rub gently into invisibility. The effect lasts a surprisingly long time.

A new solution to the fogging problem has now surfaced. In Hydron lenses (see Eastern Mountain Sports catalogue), an inner coating absorbs moisture and spreads it uniformly, leaving your vision clear. Wrap-around goggles with interchangeable green and amber lenses and adjustable vents: 3⅓ ounces; $16. Sunglasses: 1¼ ounces; $13.

Your seeing—of all kinds—can be greatly amplified by

Binoculars.

I am always astonished that so few hikers carry them. It is
not merely that a pair of binoculars can be extremely useful—that
by leapfrogging your eyes out far ahead and disclosing the curve of
a creek or the impassability of a rockwall they can save you hours
of wasted effort; or that they might even act as an emergency fire-
starter (page 148). They are the key to many unexpected and
therefore doubly delightful bonuses.

They lift you up so close to a planing hawk that you feel you
could reach out and straighten a misplaced wing feather. They convert a small low-flying plane from an impersonal outline into a
solid construction of panels and colors and markings, even of pilot
and passengers with faces and lives of their own. They transform a
deer on the far rim of a sunlit meadow from a motionless silhouette
into a warm, breathing individual—alert, quivering, suspicious.

You can focus good binoculars down close, too—sometimes
onto one of those unimportant, utterly fascinating little cameos that
you are apt to stumble on when you are in the right place and the
right mood, with no stupidly important things to occupy your
time and attention. You can even move over into the insect world.
Early one fall, on the slopes of a desert mountain, I sat idly watching with my naked eye as a clapper-rattle grasshopper made a
series of noisy, stunted airborne journeys. In flight, with its wings
beating furiously, it looked like a small and ungainly green butter-
fly. After one flight, the creature landed near the edge of a gravel
road 8 feet in front of me, and rested. Squatting there beside a tiny
tuft of grass, it was just a small, dark smudge, barely visible. I
screwed my binocular focus adjustment fully out. The grasshopper
crystallized into view: huge, green-armored and apparently wing-
less, its front end tapering into the kind of chinless and no-brow
head that to the human mind spells vacuity. Above the head
towered a gigantic forest of grass blades. After a while the grasshopper moved. It advanced, bent-stilt leg slowly following bent-
stilt leg, until it came to a small blade of grass on the edge of the
forest. Dreamily, it reached out with one foreleg, pressed down
on the blade, manipulated it, inserted the tip into its mouth, and
clamped tight. Slowly it sidled around until its body and the grass
blade formed a single straight line. And then, still unutterably
dreamily, it proceeded to devour the grass blade as if it were a
huge horizontal strand of spaghetti. It ate very slowly, moving for-

ward from time to time with an almost imperceptible shuffle of its bent-stilt legs. All at once, when the blade of grass was about three-quarters gone, the grasshopper relinquished its grip and the truncated blade sprang back into place on the edge of the forest. The grasshopper moved jerkily away, skirting the enormous and overhanging green forest, traversing a tract of sun-beaten sand, then lumbering out over huge boulders of gravel. Suddenly, for no apparent reason, it launched once more into clapper-rattle flight and rocketed noisily and forever out of my vivid binocular world.

If you are going to carry binoculars as a matter of habit when you go walking, be sure to get the right kind. They must be light. They must be tough enough to stand up to being banged around. And they must not tire your eyes, even when used for long periods.

In choosing a pair of glasses, people tend to consider only magnification (indicated by the first of the two numbers stamped on the casing—the "7" in the average-power 7 × 35, for example). But powerful lenses magnify not only what you see but also the inevitable "jump" imparted by your hands. So, unless you can steady the glasses on something, magnification beyond a certain power—about 7 or 8 for most people—does not necessarily allow you to see more clearly. Generally speaking too, the greater the magnification, the narrower your field of view.

Again, if powerful glasses are not to darken what you see, they must have big end-lenses to let in adequate light. The second of the two numbers on the casing—the "35" in the 7 × 35—gives the diameter of the end-lenses in millimeters, and for daylight use there is no advantage to having that second figure more than five times as big as the first: except at night, the average human eye cannot use the extra light that bigger lenses let in. And big lenses mean cumbersome glasses that are too heavy for ordinary use. Once the first thrill of ownership has worn off they generally get left at home—ask anyone who has invested in a pair of those impressive looking naval-type binoculars.

It used to be said that reducing the magnification/end lens ratio to less than 5 cut out so much light that it seriously reduced clarity of vision in anything but full sunlight. This gospel has been revised. Perhaps the increased efficiency of new, coated lenses engineered the revision—or perhaps just the well-known habit of long-standing human theories to undergo sudden metamorphosis or even death. I do not know. But I do know that you can now buy first-class 8 × 30 binoculars. There are even 7 × 18's. ("Good," say some people. "More like toys," say others.)

On some binoculars, a knurled wheel on the center post

focuses both lenses, and any eye difference (except for very marked variation in long- or shortsightedness) is corrected with the right eyepiece. In other models, each eyepiece focuses independently. Both systems have advantages. For quick refocusing at short range, as in birdwatching, you need center focus. But individual-focus glasses, more simply constructed, will stand up to rougher use.

A pair of 14-ounce individual focus 6 × 30's, pre–World War II Zeiss, appropriated from the German army, lasted me more than twenty years and traveled an utterly unreasonable mileage hanging and banging on my packframe (page 326). Because I wanted a center-focus pair for game-watching in East Africa (and because my old ones had at last grown tired, optically, and I was also passing through Hong Kong, the cheapest place in the world to buy binoculars), I at last replaced them with Nikon 7 × 35's (17 ounces). By the time a jeep attack on them three years later inflicted irreparable internal injuries, I was into birdwatching (page 366) and therefore bought another center-focus pair—Nikon 8 × 30's that were no bigger or heavier but even better. After three years' manhandling they seem as good as new.

My personal opinion is that good 8 × 30's such as these are probably best for average backpacking use. But there is glorious scope for disagreement. Various readers extol the surprising efficiency of pocket-size 7 × 20's and 8 × 21's, and also monoculars. (There is, for example, a Zeiss 8 × 20 monocular that weighs only 1½ ounces—but costs $80.) And some catalogues now feature compact, lightweight Bushnell and Nikon models said to be very tough (8.2–14.3 ounces; $60–$92.50). But note that because these compacts—like the new-style Leica and Zeiss models—have the center bar concealed, you cannot attach a clampocular (page 332) for binophotography.

Fifteen years ago, worthwhile binoculars were expensive luxuries. Then Japan began to produce good instruments at low prices. Today, very good-quality glasses need cost no more than $75. You can buy an adequate pair for $35 or $40.

Secondhand glasses are always a risk—unless you know exactly what you are doing. Even new ones should be bought only from reputable dealers who really understand their wares. New or old, make sure you test several pairs outside the store, in sunlight and shadow. Better still, insist on a cast-iron money-back guarantee in case you are not satisfied after, say, three days' trial. Misaligned or unsuitable binoculars can cause eyestrain, and they will probably, like too-heavy models, soon get left at home.

To get the most out of your binoculars, you must learn to use them automatically, almost without thought. First, set the barrels at the widest angle that gives you a circular field of view. Note the reading on the small center dial. Next, focus. Do not shut one eye while you do so: you may alter the normal muscle positions of the open eye. Instead, keep both eyes open, cover the right exit lens with one hand, and move the focus adjustment on the center post (or on the left eyepiece in individual-focus models) until a selected object is as sharp as you can make it. Shift your hand to the left exit lens and, still with both eyes open, move the adjustment on the right eyepiece until the *same* selected object is again sharp. Then look through both eyepieces at once: the object should still be critically sharp. With center-focus binoculars, memorize the reading on the right eyepiece adjustment: it will be correct for your eyes at any distance. It is also convenient if you can memorize the long-distance reading on the center-post adjustment (or, in individual-focus models, on each eyepiece).

Some people tend to screw their eyes up just because they're looking through a strange instrument. Naturally, their eye muscles soon tire. But if the binoculars' two barrels are properly aligned, anyone can, with practice, look through them for protracted periods without strain. After all, seamen and birdwatchers do, hours at a stretch. And there is never any reason for saying, "Oh, but my eyes are too old for binoculars." Given proper eyeglasses, age need make no difference.

If you wear eyeglasses you may have found that you see only a very restricted field of view when you look through binoculars. This is because normal eyepieces keep your eye too far back from the lens. Some manufacturers now supply special shallow eyepieces for eyeglass wearers. Others make adjustable cups that screw down out of the way. (Some such device is a great advantage under snow-and-sunlight conditions, when you have to wear goggles all the time.) Frankly, though, I find I nearly always take off eyeglasses, if I'm wearing them, before looking through binoculars.

Some people experience difficulty at first in getting what they want into the field of view. One way is to fix your eyes on the target and simply bring the glasses into position. Another method is to draw your eyes back a few inches and align the center bar on the target; then, without moving the instrument, shift your eyes to the eyepieces. The target should be dead center in your field of view.

Once you are so used to your binoculars that you use them without a thought for technique, you will probably find yourself taking them along whenever you go walking. And they will always be opening up new possibilities. I still have a couple of unfulfilled wishes on my conscious waiting list. I want to examine a nearby rainbow's end. And one day I'd like to look from a respectful distance straight into the eye of an ill-humored rattlesnake.*

Carrying binoculars

For many years now I have—except in rain and across very rough country—carried my binoculars slung by their leather or nylon harness over the projecting tubular top of one side of the packframe. (For bump pad to reduce noise, see page 84.) But my most recent packbag (illustration, page 69) reaches almost to the top of each tube, and so little projection is left that the binoculars (and the camera, which hangs on the other side) are liable to bounce off at any marked jerk or forward lean. More than five years ago, as a temporary measure, I knotted a length of nylon cord to the top securing ring bolt on each side of the packframe (for knots in nylon, see page 369). To the free ends of these cords I tied belt clips (page 371) that snap onto the carrying straps of binoculars and camera case. The cords are just long enough to let me bring the instruments forward in front of my eyes to the "use" position, but if either instrument jerks loose the cord normally prevents it from crashing down onto the ground. This device is clumsy, rather complicated, and not totally efficient: on very steep slopes or among big boulders, binoculars and camera can still fall far enough to be damaged. But after five years I have still, to my considerable surprise, come up with nothing that suits me better.

Naturally, other devices suit other backpackers better: for one thing, many packframes have no projections. One friend of mine always carries his binoculars slung around his neck. A reader recommends doing so but taking that nagging weight off your neck by resting the instrument in an open leather binocular case sewn on the pack's shoulder strap, much as I sew my "office-on-the-yoke" (page 83). Another reader has fixed a flat, ½-inch-wide clip ("made from the handle of a can opener—but aluminum would be better") to the "camera mount" on his binoculars. This clip slips into a slim pocket sewn on the pack's shoulder strap. For protection against slipouts (though "they don't happen") he ties an 18-inch cord to one of the binoculars' strap rings, attaches a small

---

* Just the other morning I looked out of my bedroom window soon after sunrise and saw a rainbow curving down into the foot of the hills opposite my house, barely half a mile away. I immediately turned and began hurrying for my binoculars. But halfway to the bedroom door I stopped. Faced with the impending reality, I knew that if I went ahead and looked, as I had so long thought I intended, I would find . . . nothing. So I turned and went back to the window, my dream intact. Well, almost intact.

clip to the free end of the cord, and clips this spring to a D-ring sewn on the shoulder strap beside the pocket. The binoculars hang close at hand and reasonably warm "so that they don't fog too badly." Cunning.

You can also buy harnesses of adjustable, 1-inch-wide elastic strap that encircle neck and back and hold binoculars (or camera) on your chest and prevent it from bouncing (4½ ounces; $7).

It is less well known than it ought to be that binoculars can be used not only for seeing but as a worthwhile aid to

RECORDING YOUR MARVEL.

Nowadays, most of us tend to accept that we are failing in some kind of duty if we do not record our outdoor doings on film. Chalk up another victory to advertising. But, brainwashing aside, we all want on at least some occasions to carry back home a thin facsimile of the marvel we have discovered.

Movie cameras and their accessories are heavy, bulky, expensive and a perishing nuisance, so most people record their backpacking highlights (not to mention the lowlights and midlights) by means of

Still photography.

The important thing is to choose equipment that is light, compact, light, simple, light, tough and light.

The *camera* can be simple or fancy, as your pocket and inclinations dictate, but it must be small. For ten years I carried an Ansco Super Regent 35 mm. rangefinder model (1 pound 10 ounces) that was tough as nails and had a gem of a lens. When tripod and camera blew over one gusty Grand Canyon afternoon and the faithful old Super Regent gave up the ghost, I replaced it, sadly, with a single-lens reflex Zeiss Contaflex that was a much finer instrument but weighed 2 pounds 7 ounces. Five years ago I bought a Pentax, with through-the-lens exposure meter, that weighs 2 pounds 6 ounces, with case. (I'd previously carried a separate 6-ounce exposure meter.) My Pentax has withstood the years without murmur, and is a joy to use; once you've experienced the convenience and accuracy of a complete through-the-lens system, you're spoiled for other cameras.

A skylight (or UV) filter stays more or less permanently on the lens.

One advantage the Pentax holds over most cameras is the smallness and lightness of its lenses. For more on auxiliary lenses, see page 330.

Readers have written suggesting various smaller and lighter cameras—ranging from half-frame single lens reflexes (24 ounces) down to Minox- or Minolta-type subminiatures (5 ounces). Although you lose some quality and flexibility with each paring of weight, many people take this route. On the increasingly rare occasions I carry a camera it is normally for professional use—and 35 mm. is the smallest acceptable size. But I see there are now "ultracompact" 35 mm. cameras that seem to have been designed especially for backpacking, ski touring, rock climbing and the like (Rollei 35: 13½ ounces; $200. Rollei 35B: 9½ ounces; $100. Petri Color 35: 13¾ ounces; $90).

For ways of carrying a camera, see page 326.

Ancillary photographic equipment should be as light and simple as your needs permit.

Tripod. At 14 ounces, the lightest I can find. Folded: 8¾ inches long, 2½ inches wide. Telescopic legs extend to 3 feet 8 inches. The legs on such light models soon develop signs of palsy, but they'll work for several months, solid, before becoming seriously crippled.

Check that the feet of any tripod you buy have large rubber toes, not just little pimples of rubber that quickly wear out and leave you with metal tips that slip on any rocky surface.

My tripod travels, along with most of the photographic equipment, in the top left-side pocket of my pack (page 376). On packless sidetrips, its ball-and-socket screw fitting snaps into a belt clip (page 371).

As a substitute camera stand, a walking staff forms a rough but very ready monopod. And years ago I bought a light-alloy C clamp (4 ounces) that purported to be a tripod substitute. It clamped to "anything" and even had a detachable screw for use in wood; and a ball-and-socket screw attachment meant you could attach the camera at any angle. I carried this crafty device for months, if not years. But taking a good photograph involves positioning the camera in exactly the place and at exactly the height you want—and at that magic spot there is never, ever, any place, anything within yards or even miles to which you can by any means short of levitation attach that besotted clamp. It is a long time since I carried it. I see that versions now exist (5¼ and 11 ounces) with "collapsible tripod legs." Uh-huh . . .

You more or less have to carry a tripod—or usable substitute—if you walk alone: continuous shots of scenery without a human figure grow horribly monotonous. And it is amazing what you can learn to do in the way of running and positioning yourself in the ten seconds that elapse between pressing the self-timer and the shutter's action.

Camel's-hair lens-cleaning brush. Screw-down metal-cased type that looks just like a lipstick and is always good for a laugh on that score (¾ ounce). Travels in pants ticket pocket. A pocket-clip type should be more convenient, but I've yet to find one that's strong or dirt resistant enough.

Lens tissue. One virtually weightless packet, protected by the inevitable plastic bag, that goes into the flap pocket of the pack, where it won't get crushed.

Two close-up attachments (together, 2 ounces). Normally they live in a double plastic bag in a side pocket of the pack. If it seems likely they'll be needed, I transfer them either to the flap pocket of the pack or to a pants pocket.

Cable release. Useful both for "binophotography" (page 331) and for long-exposure shots in which the camera must be kept still. My 8-inch cable weighs ½ ounce. It travels—held in place by two or three rubber bands—tucked in beside the flange of the flash-fitting that I use for mating binoculars and camera (page 331; illustration, page 332).

Film. It pays, I think, to get used to one kind of film, so that you use it with very little thought. But it's good to experiment occasionally with new kinds, to make sure that your personal preferences, which are all that count, have not changed. These days, I rarely shoot black and white. In color, I used Ansochrome for many years but now prefer Kodachrome II (ASA 25). Kodachrome X is 1¼ stops faster and has its uses when speed becomes important in bad light or for high-power magnification; but this film gives you less latitude and definition. High Speed Ektachrome is very fast (ASA 160) but I dislike it for any but special subjects. Agfachrome (ASA 50) might claim to be the best all-around film; and overseas, where it is called Agfacolor, there is sometimes the advantage that you can get it developed locally and quickly—though the quality of the work is not always dependable.

One truly objective criterion for judging film is its stability. Exposed color film is sensitive to high temperatures, especially when the humidity also runs high. And remember that even weak sunshine can soon raise the temperature in an outside pocket of your pack well above the possibly critical 75° F. mark. In anything but really cool weather take precautions. Replace exposed film in a can without delay and screw tight shut. Wrap all film cans in a plastic bag or even in one of those insulated ice-cream bags that stores provide. Except in really cool weather, keep this bag deep in the center of the main section of your packbag, where the temperature changes less than anywhere else in the house. And get film processed as soon as possible.

You won't have trouble with heat damage to film very often, but if you do you won't forget it. One June, I spent a week in the bowels of Grand Canyon researching and shooting a photo story on assignment for a magazine. I used Kodachrome II, Kodachrome X (for close-up high-speed action shots), and Anscochrome (which perhaps penetrates shadow more effectively). Although humidity remained low all that week in Grand Canyon, the temperature exceeded 100° F. every day. High was 109°. These are shade readings and I was rarely photographing in the shade, so I took reasonable precautions. But not one frame of Anscochrome was usable: all had faded sadly and taken on a pale green overcast. The Kodachrome II and Kodachrome X came out perfectly.

Spare camera lenses. Most popular—and a virtual necessity for animal photography—are telephoto lenses. But they're heavy. My 11-ounce Pentax 150 mm. is a bantam of the breed.

Small, lightweight magnifying lenses called "converters" are a tempting alternative. I have two- and three-power converters (4½ and 6½ ounces, with cases) and have achieved occasional spectacular successes with them. But they make focusing a highly critical operation, severely cut available light, and—worst of all—rarely give crisp definition. They certainly demand a high-quality lens in the camera. But some people swear by them—especially the two-power versions. Still, it would be wise to approach them with suspicion as well as hope.

Some people extol the virtues of short-focus or wide-angle lenses, especially for scenery.

Unfortunately, most spare lenses are not only heavy—and also cumbersome, fragile and expensive—they're dangerous. The danger lies in temptation. Once you start carrying them it is fiendishly difficult to avoid becoming involved, far too often, in physical juggling and technical expertise.

For many years I shielded myself from such confusions and time-wasting by the simple device of not owning spare lenses. But when I bought my Pentax I was going game-viewing in Africa, and I knew it would be criminal to take only a standard lens. I've only backpacked the telephoto lens, though, on those rare occasions I knew there was a good chance of such special subjects as bighorn sheep.

Interchangeable lenses certainly feed the maggot inherent in all photography (page 334), and I'm by no means convinced that, for the wilderness walker, they do not get in the way of the very best pictures. If you stick to a standard lens you will never have to stop and debate whether to fiddle about with a wide-angle or telephoto lens and will therefore always be ready to slip the camera off your packframe and capture, before the opportunity is lost, that superb but fleeting moment when a shaft of sunlight breaks through the storm clouds and arches a double rainbow across a somber mountain tarn; or ready to freeze for the future a pale but still evocative glimmer of the poetry that halts your breath when you look up the rocky trail and see once again the always new and wonderful and calming and cooling magic of sunset on fiery desert hills.

On the other hand, there is no denying that a telephoto lens will record those vivid marvels—and especially the animal marvels—that you can see only through your binoculars.

The exit from this dilemma lies, logically enough, through your binoculars. It's called

Binophotography.

Now even the best pictures taken through binoculars are not quite as sharp as those taken with a telephoto lens. But if you do the job properly they can be effective close-ups—exact records of what you saw through the binoculars. My Grand Canyon trip was the first on which I tried binophotography in the field, and in the course of it I managed to capture presentable color bino shots of deer, wild horses, wild burros, beaver and a bighorn sheep. The shots of wild burros and of the bighorn sheep were good enough to appear as black-and-whites in the book about that trip.

By far the most suitable camera for binophotography is a single-lens reflex: you look directly through camera and binocular lenses and see exactly what you photograph. But with practice, patience, determination and luck it is possible to achieve tolerable results even with a rangefinder model: my Grand Canyon shots of wild horses and the bighorn sheep were taken with the range-finder-type Super Regent.

Ideally, the binoculars should be held rigidly in front of the camera, but the proper attachments are bulky and heavy, not to mention expensive. As a backpacking compromise I use the small and rather flimsy flash attachment shown on page 332 (3 ounces). Any good photographer would scoff at its inefficiency. But any backpacker will appreciate its lightness.

The binoculars are attached to the fitting by means of a

clampocular—a small device, weighing a fraction of an ounce, that stays on the binoculars, folded down out of the way so that you almost never notice it.

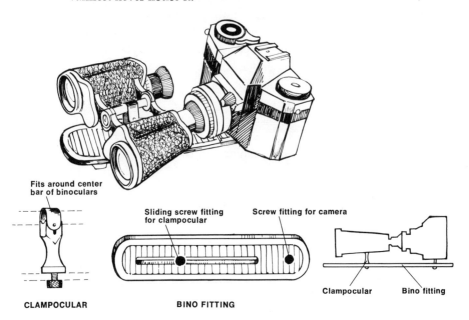

Fits around center bar of binoculars

Sliding screw fitting for clampocular

Screw fitting for camera

Clampocular   **Bino fitting**

CLAMPOCULAR   **BINO FITTING**

This is no place to go into the fine detail of binophotography with different kinds of cameras and binoculars.* But the fundamentals that you just have to grasp are focus and exposure.

With a single-lens reflex you can focus with either camera or binoculars, directly through the camera lens. In practice, I find it best to set the camera at minimum range, then focus with the binoculars. With viewfinder cameras, focusing is more complicated, but in general you set your camera at minimum range, then focus by eye through the free lens of the binoculars.

With a through-the-lens-exposure-meter camera, such as a Pentax, exposure presents no problem: you simply open the aperture wide (i.e., set at the lowest f.-stop number), then turn the shutter speed dial until the exposure meter arrow stops in the right place. For other cameras (except subminiatures such as the Minox, and certain 8 mm. movie cameras) the formula for calculating exposure is:

$$\text{Exposure} = \frac{\text{Focal length of camera} \times \text{magnification of binoculars}}{\text{Diameter of objective aperture of binoculars}}.$$

* One source of information is *Binoculars and Scopes: How to Choose, Use and Photograph Through Them* (2nd edn.), by Robert and Else Reichert—a paperback published by American Photographic Book Publishing Company, New York ($2.50).

Mercifully, this sum simplifies, with a standard 50 mm. focal length camera lens and 6 × 30 binoculars, into

$$\text{Exposure} = \frac{50 \times 6}{30} = 10.$$

With that combination of instruments, in other words, the binoculars have reduced the camera aperture to a maximum of f.10. So you always calculate for that aperture setting, and control exposure by varying the shutter speed. (To remind myself of the constant f.10 setting, I scratched "10" on my clampocular with a pin.) But you do *not* set the camera aperture at f.10; you open it up as far as it will go (i.e., set it at the lowest possible f. number). Unless you do so you will subject your pictures to vignetting. That is, their edges will be blacked out, and the subject held within a circular black frame. (As a matter of fact, vignetting can sometimes be very effective, especially in animal photography, as it conveys the impression of looking through a telescope. A cheetah-on-prey shot I took in Kenya achieved this effect beautifully.)

Because of the long focal length of your combined instrument, the slightest vibration will blur your picture. Hand-holding rarely produces satisfactory results, though I've often got by with resting the rig on a rock and pressing the release manually. See also "Walking staff," page 49. But where possible use a tripod and a cable release.

The most vital element in learning binophotography is practice. Before attempting to operate under the dirt, disorder and excitement of wilderness conditions I ran off several rolls on distant shots of my car (because it had easily focused straight lines and could be moved into various lights), and I did not consider myself ready for action until I had successfully caught Willie Mays in the act of hitting a home run. (I like to say it was a home run. The way the ball is taking off, it could easily have been one. To be honest, it was just a long out.)

I have described in my other books some of the less obvious and more dubious delights you can achieve with a camera.

Photography of any pretension at all eats up time at a rate that is rarely grasped by people who do no more than take snapshots of friends. And wilderness photography, even without interchangeable lenses, has its own special time-consuming idiosyncrasies. It is not just that exasperation and loving care have to fight their usual battles—first against each other, then as allies against form-balance, shadows, depth of focus, fluctuating light, parallax problems, and a wobbly tripod. You also have to cope with the irresistible beckonings of more and yet more brilliant wild flowers every time you move forward for a shot of an especially magnificent display; with the flimsy psyches of lizards; with the pathologically antisocial attitude of bighorn sheep; and with a 50-pound pack that has to come off for almost every shot and then, by God, has to go back on again.

Now this kind of in-fighting has its merits. Up to a point it can be instructive, diverting and satisfying. Up to a point.

Not until my Grand Canyon walk did I grasp, by sheer accident, that one of the great bonuses walking has to offer is

The delight of nonphotography.

The accident that opened my eyes was the demise of that faithful old Super Regent camera.

At first, when I discovered that its shutter refused to function, I simmered with frustration. I was carrying only the one camera, and I knew that it would be at least a week before I could get word out that I urgently needed a replacement—a week in which I would walk through a spectacular, rarely visited landscape that I would almost certainly never visit again. It promised to be a bitter week. But within an hour I discovered that I had escaped from something I never quite knew existed: the tyranny of film. Photography, I suddenly understood, is not really compatible with contemplation. Its details are too insistent. They are always buzzing around your mind, clouding the fine focus of appreciation. You rarely realize this painful fact at the time, and you cannot do much about it even if you do. But that day in Grand Canyon, after the camera had broken, I found myself savoring in a new way everything around me. Instead of stopping briefly to photograph and forget, I stood and stared, fixing truer images on the emulsion of memory. And the week, set free, became a carnival.

I learned my lesson. These days, I rarely take a camera. And if I want my walking to be, above all, carefree and therapeutic, I make sure I leave it at home—or at least carry only a roll or two of film. I find that, by and large, it works. Liberated, I have more time to stand and stare.

To nurture the holiday spirit on a minor trip I occasionally exercise similar self-denial in another, much more necessary, activity:

ROUTE-FINDING.

On such occasions I may deliberately go without

Maps.

Or I may take only rudimentary ones (page 336). In part, this stratagem works: it injects into each day a steady stream of that titillating element, the unexpected. But sometimes I find that traveling without a map becomes so inefficient that it diminishes my freedom rather than amplifies it. And when it is important that you get to the right place at more or less the right time, maps become indispensable. They're also a help in deciding what places you most want to see.

But maps are not merely for route-finding. They can radically influence many facets of your outdoor life. They act as aids not only to keeping going and to accurate estimating (page 65), but in water logistics, foot comfort, warmth, and choice of campsites. Without a map to tell you where to find the next water—even though not always with certainty—you are liable to labor along under an unnecessary canteen load, or to walk for long, half-lived hours with your awareness clogged by the gray scum of thirst. If your feet are beginning to get sore a map may help you ward off real trouble by avoiding a route that involves a long, steady, down-hill, blister-inducing trek. On a day lacerated by icy winds you can with luck and a map select trails that slink along in compara-tive coziness under the lee of a steep ridge. And with practice you can choose good campsites, hours or even days ahead—and in doing so may even collect one of walking's unexpected and de-lightful little bonuses (page 280).

In the United States, the only maps that really convey much detailed information of the kind useful to a walker are the U.S. Geological Survey topographical series. These maps come in vari-ous sizes and scales, though most new ones are either 15-minute quadrangles (covering 15 minutes of both latitude and longitude; scale, 1:62,500, or roughly 1 inch to 1 mile; contour interval usually 80 feet) or 7½-minute quadrangles (scale: 1:24,000; con-tour interval usually 40 feet). Both kinds of "quad" are so detailed that you sometimes feel they would be adequate to guide you on a prowl around on hands and knees. But don't be misled: although the contours rarely prove inaccurate, trails all too often do—and sometimes badly so.

A selection of local quads is often available at mountain shops and in certain book stores. The price is likely to be around $1. Direct from any U.S. Geological Survey map office, the quads are $.75 each.

The central distribution agency for maps covering areas east of the Mississippi River is: Distribution Section, USGS, Washington, D.C. 20242. For maps west of the Mississippi: Distribution Section, USGS, Federal Center, Denver, Colorado 80225. For Alaska: USGS, 301 First Avenue, Fairbanks, Alaska 99701.

There are subsidiary map distribution offices in Dallas, Texas; Salt Lake City, Utah; Spokane, Washington; Menlo Park, San Francisco, and Los Angeles, California; and Anchorage and Juneau, Alaska.

Any map office or distribution center will supply you, free, with an index map of your state or area. This map enables you to find the name of the quad or quads that cover the slice of country you are interested in. It also lists places within the state from which you can buy USGS topo maps.

In most big cities you can find out from the local USGS office (check in phone book) where to buy topo maps. Even if the office does not sell them itself, the staff will know the local retail outlets.

The Canadian equivalent of the USGS maps is the National Topographical Series, scale 1:50,000 (1¼ inches to 1 mile). For these maps, and for information about their distribution, write: Canada Map Office, Department of Energy, Mines and Resources, 615 Booth Street, Ottawa, Ontario, Canada, KIA OE9.

U.S. Forest Service maps generally show roads, rivers and trails but little else. It's often worth picking one up from a ranger station to check that the trail details shown on a USGS topo map are accurate and up to date. And I sometimes use one on a minor trip when I want to know roughly where I'm going but also want to conserve that titillating element of the unexpected.

Another way to achieve that end is to take along only an ordinary road map of the kind you can pick up at any gas station. Between roads, these maps are mostly blank space. At the most, they offer some rather speculative hachuring—a light shading that indicates the slope and direction of hill and valley. With such a map you can easily set yourself the vague sort of target that seems necessary to almost any kind of walk. (As someone has said, "Every journey must have a soul.") You just find a big blank space that intrigues you, drive to the edge of it, park the car, and walk in and find out what's there. Such an expedition can take an hour, an afternoon, a weekend or a week. With a little experience, local knowledge and luck, you may be able to burst clear not only of roads but of the last vestiges of any kind of a trail.*

Occasionally, if I expect much rain or drizzle, I'll carry the map I'm currently using in a light vinyl mapcase (1 ounce; $.45)

---

* Do not underestimate the importance of such a bursting free. There is a cardinal rule of travel, all too often overlooked, that I call *The Law of Inverse Appreciation.*

It states: "The less there is between you and the environment, the more you appreciate that environment."

Every walker knows, even if he has not thought very much about it, the law's most obvious application: the bigger and more efficient your means of transportation, the further you become divorced from the reality through which you are traveling. A man learns a thousand times more about the sea from the *Kon Tiki* than from the *Queen Mary;* euphorically more about space at the end of a cord than from inside a capsule. On land, you remain in closer touch with the countryside in a slow-moving old open touring car than in a modern, air-conditioned, tinted-glass-window, 80-miles-an-hour-and-never-notice-it behemoth. And you come in closer touch on a horse than in any car; in closer touch on foot than on any horse.

But the law has a second and less obvious application: your appreciation varies not only according to what you travel *in* but also according to what you travel *over.* Drive along a freeway in any kind of car and you are in almost zero contact with the country beyond the concrete. Turn off onto a minor highway and you move a notch closer. A narrow country road is better still. When you bump slowly along a jeep trail you begin at last to sense those vital details that turn mere landscape into living countryside. And not long ago, on the East African savanna—where it was at that time not considered destructive to drive cross-country over the pale grasslands—I discovered an extending corollary to my law: "The further you move away from any impediment to appreciation, the better it is."

It is less obvious that these same discrepancies persist when you are traveling on foot. Any blacktop road holds the scrollwork of the country at arm's length: the road itself keeps stalking along on stilts or grubbing about in a trough, and your feet tread on harsh and sterile pavement. Turn off onto a dusty jeep trail and the detail moves closer. A foot trail is better still. But you do not really break free until you step off the trail and walk through waving grass or woodland undergrowth or across rock or smooth sand or (most perfect of all) over virgin snow. Now you can read all the details, down to the finest print. Drifting snow crystals have barely begun to blur the four-footed signature of the marten that padded past this lodgepole pine. Or a long-legged lizard scurries for cover, kicking up little spurts of sand as it corners around a bush. Or wet, glistening granite supports an intricate mosaic of purple lichen. Or you stand in long, pale grass and watch the wave patterns of the wind until, quite suddenly, you feel seasick. And always, in snow or sand or rock or seascape grass, there is, as far as you can see in any direction, no sign of man.

That, I believe, is being in touch with the world.

that travels in my "yoke office" (page 83) and not only protects the map from moisture and dirt and general wear and tear but also seems to collect from time to time a pencil, a book of matches, camera lens tissue, and even (in heavy rain) my notebook.

You can also buy transparent plastic sheeting, adhesive on one side (with removable backing: 4 ounces per yard; 18 inches wide; $.55 a yard) that is designed to "protect maps against damage from water or wear." I tried it once, and it works. Yet I've never tried it again. You can probably attribute this failure, with considerable confidence, to laziness.

But mostly I just fold the map that I am using rather loosely and stuff it into my shirt pocket or the "yoke office." The practice often strikes me as dangerously slapdash, but the spring of the loosely folded map seems to hold it in place. I can remember only one occasion on which I lost a map, and that was when I needed just one small corner of a large map and had cut it down to postcard size so that there was none of the usual fold-pressure to hold it in my pocket.

I tend, especially if carrying many maps, to cut off their margins and also any areas that I know for sure I will not need, even for locating an escape route in an emergency. The actual weight saving may not amount to much, but with a really heavy load I find insupportable the knowledge that I'm carrying even one unnecessary dram.

Maps can furnish many bonuses that have nothing to do with efficiency. All you need to contribute is competence in using them and a certain quirky curiosity. At least, I think that is all I contribute, and I know I collect the bonuses. Map reading is one of the few arts I have been fairly competent at ever since I was a child—no doubt because I was fascinated from the start by wriggling blue rivers and amoeboid blue lakes and rhombic green woods and, above all, by the harmony and mystery of patterned red contour lines. These fascinations have never withered. I would not like to say for sure that I ever walked twenty miles simply because I wanted to see the three-dimensional reality represented on my map by a dragon's-head peninsula or a perfect horseshoe river bend or an improbably vermiform labyrinth of contours. It is certainly many years since I did such a thing openly. For now that I am a man I have carefully put away such childish motives. In self-defense, I dig up more momentous reasons.

I am aware that, for many people, a map holds neither meaning nor mystery. I can only hope, compassionately, that the rest of their existence is not equally poverty-stricken.

Map measurer

A map measurer is a cunning little instrument with a tiny
wheel that can follow any route, no matter how snaky, and which
registers on its circular dial with many scales the mileage represented by the distance the wheel has rolled. Remember, though,
that—except along absolutely straight roads or trails (come to
think of it, who ever heard of an absolutely straight trail?)—your
feet always slog a great deal further than the wheel indicates (page
31). Still, a measurer can be a useful guide. I occasionally use
mine for planning, but have never carried it in the pack (1 ounce;
$3).

Trail guides

Trail guides have in the last few years become immensely
popular. They now line a shelf or two in every mountain shop, a
column or three in most catalogues. And they continue to burgeon.

Their success is understandable. Armed with a trail guide you
can plan a trip sensibly and logically, leaving very little to chance.
You can strike camp each morning with a clear, numbered and
verbalized picture of what the day will unfold: its mileages,
gradients, difficulties, rewards. You can rest confident that you need
not miss a single important geological, botanical or historical land-
mark. You will even know where to look for beauty.

My intellectual recognition of trail guides' usefulness
prompted the mildly informative paragraph on them in the first
edition of this book. After all, I told myself, the guides clearly met
a need—or at least gave people what they thought they wanted.
And some of them seemed excellent productions. But, I'm sorry,
now, that in an attempt to be tolerant and "reasonable" I corked
my true feelings. And I'm damned if I'll pussyfoot around any
longer.

I loathe trail guides, strong and sour from the bottom of my
gut. They gnaw at the very roots of what I judge wilderness walking (or any kind of sane walking) to be all about. The whole
idea, surely, is to cast off the coordinates of civilization. You want

to "get away from it all." And less consciously perhaps, you want to "get back to it all." To get back to old roots, that is, and renew them. So once you have sprung yourself free from roadhead, the heart of traveling ceases to be the civilized one of getting from A to B: it becomes finding out what lies between. Finding out, mark you. Not confirming mere intellectual lessons, strung out along a numbered and verbalized white line. Certainly not piling up sweaty records, mile and minute, for retail to the less stalwart. Simply finding out. Simply.

The very nature of the trail guide beast cuts clear across this grain: the "sensible" subordination of doubt and chance; the mile-by-mile scheduling and checking; the rule of the written word. It is all inapplicable, stupid. It walls off, before you have even begun, the values you came so far to retrieve.

As I said, my aversion is a gut reaction. And I am weightily aware that my attitude gapes with inconsistencies. After all, I recommend meticulous planning. I carry maps. And how come a writer rails against the rule of the written word? Above all, how come the writer of this how-to book—even though he has admitted misgivings (Preface, page xv, and footnote, page 14)—inveighs against written instruction? And do we not depend, all of us, every moment, on such stiff, technological cushions as aluminum packframes and gasoline stoves and polyurethane pads? I admit these impeachments. But almost all the carefulnesses I recommend impinge only on ourselves and on the little worlds we carry on our backs. They do not blight the broader world we are traveling through. And if you use the props wisely they need not curdle your appreciation of that world. Given time to break free from accustomed channels of thought, you can establish new coordinates and so move on to discovery, wonder and illumination. But trail guides—these sensible, convenient, efficient tools—impose the old, straight-line, "civilized" coordinates, and so hold you at arm's length from the new, wilderness grid of meaning. It is, as I say, stupid. But it is hardly surprising, really. One of our common current stupidities is applying the criteria and then the tools of one realm to the exploration and exploitation of another.

Trail guides also do an altogether different damage. They bring people in by the goddam horde. If I learn a once-attractive place has been trail-guided, I sadly stay away. Most horrible of all are the now-mushrooming guides to the fragile desert. The disease has even spread to ski touring. An experienced backpacker and ski tourer said to me recently, "Crazy! And you know what it'll lead to? It's the old business of the cow that wandered through the bush, and the man that followed it, and then other men—and before long the engineer was following too, putting his road in." Exactly. And trail guides are engineers working on your thoughts. You know what happens when engineers lay their hands on a river and channelize it: they make it safer, easier to control, and thereby more convenient, more efficient. They also kill it.

After this little tirade—which has already made me feel a good deal better—I shall no doubt be berated as quirky, going on cranky. It'll hardly be the first time. And I remain unrepentant. I'm damned if I will, this edition, recommend any guide books for the blind. All you've got to do if you want one, unfortunately, is browse in a catalogue or mountain shop. And bad luck to you.*

---

* I have actively sought criticism of and counter-arguments to this section. On the whole I am pleasantly surprised. For example, the two friends who rose up in arms against my open-fires denunciation (p. 151) both endorsed this one. "It rests in my gut warmly and well," wrote one of them. "At this time, when the regulatory agencies—Park Service, Forest Service, etc.—are progressing rapidly towards a requirement of designated campsites and rigid itineraries, the philosophy you present here and in the section on maps very much needs equal time."

A request for counter-arguments to a leading publisher of trail guides—before the piece was written—unfortunately elicited only points that to me seem either to apply to backpacking books rather than trail guides ("guides raise the level of hikers' ecological awareness . . . help develop a reverence for the wilderness . . . help in the fight to defend the land") or to cling blindly to the straight-line, man-world coordinates ("guides help hikers enjoy the country more by acquainting them with the flora, the fauna, the geology, the history, etc., of the places they go . . . help the Park and Forest Service get their messages to users of their lands by listing rules and regulations"). Another argument was: ". . . guides spread out hikers . . . help prevent the ruination of the best-known places by all these new people."

Another author of trail guides made a cogent point. "I spent a great deal of deliberating time before writing the first guide," he wrote. "I ultimately concluded the choice lay between the North Cascades being logged, mined and otherwise resource-extracted vs. being used or, if you will, overused recreationally. . . . It seems that most of our current decisions involve choosing the lesser of two evils rather than choosing between black and white. . . . In my opinion, only enough people who are aware of an area have the political clout to keep it reasonably safeguarded."

An Easterner protested that trail guides perform a necessary function in such places as the Appalachians, where trails mostly follow crests and water is rare and secretive. Maybe. But surely a map would do the job at least as well? And a map, though undeniably based on man-world coordinates, can be a wonderful and tickling thing.

Two friends suggested—with reason, I think—that a trail guide is a boon to a family on its first trail trip. But "perhaps daddy could use the suggestion that he keep his burden of information under his own hat so as not to diminish the joys of exploration and discovery for the small fry."

Finally, a stern but valued critic wrote: "It seems to me here that you fall into a particular trap: you're confusing the elements of a how-to book with your own idiosyncratic way of dealing with the world." Sure.

I never walk far without

A compass.

Yet I can remember using mine only once for its primary emergency task: showing me which way to go when I'm unable to decide on or maintain direction by any other means. On that occasion I woke up one morning in broken hill country to find that a dense fog had settled down overnight, cutting visibility to about 15 feet. I needed to get back to the car that day, I had no map, and there was no general slope to the ground to show me which way to go—only a confusion of huge rocky outcrops. And I could detect nothing that might help me hold whichever line I chose to take—not the slightest breeze, and no hint through the gray fog of where the sun lay. Fortunately I knew that only a couple of miles to the north a road ran roughly east and west. So after breakfast I struck due north by the compass. Every hundred yards or so I had to change direction as another huge black outcrop of rock loomed up out of the fog. Under such conditions I doubt if I could have held any kind of course without the compass. But in little more than an hour I stepped onto the road.

Because of such possibilities, I would feel dangerously naked without my compass. But the only purpose I use it for at all often is siting a nightcamp so that it will catch—or avoid—the earliest sun (page 279). It also serves, once in a while, to check my map orientation if I have not been following the detail closely enough. And I once made a pace-and-compass march out across the featureless salt flats of Death Valley to the genuinely lowest point in the Western Hemisphere. (For a pace-and-compass march you calculate from a map the magnetic bearing and the distance from starting place to invisible target. You follow this bearing—either by repeatedly checking your compass or by selecting a distant point on the bearing and homing on it; and after working out how many of your paces, across that kind of terrain, will take you to the target, you count each pace taken until that number is reached. Carefully calculated and executed, it is a surprisingly accurate method, day or night.)

My compass is an ex–U.S. Marine Corps model with a fold-over alloy cover built to withstand brutal treatment. It does. The instrument is not liquid filled and therefore cannot develop that common and infuriating compass scourge, bubble trouble. But its dial stops oscillating within three seconds. It is fitted with a declination offsetting device. Weight: 4½ ounces. I have no idea how much it costs (it was given to me), but catalogue equivalents seem to run about $18.

Catalogues often display a wide range of compasses, basic through fancy, from ½ to 5 ounces, from $.98 to $18. Get one that's tough: it may lie around in your pack for months or even years, but it must be functioning perfectly when the testing time comes. (*Note:* The advice given in earlier printings of this book about checking for 'shielding' was ill-informed drivel. My apologies —and blushes.) Choose a model designed to perform the fanciest function you expect to use it for.

Most people, I think, want a compass only for unfancy functions. Those functions are very simple. For the basic emergency use of holding a given line, just see where the needle or north arrow points, then walk in the direction you have decided is the one to take. Base your decision about direction on the map, knowledge of the country, intuition, guesswork or desperation, in that order of preference; but stick with it. At night or in fog you must keep checking the compass, and hold dead on line. In good visibility, a quicker and much more accurate method is to pick out a distant and distinctive point that lies on the required line, put your compass away, and head for the distant point. Provided there is no danger of your losing track of the point, you can detour as widely and as often as you like.

If you want to move in a given compass "direction" ("due north," say, or "south-southeast"), it is important to remember that "true north" and "compass north" are not the same. The difference is known as magnetic declination. Because the magnetic north pole presently lies among the Canadian Arctic Islands, about a thousand miles below the true north pole (it moves, slowly), the declination is different in different places. Along the West Coast of the United States, for example, it is now 15–20 degrees east (that is, the compass needle points well east, or right, of true north). Along the East Coast it is 15–20 degrees west. (The further north you go, the greater the declination.) The declination for an area is normally given on good maps, such as USGS topos. Unfortunately, the mean annual variation is not. But for most rough-and-ready purposes all you need know is a round figure and the direction of error. Make sure, though, that you get the direction of error firmly in your mind. I sometimes pencil the magnetic variation for a given area on the back of my compass before a trip, as well as the bearing of sunrise (page 280).

For fancier uses—for which you will need to work out your individual compass error—consult one of the little paperback how-to books on the subject. I am told that a good one is the 144-page handbook *Be Expert with Map and Compass,* by Bjorn Kjellstrom, sold by the compass makers Silva, Inc., 2466 North State Road 39, La Porte, Indiana 46350 ($3.50).

I suppose I should have a lot more to say about route-finding. But, beyond map reading, it is mostly common sense, and I am not very conscious of any particular techniques. Once or twice I have become aware that I was not where I thought I was because the sun hung in the wrong place or the wind blew from the wrong direction, so I suppose I must take some cognizance of such direction checks. Otherwise, route-finding is largely a matter of obeying that sturdy old adage, "Never lose elevation unnecessarily," and of getting to know the idiosyncrasies of the country you are in—the pattern its ridges tend to follow, or the way its southern slopes tend to be covered with impassable scrub, or the tendency of its northern slopes to drop away in unclimbable cliffs.

Failing your compass, you can check your bearings on a clear night by the North Star (Polaris). Pick it out by projecting the line formed by the two stars that constitute the outer lip of the Big Dipper's bowl, for about five times the distance between those stars, and look a touch to the left. If you can't recognize the Big Dipper, go home.

Provided you know the time, the sun's position will give you a rough, commonsense bearing.* For a more accurate estimate of direction from the sun, point the hour hand of your watch at it (use standard time, not daylight saving): true south lies along a line drawn halfway between the hour hand and twelve o'clock.

With experience you will in unfamiliar country come to note without much thought the landmarks and the general lay of the land that will enable you to backtrack, should that become necessary; but I occasionally stop at points that may cause confusion—such as a junction of several valleys, or a watershed with diverging drainage systems—and look back in order to memorize the way I have come. This is certainly a worthwhile precaution at any unposted trail junction.

In certain kinds of country, the question of scale can become

* "Yes, Aunt Josephine, the sun rises in the east. Well, kind of in the east. In summertime, if you're well north of the Equator, it'll actually rise quite a ways north of east. And in the winter, quite a ways south of east. In flat country, anyway. But at noon—standard time, not daylight saving—it's always due south. Unless, of course, it's overhead. No, that isn't very helpful, is it? And if you're in the Southern Hemisphere it'll naturally be due north at noon. . . . Yes, Auntie, unless it's overhead. . . . And yes, you're right again, it always sets in the west. Well, kind of in the west. In summertime, if you're well south of the . . ."

crucial to route-finding. Among the repetitive rock patterns of Grand Canyon I at first found that it was often impossible to tell from a distance, even through binoculars, whether a sheer rockface was an inconsequential 3 or an unclimbable 30 feet high. But eventually I realized that the agaves or century plants that grew almost everywhere were a consistent 3 or 4 feet high, and from then on I used them as gauges.

In some kinds of country, particularly desert, game trails can be a tremendous help in route-finding. Decide by map, eye and cogitation what seems to you the best cross-country route. Then canvass it for game trails. Look first from a distance, through binoculars. It's often easier to spot them that way than close up. If you have no luck, search carefully at constricted places such as canyon narrows, breaks in wash walls, isthmuses between lakes. In burro-traveled desert, this search can be the most important thing you do all day. Once you hit a trail, latch onto it: route-finding apart, it is likely to afford far easier going than cross country. But keep firmly and continually and questioningly in mind that the animals may or may not be going the same place you are.

Wild burros are first-class trail makers. So are elk, I'm told. Wild horses are good; deer, fair; independent-minded bighorn sheep, next door to useless. The burros and horses, and to a lesser extent the deer, make excellent instructors. If you follow their trails and think, you'll soon turn from a tyro at route-finding in their particular kind of country into a quick and confident pro.

Local human knowledge can also be an invaluable aid to route-finding, or at least to finding the most convenient route. But local humans are not always crystal-pure sources of information, and if you are going to travel in strange country you must command a certain proficiency in the art of sifting fact from embroidery. The only reliable informant is the man who both knows what he is talking about and is not afraid to admit he doesn't know everything. You don't meet such men every day. The surest way of finding out if you have just met one is to ask questions to which you know the answers.

As I approached Death Valley on my summer-long California walk I passed through Baker, a populated road junction of the gasoline age. While I was there, one self-satisfied little man fixed me with beady eyes. "What's that?" he said. "Going through Death Valley? Huh, your feet must be stronger than your head. It'll be a hundred and ten up there by now. And climbing every day. I spent years right in the Valley, all summer too, so I know. I'm a real Desert Rat, I can tell you, a real Desert Rat."

346 House on Your Back

"Oh, what sort of temperatures do they get on the floor of the Valley?" I asked—and waited.

I knew the Death Valley temperature position accurately. All-time high is a questionable 134° F., set in July 1913, that for many years held the world record. Later and more dependable readings have never risen above 127°. Most years, the limit is 124° or 125°.

The Baker Rat pounced on my bait. "Summer temperatures in the Valley?" he squeaked. "Well, I can't quote exact figures, but it gets hot, believe me. Here in Baker we have summer highs of a hundred and twenty-five or thirty. And sometimes"—he turned to his wife—". . . sometimes we run to a hundred thirty-five, don't we?"

"Oh, not very often, dear."

"No, not too often. But it happens. And you can add a good twenty degrees for the Valley. So you'd best get ready to sweat a bit, my lad."

I did not bother to ask the Baker Rat any of the other questions I had on my mind.*

A friend of mine who is a connoisseur of human foibles was delighted when I reported this conversation. "Now there's a beautiful example of the dedicated weather exaggerater at work," he said. "The real artist often uses that ploy—provoking something that seems close to dissent from one of his in-group so as to thicken the background."

It is not always so easy to winnow worthless information. Often, you have to fall back on mere confirmation of details from several sources. But this technique can backfire. Several years ago I was wandering in leisurely fashion across the Coast Range in central California, aiming broadly for the Pacific. One afternoon I emerged from forest into ranchland and almost at once met the rancher—a pleasant-faced man wearing a ten-gallon hat and a red shirt and driving a green pickup truck. We chatted cordially for some time, discussing how far it was down to the ocean, and what the best routes were. An hour later, far down the hill, I came to a cattle chute. A tall, baldheaded man wearing blue overalls was inoculating a herd of heifers. When he had finished he turned and walked toward me. Partly as an opening pleasantry, partly to confirm the figures and routes that the rancher in the green pickup had given me, I said, "Say, can you tell me how far it is down to the sea?" The man stopped and looked at me closely. Then, to my astonishment, he turned on his heel and walked back toward the

* If this little scene seems familiar, maybe you've read *The Thousand-Mile Summer* (p. 77).

chute. After a while I wandered away, wondering, through a belt of trees. Suddenly, beyond a small outbuilding, I almost walked into the green pickup. On its seat sat a familiar-looking ten-gallon hat.

Even now, all these years later, I still feel embarrassed whenever I remember that rancher.

KEEPING YOURSELF CLEAN AND COMFORTABLE

Toilet gear

A highly personal department that every individual will stock differently, and which he will vary to meet varying conditions.

My list expands and contracts within rather wide limits, mostly in response to how crippling the load looks like being, but also according to whether I expect to touch civilization at all. The full selection includes:

Soap. I used to carry a half or quarter bar, in either a small plastic bag or a light polyethylene container with built-in nailbrush. But there are now more convenient alternatives. I use Trak, a biodegradable all-purpose cleanser that its makers anoint with the subtitle "Soapless Supersoap." The stuff comes in 1-ounce and 3.2-ounce tubes—designed to last one person, for all uses, two weeks and six weeks respectively ($1.25 and $2). It is said to have $2\frac{1}{2}$ times the cleansing power of ordinary soap, and to lather and rinse equally well in any water—cold, hard or even salt. It is recommended not only for washing all parts of the body (its pH conforms to that of human skin) and for shaving and shampooing but also for washing cuts and bruises and removing makeup and as a—wait for it—"mustache deodorant." Also, of course, for washing both dishes and clothes (including white kid gloves). The funny thing is that, although I can't yet claim to have assayed this whole spectrum, it seems to work. And to work well. For $3 you can buy a 3-ounce backpacking size, plastic-pouched Mini-Trak Kit that includes a one-ounce tube of Trak, a small vial of excellent dentifrice (see page 348), a folding toothbrush and a plastic-reinforced all-purpose paper towel. You can buy these kits—and also the separate components—from certain stores or direct by mail (minimum order $2) from Freeman Industries (see Appendix II, New York).

My one small objection to Trak is that it comes in an opaque white plastic tube: though it's easy to see if left lying around, you have to judge how much is left by the uncertain squeeze-and-watch method.

Paket—"a mild biodegradable soap for hands and face"—comes

in a ⅔-ounce tube ("contains 50 to 60 washings") that is translucent, and therefore avoids this minor problem. But its uses are limited. (3 tubes for $1.)

There are other convenient, biodegradable cleansers on the market now, and I'm sure each has its band of devoted users.

Washcloth. I used to take one occasionally but don't seem to have done so for years. Can double as a towel.

Small towel. Occasionally useful when much swimming or washing is expected and either the weather looks like being too cool or the privacy too porous to let the sun do the drying. The towel in a Trak kit will do. So will a diaper, I'm told.

Toothbrush. Most convenient are those with a detachable brush that fits inside its own handle. Various models. Average: ½ ounce; $1.20. You get a Hong Kong one in each Mini-Trak Kit.

Tooth cleanser. I used to use salt—and somehow rarely cleaned my teeth. Since discovering Trak dentifrice (½-ounce and 1½-ounce plastic vials, $1.25 and $2), I find to my surprise that I actually enjoy the operation, and therefore do it more often. (I even use the stuff for ordinary traveling.) Trak dentifrice can also be used to brush or soak dentures. It's a mouthwash too. See also dental floss, page 370.

Deodorant, comb, even a brush. Taken if the social standards of a trip demand it. That is, damned rarely.

Toilet roll. A roll, mark you, not one of those interleaved packs that in a high wind explode like bombs. For use, see, at some length, pages 385–8. I understand that some people, when they know that washing is going to be a problem, take along a few pads of "Tucks"—a medication-impregnated toilet paper.

Scissors. Kept protected in moleskin package, in "office" (page 359). A new, folding pair (1 ounce; $4) that I recently tried out are safer and more convenient. They cut well; but less well than a good standard pair.

Razors. Although it is twenty years since I used one of these barbarous instruments, I'm aware that they still exist, and I note that there is a Mallory electric model, "no larger than a pack of cigarettes . . . [that] will run for six months on two Mallory Duracell Penlight batteries" (8 ounces; $12.75).

Items classifiable as "toilet gear" but discussed elsewhere:

Mirror. For signaling rather than primping. See page 354. If your hand falls on the mirror a few washless days out and, by reflex action, you look into it, you may be in for a shock. My mirror goes into the moleskin package, between the pads, where it protects the curved points of the nonfolding scissors.

Foot powder and rubbing alcohol. See page 58.

Washing yourself is your business—except when it comes to

polluting the water. For factors to consider—and a solution in inhabited country—see "Care of clothing," page 308.

Occasionally you get sensuously delightful washing surprises. I particularly like to remember finding, a couple of hundred feet below the peak of Mount Shasta, at 14,000 feet, a bubbling hot spring. The sulphurous water smelled vile. But it was very hot. And, although the sun was already low, the air felt astonishingly warm for that elevation. So I filled both my cooking pots with snow and immersed them in the spring, which bubbles out of the ground over a fairly large area. I waited until the snow had become hot water. Then I stripped off and poured both potfuls over my head. It was a lusciously hedonistic rite.

I learned later that John Muir, the Scot who around the turn of the century did so much for the conservation of wild California, was apparently saved by this spring when caught up there in a blizzard. By lying on the hot earth and moving his body from time to time, Muir was able to keep himself comfortably warm. Well, safely warm, anyway.

There are several additional items, not strictly speaking toilet gear, that you'll often need in order to keep comfortable:

Fly dope. With luck you won't often have to use it, but once you have suffered helplessly from mosquitoes or their like you'll rarely travel without it. New and possibly better formulas appear regularly. The two I find best at present are the Insect Repellent accurately described by the makers, Cutter Laboratories, as "outlandishly expensive . . . incredibly effective and economic to use" (1½-ounce plastic vial; $1.49) and Off, which can be sprayed on clothing as well as skin (1½-fluid-ounce vial: 4 ounces; $.90). Occasionally I even carry the 6½-fluid-ounce aerosol (9 ounces; $1.29). The stuff is good but, like all repellents, not perfect. Resign yourself to meeting the occasional swarm of semi-literate insects that persists, en masse, in reading Off as On.

Though I've never experienced trouble, I understand that prolonged use of insect repellent can irritate the skin. In such cases, if the insects become unbearable, it may be necessary to wear long pants, gloves, and a face net.

Suntan lotion. Indispensable for those who sunburn easily, recommended for those who rather think they don't. The mountains are always full of people who did not realize how quickly skin burns at high altitudes, where there is less atmosphere to screen off the sun's ultraviolet rays. Don't underestimate the effects of such sunburn, especially if you have partly or wholly stripped off. It can incapacitate you (see the story of a fool on Fujiyama, page 290). And remember, if your skin happens to be halfway black, don't imagine you're immune.

Up high, almost everyone needs some kind of skin protection, especially in windy weather, and under such conditions many popular brands are ineffective. Among the specialist preparations you can now buy:

To screen sun—and so prevent burn and tan: Pabafilm (4-ounce unbreakable bottle; $3). Skreen cream, heavily applied (1¾ ounces; $1.50).

To screen sun partially, moisturize skin well—and so reduce chance of burn but permit tan: Glacier Creams (1-ounce tubes: red for high altitude [$.85]; green for lower [$.75]). Also SunSwept (2-ounce tube; $1.50).

To moisturize skin after exposure to sun: Lubriderm Lotion (5-ounce plastic bottle; $1.25).

Lip salve. Some people need it in cold and windy or hot and dry weather. Just about everyone needs it for prolonged living above 12,000 feet. Again, well-known brands are often ineffective under bad conditions. Recommended: A-Fil Sun Stick (1 ounce; $1) and Labiosan cream (1-ounce tube; $1).

Hand lotion. For places where the water is heavily alkaline. On the first half of the Grand Canyon trip my hands began to get raw from frequent use of Colorado water, and I was thankful to be able to get a tube of lotion at the halfway mark. Ignore jibes about effeminacy. I once heard a modern-day pioneer who ranched beside an almost untouched stretch of the Colorado River, and was about as masculine a man as you'll find anywhere, say to his wife as he pulled off his boots at the end of a long day, "Better throw over the hand lotion, honey. Had my arms in that damned river half the afternoon."

Lubriderm Cream (1½-ounce plastic tube; $1.38) lubes my derma.

Heaters

It seemed unlikely that even we effete, equipment-bombarded backpackers would be tempted by heaters; but two quite different kinds are now being dangled.

Space heaters that work off stove cartridges might just be worth carrying, I suppose, for use in a tent in very cold, calm weather. Gerry's infrared heater is reportedly not yet unbugged (page 169). But the Primus 2228 heater (14 ounces; $17)—rated to burn full-on for 7 hours on one of the 2201 cartridges that power the Ranger stove certainly gives off a lot of heat and seems a practical rig.

The other newcomers—new to me, anyway—are a series of "flameless catalytic pocket, hand and body warmers" now being marketed by Optimus. The smallest (model 301w; $2.95) is 3½ by 2¼ by ¾ inches and weighs only 1½ ounces. Slightly larger models have temperature controls. All burn white gas (or lighter fluid or catalytic heater fuel) with *no* flame. They work in any position, and are said to light anywhere with a match in less than 15 seconds, to be windproof, and to burn all day on a single filling —which is precious little white gas. I have a 301w in my trousers pocket as I write, inside its little felt bag and a multi-folded handkerchief, and it is soothing me without causing apprehension.

In bitter weather, one of these little heaters in each glove, or strategically sited elsewhere and properly padded, might possibly prevent frostbite or worse. And even one of them, particularly if it's a thermo-adjustable model, might in a sleeping bag bring joy to a cold sleeper—and the very stuff of life to someone suffering from hypothermia (page 413).

MEETING EMERGENCIES

First aid

The contents of any individual's personal first-aid kit will depend on terrain, length of trip, and—most of all—his temperament.

My kit, which these days seems to vary very little, includes:

1 roll 1-inch adhesive tape (either cloth tape, with metal outer cover discarded, to save weight, or thin, ultralight plastic tape—which I've now carried for some time without using or really evaluating)
1 roll 3-inch gauze (or gauze compresses)
A dozen Band-Aids
½-ounce tube Spectrocin or similar antibiotic ointment (replace at expiration date, stamped on crimp of tube)
6 headache tablets (you may need more at high elevations)
12 codeine tablets (see page 352)
12 broad-spectrum antibiotic tablets, such as Tetracycline (see page 352)
2 segments chocolate laxatives (sometimes needed at the beginning of a trip, to combat radically altered routine and diet)
Half a dozen needles. For removing thorns, breaking blisters, etc. Kept with matches in waterproof matchsafe. See also pages 147 and 363.
Scissors (page 348)

My kit travels in doubled plastic bags, averages around 4 or 5 ounces.

Mistrusting my judgment, I once asked an Everest-climbing doctor his opinion on the adequacy of the items I then carried. To my surprise and relief he suggested adding only the codeine and antibiotic tablets.

The codeine is a safe but effective pain killer. The doctor cited a recent occasion on which, coming down off a mountain, he twisted a knee rather badly. Without treatment he would have been able to keep going very slowly, if at all. But a shot of morphine killed almost all the pain, and with the help of his companions he was able to get out to civilization without difficulty. Morphine may be a shade tricky for inexperienced laymen to use, but codeine tablets are almost as good. A dozen is a reasonable stock. In getting a prescription, make sure that your doctor puts you wise to the pitfalls of usage. Pure codeine tablets, if properly sealed (all my tablets travel in 35 mm. film cans), should last for years; but if they get to look mottled, replace. Most codeine tablets now contain aspirin, which will in time deteriorate. Check occasionally for "a smell like vinegar." If detected, replace tablets.

The broad-spectrum antibiotic tablets are in case of general infection from an injury, or from some illness such as pneumonia. Again, check for pitfalls in usage when you get a prescription. Also for allergy. And take care you replace at expiration date.

Sometimes you can improvise. A hiking pamphlet recently recommended meat tenderizer (unseasoned), dissolved in water, as a pain killer for insect bites. I'm sure you'll value this brainstorm; after all, who ever heard of a backpacker worth his salt that did not carry, every trip, a plentiful supply of meat tenderizer (unseasoned)?

In a party, individual first-aid kits are normally supplemented, but *not* replaced, by a group kit. Contents will vary widely with size of party, terrain, length of trip and philosophy of leader. Candidates include:

Inflatable vinyl air splints (now almost standard; weights and prices vary riotously; for use as pillows, see page 274)
Anti-venin kit (page 405)
Oral thermometer
Some rather fancier drugs, such as morphine and Dexedrine, that are reasonably safe when given with an outsider watching the patient's reactions

For makeshift stretcher suggestions, see "Sleeping-bag covers," page 272, "Hammocks," page 249 and "Space blankets," page 419.

For those who fancy prepacked first-aid kits, the choice is now wide enough to satisfy a hypochondriacs' union. Study the catalogues (especially Eastern Mountain Sports'). Johnson and Johnson make several kits, from expedition to day's-jaunt-personal. So do Alpine Aid of Riverside, California, who offer a good range of individual items, tailored for mountaineers. Survival Research Laboratories of Colorado Springs, Colorado, plastic-pouch a mini. (Range of all these: 1½ pounds to less than an ounce; $26.50 to $.89.) See also, in Appendix II, Nicolet Products of Phoenix, Arizona, and Colorado Mountain Industries of Cincinnati, Ohio.

The best of these pre-packed kits include a small first-aid instruction booklet, and even if you do not carry one of the kits you should probably—unless you're a highly competent first-aid man—carry some such lightweight instructions. You may not look at them for years on end, but in an emergency, when you find you simply don't know the correct response to the situation, they could save your life. Any Red Cross chapter office (in the United States, see under American National Red Cross in phone book) will be pleased to supply you, free, with a useful advice sheet, "First Aid at a Glance." It is printed on both sides, weighs almost nothing, and gives some clear, basic information. My "office" (page 359) always holds one of these sheets, and also a compact little 1½-ounce, 48-page booklet called "Mountaineering Medicine," by Dr. Fred T. Darvill, Jr., an experienced outdoorsman. ($1 from some mountain shops or from Skagit Mountain Rescue Unit, Inc., P.O. Box 2, Mount Vernon, Washington 98273. All profits are used to promote the rescue activities of the unit.) This booklet is kept continually up-to-date. It is now in its sixth edition—and has sold over 30,000 copies. It gives practical advice on everything from "altitude sickness" through "fish hooks, removal of" to "ticks." I've recently been able to browse briefly through the typescript of a larger book, due for publication in mid-1974, that promises much of value for backpackers. It is *The Outdoorsman's Medical Guide: Health Care for Campers, Hikers and Backpackers,* by Alan E. Nourse, M.D. (Harper & Row; 128 pages; 4 ounces; $3.95). For a short extract, see page 412. A more comprehensive medical manual—one that goes well beyond first aid—is *Medicine for Mountaineering,* edited by Dr. James A. Wilkerson (The Mountaineers, Seattle, Washington, 1967; $7.50). It's often recommended for leaders of backpack parties.

If you are going higher than about 9000 feet, and especially if you are poorly acclimatized, read up in advance on pulmonary edema (fluid accumulation in the lungs), which can kill you but quick.

For first aid to people struck by lightning see page 416.

For treatment of snakebite see page 405; of rashes from poison oak, ivy and sumac, page 411.

Don't forget that when there is no one around to appraise your condition objectively, from the outside, it can be difficult to judge whether you need something more drastic than first aid.

Not long ago I tackled a doctor friend on the subject.

"Would it be true to say," I asked, "that one kind of disease arises when you have many species of germs or other organisms living in or on a body in a state of mutual balance and equilibrium, and then some quite slight change occurs and one species gains the upper hand and before long becomes, by its sheer weight of numbers, a danger to the parent body?"

"Yes, I think that's a fair description of a certain kind of disease."

"Well, if you had a planetary body with many species living on it in a state of mutual balance and equilibrium, and then some slight change occurred in the head properties of one species and it gained the upper hand so that by its sheer weight of numbers it became a danger to the planet—not to mention to itself, of course—would you not call that condition a disease of a certain . . . ?"

"Oh my God, I take the Fifth Amendment."

Signaling mirror

I now carry (with my moleskins; see page 60) an ordinary 3-by-3¾-inch metal mirror, the kind you can pick up for thirty-five cents in any variety store (1 ounce). In an emergency it could attract the attention of people on the ground or in the air by reflecting sunlight. Makeshift substitutes include almost anything that will shine: aluminum foil, a metal windscreen (page 180), sunglasses, even a watch. For details of use in rescues or airdrops, see pages 392–4 and 396.

Smoke bomb or flare

I always have one down in the bottom of my pack, for signaling in an emergency. For details of flares, see footnote, page 394.

For uses and alternatives, especially in airdrops, see pages 395 and 396.

Whistle

"A must for safety in the mountains," say some catalogues. Nowadays I always carry one (½ ounce; $.30).

Flint stick

For emergency fire-lighting. See page 148—also for possible alternatives: prospector's magnifying glass, camera lens, binoculars.

Emergency fishing tackle

The only living off the land that I normally do is fishing, and in almost any country I carry a tiny survival kit that weighs about ¼ ounce and contains:

1 spool (60 feet) 6-pound nylon
Half dozen hooks, assorted sizes
Half dozen lead shot
Half dozen trout flies

The whole kit wraps into a small, tough, polyethylene bag and travels, almost unnoticed, in the "office" (page 359).

Such a kit can often augment and vary a dehydrated diet, and might even help keep you alive.

In Grand Canyon I took along a 35 mm. film can of salmon eggs. They worked well. Using my staff as rod, I caught many small catfish and one carp of about 1½ pounds. Small fish of any kind demand considerable cooking effort for rather little substance, but bigger fish are rewarding. Carp need only be laid on hot embers, as their thick skins act as aluminum foil. A little aluminum foil is sometimes worth taking along for less obliging species.

For more elaborate fishing tackle, see "Enjoying extra-perambulatory activities" (page 364).

Rope

In really rough country, when there are two or more of you, a rope is often worth carrying as a safety measure. Alone, you'll rarely find much use for it, unless you expect to rappel down a cliff (that is, to pass the rope around your body in such a way that you can lower yourself at any desired speed by controlling with one hand the friction the rope creates on your body as you descend).

You need at least two people for a belay (that is, for tying yourself to rock or tree so that should your partner fall you can hold him with the rope)—or for a rescue.

The only time I have carried a rope was in Grand Canyon. I knew that for weeks on end I would be walking two or three thousand feet above the river, with my way down to it barred by a series of sheer cliffs. But there were places where most of the cliffs had eroded nearly through, and it seemed to me that in dire emergency a rope might just allow me to rappel down an otherwise impassable barrier to the lifesaving water of the river. On short rappels I might be able to retrieve the rope for reuse by doubling it and pulling it down after me through some form of loop. (Rather than carry the orthodox carabiner—or metal spring loop—for this unlikely eventuality, I decided to rely on a multiple loop of nylon cord, or perhaps a convenient tree. On long rappels I would have to use the rope single and leave it behind.) After much balancing of usefulness against weight, I took a 100-foot length of ¼-inch laid nylon rope, about 1900 pounds test (1 pound 14 ounces; $6).

No dire water emergency arose. But once, reconnoitering a tricky route, I found a rather steep 10-foot rockface that I knew I could get down but did not feel sure I could reclimb should the way ahead prove impassable. So I fastened the rope to a convenient rock pillar and handlined down. The route proved impassable all right, and I duly and thankfully handlined back up again.

I also used the rope several times to lower the pack down pitches I could manage quite confidently unladen but didn't fancy tackling with a pack. Nylon cord (page 368) will do this job, but rope is easier on the hands and waist or shoulders, which should be used for braking. Rope also gives you a better chance of pulling a pack up—though once you have tried this game with a 60-pound pack and seen how adept the frame ends are at grabbing the rock, you will go to some lengths to avoid a replay.

The best modern ropes are Perlon rather than nylon.

One reader says he regularly carries a 40-foot length of ⁵⁄₁₆-inch braided Dacron rope, for much the same reasons I did in Grand Canyon (pack-hauling and handlining at difficult rock pitches) and also for hauling food up out of bear-reach, over a tree bough, or whatever. He finds this rope far better than thin nylon cord because it "doesn't stretch like a nylon rubber band," cuts hands less, and does not create undue friction on tree boughs.

IMPROVING THE MIND

Reading matter

For me, the book should be light in weight and not too leaden in content. If your natural-history knowledge is as sketchy as mine, one of those little identification books on trees or reptiles or mammals or such would seem a good choice. For bird books, see page 367. Generally, I find myself taking books that are relevant to some aspect of my journey but which do not deal too closely with the detail around me. On the California walk I browsed slowly through a five-book paperback Mentor series on philosophy (the books were mailed ahead singly to post offices along the route). In Grand Canyon I extracted many seminal thoughts from a paperback that dealt discursively rather than didactically with present geological knowledge (*The Crust of the Earth,* edited by Samuel Rapport and Helen Wright, Signet Science Library, 1955 [5 ounces; $.60]). Poetry is good too: wilderness can open new windows into old lines.

Today, a good choice would be *The Limits to Growth,* The Club of Rome's project on the predicament of mankind (Meadows *et al.,* Potomac Associates, 1972; paperback; 9½ ounces; $2.75) —a little book that should be required reading for all literates over thirteen. If you have walked properly, with your eyes open, sometimes breaking free from the confines of your own species and standing outside it, then the message the book conveys (roughly, that the astonishing human bubble has just about reached bursting point) will not come as a shock and surprise to you—will not be something you try to reject, out of fear: you will see it as a sharp mathematical confirmation of something you had already learned esthetically from the green world, and had accepted, utterly. (I do not mean, by the way, that you will agree with the authors' conclusions—only with their frame of thought.) The book does not ask, let alone try to answer, a question you may have pondered on mountaintops: "Would it be better for the world as a whole if the human species gets itself back in hand or if it lets itself burn out?" And the book certainly does not suggest what I did on page 354. Not openly, anyway.

If you read *The Limits to Growth* remember that although it may say things that are new in a logical or at least mathematical sense, it represents no radical innovation in human thought. Even men of science have for some time been riding this road. And, at their moments, Arnold, Eliot, Picasso, Mahler and other Travellers have long ago knocked on this same moonlit door. But never the least stir made most of us Listeners.

There is, by the way, an "optimistic" statement, opposing the whole *Limits to Growth* view, that you may care to try as an antidote: *The Doomsday Syndrome,* by John Maddox (McGraw-Hill, 1972; unfortunately hardback and therefore 1 pound 6 ounces and $6.95).

Notebook

If you intend to take notes of some sort on a trip but have not yet tried it, I sound a warning: time is the trouble (table, page 32). Note-writing always seems to be among the activities that get consistently crowded out. I used to assume that this was a personal inefficiency, but I gather it's an occupational hazard among geologists, naturalists, and others committed to wilderness notetaking. I offer no solution other than determination. Don't kid yourself, as I used to, that you will just jot down a word or two for each thought, more or less as you go, and will spend each evening —or long midday halt—expanding it. The expansion rarely happens. Certainly not if you're having to push at all hard, physically. The best I've been able to do is to jot down as much as I can in my notebook *at the time* and then attack the fuller and more discursive stuff as opportunity offers. Mostly, that means on rest days.

I generally use a plastic-covered, spiral-backed, loose-leaf notebook that fits conveniently into shirt pocket or "yoke office" (page 83). One nineteen-cent book lasts at least a week. The spirals should be at the top rather than the side, so that they do not catch in pocket or office. To make it easy to open the notebook at the current pages, I slip rubber bands over both front and rear covers, halfway down, and slide each page under its band as I finish using it.

Pens and pencils

Ballpoint pens, with refills. Pencils—two of them with pocket clips (preferably the spring-loaded kind that you open up with a fingertip as you remove or replace the pencil). Don't sharpen pencils too fine, they'll only break. And sharp points can savage you. Both pens and pencils should be a bright, conspicuous color.

Onionskin paper

I often take onionskin paper for fuller, more discursive notes —and back it with a rectangle of stiff cardboard, to which I secure the paper, top and bottom, with rubber bands.

The office

My office is a specially made 12-by-16-inch envelope of coated nylon fabric, zippered at the top (4 ounces). Designed primarily for the cardboard-backed onionskin paper (see above), it has become home for many items that need to be kept flat or otherwise protected and for small items of the kind that just ache to get lost: spare pens and pencils, paperback book, stove-nozzle cleaner, Rip-stop patching material, moleskins with mirror and scissors, spare flashlight batteries, miniature can opener, rubber bands, maps not in use, car key, spare sunglasses, and survival fishing tackle.

I imagine that few backpackers feel the need of a special office, but at least one reader has liked the idea.

FIGURING

It would seem reasonable to suppose that you can escape from the man-world more easily if you walk out into wilderness without a

Watch.

But the stratagem may backfire. Without a watch (as can happen if you go without maps), you may find yourself operating so inefficiently that ways and means begin to obscure the things that matter. It is not simply a question of knowing the time of day. (Provided the sun shines, you can gauge that kind of time accurately enough—though in dank or snow-clogged weather or in country so precipitous that the sun sets soon after noon, even that may prove a problem.) But you have lost the sharp instrument that keeps prodding you forward. That is what I find, anyway, because if time and distance are important I often mark on my map (page 65) the time I stop for each halt—or at least note the time mentally. Without a watch, too, I cannot work out times and distances for the way ahead. And that, for me, means a loss rather than a gain in freedom. Some people find the precise opposite. But the fact remains that after a single week-long trip without a watch I have gone back to wearing one.

If you decide to take a watch it is probably a good thing if it bears the words "waterproof and shock resistant" or some other encouraging legend. And check before you go on a trip that the crystal, or glass, is in first-class condition. Also that the strap (assuming you wear a wristwatch) is not only in good repair but of a suitable kind. Plastic is useless: under wilderness conditions, even more quickly than at home, sunlight and cold and wear will cause dangerous cracks. Leather is better, though sweat may rot the stitching. For some reason I do not like metal straps: I have an idea, possibly erroneous, that they can get uncomfortably hot and cold; and the links certainly catch the hairs on my wrist. Woven nylon straps, I find, are ideal: they do not rot; it takes years for them to show any appreciable wear; and, although they tend to reek of sweat, they can be easily washed and dried. The only safe strap, of any material, is the one-piece kind that passes under your watch.

Not long ago I at last bought myself an alarm wristwatch. (The trick, apparently, is to find one that is also a really good timepiece. You can do so, but it costs.) I have not yet thoroughly worked out the best way to make it do its prime job: rousing me early, especially on those days I want to eat breakfast before sunrise. The difficulty is finding a sensitive part of the body for it to vibrate against (the sound is not very loud). On my wrist, down in the sleeping bag, it does not always wake me. Held against my largely unhaired cranium, inside a balaclava, it would surely do so. In a shirt breast pocket it communicates effectively with my chest; but I don't often wear a shirt in the sleeping bag. Of course, if you habitually wear underpants in the sack. . . . An alternative, if you are not going to cocoon yourself deep and mummylike in your mummy, is to put the watch in a cup or pot, metal-to-metal, and rely on the racket. It seems a pity, though, to start a wilderness day like that, especially as you'd scare every animal within earshot.

My new watch is automatic (a convenience, since if you forget to wind a manual you have to wait for sunrise or sunset to reset it with even reasonable accuracy). It's also said to be about as waterproof as they come. But no matter how much faith you choose to put in that word, it is always worth protecting your watch when you have to swim across a river, or feel that you may fall in—such as when you wade deep or venture out on a narrow log. Doubled plastic bags, knotted, should do the job. Another safe method, I'm told, is to tie your watch into a condom. For swimming across a river with a pack, my watch goes into the well-protected sanctum sanctorum (page 380).

A cruder kind of time-figuring is almost always essential:

Keeping check on the days.

Even if you have no vital commitments to meet in the outside world, you should before leaving roadhead give somebody a time and a date beyond which it can be assumed that, if you have not shown up, you are in trouble (page 33). Or you may have arranged an airdrop, or a meeting with packers or other walkers. In any of these cases, a mistake in the day can cost you dearly. And the mistake is remarkably easy to make.

I always prepare a table on a page near the end of my notebook (not the last page, because it may pull out). I block out the days and leave room for writing in the name, actual or fancied, of the place at which I camp each night. This detail, I find, is the one that my mind distinguishes most clearly in identifying the days. Without my calendar table I would often—perhaps most often —not know for sure what day it was. The table also makes it much easier to figure out, days ahead, whether I really need to hurry or can afford to amble luxuriously along.

I find that having a watch that shows the date has not made me forego the calendar-table habit. But then, I'm a cautious s.o.b.

Pedometer

Theoretically this instrument is a valuable item (2 ounces; $8). But although I own one I've never got past the finicky job of trying to calibrate it to my normal stride. Perhaps that's because I question how useful such calibration would be over any but smooth, level ground—and because I regard wilderness mileage figures as being, in most cases, singularly meaningless (page 31).

Thermometer

It is many years now since I began taking a thermometer on walks, and I still have no reasoned explanation of why it makes such a beguiling toy. I have to admit, I suppose, that it is primarily a toy. It has taught me any number of intriguing facts: the remarkably tenuous relationship that exists between air temperature and what the human body feels (page 260); the astonishingly hot surfaces your boots often have to walk on and can sometimes avoid (page 59); and the actual temperature of a river I had to swim in (the body is a miserable judge here too, and the temperature can be critical if you have to swim far [page 385]). But the sort of information my thermometer has given me has more often been interesting than practical.

One February I took a three-day hike along Point Reyes National Seashore, just north of San Francisco. On the last day a cold, damp wind blew in from offshore fog banks. At lunchtime I sheltered from the wind in a little hollow on the edge of the sand dunes bordering the beach. Down in the hollow, the wind barely rustled the thin, tough blades of beach grass. And the sun's reflected warmth beat up genially from pale sand. After a few minutes I felt sweat beginning to trickle down my face. Idly, I checked the temperature in the shady depths of the densest grass: 64°. Then I moved the thermometer out into the sun, on open sand. The mercury finally stopped at 112°.

For no clear or logical reason, I'm always checking and noting temperature readings: in shade and sun; in the air, on and below the surface; above, on, and below different neighboring surfaces; in rivers and hot springs. Once, I found myself delighted by the singularly useless information that it was still 55° in my boots half an hour after I had taken them off, when the ground temperature had already fallen close to freezing.

I suppose I gradually gain from such readings, in an untidy and diffuse sort of way, some new and rather tangential understandings of how our fascinating world works, but I doubt that this is really why I go on with the measuring and figuring. Mostly, I think, it's just that I enjoy my thermometer. I never think of leaving it behind. It travels in my "office-on-the-yoke" (page 83).

It is an ordinary mercury thermometer that comes in a pencil-size case (⅜ by 6¼ inches) with a strong pocket clip and a carrying ring at the top. Plastic cases have recently replaced the old-style metal ones. Range: −30° F. to 120° F. (which is really too low if you want to play) (1½ ounces; $3). These thermometers are reasonably tough; but I assure you that they'll break if you drop them far enough. I guess I go through about one a year.

Practical hints: Try to calibrate a new thermometer against a reliable and preferably official one. For a quick "shade" reading when there is no shade, twirl the thermometer around on the end of a length of string or nylon cord that you leave knotted to the carrying loop; but check the knot first (see knots, nylon cord, page 369). In hot weather, be careful where you leave the thermometer; in the sun, surface temperatures can easily exceed 130° F., and much beyond that you may find yourself with an empty glass stem and a blob of free-lance mercury.

A reader writes: "You can save weight by buying a skin

divers' watch-band thermometer. You wear it on your watch band. Pressure-proofed, and about the size of a nickel, it is within 2 degrees of true temperature and costs about $5." Maybe; but in air, what about the effect of my sweaty little wrist?

MENDING

Rip-stop repair tape

For repairing sleeping bags, tents or pack bags—in fact, almost any kind of equipment—there is nothing I know of to compare with this strong, lightweight, self-adhesive nylon fabric that comes in 2-inch-by-25-foot rolls in red, blue and green (5 ounces; $2.25 per roll; $.10 per foot), and also in ¾-ounce packs (3 feet of 3-inch-wide tape; $.50). You simply peel off the protective paper from its adhesive side and press the fabric in place. No heating, no nothing. And it sticks—though I'm convinced it sticks less well than it used to (page 276). Repairs seem to withstand a fair amount of washing but not dry cleaning. To make a patch permanent, sew around the edges. I always carry a length of Rip-stop tape in my office (page 359)—up to 2 feet, according to the length of the trip. Unexpected uses include repairing the split lens of a pair of snow goggles, binding the splintering end of my staff (page 51), and stopping the reek of butane gas from the empty cartridge of a Bleuet stove by simply sealing off the hole (page 166).

Needle and thread

For reinstating buttons and repairing anything from tent tabs to "yoke office." (They also puncture blisters. See page 61.) Half a dozen needles travel in my matchsafe (page 147). Short lengths of strong thread are threaded through three or four of these needles, and are wrapped around them like pythons. A longer reserve of thread, wrapped around a small piece of paper, goes into the "odds and ends" can (page 371).

Spare parts for pack

Every pack has certain small attachments whose loss or damage could disrupt a trip. In the "odds and ends" can (page 371) I carry at least one spare end-button for the frame (page 76), and three of the aluminum eyebolts that hold packbag to frame (page 81)—though I must admit I've never had to use one.

Into a separate small plastic bag goes a spare set of the buckles, with bars and split rings, that attach the yoke to the foot of the packframe (illustration, page 69).

Makeshift repairs

Substitutes for Rip-stop tape include adhesive medical tape (page 351) and moleskins (pages 60 and 48).

Occasionally, for such unexpected tasks as tying on a wrenched-off zipper tab, I've used nylon fishing line (page 355).

For epoxy, see "Air mattress," page 243.

For "Dental floss," see page 370.

ENJOYING EXTRAPERAMBULATORY ACTIVITIES

For many people, perhaps for most, a walk is rarely a self-fulfilling operation, whether it lasts an hour or a summer. Alone, with an agreeable companion, or in a group, they walk as a means to some such specific end as hunting, fishing, photography, bird watching, sex or geology.

Generally speaking, I regard the equipment for such activities as outside the scope of this book. There are two exceptions.

Fishing

An orthodox 2- or 3-piece rod is a perishing nuisance on a backpack trip. (I am thinking primarily of trout fishing, because that is what you usually find in the wilder areas still left for backpacking. And I am thinking above all of fly fishing, because in most remote areas that is the way to get the most pleasure from your fishing—and sometimes to catch the most trout. But what I have to say applies to most kinds of rods.)

If you lash an orthodox rod to your packframe—the best place for it—the risk of damage is high. If you tote along an aluminum rod case, the wretched thing tends to get in the way. When fishing is your overriding object, the inconvenience may be worth it; but if fishing is really an excuse for escape, and even more if it is just a possible bonus, the solution lies in a portmanteau rod—4- or even 6-piece.

The difficulty with this kind of rod is always its action: the perfect rod is a 1-piecer, and every metal ferrule marks another step down from perfection. Each ferrule also used to add critically to the weight, but new alloys have pretty well solved that problem. On this count even some cheaper fiberglass rods now score high. And the very best dispense with metal ferrules: fiberglass fits into hollowed fiberglass. The results are featherweight wands with smooth, lively actions.

Portmanteau rods now appear in outdoor catalogues at around $20. Shoff of Kent, Washington, make a good 4-piece 7½-footer (4½ ounces) that I used for years. But remember that with all these little rods there may be marked differences in action between half a dozen shop samples of the same model. Among the ferrule-less rods, the best known are Fenwick, said to be very good indeed. And if you are willing to spend around $70 you can have a ferrule-less beauty custom-made by R. L. Winston's of San Francisco. His 4-piece 7½-footer weighs 3 ounces. At the other extreme, see *Field & Stream*, August 1973, p. 18, for building your own ferruleless fiberglass rod.

I carry my rod inside the pack, fitting snugly down one side, close against the packframe. With no protection except a flimsy cloth cover, it has never come to any harm. Kelty now sells a "pole sock" (½ ounce; $.55)—a little bag that ties to the pack side-member and takes the rod's weight. Secure the upper end with a rubber band.

The rest of my backpack fly-fishing tackle fits into a small leather reel bag: the reel itself, six spools of nylon (2-, 3-, 4-, 6-, 8- and 10-pound test), a small can of flies, line grease, and fly flotant. Total: 11 ounces.

Anyone with enough wit to resist the widespread fallacy that you go fishing mainly in order to catch fish will understand that spinning is a barbarous way to catch trout. But I have to admit that there are places, such as high mountain lakes, where fly fish-ing may often be useless. And there are times, of course, when you'll want to fish purely for food. For such occasions I have once or twice carried a little closed-faced abomination of a spin-ning reel (9 ounces) that takes most of the pleasure out of fishing but does not demand a large butt ring on the rod and can there-fore be used with a fly rod. Into the abomination's little bag went some lead shot and weights, a few lures and bait hooks, and a bobber.

There are times when fly fishing is plainly impossible. (Often, for example, when the fish are not trout.) So I have a 4-piece, 4-ounce, 6-foot spinning rod that breaks down to 20 inches. It was made to my specifications from a hollow-glass blank that I selected from stock. It cost $12—in 1955. My other spinning tackle is standard.

You can fish purely for fun—and get it—with emergency tackle (page 355) and a light switch cut from the river bank—if cutting it seems acceptable in that place.

I'm aware that many people condemn fishing as a barbarous pursuit, lumpable with hunting. Seen from the outside, it may be—especially if the view includes close-ups of those pitiless—or, more likely, unthinking—rodmen who wrench their catch off the hook and leave it to gasp to death by inches. Even intellectually, though, I think it is possible to unlump fishing from hunting. Fish, for example, have simple nervous systems that do not seem to register pain as we mammals know it: I once hooked a small brook trout, brought it in almost to my feet before it came off the hook, and watched it swim back a few yards to its original position, then take my fly again within a minute or so. But hunters shoot birds or fellow mammals, with fellow nervous systems: a shot rabbit that just makes it back down its burrow, shattered leg gushing blood, is hardly likely to come back, like my brook trout, for another sample. Again, provided you wet your hands first and then work gently, you can, especially when fly fishing, return without harming it almost any fish you do not want for food. (Dry hands remove protective slime and leave a fish vulnerable to disease.) But you cannot by any known means set free a doe once it is lying there with its eyeball hanging and brains spattered—even if you had thought it was a buck, or if your natural hot hunter's blood has drained away and left only chill once you stand over your twitching victim. Furthermore, I see a fly rod as a delicate wand, a gun as an instrument of war. And here we may be closing on the nub. In the end, I think the difference is esthetic. I find fishing a gentle and artistic pastime that calms me. I see hunting otherwise. But I am aware that certain men whom I like and respect, men whose knowledge of and even veneration for wildlife is at least as great as mine, find hunting a satisfying and natural pursuit consonant with their veneration. See, further, the footnote on page 410. It is all very difficult.

Birdwatching

For the first forty-four years of my life I thought of birdwatchers, when I thought of them at all, as a frustrated and ineffectual bunch of fuddy-duddies, almost certainly sex starved, who funneled their energies into an amiable but pointless pursuit. My competence in their field was naturally close to zero. ("Naturally," because the firmest and most comfortable base from which to make sweeping judgments about any group of people is total ignorance.) But a few years ago, on a return visit to East Africa, I bought an identification book of the astonishingly prodigal birdlife of that astonishingly prodigal land. And at once I began to understand about birdwatching. It was not merely that birds, really looked at, turn out to be startlingly beautiful, nor even that individual birds, like individual humans, engage in funny, solemn, bitchy, pompous, brave, ludicrous, sexy, revolting and tender acts; after my first real attempt to identify individuals from the book I wrote, excitedly: "Fascinating. Not just collecting species. This business makes you see." Within days I was a full-fledged convert, always eager to try out the new plumage by reaching for my birdbook.*

My conversion has stuck. And the new creed, I find, has not only dented a lifelong conviction that I am simply not a namer of things—it has made me look at many things more closely.

From a practical backpacking point of view, a convert to birdwatching will find that if he did not take binoculars before, he will certainly do so now; that he will have even more difficulty than before in not stopping and staring when he should be pounding along; and that, everywhere for a while, and in new country forever after, he will at least consider carrying a birdbook. The U.S. "standards" are *A Field Guide to the Birds* (for east of the Mississippi) or *A Field Guide to Western Birds,* both by Roger Tory Peterson (Houghton Mifflin: hardbound—1 pound 1½ ounces each; $5.95; and paperback—1 pound even; $3.95). You can buy strong protective plastic covers for these books for $1, postpaid, from O. B. Enterprises, P.O. Box 21C, Celina, Ohio 45822. There are other bird books, of course. *Birds of North America,* by Chandler S. Robbins *et al.* (Golden Press paperback: 13 ounces; $2.95), has excellent range maps.

I have not yet fully solved the problem of how to carry a bird book safely yet ready for instant reference. The best method I've so far devised—and it's lousy—is to make a nylon-cord sling with one end tied in a fixed loop that goes over your arm and hangs from the shoulder, and the other end slip-noosed around the book. If you do something like this—or, for that matter, if you don't—stick bright red Rip-stop tape around at least half the cover of the book, so that it will, if lost, stand out from surrounding vegetation. I learned this lesson a couple of years ago, the hard way. At 4:00 P.M. one day I discovered that the birdbook had slipped from its sling somewhere in the course of a long, rough traverse across a desert slope; at 2:00 P.M. the following day, after many sweaty retraverses, I found the book lying in the open, green

---

* Echo trouble, you say? Maybe. See *The Winds of Mara,* p. 190.

and inconspicuous, in a place I had already passed at least four times. Note that I not only learned about putting red Rip-stop on green books but also confirmed yet again that ancient proverb: "a birdbook in the hand is worth twenty-two hours in the bush."

The remaining furniture and appliances can best be departmentalized:

ALWAYS-COMING-IN-USEFUL-AND-IN-FACT-QUITE-INDISPENSABLE DEPARTMENT

Nylon cord

Braided nylon cord, sometimes called "parachute cord" (⅛-inch diameter, 550-pound breaking strain), is to a backpacker what adhesive tape is to a doctor: an indispensable maid-of-all-work. I always carry half a dozen hanks, in lengths from 2 to about 15 feet; and occasionally a half or whole 100-foot hank (6 ounces; $1.50). Finer cord saves a gram or two but tangles without provocation.

No matter what lengths and thicknesses you find it best to carry, remember that cut cord always frays at the ends. To prevent fraying simply fuse the ends into unravelable blobs by holding them briefly in the flame of match or stove. Hanks of all sizes can travel, easily available, in an outside pocket of your pack.

Among their proven uses:

1. Rigging tents and allied shelters (pages 226–38)
2. Clotheslines
3. Fish stringers
4. Measuring lengths of fish and snakes, for later conversion to figures (mark with a knot)
5. Tying socks to pack for drying (page 47)
6. Securing binoculars and camera or hat to pack by clip spring, so that if dislodged they cannot fall far (pages 326 and 304)
7. Belt for pants (page 292) or for flapping poncho in high wind (page 298)
8. Lowering pack down difficult places (page 356) or even pulling it up (Don't try to pull hand over hand; bend knees, pass cord belay-fashion around upper rump, straighten legs, take in slack, and repeat and repeat and repeat....)
9. Replacement binocular strap
10. Chin band for hat (page 303)
11. Lashing tent poles to packframe (page 219)

12. When there's no wire, hanging cooking pots over a fire, from a tree, for melting snow for water (This way you can build up a really big fire and keep warm at the same time. You do so, of course, in the uneasy knowledge that the cord may burn; but in practice it doesn't seem to.)

13. Wrapping around camera case screw fitting, pulling, and so unjamming the screw for film changing

14. On packless sidetrips, tying poncho into lunch bundle (food, photo accessories, compass, etc.) and securing around waist (page 298)

15. Loop sling for birdbook (page 367)

16. On river crossings:
    (a) Lashing air mattress to pack (page 382)
    (b) Lashing plastic sheet into virtually watertight bundle for protection of valuables, either as sanctum sanctorum of pack (page 382) or as lone floating bundle to be pushed ahead or towed on packless crossings (page 379), and
    (c) Towing walking staff along behind

17. Attaching flashlight to self at night with loop around neck (page 281) (For securing nylon to un-holed flashlight, see "Dental floss" [page 370].)

Among uses I've had in mind for years but have still not had occasion to try:

1. Spare bootlaces
2. Lifting water from well
3. Doubled or tripled or quadrupled, as "carabiner-type" loop for ensuring that doubled climbing rope used for rappelling (or roping down) can be recovered from below (page 356)
4. As main rope for roping down cliff (in extreme emergency only, as cord might be weakened to danger point by knotting at top and by possible wear, and would in any case be viciously uncomfortable even if used doubled or quadrupled)
5. In river work, for pulling yourself back up against slow-to-medium river current—in case you find it necessary to float a short way past a blind headland to see if a safe land route lies ahead around dangerous rapids

Most ordinary knots in nylon eventually slip. The only safe knot I know—and it is less difficult to tie and less bulky than it looks—is the fisherman's blood knot:

For permanent knots, burn-fuse all ends.

Several readers have extolled the virtues of waxed nylon

Dental floss.

Acclaimed uses include: "most everything that nylon cord can be used for plus fishing line"; attaching line guides to fishing rods; binding around-the-neck nylon cord loop to flashlight that lacks convenient hole (page 282); sewing thread; and toothbrush-eliminating dental care.

The only cavil: "low resistance to abrasion."

Carry either wrapped around a card or in the tube (1 ounce; $.69) that it comes in—and which makes good home for needles. To prevent slippage, burn-fuse knot ends.

Rubber bands

For all-round usefulness, rubber bands rank second only to nylon cord. Their most vital function in my regimen is as weak and nonrestrictive garters for my turned-down socks, to keep stones and dirt out of the boots. Other uses: resealing opened food packages; closing food bags that are too full to be knotted at the neck; holding sugar-container lid firm; battening down the moleskin package with its added contents of nail scissors and metal mirror (page 348); securing camera cable release conveniently to binophotography bracket to prevent damage in the pack (page 329), and also for attaching the bracket to waist belt on packless sidetrips; holding onionskin paper (for notes) to its rectangle of stiffening cardboard; and keeping notebook instantly openable at the current pages, front and rear (page 358).

Rubber bands have a habit of breaking and also of getting lost, and I recommend that if your packframe has protruding arms you wrap around them as many bands as you think you need ready for immediate use. Then add the same number again. Then put into a small plastic bag about ten times as many as are on your packframe, and put this reserve safely away inside the pack. Mine go into my "office" (page 359).

Plastic bags

I sometimes wonder what backpackers used as the interior walls of their houses before the days of plastic freezer bags. I use them, in various sizes, not only for almost every food item (page 187) but also, copiously and often double thickness, for wrapping many other things: camp moccasins, underclothes, dirty socks, cooking pots, frying pan, book, rubber bands, stove, matches, toilet gear, first-aid kit, film, camera accessories, toilet paper, spare flashlight cells, can opener, stove nozzle cleaner, signal flare, fishing tackle, certain spare pack attachments, Visklamps and rubber balls for plastic shelter, car key, and unburnable garbage. Also, sometimes, as a wallet. I always take along a few spare bags.

For details of sizes and uses, and hints on packing, see pages 187–9.

35 mm. film cans

These cans are the best containers I know for salt tablets, water-purifying tablets, salmon eggs for bait, and coconut oil for lube jobs on hair and beard and even boots, not to mention for cooking. I also carry one can for "odds and ends": spare plastic end buttons and three spare aluminum eyebolts for packframe; two spare flashlight bulbs; and some strong button thread wound around a small piece of paper. At one time I also carried, with what struck me as a masterly stroke of foresight, several small screws for repairing separated boot soles; but the only time a loose sole did develop, the screws proved starkly ineffective.*

Film cans for 120 film are said to make useful makeshift matchsafes.

Belt clips

Swivel-mounted snap hooks (1 ounce; $.60) on small leather, or better still, woven nylon loops are useful for carrying certain items suspended from either your belt or the built-in waistband of your pants: a cup, in good drinking country (page 143); occasionally, your hat; the camera tripod or other light equipment on packless sidetrips.

If you use a belt clip while carrying the pack (for a cup, say), make sure you pass the belt *inside* the clip; otherwise the belt's pressure may force the clip open. After a little while you find yourself flipping the cup outside automatically every time you put the pack on.

* I'm amused—well, sort of—to hear from an Ann Arbor, Michigan, law firm that they quoted this paragraph in The Great Film Can Marijuana Case. Police stopped a student for a minor traffic offense, saw a 35 mm. film can on the floor of his car, asked to be given it, duly were, opened it, found marijuana. One legal point at issue was the right to "search": if the object was in plain view and "an obvious instrumentality of crime," then search was legal. The police contended that 35 mm. film cans were standard stash points for counter-culture marijuana and therefore suspicious. Defendant quoted this paragraph to establish legitimacy of such cans as containers for objects other than film or weed. Case dismissed. Hm.

I use two belt clips on my five-year, makeshift safety lines for binoculars and camera (page 326).

LINKS-WITH-CIVILIZATION DEPARTMENT

Generally, the last thing you want to do out in wild country is to carry any item that helps maintain a link with civilization. But there are exceptions. For example, it is sometimes more convenient and even cheaper to fly rather than drive to and from your chosen wilderness. And then you have to carry, all the way, some kind of suitable lightweight

Wallet.

The simplest and lightest is a small plastic food bag. Into it you may want to put, according to the needs of the moment, some form of identification (driver's license is best, in case you need to drive), fishing license, and fire permit. Also some money (although it's the most useless commodity imaginable once you're actually out in the wilderness). Consider both ready cash and traveler's checks, and perhaps one or two bank checks as reserve. A gasoline credit card may be worthwhile too: I once used mine to pay in advance for a short charter flight that put me down on a remote dirt road, and also for an airdrop of food that was to follow a week later.

A little cash may be worth taking along even when you are coming back to your car: late one fall, after a week in the mountains that ended with a fast, steep, 10,000-foot descent, I emerged with very sore feet onto a road 50 miles from my car, quickly hitched a ride in the right direction, and managed to persuade my benefactor that it was worth $5 for him to drive me several miles up a steep mountain road to where my car was parked.

Nowadays I always carry a dime taped to the cardboard stiffener of my "office" (page 359): few things are more frustrating than to emerge into man-country at last with a message heavy on your chest and find yourself at a remote telephone booth, dimeless and therefore mute.

Car key

The obvious place to leave your car key is at the car—taped or magnet-attached to some secret corner of it, or simply hidden close by. But I once came back from a winter mountain trip and found the rear bumper of my car, with the key craftily magnet-attached inside it, buried under a 10-foot snowdrift. Fortunately, a freak of the wind had left a convenient alley along one side of the car and I was able to get at the key without too much difficulty. But since then I find, rather to my surprise, that I tend to avoid vague worries about snow and torrential rain and landslides and thieves (human and other) by packing the key along with me. Cached or carried, the key gets wrapped in the inevitable plastic bag.

Radio

Believe it or not, I am regularly asked, "But don't you carry a transistor radio . . . so that you can keep in touch . . . or for the weather . . . or anyway for company?" You're allowed one guess.

STRICTLY-PERSONAL-BUT-YOU'LL-PROBABLY-HAVE-YOUR-OWN DEPARTMENT

Everyone, I imagine, has one or two little personal items that go along. They'll vary according to individual interests and frailties. Two very experienced friends of mine always carry small pliers. In addition to items I've already mentioned, such as office and pros-pector's magnifying glass, my list includes spare eyeglasses (some-times), and two Ace bandages (always). The bandages are primarily for a troublesome knee and for emergency use in case of a sprained ankle but they have seen most use in thornbush and cactus country, wrapped puttee fashion around my bare and vul-nerable lower legs (page 292).

Housekeeping and Other Matters

ORGANIZING THE PACK

The best way to stow your gear into your pack is to pursue, all the time, a reasonable compromise between convenience and efficient weight distribution.

For the main considerations in weight distribution—loading high and close to the back—see pages 89 and 90. Common sense and a lick or two of experience will soon teach you the necessary refinements: after some angular item such as the stove has gouged into your back a couple of times you'll make sure, almost without thinking, that flat or soft articles pad the forward surface of the packbag's main compartment; and once you've put both the full canteens that you're carrying on the same side of the bag and found that the load then rides like a one-armed gorilla, you're unlikely to repeat the mistake.

If you use a compartmented packbag, your ideas on where things should go will clearly be different from those of a bloody-great-sack addict like me. But as my experience is almost entirely sackish, and because on the rare occasions I've used compartmented bags I found that the general principles held good, I'll speak purely from experience.

The most convenient way to stow gear varies from trip to trip, from day to day, from morning to evening. Obviously, the things you'll want first at the next halt should go in last. So the groundsheet will normally travel on top. In dry country, so will one canteen—though in sunny weather it should be covered with a down jacket or some other insulator (page 139). And the balance-of-the-week's-ration bag, the signal flare, reserve or empty canteens, and refill cartridges for the Bleuet stove should—on the score of sheer convenience—languish down in the basement. Otherwise, the important thing is not where each item goes but that you always know where it is.

374

There will be variations of course. If rain threatens, the poncho must be on top and perhaps even sticking out, ready to be plucked into use. On cold evenings, have your heavy clothing ready to put on even before you start to make camp. If it looks as though you are going to have a long, torrid midday halt, make sure you don't have to dig down to the bottom of the packbag for plastic sheet or poncho before you can rig up an awning. But all this is just plain common sense.

So are the compromises you are always making between maximum convenience and fully efficient weight distribution. In time, every backpacker works out a way of stowing things that suits him best. But the inexperienced may be able to find some guidelines in the solutions that I have evolved. (A good deal of this information has been scattered around in earlier chapters, but it seems worthwhile to summarize it here. By and large, I shall let the first edition text stand: it's irrelevant that my present pack has neither inside nor flap pocket. The next may have both. And my old arrangements, taken together with new ones now mentioned elsewhere in the text, may suggest alternatives for different bags. The point, anyway, is to suggest guidelines, not perpetuate idiosyncrasies.)

I always pad the forward side of my packbag with the office, and sometimes with camp moccasins (soles facing out). A scarf and the spare plastic bags also go into the inside pocket and so increase the padding effect. The flashlight travels there too—safe from being pulled out accidentally, well protected against damage, and so situated that even after dark I can reach in and find it without fumbling. Put in at the right angle, it never gouges my back, though I can't quite understand why. In one forward corner of the main sack, fitting snugly against the packframe, go the gasoline container and, on top of it, the stove. If I'm carrying a portmanteau fishing rod or a cloth stove screen or both, they fit into the opposite and similar corner.

There are few other firm rules for the main sack. Cooking pots and the food-for-the-day bag normally go side by side on the same level, because when I want one I want the other, but otherwise the packing arrangements depend largely on what items I expect to need next. Generally, though, I try to pack heavy articles close to the packframe (see pages 89 and 90).

For stuff bags, see page 274.

For the various sleeping-bag carrying systems, see page 77.

My present pack has five outside pockets: two on each side and one amidships, aft (see page 81, and illustration, page 69).

For the moment, we'll "add" the flap pocket I used to have—and still covet.

Into the shallow flap pocket—which is the easiest of all to get at—go spare clean socks, or damp or dirty socks (in plastic bags) when for some reason such as rain or grabbing thorns it is inadvisable to leave them airing on the outside of the pack. Also camera lens tissue and camera close-up attachments, if it seems likely they'll be needed in a hurry. And, from time to time, small items—such as water-purifying tablets in a 35 mm. film can—that are temporarily in frequent use.

The upper starboard pocket is the "nibble pocket"—the most often used of all. Into it go the quick-boost foods I nibble at almost every halt (page 115). One meat bar lives there too, so that if there's no time to stop for a regular lunch I need not unpack the main food.

The lower starboard pocket holds foot powder and rubbing alcohol (page 58), the small plastic baby-bottle canteen (page 140), one package of fruit-drink mix and, sometimes, the water-purifying tablets. Also, when they're carried, fly dope and sun-tan lotion.

On the rare occasions I still carry a camera, the upper port pocket is the photography room: tripod, close-up attachments, binophotography bracket, cable release, strap extension for camera case (the camera hangs on a short strap; the extension is needed for slinging camera over shoulder on packless jaunts), and in really cool weather, film (page 329). When I'm cameraless, this pocket fills with junk as quickly as a spare room back home. The commonest squatters: scarf, balaclava, flashlight, soapless soap and hand lotion.

The lower port pocket is for other miscellaneous items that must be get-at-able in a hurry or are too small and losable to travel in the main sack: first-aid kit, compass, belt clip, carborundum stone, stove-cover handle (from Svea), odds-and-ends can, and spare pack fittings.

Because a pack can face two ways, I find I often confuse the side pockets. Some Jan Sport packs have one upper sidepocket a distinguishing color: it's a simple and efficient antidote to confusion.

Into the big central pocket go toilet paper and trowel, sheath knife, hanks of nylon cord, and unburnable garbage (in plastic bag).

Tent poles, when carried, are lashed to the packframe (page 219).

The only radical changes in organizing the pack come at

RIVER CROSSINGS.

Simple crossings raise no problems. Failing a natural log bridge or steppingstones, you just take off your boots and wade. At least, I do. Some people keep their boots on, but I mistrust the effect on boots and feet. Or perhaps I just mean that I abhor the idea of squelching along afterwards. On easy crossings, carry your boots, with socks pushed inside. Knot the laces together and twist them around one wrist. On deeper crossings, hang the lace-linked boots on the packframe. In really difficult places it's safer to stuff them inside the packbag.

A friend once suggested a method he uses regularly and which, for fast and rocky rivers, sounds obvious enough and well worth a trial: take off socks, replace boots, wade river with well-protected feet, replace socks, and go on your happy and reputedly unsquelching way. Somehow, I've yet to try it out.

Provided you choose the right places, you can wade surprisingly large rivers. (Fast rivers, that is, where the depth and character vary; slow, channeled rivers are normally unwadable.) It often pays to make an extensive reconnaissance along the bank in order to select a good crossing point. You may even need to detour for a mile or more. Generally, the safest places are the widest and, up to a point, the fastest. Most promising of all, provided the water is shallow enough and not too fierce, tend to be the fanned-out tails of wide pools. Boulders or large stones, protruding or submerged, in fairly shallow water may also indicate a good crossing place: they break the full force of racing water, and you can ease across the most dangerous places on little mounds of stone and gravel that have been deposited by the slack water behind each boulder. But always, before you start across, pick out in detail, with coldly cynical eyes, a route that looks tolerably safe—all the way. And don't get into a position you can't retreat from.

Experience is by far the most important aid to safe wading (I wish I had a lot more), but there are a few simple rules. Use a staff—particularly with a heavy pack. (It turns you, even more crucially than on dry land, from an insecure biped into a confident triped.) In fast current, the safest route for walking, other things being equal, is one that angles down and across the current. The faster and deeper the water, the more sharply downstream you should angle. The next best attack is up and across. Most hazardous of all—because the current can most easily sweep you off balance—is a directly-across route.

Unless you are afraid of being swept off your feet (and in that case you'd almost certainly do better to find a deep, slow section and swim across), wading does not call for any change in the way you pack. But before you start across you should certainly undo your waistbelt. Always. The pack (at least until it fills with water) is much more buoyant than your body and should you fall in, it will, if held in place by the belt, force you under. It is easy enough to wriggle out of a shoulder yoke, particularly if it's slung over only one shoulder. At least, I have always liked to imagine so—and a reader's letter confirms my faith. She and her husband were wading a turbulent stream in Maine—waistbelts undone and hanging free—when she lost her bare footing and was swept downstream. She quickly squirmed free of the harness and within fifty feet, still hanging onto the pack, grabbed a boulder and pulled herself to safety. Afterward, she realized that having her waistbelt undone had been "a great thing."

The only other precaution I sometimes take when wading, and then only at difficult crossings, is to unhitch camera and binoculars from the packframe and put them inside the pack.

But if you have to swim a river you must reorganize the pack's contents.*

The first time I tried swimming with a pack was on my Grand Canyon journey, in 1963. Because of the new Glen Canyon Dam, a hundred miles upriver, the Colorado was then running at only 1200 cubic feet per second—far below its normal low-water level. Even for someone who, like me, is a poor and nervous swimmer, it seemed comparatively easy to swim across a slow, deep stretch with little danger of being swept down over the next rapids. I adopted the technique developed by the one man who had been able to help me with much information about hiking in remote parts of the Canyon. He was a math professor at Arizona State College in Flagstaff; and he was also, his wife said, "like a seal in the water." He had found that by lying across his air mattress with the pack slung over one shoulder, half floating, he could, even at high water, dog-paddle across the Colorado—which is the third longest river in the United States, and is muscled accordingly. I tried his

---

* I have been taken to task for not warning you that my swimming lessons mostly apply to large desert rivers. Fast mountain rivers are generally too cold for this kind of thing. The warnings were there all right in the first edition, at the end of this section. But this time I'll play safe and inject a reference to it here at the start: please read p. 385 with care.

method out on several same-side detours, when sheer cliffs blocked my way, and by degrees I gained confidence in it.*

The air mattress made a good raft. Inflated not too firmly, it formed a reassuring V when I lay with my chest across it. I used it first on a packless reconnaissance. Remembering how during World War II we had crossed rivers by wrapping all our gear in waterproof anti-gas capes and making bundles that floated so well we could just hang on to them and kick our way forward, I wrapped the few clothes and stores I needed into the white plastic sheet and lashed it firmly with nylon cord. It floated well. I found that by wrapping a loose end of cord around one arm I could tow it along beside me and dog-paddle fairly freely.

---

* My professorial informant, after reading the first edition of this book, wrote: "I never intended to let the pack hang from one shoulder floating in the water. This happened only by accident on two or three occasions, when I was upset. Intentionally, I have only two positions on the air mattress: crosswise— as you used your shortie—when in rough water; and lengthwise under me in calm water. If I switch positions before reaching the waves, I am reasonably sure of keeping the pack in position."

I'm glad, though, that I got it wrong. The prof specializes in two- and three-day trips, carrying relatively light packs. I found my heavy burden an impossible shoulder-load when I was waterborne. But you might like to try a light pack that way.

With the pack, dog-paddling turned out to be a little more restricted but still reasonably effective. The pack, slung over my left shoulder and half-floating, tended at first to keel over. But I soon found that I could hold it steady by light pressure on the lower and upper ends of the packframe with buttocks and bald patch. It sounds awkward but worked fine.

My staff floated along behind at the end of three feet of nylon cord tied to the packframe. Everything else went into the pack. I had waterproofed the seams of the packbag rather hurriedly, and I found that water still seeped through. So into the bottom of the bag went bulky and buoyant articles that water could not damage: canteens, cooking pots, and white-gas container. Things better kept dry went in next, wrapped in the white plastic sheet. Items that just had to stay dry went on top, in what I thought of as the sanctum sanctorum: camera and accessories, flashlight and spare batteries, binoculars, watch, writing materials, and toilet paper. I tied each of these items into a plastic bag, rolled them all inside the sleeping bag, and stuffed it into the big, tough plastic bag that usually went around the cooking pots. Then I wrapped the lot in my poncho. Before strapping the packbag shut I tied the ends of the poncho *outside* the white plastic sheet with nylon cord. (On one trial run the pack had keeled over and water had run down inside the plastic sheet, though the sanctum had remained inviolate.) On the one complete river crossing that I had to make, nothing got even damp.

This system, or some variation of it, should prove adequate for crossing almost any river that is warm enough, provided you do not have to go through heavy rapids. I am more than half-scared of water and a very poor swimmer, and if I can succeed with it almost anyone can. The great practical advantage of this method is that you do not have to carry any special equipment. All you need is an air mattress, a poncho and a plastic sheet or a ground-sheet.

Heavy rapids present a different problem. In May 1966 I took a two-week hike-and-swim trip down 70 miles of the Colorado, in lower Grand Canyon. Although many people have run the Colorado by boat, it seemed that everyone had until then had the sense to avoid attempting this very enclosed stretch on foot; but I knew from boatmen's reports that even if the route proved possible I would almost certainly have to make several river crossings. I also knew that, with the reservoir now part-filled behind Glen Canyon Dam, the river was racing down at an average of about 16,000 cubic feet per second—more than twelve times its volume on my 1963 trip. That meant I would almost certainly be carried far downstream each time I attempted a crossing. Even the calmer stretches would be swirling, whirlpooled horrors, and I would probably be carried through at least some minor rapids. Under such conditions I wasn't willing to risk the lying-across-an-air-mattress technique, and I evolved a new method, more suitable for a timid swimmer.

Just before the trip I bought an inflatable life vest (Stebco Industries Inc., Model LP 31; 1 pound 2 ounces; now $22.95). It is made of bright yellow rubberized cotton fabric, and there is a valve for inflation by mouth and also a small metal cartridge that in an emergency fills the vest with carbon dioxide the instant you pull a toggled cord. The vest yokes comfortably around the neck so that when you float on your back your mouth is held clear of the water. When I tried it out in a sidecreek as soon as I reached the Colorado, I found that I could also swim very comfortably in the normal position. From the start, I felt safe and confident.

I had already decided that, rather than lie across the air mattress, I would this time rely solely on the life vest to keep me afloat—partly because I was afraid the vest's metal cartridge or its securing wire might puncture the mattress (which in the current model they will not do: they are concealed), but even more because I did not fancy my chances of staying on the mattress in swirling water. (A young fellow crossing the Colorado on a trip with my math professor friend had been swept off his mattress by a whirlpool and had drowned.) I decided that in fast water the trick would be to make the pack buoyant in its own right, and just pull or push it along with me.

The coated nylon fabric of the packbag was fully waterproof but, although I had applied seam sealant, water still seeped in. So I decided to try to keep the pack as upright as I could in the water and stow the really vital gear, well protected, up near the top. First, for extra buoyancy high up, I put one empty plastic quart-size canteen in each of the upper sidepockets. Into the bottom of the bag as ballast went the two cooking pots and two ½-gallon canteens, all filled with water. Next I lined the remaining space in the main sack with my transparent polyethylene ground-sheet and left the unused portion hanging outside. Like all ground-sheets, mine had developed many small holes, but I figured it would ward off the worst of any water that might seep in from the upper seams or under the flap, and that what little did get through would collect harmlessly in the bottom of the pack. The items that water couldn't damage (page 380) went in first. Next, those preferably kept dry. Then I made the sanctum sanctorum. Into the white plastic sheet (because rain was unlikely, I carried no poncho this trip) went all the things that just had to stay dry (as on page 380). Most of them were additionally protected inside an assortment of plastic bags. I lashed the white bundle firmly with nylon cord, put it on top of everything else, then folded over the unused portion of the groundsheet that was still hanging outside and carefully tucked it in between the main portion of the groundsheet and the packbag itself. I knotted down the pack flap, tight. Then I partially inflated my air mattress and lashed it securely with nylon cord to the upper half of the pack, taking care to keep it central. Finally I took the four-foot agave-stem walking staff that I had cut at the start of the trip (page 53) and wedged it down into the cross-webbing of the packframe, close beside one upright.

I held the pack upright in the water for several minutes, forcing it down so that water seeped in and filled the bottom 7 or 8 inches—thereby helping, I hoped, to keep the pack upright. Then I slid down into the river beside it. With my left hand I grasped the lowest cross-rung of the packframe and pulled downward. Provided I maintained a slight downward pressure (see illustration) the pack floated fairly upright, though tending to lean away from me, and I was free to swim in any position with one arm and both legs.

In addition to the inflatable vest, I wore my ultralightweight nylon swimming trunks (page 302). I'd brought them because at the start, at the sidecreek in which I practiced, there was a possibility of meeting people. But I found that I actually wore the trunks on all crossings, so that I would have at least some protection from the sun if I became separated from the pack. And so that I could still light a fire in that unlikely event, I tied the waterproof matchsafe (page 147) onto the vest.

The whole rig worked magnificently. I made four crossings.

The white plastic sheet hardly ever got damp, even on the outside, and the sanctum remained bone dry, every time. So, mostly, did all other items stowed near the top of the pack. Because I could swim freely, I always got across the river reasonably fast. Each time I could have landed within half a mile of my launch site; but twice I allowed myself to be carried a little farther down to good landing places. (And as I floated down the calmer stretches on my back, with both feet resting on the packframe in front of me—my mind and body utterly relaxed, and an integral part of the huge, silent, flowing river—I found that I had discovered a new and serene and superbly included way of experiencing the Grand Canyon of the Colorado.)

I also made two same-side river detours around impassable cliffs. And one of these detours was the high point of the trip.

For the first 50 feet of the rapids I had to go through, the racing water battered on its left flank into a jagged rockwall. I knew that the one thing I absolutely had to do was to keep an eye on this rockwall and make sure that if I swung close I fended off in time with arm or pack or legs. From the bank, the steep waves in the heart of the rapids didn't look too terrifying: not more than 3 or 4 feet high at the most. But throughout the double eternity during which I swirled and wallowed through those waves—able to think of nothing except "Is it safe to grab a breath now, before I go in under that next one?"—I knew vividly and for sure that not one of them was less than 57½ feet high. And all I saw of the rockwall was a couple of split-second glimpses—like a near-subliminal inner-thought flash from a movie.

I missed the rockwall, though—through no effort of mine—and came safely through the rapids. A belch or two in midriver cleared the soggy feeling that came from the few mouthfuls of Colorado that I had shipped; and once I got into calmer water and

had time to take a look at the pack it seemed serenely shipshape. (In the rapids, frankly, I hadn't even known that I was still hanging on to it.)

The only problem now, in the fast water below the rapids, was getting back to the bank. It took me a full mile to do so.

At first I had to stay in midriver to avoid protruding rocks at the edge of some more and only slightly less tumultuous rapids. Then, after I'd worked my way close to the bank, I was swept out again by tailwash from a big, barely submerged boulder. Almost at once I saw a smooth, sinister gray wave ahead, rising up out of the middle of the river. I knew at once what it was. Furiously, I swam toward the bank. A few strokes and I looked downstream once more. The wave was five times closer now, ten times bigger. And I knew I could not avoid it. Just in time, I got into position with the pack held off to one side and my legs out in front of me, high in the water and slightly bent. Then I was rising up, sickeningly, onto the crest of the wave. And then I was plummeting down. As I fell, my feet brushed, very gently, over the smooth, hard surface of the hidden boulder. Then a white turmoil engulfed me. But almost instantly my head was out in the air again and I was floating along in calmer water. For a moment or two the pack looked rather waterlogged; but long before I made landfall, a couple of hundred yards downstream, it was once more floating high. When I unpacked, I found the contents even drier than on some of the earlier and calmer crossings.

After those rapids and that boulder, I feel I can say that my fast-water river-crossing technique works.

That trip was something of a special case, but it has taught me a useful lesson: if you have to swim a river, and have no air mattress and no inflatable vest, rig your pack somewhat after the manner I did. It will float buoyantly, and vital items will travel safely in the sanctum sanctorum. (I'm fairly sure my air mattress did not "float" the pack, but only helped hold it upright at stressful moments.) Pull down on the bottom crossbar of the frame and swim alongside or in front or behind (in swirling water you'll do all three within seconds). A fair swimmer would have no difficulty, I imagine, in any reasonably unbroken water. And if, like me, you are a weak swimmer you could almost certainly keep yourself afloat and moving across the current by just hanging onto the pack and kicking. But if it's at all possible, try out unproven variations like this beforehand—preferably well ahead of time; or failing that, in calm, safe water before the main attempt.

A reader suggests that for short emergency swims "a pair of tough (3 mil) plastic bags, blown up and tied or secured with rubber bands or nylon string, are very handy" for pack or person.

For crossing any but the widest rivers, parties of hikers have it easier than a man on his own—provided they are carrying enough rope or cord. Only one man need swim across under his own power. The others, after paying out a cord or rope attached to his body, can be pulled across by him. At least, I guess so.

Don't forget that water temperature can be treacherous in river crossings. Even when you're wading, cold water can numb your feet and legs to danger point with astonishing speed. And no one can swim for long in liquid ice—cannot even live in it for very long. Yet your body will work efficiently for a considerable time in 50° water. During my 1963 Grand Canyon journey, the Colorado River temperature was around 60°. On the 1966 trip it averaged about 57°, and although the water always felt perishing cold when I first got into it (which was hardly surprising, with shade temperatures rising each day to over 100°, and precious little shade anywhere), I was never once, even on the longest swim, at all conscious of being cold.

SANITATION

(Note: Except for a new paragraph on trowels, this section stands much as I wrote it five years ago. But it is now ten times as important: our burgeoning numbers have had hideous impact. And the ignorance of some newcomers about how to operate in wilderness has made a sad, self-righteous mockery of my words about the respect normally accorded the earth by those who undertake demanding journeys. I shall let the words stand, though, as a goad.)

Sanitation is not a pleasant topic, but every camper must for the sake of others consider it openly, with his mind unblurred by prudery.

At one extreme there is the situation in which permanent johns have been built. Always use them. If they exist, it means that the human population, at least at certain times of year, is too dense for any other healthy solution. (The National Park Service calculates that 500 people using a leach-line-system permanent john will pollute a place no more than one person leaving untreated feces, even buried.)

A big party camping in any kind of country, no matter how wild, automatically imposes a dense population on a limited area. They should always dig deep latrine holes and, if possible, carry lime or some similar disinfectant that will counteract odor, keep flies away, and hasten decomposition. And they must fill holes carefully before leaving.

A party of two or three in a remote area—and even more certainly, a man on his own—must make simpler arrangements. But with proper "cat sanitation" and due care and consideration in choice of sites, no problem need arise.

Cat sanitation means doing what a cat does, though more efficiently: digging a hole, and covering up the feces afterward. But it must be a hole, not a mere scratch. Make it at least 4 or 5 inches deep, and preferably 6 or 8. But do not dig down below topsoil into inert-looking earth where insects and decomposing bacteria will be unable to work properly. In some soils you can dig easily enough with your boots or a stick. I used to carry my sheath knife along whenever I went looking for a cat-john site, and used it if necessary for digging. Then I came across one of the plastic toilet trowels (10 inches long; 2 ounces; $.79) that now appear in some catalogues. At first I was merely amused. But I found that the trowel digs quickly and well and means you can cat-sanitate effectively in almost any soil. Now I always pack it along. Because these little trowels remind as well as dig, I'm tempted to suggest they be made obligatory equipment for everyone who backpacks into a national park or forest. But I resist the temptation—not only because human nature being what it is, thank God, any such ordinance would drive many worthy people in precisely the undesired direction but also because blanket decrees are foreign to whatever it is a man goes out into wilderness to seek, and bureaucratic decrees are worst of all because they tend to accumulate and perpetuate and harden when they're administered, as they so often are, by people who revel in enforcing petty ukases. Anyway, a rule that's impossible to enforce is a bad rule. And this one has been tried: a young reader of eighty-nine recently drew my attention to Deuteronomy 23, verse 13 (see Appendix IV, page 464).

Your kosher plastic paddle can come in useful, by the way, when you have to melt snow for water (page 201). Conversely, a 10-inch, angled aluminum snow-peg (page 222) makes a fair toilet trowel: for digging in hard soil, pad it at the top with your ubiquitous bandanna.

In the double plastic bags that hold my roll of toilet paper lives a book of matches. I tear one match off ready beforehand and leave it protruding from the book, so that I need handle the book very little; and unless there is a severe fire hazard, when I have finished I burn all the used paper. The flames not only destroy the paper but char the feces and discourage flies. Afterward I carefully refill the hole. Unless the water situation is critical, I have soap and an opened canteen waiting in camp for immediate hand washing.

A hardy friend of mine suggests as substitutes for paper "soft grass, ferns and broad leaves, and even the tip of firs, redwoods, etc."

In choosing a john site, remember above all that you must be able to dig. Rock is not acceptable. Rock is not acceptable. Rock is not acceptable. I am driven to reiteration by the revolting memory of a beautiful rock-girt creek in California, a long hour from roadhead but heavily fished and traveled. And that raises the only other absolute rule: always go at least 50 feet, and preferably 500, from any watercourse, even if currently dry. Soil filters; but it demands time and space. The rest is largely a matter of considering other people. Wherever possible, select tucked-away places that no one is likely to use for any purpose. But do not appropriate a place so neatly tucked away that someone may want to camp there. A little thoughtful common sense will be an adequate guide.

All other things being equal, choose a john with a view.

In deep snow there is unfortunately nothing you can do except dig a hole, burn the paper, cover the hole and afterward refuse to think about what will happen come hot weather. There is not much you can do, either, about having to expose your fundamentals to the elements. Actually, even in temperatures well below freezing, it turns out to be a surprisingly undistressing business for the brief interval necessary, especially if you have a tent to crawl back into. Obviously, blizzard conditions and biting cold may make the world outside your tent unlivable, even for brief intervals, but a cookhole in the tent floor (page 213) would solve this problem. For footwear when scrambling out of a tent in snow, see page 224.

It is horrifying how many people, even under conditions in which cat sanitation is easy, fail to observe the simple, basic rules. Failure to bury feces is not only barbaric; it is a danger to others. Flies are everywhere. And the barbarism is compounded by thoughtless choice of sites. I still remember the disgust I felt when, late one rainy mountain evening, several years ago, I found at last what looked like an ideal campsite under a small overhanging rockface—and then saw, dead center, a cluster of filthy toilet paper and a naked human turd.

That rockledge was in a fairly remote area. The problem can be magnified when previously remote countryside is opened up to people unfit to use it. Power boats now cruise far and wide over Lake Powell, which is backing up fast behind the Colorado's new Glen Canyon Dam, and the boats' occupants are able to visit with almost no effort many ancient and fascinating Indian cliff dwellings. Previously, these dwellings could be reached only by extensive foot or fast-water journeys. Now people who undertake such demanding journeys have usually (though not always) learned, through close contact with the earth, to treat it with respect—and power boats do not bring you in close contact with the earth. I hear that most of the cliff dwellings near Lake Powell have already been used as toilets.

Urination is a much less serious matter. But dense and undisciplined human populations can eventually create a smell, and although this problem normally arises only in camping areas so crowded that you might as well be on Main Street, it can also do so with locally concentrated use, especially in hot weather and when the ground is impervious to liquids. During my first Grand Canyon journey I camped on one open rockledge for four days. As the days passed, the temperature rose. On the fourth day, with the thermometer reaching 80° in the shade—and 120° in my unshaded camp—I several times detected whiffs of a stale odor that made me suspect I was near the lair of a large animal. I was actually hunting around for the lair when I realized that only one large animal was living on that rockledge.

But urination is usually no more than a minor inconvenience—even for those who, like me, must have been in the back row when bladders were given out. An obvious precaution is to cut down on drinking at night. No tea for me, thank you, with dinner. But I rarely manage to get through a night undisturbed. Fortunately, it is surprising how little you get chilled when you stand up for a few moments on quite cold nights, even naked. I go no farther than the foot of my sleeping bag, and just aim at the night (hence the "animal lair" at that rocky Grand Canyon campsite). A distaff reader has written asking if I have any useful advice for her on this subject. Regretfully, I can offer only commiseration. And a man wrote reminding me of the Eskimo who "reaches for his urinal and without leaving the bag captures another increment for tomorrow's emptying ceremony." I duly bought a wide-mouthed plastic bottle. But a funny thing happened: I failed. I guess I'm just too well house-trained. I gather that such a block is not uncommon.

REPLENISHING SUPPLIES

On extended trips you always face the problem of how to replenish your supplies. Generally speaking, you can't carry food for more than a week or two (page 23). Other items also need replacement: powder and rubbing alcohol for your feet, toilet paper, other toilet articles. You'll probably need additional film too, and new maps and replacement equipment and perhaps special gear for certain sections of the trip.

Outposts of civilization

On my six-month California walk I was able to plan my route so that I called in every week or ten days at remote country post offices. Before I started the trip I had mailed ahead to each of these post offices not only a batch of maps for the stretch of country ahead but also items of special gear, such as warm clothing for the first high mountain beyond the desert. At each post office I mailed to The Ski Hut, back in Berkeley, a list of the food and equipment I wanted to pick up two weeks later; and a list of film and personal requirements went to a reliable friend. So at each post-office call-in I found waiting for me everything I needed for the next leg of the journey.

These calls at outposts of civilization provided a change of diet too: there was always a store near the post office, and usually a café—and a motel. I often stayed a day or two in the motel to write and mail a series of newspaper articles (and also to soak in several hot showers and cold beers). Exposed film went out in the mails, and completed notes, and sometimes equipment I no longer needed. All in all, the system worked very well. It could probably be adapted, with modifications to suit the needs of the moment, for many kinds of walking trips.

For firms that offer such a supply service along the Appalachian Trail, see page 16.

In wild areas you have to replenish by other means. One way is to make

Caches.

On the California walk I put out several water caches at critical points and at one or two of them I also left a few cans of food. Later I realized that I should have left at least a day's non-dehydrated food, for a treat—and possibly some dehydrated food for the way ahead, so that I could have cut down my load.

I was able to put those caches out by car, on little-used dirt roads, but on most wilderness trips you have to pack the stuff in ahead of time. On the two-month Grand Canyon trip I put out two caches of water, food, and other supplies. From the purely logistic standpoint I should have carried these caches far down into the Canyon so that on the trip itself I would not have to detour. But there is, thank God, more to walking than logistics. I had been dreaming about the Canyon for a year, and one of the prime concerns in all my planning was to shield the dream from famili-arity—that sly and deadly anesthetic. As I wrote in *The Man Who Walked Through Time*, "I knew that if I packed stores down into the Canyon I would be 'trespassing' in what I wanted to be un-known country; but I also knew that if I planted the caches out-side the Rim I would in picking them up break both the real and symbolic continuity of my journey. In the end I solved the dilemma by siting each cache a few feet below the Rim."

Such delicate precautions should, I think, always be borne in mind when one of the aims of a backpacking trip, recognized or submerged, is to explore and immerse yourself in unknown coun-try. You must avoid any kind of preview. Before my Grand Can-yon trip, several people said, "Why not fly over beforehand, low? That's the way to choose a safe route." But I resisted the tempta-tion—and in the end was profoundly thankful I had done so.

The best way to make, mark, and protect a cache will depend on local conditions. Rain and animals pose the most obvious threats. But extreme heat has to be avoided if there is film in the cache, and extreme cold if there is water. (For the protection and re-finding of water caches, and the best containers, see page 136. For precautions when caching dehydrated food in damp climates, see page 121.)

A cave or overhanging rockledge is probably the best pro-tection against rain. Burying is the simplest and surest protection, especially in sandy desert, against temperature extremes and also against animals. For animals that can read, leave a note. On the California walk I put one with each cache: "If you find this cache, please leave it. I am passing through *on foot* in April or May, and am depending on it." Similar notes went on the Grand Canyon caches. But I doubt if any of them was ever read.

At each Grand Canyon cache, all food and supplies went into a metal 5-gallon can. These cans are ideal for the job. Provided the lid is pressed firmly home, the cans are watertight, something close to airtight, and probably proof against all animals except bears and humans. I find that by packing the cans very carefully I can just squeeze in a full week's supply of everything. They are useful, too, for packing water ahead (page 137). They are also excellent for airdrops—and having them interchangeably available for caches or airdrops may help keep your plans conveniently fluid until the last possible moment.

Airdrops

Prearranged parachute airdrops are a highly efficient means of replenishment. But they are noisy. And I feel that in today's heavily used wilderness areas they should be banned as a normal supply method—as should all administrative, nonemergency over-flights. After all, an object of going into such places—perhaps *the* object—is "to get away from it all"; and surely no one in his senses would want to inject "it" routinely in the form of low-flying aircraft. I have found, oddly enough, that the disturbance you suffer personally by having an airdrop is very small indeed, but once low-altitude flights—for any purpose at all—became anything more than very exceptional incursions they would disturb for everyone the solitude and sense of freedom from the man-world that I judge to be the essence of wilderness travel. As with sanitation, it is a matter of density.

But there are still places in which an occasional airdrop remains a reasonable supply method as well as the only practical one. So I retain this section from the first edition.

Although airdrops are efficient, they are not perfect. On the ground, a practical disadvantage is that they tie you down to being at a certain place at a certain time. They are more dependable than most people imagine, but uncertainties do exist—above all, the uncertainty of weather—and I am not sure I would rely on an airdrop if there were any considerable danger that the plane might be delayed more than a day or two by storms or fog.

Airdrops have one important advantage over other means of supply: they act as a safety check. Once you've signaled "all's well" to the plane, everyone concerned soon knows you are safe up to that point. And if the pilot fails to locate you or sees a prearranged "in trouble—need help" signal, then rescue operations can get under immediate and well-directed way. (See page 420.)

Airdrops are not cheap—but neither are they ruinous. Most small rural charter outfits seem to charge around $30 for each hour of actual flying. If the base airport is within, say, 50 miles of the drop site, you ought to get by on about 1¼ hours flying time, or about $40—provided the pilot has no trouble locating you. But you may have to add the cost of the parachute.

Establishing contact is the crux of an airdrop operation.

First, make sure you've got hold of a good pilot. Unless there was no alternative, I'd hesitate to depend on a man who had never done a drop before. It is essential too that he can map-read efficiently. (I suppose all pilots are more or less competent for the conditions they're used to; but that does not mean they can all pinpoint an agreed drop zone accurately enough in roadless wilderness.) Above all, satisfy yourself that you've got a careful and reliable man. Make local inquiries. And try to assess his qualities when you talk to him. Distrust a slapdash type whose refrain is "Just say where and when, and leave the rest to me." Feel reassured if he wants to cross all t's meticulously and to dot every last i and to have clear in his mind all alternative actions in case of delay for weather, failure to make contact with you, or some such snafu as supplies falling into a river or smashing to pulp on rock because the parachute failed. I admit that it's a problem to know what to do if you decide, after discussing the minutest details with a pilot, that you just don't trust him. It's not easy to extricate yourself without gashing the poor fellow's feelings. The solution is probably to approach him first on a conditional basis: "Look, I find that I *may* need an airdrop at—" But perhaps you can dream up a better gambit.

Success in making contact depends only in part on the pilot. The man on the ground has a lot to do with it too. So make sure you know what the hell you are doing.

The first time I arranged an airdrop I was very conscious that I had no idea at all what the hell. The occasion* was the long Grand Canyon trip. I wanted three airdrops. The pilot and I, talking over details beforehand, decided that under expected conditions the surest ground-to-air signal was mirror-flashing. I would carry a little circular mirror, about 2 inches in diameter—the kind you can pick up for 15 cents in any variety store. The pilot, who had been an Air Force survival instructor, assured me that such a mirror was just as good as specially made mirrors with cross-slits— and, at barely an ounce, was also appreciably lighter. The trick was to practice beforehand. I soon picked up the idea. You hold the mirror as close to one eye as you can and shut the other eye. Then you extend the free hand and aim the tip of the thumb at a point (representing the plane) that is not more than about a hundred yards away. You move the mirror until the sun's reflection, appear-

---

* Described in rather different detail in *The Man Who Walked Through Time*, pp. 81–4.

ing as a bright, irregular patch of light, hits the top of your thumb. Then you tilt the mirror up a bit until only the lowest part of the patch of light remains on your thumb. The rest of it should then show up exactly on the object that represents the plane. If it does not, keep practicing with fractional adjustments of mirror and thumb until you know exactly where to hold both so as to hit your target. You are now ready for the real thing. Ready, that is, to flash sunlight into the pilot's eyes.

"It's the surest way I know," said my Grand Canyon pilot. "On survival exercises I've located guys that had nothing to flash with except penknife blades or even just sunglasses. When that flash hits my eye, just once, the job's done. That's all I need to know: where to look. But without something to start me off, the expanse of ground I can see, especially in broken country like the Canyon, is just too damned big."

After a few minutes' practice I had complete confidence in the mirror routine; but we also arranged that I should spread out my bright orange sleeping bag as a marker, and would have a fire and some water ready so that when the plane had located me and came over low on a trial run I could send up a plume of smoke to indicate wind direction.

Because I was not sure how far I could travel across very rough country in a week, and because I did not want to be held back if I found I could move fast, we arranged primary and alternate sites for the first drop. We set zero hour at 10:00 A.M. on the eighth morning after I left an Indian village that would be my last contact with civilization. The chances were good that at ten o'clock no clouds would obscure the sun and that the day's desert winds would not yet have sprung up.

I made the alternate site in time and, with complete confidence in the mirror signaling technique, decided for various reasons to take the drop about two miles from the prearranged place, out on a flat red rock-terrace. The plane arrived dead on schedule. But it failed to see my frantic flashings, and after an hour's fruitless search around the prime site and back along the way I'd come was heading for home and passing not too far from me when I poured water on the waiting fire and sent a column of smoke spiraling up into the clear air. Almost at once, the plane banked toward me, and within minutes my supplies were sailing safely down, suspended from a big orange parachute.

Later, a park ranger in the plane told me that he'd seen the smoke the moment it rose in the air. "But we didn't see the flashing until we were almost on top of you. At a guess, I'd say you didn't shake the mirror enough. You've got to do that to set up a good flashing. Oh, and your orange sleeping bag didn't show up at all against the red rock. We could hardly see it, even on the drop run."

So my first airdrop taught me a valuable lesson: unless it is absolutely unavoidable, don't change your prearranged drop site, even by a short distance. For the two later drops on that trip we had picked only one site, and each time I was in exactly the right place. I also had the white 8-by-9-foot plastic sheet (page 228) in my pack, and I spread it out beside the sleeping bag. Each time, the pilot saw the white patch as soon as he came within range, and although I had begun to flash with the mirror, the plane rocked its wings in recognition and I therefore stopped flashing before there was time to assess the mirror's worth. Both these later drops went off without a hitch.

A reader writes that flashing is a much surer business with a double-sided mirror that has a central hole or cross-slits. You look at the plane through the hole. The sun, shining through the hole, casts a bright spot on your nose or face or maybe even hand. You adjust the mirror until the reflection that you see of this bright spot in the back of the mirror coincides with the hole—and is seen right on the plane. At that moment, the mirror is flashing at the plane. I guess so. But I'd still waggle it about a lot.

I didn't have a chance to test my mirror technique again on the only other airdrop I have taken. That was on the seventeen-day hike-and-swim trip down the Colorado. The pilot this time was a young man named Jack Westcott whose father before him had flown the whole Grand Canyon region. The drop had to be down in the Inner Gorge, between rockwalls more than 2000 feet high and, at their foot, barely 200 yards apart. From the map we selected a clearly defined ledge for the drop site; but, because my route was untried, there was no certainty I could make it that far down in time. So we agreed that if Jack did not see me at the appointed place he would fly on upriver to the point at which I started and then would return, still low. He would come between 5:30 and 6:00 in the morning, before any wind was likely to spring up. At that hour there would be no sun to reflect with a mirror, but I would have a fire ready and would signal with smoke. If Jack missed me on the upriver flight, I would on his return sortie signal not only with natural smoke but also with the "day" end of a day-and-night signal flare.*

* Each end of this flare burns for 45 seconds—one as a red flame for night use, the other in dense orange smoke. (Weight, 7 ounces; cost unknown—it was a naval flare, given to the man who gave it to me.) The flare I'd recommend for purely daytime use was not available at that particular time. It burns for 1 minute, emitting a cloud of dense and persistent orange smoke (1½ by 5

In spite of pushing as fast as I could, I failed to reach the drop site in time. At dusk the day before our scheduled rendezvous, I was still three miles upriver. In that country, three miles meant three or four hours' hard slogging, even in daylight—and night travel is just about impossible. So I camped on the most obvious and open ledge I could find—though it was neither very obvious nor very open. Before cooking dinner I collected a healthy pile of dry driftwood (working at the end by flashlight). I set two full canteens beside the wood and spread out my white plastic sheet and weighted down its corners with stones.

In the morning I had the fire alight by 5:25. The minutes ticked past—5:45 . . . 5:55 . . . 6:00. A couple of centuries later my watch read 6:30. A millennium more, and it was seven o'clock. Now I should warn you that if you are waiting for an airdrop and the plane is late, your mind conjures up the most dire explanations. At least, mine does. (The same thing happened when the plane was late for one of the earlier Grand Canyon drops.) By 7:25, the only doubt left was whether the failure was due to Jack Westcott's having crashed or to the beginning of World War III. The plane came at 7:30. It came low, so that the sound of its motor gave me little warning, but I managed to pour the contents of both canteens onto the fire just as it appeared. Now desert driftwood burns very quickly and you can't keep a big blaze going for two hours without a truckload of logs, so the fire had burned pretty low and when I poured the water on all it produced was a feeble little puff of smoke that rose barely 6 feet. The plane passed slowly by, way out over the river, with no sign of having seen me. (By this time, sunlight was streaming obliquely across the gorge just above my camp, and Jack told me later that as he flew upriver it shone directly into his eyes. It was all he could do to see the rockwalls, he said, let alone shadowy details down beside the river.)

By the time the plane came back downriver I had the fire blazing again, and plenty of water ready. The signal flare lay beside the waiting canteens and cooking pots. The moment I heard the plane's motor I emptied both cooking pots onto the fire. A column of dense smoke rose high into the air. I picked up the signal flare and tugged at the metal loop of the friction igniter at the "day" end. For a moment nothing happened. I pulled harder. Suddenly the tab pulled free and dense orange smoke gushed out and up. And then, before this smoke had risen more than a few

---

inches; 3 ounces; $2.50). Eastern Mountain Sports now sells "distress signals" that shoot brilliant red flares up 150 to 200 vertical feet; but they burn for only 7 seconds ($\frac{3}{4}$ by $4\frac{3}{4}$ inches; 1 ounce each; package of 3, $7).

feet, the plane was thundering directly overhead, very low. It did not rock its wings in recognition, but I felt fairly confident from the angle at which it came that it had turned in toward me from out over the river. And when it somehow managed to turn, deep within the gorge, just a few hundred yards downriver, I knew that Jack had seen me. The plane came back somewhat higher—perhaps 300 feet up—with the motor running very slowly. As it passed overhead a dark blob dropped clear. Almost at once, the parachute opened. It was a makeshift parachute that Jack, to save me unnecessary expense, had made by stitching together two plastic windsocks. It worked perfectly. The unprotected metal can landed about 50 feet from my white marker. It landed, rather heavily, among some angular rocks. One corner of the can was dented, but when I had cut free the nylon cords and had pried off the lid, everything looked fine. Above all, there was no smell of butane from the two refill cartridges for the Bleuet stove (page 166). Before I had checked all the can's contents the plane came by again, heading back downriver. I butterflied "all's well" with my arms. The plane vanished. In the suddenly very silent silence, I finished my check. The damage was minor: a couple of food bags had burst, with no serious effects.

Later, Jack told me that on his second run he had seen the smoke from the fire, clear and unmistakable, from far upriver. It rose well above the rocks and trees that hemmed in my little ledge. He did not think he had seen the orange smoke on that run (probably because the flare had only just begun to burn); but on the drop run, when he was once more heading into the blinding sun, the big orange cloud, which persisted very effectively, had shown up well.

So from my limited experience with airdrops I have come to the following tentative conclusions: The easiest and surest way to attract a pilot's attention under suitable conditions is by a fire-and-water smoke column. A good day flare may be even better, but is perhaps too valuable in an emergency (page 420) to be used in supply drops except when other methods have failed. Obviously, there are conditions under which any smoke signal may be ineffective: among very tall trees (where you'd hardly choose to take a parachute drop anyway), and probably in very high winds. For me, mirror-flashing remains an unproven but potentially valuable method. (I always carry a mirror nowadays, mainly for emergency use.) As for markers, I suspect that white is better than orange on most backgrounds other than snow. Finally, I grant now that it is dangerous to change your drop site unilaterally; but if you are going to be somewhere along an unmistakable line, such as a river, and the pilot is prepared to search along it, you can with reasonable safety leave a lot of latitude.

Several people have written asking what I did in the Canyon with the parachutes and other garbage. I packed the chutes and everything else into the metal 5-gallon cans that the supplies had been packed in (page 390); and I tucked the cans away out of sight.

Helicopters

Useful as they may be, helicopters are—at least in wilderness—disgusting bloody machines. And I feel sure that having one land and offload supplies—and also bring you into contact with "outsiders"—would be a far more disruptive event than an airdrop. What's more, the 'copters' fiendish clatter and the way they can mosey into every corner make them even less desirable as wilderness suppliers than conventional planes. Still, I suppose there are times and places . . .

Average charter rates for a small helicopter operating no higher than about 5000 feet run around $100 an hour. Supercharged 'copters for mountain work may cost $130 an hour, and the newer light-turbine versions as much as $250. (Comparable rates for small conventional plane: around $30.)

It's worth knowing—not so much for supply purposes, but because most wilderness rescue work is now carried out by helicopters—that they cannot put down just anywhere. A slope of more than about 10 degrees is not a feasible landing place for even a small machine. In good conditions, though, on a clear surface, an expert pilot may be able to hover with one skid on a steeper slope long enough to pick up a casualty. But even for this method the slope cannot be more than about 25 degrees.

Pack animal or support backpacker

I have never tried replenishing supplies by either of these methods. Obviously, though, you must make cast-iron arrangements about the meeting place—and hardened-steel arrangements if someone else is going to plant a cache for you.

Auxiliary pack animal

Indoorsmen often ask why I never use a pack animal such as a burro on any of my long walks. Blame for the thought probably lies with Robert Louis Stevenson and his *Travels with a Donkey*—

or maybe with TV prospectors who amble across parched western deserts escorted by amiable burros.

Frankly, I've never even been tempted. For one thing, I can go places a burro can't. And I blench at the prospect of looking after a burro's food and water supply. Also, although I know nothing at firsthand about managing the beasts, I mistrust their dispositions. Come to think of it, I do not seem to be alone in my distrust. Precious few people use burros these days. It is perhaps significant that on the one occasion I can remember coming across the man-beast combination, the man was on one side of a small creek pulling furiously and vainly at the halter of the burro, and the burro was planted on the far bank with heels dug resolutely in.

DANGERS, REAL AND IMAGINED

For many wilderness walkers, no single source of fear quite compares with that stirred up by

Rattlesnakes.*

Every year, an almost morbid terror of the creatures ruins or at least tarnishes countless otherwise delightful hikes all over the United States and Canada. This terror is based largely on folklore and myth, hardly at all on fact.

Now rattlesnakes can be dangerous, but they are not what so many people fancy them to be: vicious and cunning brutes with a deep-seated hatred of man. In solid fact, rattlers are timid and retiring. They are highly developed reptiles, but they simply do not have the brain capacity for cunning in our human sense. And although they react to man as they would to any big and threatening creature, they could hardly have built up a deep-seated hatred: the first man that one of them sees is usually the last. Finally, the risk of being bitten by a rattler is slight, and the danger that a bite will prove fatal to a healthy adult is small.†

---

* Only two distinct kinds of poisonous snakes occur in the United States: the coral snakes and the pit vipers—a group that includes rattlesnakes, cottonmouths (or water moccasins) and copperheads.

Coral snakes, though highly poisonous, rarely bite humans; and they are restricted to the southeast corner of the country plus one sector of Arizona.

† In the United States, more people are killed and injured in their bathtubs than by snakebite. Of 210 million Americans, perhaps 1200 will be bitten this year. Twelve of these (or 1 percent) may die; but this figure includes people who have been badly frightened, those with weak hearts, and small children whose bodies cannot absorb the venom. Even without treatment, odds on survival are long.

In other words, ignorance has as usual bred deep and unreasoning fear—a fear that may even cause more harm than snakebite. Not long ago, near San Diego, California, a hunter who was spiked by barbed wire thought he had been struck by a rattler—and very nearly died of shock.

The surest antidote to fear is knowledge. When I began my California walk I knew nothing about rattlesnakes, and the first one I met scared me purple. Killing it seemed a human duty. But by the end of the summer I no longer felt this unreasoning fear, and as a result I no longer killed rattlers—unless they lived close to places frequented by people.

Later I grew interested enough to write a magazine article about rattlesnakes, and in researching it I read the entire 1500-odd pages of the last-word bible on the subject. As I read, the fear sank even further away. Gradually I came to accept rattlesnakes as fellow creatures with a niche in the web of life.

The book I read was *Rattlesnakes: Their Habits, Life Histories and Influence on Mankind,* by Laurence M. Klauber (2 vols.; University of California Press, 2nd edn., 1973; $50). Dr. Klauber was the world's leading authority on rattlesnakes, and in the book he sets out in detail all the known biological facts. But he does more. He examines and exposes the dense cloud of fancy and folklore that swirls around his subject. I heartily recommend this fascinating book to anyone who ever finds his peace of mind disturbed by a blind fear of rattlesnakes—and also to anyone interested in widening the fields in which he can observe and understand when he goes walking. The book should be in any university library, and in any medium-size or large public library.

Among the many folklore fables Dr. Klauber punctures is the classic "boot story." I first heard this one down in the Colorado Desert of Southern California—and believed it. "There was this rancher," the old-timer told me, "who lived not far from here. One day he wore some kneeboots belonging to his father, who had died ten years before. Next day, the rancher's leg began to swell. It grew rapidly worse. Eventually he went to a doctor—just in time to avoid amputation from rattlesnake poisoning. Then he remembered that his father had been struck when wearing the same boots a year before he died. One of the snake's fangs had broken off and lodged in an eyehole. Eleven years later, it scratched the son."

Essentially the same story was read before the Royal Society of London by a New World traveler on January 7, 1714. That version told how the boot killed three successive husbands of a Virginia woman. Today the incident may take place anywhere, coast to coast, and the boot is sometimes modernized into a struck and punctured tire that proves fatal to successive garagemen who repair it. Actually, the amount of dried venom on the point of a fang is negligible. And venom exposed to air quickly loses its potency.

Then there is the legend of the "avenging mate": Kill one rattler, and its mate will vengefully seek you out. Pliny, the Roman naturalist who died in A.D. 79, told this story of European snakes, and it's still going strong over here. In 1954, after a rattlesnake had been killed in a downtown Los Angeles apartment, the occupant refused to go back because a search had failed to unearth the inevitably waiting mate.

The legend probably arose because it seems as though a male may occasionally court a freshly killed female. Some years ago, a geographer friend of mine and a zoologist companion, looking for specimens for research, killed a rattler high in California's Sierra Nevada. The zoologist carried the snake 200 yards to a log and began skinning it. My friend sat facing him. Suddenly he saw another rattler crawling toward them. "It was barely four yards away," he told me later, "and heading directly for the dead snake; but it was taking its time and seemed quite unaware of our presence. We killed it before it even rattled. It was a male. The first was a female." An untrained observer might well have seen this incident as proof positive that the second snake was bent on revenge.

Toward the end of my seventeen-day trip down the Colorado I saw with my own eyes just how another myth could have arisen. I was running very short of food, and after meeting four rattlers within four days I reluctantly decided that if I met another I would kill and cook it. I duly met one. It was maybe 3 feet long— about as big as they grow in that country. I promptly hit it with my staff a little forward of the tail, breaking its back and immobilizing it; but before I could put it out of its pain by crushing its head, it began striking wildly about in all directions. Soon— and apparently by pure accident—it struck itself halfway down the body. It was a perfect demonstration of how the myth arose that wounded rattlers will strike themselves to commit suicide. (Quite apart from the question of whether snakes can comprehend the idea of a future death, rattlesnakes are little affected by rattlesnake venom.)

After I had killed that snake I cut off the head, wrapped the body in a plastic bag, and put it in my pack; but I could not for the life of me remember what Dr. Klauber had said about eating rattlers that had struck themselves. As I walked on, thinking of the venom that was probably still circulating through the snake's blood system, I grew less and less hungry. After half an hour, feeling decidedly guilty about the unnecessary killing, I discarded the corpse.

Later, I found that although people are often warned against eating a rattler that has bitten itself there is in fact no danger if the meat is cooked: the poisonous quality of snake venom is destroyed by heat. It's as well to cut out the bitten part, though, just as you cut away damaged meat in an animal that has been shot. Back in the 1870s, one experimenter got a big rattler to bite itself three or four times. It lived 19 hours and seemed unhurt. The man then cooked and ate it without ill effect!

According to Dr. Klauber, rattler meat has been compared with chicken, veal, frog, tortoise, quail, fish, canned tuna, and rabbit. It is, as he points out, useful as an emergency ration because it is easily hunted down and killed, even by people weakened by starvation. But there's only 1 pound of meat on a 4-foot rattler, 2½ pounds on a 5-footer, and 4½ on a 6-footer.

Even straightforward information about rattlesnakes often gets hopelessly garbled in the popular imagination. For example, the only facts about rattlers that many people know for sure are that they grow an extra rattle every year, revel in blistering heat, and are fast and unfailingly deadly. Not one of these "facts" is true. Number of rattles is almost no indication of age. A rattler soon dies if the temperature around it rises much over 100°. It crawls so slowly that the only dangerous rattler is the one you don't see. Even the strike is not nearly as fast as was once thought. Tests prove it to be rather slower than a trained man's punching fists. If you move first—as fast as you can, and clean out of range—you may get away with it, though avoiding the strike, even if you're waiting for it, borders on the impossible.

Accurate knowledge will not only help dispel many unreasoning fears (it is nearly always the unknown that we fear the most), but can materially reduce the chances that you will be bitten.

Take the matter of heat and cold, for example. Rattlesnakes, like all reptiles, lack an efficient mechanism such as we have for keeping body temperature constant, so they are wholly dependent on the temperature around them. In cold climates they can hibernate indefinitely at a few degrees above freezing, and have fully recovered after four hours in a deep freeze at 4° F. Yet at 45° F. they can hardly move, and they rarely choose to prowl in temperatures below 65°. Their "best" range is 80–90° F. At 100° they're in danger, and at 110° they die of heat stroke. But these, remember, are *their* temperatures—that is, the temperatures their bodies attain through contact with the ground over which they are moving and with the air around them. These temperatures may differ markedly from official weather readings taken in the shade, 5 feet above ground level. When such a reading is 60°, for example, a thermometer down on sunlit sand may record 100°, and in the lowest inch of air about 80°. (See pages 59 and 362.) In other words, a rattler in the right place may feel snugly comfortable in a weather temperature of 60°. On the other hand, in a desert temperature of 80° in the shade the sunlit sand might be over 130° and the lowest inch of air around 110°, and any rattler staying for long in such a place would die.

Once you know a few such facts, you find after a little practice that your mind almost automatically tells you when to be especially watchful, and even where to avoid placing your feet. In cool early-season weather, for example, when rattlers like to bask, you will tend to keep a sharp lookout, if the sun is shining but a cold wind is blowing, in sunlit places that are sheltered from the wind. And in hot desert weather you will know that there is absolutely no danger out on open sand where there is no shade. On the other hand, the prime feeding time for rattlers in warm weather is two hours before and after sunset, when the small mammals that are their main prey tend to be on the move; so if you figure that the ground temperature during that time is liable to be around 80° to 90°, you keep your eyes skinned. I do not mean that you walk in fear and trembling. But you watch your step. Given the choice, for example, you tend to bisect the space between bushes, and so reduce the chances of surprising a rattler resting unseen beneath overhanging vegetation. Once you're used to it, you do this kind of thing as a natural safe operating procedure, no more directly connected with fear than is the habit of checking the street for traffic before you step off a sidewalk.

You'll also be able to operate more safely once you understand how rattlesnakes receive their impressions of the world around them. Their sight is poor, and they are totally deaf. But they're well equipped with other senses. Two small facial pits contain nerves so sensitive to heat that a rattler can strike accurately at warm-blooded prey in complete darkness. (Many species hunt mainly at night.) They're highly sensitive to vibration too, and have rattled at men passing out of sight 150 feet away. (Moral: in bad rattler country, at bad times, tread heavily.) Two nostrils just above a rattler's mouth furnish a sense of smell very like ours. And that's not all. A sure sign that a snake has been alerted is a flickering of its forked tongue: it is "smelling" the outside world. The tongue's moist surface picks up tiny particles floating in the air and at each flicker transfers them to two small cavities in the roof of the mouth. These cavities, called "Jacobson's organs," interpret the particles to the brain in terms of smell, much as do the moist membranes inside our noses.

In Biblical times, people wrongly associated snakes' tongues with their poison. Nothing has changed. Stand at the rattlesnake cage in any zoo and the chances are you'll soon hear somebody say, "There, did you see its stinger?" or even, "Look at it stick out its fangs!" It is true, though, that an alarmed snake will sometimes use its tongue to intimidate enemies. When it does, the forked tips quiver pugnaciously out at their limit, arching first up, then down. It's a chillingly effective display. But primarily, of course, a snake reacts to enemies with that unique rattle. Harmless in itself, it warns and intimidates, like the growl of a dog.

The rattle is a chain of hollow, interlocking segments made of the same hard and transparent keratin as human nails. The myth that each segment represents a year of the snake's age first appeared in print as early as 1615. Actually, a new segment is left each time the snake sheds its skin. Young rattlers shed frequently, and adults an average of one to three times each year. In any case, the fragile rattles rarely remain complete for very long.

In action, the rattles shake so fast that they blur like the wings of a hummingbird. Small snakes merely buzz like a fly, but big specimens sound off with a strident hiss that rises to a spine-chilling crescendo. Someone once said that it was "like a pressure cooker with the safety valve open." Once you've heard the sound, you'll never forget it.

The biggest rattlers are eastern diamondbacks: outsize specimens may weigh 30 pounds and measure almost 8 feet. But most of the thirty different species grow to no more than 3 or 4 feet.

People often believe that rattlers will strike only when coiled, and never upward. It is true that they can strike most effectively from the alert, raised-spiral position; but they are capable of striking from any position and in any direction.

Rattlers are astonishingly tenacious of life. One old saying warns, "They're dangerous even after they're dead"—and it is true. Lab tests have shown that severed heads can bite a stick and discharge venom for up to 43 minutes. The tests even produced some support for the old notion that "rattlers never die till sundown." Decapitated bodies squirmed for as long as 7½ hours, moved when pinched for even longer. And the hearts almost always went on beating for a day, often for 2 days. One was still pulsating after 59 hours.

A rattlesnake's enemies include other snakes (especially king snakes and racers), birds, mammals, and even fish. In Grand Canyon I found a 3-foot rattler apparently trampled to death by wild burros. Torpid captive rattlers have been killed and part eaten by mice put in their cages for food! Not long ago, a California fisherman caught a big rainbow trout with a 9-inch rattler in its stomach. But only one species of animal makes appreciable inroads on the rattlesnake population. That species is man—to whom the warning rattle is an invitation to attack. If man had existed in large numbers when rattlesnakes began to evolve, perhaps 6 million years ago, it is unlikely the newfangled rattlebearers would have succeeded and flourished.

In spite of stories to the contrary, a rattlesnake meeting a large animal such as man does not attack so long as the potential enemy stays outside its striking range. (Very rarely, when courting, it may just possibly attack; but then, so may a deer or even a rabbit.) It may move toward you, but that will be for other reasons, such as the slope of the ground. Its first reaction will most likely be to lie still and escape attention. Then it may crawl slowly for safety. Detected or alarmed, it will probably rattle and rise into its menacing defensive coil—a vibrant, open-spiral quite distinct from the tightly wound pancake resting position. It may also hiss. Finally, it may strike. Usually, though by no means always, it will rattle before striking. Of course, none of these comments necessarily applies if a man treads on a snake or comes suddenly and alarmingly within its restricted little world. Then, not unnaturally, it will often strike without warning.

But it's important to remember that rattlesnakes are as moody as men, as unpredictable as women. A man who for many years was rattlesnake control officer of South Dakota concluded that they simply "are not to be trusted, for some will violate all rules." Certain individuals, even whole species, seem to be always "on the prod." A few habitually strike without warning. Others seem almost amiable.

Defense is not, of course, the main purpose of a rattler's venom and fangs. Primarily, they're for securing food.

The fangs, regularly replaced, are precision instruments. One slender, curving tooth on each side of the snake's upper jaw grows almost five times longer than its fellows. In large rattlers it may measure ¾ inch. A cunning pivot-and-lever bone structure ensures that when the mouth is closed these fierce barbs lie flat; but as the jaw opens wide to strike they pivot erect. Each fang is hollow. Its cavity connects with a venom sac beneath the eye, equivalent to our salivary gland. When the fangs stab into a prey, the snake injects a controlled dose of venom through the cavity and out of an aperture just above the fang's point. In the small mammals that rattlers mostly feed on, the venom causes almost instant paralysis and rapid death.

A rattlesnake's venom—present from birth—is as unpredictable as its temperament. Quantity and toxicity seem to vary widely from species to species, from individual to individual. In general, though, the bigger the snake the greater the danger: a big snake stabs deeper with its fangs and generally injects more venom. But there are other, quite unpredictable, factors in any case of snakebite. It's not just that a rattler can control, at least to some degree, the amount of venom it injects; the quantity in its sacs will vary markedly according to whether it has or has not expended venom recently in killing prey.

Treatment of snakebite

The greatest danger is probably hysteria; people bitten by harmless snakes have come close to dying from fright. What many snakebite patients need most, in fact, is rest and reassurance. But there is no doubt that in genuine cases of snakebite *quick* physical treatment can save lives.

Some doctors hold that the only emergency treatment worth a damn is cryotherapy: making the site of the bite so cold that the body absorbs the venom slowly enough to neutralize the most serious effects. For use in the field, where more elaborate treatment will not normally be available, they recommend carrying ethyl chloride. Applied to the skin, it evaporates quickly and cools the immediate area.

This method enjoyed a recent vogue but seems to be losing favor. Most doctors now recommend the old cut-and-suck method: removing as much venom as you can, *as soon as possible.* The first few seconds and minutes are the critical time, before the bulk of the venom has a chance to circulate. I find myself inclined to believe the cut-and-suck experts—possibly because theirs was the first method I learned. Anyway, I always carry a Cutter Compak Suction Kit in my pocket: One of these neat little devices (new, flattened version: 1 ounce; $2.40) is no bigger than a 12-gauge shell. It includes three rubber suction cups. Two of these cups form the kit's outer shell and are indented on the outside so that they grip the bottom of your pants pocket. I have never had one even hint that it might fall out. The interlocking suction cups contain a small, very sharp blade, a vial of sterilizing liquid, a tourniquet, and full instructions. Memorize at least the essence of the instructions. And always remember that in the unlikely event of your being bitten it's the first few seconds and minutes that count.

The "cryotherapists" tend to decry the effectiveness of cut-and-suck. "Cut-and-suckers" reciprocate. This is known as human nature. It may well be that the practical answer is to do the best you can with both methods. Meanwhile, I shall continue to carry my little rubber lozenge. There may be some element of doubt about its effectiveness, but I can assure you that in snake country its presence in your pants pocket is highly reassuring. A less purely psychological consideration is that, unlike ethyl chloride, it is always with you—unless you take off your pants.

The one emergency treatment that everyone now agrees is not merely useless but positively dangerous—because it stimulates your metabolism and therefore spreads the venom more quickly—is the old-timers' "snakebite cure": alcohol.

Any snakebite kit you carry (unless it contains an antivenin, and that can be dangerous for an inexperienced layman to use) is essentially an emergency measure. Whenever possible, get the patient (whether yourself or a companion) to a doctor as quickly as possible. He will be able to administer one of the modern, highly efficient antivenins. But the advantages of medical treatment have to be balanced against the dangers of rapid movement that will spread the venom quickly. If you are many miles from the nearest help, particularly if alone, the safest thing to do after applying suction treatment may be to rest in a cool place, keep the site of the bite as cold as possible (perhaps with creek water), immobilize that part of the body, and prepare for a forty-eight-hour siege—during which you are likely to vomit and retch and feel feverish and generally pretty damned bad.

I must accent that what I have said applies only to rattle-snakes and the other pit vipers of the United States and Canada (first footnote, page 398). All have comparatively low-toxicity venom. Where the snakes are much more deadly—as in Africa and, I understand, Central and South America—the only worthwhile snakebite kit is antivenin and a syringe. Some antivenins are now made with human serum; but remember that some people are very seriously allergic to the horse serum commonly used. If you plan to carry a kit, consider checking your reaction with an allergist.

I hope this rather long discourse has convinced you that rattle-snakes, although dangerous, are not the vicious and deadly brutes of legend. If you have in the past felt, as so many people do, a deep and unreasoning fear of them, then I hope I have helped just a little in dispelling that fear—and have left you free to walk almost anywhere with enjoyment.

You may even find that your understanding of rattlesnakes passes at length beyond mere factual knowledge. I have described in *The Man Who Walked Through Time* (p. 166) how I was sit-ting naked one afternoon on a sandbar at the edge of a willow thicket when I saw a pale-pink rattlesnake come gliding over the sand, barely six feet away from me, clearly unaware of my pres-ence. Sitting there watching it, I found that I felt curiosity rather than fear. Slowly, gracefully, the snake threaded its way through a forest of willow shoots. As its flank pushed past each stem I could see the individual scales tilt under the stem's pressure, then move back flush. Four feet from my left buttock the snake stopped, its head in a sun-dappled patch of sand beside a cluster of roots. Un-hurriedly, it drew its body forward and curled into a flat resting coil. Then it stretched and yawned. It yawned a long and unmistakable yawn. A yawn so uninhibited that for many slow seconds I seemed to see nothing but the pale lining of its mouth and two matching arcs of small, sharp teeth. When the yawn was over at last the snake raised its head and twisted it slowly and luxuriously from side to side, as a man or a woman will do in anticipation of rest and comfort to come. Finally, with such obvious contentment that I do not think I would have been altogether surprised to hear the creature purr, it laid its head gently on the pillow of its clean and beautifully marked body.

And all at once, for the first time in my life, I found that I had moved "inside" a rattlesnake. Quite unexpectedly, I had shared its sleepiness and anticipation and contentment. And as I sat looking down at the sleeping snake coiled in its patch of sun-dappled shade, I found myself feeling for it something remarkably close to affection.

Frankly, the feeling has not lasted. I am still no rattlesnake aficionado. But my fear, helped by the moment of understanding, has now contracted to vanishing point. On my 1966 trip down lower Grand Canyon I met five rattlesnakes in five days. One small specimen even struck from under a stone and hit my boot (no damage done). Yet even at that moment I do not think I felt much fear: it was more a matter of interest and curiosity. But— and it may be a very big "but"—the rattlesnakes of Grand Canyon do not grow more than about 3 feet long. Whether I would have been so consistently calm in country thick with big diamondbacks, I just don't know. I'm afraid I can guess, though.

Scorpions

A friend of mine who does a great deal of hiking in Arizona once told me that he worried more about scorpions than about rattlesnakes. "You can see the rattlers," he said.

In Arizona there is good reason for respecting scorpions: the sting of two quite small, sand-colored species that are found in that state—and only there—is always serious and can prove fatal. But the sting of other scorpions found in North America (except Mexico) is rarely much more serious than a bee sting. (Remember, though, that some people react violently to almost any venom. For them, even a bee sting may be fatal.)

But unless you go around turning up stones you are not very likely to see a scorpion. I have only come across two in the United States: one, rather surprisingly, was at an elevation of over 10,000 feet; the other, in my garden.

There is a well-known desert tradition that in scorpion country you always turn out your boots before putting them on in the morning. Before I went down into Grand Canyon I asked an experienced park ranger about it. "Oh, it always sounds to me like an old wives' tale," he said. Then a smile leaked slowly out over his face, and he added, "But I still do it."

Tarantulas and black widows

The chance of being bitten by either of these spiders is small. And the tarantulas that occur in the United States do not, in spite of their evil aspect and matching reputation, inflict a serious bite. No more serious, again, than a bee sting.

But black widows are dangerous. Although they're very much smaller, their bites are always serious and can prove fatal, even to adults. Cut-and-suck treatment is ineffective: there's simply not enough venom (which is of a neurotoxic type). Cryotherapy, or cooling of the site (page 405), is the best first aid. Keep the victim (whether you or non-you) quiet, and if possible get him to a doctor as soon as possible. At first, the only sensation may be as of a pinprick—though the spider may still be adhering to the skin. But after a few hours the pain may become severe.

Black widows have spherical bodies about the size of a marble. They do not have particularly noticeable legs. They are entirely black except for a red patch on the underside, shaped like an hourglass.

Other animals

Contrary to popular indoor opinion, there is almost no danger from such large and reputedly ferocious mammals as mountain lions and bobcats. Mountain lions (also called cougars) may follow you at a safe distance out of curiosity, but they will not attack—unless, possibly, you have a dog with you. I have woken up to find fresh bobcat tracks within 6 feet of my sleeping bag. And during a recent breakfast a bobcat inspected me warily from 30 paces, then turned and trotted away.

It is fairly safe to say that no healthy American animal will attack you unless provoked.* But it can be provoked unintentionally. If you stumble on almost any animal and surprise and frighten it, it may react ferociously in self-defense. Again, thirst or hunger or the sex urge or mother love may turn a normally peaceful beast into a potentially dangerous one. The best-known example is probably the black bear mother with cubs. But even rabbits, when courting, have been known to attack an interfering intruder.

Another possible but extremely slight risk is from attack by rabid animals. I have seen only one animal that I assumed was rabid: a jackal that in broad daylight walked openly across a wheat field we were harvesting in Kenya. It seemed to be walking in a self-contained little world of its own, and it took no notice at all of either a combine or several people standing alongside. As it walked it kept twitching its head in a regular and demented fashion. It was, in other words, "acting contrary to general behavior patterns"— which is what rabid animals are described as habitually doing.

Naturally, you just have to take your chances over these very slight risks from attack by wild animals. Provided you behave sensibly, the danger is probably a great deal less than that involved in getting to the wilderness, when some unprovoked animal traveling rapidly in the opposite direction may fall asleep or suffer a heart attack or a burst tire and slew across the dividing line and write an abrupt "finis" to your little game.

There seems to be some doubt about how far you can trust grizzly bears; but grizzly bear country is now pretty accurately defined, so you can take precautions:

1. Stay away; or
2. Walk alertly and carry a big gun. (Except in rare cases, this is a poor solution that could turn out to be the most dangerous of the lot); or

* Two well-publicized cases in each of which a person sleeping in the open in a sleeping bag was killed by a black bear, apparently while asleep, cast doubt on this statement. I let it stand, though, as overwhelmingly true.

3. Accept the risk (knowing that it's likely to be less in really remote areas than in places the bears have been harassed by humans); or
4. Follow the advice of a reader who points out that grizzlies, "like most bears, are extremely shy animals. If in grizzly territory, a hiker can travel with more peace of mind by making a noise either by 'singing loudly' (35 calories per 100 pounds per hour) or perhaps by making a rattle out of a tin can and some stones and tying it to his foot (around the ankle). Some [people] fix bells to their horses and even carry transistor radios for this purpose." He goes on to tell of being chased by a grizzly with two cubs while hiking in the Canadian Rockies. "The poor bears had been surprised while taking a bath in a river; we had made no sound coming into their territory and there was little bush. I now always use a tin can rattle when in grizzly country." And he concludes: "The grizzly bear, which once ranged as far south as Mexico is gradually becoming a rare animal indeed. It would be nice to build up a feeling of understanding and tolerance toward this animal, but it has a reputation, either rightly or wrongly, to fight."

Another reader alerts me to a less serious danger. Backpacking in the Catskills, he became aware of a camp robber about four o'clock in the morning. "I moved slowly to check it out, and it's just as well, because it was a rather large skunk. Right at my elbow. The disaster of a sudden move cannot be stressed too hard."

There is one other animal that puts the fear of God into me: *Homo sapiens nimrodamericanus,* the red-breasted, red-blooded, North American hunter. Every year, in the fall, the woods are alive with hunters, and every year a few more hunters fall dead. I am aware that some of the massacre stories are probably apocryphal, but I play it safe: when the calendar springs the hunters loose, I stay at home.*

Outside North America, the general animal situation can be less reassuring. In East Africa, for example, many rhinos and some elephants and even perhaps a rare buffalo will charge without apparent provocation. (Or does trespass on another animal's territory constitute provocation? Remember Cuba.) Lions, if surprised, may also attack. See also page 213.

---

* This statement must not be construed as an attack on hunters as individuals (p. 366). I find to my surprise that I often feel more comfortable in the company of men whom I know are hunters—even though I deplore what they do in that role—than I do in the company of many "ecologically aware individuals" who share my concerns but who never for one moment, by God, let you forget that they are the Chosen Defenders of the Earth.

The only vegetable dangers you're likely to meet (assuming no gigantic Venus flytraps) are

Poison oak, ivy and sumac.

All these closely related plants cause rashes on some people—perhaps most people—if oil from leaf or stem comes in contact with the skin, directly or through transfer by clothes or other agents. The sooner you start treatment after exposure, the less severe the reaction is likely to be. But if you're susceptible and get a bad case, you may spend three ghastly weeks in the hospital. (And never assume you're safe: one experienced friend of mine maintains that "the hospitals are full of people who thought they were immune.") In less serious cases, affected skin reddens, swells and develops blisters. The rash—which can appear one to nine days after exposure—is always liable to spread. And it itches like crazy. Scratch, and you increase the irritation.

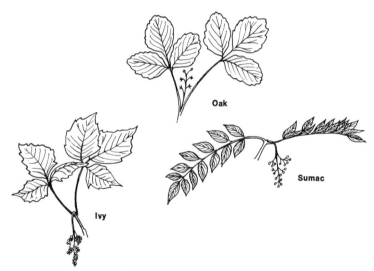

Oak

Sumac

Ivy

Folklore, purveyed by hearty souls with loud voices and doubtless with total immunity as well, goes something like this: "Can't understand what all the fuss is about. Just a good wash down with soap and hot water afterward and you'll never get any rash worth talking about. Why, I've waded thigh deep through the stuff and never had any kind of a rash at all."

Washing is indeed the recommended first step in treatment for known contact with any of the three. But only the first step. The little booklet that comes with Alpine Aid first-aid kits (page 353) says: ". . . wash with strong laundry soap and warm water, then with rubbing alcohol, if available. Apply calamine lotion. In severe cases, consult a physician." Alan Nourse's *Out-doorsman's Medical Guide* (page 353, this book) recommends washing "the exposed area *thoroughly* with soap and warm water to remove as much of the irritating oil as possible. If the area is already blistering or itching intensely, use cold wet compresses of saline solution (six or seven salt tablets dissolved in a pint of water) to help relieve the itching. In addition, any potent anti-histamine (Benadryl, pyrabenzamine, Chlortrimeton, Teldrin or the like) taken by mouth will help temper the allergic reaction, and aspirin will help the victim get a night's sleep. If the skin is not broken, a cortisone cream such as Kenalog can be applied between soaks to help relieve the itching and irritation."

I have found another cortisone cream—Synalar, a prescription drug—a valuable suppressant for poison-oak rash. Applied soon and often, but sparingly, it seems to hold the reaction down, prevent spread, and almost eliminate itching. A mild rash may still persist for as long as three weeks, but it never gets out of hand. Nowadays I always try to remember to carry a tube in poison-oak country.

Various prophylactics for poison oak now smile at you from pharmacy shelves. Opinion on their effectiveness covers the whole spectrum from "useless" to "miraculous," so I guess it depends on the individual. Note that people who react violently to poison oak may get some reaction to a prophylactic medicine.

Many easterners now come West to backpack, and they're often confused about where to expect and how to recognize poison oak. No wonder. It's ubiquitous stuff. Although primarily a plant of low-altitude grasslands and forests, I've found it at nearly 7000 feet in the Sierra Nevada and, once, beside a desert creek in Southern California. And it's a botanical chameleon. Leaves are normally indented and oaklike; but they're variable. Their color is normally green; but they can be red, even in spring. Their surface is often shiny; but not always. The plant may be a single small stalk, standing on its own or lurking among others; it may climb, vine-like, far up a tree; or it may mass into dense clumps, a dozen feet high and covering acres. Almost the only constant you can verbalize, in fact, is that its leaves, like those of poison ivy, *always* grow in clusters of three. Yet once you're familiar with the stuff you can recognize it readily enough; and in suspect country you soon learn to keep your eyes skinned in a barely conscious safe-operating procedure akin to that you adopt in rattler country (page 402).

Hypothermia

A little booklet called *Hypothermia: Killer of the Unprepared* (Dr. Theodore G. Lathrop, The Mazamas, Portland, Oregon [see Appendix III]; paperback; 23 pages; 2 ounces; $1) recently taught me that I was at best only partly prepared for one of wilderness walking's most real dangers. I suspect that many other people are equally unprepared, and I recommend the booklet as required reading for everyone who ventures out beyond the sidewalks, possesses an ounce of wisdom, and genuinely wishes to remain among the quick.

To summarize some of its salient points:

Hypothermia (= subnormal body temperature; often called "exposure") is not a danger restricted to high altitudes or bitter cold. Under certain conditions—wind, wetness, and a victim who is exhausted or unprepared to protect himself—deaths have occurred at sea level and in temperatures no lower than 42° F.

Wind drastically increases chilling effect—and two-thirds of the maximum increase occurs when the wind is blowing at only 2 mph. The chart overleaf gives values for almost the whole human operating range. To use it, join with a ruler the wind velocity on left scale and the temperature on right scale, then read off windchill factor on diagonal—and learn that absolutely calm air at 30° F. means a chill factor of 350 (cool, going on pleasant) and is the equivalent of a 2 mph wind at 58° F. (page 262). Play with the chart—and meditate.

Wet clothing can increase chill just as drastically. Clothing protects you by trapping body-warmed air between its layers and your skin. Water eliminates these airspaces—and conducts heat away from your body *up to 240 times as fast* as still, dry air. Wool is by far the best material when wet; but a soaked-through set of light hiking gear that includes a wool jersey, wool-cotton shirt, and string vest but is unprotected by a windproof outer garment will, in a 9 mph wind, afford less than 10 percent of its dry insulating value.

A person who is exhausted—from overexertion, sickness, lack of food or even extreme apprehension—and who becomes cold in wet, windy conditions may very quickly become colder, and lose the capacity to rewarm himself. To generate heat, a cold body starts shivering—which in turn consumes a great deal of energy (page 101). Even apart from that, a cold body greatly elevates its metabolic demands (for oxygen and energy) and only a very fit person

"Windchill"

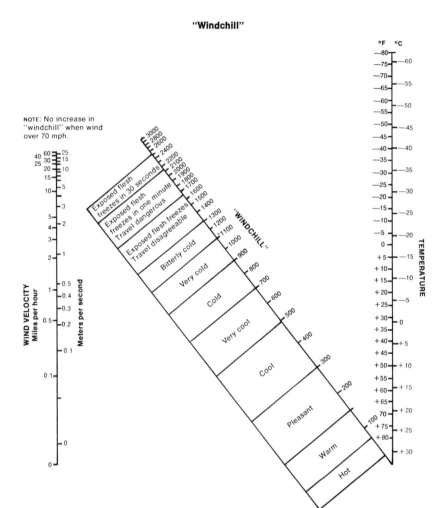

Line chart showing "windchill" and state of comfort under varying conditions of temperature and wind velocity. From Consolazio *et al.*, *Metabolic Methods* (St. Louis: C. V. Mosby Company, 1951)

can meet them for long. In addition, hypothermia, like dehydration (page 126), quickly impairs judgment and so reduces chances of effective remedial action.

Treatment. First, reduce heat loss. Try to get out of wind and put on dry clothes, or at least a windproof shell. Above all, protect the head and back of the neck: at 40° F. an unprotected head may lose up to one-half of total body heat production; at 5° F., up to three-quarters. If stationary, insulate body from ground.

Second, produce heat by exercise, if that is possible (hiking uphill with a heavy pack may increase heat output sixfold); or apply it by sun, fire, food (especially hot sweet drinks, but *not* alcohol—Saint Bernard's kegs notwithstanding), or close contact with other people's bodies.

But remember, this is only a brief summary. To be properly prepared, read *Hypothermia: Killer of the Unprepared.*

Lightning

Lightning is a low-risk danger worth learning something about: knowledge can reduce the hazard to vanishing point.

For walkers, mountains are the dangerous places. American Alpine Club statistics show that in the past 22 years there have been 14 lightning accidents on U.S. mountains. Twenty-eight people were involved. Seven died. (In the metal-rich man-world, the risk is surprisingly high: lightning kills about 150 Americans a year—more than tornadoes or hurricanes—and injures about 250.)

If you are caught up high in a storm, the first thing to remember is the old mountaineering maxim: "In a storm, get off peaks and ridges." Avoid steep inclines (where the current flows fastest) and seek out flat ledges or gentle slopes. If possible, get near a pinnacle that will act as a lightning rod. Stay a little way out from its base but not farther away than its height. Crouch low, touching the ground only with your feet, or sit on some insulator such as a coiled climbing rope. Keep clear of metal, such as your packframe. A cave, though the obvious shelter, is probably the most dangerous place of all unless it is very deep and high-roofed. Stay resolutely clear of shallow, low-roofed caves that are really no more than overhanging ledges. On August 4, 1948, a party of four California climbers was surprised by a storm near the summit of Bugaboo Spire in British Columbia and took shelter in just such a "cave." Almost at once, a bolt of lightning struck outside the entrance. Two of the party died; the other two, dazed and burned, barely managed to make their way down safely.

No matter how careful you are, of course, the element of luck remains. On Bugaboo Spire, it was the chance positioning of the four members of that party at the moment of the strike that determined who would live and who would die. Remember, though, that near-strikes such as the Bugaboo party suffered are not always serious. That day, three other parties of the same expedition were all "hit," out in the open, with no ill effects. And mountains are by no means the only dangerous places. On the same day as the Bugaboo accident, two children were killed by lightning in an open field in Oklahoma.

Useful facts: To estimate the distance in miles to a thunderstorm (and gain some idea of how much time you have to get the

hell out of there) count the number of seconds between lightning
and thunder and divide by 5.

At roadhead, the inside of your car is almost certainly the
safest place around.

First aid. Persons struck by lightning receive a severe electrical shock and may be burned, but they carry no electrical charge
and can be handled safely. A person "killed" by lightning can often
be revived by prompt mouth-to-mouth resuscitation, cardiac mas-
sage, and prolonged artificial respiration. In a group struck by
lightning, the apparently dead should be treated first; those who
show vital signs will probably recover spontaneously, although
burns and other injuries may require treatment. Recovery from
lightning strikes is usually complete except for possible impairment
or loss of sight or hearing. (Source: "Death from Lightning—and
the Possibility of Living Again," by H. B. Taussig, *Annals of
Internal Medicine,* Vol. 68, No. 6 [June 1968].)

Many experienced outdoorsmen—and all reasonable hiking
organizations—contend that one of the greatest dangers in wilderness travel is a practice that permeates this book:

Walking alone.

They may have something too. But once you have discovered
solitude—the gigantic, enveloping, including, renewing solitude of
wild and silent places—and have learned to put it to creative use,
you are likely to accept without a second thought such small additional dangers as the solitude imposes. Naturally, you are careful. You make darned sure that someone always knows where you
are, and when you will be "out." You leave broad margins of safety
in everything you do: hurrying (or not hurrying) over rough
country to make up time; crossing (or not crossing) the creek on
that narrow log; inching past (or not inching past) that perilously
perched boulder. And when it comes to the all-important matter of
luck, you keep firmly in mind the Persian proverb I have already
quoted: "Fortune is infatuated with the efficient."

But if you judge safety to be the paramount consideration in
life you should never, under any circumstances, go on long hikes
alone. Don't take short hikes alone either—or, for that matter, go
anywhere alone. And avoid at all costs such foolhardy activities as
driving, falling in love, or inhaling air that is almost certainly rid-
dled with deadly germs. Wear wool next to the skin. Insure every
good and chattel you possess against every conceivable contingency
the future might bring, even if the premiums half-cripple the pres-

ent. Never cross an intersection against a red light, even when you can see that all roads are clear for miles. And never, of course, explore the guts of an idea that seems as if it might threaten one of your more cherished beliefs. In your wisdom you will probably live to a ripe old age. But you may discover, just before you die, that you have been dead for a long, long time.

A book like this should obviously have something to say about

SURVIVAL.

But I find to my surprise that I can rake up precious little—and that I've never really given the matter the thought it seems to deserve.

Hoping to fill this awkward and humiliating gap in my knowledge, I asked a friend of mine—an experienced hiker, a cross-country skier of repute and an expert climber who has been on Alaskan and Himalayan expeditions—for suggestions about books to read. "Oh, I dunno," he said. "I never read them. And I guess I never give the matter much thought."

Somewhat relieved but still uneasy, I turned for counsel to a practical outdoorsman who is in heavy demand as an instructor of survival and associated crafts. We talked for some time, but with each subject he brought up—water sources, signal flares, first-aid and snakebite kits, loosening waistbelt when wading rivers, and so on—I found myself saying, "Oh, but I've discussed that in the book as part of normal operating procedure."

After four or five such answers my counselor paused. "Yes," he said slowly. "Come to think of it, I guess you could say, really, that if you know how to operate properly in wilderness, then you know most of what there is to know about survival.

"What it generally amounts to, anyway, with inexperienced people, is simply not giving in to terror. That's what usually happens: ignorance—then panic. If your partner breaks a leg, for instance, you're in bad shape if you start thinking, 'Is it safe to leave him here, with all these wild animals around?' Of course it's safe —provided he's warm and comfortable. But if you don't know that, and feel suddenly overwhelmed and alone, you're liable to give way to panic. Naturally, you must be able to find your way out to civilization, or the nearest help, and then guide rescuers back unerringly to the right place . . . but here we're back with plain competence in operating. And this is the kind of survival problem that's most likely to arise with walkers in the United States. Almost anywhere, outside of Alaska, you can get out to civilization—if you can walk —within two days at most. The old idea of survival as the problem of having to look after yourself for six months, completely cut off, when you're in good physical shape, just doesn't apply here any more. And the rest amounts in most cases to medical knowledge and common sense."

In other words, this kind of "survival" mostly amounts to "experience." But "experience" is not easy to assess. When I left the Mexican border at the start of my summer-long walk up California in 1958, at the age of 35, I had never spent a night on my own, away from the man-world, dependent *entirely* on what I carried on my back. (It was only some years later, I think, that I registered this fact—with considerable surprise.) I'm more than a little leary, now, of admitting my "inexperience" at that time: I might encourage tyros to attempt stupid and dangerous things. But even on the day I walked north from the Mexican border I was no tyro. Not really. I had considerable experience, in war and peace, of walking with loads and also of being alone in the bush for days on end—in cabins, for example, and canoeing around a remote lake. Also, in addition to being drum-tight with determination, I knew the limitations of my experience. I knew I had a lot to learn as I went along. That was important. People often get into trouble because they unwittingly—often unthinkingly—bite off more than they know how to chew. And sometimes, then, they do not survive.

"Survival" in the sense of living off the land (page 93) poses a different problem. It's a real one all right, but the answers are specifically local. Knowing what to eat and what not to eat in the Sierra Nevada will get you nowhere in the Adirondacks, and even less place in the Mojave Desert. In each kind of country you have to learn it all again. Sometimes there are local books or pamphlets —often listed in equipment makers' catalogues (Appendix II). Useful sources include Explorer Scouts, hiking and mountaineering clubs (Appendix III), and universities (forestry departments might be good places to start). For less local information, see Euell Gibbons's *Stalking . . .* books: *. . . the Wild Asparagus*; *. . . the Healthful Herbs*; and *. . . the Blue-Eyed Scallop*. Also the card decks of *Edible and Poisonous Plants* (page 93).

If you want reassurance on the broader questions of survival, and if you're a reader of books on such matters (and I guess you are if you've come 400 pages with me), there's plenty of material. Some of the best-known books are by Bradford Angier (*Living Off the Country*, Stackpole, 1956, $5 [with a paperback version called

How to Stay Alive in the Woods, Collier-Macmillan Books, $.95];
How to Go Live in the Woods, Stackpole, 1959, $5; and *Free
for the Eating,* Stackpole, 1966, $4.95), but the survival sections
are apparently oriented toward the North Woods and the problem of being cut off for months on end, far from help. Another
and perhaps more applicable book is *Getting Out of Outdoor
Trouble,* by W. K. Merrill (Stackpole, 1965; $2.95). *How to Sur-
vive on Land and Sea,* by Frank C. and John J. Craighead (Arlo
Publishing; $5), has for years been the survival bible. I understand,
though, that it's now regarded as the old testament—and that the
new testament does not yet seem to have been written. *The Survival Book,* by Nesbitt, Pond, and Allen (Funk and Wagnalls;
paperback; 9 ounces; $1.95), is specifically for survivors of aircraft
downed in remote places, but it offers some useful information—
and some that is utterly fascinating ("Article 39 of the Saudi
Arabian laws prohibits you from striking a person, using abusive
language or treating him with scorn or contempt"). For other
books, see *The Whole Earth Catalog* (page 18, this book).

But perhaps, like me, you're lazy or a touch skeptical about
such reading. If so, just remember, comfortably, that survival is
80 percent competence, 20 percent local knowledge, and 100 percent keeping your cool.

"The best single survival item you can carry," an experienced
backpacker said to me recently, "is a

Space blanket."

These ultralightweight, aluminized mylar sheets (56 by 84
inches; 2 ounces; $1.60) certainly have a lot going for them.
Wrapped around as makeshift blanket, "they reflect up to 90%
of a person's body heat back to him." They are wind- and waterproof. They remain flexible at 60° below. They are very difficult
to tear. And they fold down to 1½ by 2 by 4 inches. Proclaimed
uses include: emergency blanket; lean-to protection against wind,
rain or snow; sun awning; short-term groundsheet (though they'll
soon puncture); litter for carrying injured person; heat reflector
behind your back at campfire; reflector for ovens; and a signal
to aircraft or ground (sun-reflection with the silver side, or color-
contrast with the orange side). All this sounds very impressive.
But after carrying one in my pack for a year or so I found that I
had never used it: for all the uses I might put it to, I carried something else that it would not fully replace. Somewhat to my surprise,
I have stopped taking it. But it is certainly worth considering—even

if only as insurance on away-from-the-pack sidetrips. And I testify that as a pocket-stuffable item for covering your legs in frigid ball-parks nothing I know of can hold a candlestick to it.

A heavier, more durable space blanket (also 56 by 84 inches, but 12 ounces and $6) is a multiple laminate of polyethylene, aluminum and fiberglass, grommeted at each corner. One side is silvery metalized plastic, the other red or blue. Properties and uses as above. Very much tougher than the lightweight version, it makes a really viable groundsheet and also a reasonable makeshift over-the-shoulders poncho around camp.

Emergency signals

These days, almost any search operation for people believed lost in wild country is carried out, at least at first, from the air. So it pays to carry something that will enable you to signal to a search plane even if you are injured and can move very little or not at all. A mirror and a smoke flare are obvious candidates. But if you are able to build a fire and have water available, natural smoke may be the best bet. For details of flares and distress signals, see footnote, page 394. For use and usefulness of mirror, flares and smoke, see pages 392–6. For makeshift mirror-substitutes, see page 354.

The same signals can, of course, be used for establishing con-tact with search parties on the ground. So can a whistle (page 355).

For places a helicopter can and cannot land, see page 397.

PRESERVING THE WILDERNESS

Once you become a walker, you become a conservationist: no one can walk for days on end through wild and unspoiled country and then stumble on some man-perpetrated horror without having his blood start to boil.*

Please do not misunderstand me. On balance, I am in favor of man. But there have been moments when my vote might have gone the other way—and such moments have mostly come when I have stumbled on the atrocities of the feeble-minded. I still remember vividly, from many years ago, walking across a secluded forest glade and all at once finding myself standing stock-still beside an old campsite that was a carnage of beer cans and cardboard boxes and torn plastic sheeting and dirty aluminum-foil plates and crumpled, soggy newspapers. Once, deep in a sidecanyon that led

---

* At least, I used to think this was so. I'm afraid I am no longer so sure.

to the Inner Gorge of the Colorado River, I passed half a dozen pale pink boulders that the ages had worn into smooth and sensuous sculpture but which had recently been overprinted with crude black drawings and the timeless legend "Batman." Such droppings of bat-witted individuals are bad enough, but it angers me far more when a whole segment of society goes in for large-scale desecration. Years ago, for two long and satisfying summers, I walked the virgin forests of western Vancouver Island, British Columbia, prospecting and staking claims for a mining company (and hoping, with some confidence, that the claims would never be developed). All through those two summers, with increasing and appalling frequency, I would emerge without warning from the coolness and cloistered calm of huge trees and green undergrowth into the glare and heat and desolation of gouged earth and splintered wood. (I have never recovered from those summers: logging is still the one provocation that I acknowledge might drive me to murder.) But most of all, now, I fear the deadly tentacles of the engineering mind. More and more, it seems, the engineers are gathering up the reins of power. And they are little men, most of them, with no concept at all of what their projects are doing to the face of the earth. They will, if it serves any half-baked economic purpose, slash a freeway through irreplaceable redwood groves. Driven by a perfectly understandable professional challenge and an equally understandable desire to have plenty of work in the years ahead (and also driven, even less consciously, by the built-in self-aggrandizement mechanism that rots into the structure of almost all our human institutions) they will concoct plans for gigantic, unnecessary dams. If they have their way, every yard of the Colorado River that I followed on my trip through lower Grand Canyon will be drowned by a 93-mile reservoir that will form behind "the tallest dam in the Western Hemisphere." That inundation would be only a preliminary in the slow destruction of the glory that is Grand Canyon. And after that would come Alaska and the huge and horrendous Rampart Dam.*

* I have let those last ten lines, and the text that follows, stand unchanged from the first edition. But none of the engineering projects has happened. And that is comforting. I hear less often, now, the old shibboleth: "You can't stop progress." So I don't so often have to reply, "Sure; but you can redefine it." At times it seems as if we have really begun the long, grinding task of redefinition. But sometimes it seems that nothing has changed. Yesterday it was Rampart Dam; today, the Alaska Pipeline.

(I shall also let that footnote stand. But it was written in the summer of 1973. Now, in November 1973, sanction for the pipeline seems final.

This outcome was almost inevitable once people and politicians at last accepted as real the iceberg tip that is currently labeled "the energy crisis." At the same time, the temporary villains in the case—joining the oil companies, the

But I said that these things would happen if the engineers had their way—and there are plenty of signs that they will not always have their way. Of course, they have not always had their way in the past. Even now, you cannot help but feel hopeful of real progress when you cease to take for granted the vast and in some cases still unspoiled national parks and wilderness areas that man has had the wisdom to shield from progress. And it is comforting to reflect that even as the menace and arrogance grow, so does the wisdom. It looks as though sanity may still . . .

But wait a minute. I did not mean to write these last two paragraphs. After all, I had made my point: once you become a walker, you become a conservationist. The rest follows. And I had intended to move on without delay to a warning. But I think I shall let the intruding paragraphs stand. It's not just that I needed to get them off my chest. Much more importantly, they are a shining example of what I wanted to sound a warning about. They are self-righteous. And self-righteousness is an occupational hazard for conservationists—or, if you must, "ecologists."

Now, it does not matter much that self-righteousness begets crashing bores—the sort of people you're always slipping away from at cocktail parties. What does matter is that as soon as we raise our self-righteous banners we lose our effectiveness. The Sierra Club, of which I am a member and a strong supporter, is probably today's most effective conservationist voice in the United States. It has, for example, fought more stoutly than anyone in the battle to save Grand Canyon. But, like cooperative societies and organized religious bodies, it tends to be a holier-than-thou organization. The

---

ecology lobby and then the Nixon administration—became the Arabs. . . .

Such responses typify the bind in which we, homo sapiens, now find ourselves.

By any short-term, old-style accounting, the decision to push ahead with the Alaska pipeline was pragmatic and sensible. After all, we—we Americans, that is, as opposed to we Arabs or Japanese or Dutch or even Canadians—clearly need our own secure, internal oil sources: otherwise, the whole complicated machinery that supports our lives might soon be threatened with slowdown.

By any long-term accounting, this decision to slash through the heart of the last big unmammonized oasis left under U.S. control was stupid as well as criminal: pragmatic responses to these first quivers of our human bubble should surely involve at least trying to retain some semblance of harmony between ourselves and the non-human world. Disruption of that harmony is, after all, the root of the trouble. But by the time we wake up to what is going on and convene a new Nuremberg to indict pipeline-voting politicians for crimes against the planet, it will be too late: much of the complicated machinery that now supports our lives could by then indeed be grinding to a halt. In any case, the politicians are not the guilty ones. The enemy, as usual, is us—the whole damned clutch of homo insapiens.

And now read on in the text, marking with amusement my sapient warnings against self-righteousness.)

maggot is built in. As a result, the words "Sierra Club" are liable to raise, in certain neutral circles, a chorus of groans. A meeting of suburban housewives once became thoroughly aroused by a conservationist slide show to the dangers of blind industrial "progress"; but then a Sierra Club member, in an uninvited "speech from the floor," laid the line on too thickly. It was as if a fog had blanketed the hall. The audience, which had been asking keen and probing questions, began to subside. First the mood changed to apathy. Soon it became a resentful and almost tangible hostility. The same kind of reaction occurs, I think, when we who are rabid antilitter fiends forget that we are human (see, pointedly, page 190) and start throwing our holy weights around. The result may well be a hostile group strewing their every last can and food wrapper about the landscape, deliberately and gleefully.

Now, the last thing I want to do is condone such barbarism. The point is that incidents of this kind have happened—and are desperately understandable. The lesson to be learned from them is that we conservationists must strive to suppress our self-righteousness. It is difficult, I know. I too am pretty damned sure that we *are* holier than the litterlouts and the engineers. But we must not let the conviction show. Not because it is bad for our souls or something, but because it reduces the chances that we will achieve what we desperately want and need to achieve.

It would be good to write that since this book first appeared we have made progress in our war against self-righteousness. I would particularly like to say warm and hopeful things about the youth movement "into the woods"—the movement that seemed to hold such high promise (and is, I guess, largely responsible for the extraordinary and continuing success of the first edition of this book). I rejoice at much of what the young have to say: they are at least asking the right questions. But as my years pass I find I judge people less and less by what they say they believe, more and more by the way they believe. "Ecology" is now in what Eric Hoffer called "the active, revivalist stage of a world movement," and so is no doubt bound to spawn pewsful of "true believers," but that does not make them any easier to stomach. I used, for example, to give rides in my car to almost all young roadside pack-toters; but a horrendous majority of them turned out to be thoroughly human—arrogant, self-righteous, clamped tight against the thought that a stranger might lead a reasonably moral life by his own standards. And until that changes it will be difficult to feel very hopeful.

LEARN OF THE GREEN WORLD

Learn of the Green World

Learn of the green world what can be thy place.
Ezra Pound

When I began this book it was my intention to examine, here at the end, the delights of walking in different kinds of country. For I was afraid that in the course of 400 fundamentally how-to pages we might have forgotten the feel-how—that the ways and means might have masked the joys and insights that can come, in the end, from the simple act of walking. I am still afraid that such an eclipse may have occurred. But I see now that the delights of different places are not what I must write about. They too are only means to an end.

Now I am the last person to deny that each kind of country—and also each season of the year and each hour of the day—has its own very special enchantments.

Mountains offer the slow unfolding of panoramas and the exhilaration of high places. Their summits, even the humble ones, are nearly always pinnacles of experience. And afterward you come back down. You ease back, step by step, from stark rock and snow into the world of seething life: first, a single tuft of vegetation in a windswept saddle; then the tracks of a small mammal; two hours later, the first tree; then the first tree that can stand upright against the wind; then the tracks of a large two-footed animal that was wearing cleated boots; then undeniable soil; soon, trees that would be trees in any company; finally, thick undergrowth beneath the trees—and you pat your pocket to make sure the snakebite kit is still there.

In the desert you rediscover, every time you go back, the cleanness that exists in spite of the dust, the complexity that underlies the apparent openness, and the intricate web of life that stretches over the apparent barrenness; but above all you rediscover the echoing silence that you had thought you would never forget.

Then there is untrodden snow country, silent with its own

427

kind of silence. And the surging seashore. And other dominions too, each with its own signature: estuaries, the river worlds, marshland, farmlands, moors, and the open plain.

But in the course of time the memories meld. For they come, all of them, from the green world.

When I open my own mind and let the memories spill out, I find a many-hued mosaic. I remember the odd excitement and the restricted yet infinitely open world I have moved through several times when I have clambered up—very late at night, and following the little pool from my flashlight beam—to the flat, grassy summit of the hill on which I wrote at last the opening chapter of this book. I remember a three-day walk along an unspoiled beach with the wind always barreling in from the Pacific and the sand dunes always humping up on my left; and I remember the ceaseless surging and drawing back of the sea, with its final, curving excursions into smooth sand—excursions that sometimes left stranded, high and almost dry, little fragments of transparent protoplasm (which set me thinking, "This is the stuff we came from") and sometimes cast up a bottle that I could peer at (laughing at myself for being so childlike) in the hope that it might contain a message. I remember standing on snowshoes outside my half-buried tent after a four-day storm, in a newly gleaming white world, and watching the guilty, cloud-bearing southwest wind trying to reassert itself; I remember feeling a northeast breeze spring up, and almost hearing it take a deep breath and say, "They shall not pass," and then begin to blow in earnest; and I remember watching, thankfully, as the line of dark clouds was held along a front, horizon to horizon, and then was driven back, slowly but inexorably, until at last it retreated behind the peaks and the sky was left to the triumphant northeast wind and the warm and welcome sun. I remember trying to clamber up a steep woodland bank after dark, somewhere in the deep South (I think it was in Alabama), and finding myself in an enchanted world of fireflies and twisted tree roots and fireflies and clumps of grass and fireflies and wildflowers and fireflies and fireflies and fireflies—a world suddenly filled with a magic that I had not glimpsed since I was ten, and had almost come to disbelieve in. I remember striding down a desert road as dusk fell, with the wind catching my pack and billowing out the poncho like a sail and carrying me almost effortlessly along before it; and I remember how, when the rain came, it stung my bare legs, refreshing without hurting. I remember, in a different, sagebrush desert, coming to the edge of a village and passing a wooden building with three cars and a truck parked outside, and a battered sign that said PENTECOSTAL

CHURCH OF GOD, EVERYONE WELCOME; I remember that the church door stood open to the warm evening, and that I could hear a piano and the congregation following along, with only a hint of exasperation, a half-beat behind a contralto whom nature had endowed with the volume, tempo, rigidity, and determination of a brass band. In another desert village—a long-dead ghost town, this one—I remember a clump of wild blue irises growing inside the worn wooden threshold of a once busy home. I remember red, red sunsets in a small desert valley when I was not alone. I remember, further back, a dead native cow in a clearing in the dry African bush; and, in the blood-softened soil beside its torn-out entrails, a single huge paw mark. I remember the small, round furry heads of the hyraxes that would solemnly examine us from the boulders just behind our 13,000-foot camp, up near Lewis Glacier on Mount Kenya. Further back still, I remember three otters cavorting across a moonlit Devonshire meadow; and a stag on a Scottish moor, silhouetted, elemental; and a shoal of small fish swimming slowly over a sloping bed of brown gravel that I can still see, stone fitting into stone, down the tunnel of thirty-five years. And now, vaulting back into yesterday, I find I am remembering an elk that stands regally among redwood trees and the last tendrils of morning mist, and a surprised beaver that crouches almost at my feet and eyes me for clues, and a solitary evening primrose that has prospered in a desolation of desert talus, and a rainbow that arches over a dark mountain tarn, and the huge and solemn silence that encompasses, always, the buttes and mesas and cliffs and hanging terraces of the Grand Canyon of the Colorado.

Everyone who walks has his own floodlit memories—his own fluttering windwheel of scenes and sounds and scents. (It is often the scents that linger longest, though you do not know it until they come again.) But no matter what the hue of the individual memories, they all come from the green world. And in the end, when you have learned to connect—only to connect—you understand that it is simply the green world that you seek.

I suppose you could say that going out into this older world is rather like going to church. I know that it is in my case, anyway. For me, praying is no good: my god is not interested in what happens to me personally. But by walking out alone into wilderness I can elude the pressures of the pounding modern world, and in the sanctity of silence and solitude—the solitude seems to be a very important part of it—I can after a while begin to see and to hear and to think and in the end to feel with a new and exciting accuracy. And that, it seems to me, is just the kind of vision you should be hoping to find when you go to church.

Now I do not want to suggest that out in the wilderness my mind—or, I suspect, anyone else's mind—is always soaring. Most of the time it operates on a mundanely down-to-earth level. In the course of a four-day hike taken primarily so that I could sort out ideas and directions for the second half of this book, I tried to write down before they had faded away the thoughts that had run through my head while I was climbing one afternoon up a long and fairly steep hill. What I scribbled down was, in part: "Wonder how far now, over top and down to next creek. Maybe should have half-filled canteen from that last spring. . . . Oh hell, left heel again! Hope it's not a blister. Moleskin? No, not yet. Oh, look at that squirrel! Sun caught it beautifully, coming in from behind at an angle. Hm, horse tracks. Wonder how old. . . . Phew! Pretty damned hot for January. Better take off shirt at next halt. Almost time for rest anyway. Only five minutes. That should just get me to top of hill. . . . Hey, what's that on my leg? Oh, just water dripping off wet socks, on pack. . . . Oh my God, look! It'll be at least ten or fifteen minutes to top of bloody hill. Maybe more. . . . Say, your thoughts really do run on, don't they? Normally, don't notice it much, but . . . wait a minute, better jot down what I've been thinking, as accurately and as far back as I can. Might just be worth using in the walking book. Yes, out notebook right now . . ."

Twice more on that four-day trip I jotted down odd islets of thought that jutted up from what was no doubt a continuous stream. Once, on a slightly less mundane but still distinctly un-soaring level, I found that as I walked I had concocted a mnemonic sentence ("King Philip, come out, for God's sake!") for a sequence that often leaves me groping: the hierarchy of categories into which biologists divide the living world (kingdom, phylum, class, order, family, genus, species). And one evening I was warming myself by a campfire and looking up at the dark pine trees silhouetted against a quarter moon and beginning to think of beauty and life and death (or so my notes assure me) when I realized with some surprise that I was at the same time singing quietly to myself the soulful and almost immortal refrain from a song that was implanted in my mind somewhere deep in half-forgotten childhood: "And the captain sat in the captain's chair, and he played his ukulele as the ship went down."

But in trying to remove a false impression, I must not over-compensate. There are, of course, times when your mind soars or floats or hangs free and impartial—or dives into the depths.

For even in wilderness you may, very occasionally, plunge into despair—into the blackness that exists, I suppose, deep down in all our lives, waiting to blot out the underpinnings and so keep us honest. I remember a desert canyon in which, as I lay quiet beneath the stars, man was a pointless impostor on the bleak and ancient surface of the earth, and I knew I would never hope again. And I remember a night on a mountain when all that existed out in the blackness beyond my campfire was a small hemlock, and even the hemlock only flickered into and out of existence at the mercy of the fickle firelight; a night on which, for an endless, empty span, that little tree with its dark, stark needles was more lasting and more real than I was, and so claimed a crushing victory; a night on which, above all, the blackness beyond the tree was tragically and incontestably more real than the fragile tree, and therefore claimed the final, aching, desolate victory. Such interludes—in which the keepers of the void ensnare you and all, all is vanity—are rare in wilderness. But they happen. And, although I would like to deny it, they are worse than in the city. While they last, the blackness is blacker, more hopeless, more desolately victorious. This time, you cannot appeal to a more profound reality.

But, far more often than despair, you find elation. A squirrel leaps across a gap in the trees, a hundred feet above your head, and your mind, caught by the beauty, leaps too—across the gap between the dragging everyday world and the universals. Two swallows, bound head to tail in tight and perfect formation, bank up and away from a cliff face in a joyous arc of freedom. A quartet of beavers browses by the margin of a backwater, silent and serene, a tableau from a calmer age. Or you sit, triumphant, on a rocky peak and look and look at the whole world spread out below; and for a while, though still a man, you are no longer merely a man.

At such moments you do not "commune with nature" (a trite phrase that seems to classify nature as something outside and separate from us men). At such moments you know, deep down in your fabric, with a certainty far more secure than intellect can offer, that you are a part of the web of life, and that the web of life is a part of the rock and air and water of pre-life. You know the wholeness of the universe, the great unity. And if you keep walking long enough—for several weeks or for several months—you may with care and good fortune experience whole days or even series of days during which you exist in this happy, included state.

They do not last, of course, these rich cadenzas. But their echoes linger. When you first return to the world of man there is a period of readjustment, just as there was when you left it and went out into the wilderness. After that first glorious hot shower (which is always—and always to your new surprise—a great experience in itself) you live for a day, or perhaps three days, or even a week, an unreal, cut-off-by-a-screen-of-gauze sort of existence. But once you have readjusted to hot showers and radios and orthodox beds and automobiles and parking meters and sidewalks and elevators and other people and other people's points of view, you begin to find that you have regained thrust and direction and hope and wonder and other such vital intangibles whose presence or absence color so indelibly the tenor of our lives, but which are very difficult to discuss without sententiousness. You find yourself refreshed, that is, for the eternal struggle of trying to see things as you more or less know they are, not merely as other people tell you they are. Above all, you find that you have recomprehended— totally, so that it is there behind every thought—the knowledge that we have arisen from everything that has gone before. You know, steadily, that we are more than just a fascinating and deadly and richly promising species that has begun to take over the face of the earth. You know again, fully, that this species you belong to is the current spearhead of life—and that your personal meaning is that you are a part of the spearhead. And so you find that you can take up once more the struggle we all have to make in our own several and quirky ways if we are to succeed in living lives that are truly human—the struggle to discern some glimmering of sense in the extraordinary phenomenon that is man.

And that, I guess, is quite a lot to get out of such a simple thing as walking.

Check List of Equipment

Note: the jacket photo is keyed to this list. For an explanation, see back flap of jacket.

Everyone should in the end develop his own check list (see page 26), but this may be a useful starter.

Suggestion: photostat the following list of items, rule columns in both margins, and before a trip check off each item as you put it on one side, as you pack it at home, and again when you finally strike out and away from civilization. At the end, add your own idiosyncratic items and perhaps some of the minor items I have mentioned in the text but chosen to exclude, such as bootwax, polysqueeze tubes, scouring pad, frost liner and snow anchors for tent, hammock, sleeping-bag liner and cover, razor, meat tenderizer (unseasoned), dental floss, and even, by God, trail guide and doggie pack.

This is a reasonably exhaustive list, including most items the average backpacker will want to consider taking along on any kind of trip. What he actually takes will always, of course, be a great deal less. For samples of gear that the author carried under specific conditions, see *The Thousand-Mile Summer,* photographs between pp. 32 and 33, and *The Man Who Walked Through Time,* Appendix, p. 235.

Weights are for author's own equipment or, where no such item is owned, an average.

Foundations

Page		Lbs.	Oz.
38	Boots	5	12
46	Socks (3 pairs)	0	13½
48	Moccasins	0	17
51	Staff	0	15½
54	Ice ax	2	0
54	Crampons	1	5
56	Snowshoes	6	0
58	Rubbing alcohol	0	2
58	Footpowder	0	3
60	Moleskins	0	1

Walls

Page		Lbs.	Oz.
81	Pack	4	1
88	Belt bag	0	6

Kitchen

Page		Lbs.	Oz.
122	Food (see table, pages 122–3)	15	3
120	Booze bottle	0	8
131	Water purification tablets	0	½

433

Page		Lbs.	Oz.
136	Solar still kit	0	5½
139	Canteen(s) (empty)	0	15½
141	Rubber tubing	0	2
141	Frying pan	0	12
142	Cooking pots	1	4
143	Pot lifter	0	1
143	Cup	0	3
144	Spoon	0	2
145	Sheath knife	0	6
145	Carborundum stone	0	1
145	Salt-pepper shaker	0	1
146	Sugar container	0	2
146	Margarine container	0	1
146	Milk squirter	0	1
147	Bookmatches (7)	0	1
147	Matchsafe	0	1
148	Magnifying glass	0	2
148	Flint stick	0	1
147	Can opener	0	⅛
148	Dish cloth	0	½
165	Stove (full)	1	5½
173	White gas bottle(s)		
	(full) (or cartridges)	1	4½
174	Funnel/Canedy cap	0	½
176	Eyedropper	0	⅛
179	Stove windscreen	0	4
180	Foam pad for stove	0	¼
180	Wundergauze	0	1

Bedroom

Page		Lbs.	Oz.
213	Tent	2	14
218	Fly sheet	1	10
218	Tent poles	1	6
219	Tent pegs	0	6
228	Polyethylene sheet	1	5
229	Visklamps (5)	0	4
241	Groundsheet	0	9
242	Air mattress patch kit	0	4
244	Air mattress	1	14
248	Foam pad	1	4
265	Sleeping bag	3	3½

Clothes Closet

Page		Lbs.	Oz.
287	String vest	0	6
288	String longs	0	6
289	Long johns	0	9
289	Undershorts (? spares)	0	2
289	Shirt (? spare)	0	9
290	Sweater	0	10
291	Short pants	1	9
292	Long pants	1	10
292	Belt	0	4
292	Gaiters	0	3½
293	Down jacket (light)	1	1
294	Down jacket (heavy)	2	0
294	Down pants	1	0
295	Down booties	0	8
296	Parka	1	4
297	Rain jacket	0	9
297	Rain pants	1	2
297	Rain chaps	0	5
297	Poncho	0	14
299	Cagoule	0	11
299	Cagoule footsack	0	6
300	Gloves	0	12
301	Inner gloves (? spares)	0	¼
302	Scarf	0	1
301	Balaclava	0	3
302	Swimsuit	0	2½
302	Bandanna	0	1
302	Hat	0	6
308	Bucket and bowl set	0	8

Furniture and Appliances

Page		Lbs.	Oz.
312	Flashlight, with batteries	0	2½
314	Spare batteries	0	3
317	Spare bulb(s)	0	0
318	Candle lantern	0	3¾
318	Candles	0	3
319	Cartridge lantern	0	9
320	Sunglasses (? spares)	0	1
320	Goggles	0	2½

Page		Lbs.	Oz.	Page		Lbs.	Oz.
321	Anti-fog preparation	0	½	355	Emergency fishing		
324	Binoculars	0	17		tackle	0	¼
	Photography:			355	Rope	1	14
327	Camera	2	6	357	Reading matter	0	5
330	Spare lens(es)	0	11	358	Notebook	0	2
328	Tripod	0	14	358	Pencils, pens, refills	0	¾
329	Lens brush	0	¾	359	Paper for notes	0	2
329	Lens tissue	0	0	359	Office	0	4
329	Close-up at-			360	Watch	0	2
	tachments	0	2	361	Pedometer	0	2
329	Cable release	0	½	362	Thermometer	0	1½
329	Film	0	3	363	Rip-stop tape	0	¼
331	Bino-attachment	0	3	363	Needles and thread	0	0
335	Maps	0	3	363	Spare pack parts	0	2
337	Mapcase	0	1	365	Fishing tackle	0	14
339	Map measurer	0	1	368	Nylon cord	0	4
342	Compass	0	4½	370	Rubber bands	0	0
347	Soap/Detergent	0	1	370	Spare plastic bags	0	1
348	Towel	0	2	371	Odds-and-ends can	0	¼
348	Toothbrush	0	½	371	Belt clip(s)	0	1
348	Dentifrice	0	½	372	Wallet	0	½
348	Comb	0	⅛	372	Dime	0	0
348	Toilet roll	0	7	372	Car key	0	¼
348	Scissors	0	1				
349	Fly dope	0	1½				
350	Suntan lotion	0	1				

Housekeeping

Page		Lbs.	Oz.
350	Lip salve	0	1
350	Hand lotion	0	1½	381	Life vest	1	2
351	Heater	0	1½	386	Toilet trowel	0	2
351	First-aid kit	0	5	394	Signal flare	0	3
354	Signaling mirror	0	1	404	Snakebite kit	0	1
355	Whistle	0	½	419	Space blanket	0	2

Retailers of Backpack Equipment and Foods Who Operate Mail-Order Services

This list is as complete and current as I can make it. But please remember (from page 17) to treat it as a guide, not a gospel.

Many retailers report that they "accept mail orders" but do not issue catalogues. Space unfortunately demands that I omit them.

The *star grading* is an attempt, inevitably fallible, to indicate the *range* of equipment that each firm offers (in its catalogue, not necessarily in its store). For example, **** means "just about everything a backpacker could want, and a wide choice of models." The stars do not necessarily reflect *quality* of stock.

Additional symbols:

† Firms that specialize in a certain branch or branches of equipment—usually, though not always, of high quality.

‡ Firms that operate a general-merchandise mail-order service, of which backpacking equipment typically forms only a minor part—though in recent years the space their catalogues devote to it has in most cases been given a considerable hike.

Where both a street address and P.O. Box number are given they indicate, respectively, a retail store location and a mail-order address.

UNITED STATES

Coast-to-Coast
Montgomery Ward.
Sears, Roebuck.

Arizona
† Camp Trails, 4111 West Clarendon, P.O. Box 14500, Phoenix, 85063.
(Packs and tents.)

† Nicolet Products, 42 South 42nd St., Phoenix, 85034.
(Specialty: survival and first-aid kits. But also some foods and equipment.)

California

† Alpenlite, P.O. Box 851, Claremont, 91711.
(Packs.)

‡ Abercrombie and Fitch: see New York.

† Adventure Horizons, P.O. Box 6085, San Diego, 92106.
(Aluminum walking staffs.)

† Adventure 16, 656 Front St., El Cajon, 92020.
(Packs, tents, sleeping bags.)

† Airlift, 2217 Roosevelt Ave., Berkeley, 94703.
(Air mattresses.)

† Alpine Aid, 3920 Beechwood Pl., Riverside, 92506.
(Lightweight first-aid kits and items.)

† Antelope Camping Equipment, 21740 Granada Ave., Cupertino, 95014. Additional retail outlet: Sacramento.
(Mainly packs.)

Backpacker Shop, The, 743 E. Foothill Blvd., Claremont, 91711.
Additional retail outlets: Pasadena and Santa Ana.
(Unrated: supply own mail-order lists for foods and books, but suppliers' catalogues for most equipment.)

† Beck Outdoor Projects, P.O. Box 3061, South Berkeley, 94703.
(Neoprene-nylon snowshoe bindings and crampon straps.)

† Black Forest Enterprises, P.O. Box 1007, Nevada City, 95959.
(Aluminum-frame snowshoes.)

† Bugaboo Mountaineering, 170 Central Ave., Pacific Grove, 93950.
(Down-filled sleeping bags and jackets, made to personal specifications. Catalogue: $.10.)

† Chouinard Equipment: see Great Pacific Iron Works, below.

† Class 5, 2010 7th St., Berkeley, 94710.
(Sleeping bags, down garments, tents, packs.)

*** Co-op Wilderness Supply, 1432 University Ave., Berkeley, 94702.

† Denali, 2402 Ventura, Fresno, 93721.
(Packs; some clothing and climbing equipment.)

† Down Depot, The, 431 Belvedere St., San Francisco, 94117.
(Counter-service and mail-order dry cleaning of down sleeping bags and clothing.)

** Eddie Bauer: see Washington.

† Great Pacific Iron Works, The (formerly Chouinard Equipment), P.O. Box 150, Ventura, 93001.
(Primarily climbing equipment, but a small range of good backpacking items. Catalogue: $1.)

** Highland Outfitters, 3579 University Ave., P.O. Box 121, Riverside, 92502.

*** Kelty, 1801 Victory Blvd., Glendale, 91201.
(Specialty: packs. But now a good range of other equipment.)
† Mountain Equipment, 3208 E. Hamilton, Fresno, 93702.
(Packs and tents.)
*** Mountain Shop, The, 228 Grant Ave., San Francisco, 94108.
(Specialty: equipment by Gerry. But now a wide range by other makers.)
† Mountain Traders, 1702 Grove St., Berkeley, 94709.
(See page 16.)
** North Face, The, 1234 Fifth St., P.O. Box 2399, Station A, Berkeley, 94702. Additional retail store: Palo Alto.
(Specialties: sleeping bags, down clothing, tents.)
† Pinnacle, The, P.O. Box 4214, Mountain View, 94040.
(Down sleeping bags. Mail order only; no store.)
† Reyco, P.O. Box 914, Sonoma, 95476.
(Six "outdoor creams" designed to afford protection against sun, wind, insects, cold, skin-drying, and such "toxics" as poison oak and ivy.)
*** Sierra Designs, 4th and Addison Sts., Berkeley, 94710.
(See page 15. Offers a wider selection than recent rather fey catalogues suggest. 1974 catalogue: $.50.)
Sierra Equipment, 747 Polk St., P.O. Box 15251, San Francisco, 94109.
(Unrated: catalogue due 1974. A "backroom" operation now expanded to a store.)
**** Ski Hut, The, 1615 University Ave., Berkeley, 94703.
(See page 14. Makers of Trailwise equipment.)
*** Smilie Company, The, 575 Howard St., San Francisco, 94105.
(Tends to specialize in economically priced equipment. Catalogue: $.10 plus $.15 postage.)
† Snow Lion, 1330 9th St., P.O. Box 9056, Berkeley, 94710.
(Sleeping bags and down clothing.)
† Stephenson's, 23206 Hatteras St., Woodland Hills, 91364.
(Makers of Warmlite tents, sleeping bags, packs, no-sweat shirt.)
† Sunbird Industries, 5368 N. Sterling Center Dr., Westlake Village, 91301.
(Packs.)
** Swiss Ski Sports, 559 Clay St., San Francisco, 94111.
(Ski specialists. But offer a good range of backpacking gear.)
† Tanasol Company, The, 2848 Derby St., Berkeley, 94705.
(Neva-Mist anti-fogging agent: see page 321.)
**** Trailwise: see Ski Hut, above.
† Universal Field Equipment Company, Mira Loma Space Center, Building 811A, Mira Loma, 91752.
(Packs.)
† Warmlite: see Stephenson's, above.

Wilderness West, P.O. Box 1841, Monterey, 93940.
(Mail order only. Unrated: catalogue due 1974.)
† World Leisure Products, P.O. Box 77343, San Francisco, 94107.
(New Zealand–made sleeping bags, jackets, polar equipment.)
† Yeti Enterprises, P.O. Box 6170, Topanga, 90290.
(Down-filled sleeping bags and jackets, made to personal specifications. A "cottage industry.")

Colorado

‡ Abercrombie and Fitch: see New York.
Alpine Designs (formerly Alp Sport): see Ohio—Wilderness Ways.
** Alpine Outfitters, 328 Link Lane #5, Fort Collins, 80521.
(A good selection of major items by leading makers. Have a 10 percent "Participation Bonus System" for repeat orders.)
** Eddie Bauer: see Washington.
† Forrest Mountaineering, P.O. Box 7083, Denver, 80207.
(Frameless packs. Also climbing ironmongery.)
† Frostline Kits, P.O. Box 9100–F, Boulder, 80301. Retail store: Crossroads East Shopping Center, Boulder.
(Do-it-yourself kits for a wide and increasing range of equipment.)
Gerry: no longer sell retail, direct; only through dealers.
**** Holubar Mountaineering, 1975 30th St., P.O. Box 7, Boulder, 80302. Additional retail stores: Denver and Colorado Springs.
(Embracing Carikit do-it-yourself equipment kits.)
† Lowe Alpine Systems, P.O. Box 151, Louisville, 80027.
(Specialists in exceptional "alpine"-style climbing gear. But some items might interest extreme-cold-weather backpackers: tents, mitts, overboots, down jacket, etc.)
*** Mountain Sports, 821 Pearl St., Boulder, 80302.
† Sportsmen Products, P.O. Box 1082, Boulder, 80302.
("Snowtreads" plastic snowshoes.)
† Steve Komito, P.O. Box 2106, Estes Park, 80517.
(Specialist boot repairs and sales. See page 16. Now has catalogue. Current wait for repair appointment: about 5 months.)
† Survival Research Labs, 17 Marland Rd., Colorado Springs, 80906. Canadian Branch: see Alberta.
(Safety and first-aid equipment for outdoorsmen, including some for backpackers.)

Connecticut

† Cannondale Corporation, 35 Pulaski St., Stamford, 06902.
(Packs.)
Ski Hut, The, Keeler Bldg., Wilton, 06897.
(Unrated: catalogue due 1974.)

Florida
‡ Abercrombie and Fitch: see New York.

Illinois
‡ Abercrombie and Fitch: see New York.
** Eddie Bauer: see Washington.
   Erewhon Mountain Supply, 1252 W. Devon Ave., Chicago,
      60626. Additional retail outlet: Madison, Wisconsin.
      (Unrated: catalogue due 1974.)
† Todd's, 5 S. Wabash Ave., Chicago, 60603.
      (Boots and shoes.)
** Wilderness Shack, 515 La Grange Rd., La Grange, 60525.
      (Catalogue: $1.)

Iowa
‡ Herter's: see Minnesota.

Kansas
   Voyageur Enterprises, P.O. Box 512, Shawnee Mission, 66201.
      Retail store: 5935 Merriam Dr., Merriam 66202.
      (Unrated: full catalogue due 1974. Canoeing and backpacking
      gear. Specialty: Camp-Pak waterproof plastic bags.)

Maine
** L. L. Bean, Main St., Freeport, 04032.
      (Specialty: Maine Hunting Boots. But the catalogue—a long-
      standing institution—now lists increased stock of backpacking
      gear. Store open 24 hours a day.)
† Burgess Shoe Store, Wilton, 04294.
      (Boots and shoes. "Official" Bass factory outlet.)
† Sugarloaf Ski Specialists, Kingport, 04947.
      (No retail mail-order service—but walkers along Appalachian
      Trail in Maine, see page 16.)

Maryland
   Appalachian Outfitters, 8563 Baltimore National Pike, Ellicot
      City, 21043.
      (For details, see Virginia.)
† Bishop's Ultimate Outdoor Equipment, 6804 Millwood Rd.,
      Bethesda, 20034.
      (Tents. See page 216.)
**‡ H & H Surplus and Camper's Haven, 424 N. Eutaw, Baltimore,
      21201.
      (Emphasis on car-camping, but now lists good stock of back-
      packing gear. Catalogue: $.50.)

Massachusetts

† Corcoran Inc., Stoughton, 02072.
(Clothing and heavy hunting gear.)
**‡ Don Gleason's Camper's Supply, 9 Pearl St., Northampton, 01060.
(Emphasis on car-camping, but now lists good stock of backpacking gear. Catalogue: $.25.)
**** Eastern Mountain Sports, 1041 Commonwealth Ave., Boston, 02215. Additional retail outlets: Wellesley and Amherst, Massachusetts; North Conway, New Hampshire; Ardsley, New York; and St. Paul, Minnesota.
(Catalogue: $1—but see page 17.)
† Fabiano Shoe Company, South Station, Boston, 02110.
(Italian boots.)
*** Moor and Mountain, 63 Park St., Andover, 01850.
(For details, see page 17.)
*** Stow-A-Way Sports Industries, 166 Cushing Hwy., Cohasset, 02025.
(Still specializes in foods, but now carries a full range of equipment. Mails packages of food and other equipment to designated post offices along Appalachian and other eastern trails according to schedules of long-distance walkers.)
* Tight Lines, 220 S. Main St., West Bridgewater, 02379.
(Emphasis on hunting and fishing, but some backpacking items.)

Michigan

‡ Abercrombie and Fitch: see New York.

Minnesota

**** Eastern Mountain Sports: see Massachusetts.
** Eddie Bauer: see Washington.
*‡ Gokey Company, 21 W. 5th St., St. Paul, 55102.
(Increased backpacking listings.)
‡ Herter's Inc., Rural Route 1, Waseca, 56093. Additional retail outlets: Iowa Falls, Iowa; Beaverdam, Wisconsin; and Olympia, Washington.
(650-page catalogue: $1. Primarily for hunters and fishermen.)

New Hampshire

† Booted Shepherd, The, 101 Main St., Francestown, 03043.
(Clothing, especially sheepskin jackets. But some items—boots, moccasins—for backpackers.)
**** Eastern Mountain Sports: see Massachusetts.
† Peter Limmer and Sons, Intervale, 03845.
(Custom climbing boots; some general equipment.)
*** Skimeister Sports Shop, Main St., North Woodstock, 03262.

New Jersey
Wooden Nickel, The, 150 Main St., Flemington, 08825.
(Unrated: catalogue due 1974.)

New Mexico
River and Ridge Suppliers, P.O. Box 5218, Santa Fe, 87501.
(Apparently to handle all "direct sales" of Ocaté equipment—
and other products too. But they are, like Ocaté, very difficult
to squeeze information from.)

New York
‡ Abercrombie and Fitch, Madison Ave. at 45th St., New York,
10017. Additional retail outlets: Chicago and Oak Brook, Illi-
nois; San Francisco, California; Troy, Michigan; The Broad-
moor, Colorado; and Bal Harbor and Palm Beach, Florida.
(Some retail stores seem to carry a fair backpacking stock, but
the mail-order catalogue holds few relevant items, especially
for unbeautiful people.)
*** Black's: Thomas Black and Sons, 930 Ford St., Ogdensburg,
13669. Canadian branch: see Ontario.
**** Eastern Mountain Sports: see Massachusetts.
† Eureka Tent and Awning, 625 Conklin Rd., P.O. Box 966,
Binghamton, 13902.
(Tents. Some other equipment.)
† Freeman Industries, Tuckahoe, 10707.
("Trak Soapless Supersoap." See page 347.)
* Gloy's, 12 E. 22nd St., New York, 10010.
(Mostly boating and car-camping equipment.)
* Hudson's, 105 Third Ave., New York, 10003.
(Primarily car- and boat-camping, but considerable backpacking
list.)
*** Kreeger & Son, 30 W. 46th St., New York, 10036.
(Rating tentative, based on store stock: comprehensive catalogue
due 1974.)
‡ Outdoor Outfitters, P.O. Box 56, New Hartford, 13413.
(Duxbak clothing, including some for backpackers.)
Rock and Snow, 44 Main St., New Paltz, 12561.
(Unrated: catalogue due 1974.)
† Trail Tech, 108–02 Otis Ave., Corona, 11368.
(Foam sleeping bags. Some other items.)
† Walking News, P.O. Box 352, New York, 10013.
(See *The Great Outdoors Book List,* page 18, and Dale Vent O
Soles, page 40.)
† Woods Bag and Canvas Company, 90 River St., P.O. Box 118,
Ogdensburg, 13669.
(Sleeping bags, down clothing.)

North Carolina

** Hi-Camp, P.O. Box 17602, Charlotte, 28211.
(Strictly mail order. No retail store.)
Pack & Paddle, 4240 Kernersville Rd., Winston-Salem, 27107.
(Branch of Appalachian Outfitters: for details, see Virginia.)

Ohio

† Springhart Corporation, 5988 Executive Blvd., Dayton, 45424.
(Wauk-O-Long staffs. See page 53.)
† Colorado Mountain Industries, 1896 Reading Rd., Cincinnati,
45215.
(Mainly mountaineering equipment, but also first-aid kits.)
*** Wilderness Ways, 12417 Cedar Rd., Cleveland Heights, 44106.
(National mail-order outlet for Alpine Designs, but also carries
other well-known brands.)

Oklahoma

‡ P & S Sales, P.O. Box 45095, Tulsa, 74145.

Oregon

** Beckel Canvas Products, P.O. Box 20491, Portland, 97220.
(A fair range of mostly custom-made equipment—*not* only can-
vas—including some for pack animals.)
† Life Support Technology, Inc., P.O. Box 13, Manning, 97125.
(Manuals and movies on survival and "wilderness appreciation."
Movies for sale or rental.)
† Norm Thompson, 1805 N.W. Thurman, Portland, 97209.
(Clothing and footwear, including some for backpackers.)

Pennsylvania

*** Co-op Wilderness Shop, 122 Meyran Ave., Pittsburgh, 15213.
(Cheerful catalogue free. Claims to discount "as much as 10–20
percent.")
‡ I. Goldberg, 902 Chestnut St., Philadelphia, 19107.
(Exceptionally good selection of packs.)
Mountain Trail Shop, The, 5435 Walnut St., Pittsburgh, 15232.
(Unrated: catalogue due 1974.)
† Pak-Lite, P.O. Box 583, Berwyn, 19312.
(Foam pads. No catalogue.)

Tennessee

† Appalachian Designs, P.O. Box 11252, Chattanooga, 37401.
Retail store: 3419 Chapman Hwy., Knoxville, 37920.
(Sleeping bags, tents, packs—and apparently expanding.)
*** Camp and Hike Shop, The, 4674 Knight Arnold, Memphis,
38118.
(Car-camping as well, but a wide backpacking selection.)

Utah

** AAA Tent and Awning Company, 24 W. 5th South, Salt Lake City, 84101.

(Specialty: tents. But many other items.)

Vermont

‡ Orvis Company, The, Manchester, 05254.

Virginia

Appalachian Outfitters:

(1) 2930 Chain Bridge Rd., P.O. Box 248, Oakton, 22124; (2) 215 N. Main St., Blacksburg, 24060; (3) 7832 Plantation Rd. N.W., Roanoke, 24019. See also Maryland and North Carolina.

(Unrated, because no catalogue of own; but all five stores accept mail and phone orders for equipment of following manufacturers—whose catalogues are furnished on request: Alpine Designs, Black's, Camp 7, Gerry, North Face, Sierra Designs.)

Washington

** Eddie Bauer, 1737 Airport Way South, Seattle, 98134. Seattle retail store: Third and Virginia. Others: Chicago, Illinois; Denver, Colorado; Minneapolis, Minnesota; and San Francisco, California.

(Catalogue emphasis is on clothing, some for backpackers; but a fair range of other backpacking items. Stores carry wide range. Mail orders taken at any store are teletyped to Seattle. Orders can also be mailed there or telegraphed or phoned [24-hour service].)

‡ Herter's: see Minnesota.

† Mountain Safety Research, 631 S. 96th St., Seattle, 98108.

(Stoves, packs, parkas. Details appear in irregular newsletters.)

** Northwest Recreational Supply, P.O. Box 70105, Seattle, 98107.

(Mail order only.)

**** Recreational Equipment Inc., 1525 11th Ave., Seattle, 98122.

(A cooperative. Prices often very competitive.)

† Rivendell Mountain Works, P.O. Box E, Snoqualmie, 98065.

(Packs and tents.)

† Seattle Tent and Fabric Products Company, 900 N. 137th St., Seattle, 98133.

(Tents, tarps.)

Wisconsin

Erewhon Mountain Supply: see Illinois.

**‡ Laake and Joys, 1432 N. Water St., Milwaukee, 53202. Additional retail store: Brookfield.

‡ Gander Mountain, P.O. Box 248, Wilmot, 53192.
(Primarily for hunters, fishermen.)

‡ Herter's: see Minnesota.

† The W. C. Russell Moccasin Company, 285 S.W. Franklin St.,
Berlin, 54923.
(Handcrafted, custom-fit moccasins, boots, and shoes.)

Wyoming

† Powderhorn Mountaineering, P.O. Box 1228, Jackson Hole,
83001.
(Down jackets, parkas.)

† Paul Petzoldt Wilderness Equipment, P.O. Box 78, Lander,
82520.
(Specialty: Fiberfill II sleeping bags. Also tents, packs, clothing,
foods, and climbing gear.)

CANADA

Please note that various financial impediments prevent most Canadian
firms from being able to supply individual U.S. residents economically.
Indeed, it's hardly reasonable to expect replies to other than exceptional
U.S. mail orders.

Coast-to-Coast

‡ The T. Eaton Company. Head office: 190 Yonge St., Toronto 1,
Ontario.

‡ Simpson-Sears. Head office: 22 Jarvis St., Toronto, M5B 2B8.

Alberta

‡ Woodwards: see British Columbia.

† Survival Research Laboratories, P.O. Box 1288, Peace River.
(For details, see Colorado.)

British Columbia

*** Arlberg Ski Hut, 2401 Cambie St., Vancouver 9.
(Mail-order service for *Canada only*. No catalogue of own, but
works from that of Black's and other suppliers.)

Mountain Equipment Co-operative, 2068 W. 4th Ave., Vancouver 9.
(A new co-op. $5-share entry requirement. Varying stock of new
equipment. Also sells members' used gear on consignment,
keeping one sixth of price.)

‡ Woodward's. Head office: Hastings and Abbot Sts., Vancouver 3.
Branches elsewhere in British Columbia and in Alberta.
(No catalogue; but has "country shopping," a telephone ordering
system.)

Ontario

*** Black's: Thomas Black & Sons, 225 Strathcona Ave., Ottawa, KIS 1X7. Also in Ogdensburg, N.Y.

*‡ Margesson's, 17 Adelaide St. East, Toronto.
(Long-established coast-to-coast general merchandise mail-order service. Recently issued first backpacking-and-canoeing catalogue, and plans to expand it.)

Lightweight Foods

Many of the retailers listed above (and especially those rated ******** or *******) offer a wide range of lightweight foods for backpackers. Most of the foods are made by a few specialist firms. Some of these firms—including Wilson's and Oregon Freeze Dried Foods (Mountain House and Tea Kettle products)—will advise you of the major retail outlets handling their merchandise but do not themselves operate retail mail-order services. Others do. And the field now boasts several specialist retailers.

Some of the firms listed will mail only case lots. Others, understandably, find they cannot fill orders totaling less than $10. So study catalogues before ordering.

I had hoped to compile a separate and meaningful list of "organic" food suppliers; but they tend, overnight, to fold their tents, like the Arabs, and as silently steal a whey.

UNITED STATES

California

Dri-Lite Foods, 11333 Atlantic, Lynwood, 90262.

FSP Foods, P.O. Box 929, El Cerrito, 94530.
(Price lists for Rich-Moor, Mountain House, and Wilson.)

Inter-Mountain Trading Company, P.O. Box 938, Berkeley, 94701. (See page 116.)

Kamp Pack Division, Bernard Food Industries, P.O. Box 487, San Jose, 95103.
(25-percent "organizational discount" for Scout units, hiking and conservation clubs, and the following groups: church, youth, educational, military.)

Rich-Moor, P.O. Box 2728, Van Nuys, 91401.
(Current order form/brochure lists nutritional values for almost every item.)

Trail Chef, P.O. Box 60041 Terminal Annex, Los Angeles, 90036.

Illinois

Ad. Seidel & Son, 2323 Pratt Blvd., Elk Grove Village, 60007.
(Nothing smaller than case lots: sells direct, primarily to summer
   camps. But most products available in small quantities from Recreational Equipment [see Washington, above] and National Packaged
   Trail Foods [see Ohio, below].)

Massachusetts

Chuck Wagon, Micro Drive, Woburn, 01801.
(Has abandoned long-standing policy of inflated prices with big group
   discounts.)
Stow-A-Way Sports Industries, 155 Cushing Hwy., Cohasset, 02025.
(Food specialists. But see also in equipment listing, above.)

New Jersey

S. Gumpert & Co., 812 Jersey Ave., Jersey City, 07302.
(For details, see Ontario, below.)

New York

Freeze-Dry Foods. Sole U.S. mail-order distributor: Black's (see New
   York, in equipment listing, above). See also Ontario, below.

Ohio

National Packaged Trail Foods, 632 E. 185th St., Cleveland, 44119.
(Seidel and Wilson products.)

Utah

Camplite Foods, 40 E. 2430 South, Salt Lake City, 84115. Also retail
   store.
(Perma-Pak brand. Special pricing on Scout-troop and summer-camp
   orders.)

CANADA

Ontario

Freeze-Dry Foods, 579 Speers Rd., Oakville, L6K 2G4. See also New
   York, above.
S. Gumpert & Co. of Canada, 31 Brock Ave., Toronto M6K 2L1. See
   also New Jersey, above.
(Trip-Lite foods. Case lots only. Minimum order: $30.)

Organizations That Promote Walking

Although the groups I've listed vary in size from a handful to the 140,000 of the Sierra Club and 270,000 of the Audubon Society, all of them, as far as I can confirm, include communal hikes among their activities—even when their names suggest otherwise. And you may, in spite of pages 5 and 416, sensibly prefer to walk in company. In any case, communal hikes are a safe way of getting to know the ropes—for an afternoon nature stroll or a month's wilderness backpacking.

No amount of research is going to dredge up the name of every walking group in the country; and secretaries, not to mention entire organizations, come and go. So any list like this is sure to be incomplete, and it begins to die before it is born. But it should at worst offer leads for earnest seekers. If an address proves "dead," inquire for the current version from local libraries, newspapers, chambers of commerce, or other sources your ingenuity smells out.

Please remember that secretaries—particularly of small local clubs —tend to be starved of funds and inundated with mail. If you write, it is only courteous to enclose a stamped, self-addressed #10 envelope.

UNITED STATES

Coast-to-Coast

The National Audubon Society.

Headquarters: 950 Fifth Ave., New York, N.Y. 10028.

Western regional office: 555 Audubon Way, Sacramento, Calif. 95825.

Nationwide: 600 branches and affiliates.

The society's walks are always nature walks and normally accent birdwatching; but do not forget that they are walks.

The Sierra Club.

Headquarters: 1050 Mills Tower, 270 Bush St., San Francisco, Calif. 94104.

Chapters in the following (see listings under each): Alaska, Arizona, California (11 chapters), Connecticut, Colorado, District of Columbia, Florida, Georgia, Hawaii, Idaho, Illinois, Iowa, Kentucky, Louisiana, Massachusetts, Michigan, Minnesota, Missouri, Nevada, New Jersey, New Mexico, New York, North Carolina, Ohio, Oklahoma, Oregon, Pennsylvania, Texas, Utah, Washington, and Wisconsin. (Many chapters embrace neighboring states; almost the entire country is covered.) For Canada, see pages 460–1. There are also territorial groups in American Samoa and the Canal Zone.

National Campers and Hikers Association.
   7172 Transit Rd., Buffalo, N.Y. 14221.
   Primarily for car-campers, but also for walkers. Has 2900 chapters and 525 Teen Chapters.

National Hiking and Ski Touring Association (NAHSTA).
   P.O. Box 7421, Colorado Springs, Colo. 80907.
   Prime object: "To help rebuild America's trails." Official journal: *Better Camping* Magazine (see page 18). Individual annual membership: $10. Students: $7.

Many colleges and universities—perhaps most—have hiking clubs. If local inquiries prove fruitless, consider asking: Association of College Unions–International, P.O. Box 7286, Stanford, Calif. 94305.
   And for possible local walking activities, do not forget: American Youth Hostels, Boy Scouts, Campfire Girls, Four-H Clubs, Girl Scouts, Young Life Campaign, YMCA and YWCA; also churches, parks and recreation departments of some big cities, and national and state parks.

Regional
The Appalachian Trail Conference.
   P.O. Box 236, Harpers Ferry, W. Va. 25425.
   Thirty-four trail clubs affiliated to this conference maintain the 2035-mile, Maine–Georgia Appalachian Trail; 40-odd other clubs are non-maintenance affiliates. The conference is the surest source of up-to-date information on eastern-seaboard walking activities. Listed clubs affiliated to the conference are marked ■.

The Federation of Western Outdoor Clubs.
   Secretary: Edgar D. Bauch.
   16603 53rd Ave. S., Seattle, Wash. 98188.
   The secretary will supply information on club addresses or membership but unfortunately cannot answer questions on trails or hiking details. Member clubs are marked ♦.

The New England Trail Conference.
   Secretary: Anne Mausolff.
   P.O. Box 145, Weston, Vt. 05161.

A valuable source of hiking activities in the area. List of member clubs: $.10. Publishes annual *New England Trails* and irregular updates.

Alabama
See Tennessee: Tri-State Hiking Club.

Alaska
Sierra Club: Alaska chapter, P.O. Box 2025, Anchorage, 99501.
♦ South Eastern Alaska Mountaineering Association, P.O. Box 1314, Ketchikan, 99901.

Arizona
♦ Sierra Club: Grand Canyon chapter, 2950 N. 7th St., Phoenix, 85014.
Southern Arizona Hiking Club, P.O. Box 12122, Tucson, 85711.

California
Berkeley Hiking Club, P.O. Box 147, Berkeley, 94701.
♦ California Alpine Club, 821 Market St., San Francisco, 94103.
♦ Contra Costa Hills Club, 306 40th St., Oakland, 94609.
♦ Desomount Club, 2406 S. 4th Ave., Arcadia, 91006.
♦ Regional Parks Association, 1097 Creston Rd., Berkeley, 94708.
♦ Roamer Hiking Club, 3533 W. 74th Pl., Inglewood, 90305.
♦ Sierra Club chapters:
  Angeles, 2410 Beverly Blvd., Suite 2, Los Angeles, 90057.
  Kern Kaweah, P.O. Box 3295, Bakersfield, 93305.
  Loma Prieta, 190 California Ave., Palo Alto, 94306.
  Los Padres, P.O. Box 30222, Santa Barbara, 93105.
  Mother Lode, P.O. Box 1335, Sacramento, 95806.
  Redwood, c/o White, 3144 Valley Green Lane, Napa, 94558.
  San Diego, 1549 El Prado, San Diego, 92101.
  San Francisco Bay, 5608 College Ave., Oakland, 94618.
  San Gorgonio, P.O. Box 1023, Riverside, 92502.
  Santa Lucia, c/o Bracken, 765 Highland Dr., Los Osos, 93401.
  Tehipite, P.O. Box 5396, Fresno, 93755.
  Ventana, P.O. Box 5667, Carmel, 93921.
♦ Tamalpais Conservation Club, 821 Market St., San Francisco, 94103.

Colorado
Colorado Mountain Club, 1723 E. 16th Ave., Denver, 80218.
♦ Sierra Club: Rocky Mountain chapter, P.O. Box 6312, Cherry Creek Station, Denver, 80206.
The Wilderness Society, Western Office, 4260 E. Evans Ave., Denver, 80222. See also District of Columbia, below.

Connecticut
■ Connecticut chapter, Appalachian Mountain Club, Bertha Guros, 37 Play St., Thompsonville, 06082.
Connecticut Forest and Parks Association, Secretary: John E. Hibbard, 15 Lewis St., Hartford, 06103.
Sierra Club: Connecticut chapter, P.O. Box 153, Storrs, 06268.

Delaware
■ Brandywine Valley Outing Club, P.O. Box 7033, Wilmington, 19803.
■ Wilmington Trail Club, P.O. Box 1184, Wilmington, 19899.

District of Columbia
Capital Hiking Club, President: George K. Ashenden, 1608 Preston Rd., Alexandria, Va. 22302.
Center Hiking Club, President: Bob Semenoff, 906 Domer Ave., Takoma Park, Md. 20012.
■ Potomac Appalachian Trail Club, 1718 N St. N.W., Washington, 20036.
Sierra Club: Potomac chapter, 324 C Street S.E., Washington, 20003.
■ Wanderbirds Hiking Club, Secretary: Miss Jeannie Allan, 2122 California St. N.W., Washington, 20008.
The Wilderness Society, 1901 Pennsylvania Ave. N.W., Washington, 20006.

Florida
Florida Trail Association, 33 S.W. 18th Ter., Miami, 33129.
Sierra Club: Florida chapter, c/o Winchester, 2405 Delgado Dr., Tallahassee, 32304.

Georgia
■ Georgia Appalachian Trail Club, Inc., Box 43A, Rt. #2, Hwy. 92, Fayetteville, 30214.
Sierra Club: Chattahoochee chapter, P.O. Box 19574, Station N, Atlanta, 30325.
See also Tennessee: Tri-State Hiking Club.

Hawaii
Hawaiian Trail and Mountain Club, P.O. Box 2238, Honolulu, 96804.
♦ Sierra Club: Hawaii chapter, c/o Bishop Museum, P.O. Box 6037, Honolulu, 96818.

Idaho
♦ Idaho Alpine Club, P.O. Box 2885, Idaho Falls, 83401.

♦ Sierra Club: Northern Rockies chapter, c/o Meiners, 7717 Ustick Rd., Boise, 83704.

Illinois

Prairie Club, Room 1010, 38 S. Dearborn St., Chicago, 60603.
Sierra Club: Great Lakes chapter, 616 Delles, Wheaton, 60187.
Tazewell-Peoria Hiking Club, Glen Oak Park Pavilion, 2500A N. Prospect Road, Peoria, 61603.

Iowa

Iowa Mountaineers, P.O. Box 163, Iowa City, 52240.
Sierra Club: Iowa chapter, P.O. Box 171, Des Moines, 50301.

Kansas

Backpack Club, Johnson County Outdoor Society, c/o Johnson County Park and Recreation District, 6501 Antioch, Shawnee Mission, 66202.

Kentucky

Louisville Hiking Club, Secretary: Carlyle Chamberlain, 2112 Eastview Ave., Louisville, 40205.
Sierra Club: Cumberland chapter, c/o Geralds, 320 Mariemont Dr., Lexington, 40505.
See also Tennessee: Tri-State Hiking Club.

Louisiana

Sierra Club: Delta chapter, c/o Osborne, 1006 National Bank of Commerce Bldg., New Orleans, 70112.

Maine

■ Maine Appalachian Trail Club, Inc., Sam Butcher, Box 1080, Hillside Rd., Brunswick, 04011.

Maryland

■ Maryland Appalachian Trail Club, Robert Rice, R.F.D. #1, Box 145, Clear Spring, 21722.
■ Mountain Club of Maryland, c/o Thurston Griggs, 5128 Rolling Rd., Baltimore, 21227.
■ Terrapin Trail Club, Box 67, Univ. of Maryland, College Park, 20742.
■ Wanderbirds Hiking Club: see District of Columbia.

Massachusetts

■ Appalachian Mountain Club, 5 Joy St., Boston, 02108.

■ Metawampe (University of Massachusetts Faculty Outing Club), Univ. of Massachusetts, Amherst, 01002.

■ Mt. Greylock Ski Club, Inc., P.O. Box 478, Pittsfield, 01201.

Sierra Club: New England chapter, Room 719, 14 Beacon St., Boston, 02108.

Michigan

Sierra Club: Mackinac chapter, 409 Seymour St., Lansing, 48933.

Minnesota

Sierra Club: North Star chapter, P.O. Box 80004, St. Paul, 55108.

Missouri

Sierra Club: Ozark chapter, P.O. Box 12424, Olivette, 63122.

See also Kansas: Backpack Club, Johnson County Outdoor Society.

Montana

◆ Montana Wilderness Association, P.O. Box 548, Bozeman, 59715.

◆ Rocky Mountaineers, P.O. Box 1575, Missoula, 59801.

Nebraska

Omaha Walking Club, 3261 Farnam St., #3, Omaha, 68131.

Nevada

◆ Sierra Club: Toiyabe chapter, P.O. Box 8096, University Station, Reno, 89507.

New Hampshire

■ Dartmouth Outing Club, Box 9, Robinson Hall, Dartmouth College, Hanover, 03755.

Lumberjack Outing Club, c/o Skimeister Ski Shop, North Woodstock, 03262.

Wonalancet Outdoor Club, c/o Mrs. Elizabeth McKey, Wonalancet, 03897.

New Jersey

Adirondack Mountain Club: North Jersey chapter, P.O. Box 185, Ridgewood, 07451.

College Alumni Hiking Club, Jeannette E. Brown, 13 Dennis Pl., Summit, 07901.

Cosmopolitan Club of Montclair, Pierre Deleener, 32 Normal Ave., Upper Montclair, 07043.

■ Interstate Hiking Club, Herbert E. Snider, 6 Carl Dr., Fairfield, 07006.

■ New York–New Jersey Trail Conference—many New Jersey clubs: see New York.

Sierra Club: New Jersey chapter, 360 Nassau St., Princeton, 08540.

Wanderbirds Hiking Club, P.O. Box 98, Uptown Station, Hoboken, 07030.

Woodland Trail Walkers, Catherine Servas, 142 Lake Ave., Clifton, 07011.

New Mexico

♦ Sierra Club: Rio Grande chapter, P.O. Box 351, Los Alamos, 87544.

New York

Adirondack Forty-Sixers, Adirondack, 12808.

Adirondack Mountain Club, R.D. 1, Ridge Rd., Glens Falls, 12801.

Adirondack Trail Improvement Society, Saint Huberts, 12943.

American Youth Hostels: Metropolitan New York Council, 535 West End Ave., New York, 10024.

■ Appalachian Mountain Club: New York chapter, Mrs. Elizabeth Burton, 190 Columbia Hts., Brooklyn, 11201.

Buffalo Hiking Club, Buffalo Museum of Science, Buffalo, 14211.

College Alumni Hiking Club: see New Jersey (includes New York).

Finger Lakes Trail Conference, Rochester Museum of Arts and Sciences, Rochester, 14600. (Trail Chairman: Ervin H. Markert, 22 Sturbridge Lane, Pittsford, 14534.)

Formed in 1961 to build a foot trail across southern New York state, from the Catskills to the Alleghenies, connecting the Bruce Trail of Canada with the Appalachian Trail. Still building.

Builder organizations:

Adirondack Mountain Club, Finger Lakes chapter, Ithaca.

Adirondack Mountain Club, Niagara Frontier chapter, Buffalo.

Adirondack Mountain Club, Onondaga chapter, Syracuse.

Cayuga Trails Club, General Delivery, Ithaca, 14850.

Cornell Outing Club, Willard Straight Hall, Cornell University, Ithaca, 14850.

Cortland County Bird Club, Cortland.

Finger Lakes Regional Group, c/o Sierra Club, P.O. Box 864, Ithaca, 14850.

Foothills Trail Club, Buffalo.

Genesee Valley Hiking Club, Rochester Museum of Arts and Sciences, Rochester, 14600.

Otetiana Council, Boy Scouts of America, Rochester.

Seven Lakes Girl Scout Council, Geneva.

Southern Tier Girl Scout Council, Corning.

Triple Cities Hiking Club, Johnson City.

Tri-Town Trail Club, Sydney.

U.S. Forest Service, 208 Broadway, Mountour Falls, 14865.

■ Green Mountain Club: New York section, W. Fred Rousseau, 65 Concord Ave., Glen Rock, N.J. 07452.

■ Nassau Hiking and Outdoor Club, Rodger W. Junk, 3 Rosedale Rd., Valley Stream, 11560.

■ New York Hiking Club, Harold Diamond, 404 E. 18th St., Brooklyn, 11226.

■ New York–New Jersey Trail Conference, G.P.O. Box 2250, New York, 10001.

Fifty member organizations, including sub-units of the Adirondack Mountain Club, Appalachian Mountain Club, American Youth Hostels, Boy Scouts of America, and Sierra Club. Also several clubs listed separately; and the following independent clubs, whose presidents and even membership in the conference "are continually changing":

New York

Catskill 3500 Club, Hudson.

City College Outdoor Club, New York.

Fresh Air Club, Coram.

Inkowa Outdoor Club, Woodhaven.

Metropolitan Intercollegiate Outing Club Association, Bronx.

Neophyte Explorers, Brooklyn.

Open Road Club, Brooklyn.

Protectionists and Trail Hikers, Dobbs Ferry.

RENEW, Bellvale.

New Jersey

Metropolitan Recreation Association, Paterson.

Nopco Hiking Club, Hackettstown.

Ramapo Hiking Club, Ocean.

Rutgers University Outdoor Club, New Brunswick.

Short Hills Outing Club, Union.

Union County Hiking Club, Summit.

University Outing Club, Somerset.

Windbeam Outdoor Club, Wanaque.

New York State Department of Environmental Information, 50 Wolf Rd., Albany, 12226. (Hiking information.)

New York State Department of Parks and Recreation, S. Swan St. Building, South Mall, Albany, 12223. (Hiking information.)

Sierra Club: Atlantic chapter, 50 W. 40th St., New York, 10018.

Suffern Historical Hikers, Gardner F. Watts, 15 Beech Rd., Suffern, 10901.

Taconic Hiking Club, Anita Rioux, 30 Continental Ave., Cohoes, 12047.

■ New York Ramblers, Anne H. Blumenstein, 4523 Broadway, Apt 3-C, New York, 10040.

■ Torrey Botanical Club, Grace A. Dietz, New York Botanical Garden, Bronx, 10458.

■ Tramp and Trail Club of New York, Robyn Stockton, 229 E. 52nd St., New York, 10022.

Wanderbirds Hiking Club: see New Jersey.

■ Westchester Trails Association, Linda Heilmann, 632 Warburton Ave., Apt 6-K, Yonkers, 10701.
■ Woodland Trail Walkers, John J. Cotter, 350 E. 65th St., New York, 10021.

North Carolina
■ Carolina Mountain Club, P.O. Box 68, Asheville, 28802.
■ Nantahala Hiking Club, John J. Brown, Highlands, 29741.
■ Piedmont Appalachian Trail Hikers (PATH), President: Mrs. Don Chatfield, 124 Laurence St., Greensboro, 27406.
■ Sierra Club: Joseph LeConte chapter, c/o Kohl, 807 Gardner, Raleigh, 27607.
See also Tennessee: Tri-State Hiking Club.

Ohio
Akron Metropolitan Park Hiking Club, Don Vogt, 1141 Janis Ave., Akron, 44314.
American Walkers Association of Cincinnati, Irwin J. Carroll, 6221 Robison Rd., Cincinnati, 43213.
Athens Ecology Group, 413 Baker Center, Ohio University, Athens, 45701.
Buckeye Trail Association, Inc., P.O. Box 8746, Columbus, 43215.
Central Ohio Hiking Club, YMCA, 40 Long St., Columbus, 43215.
Cleveland Hiking Club, James D. Hedberg, 2851 Southington St., Cleveland, 44120.
Sierra Club: Ohio chapter, 9900 Grass Creek Court, Cincinnati, 45231.
■ Tri-County Trail Association, Mrs. Jerri Fitch, 7011 Dueber Ave. S.W., East Sparta, 44626.
■ Washington County Hiking Club, William Ortt, 301 Colegate Dr., Marietta, 45750.

Oklahoma
Sierra Club: Oklahoma chapter, P.O. Box 53401, Oklahoma City, 73105.

Oregon
♦ Angora Hiking Club, P.O. Box 12, Astoria, 97103.
♦ Chemeketans, 360½ State St., Salem, 97301.
♦ Crag Rats, 417 May St., Hood River, 97031.
Mazamas, 909 N.W. 19th, Portland, 97209.
♦ McKenzie Guardians, c/o James Baker, President, Blue River, 97413.
♦ Obsidians, Inc., P.O. Box 322, Eugene, 97401.
♦ O.S.U. Mountain Club, Memorial Union Bldg., Corvallis, 97331.

♦ Reed College Outing Club, Box 186 (or Box 555), Reed College, Portland, 97202.

♦ Santiam Alpine Club, Inc., P.O. Box 1013, Salem, 97308.

♦ Trails Club of Oregon, P.O. Box 1243, Portland, 97207.

♦ Wy' East Climbers, 4929 N.E. Fremont, Portland, 97213.

Pennsylvania

American Nessmuk Society, Harry L. Hart, 109 N. Furnace St., Birdsboro, 19508.

Central Allegheny Trail Hikers, R. B. Sumantri, P.O. Box 28, Lemont, 16801.

■ Keystone Trails Association, Richard Kimmel, 1020 Martin St., Lebanon, 17042. An association of 28 hiking clubs, including the following in Pennsylvania:

■ Allentown Hiking Club, 3000 Parkway Blvd., Allentown, 18104.

Alpine Club of Williamsport, P.O. Box 501, Williamsport, 17701.

■ Appalachian Mountain Club: Delaware Valley chapter, Winfield W. Howe, 422 Dudley Ave., Narberth, 19072.

■ Back To Nature Hiking Club Of Philadelphia (Batona), John W. Kirker, 238 Taylor Rd., Springfield, 19064.

■ Blue Mountain Eagle Climbing Club and Wilderness Park Association, P.O. Box 3523, Reading, 19605.

Boondockers Hiking Club, Bernie McKenna, 553 Midland St., Pittsburgh, 15221.

■ Horse Shoe Trail Club, Dr. John A. Goff, 623 Righters Mill Rd., Narberth, 19072.

■ Lancaster Hiking Club, Roy K. Albright, 45 Petersburg Rd., Neffsville, 17601.

■ Philadelphia Trail Club, Mrs. A. Peers Montgomery, 520 Fox Rd., Glenside, 19038.

■ Springfield Trail Club, John W. Kirker, 238 Taylor Rd., Springfield, 19064.

■ Susquehanna Appalachian Trail Club, Warren Sleighter, 102 Fifth St., New Cumberland, 17070.

■ York Hiking Club, Mrs. Frank V. Senft, 1957 Woodstream Dr., York, 17402.

■ Lebanon Valley Hiking Club, Richard C. Kimmel, 1020 Martin St., Lebanon, 17042.

Penn State Outing Club, H. White, 60 Recreation Bldg., University Park, 16802.

Reading Community Hiking Club, 410 Douglass St., Reading, 19601.

Sierra Club: Pennsylvania chapter, c/o Lockwood, 2015 Land Title Bldg., Philadelphia, 19110.

Susquehanna Trailers Club, Mrs. Irene Stawicki, R.211 Bowman St., Wilkes-Barre, 18702.

Warrior Trail Association, 202 County Office Bldg., Waynesburg, 15370.

South Carolina
■ Sierra Club: Joseph LeConte chapter—see North Carolina.

Tennessee
Bowaters Southern Paper Corporation, Public Relations Department, Calhoun, 37309. ("Pocket wilderness areas.")

Cumberland Hiking Club, David Fulmer, 428 Booth Rd., Chattanooga, 37411.

Sierra Club: Tennessee chapter, c/o Gray, 708 Georgetown Dr., Nashville, 37205.

■ Smoky Mountains Hiking Club, Ken Roberts, 5419 Timbercrest Trail, Knoxville, 37901.

■ Tennessee Trails Association, Donald Todd, P.O. Box 331, Wartburg, 37887. (Or—southern section—Mrs. Dorothy Y. Ventress, 4901 Guild Trail, Chattanooga, 37409.)

■ TERC Hiking Club, c/o Tennessee Eastman Recreation Club, B-89, Kingsport, 37662.

Tri-State Hiking Club, William Stultz, 1806 Oak St., Chattanooga, 37404. (For Tennessee, Alabama, Georgia, Kentucky, and North Carolina.)

Texas
Sierra Club: Lone Star chapter, 27190 Lana Lane, Conroe, 77301.

Utah
♦ Sierra Club: Uinta chapter, P.O. Box 8393, Foothill Station, Salt Lake City, 84108.

Wasatch Mountain Club, 2959 Highland Dr., Salt Lake City, 84106.

Vermont
■ Green Mountain Club, Inc., P.O. Box 94, Rutland, 05701.

Virginia
■ Mt. Rogers Appalachian Trail Club, David Thomas, Route 1, Box 168-A, Abingdon, 24210.

■ Natural Bridge Appalachian Trail Club, P.O. Box 3156, Lynchburg, 24503.

■ Old Dominion Appalachian Trail Club, John Fisher, 711 Trevor Ter., Richmond, 23226.

■ Roanoke Appalachian Trail Club, Dr. Wm. N. Gordge, 1201 Third St. S.W., Roanoke, 24016.

■ Tidewater Appalachian Trail Club, Mrs. W. R. Nelson, 612 Timberland Trail, Virginia Beach, 23452.

■ University of Virginia Outing Club, P.O. Box 101X, Newcomb Hall Station, Charlottesville, 22903.

■ Virginia Tech Outing Club, Dr. Carlton N. Newton, College of Agriculture, VPI, Blacksburg, 24601.

Washington

♦ Alpine Roamers, 1500 N. Eastmont, East Wenatchee, 98801.

American Camping Association, John B. Heisell, 4601 91st Pl. N.E., Bellevue, 98004.

♦ Boeing Employees Alpine Society, P.O. Box 3707 M.S.4H-96, Seattle, 98124.

♦ Cascade Wilderness Club, P.O. Box 194, Bellingham, 98225.

♦ Cascadians, P.O. Box 2201, Yakima, 98902.

♦ Hobnailers, P.O. Box 1074, Spokane, 99202.

Institute for Survival Education, D. T. Kneeland, P.O. Box 1466 Greenwood Station, Seattle, 98103.

♦ Intermountain Alpine Club, P.O. Box 505, Richland, 99352.

♦ Klahane Club, P.O. Box 494, Port Angeles, 98362.

♦ Mountaineers, The, P.O. Box 122, Seattle, 98111.

♦ Mt. Baker Club, P.O. Box 73, Bellingham, 98225.

♦ Mt. St. Helena Club, P.O. Box 843, Longview, 98632.

♦ Olympians, Inc., P.O. Box 401, Hoquiam, 98550.

♦ Ptarmigans, P.O. Box 1821, Vancouver, 98663.

Puget Sound Mycological Society, c/o Pacific Science Center, 200 Second Ave. N., Seattle, 98109.

♦ Rimrock Mountaineers, c/o Albert Carlson, Star Route, Coulee Dam, 99116.

♦ Seattle Audubon Society, 712 Joshua Green Bldg., Seattle, 98101.

♦ Sierra Club: Pacific Northwest chapter, 4534½ University Way N.E., Seattle, 98105.

Signpost Magazine, 16812 36th Ave. W., Lynnwood, 98036. Maintains formidable card index of hiking and similar clubs. See also page 18.

♦ Skagit Alpine Club, P.O. Box 513, Mt. Vernon, 98273.

♦ Spokane Mountaineers, Inc., P.O. Box 1013, Spokane, 99210.

♦ Wanderers, 1311 N. Quince, Olympia, 98506.

♦ Washington Alpine Club, P.O. Box 352, Seattle, 98111.

Washington Recreation and Trails Unlimited, P.O. Box 542, Bellevue, 98004.

Wisconsin

Sierra Club: John Muir chapter, 14660 Golf Pkwy., Brookfield, 53005.

Wisconsin Go-Hiking Club, Gertrude Kantzer, 3863 N. 37th St., Milwaukee, 53216.

Wisconsin Hoofers, The Wisconsin Union, 770 Langdon St., Madison, 53706.

CANADA

Coast-to-Coast

Alpine Club of Canada.
    Club Manager: P. A. Boswell.
    P.O. Box 1026, Banff, Alberta ToL oCo.
    (Please note that this is essentially a *climbing* club—though rather more like the Sierra Club than the American Alpine Club.) Sections in Banff, Calgary, Edmonton, Montreal, Ottawa, Toronto, Vancouver, Vancouver Island, Winnipeg. U.S. sections in East, Midwest, and West.

Canadian Youth Hostels Association.
    National office: 333 River Rd., Vanier City, Ottawa, K1L 8B9.
    Regional offices in Alberta (two), British Columbia, Nova Scotia, Ontario, and Quebec. See provincial listings.

National Campers and Hikers Association (see United States, Coast-to-Coast).
    Canadian Regional Directors: Mr. and Mrs. Roy Williamson.
    51 W. 22nd St., Hamilton, Ontario.

Alberta

Canadian Youth Hostels Association: Mountain Region, 455 12th St. N.W., Calgary. Northwest Region, 10922 88th Ave., Edmonton.
Skyline Trail Hikers of the Canadian Rockies, 622 Madison Ave. S.W., Calgary.

British Columbia

British Columbia Institute of Technology Outdoor Club, 3700 Willingdon, Burnaby.
British Columbia Mountaineering Club, P.O. Box 2674, Vancouver 3.
Canadian Youth Hostels Association, Pacific Region, 1406 W. Broadway, Vancouver 9.
Federation of Mountain Clubs of British Columbia, P.O. Box 33768, Station D, Vancouver 9.
Island Mountain Ramblers, P.O. Box 691, Nanaimo, Vancouver Island. (District Representatives in Victoria, Duncan, Ladysmith, Nanaimo, Port Alberni, Ucluelet, Courtenay, and Campbell River.)
Kamloops Outdoor Club, Secretary: George Eldridge, 925 Douglas St., Kamloops.
North Shore Hikers, P.O. Box 4535, Vancouver U6B 4A1.
Northwest Wilderness Society, 949 W. 49th Ave., Vancouver 13.
Outdoor Club of Victoria, Robert Spearing, 14 Linden Ave., Victoria.
Sierra Club, Western Canada chapter, 444 Robson St., Vancouver, V6B 2B5.

Simon Fraser University Outdoor Club, Burnaby.
South Vancouver Island Rangers, P.O. Box 341, Victoria.
Varsity Outdoor Club, University of British Columbia, Vancouver 8.

Nova Scotia
Canadian Youth Hostels Association, Maritime Region, P.O. Box 2332, Halifax.

Ontario
Bruce Trail Association, Secretary: Ray Lowes, 33 Hardale Cres., Hamilton, L8T 1X7.
Canadian Youth Hostels Association, Great Lakes Region, 86 Scollard St., Toronto 5.
Greb Hiking Bureau, 1 Adams St., Kitchener.
Niagara Escarpment Trail Council, P.O. Box 1, St. Catharine's.
Sierra Club: Ontario chapter, 47 Colborne St., Toronto, M5E 1E3.
Toronto Hiking and Conservation Club, P.O. Box 121, Postal Station F, Toronto 5.

Quebec
Canadian Youth Hostels Association, St. Lawrence Region, 754 Sherbrooke St. W., Montreal 2.
Club Aventure, 39-A rue Prince, Drummondville.
Club de Grande Randonnée Sutton, 30 rue Western, Sutton.
Club de la Montagne Canadienne, 11, 215 Ste-Gertrude, Montréal Nord 460.
Kiak, 1065-A, St-Jean, app 2, Québec 4.
Montreal Ski and Outing Club, 1619 Selkirk Ave., app 101, Montreal 109.
Quebec Hiking Clubs Association (Association des Clubs de Randonnée Pédestre du Québec), 2322 Est, rue Sherbrooke, #1, Montréal 134.

WORLDWIDE WALKING

Some of the more ambitious American organizations, including the Sierra Club, now organize walking trips in faraway places. So do at least two commercial firms (free brochures available):

Mountain Travel, 1398 Solano Ave., Albany, Calif. 94706. (Pioneers in the field, operating since 1968.)
Wilderness Expeditions, 230 Park Ave., New York, N.Y. 10017. (Since 1971. Works closely with Friends of the Earth. Specialty: ecologically threatened places.)

Under such auspices you can now walk in small groups in Africa, Asia, Europe, South America, Australasia, even Antarctica. Bearers or pack animals often carry your gear.

Pleasant Quotes for Contemplative Walkers

I nauseate walking.

WILLIAM CONGREVE

Today I have grown taller from walking with the trees.

KARLE WILSON
(Mrs. Thomas Ellis Baker)

The longing to be primitive is a disease of culture.

GEORGE SANTAYANA

I like to walk about amidst the beautiful things that adorn the world.

GEORGE SANTAYANA

If you pick 'em up, O Lord, I'll put 'em down.

ANON.
The Prayer of the Tired Walker

Our mental make-up is suited to a life of very severe physical labor. I used, when I was younger, to take my holidays walking. I would cover 25 miles a day, and when the evening came I had no need of anything to keep me from boredom, since the delight of sitting amply sufficed. . . .

When crowds assemble in Trafalgar Square to cheer to the echo an announcement that the government has decided to have them killed, they would not do so if they had all walked 25 miles that day.

BERTRAND RUSSELL
Nobel Prize Acceptance Speech

I drew my bride, beneath the moon,
Across my threshold; happy hour!
But, ah, the walk that afternoon
We saw the water-flags in flower!.
                    COVENTRY PATMORE

I want a divorce.
                    BARBARA BAILEY MARCUS
          Response suggested for Mrs. Coventry Patmore

The civilized man has built a coach, but he has lost the use of his feet.
                    EMERSON

Huh, your feet must be stronger than your head!
                    STRANGER
          To Colin Fletcher, during thousand-mile walk

For my part, I travel not to go anywhere, but to go.
                    STEVENSON
                    Travels with a Donkey ...

There is more to life than increasing its speed.
                    GANDHI

The swiftest traveler is he that goes afoot.
                    THOREAU

He that riseth late must trot all day.
                    BEN FRANKLIN

Walk while ye have the light, lest darkness come upon you.
                    ST. JOHN, XII:35

And the Lord said unto Satan, Whence comest thou? Then Satan
answered the Lord, and said, From going to and fro in the earth,
and from walking up and down in it.
                    JOB I:7

One big vice in a man is apt to keep out a great many smaller ones.
BRET HARTE

Thou shalt have a place also without the camp, whither thou shalt go forth abroad: and thou shalt have a paddle upon thy weapon; and it shall be, when thou wilt ease thyself abroad, thou shalt dig therewith, and shalt turn back and cover that which cometh from thee.
DEUTERONOMY XXIII: 13

He travels the fastest who travels alone.
KIPLING

Can two walk together, except they be agreed?
AMOS III: 3

The true male never yet walked
Who liked to listen when his mate talked.
ANNA WICKHAM
(Mrs. Patrick Hepburn)

I was never less alone than when by myself.
EDWARD GIBBON

In solitude
What happiness? Who can enjoy alone,
Or all enjoying, what contentment find?
MILTON
Paradise Lost

That inward eye which is the bliss of solitude.
WORDSWORTH

Solitude is as needful to the imagination as society is wholesome for the character.
JAMES RUSSELL LOWELL

O Solitude! where are the charms
That sages have seen in thy face?

> COWPER
> *Verses Supposed to Be Written*
> *by Alexander Selkirk*

Fraternity is the State's bribe to the individual.

> PALINURUS

He went back through the Wet Wild Woods, waving his wild tail,
and walking by his wild lone. But he never told anybody.

> KIPLING
> *The Cat That Walked by Himself*

O why do you walk through the fields in gloves,
Missing so much and so much?

> FRANCES CORNFORD
> *To a Fat Lady Seen from the Train*

Oh, he's a genuine backpacker all right. He's got a filed-down toothbrush.

> Overheard by Colin Fletcher

Who walks with beauty has no need of fear;
The sun and moon and stars keep pace with him;
Invisible hands restore the ruined year,
And time, itself, grows beautifully dim.

> DAVID MORTON

Mountains are earth's undying monuments.

> HAWTHORNE

"I'm sure nobody walks much faster than I do."
"He can't do that," said the King, "or else he'd have
been here first."

> LEWIS CARROLL
> *Through the Looking-Glass*

The Promised Land always lies on the other side of a wilderness.

> HAVELOCK ELLIS

The walking stick serves the purpose of an advertisement that the bearer's hands are employed otherwise than in useful effort, and it therefore has utility as an evidence of leisure.

THORSTEIN VEBLEN
The Theory of the Leisure Class

Dear Uncle Colin: I'm haveing fun at camp My counselors he Read one of your Books anb he said it gave him sore Feet.

Postcard from honorary nephew

Hi-Rise Campsites, Inc., has announced plans to construct a 20-story campground in downtown New Orleans . . . Plans for the $4 million project call for eight lower floors of parking and 12 upper stories with 240 individual sites equipped with utility hookups for campers . . . [and] campsites carpeted with artificial turf, and a rooftop pool.

"This will be unique—the first of its kind anywhere," said Wesley Hurley of Hi-Rise. "It is designed for today's different kind of camping. People don't want the woodsy bit now; they want to camp in comfort near the city."

Associated Press report

. . . the brisk exercise imparts elasticity to the muscles, fresh and healthy blood circulates through the brain, the mind works well, the eye is clear, the step is firm, and the day's exertion always makes the evening's repose thoroughly enjoyable.

DR. DAVID LIVINGSTONE

All men who explore
Deplore
That frustrating hurdle,
The girdle.

COLIN FLETCHER
(Unpublished)

I find that the three truly great times for thinking thoughts are when I am standing in the shower, sitting on the john, or walking. And the greatest of these, by far, is walking.

COLIN FLETCHER
(Unpublished)

When I am not walking, I am reading; I cannot sit and think,
[but] books think for me.
                                        CHARLES LAMB

Man is a thinking reed but his great works are done when he is not
calculating and thinking.
                                        DAISETZ T. SUZUKI

Thou canst not stir a flower
Without troubling of a star.
                                        FRANCIS THOMPSON

To a person uninstructed in natural history, his country or sea-side
stroll is a walk through a gallery filled with wonderful works of art,
nine-tenths of which have their faces turned to the wall.
                                        THOMAS HUXLEY

The book of nature is that which the physician must read; and to do
so he must walk over the leaves.
                                        PARACELSUS

No bird soars too high, if he soars with his own wings.
                                        WILLIAM BLAKE

Solvency is entirely a matter of temperament and not of income.
                                        LOGAN PEARSALL SMITH

He likes the country, but in truth must own,
Most likes it when he studies it in town.
                                        WILLIAM COWPER

Man is an animal, and his happiness depends on his physiology more
than he likes to think. . . . Unhappy businessmen, I am convinced,
would increase their happiness more by walking six miles every day
than by any conceivable change of philosophy.
                                        BERTRAND RUSSELL

Man . . . walks up the stairs of his concepts, [and] emerges ahead of his accomplishments.

JOHN STEINBECK

The best definition of man is that he is the one creature capable of reflection, of seeing himself in the frame of reference of the surrounding universe.

KONRAD LORENZ

Man discovers that he is nothing else than evolution become conscious of itself.

JULIAN HUXLEY

. . . man, in his paranoid arrogance, has perpetrated the greatest blasphemy of all time by stating in the Bible, "So God created Man in his own image." . . . There is a God all around us which man has refused to accept but he abuses and exploits her forgetting that she of all deities is our own true God. . . . Man's greatest enemy is his own kind and upon an understanding of this fact depends his chances of survival in the future.

DR. PHILIP E. GLOVER,
Director, Tsavo Research Project,
Kenya

Men and their works have been a disease on the surface of their planets before now. . . . Nature tends to compensate for diseases, to remove or encapsulate them, to incorporate them into the system in her own way.

FRANK HERBERT
In *Dune,* a story set in the far future

Polish comes from the cities, wisdom from the desert.

FRANK HERBERT
Dune

Three things there are that ease the heart—water, green grass, and the beauty of woman.

FRANK HERBERT
Dune

Let a man once overcome his selfish terror at his own finitude, and his finitude is, in one sense, overcome.

GEORGE SANTAYANA

To understand life man must learn to shudder.
>   Quoted by Loren Eiseley

There is no cure for birth and death save to enjoy the interval.
>   GEORGE SANTAYANA

Comedy is tragedy plus time.
>   Attributed to Carol Burnett's mother

Humor and knowledge are the two great hopes of civilization.
>   KONRAD LORENZ

I went to the woods because I wished to live deliberately, to front
only the essential facts of life, and see if I could not learn what it had
to teach, and not, when I came to die, discover that I had not lived.
>   THOREAU

Early and provident fear is the mother of safety.
>   EDMUND BURKE

The beginning of wisdom is a salutary shock.
>   ARNOLD TOYNBEE

Two roads diverged in a wood, and I—
I took the one less traveled by,
And that has made all the difference.
>   ROBERT FROST

All paths lead nowhere, so it is important to choose a path that has
heart.
>   CARLOS CASTAÑEDA

Improvement makes straight roads; but the crooked roads without
improvement are roads of genius.
>   WILLIAM BLAKE

The concept of progress acts as a protective mechanism to shield us from the terrors of the future.

FRANK HERBERT
Dune

The . . . scientists were wrong . . . the most persistent principles of the universe were accident and error.

FRANK HERBERT
Dune

If one advances confidently in the direction of his dreams, and endeavors to live the life which he has imagined, he will meet with a success unexpected in common hours.

THOREAU

Grow up as soon as you can. It pays. The only time you really live fully is from thirty to sixty. . . . The young are slaves to dreams; the old servants of regrets. Only the middle-aged have all their five senses in the keeping of their wits.

HERVEY ALLEN

I speak truth, not so much as I would, but as much as I dare; and I dare a little the more, as I grow older.

MONTAIGNE

Growing old isn't so bad—when you consider the alternative.

MAURICE CHEVALIER

We will go no more to the woods, the laurel-trees are cut.

THÉODORE DE BANVILLE

And as I turn me home,
My shadow walks before.

ROBERT BRIDGES

Index

A NOTE ON THE TYPE

The text of this book was set on the Linotype in Garamond (No. 3), a modern rendering of the type first cut in the sixteenth century by Claude Garamond (1510–1561). He was a pupil of Geoffroy Troy and is believed to have based his letters on the Venetian models, although he introduced a number of important differences, and it is to him we owe the letter which we know as Old Style. He gave to his letters a certain elegance and a feeling of movement which won for their creator an immediate reputation and the patronage of the French King Francis I.

This book was composed, printed and bound by The Book Press, Brattleboro, Vermont.

Typography and binding based on designs by Winston Potter